Software Development Techniques for Constructive Information Systems Design

Khalid A. Buragga
King Faisal University, Saudi Arabia

Noor Zaman
King Faisal University, Saudi Arabia

Information Science
REFERENCE

Managing Director:	Lindsay Johnston
Editorial Director:	Joel Gamon
Book Production Manager:	Jennifer Yoder
Publishing Systems Analyst:	Adrienne Freeland
Development Editor:	Austin DeMarco
Assistant Acquisitions Editor:	Kayla Wolfe
Typesetter:	Erin O'Dea
Cover Design:	Jason Mull

Published in the United States of America by
Information Science Reference (an imprint of IGI Global)
701 E. Chocolate Avenue
Hershey PA 17033
Tel: 717-533-8845
Fax: 717-533-8661
E-mail: cust@igi-global.com
Web site: http://www.igi-global.com

Library of Congress Cataloging-in-Publication Data

Software development techniques for constructive information systems design / Khalid A. Buragga and Noor Zaman, editors.
       pages cm
  Summary: "This book focuses on the aspects of information systems and software development as a merging process, paying special attention to the emerging research, trends, and experiences in his area"-- Provided by publisher.
  Includes bibliographical references and index.
  ISBN 978-1-4666-3679-8 (hardcover) -- ISBN 978-1-4666-3680-4 -- ISBN 978-1-4666-3681-1 (print & perpetual access) 1. Software engineering. 2. System design. 3. Computer software--Development. I. Buragga, Khalid A., 1965- editor of compilation. II. Zaman, Noor, 1972- editor of compilation.
  QA76.758.S6446 2013
  005.3--dc23
                                     2012046051

British Cataloguing in Publication Data
A Cataloguing in Publication record for this book is available from the British Library.

All work contributed to this book is new, previously-unpublished material. The views expressed in this book are those of the authors, but not necessarily of the publisher.

This book is dedicated to our beloved Family, who bear with us and friends who support us.
Dr. Khalid A Mohsin Buragga and Dr. Noor Zaman

Table of Contents

Section 2
Advanced Topics in Software Engineering

Detailed Table of Contents

Section 1
Software Development Methodologies and Techniques

Chapter 1

Tanya Bondarouk, University of Twente, The Netherlands
Huub J. M. Ruël, Windesheim University of Applied Sciences, The Netherlands
Paul Timmermans, University of Twente, The Netherlands

This chapter describes the requirements for e-selection technology to be of practical use for any company. It focuses on different e- techniques, and identified related e- hiring issues. The chapter further provides a conclusion to focus e-techniques web-based technologies and states that web-based technologies should primarily support the core day-to-day work activities rather than be user-friendly or provide additional functionality.

Chapter 2

Elvira Locuratolo, ISTI Consiglio Nazionale delle Ricerche, Italy

This chapter focuses on the conceptual database design evolution, by introducing concepts which are common to both information systems and software engineering researches. An optimization algorithm of partitioning, based on the decomposition of objects and on the inheritance of attributes, is proposed and extended. The extended algorithm, which defines a formal constructive mapping from conceptual to logical database models, aims to show how some updates reflecting modifications occurring in the real life can affect the conceptual database design.

Chapter 3

José Fonseca, DEI/CISUC, University of Coimbra/UDI, Polytechnic Institute of Guarda, Portugal
Marco Vieira, DEI/CISUC, University of Coimbra, Portugal

This chapter presents a survey on the most relevant software development practices that are used nowadays to build software products for the web, with security built in. It starts by presenting three of the most relevant Secure Software Development Lifecycles, which are complete solutions that can be adopted by development companies: the CLASP, the Microsoft Secure Development Lifecycle and the Software Security Touchpoints. This chapter also discusses other relevant initiatives that can be integrated into existing development practices, which can be used to build and maintain safer software products: the OpenSAMM, the BSIMM, the SAFECode, and the Securosis.

Chapter 4

This chapter describes suitable quality practices which could not only support development of a good quality software product but also linked up well with the strategic needs of the organizational business. It focuses industry requirements for quality practices of software development, and then presents a framework that links Information System's development process improvement with strategic needs of an organization. It also covers the process improvement plan and use of different software development methodologies in multimodal process improvement scenarios.

Chapter 5

Project management is a key activity to manage project's objectives, timeline, cost, roles of the participants, and other challenges like estimating, planning, scheduling, budget monitoring, resource management, and documentation. This chapter briefly discusses issues related to project management and provides knowledge about different software that can be used in project management and diagramming to overcome project management issues.

Chapter 6

This chapter focuses the emerging role of cloud computing and its impact on software development methodologies. It briefly talks about the trend of cloud computing and new responsibilities which are linked with software development methodologies with respect to this new change of cloud computing environment from client server architecture.

Chapter 7

This chapter provides knowledge of the features and purposes of information. It also discusses the role of information system for developing a new system using System Development Life Cycle (SDLC). It also analyzes the concept of information quality to make a new system uses the different phases of SDLC.

In this chapter, author proposes a "Cybernetic Planning Framework" (CPF), which combines the diversity of educational theories and practices, yielding in a common basis for their inclusion. The chapter focuses on Second Life's qualitative characteristics that can utilize to construct a "teaching-organizational" framework, which is essential for planning effective and meaningful distance learning courses. This gain averred a "cybernetic model," in which enhanced pedagogical authorities and principles of Contemporary Learning Theories previous studies carried out in Second Life.

The author describes Information Systems' complexity and importance. Though Information Systems use the most advanced development tools and methodology, they must be simple for the users to understand, comprehend, and use, and they should be capable of performing all the functions necessary to perform a tasks efficiently.

This chapter describes Agile Interactive Software Development Process Models for Crowd Source Projects, which are very flexible in considering previous project parameters assume somewhat stable team and project structures. The author investigates all traditional project characteristics, elaborate on all those elements that should be modified to fit the open competition agile structure. Author use several case studies to demonstrate management issues related to managing software projects in open competitions.

Chapter 11

This chapter discusses the Software Engineering lifecycle, history, and software architecture as well as foundation of Information Engineering and Information System. It describes the software lifecycle phases and how to make effective use of various technical methods by applying effective technical and other efficient methods at the right time. This chapter shows the Information Engineering Life Cycle and discusses the key phrases for Information Engineering as well as Information System.

Section 2
Advanced Topics in Software Engineering

Chapter 12

Issa Traore, University of Victoria, Canada
Isaac Woungang, Ryerson University, Canada

In this chapter, authors introduce a novel model-driven perspective on secure software engineering, which integrates seamlessly software security analysis with traditional software development activities. A systematic security engineering process that starts in the early stages of the software development process and spans the entire software lifecycle is presented. Fundamental software security concepts and analysis techniques are also introduced, and several illustrative examples are presented, with focus on security requirements and risk analysis.

Chapter 13

Issa Traore, University of Victoria, Canada
Isaac Woungang, Ryerson University, Canada

This chapter explains the major objectives of a security policy, with focus on how applications that can protect data at all access points can be developed. Access control models and their known issues are discussed. From a security policy prospective, the security design principles and modeling using the UML are also discussed. In addition, an informal discussion on potential software security metrics that can be used for security measurement and finally, a discussion on security testing involving the use of metrics, are discussed.

Chapter 14

Muneer Ahmad, King Faisal University, Saudi Arabia
Low Tang Jung, University Technology PETRONAS, Malaysia
Noor Zaman, King Faisal University, Saudi Arabia

In this chapter, a comparative analysis has been presented for sequence analysis and comparative analysis best approaches has been reported along with some notions about tools, techniques, methodologies, and algorithms used for sequence analysis. The overall objective is to highlight the significance of underlying problems and existing solutions for analysis. Best approximation can only be achieved by comparing and identifying the optimal pathway for destination. It is commonly observed that one computational solution can't be guaranteed as an optimal solution for sequence NP hard problems, different and diverse solutions can lead to more significant result.

Chapter 15

Jaffar Ahmad Alalwan, Institute of Public Administration, Dammam, Saudi Arabia

Enterprise systems development approaches can be classified into development-centric and procurement centric approaches. Based on the component-based system development methodology (CBSD), the chapter proposes a procurement-centric framework to develop enterprise content management (ECM) system. Adopting CBSD to develop ECM system avoids the drawbacks of the development-centric approaches, and remedies the ECM field lacks where there is no system development method that helps in selecting and implementing the ECM system. A case study is applied to validate the proposed framework.

Chapter 16

Fausto Pedro García Márquez, University of Castilla-La Mancha, Spain
Alberto Pliego Mangurán, University of Castilla-La Mancha, Spain
Noor Zaman, King Faisal University, Saudi Arabia

A fault tree analysis (FTA) is presented as a qualitative method for studying the state of the WT as a system considering to its different sub-systems. The quantitative analysis of the FTA is done by Binary Diagram Decision (BDD). The size of the BDD generated by the transformation from FTA to BDD will depend of the ordering of the FTA events. This work employed the top-down-left-right, the level, and the "and" methods for listing the events. Finally, a classification of the events is done based on their importance measures. The importance measures has been calculated by the Birnbaum (1969), Critically and Structural heuristic methods. A comparative analysis is done, and the main results are presented.

Chapter 17

Qazi Mudassar Ilyas, King Faisal University, Saudi Arabia

This chapter describes the semantic approach: Semantic Web applications which promise to make the content on the World Wide Web understandable, thus enabling creation of an agent based web where automated programs can accomplish a variety of tasks that involve interpretation of the content and are not possible with existing web technologies. The chapter also gives a brief introduction to the Semantic Web and components common to all Semantic Web applications.

Chapter 18

Arshad Siddiqi, Institute of Business Administration, Pakistan

This chapter describes about knowledge management, the methodological formulation of strategies and practices which are deployed by the businesses and organizations. The chapter also identifies, defines, develops, and utilizes the Tacit and Explicit information within the organization for better use of developing and marketing new products and ideas.

Chapter 19

Muneer Ahmad, King Faisal University, Saudi Arabia
Noor Zaman, King Faisal University, Saudi Arabia
Low Tang Jung, University Technology PETRONAS, Malaysia
Fausto Pedro García Márquez, University of Castilla-La Mancha, Spain

This chapter discusses access control to multi level security documents, as well as how organizations around the globe intend to apply security levels over their confidential documents to protect from unauthorized use. Some numbered access control approaches have been proposed within this study, and the chapter also presents an overview of a robust software engineering approach for access control to multi-level security documents. The access control system incorporates stages including data refinement, text comprehension, understanding of multi-stage protection, and application levels.

This chapter looks into evolution of information security, the current impetus towards boundary-less enterprises, federated identities, the contemporary standards, need for federal governments to be involved in information security, ethics, and privacy concerns. With such a gamut of influencing forces, information security needs to be inbuilt with SDLC as a natural process rather than as an afterthought. The chapter also covers information security trends in relation to cloud, mobile devices, bring your own device.

In this chapter, two important trends are discussed in modern software engineering (SE) regarding the utilization of Knowledge Management (KM) and information retrieval (IR). The chapter also introduces the fundamental concepts of KM theory, practice, and mainly describes the aspects of knowledge management that are valuable to software development organizations and how a KM system for such an organization can be implemented. The chapter further describes how information retrieval (IR) can plays a vital role in SE.

This chapter discusses the ethical issue of transparency. Transparency is being considered an indispensable ingredient in social accountability and necessary for preserving and guaranteeing ethical and fair processes. The chapter describes importance of transparency issues and challenges faced to implement transparence in software systems for distributed work groups.

Semantic Web was proposed to make the content machine-understandable by developing ontologies to capture domain knowledge and annotating content with this domain knowledge. The author is focusing the Semantic Web role for several domains in general and specially about ontologies. This chapter discusses how ontologies can be used in various stages of system development life cycle.

Preface

INTRODUCTION

Information Systems and Software Development is a very dynamic, grooming, and important research area of today's technology. It provides the finest and the fastest way for solving the typical problems. Designing, developing, implementing, and functioning a system involves a wide range of disciplines and many application-specific constraints. To make sense of and take full advantage of these systems, an excellent approach is needed, as software development plays a major role for successfully run of information systems and also a good segment of researchers are focusing on this area. Although this field is mature in many aspects, the main issue with this technology is related to its concrete link between software development and information systems, as it is a highly important factor as all functional requirements are based on it. Researchers have suggested so many different ways for the best use of information systems and software developments. But it still need to be consider more, for getting more accurate and precise results by applying new trends and techniques including merging the concepts of both.

This book aims to provide a comprehensive reference for Information Systems and Software Developments by covering all important topics including introduction, information systems and software development life cycle, systems and software processes, functional and non-functional requirements, managing software development and software quality, metrics and technology. In addition *Software Development Techniques for Constructive Information Systems Design* will focus on research and experience that could contribute to the improvement of information systems and software development practices. The book's scope includes methods, techniques, and technology to better engineer software and manage its development. It is divided into two sections and with each section, extends the growing literature on the emerging technologies and innovations would be covered in the field of Software development techniques and Information System Design. Thus, it would not only serve as a reference for information systems and software development area, but it would also become a reference for new innovations in Software Development and Information System Development.

This book contains 23 excellent chapters authored by a group of internationally experienced professionals and researchers in the field of software engineering, information system, and system analysis and design. Contributors also include industry experienced and younger authors, creating a value-added constellation of dynamic authors. Concerning the environments from which the contributions are presented, the chapters came from academia, research institutions, and industry.

ORGANIZATION OF BOOK

This book is designed to cover a wide range of topics in the field of software engineering and information systems. It includes two sections that provide a comprehensive reference for software engineering and information systems by covering all important topics, including an introduction, Introduction and Overview of Information Systems and Software Development, information systems and software development life cycle, systems and software processes, functional and non-functional requirements, diagrams and representations, managing software development, software quality, metrics and technology, Structural (non functional) Testing, Ethics Privacy and Information Security, Data and Knowledge management and Project Planning. Each chapter is designed to be as a stand-alone as possible; the reader can focus on the interested topics only. The chapters are described briefly as follows.

Section 1: Software Development Methodologies and Techniques

Chapter 1 describes the requirements for e-selection technology to be of practical use for any company. Chapter focuses on different e- techniques, and identified related e- hiring issues. The chapter further provides a conclusion to focus e-techniques web-based technologies and stated that web-based technologies should primarily support the core day-to-day work activities rather than be user-friendly or provide additional functionality.

Chapter 2 focuses on the conceptual database design evolution, by introducing concepts which are common to both information systems and software engineering researches. An optimization algorithm of partitioning, based on the decomposition of objects and on the inheritance of attributes, is proposed and extended. The extended algorithm, which defines a formal constructive mapping from conceptual to logical database models, aims to show how some updates reflecting modifications occurring in the real life can affect the conceptual database design.

Chapter 3 presents a survey on the most relevant software development practices that are used nowadays to build software products for the web, with security built in. It starts by presenting three of the most relevant Secure Software Development Lifecycles, which are complete solutions that can be adopted by development companies: the CLASP, the Microsoft Secure Development Lifecycle and the Software Security Touchpoints. This chapter also discusses other relevant initiatives that can be integrated into existing development practices, which can be used to build and maintain safer software products: the OpenSAMM, the BSIMM, the SAFECode and the Securosis.

Chapter 4 describes suitable quality practices which could not only support development of a good quality Software product but also linked up well with the strategic needs of the organizational business. It focuses industry requirements for quality practices of software development, then presented a framework which links Information System's development process improvement with strategic needs of an organization. It also covers the process improvement plan and use of different software development methodologies in multimodal process improvement scenarios.

Chapter 5 Project management is a key activity to manage project's objectives, timeline, cost, roles of the participants and other challenges like estimating, planning, scheduling, budget monitoring, resource management, and documentation. This chapter briefs about issues related to project management and provides knowledge about different software that can be used in project management and diagramming to overcome project management issues.

Chapter 6 focuses the emerging role of Cloud computing and its impact on software development methodologies. It briefs about the trend of cloud computing and new responsibilities which are linked with software development methodologies with respect to this new change of cloud computing environment from client server architecture.

Chapter 7 provides knowledge of the features and purposes of information. It also discusses the role of information system for developing a new system using System Development Life Cycle (SDLC). It also analyzed the concept of information quality to make a new system uses the different phases of SDLC.

Chapter 8 author propose a "Cybernetic Planning Framework" (CPF), which combines the diversity of educational theories and practices, yielding in a common basis for their inclusion. Chapter focuses on Second Life's qualitative characteristics that can utilize to construct a "teaching-organizational" framework, which is essential for planning effective and meaningful distance learning courses. This gain averred a "cybernetic model," in which enhanced pedagogical authorities and principles of Contemporary Learning Theories that previous studies carried out in Second Life.

Chapter 9 describes about Information Systems its complexity and importance. As the Information Systems are to be using the most advanced development tools and methodology, it must be simple for the users to understand, comprehend and use they should be capable of performing all the functions necessary to perform a tasks efficiently.

Chapter 10 describes Agile Interactive Software Development Process Models for Crowd Source Projects, which are very flexible in considering previous project parameters assume somewhat stable team and project structures. Author investigate all traditional project characteristics, elaborate on all those elements that should be modified to fit the open competition agile structure. Author use several case studies to demonstrate management issues related to managing software projects in open competitions.

Chapter 11 discusses 'Software Engineering life cycle, history and software architecture' as well as foundation of Information Engineering and Information System. It describes the software lifecycle phases and how to make effective use of various technical methods by applying effective technical and other efficient methods at the right time. This chapter shows Information Engineering Life Cycle' and discuss the 'key phrases' for Information Engineering as well as Information System.

Section 2: Advanced Topics in Software Engineering

Chapter 12 author introduce a novel model-driven perspective on secure software engineering, which integrates seamlessly software security analysis with traditional software development activities. A systematic security engineering process that starts in the early stages of the software development process and spans the entire software lifecycle is presented. Fundamental software security concepts and analysis techniques are also introduced, and several illustrative examples are presented, with focus on security requirements and risk analysis.

Chapter 13 explains the major objectives of a security policy, with focus on how applications that can protect data at all access points can be developed. Access control models and their known issues are discussed. From a security policy prospective, the security design principles and modeling using the UML are also discussed. In addition, an informal discussion on potential software security metrics that can be used for security measurement and finally, a discussion on security testing involving the use of metrics, are discussed.

Chapter 14 a comparative analysis has been presented for sequence analysis and comparative analysis best approaches has been reported along with some notions about tools, techniques, methodologies and algorithms used for sequence analysis. The overall objective is to highlight the significance of underlying problems and existing solutions for analysis. Best approximation can only be achieved by comparing and identifying the optimal pathway for destination. It is commonly observed that one computational solution can't be guaranteed as an optimal solution for sequence NP hard problems, different and diverse solutions can lead to more significant result.

Chapter 15 Enterprise systems development approaches can be classified into development-centric and procurement centric approaches. Based on the component-based system development methodology (CBSD), chapter proposed a procurement-centric framework to develop enterprise content management (ECM) system. Adopting CBSD to develop ECM system avoids the drawbacks of the development-centric approaches, and remedies the ECM field lacks where there is no system development method that helps in selecting and implementing the ECM system. A case study is applied to validate the proposed framework.

Chapter 16 A fault tree analysis (FTA) is presented as a qualitative method for studying the state of the WT as a system considering to its different sub-systems. The quantitative analysis of the FTA is done by Binary Diagram Decision (BDD). The size of the BDD generated by the transformation from FTA to BDD will depend of the ordering of the FTA events. This chapter describes the the top-down-left-right, the level and the "and" methods for listing the events. Finally, a classification of the events is done based on their importance measures. The importance measures has been calculated by the Birnbaum, Critically and Structural heuristic methods. A comparative analysis is done and the main results are presented.

Chapter 17 describes about Semantic approach, Semantic web applications which promises to make the content on World Wide Web machine understandable thus enabling creation of an agent based web where automated programs can accomplish a variety of tasks that involve interpretation of the content and are not possible with existing web technologies. Chapter also gives a brief introduction to the semantic web and components common to all semantic web applications.

Chapter 18 describes knowledge management, the methodological formulation of strategies and practices which are deployed by the businesses and organization identify, define, develop and utilize the Tacit and Explicit information within the organization for better use of developing and marketing new products and ideas.

Chapter 19 briefed about an access control to multi level security documents. How organizations around the globe intend to apply security levels over their confidential documents to protect from unauthorized use. Some numbered access control approaches have been proposed with this study, and also chapter presents an overview of a robust software engineering approach for access control to multi-level security documents. The access control system incorporates stages including data refinement, text comprehension, understanding of multi-stage protection and application levels.

Chapter 20 presents evolution of information security, current impetus towards boundary less enterprises, federated identities, the contemporary standards, need for federal governments to be involved in information security, ethics and privacy concerns. With such a gamut of influencing forces, information security needs to be inbuilt with SDLC as a natural process rather than as an afterthought. chapter also covers information security trends in relation to cloud, mobile devices, bring your own device. Convergence of information security with risk management and business process continuity.

Chapter 21 two important trends are discussed in modern software engineering (SE) regarding the utilization of Knowledge Management (KM) and information retrieval (IR). Chapter also introduces the fundamental concepts of KM theory, practice and mainly describes the aspects of knowledge management that are valuable to software development organizations and how can a KM system for such an organization be implemented. Chapter further describes how information retrieval (IR) can plays a vital role in SE.

Chapter 22 discusses the ethical issue of transparency. Transparency is being considered an indispensable ingredient in social accountability and necessary for preserving and guaranteeing ethical and fair processes. Chapter describes importance of transparency issues and challenges faced to implement transparence in software systems for distributed work groups.

Chapter 23 Semantic web was proposed to make the content machine-understandable by developing ontologies to capture domain knowledge and annotating content with this domain knowledge. Author is focusing the Semantic web role for several domains in general and specially about ontologies. This chapter discusses how ontologies can be used in various stages of system development life cycle. Ontologies can be used to support requirements engineering phase in identifying and fixing inconsistent, incomplete and ambiguous requirement. They can also be used to model the requirements and assist in requirements management and validation. During software design and development stages, ontologies can help software engineers in finding suitable components, managing documentation of APIs and coding support. Ontologies can help in system integration and evolution process by aligning various databases with the help of ontologies capturing knowledge about database schema and aligning them with concepts in ontology.

Khalid A. Buragga
King Faisal University, Saudi Arabia

Noor Zaman
King Faisal University, Saudi Arabia

Section 1
Software Development Methodologies and Techniques

Chapter 1
Determining the Requirements for E–Selection in a Small Recruitment Company:
Using the Regulative Cycle

Tanya Bondarouk
University of Twente, The Netherlands

Huub J. M. Ruël
Windesheim University of Applied Sciences, The Netherlands

Paul Timmermans
University of Twente, The Netherlands

ABSTRACT

The requirements for e-selection technology to be of practical use for Company T have been investigated. Company T's main business is in identifying and seconding personnel, especially in the technical sector, and it had been anticipating a shortage in the supply of candidates. This served as the initial problem definition for this research. In order to cope with the expected situation, speed and accuracy were seen as of major importance in adopting e-selection. Using interviews, eleven issues were identified across two topics: namely, the use of web-based technologies, i.e., speed, and the use of personal characteristics, i.e., accuracy. These eleven potential problems were ranked using a focus group. Then, based on contemporary literature, solutions were proposed to counter these problems. Combining these solutions has led to a design in which it is proposed that valid psychological instruments should be applied and interpreted by skilled professionals. Further, extensive knowledge sharing is seen as vital when dealing with the large amount of tacit knowledge associated with the work at Company T. Finally, it was concluded that the web-based technologies should primarily support the core day-to-day work activities rather than be user-friendly or provide additional functionality.

DOI: 10.4018/978-1-4666-3679-8.ch001

INTRODUCTION

The application of new technologies to aspects of human resource management (HRM) has shown an increasing trend, and HRM is expected to continue to be affected by continuing technological changes (Ruël, et al, 2004; Strohmeier, 2007). However, most of such new technologies are applied to basic HRM practices (Lepak and Snell, 1998; Ruël, et al, 2004; Wright and Dyer, 2000). The reasons seen for implementing new technologies were mainly related to reducing costs, by improving efficiency and effectiveness, and to removing recruiter bias through far-reaching automation (Chapman and Webster, 2003; McManus and Ferguson, 2003).

These trends were being experienced at a small recruitment company in the eastern part of the Netherlands, referred to here as Company T. Their main business is in the secondment of personnel, especially in the technical sector (especially mechanical and electrical engineers). In addition, they offer a wide range of HRM consultancy activities to organizations, again mainly in the technical sector. With five full-time employees and two part-time employees they were considered a rather small player in the secondment business. However, by being small, they do not suffer from excessive bureaucracy. This allows them to react quickly to changes in the market, as well as being able to quickly adopt new technologies and apply them to their business processes (Anderson, 2003).

Indeed, they had already applied various web-based technologies to enhance their business processes. The first of such technologies was the use of an extensive database, and database management tools, alongside a customer relations management tool. Next, they expanded their armory to include the use of e-recruitment and web portals. However, the founder of the company was expecting difficulties in the near future; a significant shortage of appropriately educated employees, or candidates, with technical skills. Furthermore, Company T did not believe that their current set of instruments would be sufficient to cope with the expected difficulties. As such, Company T was trying to find a way to adapt and to survive.

Essentially, Company T needs to be more flexible to secure a steady supply of candidates in order to be able to stay alive and thrive (Bartram, 2000; Spector, 2008) while, at the same time, it needs to work more efficiently and effectively. It is possible that new HRM technologies could be deployed in order to assist Company T in these times of change. Secondly, an increased emphasis on the other personal characteristics (O) of candidates, beyond their technical skills, such as personality and ambition might also be beneficial. The effects of personality, and other latent individual qualities, on work-related aspects, e.g. performance, have been mapped quite extensively over recent years (Gellatly, 1996; Gevers, et al, 2006; McAdams, 2009). In addition, two work-related trends have put a greater emphasis on the softer aspects of an individual: working in teams (Keller, 2001; O'Leary-Kelly, et al, 1994); and assertive employees taking charge of their own careers (Baruch, 2004). Thus, greater emphasis is put on 'other' personal characteristics (O) in addition to the more traditional components of a candidate: their knowledge, skills, and abilities (KSA) (Spector, 2008).

These other personal characteristics were not yet being applied in the selection process in a mature way at Company T. Further, web-based technologies were not being deployed to the full extent possible to support the measurement of other personal characteristics, i.e. through psychological testing. As such, it was crucial to select technologies that would fit with the applications already running as well as with the current business process (Kehoe, et al, 2004). Here, attention was placed on e-selection. This concept was defined as the application of (web-based) information technology for the execution and support of the personnel selection process by the employee and/or the organization (Chapman and Webster, 2003; Ruël, et al, 2004; Strohmeier, 2007). The goal of this research was to explore *the requirements of an e-Selection tool that would contribute to improving the selection process at Company T.*

This research makes several contributions. Firstly, efficiency and effectiveness were *not* found to be the main drivers for applying e-selection in the context of the study; rather, the main focus was on the core functionality of the tools to be applied. Maybe reducing costs, by increasing efficiency and effectiveness, is not the true driver in implementing e-selection after all. Other factors may determine the degree to which cost reduction is a driver. In addition, the decision to deploy e-selection, notionally used to reduce recruiter bias, was also found to be influenced by other factors, and removing bias was not considered a real driver in this context. Issues such as enforced laws or the culture of a particular country can influence the extent to which e-selection is deployed to reduce recruiter bias. Another contribution made is in highlighting the continuing gap between research and practice. For example, issues such as response distortion in psychological testing were still thought to be a problem by our interviewees, whereas the contemporary literature indicates that such issues are not a major issue provided valid tests are employed. Through practice-based research, the gap between practice and theory could be reduced, at least in those isolated cases where such research is conducted.

On a practical note, a list of problems associated with e-selection at Company T was constructed, and these problems were then prioritized. With such a prioritization, Company T can allocate its resources efficiently and effectively when addressing these problems during the implementation of e-selection. Regarding the two main topics, i.e. the increased use of personal characteristics and of web-based technologies in the selection process, the recommendations made were that valid psychological tests be deployed and that specific knowledge be added to the web-based technologies in use. In addition, knowledge-sharing was found to be instrumental in the transfer of tacit knowledge, and was found to occur amongst employees in

their day-to-day work at Company T. In practical terms, it was suggested that Company T could develop in two directions to remain competitive in the future: firstly by deploying a wide array of e-recruitment and e-selection tools in order to select suitable candidates for their customers and, secondly, by offering consultancy services to their customers concerning the deployment of far-reaching e-services. Overall, the manner in which Company T makes use of digitally stored knowledge, skills, abilities and other (KSAO) measures will determine its longevity.

THEORETICAL BACKGROUND

This research was driven by a practical problem and was aimed toward improving the performance of business processes in a particular context (Heusinkveld and Reijers, 2009; Romme and Endenburg, 2006). Therefore, the approach taken was that of the problem-solving cycle, or the regulative cycle (Van Aken, et al, 2007; Van Strien, 1997). Following this regulative cycle led to covering issues of both rigor as well as relevance (van Aken, 2005; Shrivastava, 1987). However, not all the steps of the regulative cycle are reported in this paper: as is common in most business problem solving projects (Van Aken, et al, 2007), the implementation of the final design, along with its evaluation, is left to Company T.

The steps that were followed, and the corresponding actions taken, are shown in Table 1 (based on Van Aken, et al, 2007).

PROBLEM DEFINITION: RESULTS OF THE INTERVIEWS

Semi-structured interviews were used since these allow comparison between respondents as well as the possibility to clarify and extend the statements made by respondents (Kvale and Brinkmann, 2009). The interview questions were all open-

Table 1. Steps of the regulative cycle which were followed along with a theoretical description and practical application

Phase	Theoretical description	Practical application
Problem mess	Starting point of a problem solving project. This is an initial problem constructed by the organization	Anticipated shortage of employees with proper technical skills in the eastern part of the Netherlands
Problem definition	Analysis of the initial problem which leads to a formal definition of the problem to be investigated.	Using interviews to determine what kind of problems might be encountered when deploying psychological testing and web-based technologies in the selection process at Company T
Analysis and diagnosis	The actual problem will be analyzed. This leads to input for the diagnosis. Specific knowledge concerning the context and problem is created here	Using a focus group session in order to determine the relative importance of the problems identified in the problem definition
Plan of action	Based on contemporary literature and context specific information, a solution is designed. In addition, an implementation plan is constructed.	

ended in order to stimulate as much detail in the responses as possible. Before each interview, the respondents were told what the goal of the interview was, that information would be handled anonymously, and that they would receive a transcript of the interview. The respondents could then indicate if they felt their answers were interpreted correctly or if corrections were necessary.

The sample of interviewees consisted of practitioners working at Company T plus some of their business clients, as detailed in Table 2. The sample included five employees of Company T, plus an additional employee from an aligned company. In addition, three interviews were conducted with business clients of Company T.

The interviews were analyzed using the transcriptions. In interpreting the information obtained from the interviews we took into account that the information was socially and actively created, and thus inter-subjective rather than subjective or objective (Kvale and Brinkmann, 2009). Using the selective reading approach, i.e. seeking statements or phrases that were deemed of particular interest in the final transcriptions of the interviews, the contents of the interviews were examined (Van Manen, 1990). The contents of the statements or phrases were then coded, driven by the data, to create categories of information (Gibbs, 2007; Strauss and Corbin, 1990). Here, statements and phrases which included terms, or references to terms, such as selection, personality, or software packages were singled out. These terms, and other related words, were considered as relating to the central theme of this paper. Next, the statements or phrases were compressed into shorter formulations, or thoughts of the coder, in order to grasp the main point of the statement (Kvale and Brinkmann, 2009).

Table 2. Interview and background information regarding the interview respondents

No.	Date	Time	Location	Duration	Sex	Age	Education	Occupation
1	27-4	10:00 am	At work	27 minutes	M	26	HVE	Recruiter
2	27-4	11:00 am	At work	28 minutes	M	38	IVE	Recruiter
3	27-4	2:00 pm	At work	30 minutes	M	47	HVE	Recruiter
4	28-4	11:00 am	At work	35 minutes	M	46	HVE	Recruiter
5	28-4	2:00 pm	At work	25 minutes	M	30	IVE	Recruiter
6	18-5	1:30 pm	At work	26 minutes	V	27	HE	Recruiter
7	20-5	09:00 am	At work	75 minutes	M	Undisclosed	Undisclosed	Controller
8	23-5	09:00 am	At work	75 minutes	V	Undisclosed	Undisclosed	Coordinator
9	1-6	1:00 pm	At work	50 minutes	V	Undisclosed	Undisclosed	Personnel manager

As was made clear in the initial problem definition, there was a heavy reliance in Company T on the use of web-based applications. However, their usability and user-friendliness left something to be desired. Also, an emphasis was put on the more latent aspects of an individual, such as their personality, social intelligence, and intrinsic motivation, even though these aspects were not yet fully incorporated in the business processes at Company T.

From the interviews, two cause and effect diagrams were constructed in which the initial problem definition was displayed in relation to possible causes and consequences, divided into the two areas of interest. Essentially, the initial problem proved to have several consequences, as can be seen in Figure 1, concerning the use of personal characteristics, and Figure 2 concerning the application of web-based technologies. These cause and effect diagrams have been discussed with the founder of Company T. It was explained how, and why, these cause and effect diagrams were derived from the initial problem definition and the subsequent interviews. Agreement concerning these cause and effect diagrams was reached.

Personal Characteristics of Job Seekers

Other personal characteristics (O) are those aspects of an individual which do not reflect their knowledge, skills, or abilities but that are relevant to working in a job such as personality, motivation, physical characteristics, interests, and prior experiences (Spector, 2008). These characteristics have been linked to job-related aspects such as performance (Gellatly, 1996; Locke and Latham, 2002; McAdams, 2009; Peeters, 2006), the ability to work in teams (Gevers, et al, 2006), absenteeism (McAdams, 2009; Van Eerde and Thierry, 1996), and stress (Dale and Fox, 2008; McAdams, 2009). At Company T, each of the interviewees acknowledged the need for a greater emphasis on these other personal characteristics of a candidate in addition to their knowledge, skills, and abilities. This is not to imply that such personal characteristics were not being already considered, only that the degree of such usage was increasing.

The importance of these other personal characteristics became more apparent after analyzing the interviews held with the business partners. We

Figure 1. Cause and effect diagram of an increased emphasis on other personal characteristics during the selection process

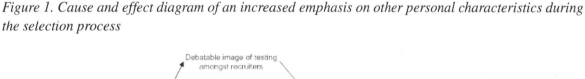

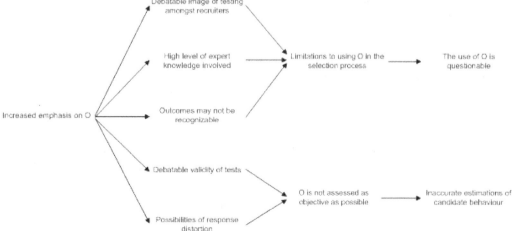

Figure 2. Cause and effect diagram of the application of web-based technologies in the selection process

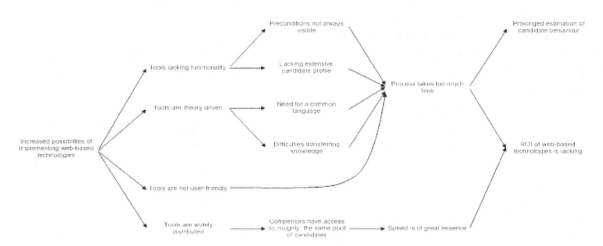

saw that the KSA qualities of an individual were regarded increasingly as prerequisites rather than as a way of distinguishing between good and excellent candidates. The other personal characteristics (O) had largely taken over the distinguishing role. However, the respondents were not deploying reliable instruments to measure these. Thus, overall, at Company T an increased use of objective measures to assess O, in response to an increased emphasis on O, was not observed.

From the interviews, it became clear that some of the respondents felt they could make a judgment similar to that of a psychological test, i.e. a self-report, or do even better. In other words, they did not see the added value of deploying such tests. The judgment of the respondents was that evaluating the impact of these other personal characteristics was tacit, i.e. such information is explicit, context specific, and difficult to share (Hislop, 2005).

Further, the interviewees feared that an increase in the use of such latent aspects would lead to an increase in the provision of socially desirable answers. Such a fear may be justified since the increased use of such aspects has been associated with increased opportunities to provide socially desired answers (Chapman and Webster, 2003;

Spector, 2008). While providing socially desirable answers may be an indication that the test taker is aware of the requirements of an organization, it is considered unlikely that one can act out of character over a lengthy period (Spector, 2008). Furthermore, a concern had been raised that the use of such personal characteristics in the selection process might lead to the exclusion of excellent individuals who are reluctant to disclose such information to organizations (Hausknecht, et al, 2004). Another aspect raised by the interviewees was that individuals might not recognize themselves in the outcome of a psychological test. Finally, we saw that rejecting candidates based solely on their other personal characteristics was more or less taboo within an organization where the emphasis had been on the technical knowledge of a candidate.

Overall, the issues raised by the interviewees were an indication that the mapping of individuals could be done in a more objective manner than was done previously. The process of selecting employees was not as objective as it could, and should, be, and there was a need to remove recruiter bias (Chapman and Webster, 2003; Stone-Romero, 2005).

Applying Web-Based Technologies

Besides the greater emphasis on other personal characteristics, there has been a general increase in the application of web-based technologies, such as databases and database management tools, and recruitment portals. These web-based technologies are replacing the more traditional methods of recruiting employees (Stone, et al, 2005) and they are changing the HRM field in both technical and developmental ways (Hempel, 2004). In other words, these new technologies are shaping our view of HRM, despite these technologies being far from foolproof.

The entry barrier to using new technologies is rather low. Deploying a database, connected to some customer relation management (CRM) tool, or to an even more extensive enterprise resource planning (ERP) tool, can easily be achieved by calling in a software manufacturer. As a result, some organizations are deploying new technologies just to have a tech-savvy look (Chapman and Webster, 2003). On the other hand, due to the ease of distributing and applying such technologies, those looking for a job can easily upload their data to numerous databases or job-boards using the internet. Even those with limited resources can gain access to a database and a website which will automatically fill in the database. Even though it takes time to grasp the possibilities of the various technologies, this will eventually lead to a situation in which competitors have access to, more or less, the same pool of candidates. While this does not inherently have to be a problem, it will force organizations to make solid decisions more quickly in order to stay ahead of competition.

Several current tools lack usability, functionality, and user-friendliness. In order to pre-select from a large pool of applicants, preconditions need to be easily accessible but this is often not the case. Especially job boards, such as monsterboard. com, either lack information within candidate profiles, or such information is hard to find. This may be due to not having a uniform method, or format, for entering data across the multitude of online tools, an observation made in several of our interviews. Also, the information provided in CVs and résumés is often tacit, and it is hard, if not impossible, to make such tacit information explicit (Hislop, 2005).

All this leads to the process taking more time than should be necessary since some information needs to be entered manually, or searched manually, and information needs to be extensively interpreted. This is despite one of the reasons for applying web-based technologies being that they will save costs and time. Thus, due to the limited usability, functionality, and user-friendliness, the applications are failing to meet expectations.

Summary of the Interview Outcomes

Based on the interviews, and the subsequent cause and effect diagrams, addressing the increased use of personal characteristics (Figure 1) and of the increased usage of web-based technologies (Figure 2), a number of problems were prioritized. Some of these problems were refined to some extent, for example a single problem "tools lacking functionality" was created combining aspects indicated in the cause and effect diagram in Figure 2. The "problems" taken forward for further research are displayed in Table 3.

ANALYSIS AND DIAGNOSIS

Focus Group

After analyzing the interview transcripts, a plenary discussion session was organized. Through this refinement, a prioritization was established, which was used in coming up with solutions for each of the problems. A focus group seemed ideal for such a goal since one of the prime concerns was to "encourage a variety of viewpoints on the topic

Table 3. Summary of the problems encountered in the selection process at Company T

No.	Issue description
1	Lacking functionality
2	Lacking user-friendliness
3	Tools are widely distributed
4	Access to a common applicant pool
5	Need for a common language
6	Difficulties transferring knowledge
7	Debatable validity of tests
8	Outcomes may not be recognizable
9	Possibilities of response distortion
10	High level of expert knowledge involved
11	Debatable image of testing amongst recruiters

in focus for the group" (Kvale and Brinkmann, 2009, p. 150). The sample in the focus group was nearly the same as for the interviews but with the absence of two external respondents and one Company T employee; thus the focus group was made up of six subjects plus a moderator.

After introducing the goal of the session, and explaining the organizational problems, the session started. The first step was for the members to rank all the identified problems. Such a ranking exercise can prove to be difficult since a large amount of information needs to be processed (Tsiporkova and Boeva, 2006). Next, these rankings were discussed. Here, the moderator highlighted several individual scores and asked the corresponding member why he or she felt the problem was, or was not, considered bothersome. In turn, the other members were asked how they felt about the issue. This resulted in lively discussions concerning each of the problems. The third step for the focus group was for the members to explain how they thought the problems could be tackled, even though this is not usually an aim for a focus group in such an exercise (Kvale and Brinkmann, 2009). Members who rated an issue either very highly or very lowly were initially asked if they could suggest a possible way of coping with the issue, after which this proposition was pot to the other members for their opinions.

Nevertheless, we had to produce a final overall ranking, based on the individual rankings, in order to discriminate between important and less important problems (Chen and Cheng, 2010). We

decided to aggregate individual rankings using the Borda rule since the members had ordered the set of problems, rather than scored them each out of ten for example (Chebotarev, 1994). This involves calculating so-called Borda scores from which an aggregated ranking can be constructed (Truchon, 2008). The first step in calculating Borda scores is to weight the rankings for each member, i.e. the highest ranked issue per member is given $(k-1)$ points, the second highest ranked issue was given $(k-2)$ points until the lowest ranked issue received zero points, with k here equal to eleven - the total number of problems. From these values, Borda scores are calculated by summing the weighted values for each issue across all members.

A final ranking was then created by putting the issue with the highest Borda score first, and so on. In Table 4, the ranking by each member, and also the weighting factor per rank, are shown. For example, R_1 is the highest rank and thus the weighing factor is 10 (11-1). The aggregated rankings are shown in Table 5.

As can be seen in Table 5, problems 4 and 7 had the same Borda score. In order to resolve this tie, we considered both their means and standard deviations. It was clear, as can be seen from Table 6, that there was a higher level of consensus on problem 4, i.e. it had a smaller standard deviation, and, further, it had a higher mean. As a result, issue 4 was prioritized ahead of issue 7.

Below, the problems are discussed based on the final, aggregated, rankings.

Table 4. Final ranking by member of the problems: M_x are the members, R_x are the rankings, and W is the weighing factor per rank

	M_1	M_2	M_3	M_4	M_5	M_6	W
R_1	7	11	3	7	7	9	10
R_2	4	10	6	9	11	9	9
R_3	3	4	5	8	10	10	8
R_4	5	3	4	10	9	11	7
R_5	11	9	11	4	8	5	6
R_6	9	6	8	3	2	6	5
R_7	6	5	10	2	1	7	4
R_8	10	1	9	11	5	3	3
R_9	8	8	2	1	4	4	2
R_{10}	2	2	1	5	6	2	1
R_{11}	1	7	6	6	3	1	0

Table 5. Aggregated ranking based on the Borda scores per issue

I_{11}	I_9	I_{10}	I_4	I_7	I_3	I_8	I_5	I_6	I_2	I_1
41	40	39	34	34	33	32	29	24	14	10

Table 6. Mean scores and standard deviations for each of the eleven problems (N = 6)

Issue description	μ	σ	Issue no.
Debatable image of testing amongst recruiters	7.83	2.483	11
Possibilities of response distortion	7.67	2.582	9
High level of expert knowledge involved	7.50	2.429	10
Access to a common applicant pool	6.67	3.011	4
Debatable validity of tests	5.00	4.899	7
Tools are widely distributed	6.50	3.619	3
Outcomes may not be recognizable	6.33	2.944	8
Need for a common language	5.83	2.639	5
Difficulties transferring knowledge	5.00	3.225	6
Lacking user-friendliness	4.00	1.897	2
Lacking functionality	2.67	1.633	1

Debatable Image of Testing amongst Recruiters

The focus group members perceived psychological testing to have an added value when mapping the personal characteristics of an individual. Thus, the viewpoint that a human resource manager could predict future behavior just as well as a psychological test could was not shared by the focus group. While people are capable of making judgments concerning the personal characteristics of another person, such judgments were thought to be less accurate and less well-founded than those from a psychological test, as was noted by one of the members: "in a global sense, I can do the same; however, I am not able to back up my claims" (Respondent 5). Also, psychological tests, and their outcomes in terms of personal characteristics, were thought to provide insight into which person might be the most appropriate in a specific context.

Further, the members felt that possible problems encountered when interacting with customers who did not believe in the usefulness of such tests were of minor importance. They believed that by demonstrating the outcomes of such tests, people would be convinced of their merit. The members did indicate however that they felt that people who have had bad experiences with psychological tests in the past would be less easily convinced. Overall, the members felt that it was important to have other people recognize the added value of such tests since that would only be beneficial if properly deployed.

Possibility of Response Distortion

The members of the focus group felt that, for the outcomes of a psychological test to be useful, it should be impossible for candidates to provide socially desirable answers. Especially when aspects such as personal characteristics are being measured, this was perceived as essential. Otherwise, "you still don't know who the person is" (Respondent 4). If the outcomes are not truthful, the use of such tools was considered a waste of time, money, and effort. It was noted that, if such tests are not as accurate as practitioners would like, their added value will be rather low in a practical context.

It was felt that if it is not possible to ban socially desirable answers from a psychological test, then the test should indicate that the answers provided are possibly socially desirable rather than truthful. Firstly, being able to detect socially desirable answers was thought to be a deterrent if this was communicated to test takers. Secondly, the members believed that indications of possible socially desired answers would allow them to engage in a constructive discussion with a test taker in order to get at the truth.

High Level of Expert Knowledge Involved

As explained at the start of the group session, the knowledge obtained from such tests has some degree of tacitness, such that high levels of conscientiousness may be attributed to a certain behavior by one individual, but to another behavior by another, even though a definition exists. One of the members commented that it was hard to grasp the idea that others may not know what you consider as common knowledge. However, this aspect was, eventually, recognized by the focus group as a genuine issue.

It transpired that the group members felt a need for practitioners who were able to interpret psychological tests and give practical advice based on such tests: "One should be able to give solid explanations concerning the outcomes of a test" (Respondent 7). Further, it was noted that a person who uses, and shares, such information needs to be careful. For some practitioners, using information from psychological tests in a negative manner was thought to lower their perceived added value.

Access to a Common Pool of Applicants

The notion of competitors deploying more-or-less identical tools was perceived as resulting in competitors having access to roughly the same pool of applicants. Even though this problem is, in essence, an effect of competitors having easy access to the same tools, the members of the focus group rated this problem as more important than that specific issue.

During the discussion, the members reached agreement once when one of them commented that it was not the access that matters, but rather what is done with the pool of applicants. For example, as was noted by one of the members, an applicant may register at several secondment agencies and, if others can "provide a superior service" (Respondent 6), they will likely make the money for getting the jobseeker work. In other words, the relationship established between a jobseeker and an agency was perceived as more important than just having candidates in the database.

Debatable Validity of Tests

Rather than considering the more traditional trade-off between validity, reliability, and costs when considering what kind of psychological test to use, the members of the focus group considered the goal of deploying psychological tests to be critical. Initially, some members felt that less objective tools could be used when the goal is to obtain only somewhat superficial insights into a person. The outcomes of a test could be then used to trigger an applicant into expressing themselves more freely in a conversation. On the other hand, when the intention is to make decisions based on a personality inventory or intrinsic motivation test, for example, then a tool needs to be as objective as possible. Other members however argued that, even where the objectives do not have far-reaching consequences, it is dangerous to apply poorly validated tools. Overall, it was believed that, regardless of levels of validity, "a test should be followed by a personal conversation in order to make the person feel good about the test and its outcomes" (Respondent 2).

Further, using personality inventories in order to decide whether an applicant was suitable for a job was perceived as legitimate only when it was clear what kind of personality was required and when the personal characteristics had been measured using objective tools. Moreover, the members felt that one of the most important aspects of psychological testing was discussing the test outcomes with the test taker.

Tools are Widely Distributed

The central thought of the members of the focus group was that this problem should be seen as a given: and it is not about what technologies are applied, but how they are applied. It was felt that "everything can be copied, given enough time" (Respondent 4).

However, even though competitors were seen as having easy access to the same tools, it was still felt that new technologies were needed in order to stay ahead of the competition. Competitive advantage was perceived as being gained in two ways: by deploying state-of-the-art technologies and by devising innovative ways to exploit such technologies to the fullest.

Outcomes May Not Be Recognizable

An important aspect of deploying psychological testing should be, according to the focus group, that the test takers recognize themselves in the outcomes of a test. The members of the focus group thought something would be amiss if such recognition did not materialize. A number of situations were proposed where this could happen including the applicant not understanding the questions, not answering the questions truthfully, and the picture one had of oneself being inaccurate.

Discussing the outcomes of a test with the test taker was thought to be the first step in uncovering what had gone wrong. One of the members commented that, if an applicant did not recognize themself, then this might be an indication that this person is not appropriate for the vacancy at hand: "most vacancies require the person to have at least some level of self-reflection, and such a situation might suggest this was lacking" (Respondent 2). However, this vision was not shared by the other members of the focus group. The overall perception was that, if this situation arose, using the outcomes of the test would be questionable.

Need for a Common Language

A strict and rigid way of working was thought to be one of the outcomes of deploying (web-based) technologies in order to ensure a common language,. However, the group members felt that experience with working with the technology might resolve this issue since one of the members noted that "such a systematic way of entering data becomes a way of working" (Respondent 3). Having experience with a tool was perceived as vital in gaining in-depth knowledge about the tool and, as a result, systematic entry would become a way of working. Most of the members did not believe this issue to be of great importance.

However, it was noted by some that, without experience, getting information from a database management system might be a problem. The other members did not perceive this to be an issue. Given that the tacitness of information related to psychological tests was recognized, the moderator was surprised that this issue, and the next, raised so little concern. When raising this point, all the members held to their original statement and no additional comments were made.

Difficulties Transferring Knowledge

Transferring knowledge from one employee to another was not perceived to be an issue. Even though the extent of the tacit knowledge involved in their work was considered very high, the members of the focus group did not foresee major difficulties in transferring such knowledge. Rather, they believed that a lot of tacit knowledge could be made explicit using software packages. An example was given where their current tools allow anyone to track all the communications concerning a particular vacancy or candidate. In addition, comments could be made at crucial moments when decisions are to be made in order to clarify the choices selected.

Nevertheless, as one of the members noted, trying to transfer tacit knowledge, about details and personal feelings, consumes quite some energy which could be put to more effective and efficient use. "In this business, a lot of feelings come into play when making decisions. It is hard to explain decisions based on such feelings experienced only by yourself and not by the person to whom you are explaining the situation" (Respondent 2).

Lack of User-Friendliness

Rather than focusing on problems such as user-friendliness, the main concern of the focus group was on the presence, or absence, of key functionality. Evaluating software on functionality grounds was thought to be more objective than evaluating user-friendliness, which was perceived as very subjective. It was felt that objective measures should

be first and foremost when making a purchasing decision. This was reflected in the comment of one of the members: "whether I have to double-click to open a new page, or just single-click, I don't care as long as I can do with the tools what I want to do" (Respondent 2).

It was acknowledged that a lack of user-friendliness could hamper the efficiency gained in deploying software packages. Such losses of efficiency, due to a lack of user-friendliness, were, however, not thought to be major.

Lack of Functionality

Besides a lack of user-friendliness, lacking certain functionality is also perceived as hampering the potential efficiency gains obtained by deploying software packages. However, the members of the focus group were again mainly focused on the presence of key functions. Even though "the absence of a quick overview of the preconditions of a candidate requires me to spend more time, such additional functionality is not crucial" (Respondent 1). From the discussion, it became clear that their main concern was to get a complete picture of an individual, that all the relevant information could be acquired with the tools: efficiency was not a major concern.

ADVANCED PRIORITIZING

The analysis has revealed the major importance attached to the validity and reliability of the knowledge used in (web-based) technologies. While competitors using the same tools, and having access to a similar pool of applicants, was considered a significant threat, it was also considered as inevitable, and a situation one had to deal with. New and innovative ways of applying technologies should be devised in order to differentiate oneself from the competition. Further, all the knowledge contained in such technologies, or tools, must be findable. User-friendliness and functionality are not as important as being able to find the knowledge one is looking for. Table 7 shows a summary of the problems as explained before.

PLAN OF ACTION (DESIGN)

Literature Review

Based on the findings from the interviews and the focus group, a practical design was constructed for Company T which they can then apply in order to improve their business processes (Van Aken, et al, 2007), that is, the selection process. Contemporary literature was used to find solutions to the problems identified. Here, search engines such as ScienceDirect and PsycINFO were used. Further, specific attention was given to journals such as the Journal of Applied Psychology, Journal of Personality and Social Psychology, Personnel Psychology, and the International Journal of Selection and Assessment. The literature was searched by looking for the problem topics in the title, keywords, and abstract of articles.

Group 1: "Essential" Aspects

Debatable Image of Testing amongst Recruiters

In exploring this problem, the focus was on the gap between research and practice. There are several factors that could explain why psychological tests may not be embraced by HR practitioners (Ryan and Tippins, 2004). Five major factors were identified and translated to the specific context of Company T:

- Due to the use of jargon, some practitioners may not grasp the ideas presented in papers and journals, and do not see the added value of testing.
- Research usually fails to consider context, leading to lower scores and benefits when deploying testing in practice, and subsequently to the abandonment of testing.
- Lack of time to integrate research findings into practice due to continuous pressure.
- Perceptions of practitioners incompatible with research findings.
- Confusing legal requirements leading to avoidance.

Personality inventories are regarded by applicants as the least favorable psychological test when compared with cognitive ability tests, work samples, and interviews (Hausknecht, et al, 2004). However, such perceptions by an applicant of the selection procedure are unlikely to lead to their withdrawal from the selection process (Sackett and Lievens, 2008). In addition, some managers may believe that they become increasingly capable of making sound judgments regarding the predicted behavior of candidates. This usually results in an overreliance on intuition and the rejection of psy-

Table 7. Grouped problems, in descending order of perceived importance

Group	Issue description	No.
1	Debatable image of testing amongst recruiters	11
"Must"	Possibilities of response distortion	9
	High level of expert knowledge involved	10
2	Access to a common applicant pool	4
"Should"	Debatable validity of tests	7
	Tools are widely distributed	3
3	Outcomes may not be recognizable	8
"Could"	Need for a common language	5
	Difficulties transferring knowledge	6
4	Lacking user-friendliness	2
"Perhaps"	Lacking functionality	1

chological tests as a useful aid (Highhouse, 2008). Further, managers tend not to see psychological tests as probabilistic and, as a result, they doubt they can be of use (Highhouse, 2008). Thus, "sound selection procedures are often either not used or are misused in organizations" (Sackett and Lievens, 2008). Nevertheless, in the end, it is argued that structured ways to select employees will always be better than unstructured ways (Ryan and Tippins, 2004). Moreover, when personality information is available, it can be accurately used in selection decisions (Dunn, et al, 1995).

Countering this problem was considered as inherently difficult since there are no obligations to use psychological tests in a selection process, let alone validated tests. Further, there was little need to convince the employees at Company T themselves since they acknowledged the added value of psychological testing, even though they were deploying non-validated tests. However, due to the costs associated with psychological testing, which would have to be passed on to their customers, Company T would have to convince them of the value of testing through it increasing the quality of the service provided. This could possibly be achieved by providing elaborate examples of deployed tests, as well as scientific validations, in easy to understand terms. Furthermore, given the perception that such tests are too analytical, it may be helpful to educate managers as to how psychological tests actually work, that is, that they try to predict future behavior but that they can never fully predict such behavior (Ryan and Tippins, 2004).

The solution proposed by the members of the focus group was to set a branch-wide standard. An increase was observed in the opportunities given to non-psychologists to deploy certain psychological tests, in order to increase the level of usage. As a result, it was thought unlikely that strict regulations will ever be put in place by whatever authority is able to do so. Such regulations are likely to increase the gap between research and practice.

Possibilities of Response Distortion

Response distortion is very possible in self-reporting (Barrick and Mount, 1996). Two major constructs can be distinguished when looking at response distortion (Paulhus and Reid, 1991): self-deception - the tendency to think about oneself favorably, and impression management - a deliberate attempt to create a favorable impression in others. Response distortion can be detrimental to some individuals when rankings are used to shortlist appropriate candidates. Such distortions are considered harmful when an individual is not selected for a follow-up round due to the place being taken by someone who distorted their responses (Stewart, et al, 2010). Thus, false positives may be hired and false negatives overlooked. Both situations lead to money being wasted (Spector, 2008).

In order to detect such response distortions, lie or social desirability scales can be applied. Such scales can be included in the overall personality inventory, and the responses on these scales used to determine the degree to which one has answered in a socially desirable way (Barrick and Mount, 1996). However, the effect of socially desirable answers on the predictive validity of personality inventories, including the Big Five, is actually rather small and not significant (Christiansen, et al, 1994; Hough, et al, 1990; Ones, et al, 1993). Furthermore, self-deception, which this approach would not overcome, has a roughly equal effect on the predictive validity of personality measures as impression management (Barrick and Mount, 1996).

The implications of this earlier research are that one should not determine cut-off scores based on testing current employees since they are less likely than applicants to distort their responses (Barrick and Mount, 1996). Secondly, adjusting tests to address response distortion is not worthwhile since the gain in predictive validity is negligible while the application of such techniques may be hard to defend (Barrick and Mount, 1996). Moreover, relatively few applicants will fake personality inventories in order to look socially desirable (Hough, et al, 1990). Therefore, the removal of applicants who are distorting their responses is unlikely to have a large effect on overall validity (Schmitt and Oswald, 2006). Further, unproctored internet-based testing was not found to be a unique opportunity for response distortion in personality inventories (Arthur Jr., et al, 2010).

Another solution would be to replace self-reporting with another type of measure, such as structured interviews or assessment centers, since one is more likely to misrepresent in a self-report than in a structured interview (Van Iddekinge, et al, 2005). Comparing these options, structured interviews have the danger that applicants will engage in impression management, something that is less likely to succeed in assessment centers (MacFarland, et al, 2005). However, assessment centers are quite expensive and therefore usually only used for filling senior management positions.

Thus, self-reporting would seem sufficient, with response distortion not being a major threat. Nevertheless, one could add lie or social desirability scales to the personality inventory to uncover those being less than honest. Such information could then be used in a structured follow-up interview with the applicant. Furthermore, when unproctored internet testing is used, a proctored retest should take place in order to verify that the applicant themselves took the original test (Tippins et al., 2006).

High Level of Expert Knowledge Involved

Contemporary research shows that almost all knowledge is some combination of tacit and explicit knowledge. Tacit and explicit knowledge are, at least in the practice-based view, regarded as inseparable and mutually constituted (Tsoukas, 1996; Werr and Stjernberg, 2003). Thus, people need to have some level of knowledge already present in order to grasp new knowledge (Gupta and Govindarajan, 2000). Furthermore, knowing is

linked to doing (Blackler, 1995). More precisely: knowledge is needed in order to be able to perform activities, while activities are necessary to use, develop, create, or share knowledge (Hislop, 2005).

As a consequence, it is considered impossible to completely disembody knowledge from a person (Hislop, 2005). This notion has a great impact on this problem since it mainly addresses how to handle the outcomes of psychological tests. As such, determining the outcomes of such a test and the use of such outcomes should involve only knowledgeable individuals who are active in this field. Since training Company T's employees in industrial and organizational psychology, as well as in administering and interpreting psychological tests, did not seem feasible, the proposal was that professionals should be hired or contracted when needed. However, due to the costs involved, an option might be to provide training programs and practical experiences related to a specific test (Boer, et al, 2004; Szulanski, 1996). Furthermore, follow-ups to such training would be required to ensure a certain level of activity in order to develop and create further knowledge.

On balance, it seems best to deploy a professional when working with psychological tests in order to deal with the aspects of tacit and explicit knowledge, as well as of working experience, and perhaps also with legal issues. If, instead, it is decided that an employee should hold this knowledge concerning the administration and interpretation of psychological tests, it seems best to provide educational programs as well as guided practical experiences in order to be able to create, develop, discuss, and use the knowledge provided.

This solution was in line with the ideas of members of the focus group, who felt that the tools applied for objectively mapping personal characteristics should be handled by professionals, i.e. psychologists. Such professionals have the knowledge on how outcomes are to be interpreted and what the consequences of specific outcomes, and combinations of outcomes, are when predicting future behavior. That is, they should deploy their tacit and explicit knowledge about test taking and translate the outcomes, i.e. give advice, to those who are going to make decisions based on these outcomes. Further, it was noted that one should take account of current legal regulations as well as those of the relevant union branch, the Dutch Institute for Psychologists (NIP).

Group 2: "Should" Areas

Access to a Common Applicant Pool

In the field of seconding, there is one unwritten rule: first come, first served. In other words, one can only charge a recruitment and selection fee when one has introduced an applicant to an organization, who is then hired, before other agencies have done so. As a direct result, speed is of the essence, especially since competitors have access to roughly the same pool of applicants.

When applicants are looking for a job, it is likely that they are concerned about getting a job regardless of which agency finds them one. With such an attitude, organizations fear that they might scare away the best applicants if they have a negatively perceived selection process (Ryan, et al, 2000). This notion is reflected in contemporary research on applicant reactions. Applicant perceptions, and reactions, on the selection process have been linked to, for instance, their intention to accept a job. However, these linkages are apparently weak and applicant perceptions seem to have little influence on withdrawal behavior (Ryan, et al, 2000; Truxillo, et al, 2002). However, the research in this field is relatively limited and conclusions might change.

While applicant reactions may not influence withdrawal behavior, it could influence preferences for one agency over another. Even though there is a first come, first serve rule, applicants need to agree to being introduced to a certain organization or for a certain vacancy. Whereas personal aspects, such as gender and age, do not seem to influence an applicant's view of the selection

process, the perceived procedural characteristics do, albeit marginally (Hausknecht, et al, 2004). There are several practices which may be deployed by a recruitment agency to counter an applicant's negative perceptions (Ryan and Ployheart, 2000). In particular, "applicants will not react negatively to tools that are well developed, job-relevant, and used in selection processes in which the procedures are appropriately applied, decisions are explained, and applicants are treated respectfully and sensitively – these concerns apply to all tools equally" (Ryan and Tippins, 2004, p. 315).

Countering this issue requires a twofold solution. First, the employees at Company T need to respond very quickly to market demands and this requires quick access to all relevant data. In this way, they can be the first to introduce candidates to a certain organization or for a specific vacancy, and in so doing the candidate receives the message that their application is considered important. Second, they might want to consider how to make themselves more appealing to candidates in times when the number of jobs exceeds the number of candidates. By offering, and communicating, an honest and respectful selection process, with face-to-face appointments when required, good feedback on decisions made and a clear overview of the tools which are going to be applied, and why, they may come over as more appealing than competitors (Ryan and Ployheart, 2000; Ryan and Tippins, 2004; Sylva and Mol, 2009). Company T needs to work with the reality that they share a candidate pool and act accordingly: displaying and executing an appealing and fast-paced selection process.

Debatable Validity of Tests

If using psychological tests in a selection process, it is important that such tests provide information on "who will be a good employee" (Ryan and Tippins, 2004, p. 308); that is, the test should have a high level of validity when it comes to predicting those aspects which are important for working at an organization, such as performance, motivation, and turnover. Since these aspects relate to a context, one is actually trying to achieve a fit between the person and the environment; that is the job, team, organization, and organizational culture (Greguras and Diefendorff, 2009; O'Reilly III, et al, 1991; Ostroff and Aumann, 2004; Vogel and Feldman, 2009). However, other issues are important when looking at which tool is the most appropriate for a given situation: these include the costs of developing a test, the costs and ease of administrating a test, and the likelihood of an adverse impact (Finch, et al, 2009; Ryan and Tippins, 2004). However, one should only look at these issues if there are a number of valid tools from which to choose.

Even though cognitive abilities tests have a high level of predictive validity (around 0.51, that is they can predict up to 51% of the variation in performance in future work behavior), this paper stresses that greater emphasis should be put on the other personal characteristics (O) of individuals (Ryan and Tippings, 2004; Schmidt and Hunter, 1998; Spector, 2008). Cognitive levels are increasingly considered a precondition, and these can be checked by educational level to some extent. Moreover, personality inventories have been demonstrated to be very useful in the selection process (Barrick and Mount, 1991; Bartram, 2005; Kieffer, et al, 2004; McAdams, 2009) as well as having an increased validity over cognitive ability tests (Ones, Dilchert, Viswesvaran and Judge, 2007). In particular, the conscientiousness trait has been linked to performance in numerous studies (Barrick and Mount, 1991; Kluemper and Rosen, 2009). As a result, tests based on the Big Five such as the Personality And Preference Inventory (PAPI) and the Role Diagram Approach (RDA) are considered superior to tests which are not such as the Jung Type Index (JTI) and the Meyer-Briggs Type Indicator (MBTI). Finally, motivation and ambition have been found to be important in determining future job performance. One may have the abilities to perform a particular

set of tasks but might not be fully motivated to do so and thus will not perform well (Ryan and Deci, 2000).

While such inventories currently rely on self-reporting, trends have emerged which aim to measure personality by other means (Sackett and Lievens, 2008). One interesting, and potentially practical, idea in this context is to apply structured interviews (Barrick, et al, 2000; Van Iddekinge, et al, 2005). However, while some evidence shows that structured interviews provide more valid measures of personality than self-reporting (McCrae, et al, 1998; Mount, et al, 1998), other research has criticized such claims (Murhpy and DeShon, 2000) or have found only moderate correlations between self-reporting and other ratings (Barbaranelli and Caprara, 2000). Further, research has shown that conscientiousness and emotional stability cannot easily be measured using structured interviews (Barrick, et al, 2000). The key issue here is that the interviewer has to be capable of making a sound assessment of personality measures (Schmidt, et al, 2000; Van Iddekinge, et al, 2005).

Measuring personality through the use of social networking websites is another innovative method. From such sites, a distinction can be made between high and low performers. In addition, one can get access to information which does not usually come up during an interview (Kluemper and Rosen, 2009). Also, one may gain an insight into the personality of an individual just by looking at such social networking sites (Kluemper and Rosen, 2009). While some claim this technique may counter the effects of dishonesty and false identity, we would question this. In the end, it still involves individuals providing information about themselves. Increasingly, people are becoming aware that such websites are sources of information, and there are suggestions that personal information is being modified to give a good impression.

Another trend is in the use of unproctored internet testing (UIT), that is testing without a human test administrator, something which has direct linkages with e-selection. While one could question whether internet testing would yield similar scores to traditional methods, i.e. paper-and-pencil tests, a good equivalence has been found between scores (correlations between 0.74 and 0.93, with a mean of 0.85; Lievens and Harris, 2003). However, despite the advantages of increased consistency and increased efficiency, several drawbacks are also apparent (Chapman and Webster, 2003; McManus and Ferguson, 2003; Tippins et al., 2006). Besides the issues of honesty, cheating, and applicant identification, there are also issues such as the impact of contextual factors, ethics, and adverse impacts, such as the availability of the internet, computer/internet experience, webpage loading speed, and data accuracy (Stone-Romero, 2005; Tippins et al., 2006). We would stress that UIT needs to be regarded as only a tool and that it needs to be supplemented with a face-to-face interview, rather than other means such as webcam-taped videos (Van Iddekinge, et al, 2006), in which the outcomes, as well as any issues experienced, can be discussed. Further, one might consider administering a second set of tests in order to check that potentially successful applicants have taken the online test themselves without any help.

Overall, we advised Company T to rely on traditional methods based on the Big Five, and expand such inventories with measures covering motivation and ambition. Even though one member of the focus group commented that for "generating input for a discussion" less validated tests could be applied, this was not recommended. As noted earlier, validity is key. Further, structured interviews were not considered a viable option for Company T since they lack appropriate employees capable of assessing personality traits. Hiring someone to do so would probably cost more than administering a self-report test. Lastly, given their striving to be innovative, Company T would do well to keep track of the latest developments regarding UIT. While having some drawbacks,

mainly related to cheating, this is regarded as having potential in the field of e-selection. With the addition of a second set of tests, or perhaps just a threat of this possibility, and an interview, such drawbacks could be countered.

Tools are Widely Distributed

Tools are vital to the selection process, but they can easily be obtained and used by competitors. As a result, while one needs to deploy certain tools in order to help achieve one's goals, deploying them is no guarantee of a good outcome; it is also about how you use them. Moreover, tools should be used in a manner which is hard to copy. This notion reflects the concept of a core competence (Prahalad and Hamel, 1990); that the simple application of tools will not be critical in competing with competitors. A core competence should be regarded as a skill rather than a resource (Mooney, 2007). Such skills allow organizations to define and solve problems in order to grow (Lei, et al, 1996). The fact that the current tools can be acquired by competitors with great ease needs to be taken as a given: one should aim to use such tools to define new problems and then solve them.

One such problem, which has already been defined, is the upcoming shortage of employees with appropriate technical skills. How might such tools, or perhaps new tools, help cope with such a shortage? While Company T is already trying to combine both the hard skills (KSA) and the softer skills (O) when introducing candidates to an organization or for a vacancy, they could consider also offering HRM consultancy services for mapping the existing employees of a particular organization. If one were to also map the ambitions, work motivation, and achieved performance, this would provide some quite valuable information when grouped together for that organization. Using such information should lead to more realistic planning schedules, an ability to plan successions more easily, training programs distributed more effectively, a better management of competences, and so on. Another option would be to start a branch-wide database, in which all the employees of linked organizations are present. While such a database should include all the available knowledge, it would have to be an anonymous database in order to secure privacy. Each of the linked organizations would then have access to the database and could look for suitable entries. If they find one, they could then contact the organization linked to the specific entry and seek to hire that employee.

The addition of knowledge to the tools, or using a combination of tools, was also proposed by the members of the focus group. However, they were not able to specify what type of knowledge should be added, or how the tools should be applied in order to gain a competitive advantage. Overall, solving this issue involved devising a practical e-selection application for Company T.

Group 3: "Could" Areas

Outcomes May Not Be Recognizable

Discrepancies between the perceptions of the test taker and the outcomes of a self-report test exist in most types of testing, from personality to cognitive ability testing. Furthermore, such discrepancies may occur both for those who distort their responses and for those who do not. However, it is only when feedback is provided that such discrepancies come to light, and this is one of the functional purposes of providing feedback (Bannister, 1986). While bringing discrepancies to light is one step, finding out why they occurred is the next.

Considering applicant reactions, it seems that tests, and especially personality tests, may be seen as invasive to privacy since applicants cannot, or are encouraged not to, distort the information provided and therefore also not to alter the subsequent impressions (Rosse, et al, 1994). Tests

may reveal socially undesirable information which may lead to not being selected and, as a result, one may claim not to recognize oneself in such undesirable outcomes. Besides such principles based on justice, there are also issues concerning self-serving bias in applicant characteristics (Chan and Schmitt, 2004). In other words, the motivation for test taking, and the belief in a certain test, may influence performance in a particular test (Arvey, et al, 1990; Bauer, et al., 2006; Chan, et al, 1998). Conversely, discrepancies may occur due to the test being deployed. Issues can arise related to test content and method, which may be perceived as invalid (Chan and Schmitt, 2004). Applicants may not understand the questions, or not grasp what they are meant to do, etc. Employing tests with high levels of validity may largely guard against such issues, but the type of test may still influence the test taker.

In using unproctored internet testing, some additional problems arise. First, the variations in internet speed, especially when using a timed cognitive ability test, may lead to a discrepancy between test scores and actual capabilities. In addition, without a supervisor present, there is no possibility to ask questions; and this may promote perceived unfairness and limit understanding of the test taking (Bauer, et al, 1998). A possible solution would be to retake the test with a supervisor present (Tippins et al., 2006).

Whatever the reason for perceived discrepancies, this should be understood as a signal that something is amiss and that further investigation is needed. Since no reliable solutions were found for this issue, our proposed solution would be to first discuss the findings with the test taker and dig deeper into the measured performance. Here, the applicant should be provided with an opportunity to explain why and where they feel there is a discrepancy. This could be achieved using the STAR (Situation, Task, Action, Result) interview technique in which the test taker is asked to describe situations in which they have displayed a certain behavior in contrast to the measured performance. The options would then be open to administer another test, to discard the test taker from the candidate pool, or to select the test taker based on the STAR technique. If it is decided to administer a second test, and the test taker still perceives discrepancies, one should question whether the test taker is being honest with themselves and capable of self-reflection.

Overall, if a test taker perceives discrepancies, then the test will be of little use in the selection process. Since the cause of such discrepancies may be attributed to the test taker or to the test itself, our proposal is that sound and validated tests should be applied in order to minimize the risk of the test being ambiguous. Furthermore, test feedback should be provided before the test taker is selected to proceed to the next stage or rejected (Bauer, et al, 1998). When discrepancies are discovered, we would propose engaging in a conversation in which the results are discussed in-depth. For instance, one might look for internal contradictions; such as an applicant arguing that they are a true entrepreneur while showing little preference for risk taking. Discussing such contradictions might help steer the conversation such that matters can be resolved.

Need for a Common Language

One of the main goals in using databases is to increase efficiency by increasing the speed and reach of search efforts. In order for a database to yield such gains in efficiency, queries need to function properly (Stone-Romero, 2005). However, efficiency is also dependent on the degree to which reliance is put on the systematic entry of data. If the reliance on systematic entry of data is high, there is a greater chance of input errors, and thus data which does not correspond to set standards, leading to reduced efficiency and vice versa. Furthermore, when a database is programmed in a strict sense; several queries will

be required to cover all the possible terms for a single topic. Ideally, one should avoid having to enter data in an extremely strict sense, that is educational degrees such as chemistry and chemical engineering should be seen as a match.

Our proposal was that some sort of dictionary, or taxonomy, should be devised in which terms that refer to the same theme are linked. Then, instead of searching a database based on terms, one is actually searching within themes. This results in a database management tool which is more efficient, more user-friendly, and less prone to errors (Mohamed, et al, 2001). Secondly, the systematic entry of data involves making tacit information explicit. This requires employees to be consistent in their data entry since, otherwise, tacit information will be lost in the transfer of knowledge. It might be an idea to formulate a manual on the way in which the explicit and tacit knowledge of potential workers is to be captured in order to provide a standard way of working, and this could also serve as an introduction for new employees. Such a standard way of working will aid employees in consistently adding data to their software package.

Difficulties Transferring Knowledge

In organizations, including in Company T, knowledge sharing is an important issue in day-to-day operations. Due to the large amount of tacit knowledge involved in working at Company T, an aspect highlighted by the focus group, it may be difficult for new employees, or even more experienced colleagues who do not work with a certain client, to take over tasks. Knowledge sharing provides opportunities to transfer expertise and knowledge from experts to novices (Wang and Noe, 2010).

Many factors contribute to the degree to which employees share knowledge within an organization. However, since the context of this paper is a single company in which the employees are rewarded based on both individual and team performance, it was assumed that the employees would be motivated and willing to share knowledge. Further, there was little inter-group or inter-personal conflict, trust was evident among the employees, and they were all committed to the organization. As such, they were all assumed to have traits beneficial for knowledge sharing. Furthermore, the culture of Company T is aimed at collaboration, and thus at knowledge sharing (Hislop, 2005; Matzler, et al, 2008; Yang, 2007, 2008). Naturally, one could consider rewarding separate knowledge-sharing actions since this has been found to stimulate increased knowledge sharing among employees (Yang and Wu, 2008), but we did not feel this was necessary given this particular situation.

Even though a good basis for knowledge sharing was present, the problem still stands that while explicit knowledge may be shared easily, this is not the case with tacit knowledge (Hislop, 2005). Contemporary literature indicates that one may classify knowledge transfer into structured and unstructured processes. Whereas explicit knowledge may be transferred easily using structured processes, such as formal documents, tacit knowledge usually requires less structured knowledge transfer processes (Chen and McQueen, 2009). Such unstructured processes may be seen as sharing knowledge rather than extracting it from those holding the information, i.e. as socializing in order to share information (Fernie, et al, 2003; Boh, 2007). However, in order to share such tacit knowledge, it has been argued that strong connections are required between the actors (Ahuja, 2000; Boer, et al, 2004; Boer, et al, 2011; Burt, 2000; Granovetter, 1973). Further, the context of both the origin of the tact information as well as the application of the information plays a role in its sharing (Fernie, et al, 2003). However, in Company T the context was unlikely to be an issue since all of the employees were broadly working in the same context. Furthermore, an actor trying to acquire information requires at least some level of cognitive capability in order to grasp the information (Chen and McQueen, 2009).

A solution proposed by the members of the focus group was to add commentary to their software package at each of the steps taken during a selection process. This way, the reasoning behind a choice would be made more explicit. While this may be a viable option to some extent, there is still the problem that tacit knowledge may not be communicated (Hislop, 2005).

In response, we proposed that the employees should indeed add commentary at every step of the selection process in order to share their explicit knowledge as well as noting their thoughts on why choices were made. Also, it was recommended to keep in place the tracking of all the communications between the employee and the candidate, and the employee and the organization. In addition, it was advised that employees should interact with each other when they want to share in the tacit knowledge held by others, or when they want to share their tacit knowledge with others. It was further proposed that these interactions could either emerge naturally or be set up as an intervention in which the employees are required to share their experiences and knowledge with each other. It has been argued that both routes should be available (Van den Hooff and Huysman, 2009), and the latter was already in place to some extent. When an interaction is sparked through an existing problem, collaboratively solving the problem will also contribute to the sharing of tacit knowledge (Berends, et al, 2006), and we proposed encouraging such interactions. In the given situation, a combination of rich explicit knowledge sharing and providing a basis for sharing tacit knowledge seemed the best approach.

Group 4: "Unimportant" Areas

Lack of User-Friendliness and Lack of Functionality

Since these issues were not thought to be of major importance, no solutions were proposed to the company. Missing out on some efficiency gains was not deemed to be as important as other factors provided everything was findable. Further, preferences regarding software packages are a highly subjective matter, and switching between such packages will result in a decrease in efficiency since one needs to adjust and become accustomed to new packages. Moreover, digging into the functionality would be another study in its own right, as would be seeking to improve user-friendliness.

One suggestion was made regarding a possible solution to the issue of lacking functionality: since the importance of other personal characteristics is growing, the company's software packages should be adapted to handle a more extensive personal profile, in which these aspects are more prominent, than is currently possible. Nevertheless, the knowledge, skills, and abilities (KSA) aspects need to be easily accessible since Company T is operating in a technical branch where such aspects remain highly important.

E-Selection at Company T: A Final Solution Design

With the requirement issues resolved, the next step was to determine how the individual requirements could be combined in a single design. This final design serves as a guideline for Company T which they can use when they decide to deploy e-selection in responding to the expected shortage of employees with the required technical skills, as well as in accommodating the increased use of other personal characteristics (O) in the selection process. Having discerned these two major topics, the requirements for both psychological testing as well as web-based technologies have been examined. This final design is summarized in Table 8.

Support for E-Selection

The first and foremost requirement of e-selection for it to be viable for Company T is that e-selection has to be perceived as useful. A positive perception is required of the use of advanced, web-based technologies as well as the application of validated psychological tests, and this usually starts with support displayed by higher management (Parkers, 2000). While such a positive perception was already considered present at Company T at the time of our investigation, it was less clear that this was shared by their customers. The perception of their customers is of some importance to Company T since the costs of psychological tests would likely be passed on to them. Customers might be convinced with the help of scientific research, translated into non-technical language, that demonstrated the value, or by allowing a customer to oversee a test and go through the process to demonstrate the added value.

The E-Selection Tool and Process

Once support for the concept of e-selection is in place, the next step is to tailor fit e-selection to Company T. With the increased use of web-based technologies, and this resulting in applicants being registered with competitors at the same time, the employees at Company T need to adopt an attitude of fast response while not ignoring the anticipated problems. When an applicant applies for a vacancy, they need to be able to react within a matter of minutes in order to exploit the opportunity and minimize the possibility that a competitor gets in first. Given that user-friendliness and functionality were not considered particularly important by

Table 8. E-selection at Company T; a final solution design

Problem	Solution
Debatable image of testing amongst recruiters	Deploy valid psychological tests and persuade customers, with elaborate examples when needed
Possibilities of response distortion	Add a lie scale and deploy feedback sessions with test takers. Also, deploy valid psychological tests. Another solution would be to deploy measures which do not rely on self-reports, i.e. structured interviews / social media
High level of expert knowledge involved	Hire professionals to cope with the level of expert knowledge involved with psychological testing
Access to a common applicant pool	Adopt an attitude of fast responses to changes in the market and offer, and communicate, an honest and respectful selection process
Debatable validity of tests	Deploy valid psychological tests and expand such test taking with the use of unproctored internet testing
Tools are widely distributed	Add specific knowledge to the use of various tools, see recommendations
Outcomes may not be recognizable	Deploy valid psychological tests as well as feedback sessions with test takers. In addition, omit test takers for which the test outcomes are persistently not recognizable
Need for a common language	Buy, or develop, a taxonomy which allows for easier data entry and retrieval in the database
Difficulties transferring knowledge	Set up formal knowledge sharing sessions and allow informal knowledge sharing sessions to take place. Adopt collaborative problem solving when needed. Denote, in the tools, as much information as possible in order to clarify decisions.
Lacking user-friendliness	No solution was constructed
Lacking functionality	Search for tools, or buy an add-on, which enables extensive personal profiles in the current tools, i.e. both the KSA and O.

the members of the focus group, the proposition here is to buy, or develop, a tool which fits well with the current set of tools and ways of working.

Offering a quick response was considered unlikely to be enough to attract and satisfy potential candidates. We argued that an honest and respectful selection process needed to be followed and communicated to candidates. Such a process would involve face-to-face appointments when required, feedback on decisions made, and a clear overview of the tools which are going to be applied, and why. This will help to create a positive image of the organization, something that is especially important when market conditions are favoring the job seeker.

The e-selection tool chosen should enable less rigid entry and retrieval of data. It was proposed that some sort of taxonomy should be present in the tool which would allow less rigid ways of working that would increase effectiveness and efficiency. This taxonomy would group terms belonging to a single topic, such that each of the terms would then correspond with all the others within that topic. Then, instead of having to execute multiple database queries including each of the terms in turn, a single query would be sufficient to obtain the same results.

Knowledge Sharing

Further, when looking at efficiency and effectiveness, we argued that several knowledge-sharing mechanisms should be put into place. First, it was proposed that a manual should be constructed in which the standard ways of working at Company T were described. This would help in transferring explicit knowledge, and could also help in transferring tacit knowledge, to both new and existing employees. Another mechanism proposed was to enter as much information into the tool used as possible, in order to clarify decisions made. Other employees would then be able to look at selection processes regarding older vacancies and discover what decisions were made and why. A more active variant of this mechanism would be to ask colleagues to think together, trying to uncover their reasoning and gain new insights. Moreover, it was proposed that the employees engage in both formal and informal knowledge-sharing sessions in which they could share both experiences and knowledge with each other. While limited formal sessions were already taking place on a weekly basis, informal sessions could help to share more tacit knowledge given their nature of intrinsic motivation.

The Use of Other Personal Characteristics

Given the increasing reliance on 'O', it is of vital importance that validated psychological tests are deployed to assess these. That is, psychological tests that have been validated through scientific means and reported in the scientific literature, such as tests based on the Big Five, or the NEO-PI-R. Besides such personality inventories, it was also proposed that measures of ambition, motivation, and other personal characteristics beyond the KSA confines, be included. Using validated tests helps in countering potential issues such as response distortion since the validity of psychological tests has been shown not to be significantly affected by response distortion. If considered desirable, it would be possible to add a lie scale to the personality inventory to indicate if responses are being distorted. Such information could then be used to "confront" the test taker and determine the reality. In addition, using validated tests may avoid the issue of outcomes not being recognizable by the test taker, i.e. it would reduce the chances that discrepancies are present due to an inaccurate test. When discrepancies become apparent, usually during a feedback session, it was proposed holding a structured interview in which the results would be discussed and during which the test taker could explain why the results do not apparently reflect the individual. Further, if discrepancies persist, it was suggested that the candidate be omitted from the selection process since their personality's suitability for the job was uncertain.

While most psychological tests rely on self-reporting, other measures of O exist. Although scientific support for these measures is not yet convincing, they may prove useful when self-reporting seems to be failing, such as when there are consistent discrepancies between outcomes and self-perceptions. The first proposal was to measure O through structured interviews. However, impression management may lower the validity of this method, and a professional would have to be hired in order to ensure the accuracy of the process. A second thought was to involve assessment centers but they were considered too costly unless a senior management position was to be filled. Lastly, social media such as LinkedIn and Facebook may be used. While some research suggests that such pages contain accurate information about a person, this was not considered to be consistently the case, especially with the growing awareness that potential employers look at one's social media sites.

Given the desire of Company T to be innovative, and looking at the expected future of test taking, the possibilities offered by unproctored internet testing should not be overlooked. Such tests produce similar scores as traditional paper-and-pencil self-reporting. However, issues such as identifying the true test sitter and the availability and speeds of internet access may pose a threat to this method of testing. Nevertheless, by combining unproctored internet testing with follow-up face-to-face interviews, and perhaps a second set of tests to confirm the identity of the test taker, this method was thought to have a significant potential.

Further, it was proposed that professionals should be hired to evaluate sensitive issues such as personality, motivation, and ambition. Especially when an honest and respectful selection process is being promoted, one should rely on professionals with high levels of skill and ethics rather than less experienced employees. Another possibility would be to train employees in interpreting and understanding psychological testing. However, this would consume a lot of time, energy, and money, and would require regular refreshing to remain reliable.

DISCUSSION

Through resolving the perceived problems, and constructing a final design, answers were provided to the main research question and its sub-questions, Here, the limitations are highlighted and the final conclusions drawn.

The main goal of this research was to uncover the requirements of an e-selection tool that would contribute to improving the selection process at Company T. In turn, two sub-questions were derived which aimed to directly uncover requirements for psychological testing and for web-based technologies that would contribute to improving and supporting the selection process at Company T. By taking a practical approach, and following the regulative cycle, a design was constructed that took the specific context into account. The final requirements are detailed in Table 9.

Using a validated test would largely ensure valid results. However, when deploying unproctored internet testing, it would be wise to deploy a second set of tests with an observer present in order to verify the identity of the test taker. Moreover, we advised hiring in professionals to deal with the expert knowledge encountered when deploying psychological tests. Another possibility would be to train one or two employees in the use of psychological testing, but even then their level of interpretation and linking of outcomes would fall short of a true professional, that is an

industrial or organizational psychologist. We saw that Company T wanted full information on candidates, and was keen to know when candidates distorted their responses. As a result, one of the requirements for any psychological testing was to include a lie scale through which distorting candidates could be detected, even though the effect of such distorters has been shown not to be significant.

The core functionality of the tools was found to be more important than aspects such as additional functionality and user-friendliness. As a result, the only requirement was that the new tools could be integrated with their current set of tools and with the company's way of thinking. In addition, when considering anticipated problems, it was requested that new tools should allow rapid responses to a changing environment, such as real-time information concerning new candidates, allow for extensive note taking in order to transfer knowledge, and allow integration with their current website, that is automatically process candidates applying for a vacancy through the website.

Once these e-selection requirements are met, Company T will be able to service their customers through innovative tools designed to select candi-

Table 9. Requirements for e-selection at Company T

Overall requirements	Offer an honest and respectful selection process
Requirements for psychological testing	Deployment of valid tools based on the Big Five, or another validated personality inventory
	Integration with web-based technologies, i.e. unproctored internet testing
	Innovative ways of measuring personality, e.g. structured interviews, social media
	Being able to detect response distortion
	Feedback sessions during which the outcomes of psychological tests can be discussed
	Experts capable of dealing with the expert knowledge associated with psychological testing
	Convinced customers / employees
Requirements for web-based technologies	An attitude of fast responses to changes in the market
	A taxonomy which allows easier data entry and retrieval in the database
	Establishment of standards and adoption of a standard way of working
	Storage of as much tacit information as possible, e.g. elaborate note taking tools
	Time and space for knowledge sharing, e.g. formal and informal knowledge sharing opportunities
	Integration with the current set of tools
	Integration with the mindset at Company T

dates effectively, efficiently, and in a sustainable manner (Kehoe, et al, 2005).

While the concept of e-selection was considered potentially very interesting by the founder of Company T, the originator of the initial problem definition, the drivers behind wanting to apply web-based technologies were found to be different to those suggested in the contemporary literature. In such literature, the two main drivers for applying web-based technologies, or e-HRM, were considered to be increasing the efficiency and the effectiveness of the selection process, with the ultimate goal of reducing costs (Chapman and Webster, 2003; MacManus and Ferguson, 2003). However, these drivers were not found to be the key issues in the company examined. Rather, it was crucial that employees could use the new technologies in executing the selection process: core functionality was rated as most important, with efficiency and effectiveness less so. While the respondents may have implicitly valued efficiency and effectiveness, they did not do so explicitly during the focus group meeting.

Another driver behind implementing e-selection is to reduce recruiter bias (Chapman and Webster, 2003). E-selection aims to increase the objectivity of the selection process by removing as much human intervention as possible and, as a result, applicants will be treated more equally. However, this driver was only indicated by one of interviewees. During the focus group, almost no attention was given to this potential advantage of e-selection. The employment laws in the Netherlands, compared to some other nations, already insist that protected groups are treated fairly. In addition, since the sample consisted mainly of recruiters, they may have been reluctant to discuss issues which could make much of their day-to-day work obsolete.

Although research has shown that response distortion is not a significant problem in deploying psychological tests, the respondents from Company T were reluctant to renounce their contrary beliefs. Since such beliefs could not be removed simply by displaying the literature, the addition of lie scales was proposed in order to give Company T the feeling they could detect test takers who were distorting their responses. Furthermore, the tests currently deployed at Company T were both unvalidated scientifically and administered by their own employees. This was despite the company recognizing the added value of validated tests supervised by external professionals bringing in expert knowledge on psychological testing. This situation was seen as somewhat contradictory.

Thus, the results suggest that there is a real gap between research and practice. Conducting practice-based research may help to close such gaps, at least in the isolated cases where such research is conducted. In turn, those involved may "spread the message", which should ultimately lead to a closing of the research-practice gap.

RECOMMENDATIONS

In addition to a final design, which contains proposed solutions to address the problems associated with e-selection in the context of Company T, several other recommendations were also proposed. In general terms, it was recommended that Company T should consider advancing in two, non-exclusive, directions: deploying a wide array of e-recruitment and e-selection tools in order to select appropriate candidates for their customers; and offering consultancy services to their customers that would involve deploying these far-reaching e-services. As such, these involve dealing with access to digitally stored KSAO measures (Cronin, et al, 2006).

One of the key questions in pursuing e-selection is whether to develop or buy the required software (Kehoe, et al, 2005). There are several e-selection, and related, software packages available but most of these are offered by large software manufacturers such as SAP and, as a result, such packages are very costly. Further, off-the-shelf products may be of limited attraction because of the limited possibilities to personalize them. Instead, it was proposed to search for either a modular off-the-shelf package, or to cooperate with a software manufacturer to implement the company-specific requirements. Whichever route is taken, the e-selection package has to be intertwined with other enterprise resource planning (ERP) functionalities.

Selecting Suitable Candidates

If Company T decides to deploy e-selection tools in order to select suitable candidates, it will have to take several conditions into account: the required educational level for the vacancy, the organization for which candidates are being found, perceptions of whether the vacancy is hard or easy to fill, the perceived popularity of the vacancy, etc. This will require an adaptation to the general model proposed: a partially automated multiple-hurdle system with appropriate predictors at each stage. Such a system requires each candidate to clear a number of hurdles, i.e. meet various requirements, in sequence. The remaining pool which clears all the hurdles is then invited for an interview after which the final selection is made. The general idea behind such a system is that costs are minimized and social capital utilized to its maximum (Kehoe, et al, 2005). However, when multiple hurdles are to be applied, it is important that a thorough job analysis is completed to achieve a clear profile which the successful candidate has to match.

Such a system begins with having an easy to use website on which all of the current vacancies are present along with relevant information (Gueutal and Falbe, 2005). Here, applicants can upload their CV and apply for a specific vacancy. The first step, after applicants have applied self-selection (Ryan, et al, 2000), is usually a keyword search based on the KSA attributes and, if available, the O aspects on the uploaded CV. Here, one scans for keywords essential for the job (Mohamed, et al, 2001; Stone-Romero, 2005). However, it is considered unlikely that the other personal characteristics (i.e. the O) will be available for most applicants at this stage. Only if an applicant is already in the database can a keyword search be done on aspects of O. If the CV is found to contain most of the pre-identified keywords, the candidate can be moved on to the next stage. The proposed second step is to administer a cognitive ability test since these have low costs (Ryan and Tippins, 2004). Here the proposal is to make use of a cut-off score associated with educational level. Next, one should develop a personality inventory for each potential candidate using self-reporting and unproctored internet testing, with a follow up interview to discuss the results. It was further proposed that such a test should be based on the Big Five because of its high validity. Due to the fear of response distortion, it was proposed not to make use of a cut-off score but rather to map the different personalities in the team and determine whether one is looking for a complementary or similar personality to the rest of the team. Automating this hurdle was considered difficult due to the subtle distinctions between individuals. Rather, it was proposed to partially automate this step: the test would be administered online, outcomes would be generated automatically, but then a professional would interpret the results before providing feedback to the system. A possible fourth hurdle would involve an assessment center or work sample. This test was placed last due to the high costs associated with it (Ryan and Tippins, 2004) and also because it is possibly of little use to Company T. Further, the incremental validity of such a test over a cognitive ability test and a personality inventory has been considered as rather low (Ryan and Tippins, 2004).

The number of hurdles to be applied depends to an extent on the required level of skills. The lower the required skills for a vacancy, the less sensible it would be to spend a lot of time and money in filling it (Finch, et al, 2009). In addition, the popularity of a vacancy matters. If there is little interest in a vacancy, it might be better to avoid a multi-hurdle process if this reduces the attractiveness of the vacancy even further. While cognitive ability has been shown to be a sound predictor for future performance (Ryan and Tippins, 2004), it has not been used at Company T before.

Offering Consultancy Services

While organizations currently construct planning schedules in terms of machining hours based on information in their ERP package, this can be extended to include the planning of employees. In this form, e-selection can be deployed to assist organizations in strategically deploying social capital in the longer term. Such a strategic deployment involves taking both employer and employee perspectives, and is assumed to result in a win-win situation. As such, providing consultancy advice in this area was recommended as an important and significant service that Company T could offer in the future.

Based on the notion of person-environment fit, e-selection can help to select appropriate candidates for a particular function, and it can help in planning successors in the event of an emergency or promotion. For this to be feasible, organizations need to map all of their employees, both in terms of knowledge, skills and abilities, as well as of other personal characteristics. However, this fitting process needs to be viewed as a continuous process because both the individual and the environment are likely to change over time (Caldwell, et al, 2004; DeRue and Morgeson, 2009). Moreover, addressing the person-environment fit is not restricted to selecting new employees; a fit may also be achieved through developing or retaining employees (Schneider, et al, 1997).

In more detail, one can better allocate training programs by considering the KSAO attributes of employees. It is important to look beyond the KSA qualities and take other aspects, such as ambition, interests, and motivation, into account (Ryan and Deci, 2000; Anthoney and Armstrong, 2010). Employees may request a training program while an employer may invite an employee to undertake

one. In such situations, decisions should be based on performance appraisals, ambition, and motivation, as well as the personality of the employee. All this information can be made accessible through an e-selection tool. Using the same information, one can make better informed decisions when considering promotions. It is in the best interests of both parties to appoint employees to appropriate functions, and this should as far as possible be based on objective measures.

Moving from the individual to a team setting, the KSAO qualities of an individual can form the basis for setting up a team to achieve specific goals. Depending on the level of cooperation, the goals, and the dependency upon one another (Tesluk, et al, 1997), the other personal characteristics can be critical: they may need to be in line with the rest of the team or they may need to offer complementary qualities to the rest of the team. Having a single database in which all the employees are present, along with their KSAO attributes, would ease such decisions.

The departmental level provides ample opportunities to link the planning of social capital to that of the machinery. Here, a resource-based view (RBV) was proposed (Aryee and Budhwar, 2008) with one of the key questions being the extent to which a department is able to handle the expected workload for the next month, six months, year, or two years. In order to answer this question, one needs to map the required competences to handle the expected workload and the degree to which these are available. Using an extensive database including the KSAO attributes of all employees, one can make a plan and also backup plans, and then establish future actions such as hiring new employees, assigning training programs, and also keeping employees motivated, committed, and healthy. These practices are more appropriate when pursuing a level strategy, i.e. keeping the workforce size constant, than a chase strategy, i.e. hiring and firing based on market needs (Silver, et al, 1998). The RBV suggests a need to invest in employees since they are invaluable. Following the thinking of competence management, an extensive database and appropriate investment can result in high levels of utility. Specifically, in order to assist their customers in handling their future workloads, and assuming it will become increasingly difficult to meet production schedules over time, Company T could offer services that address the following practices within competency management (Belkadi, et al, 2007; Berio and Harzallah, 2007):

- **Identification:** Identification and definition of required competencies;
- **Characterization:** Formalizing competencies and storing key features;
- **Allocation:** Division of labor according to possessed competences;
- **Assessment:** Measuring the levels of competence (e.g. in individuals, groups);
- **Acquisition:** Planning and deciding on how and when to obtain competences;
- **Development:** Training and on-the-job learning;
- **Mobilization:** Providing the right conditions for workers to fully use their competences;
- **Knowledge usage:** Actually using the identified, assessed, and acquired competences.

Then, looking at the overall organization, one could deploy the social capital in a strategic sense and in line with the KSA attributes and the ambitions, personality, interests, and motivation of the employees. A good fit is more likely to be established if it is based on objective measures rather than on the politics and goodwill of one's immediate superior. When employees are working in a suitable environment in a function that they can, should, and want to fulfill, certain positive attitudes and behaviors will result, and these in turn should lead to positive outcomes (Chen, et al, 2009). Moreover, the goal of striving for healthy and employable employees can be in-

corporated in order to enhance both the morale and the motivation of employees and so maintain production levels. The overall goal is to deploy one's employees as efficiently and effectively as possible, and not only in the short term but also into the future.

This idea could be taken a step further by expanding such a database to other organizations and to cooperate with companies within the same economic branch. In such a database, all the employees of these linked organizations would be present, along with their KSAO qualities. While the employees would, for privacy reasons, have to remain anonymous in the database, identified only by current organization and employee number, each of the linked organizations would have access to the database and could look for suitable entries for their own particular needs, or to see if other organizations had needs that they could satisfy. Where an appropriate entry was found, contact could be made to see whether one could hire in or lend out an appropriate employee.

To sum up, by taking a more personal look at employees, based on characteristics which are measured as objectively as possible, a win-win situation can be achieved by appropriately using such information. The main goal is to achieve a fit between the person and the organization, with both current and new employees. An e-selection tool would be appropriate for handling all the information involved in achieving such a fit. Here, Company T could offer consultancy services to other organizations in order to help them strategically deploy social capital.

REFERENCES

Ahuja, G. (2000). Collaboration networks, structural holes, and innovation: A longitudinal study. *Administrative Science Quarterly, 45*(3), 425–455. doi:10.2307/2667105

Anderson, N. (2003). Applicant and recruiter reactions to new technology in selection: A critical review and agenda for future research. *International Journal of Selection and Assessment, 11*(2/3), 121–136. doi:10.1111/1468-2389.00235

Anthoney, S. F., & Armstrong, P. I. (2010). Individuals and environments: linking ability and skill rating with interests. *Journal of Counseling Psychology, 57*(1), 36–51. doi:10.1037/a0018067

Arthur, W. Jr, Glaze, R. M., Villado, A. J., & Taylor, J. E. (2010). The magnitude and extent of cheating and response distortion effects on unproctored internet-based tests of cognitive ability and personality. *International Journal of Selection and Assessment, 18*(1), 1–16. doi:10.1111/j.1468-2389.2010.00476.x

Arvey, R. D., Strickland, W., Drauden, G., & Martin, C. (1990). Motivational components of test taking. *Personnel Psychology, 43*, 695–716. doi:10.1111/j.1744-6570.1990.tb00679.x

Aryee, S., & Budhwar, P. (2008). Human resource management and organizational performance. In Ashton Center for Human Resources (Eds.), *Strategic human resource management* (pp. 191-212). London, UK: Chartered Institute of Personnel and Development.

Bannister, B. D. (1986). Performance outcome feedback and attributional feedback: Interactive effects of recipient responses. *The Journal of Applied Psychology, 71*(2), 203–210. doi:10.1037/0021-9010.71.2.203

Barbaranelli, C., & Caprara, G. V. (2000). Measuring the Big Five in self-report and other ratings: A multitrait-multimethod study. *European Journal of Psychological Assessment, 16*(1), 31–43. doi:10.1027//1015-5759.16.1.31

Barrick, M. R., & Mount, M. K. (1991). The Big Five personality dimensions and job performance: A meta-analysis. *Personnel Psychology, 44*, 1–25. doi:10.1111/j.1744-6570.1991.tb00688.x

Barrick, M. R., & Mount, M. K. (1996). Effects of impression management and self-deception on the predictive validity of personality constructs. *The Journal of Applied Psychology, 81*(3), 261–272. doi:10.1037/0021-9010.81.3.261

Barrick, M. R., Patton, G. K., & Haugland, S. N. (2000). Accuracy of interviewer judgments of job applicant personality traits. *Personnel Psychology, 53*, 925–951. doi:10.1111/j.1744-6570.2000.tb02424.x

Bartram, D. (2000). Internet recruitment and selection: kissing frogs to find princes. *International Journal of Selection and Assessment, 8*(4), 261–274. doi:10.1111/1468-2389.00155

Bartram, D. (2005). The great eight competencies: A criterion-centric approach to validation. *The Journal of Applied Psychology, 90*(6), 1185–1203. doi:10.1037/0021-9010.90.6.1185

Bauer, T. N., Maertz, C. P. Jr, Dolen, M. R., & Campion, M. A. (1998). Longitudinal assessment of applicant reactions to employment testing and test outcome feedback. *The Journal of Applied Psychology, 83*(6), 892–903. doi:10.1037/0021-9010.83.6.892

Bauer, T. N., Truxillo, D. M., Tucker, J. S., Weathers, V., Bertolino, M., Erdogan, B., & Campion, M. A. (2006). Selection in the information age: The impact of privacy concerns and computer experience on applicant reactions. *Journal of Management, 32*(5), 601–621. doi:10.1177/0149206306289829

Belkadi, F., Bonjour, E., & Dulmet, M. (2007). Competency characterisation by means of work situation modelling. *Computers in Industry, 58*, 164–178. doi:10.1016/j.compind.2006.09.005

Berends, J. J., van der Bij, J. D. K., & Weggeman, M. (2006). Knowledge sharing mechanisms in industrial research. *Research and Development Management, 36*(1), 85–95.

Berio, G., & Harzallah, M. (2007). Towards an integrating architecture for competence management. *Computers in Industry, 58*, 199–209. doi:10.1016/j.compind.2006.09.007

Boer, N. I., Berends, J. J., & van Baalen, P. (2011). Relational models for knowledge sharing behavior. *European Management Journal, 29*, 85–97. doi:10.1016/j.emj.2010.10.009

Boer, N. I., van Baalen, P. J., & Kumar, K. (2004). The implications of different models of social relations for understanding knowledge sharing. In Tsoukas, H., & Mylonopoulos, N. (Eds.), *Organizations as knowledge systems: Knowledge, learning and dynamic capabilities* (pp. 130–151). New York, NY: Palgrave MacMillan.

Boh, W. F. (2007). Mechanisms for sharing knowledge in project-based organizations. *Information and Organization, 17*, 27–58. doi:10.1016/j.infoandorg.2006.10.001

Burt, R. S. (2000). Structural holes versus network closure as social capital. In Lin, N., Cook, K. S., & Burt, R. S. (Eds.), *Social capital: Theory and research* (pp. 1–30). Preprint.

Caldwell, S. D., Herold, D. M., & Fedor, D. B. (2004). Toward an understanding of the relationships among organizational change, individual differences, and change in person-environment fit: A cross-level study. *The Journal of Applied Psychology, 89*(5), 868–882. doi:10.1037/0021-9010.89.5.868

Chan, D., & Schmitt, N. (2004). An agenda for future research on applicant reactions to selection procedures: A construct-oriented approach. *International Journal of Selection and Assessment, 12*(1/2), 9–23. doi:10.1111/j.0965-075X.2004.00260.x

Chan, D., Schmitt, N., Sacco, J. M., & DeShon, R. P. (1998). Understanding pretest and posttest reactions to cognitive ability and personality tests. *The Journal of Applied Psychology, 83*(3), 471–485. doi:10.1037/0021-9010.83.3.471

Chapman, D. S., & Webster, J. (2003). The use of technologies in the recruiting, screening, and selection processes for job candidates. *International Journal of Selection and Assessment, 11*(2/3), 113–120. doi:10.1111/1468-2389.00234

Chebotarev, P. Y. (1994). Aggregation of preferences by the generalized row sum method. *Mathematical Social Sciences, 27*, 293–320. doi:10.1016/0165-4896(93)00740-L

Chen, J., & McQueen, R. J. (2009). Knowledge transfer processes for different experience levels of knowledge recipients at an offshore technical support center. *Information Technology & People, 23*(1), 54–79. doi:10.1108/09593841011022546

Chen, S., Langner, C. A., & Mendoza-Denton, R. (2009). When dispositional and role power fit: Implications for self-expression and self-other congruence. *Journal of Personality and Social Psychology, 96*(3), 710–727. doi:10.1037/a0014526

Chen, Y., & Cheng, L. (2010). An approach to group ranking decisions in a dynamic environment. *Decision Support Systems, 48*, 622–634. doi:10.1016/j.dss.2009.12.003

Christiansen, N. D., Goffin, R. D., Johnston, N. G., & Rothstein, M. G. (1994). Correction the 16PF for faking: Effects on criterion-related validity and individual hiring decisions. *Personnel Psychology, 47*, 847–860. doi:10.1111/j.1744-6570.1994.tb01581.x

Cronin, B., Morath, R., Curtin, P., & Heul, M. (2006). Public sector use of technology in managing human resources. *Human Resource Management Review, 16*, 416–430. doi:10.1016/j.hrmr.2006.05.008

Dale, K., & Fox, M. L. (2008). Leadership style and organizational commitment: Mediating effect of role stress. *Journal of Managerial Issues, 20*(1), 109.

DeRue, D. S., & Morgeson, F. P. (2009). Stability and change in person-team and person-role fit over time: The effects of growth satisfaction, performance, and general self-efficacy. *The Journal of Applied Psychology*, *92*(5), 1242–1253. doi:10.1037/0021-9010.92.5.1242

Dunn, W. S., Mount, M. K., Barrick, M. R., & Ones, D. S. (1995). Relative importance of personality and general mental ability in managers' judgments of applicant qualifications. *The Journal of Applied Psychology*, *80*, 500–509. doi:10.1037/0021-9010.80.4.500

Fernie, S., Green, S. D., Weller, S. J., & Newcombe, R. (2003). Knowledge sharing: context, confusion and controversy. *International Journal of Project Management*, *21*, 177–187. doi:10.1016/S0263-7863(02)00092-3

Finch, D. M., Edwards, B. D., & Wallace, J. C. (2009). Multistage selection strategies: Simulating the effects on adverse impact and expected performance for various predictor combinations. *The Journal of Applied Psychology*, *94*(2), 318–340. doi:10.1037/a0013775

Gellatly, I. R. (1996). Conscientiousness and task performance: Test of cognitive process model. *The Journal of Applied Psychology*, *81*(5), 474–482. doi:10.1037/0021-9010.81.5.474

Gevers, J. M. P., Rutte, C. G., & Eerde, W. (2006). Meeting deadlines in work groups: Implicit and explicit mechanisms. *Applied Psychology*, *55*, 52–72. doi:10.1111/j.1464-0597.2006.00228.x

Gibbs, G. (2007). *Analyzing qualitative data*. London, UK: Sage.

Granovetter, M. S. (1973). The strength of weak ties. *American Journal of Sociology*, *78*(6), 1360–1380. doi:10.1086/225469

Greguras, G. J., & Diefendorff, J. M. (2009). Different fits satisfy different needs: Linking person-environment fit to employee commitment and performance using self-determination theory. *The Journal of Applied Psychology*, *94*(2), 465–477. doi:10.1037/a0014068

Gueutal, H. G., & Falbe, C. M. (2005). eHR: Trends in delivery methods. In H. G. Gueutal & D. L. Stone (Eds.), *The brave new world of eHR* (pp. 226-254). San Francisco, CA: Jossey-Bass.

Gupta, A. K., & Govindarajan, V. (2000). Knowledge flows within multinational corporations. *Strategic Management Journal*, *21*(4), 473–496. doi:10.1002/(SICI)1097-0266(200004)21:4<473::AID-SMJ84>3.0.CO;2-I

Hausknecht, J. P., Day, D. V., & Thomas, S. C. (2004). Applicant reactions to selection procedures: An updated model and meta-analysis. *Personnel Psychology*, *57*, 639–683. doi:10.1111/j.1744-6570.2004.00003.x

Hempel, P. S. (2004). Preparing the HR profession for technology and information work. *Human Resource Management*, *43*(2/3), 163–177. doi:10.1002/hrm.20013

Heusinkveld, S., & Reijers, H. A. (2009). Reflections on a reflective cycle: Building legitimacy in design knowledge development. *Organization Studies*, *30*, 865–886.

Highhouse, S. (2008). Stubborn reliance on intuition and subjectivity in employee selection. *Industrial and Organizational Psychology. Perspectives on Science and Practice*, *1*(3), 333–342.

Hislop, D. (2005). *Knowledge management in organizations: A critical approach*. Oxford, UK: Oxford University Press.

Hong, D., Suh, E., & Koo, C. (2011). Developing strategies for overcoming barriers to knowledge sharing based on conversational knowledge management: A case study of a financial company. *Expert Systems with Applications, 38*(12). doi:10.1016/j.eswa.2011.04.072

Hough, L. M., Eaton, N. K., Dunnette, M. D., Kamp, J. D., & McCloy, R. A. (1990). Criterion-related validities of personality constructs and the effect of response distortion on those validities. *Journal of Applied Psychology Monograph, 75*(5), 581–595. doi:10.1037/0021-9010.75.5.581

Kehoe, J. F., Dickter, D. N., Russell, D. P., & Sacco, J. M. (2005). E-selection. In Gueutal, H. G., & Stone, D. L. (Eds.), *The brave new world of eHR* (pp. 54–103). San Francisco, CA: Jossey-Bass.

Keller, R. T. (2001). Cross-functional project groups in research and new product development: Diversity, communication, job stress and outcomes. *Academy of Management Journal, 44*(3), 547–555. doi:10.2307/3069369

Kieffer, K. M., Schinka, J. A., & Curtiss, G. (2004). Person-environment congruence and personality domains in the prediction of job performance and work quality. *Journal of Counseling Psychology, 51*(2), 168–177. doi:10.1037/0022-0167.51.2.168

Kluemper, D. H., & Rosen, P. A. (2009). Future employment selection methods: Evaluating social networking web sites. *Journal of Managerial Psychology, 24*(6), 567–580. doi:10.1108/02683940910974134

Kvale, S., & Brinkmann, S. (2009). *Interviews: Learning the craft of qualitative research interviewing* (2nd ed.). London, UK: Sage.

Lei, D., Hitt, M. A., & Bettis, R. (1996). Dynamic core competences through meta-learning and strategic context. *Journal of Management, 22*(4), 549–569. doi:10.1177/014920639602200402

Lepak, D. P., & Snell, S. A. (1998). Virtual HR: Strategic human resource management in the 21st century. *Human Resource Management Review, 8*(3), 215–234. doi:10.1016/S1053-4822(98)90003-1

Lievens, F., & Harris, M. M. (2003). Research on internet recruiting and testing: Current status and future directions. *International Review of Industrial and Organizational Psychology, 18,* 131–165.

Locke, E. A., & Latham, G. P. (2002). Building a practically useful theory of goal setting and task motivation: a 35-year odyssey. *The American Psychologist, 57*(9), 705. doi:10.1037/0003-066X.57.9.705

MacFarland, L. A., Yun, G. J., Harold, C. M., Viera, L., & Moore, L. G. (2005). An examination of impression management use and effectiveness across assessment center exercises: The role of competency demands. *Personnel Psychology, 58,* 949–980. doi:10.1111/j.1744-6570.2005.00374.x

Matzler, K., Renzl, B., Müller, J., Herting, S., & Mooradian, T. A. (2008). Personality traits and knowledge sharing. *Journal of Economic Psychology, 29,* 301–313. doi:10.1016/j.joep.2007.06.004

McAdams, D. P. (2009). *The person-an introduction to the science of personality psychology.* Hoboken, NJ: John Wiley and Sons, Inc.

McCrae, R. R., Stone, S. V., Fagan, P. J., & Costa, P. T. Jr. (1998). Identifying causes of disagreement between self-reports and spouse ratings of personality. *Journal of Personality, 66,* 286–313. doi:10.1111/1467-6494.00013

McManus, M. A., & Ferguson, M. W. (2003). Biodata, personality, and demographic differences of recruits from three sources. *International Journal of Selection and Assessment, 11*(2/3), 175–183. doi:10.1111/1468-2389.00241

Mohamed, A. A., Orife, J. N., & Wibowo, K. (2001). The legality of key word search as a personnel selection tool. *Employee Relations, 24*(5), 516–522. doi:10.1108/01425450210443285

Mooney, A. (2007). Core competence, distinctive competence, and competitive advantage: What is the difference? *Journal of Education for Business,* (November/December): 110–115. doi:10.3200/JOEB.83.2.110-115

Mount, M. K., Judge, T. A., Scullen, S. E., Sytsma, M. R., & Hezlett, S. A. (1998). Trait, rater, and level effects in 360-degree performance ratings. *Personnel Psychology, 51,* 557–576. doi:10.1111/j.1744-6570.1998.tb00251.x

Murhpy, K. R., & DeShon, R. (2000). Interrater correlations do not estimate the reliability of job performance ratings. *Personnel Psychology, 53,* 873–900. doi:10.1111/j.1744-6570.2000.tb02421.x

O'Leary-Kelly, A. M., Martocchio, J. J., & Frink, D. D. (1994). A review of the influence of group goals on group performance. *Academy of Management Journal, 37*(5), 1285–1301. doi:10.2307/256673

O'Reilly, C. A. III, Chatman, J., & Caldwell, D. F. (1991). People and organizational culture: A profile comparison approach to assessing person-organization fit. *Academy of Management Journal, 34*(3), 487–516. doi:10.2307/256404

Ostroff, C., & Aumann, K. A. (2004). Person-environment fit. In Spielberger, C. (Ed.), *Encyclopedia of applied psychology* (*Vol. 3*, pp. 19–28). doi:10.1016/B0-12-657410-3/00746-7

Paulhus, D. L., & Reid, D. B. (1991). Enhancement and denial in socially desirable responding. *Journal of Personality and Social Psychology, 60*(2), 307–317. doi:10.1037/0022-3514.60.2.307

Peeters, M. A. G. (2006). *Design teams and personality: Effects of team composition on processes and effectiveness.* Dissertation, Technische Universiteit Eindhoven.

Prahalad, C. K., & Hamel, G. (1990). The core competence of the corporation. *Harvard Business Review, 68,* 79–91.

Romme, A. G., & Endenburg, G. (2006). Construction principles and design rules in the case of circular design. *Organization Science, 17*(2), 287–297. doi:10.1287/orsc.1050.0169

Rosse, J. G., Miller, J. L., & Stecher, M. D. (1994). A field study of job applicants' reactions to personality and cognitive ability testing. *The Journal of Applied Psychology, 79*(6), 987–992. doi:10.1037/0021-9010.79.6.987

Ruël, H., Bondarouk, T., & Looise, J. K. (2004). *E-HRM: innovation or irritation? An exploration of web-based human resource management in large companies.* Utrecht, The Netherlands: Lemma Publishers.

Ryan, A. M., & Ployheart, R. E. (2000). Applicants' perceptions of selection procedures and decisions: A critical review and agenda for the future. *Journal of Management, 26,* 565–606. doi:10.1177/014920630002600308

Ryan, A. M., Sacco, J. M., McFarland, L. A., & Kriska, S. D. (2000). Applicant self-selection: Correlates of withdrawal from a multiple hurdle process. *The Journal of Applied Psychology, 85,* 163–179. doi:10.1037/0021-9010.85.2.163

Ryan, A. M., & Tippins, N. T. (2004). Attracting and selecting: What psychological research tells us. *Human Resource Management, 43*(4), 305–318. doi:10.1002/hrm.20026

Ryan, R. M., & Deci, E. L. (2000). Self-determination theory and the facilitation of intrinsic motivation, social development and well-being. *The American Psychologist*, *55*(1), 68–78. doi:10.1037/0003-066X.55.1.68

Sackett, P. R., & Lievens, F. (2008). Personnel selection. *Annual Review of Psychology*, 419–450. doi:10.1146/annurev.psych.59.103006.093716

Schmidt, F. L., & Hunter, J. E. (1998). The validity and utility of selection methods in personnel psychology: Practical and theoretical implications of 85 years of research findings. *Psychological Bulletin*, *124*(2), 262–274. doi:10.1037/0033-2909.124.2.262

Schmidt, F. L., Viswesvaran, C., & Ones, D. S. (2000). Reliability is not validity and validity is not reliability. *Personnel Psychology*, *53*, 901–912. doi:10.1111/j.1744-6570.2000.tb02422.x

Schmitt, N., & Oswald, F. L. (2006). The impact of corrections for faking on the validity of non-cognitive measures in selection settings. *The Journal of Applied Psychology*, *91*, 613–621. doi:10.1037/0021-9010.91.3.613

Schneider, B., Kristof-Brown, A., Goldstein, H. W., & Smith, D. B. (1997). What is this thing called fit? In Anderson, N., & Herriot, P. (Eds.), *International handbook of selection and assessment* (pp. 393–412). Chichester, UK: Wiley.

Shrivastava, P. (1987). Rigor and practical usefulness of research in strategic management. *Strategic Management Journal*, *8*, 77–92. doi:10.1002/smj.4250080107

Silver, E. A., Pike, D. F., & Peterson, R. (1998). *Inventory management and production planning schedules* (3rd ed.). Hoboken, NJ: John Wiley and Sons Inc.

Spector, P. E. (2008). *Industrial and organizational psychology* (5th ed.). Hoboken, NJ: John Wiley and Sons Inc.

Stewart, G. L., Darnold, T. C., Zimmerman, R. D., Parks, L., & Dustin, S. L. (2010). Exploring how response distortion of personality measures affects individuals. *Personality and Individual Differences*, *49*, 622–628. doi:10.1016/j.paid.2010.05.035

Stone, D. L., Stone-Romero, E. F., & Lukaszweski, K. (2003). The functional and dysfunctional consequences of using technology to achieve human resource system goals. In Stone, D. L. (Ed.), *Research in human performance and cognitive engineering technology* (*Vol. 3*, pp. 37–68). Greenwich, CT: JAI.

Stone-Romero, E. F. (2005). The effects of HR system characteristics and culture on system acceptance and effectiveness. In Gueutal, H. G., & Stone, D. L. (Eds.), *The brave new world of eHR* (pp. 226–254). San Francisco, CA: Jossey-Bass.

Strauss, A. M., & Corbin, J. (1990). *Basics of qualitative research*. Newbury Park, CA: Sage.

Strohmeier, S. (2007). Research in e-HRM: Review and implications. *Human Resource Management Review*, *17*, 19–37. doi:10.1016/j.hrmr.2006.11.002

Sylva, H., & Mol, S. T. (2009). E-recruitment: a study into applicant perceptions of an online application system. *International Journal of Selection and Assessment*, *17*(3), 311–323. doi:10.1111/j.1468-2389.2009.00473.x

Szulanski, G. (1996). Exploring internal stickiness: Impediments to the transfer of best practices within the firm. *Strategic Management Journal*, *17*, 27–43.

Tesluk, P., Mathieu, J. E., Zaccaro, S. J., & Marks, M. (1997). Task and aggregation issues in the analysis and assessment of team performance. In Brannick, M. T., Salas, E., & Prince, C. (Eds.), *Team performance assessment and measurement* (pp. 197–224). Mahwah, NJ: Lawrence Erlbaum.

Tippins, N. T., Beaty, J., Drasgow, F., Gibson, W. M., Pearlman, K., Segall, D. O., & Shepherd, W. (2006). Unproctored internet testing in employment settings. *Personnel Psychology, 59*, 189–225. doi:10.1111/j.1744-6570.2006.00909.x

Truchon, M. (2008). Borda and the maximum likelihood approach to vote aggregation. *Mathematical Social Sciences, 55*, 96–102. doi:10.1016/j.mathsocsci.2007.08.001

Truxillo, D. M., Bauer, T. N., Campion, M. A., & Paronto, M. E. (2002). Selection fairness information and applicant reactions: A longitudinal field study. *The Journal of Applied Psychology, 87*, 1020–1031. doi:10.1037/0021-9010.87.6.1020

Tsiporkova, E., & Boeva, V. (2006). Multi-step ranking of alternatives in a multi-criteria and multi-expert decision making environment. *Information Sciences, 176*, 2673–2697. doi:10.1016/j.ins.2005.11.010

Tsoukas, H. (1996). The firm as a distributed knowledge system: A constructionist approach. *Strategic Management Journal, 17*(winter special issue), 11-25.

Van Aken, J. E. (2005). Management research as a design science. *British Journal of Management, 16*, 19–36. doi:10.1111/j.1467-8551.2005.00437.x

Van Aken, J. E., Berends, J. J., & van der Bij, J. D. (2007). *Problem solving in organizations: a methodological handbook for business students.* Cambridge, UK: Cambridge University Press. doi:10.1017/CBO9780511618413

Van den Hooff, B., & Huysman, M. (2009). Managing knowledge sharing: Emergent and engineering approaches. *Information & Management, 46*, 1–8. doi:10.1016/j.im.2008.09.002

Van Eerde, W., & Thierry, H. (1996). Vroom's expectancy models and work-related criteria: A meta-analysis. *The Journal of Applied Psychology, 81*(5), 575–586. doi:10.1037/0021-9010.81.5.575

Van Iddekinge, C. H., Raymark, P. H., & Roth, P. L. (2005). Assessing personality with a structured employment interview: Construct-related validity and susceptibility to response inflation. *The Journal of Applied Psychology, 90*, 536–552. doi:10.1037/0021-9010.90.3.536

Van Iddekinge, C. H., Raymark, P. H., Roth, P. L., & Payne, H. S. (2006). Comparing the psychometric characteristics of rating of face-to-face and videotaped structured interviews. *International Journal of Selection and Assessment, 14*(4), 347–359. doi:10.1111/j.1468-2389.2006.00356.x

Van Manen, M. (1990). *Researching lived experience: Human science for an action sensitive pedagogy.* Ontario, Canada: Althouse press.

Van Strien, P. J. (1997). Towards a methodology of psychological practice. *Theory & Psychology, 7*(5), 683–700. doi:10.1177/0959354397075006

Vogel, R. M., & Feldman, D. C. (2009). Integrating the levels of person-environment fit: the roles of vocational fit and group fit. *Journal of Vocational Behavior, 75*, 68–81. doi:10.1016/j.jvb.2009.03.007

Wang, S., & Noe, R. A. (2010). Knowledge sharing: A review and directions for future research. *Human Resource Management Review, 20*, 115–131. doi:10.1016/j.hrmr.2009.10.001

Werr, A., & Stjernberg, T. (2003). Exploring management consulting firms as knowledge systems. *Organization Studies, 24*(6), 881–908. doi:10.1177/0170840603024006004

Wright, P., & Dyer, L. (2000). *People in the e-business: New challenges, new solutions.* Working paper 00-II, Center for advanced human resource studies, Cornell University.

Yang, H. L., & Wu, T. C. T. (2008). Knowledge sharing in an organization. *Technological Forecasting and Social Change, 75*, 1128–1156. doi:10.1016/j.techfore.2007.11.008

Yang, J. T. (2007). Knowledge sharing: Investigating appropriate leadership roles and collaborative culture. *Tourism Management*, *28*, 530–543. doi:10.1016/j.tourman.2006.08.006

Yang, J. T. (2008). Individual attitudes and organisational knowledge sharing. *Tourism Management*, *29*, 345–353. doi:10.1016/j.tourman.2007.03.001

KEY TERMS AND DEFINITIONS

Competence Management: Supports the integration of human resources planning with business planning by allowing organizations to assess the current human resource capacity based on their competencies against the capacity needed to achieve the vision, mission and business goals of the organization.

E-Selection: An application of (web-based) information technology for the execution and support of the personnel selection process by the employee and/or the organization (Chapman and Webster, 2003; Ruël, et al, 2004; Strohmeier, 2007).

Knowledge Management: A range of strategies and practices used in an organization to identify, create, represent, distribute, and enable adoption of insights and experiences.

Psychological Testing: A field characterized by the use of samples of behavior in order to assess psychological construct(s), such as cognitive and emotional functioning, about a given individual.

Chapter 2
A Constructive Approach for Conceptual Database Design

Elvira Locuratolo
ISTI Consiglio Nazionale delle Ricerche, Italy

ABSTRACT

The chapter focuses on the conceptual database design evolution, by introducing concepts which are common to both information systems and software engineering researches. An optimization algorithm of partitioning, based on the decomposition of objects and on the inheritance of attributes, is proposed and extended. The extended algorithm, which defines a formal constructive mapping from conceptual to logical database models, aims to show how some updates reflecting modifications occurring in real life can affect the conceptual database design. The chapter evidences the idea that model design, which retains quality aspects, such as maintainability and re-usability over a long lifetime, also suggests appropriate implementations which can be characterized by innovation and productivity. Algorithms of partitioning have been exploited within a database design methodology for quality, a method of re-engineering, and recently, in concept theory for digital preservation.

INTRODUCTION

Before creating an information system, the business and organizational domain in which the information system is used must be represented. This representation, called conceptual model, is a critical point for the success of the information system development. Databases and database systems play a pre-eminent role in supporting data management and in implementing engineering information (Ma, 2006). *Conceptual Database Design* (Elmasri & Navathe, 2003), defined by approaches of mappings from conceptual to logical database models, is essential in researches on *information systems* and *software engineering*. Graphs of classes representing *conceptual/logical database models* are based on concepts which are common to both these areas. New engineering

DOI: 10.4018/978-1-4666-3679-8.ch002

requirements and current technologies favor the conceptual database design evolution.

This chapter focuses on graphs of classes representing conceptual/logical database models, on methods for their construction and on algorithms of mapping from conceptual data models to logical data models. When a method engineer creates a methodology, he or she usually utilizes a given meta-model to create a specific instance, in our case to create a specific conceptual/logical database model and a corresponding mapping. Meta-models are adequate means to understand how design, development and implementation of systems concerned with different disciplines can be affected to reflect evolutions occurring in real life. In this chapter, starting from the formal approach exploited to design the model of a conceptual database design methodology (Locuratolo, 2011); a formal constructive approach of mappings from conceptual database models to logical database models is provided. The following motivations justify the approach.

Semantic data models and object database systems (Cardenas & McLeod, 1990) have similar mechanisms of abstraction; however, while semantic data models have never been implemented efficiently (Nixon & Mylopoulos, 1990), object database systems have reached a remarkable level of efficiency. On the contrary, while semantic data models are adequate for conceptual design, object database systems can display serious shortcomings in their ability to describe the dynamic nature of the real world entities. Semantic data models enhance *flexibility,* whereas object models enhance *efficiency*. The mapping from semantic data models to object systems is a means to achieve both the conflicting desiderata of *flexibility* and *efficiency*. Model *correctness* is also desired for conceptual design. Correctness can be appropriately preserved designing formal mappings based on model equivalence. Many classifications of mappings are presented in the literature, however formal methods for creating mappings are scant (Yuan, 2006).

By *partitioning* (Spagnolo, 2000; Locuratolo & Palomäki, 2008) we mean a set of properties enjoyed by algorithms which map semantic data models to object systems. Each map provides as output the same set of disjoint classes. These classes are then recomposed to define a graph of object classes. Many equivalent graphs of classes can be defined. The choice of the specific partitioning algorithm, as well as the choice of the specific graph of object classes is related with an objective to be reached. The partitioning algorithms guarantee the design correctness.

In this chapter, an optimization algorithm of partitioning is proposed. Interesting aspect of the chapter is the determination of conceptual/logical model extensions. Moreover, the optimization algorithm can be extended coherently with the determined model extensions. Specifically, the proposed extension aims to show how some modifications occurring in the real life can affect the conceptual design. The approach can be summarized as follows: a graph of classes supported by semantic data models, a notion characterizing the partitioning algorithms and an optimization algorithm of partitioning are first introduced. Then, an extension of the proposed graph and an extension of the optimization algorithm are proposed. The extended algorithm, which defines a formal constructive mapping from conceptual to logical database models, show how the conceptual database design evolution can affect also possible implementations.

The chapter encloses:

- A background section which gives an overview of the concepts related with information systems and software engineering.
- A section which presents the chapter perspective in modeling and defining constructive algorithms of conceptual database design. Specifically, an optimization algorithm of partitioning is proposed and extended.

- A presentation of new topics for future research in the perspective of the book's theme. These include an interesting topic of research based on concept theory and databases (Locuratolo & Palomäki, 2012) and new approaches to database research, including ontology for database preservation (Locuratolo & Palomäki, 2013).

BACKGROUND

In *Software Engineering*, Model-Driven Engineering (MDE) is an approach to software development that separates the specification of the system functionality from its implementation on a particular platform. The Object Management Group (OMG) model driven architecture (MDA) makes models the primary artefacts of software engineering. The MDA development consists in the definition of a platform-independent model (PIM) of a system and in the application of parameterised transformations to this PIM in order to obtain one or more specific platforms. Another important specification is Architecture Driven Modernization (ADM) which is the process of understanding and evolving existing software. It involves modifications, reuse and enterprise application integrations. An MDA approach to modernization is a way to revitalize existing applications and systems. It concerns a wide variety of models and mappings between models, allowing integration and transformation of those models. Two main categories of mapping can be distinguished:

- **Vertical mapping:** Relates system models at different abstraction levels;
- **Horizontal mapping:** Relates or integrates models at the same level of abstraction.

Over the last few years, MDA has been integrated with *enterprise information systems* and other technologies, such as Semantic Web, Se-

mantic Web services, Ontology and Knowledge representation technique. Ontology definition meta-models (ODM) join Semantic Web with MDA. Conventional paradigms for capturing conceptual knowledge, such as (UML) Entity-Relational models (E/R) and Semantic Data Models have also been considered within approaches of mapping.

In (Locuratolo, 2011), a meta-model based on horizontal mappings is proposed. Starting from an initial semantic data model based on the notions of class and is-a relationship, two gradual model extensions are considered: the former defines the basic operations, whereas the latter defines the conceptual model of ASSO, a formal database design methodology (Locuratolo, 2005). This model, called Structured Database Schema is a platform-independent model that raises the abstraction level of the B model (Abrial, 1995). Both a "qualitative measure" of information implicitly specified within the structured database schema and a "qualitative evaluation" of the consistency costs, given in terms of cost reduction of not specified classes, are provided.

Approaches of conceptual database design come from database design methodologies and from software engineering methodologies. The data-driven methodologies (Batini, Ceri & Navathe, 1992) generally consist of two steps: the conceptual schema construction and the logical schema generation. To make the conceptual schema *easy to be used*, high level abstraction models, such as *Semantic Data models* (Cardenas & McLeod, 1990) or *Entity-Relationship Models* (Chen, 1976), are employed with a diagrammatic representation. The abstraction mechanisms of these models closely resemble those used in describing the applications. To represent the complementary *dynamic aspects*, state-based and data-flow models are used; however, as the models employed to represent statics and dynamics are either informal or non-integrated formalizations, it is not possible to prove that the specified operations preserve the database consistency. The construction of the conceptual schema is followed by the generation of the logical schema. Within this step of design, the conceptual schema is mapped to a relational model; however, in the mapping process there is the possibility of introducing errors.

The *object-oriented methodologies* (Coad & Yordon, 1991; Bernard, 1993; Booch, 1994; Rumbaugh & Booch & Jacobson, 1999) proposed within the software engineering area are the more natural way to develop object systems, which nowadays are very popular because of the efficiency they provide. These methodologies focus on the identification and organizations of the objects that compose an application. The object-oriented methodologies employ the same model along the whole life cycle. This renders the mapping smoother thus reducing the risk of introducing errors. ASSO is a methodology of the database design which starts from the definition of the conceptual schema, i.e., a high level description of the database structure and behavioral independent from the particular DBMS which will be used, and provides a logical schema, i.e., a description of the database schema processable from the chosen DBMS.

An algorithm of Partitioning is one of the ASSO components. ASSO has been designed to combine easy modification of the schema with efficient implementation, whilst ensuring specification consistency and design correctness. Object oriented methodologies, however, have always been very weak when dealing with data design; an example of methodology which overcomes this problem is IDEA (Ceri & Fraternali, 1997). In this methodology, data design comes first and application design follows. For the generalization hierarchies of IDEA, no transformation is required in the passage from analysis to design. The objects of a super class are partitioned into the objects of the subclasses. This differs from the specialization hierarchy of the ASSO conceptual model, where the objects of the subclasses can overlap and a

partitioning algorithm is exploited to map the conceptual model to the logical model.

Database Models

Database models can be classified at two levels: conceptual data models and logical database models.

A survey of the current database models can be found in (Ma, 2006). This paper focuses on conceptual database design: the relationships between the conceptual and the logical database models for engineering information modeling are presented and the requirements for engineering information modeling are identified. These enclose complex objects, data exchange and data sharing, web-based applications, imprecision and uncertainty and knowledge management. New techniques, such as Web and Artificial Intelligence, have been introduced in industrial applications. Current researchers are concerned with design, development and use of information systems in organizations based on socio-technological perspective, rather than purely technological perspective. Much attention is devoted to social, organizational, cognitive, and behavioral aspects of these systems.

The partitioning algorithms define mappings from semantic data models, called *conceptual classes* to object systems, called *object classes*. These algorithms are based on the decompositions of objects and on the inheritance of attributes. In order to evidence the main differences between the conceptual classes and the object classes, let us refer to the graph of Figure 1, which is based on the following properties:

- **Classification:** Each node of the graph (*person* with attribute *income, student* with attribute *matriculation,* and *employee* with attribute *salary*) is a class. A node linked with a higher level node is a class called *specialized class*. In Figure 1 there are the specialized classes *employee* with attri-

Figure 1. Graph of classes

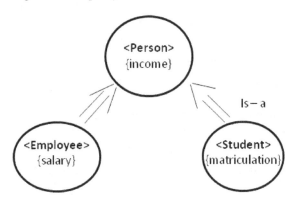

butes *income* and *salary*, and the specialized class *student* with attributes *income* and *matriculation*.

- **Attribute Inheritance:** A specialized class (for example, in our example, the specialized class *employee*) inherits all the attributes from the higher level classes (in our example, the class *person*) and may have also additional attributes.

The graph in Figure 1 can be both a graph of conceptual classes and a graph of object classes. Coherently with the perspective of the ODMG (Object Data Management Group), the difference between the conceptual classes and the object classes can be evidenced by the following properties:

- **Conceptual classes:** Each object instance can belong to any class of the graph. This enhances *flexibility* while limiting *efficiency*. In our example, the object instances of the specialized class *employee* are a subset of the class *person* instances.
- **Object classes:** Each object instance belongs to one and only one class of the graph. This enhances *efficiency* while limiting *flexibility*. In our example, the object instances of the specialized class *employee*

and the object instances of the class *person* are disjoint sets.

Object classes limit the flexibility in reflecting the changes occurring in the real life. Let us suppose for example, that *student* John becomes an *employee*. In this case, the corresponding object instance must be removed from the class *<Student>* and must be inserted into the class *<Student•Employee>*, which is the class defined by the object intersection of the two classes *<Student>* and *<Employee>*. If John later on completes his studies, the corresponding object instance must be removed from the class *<Student•Employee>* and must be inserted into the class *<Employee>*. On the contrary, in semantic data models, the object instance corresponding to John can be inserted into the class *<Employee>* when the *Student* John becomes an *Employee,* and can be removed from the class *<Student>* when John completes his studies. Semantic data models enhance *flexibility*, whereas object models enhance *efficiency*. An algorithm of partitioning is a mapping from *conceptual* classes to *object* classes which allows achieving both the conflicting desiderata of *flexibility* and *efficiency*.

Partitioning Algorithms

The first algorithm of partitioning, called *Partitioning Method* (Locuratolo & Rabitti, 1998) is based on *difficult* operators of graph decompositions and results into *disjoint classes,* which satisfy the property that each object instance belongs to one and only one class. The disjoint classes, however, have not been recomposed into a graph of object classes. The partitioning method is *correct,* that is the objects of the obtained classes are all and only the objects of the conceptual classes. Further, they have all and only the attributes defined in the conceptual classes. The partitioning method is *complete*, that is it provides as output the finest decomposition of the conceptual classes.

Differently from the partitioning method, other algorithms of partitioning (Locuratolo, 1998; Spagnolo, 2000; Locuratolo & Palomäki, 2008/2012) are based on the set theory operators. All these algorithms are composed by of two phases, called *representation* and *decomposition,* respectively. The former is related with the description of the conceptual graph, whereas the latter is related with the object decomposition process. In the *representation* phase, a label connoting the class name and denoting the class objects is associated with each graph node, whereas a list of attribute names is associated with each label. In the example of Figure 1, the class *<Person>* has the attribute *income*. This model implicitly specifies that the objects of each class are represented by a subset of a given set, whereas each attribute has been formalized by a function defined in the specified set of objects and assuming values in an implicitly specified set. The *decomposition* phase is a stepwise approach based on successive decompositions of an initial graph of conceptual classes until all and only disjoint classes are obtained. At each decomposition step, class names combined through the complement and the intersection operators of the set theory label the classes of the resulting graphs. The disjoint classes can be recomposed into a graph of object classes in many different ways. The choice of the specific algorithm as well as the choice of the specific graph of object classes is related with the objective to be reached.

APPROACH

In accordance with the partitioning perspective presented in the background section, an optimization algorithm is designed. This algorithm is a vertical mapping from a conceptual graph, i.e. a graph of conceptual classes to a corresponding objet/logical graph, i.e. a graph of object/logical classes. The conceptual graph, which is a minimal model, is extended through a horizontal mapping, and an extended conceptual graph is defined. The chapter aims to show how some updates reflecting modifications occurring in the real life can affect the conceptual design of the proposed optimization algorithm.

Box 1.

[conceptual class]: (v, V) is a conceptual class	⇔	1. v is a term denoting a subset of a given set; 2. V is finite set of distinct terms, attributes, and denoting functions from v to the power set of given sets.

Box 2.

[specialized conceptual class]: If (v, V) and (u, U) are conceptual classes, then the following class (u, U_e) is defined as enrichment of class (u, U)		
(u, U_e) is the specialized conceptual class	⇔	1. $u \subseteq v$ 2. $U_e \supseteq U$ 3. $f \in V \Rightarrow f_u \in U_e$ with f_u restriction of f to the set u 4. $g \in U_e \Rightarrow g \in U$ Or $\exists h \in V / h_u = g$

Box 3.

[is-a relationship]: (u, U) is-a (v, V)	⇔	1. (v, V) is a conceptual class;
		2. (u, U) is a conceptual class;
		3. ∃ the class (u, U_e).

Box 4.

[conceptual graph]: G_c is a graph of conceptual classes	⇔	G_c is an acyclic, oriented graph /
		1. The nodes are conceptual classes.
		2. The links are is-a relationships between conceptual classes.

The Conceptual Graph G_C

The following notions: [*conceptual class*], [*specialized conceptual class*], [*is-a relationship*], and [*conceptual graph*] define the conceptual graph G_C (Locuratolo, 2009a). Each notion is specified on the left side of the " ⇔ " symbol, whereas its characterization is specified on the right side. (see Boxes 1 though 4)

- [*Conceptual class*] is a notion given in terms of definitions: the former is related with the class objects, whereas the latter is related with the attributes associated with the objects.
- [*Specialized conceptual class*] is a notion given under hypothesis and formally defined in terms of the following properties:
    - The objects of the specialized class (u, U_e) are a subset of the *(v, V)* objects;
    - The specialized class (u, U_e) inherits all the attributes from the class *(v, V)*;
    - The specialized class (u, U_e) encloses all the attributes of the class *(u, U)*;
    - No other attributes belongs to the specialized class (u, U_e).
- [*Specialized conceptual class*] and [*is-a relationship*] are two equivalent notions.

- [*Conceptual graph*] is a notion given through the already given notions of [*conceptual class*] and [*is-a relationship*].

The Revised Partitioning Notion

The *revised partitioning* notion adds property 3 to the partitioning notion given in (Locuratolo, 2009 a). This property is exploited in the next section to introduce the optimization algorithm. (see Box 5)

In Figure 2, a decomposition step of the conceptual graph, shown in Figure 1, is presented: the root objects of the original graph are partitioned into the root objects of two conceptual graphs. The classes are labeled. Attributes are associated in order to satisfy the consistency property: only the attributes of the conceptual class *<Person>* are associated with the conceptual class *<Person-Employee>*, whereas both the attributes of the conceptual class *<Person>* and of the conceptual class *<Employee>* are associated with the conceptual class *<Person•Employee>*. The example shows that the number of object classes is greater than the number of conceptual classes. Moreover, starting from three conceptual classes four disjoint logical classes are obtained. These can be recomposed in order to define a graph of object classes, as in Figure 3. This graph defines an object/logical graph G_L.

Box 5.

[revised partitioning]	⇔	*Step-sequence of decompositions resulting in the finest partition of a given conceptual graph. At each step of decomposition, the following properties hold:*
		1. **Root Partitioning:** *The root objects of a conceptual graph G_c are partitioned into the root objects of the conceptual graphs obtained after the decomposition.*
		2. **Root Labeling:** *The root labels of the graphs obtained from decomposition represent the partition. These labels are obtained combining the root label of the decomposed graph with the labels of the root directed descendants.*
		3. **Root Structuring:** *The root labels can be decomposed into two parts separated by the "-"sign: the former on the left of this sign consists of label intersections, whereas the latter on the right consists of label unions. One of the two parts can be empty.*
		4. **Consistency:** *The following implicit information is specified through the root labels: only the attributes of class <u> are associated with a node labeled by <u-v>, whereas the attributes of all the classes <v_1>...<v_n> with the node labeled by <$v_1 \cap ... \cap v_n$>.*
		5. **Object/Logical Graph:** *The obtained disjoint classes can be recomposed into a object/logical graph G_L.*

Figure 2. Decomposition

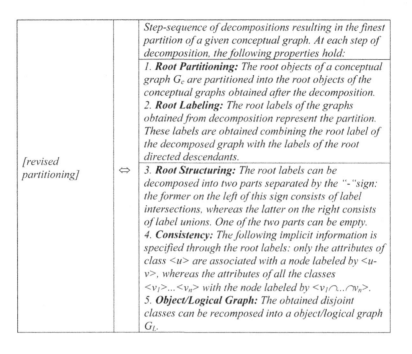

Figure 3. Object/logical graph G_L

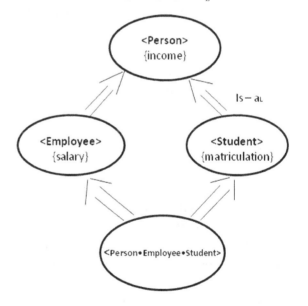

The class notion is the same in both the graphs G_C and G_L. The main difference between these two graphs is given by Property 1 of the specialized class notion, i.e. property $u \subseteq v$ in G_C is substituted by property $u \cap v = \phi$, in G_L. At the *logical/object level*, the *is-a$_L$* relationship corresponds to the *is-a* relationship, and thus it requires the existence of the logical specialized class $(u, U_e)_L$. The logical graph notion differs from the conceptual graph notion since the relationships between classes are *is-a $_L$* links. In a conceptual graph G_C, each object instance can belong to any class of the graph, thus enhancing *flexibility*, whereas in a logical graph G_L, each object instance belongs to one and only one class, thus enhancing *efficiency*. As an example, the <person> class of the conceptual graph G_C represented in Figure 1 encloses the student objects and the employee objects, whereas the student objects and the employee objects do not belong to <person> class of the logical graph G_L represented in Figure 3.

Models G_C and G_L are equivalent models. The model equivalence can easily be demonstrated proving that:

- The objects of the model G_L are all and only the objects of the model G_C,
- Each object of G_L has all and only the attributes which it has in G_C.

Each algorithm which satisfies the partitioning notion is a *correct* vertical mapping from G_C to G_L.

Optimization Algorithm

The complexity of a partitioning algorithm is defined by the number of the object classes (Locuratolo & Rabitti, 1998). This number is related with the structure of the graph and is independent from the chosen algorithm. The difference between any two partitioning algorithms is related with the number of the intermediate steps during the decomposition process. In (Locuratolo & Palomäki, 2012), an algorithm of maximum intermediate steps is provided. In this chapter, an algorithm composed by a single step is proposed. This algorithm, called *optimization algorithm*, computes the object classes without intermediate steps.

To define our approach, let us start with the optimization algorithm of a conceptual graph composed by a root $= (v, V)$ and tree directed descendents (u_1, U_1), (u_2, U_2), (u_3, U_3), and let us then generalize the approach. The former component of the couple is a label which connotes the class name and denotes the class objects. In order to determine the object classes resulting from the optimization algorithm, each node will be identified through its name, as follows: $<v>, <u_1>, <u_2>, <u_3>$. The number of the object classes resulting from a partitioning algorithm applied to the above conceptual graph is 2^3. As the optimization algorithm is composed by a single step, the *root structuring* property is substituted by the following *object node structuring* property:

Object node structuring: The 2^3 labels of the object classes are decomposed into two parts separated by the "-"operator: the former on the left of "-"operator consists of label intersections, whereas the latter on the right of the "-" operator consists of label unions. One of the two parts can be empty.

The *optimization partitioning algorithm* is an algorithm of direct computation of the class names, since it is composed by only one step. In accordance with the *object node structuring*, the optimization algorithm computes all and only the names resulting from labels connected through intersection operators on the left side of "-" sign and union operators on the right side. In accordance with the *consistency property*, also the attributes associated with the node labels can be directly computed. Finally, the obtained disjoint classes can be recomposed into an object/logical graph of classes analyzing the set-theory operators in the name labels of the disjoint classes. (See Algorithm 1)

Algorithm 1.

Optimization Algorithm $(<v>,<u_1>,<u_2>,<u_3>)$
Begin

{class names}

$<v - (\cup u_i)>,$ i={1,2,3}

$<(v \cap u_1) - \cup u_i>,$ i={2,3}

$<(v \cap u_2) - \cup u_i>,$ i={1,3}

$<(v \cap u_3) - \cup u_i>,$ i={1,2}

$<(v \cap u_1 \cap u_2) - u_3>,$

$<(v \cap u_1 \cap u_3) - u_2>,$

$<(v \cap u_2 \cap u_3) - u_1>,$

$<(v \cap u_1 \cap u_2 \cap u_3)>.$

{attributes}

V with the node label $<v - (\cup u_i)>,$ i={1,2,3}

$(V \cup U_1)$ with the node label $<(v \cap u_1) - \cup u_i>,$ i={2,3}

$(V \cup U_2)$ with the node label $<(v \cap u_2) - \cup u_i>,$ i={1,3}

$(V \cup U_3)$ with the node label $<(v \cap u_3) - \cup u_i>,$ i={1,2}

$(V \cup U_1 \cup U_2)$ with the node label $<(v \cap u_1 \cap u_2) - u_3>,$

$(V \cup U_1 \cup U_3)$ with the node label $<(v \cap u_1 \cap u_3) - u_2>,$

$(V \cup U_2 \cup U_3)$ with the node label $<(v \cap u_2 \cap u_3) - u_1>,$

$(V \cup U_1 \cup U_2 \cup U_3)$ with the node label $<(v \cap u_1 \cap u_2 \cap u_3)>.$

End

The proposed algorithm provides all disjoint classes. In order to define the *object/logical graph* G_L, the following observations can be taken into consideration:

Observation: As no intersection sign is enclosed in the label $<v - (\cup u_i)>$ i={1,2,3}, this label defines the root node of the *object/logical graph*. As an intersection sign is enclosed in the following labels: $<(v \cap u_1) - \cup u_i>,$ i={2,3}; $<(v \cap u_2) - \cup u_i>,$ i={1,3}; $<(v \cap u_3) - \cup u_i>,$ i={1,2}, these labels define the directed descendants of the root and the attributes of V are inherited. Generalizing the approach, $<(v \cap u_1 \cap u_2) - u_3>$ defines the descendant of $<(v \cap u_1) - \cup u_i>,$ and the attributes of $(V \cup U_1)$ are inherited; analogously, $<(v \cap u_1 \cap u_3) - u_2>$ defines the descendant

Box 6.

[extended conceptual class]: (v, V, Op) is an extended conceptual class	⇔	1. v is a term denoting a subset of a given set;
		2. V is finite set of distinct terms, attributes, denoting functions from v to the power set of a given set;
		3. Op is a finite set of basic operations (ADD, REM, SKIP, CHANGE) denoting functions from predicates satisfying the class-constraints to predicates satisfying the conceptual class-constraints.

Box 7.

[extended specialized conceptual class] If *(v, V, Op)* and *(u, U, Op')* are extended conceptual classes, then

(u, U_e, Op'_e) is the extended specialized conceptual class	⇔	1. $u \subseteq v$
		2. $U_e \supseteq U$
		3. $f \in V \Rightarrow f_u \in U_e$
		4. $g \in U_e \Rightarrow g \in U$ or $\exists h \in V / h_u = g$
		5. $op \in OP \Rightarrow \exists op_s \in OP' \wedge op \,||\, op_s \in OP'_e$
		6. $op° \in Op'_e \Rightarrow op° \in Op'$ or $\exists op \in OP \wedge \exists op_s \in OP' / op \,||\, op_s = op°$

Box 8.

[extended is-a relationship]: (u, U, Op') is-a (v, V, Op)	⇔	1. (v, V, Op) is an extended conceptual class;
		2. (u, U, Op') is an extended conceptual class;
		3. ∃ extended specialized conceptual class (u, U_e, Op'_e)

Box 9.

[extended conceptual graph]: G_c' is an extended conceptual graph	⇔	G_c is an acyclic, oriented graph /
		1. The nodes are extended conceptual classes.
		2. The links are is-a relationships between extended conceptual classes.

Figure 4. Extended conceptual graph

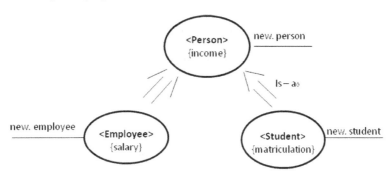

of $< (v \cap u_1) - u_2 >$ and so on. Once constructed the object/logical graph G_L, the class names can be simplified (See Figure 3).

The Extended Conceptual Graph G_C'

The extended conceptual graph G_C' adds basic operations to the notions of conceptual graph G_C. Each notion of G_C' extends a corresponding notion of G_C. The extended notion is compatible with the previous corresponding notion. The couple (G_C, G_C') defines a horizontal mapping from the initial conceptual/semantic model to the extended conceptual/semantic model. The notion compatibility allows determining an extended partitioning notion. The approach affects usefully the conceptual design evolution. The following notions: [*extended conceptual class*], [*extended specialized conceptual class*], [*extended is-a relationship*] and [*extended conceptual graph*] define G_C'. (see Boxes 6 through 9.)

Figure 5. Extended specialized conceptual class

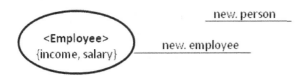

- The *extended conceptual class (v, V, Op)* enlarges the couple *(v, V)* of the initial model with the set *Op* of basic operations. The extension is "*good*" since the *(v, V, Op)* characterization is compatible with the *(v, V)* characterization. Moreover, both attributes and basic operations are defined by functions. Specifically, the basic operations are predicate transformers preserving the conceptual class constraints, i.e., functions from predicates to predicates. The weakest precondition semantics for a basic operation *op* is the following:
  [*op (v, V) (par_list)]R* ⇔ (*conceptual class-constraints(v, V)* ⇒ *conceptual class-constraints(v, V)*) ∧ R**
  where *R* is a predicate on the variables of class *(v, V)*, *conceptual class-constraints* is the predicate which formalizes the conceptual class definition and the star predicates are the mentioned predicates after the operation.

- The [*extended specialized conceptual class*] notion adds Properties 5. and 6. to the [*specialized conceptual class*] notion, making Properties 5. and 6. similar to Properties 3. and 4. Specifically, Property 5. ensures that the extended specialized class (u, U_e, Op'_e) inherits the operations from *(v, V, Op)*. The inheritance consists in the parallel composition of an operation coming from *(v, V, Op)* and a corresponding operation defined in *(u, U, Op')*, called

Figure 6. Extended logical/object graph $G_L{}'$

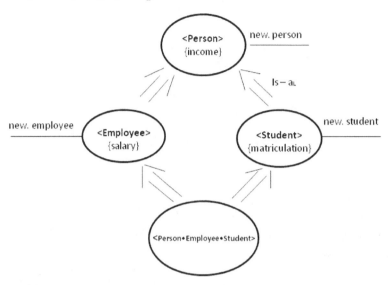

specialization. Property 6 ensures that each operation of (u, U_e, Op'_e) is either an operation inherited from *(v, V, Op)* or a specific operation of *(u, U, Op')*.

- The [*extended is-a relationship*] is given in terms of [*extended conceptual class*] notion and requires the existence of an extended specialized conceptual class.
- The [*extended conceptual graph*] is given in terms of the [*extended conceptual class*] and of the [*extended is-a relationship*] notions.

Figure 4 represents the extended conceptual graph $G_C{}'$ of the conceptual graph G_C represented in Figure 1. The operation *new.person* has been associated with the original class *<Person>*. Furthermore, the two specializations *new.employee* and *new.student* have been associated with the classes *<Employee>* and *<Student>*, respectively. Each operation/ specialization is represented in the Figures through an underlined name. A similarity holds for the inheritance of attributes and operations.

In Figure 5, the extended specialized conceptual class *<Employee>* is represented. The attribute *income* is restricted and inherited. Similarly, the operation *new.person* is restricted and inherited. To ensure the conceptual class consistency, the operation inheritance consists in the composition of the restricted operation *new.person* with the operation *new.employee* through the *//* operator presented in (Abrial, 1996).

The extended decomposition notion differs from the decomposition notion since, according to the consistency property, not only the attributes, but also the operations are associated with the classes. As far as the first decomposition step of the extended conceptual classes in Figure 4, only the operation *new.person* is associated with the node *<Person-Employee>*, whereas both the operations *new.person* and *new.employee* composed through the *//* operator are associated with the node *<Person•Employee>*.

In Figure 6, the graph of the extended logical classes corresponding to the graph of the extended conceptual classes proposed in Figure 4 is given. The multiple inheritance class *<Person•Employee•Student>* has no specific attribute/operation. The extended specialized class

<Person•Employee•Student> inherits attributes and operations from all the remaining classes. The equivalence of models G_L ' and G_C ' guarantees the vertical mapping correctness. The model equivalence can be easily demonstrated proving that:

- The objects of the model G_L ' are all and only the objects of the model G_C '.

- Each object of the model G_L ' has all and only the attributes which it has in G_C '.

- Each object of the model G_L ' is involved in all and only the operations corresponding to operations involving the objects in the model G_C '.

Starting from a correct algorithm of mapping, the approach determines extensions of this algorithm that can be incrementally extended and result to be correct without any need of proof.

Let us now extend the conceptual graph considered in the previous section, in accordance with the model extension. The extended conceptual graph is composed by a root $= (v, V, Op)$ and tree directed descendants $(u_1, U_1, Op'_1), (u_2, U_2, Op'_2),$ (u_3, U_3, Op'_3). Both attributes and basic operations are defined by functions, so as to be treated with homogeneity. As we will not start from scratch, no computation of the class manes is required and, in accordance with the *consistency property*, only the operations must be added to the listed attributes of the previous algorithm. The extension consists in adding the operations to the attributes of the optimization algorithm, as follows:

- $(V \cup Op)$ are associated with the node label $< v - (\cup u_i) >$, $_{i=\{1,2,3\}}$

- $(V \cup U_1 \cup Op'_1)$ are associated with the node label $< (v \cap u_1) - \cup u_i >$, $_{i=\{2,3\}}$

- $(V \cup U_1 \cup Op'_2)$ are associated with the node label $< (v \cap u_2) - \cup u_i >$, $_{i=\{1,3\}}$

- $(V \cup U_1 \cup Op'_3)$ are associated with the node label $< (v \cap u_3) - \cup u_i >$, $_{i=\{1,2\}}$

- $(V \cup U_1 \cup U_2 \cup Op'_1 \cup Op'_2)$ are associated with the node label $< (v \cap u_1 \cap u_2) - u_3 >$,

- $(V \cup U_1 \cup U_3 \cup Op'_1 \cup Op'_3)$ are associated with the node label $< (v \cap u_1 \cap u_3) - u_2 >$,

- $(V \cup U_2 \cup U_3)$ are associated with the node label $< (v \cap u_2 \cap u_3) - u_1 >$,

- $(V \cup U_1 \cup U_2 \cup U_3 \cup Op'_1 \cup Op'_2 \cup Op'_3)$ are associated with the node label $< (v \cap u_1 \cap u_2 \cap u_3) >$.

The next section gives the general solution of the algorithm and some recommendations related with possible implementations.

Solutions and Recommendations

The general solution to the *optimization* algorithm of partitioning is approached examining the following two cases:

1. No direct descendant of the root has further descendants.
2. Some direct descendant of the root has further descendants.

Case A

Let n be the number of the directed descendents of the root. The following formulas are introduced to directly compute the object classes.

$$< v - (\cup u_i) >_{i=\{1,2,\dots,n\}}$$

$$< (v \cap u_{i'}) - (\cup u_j) >_{i'=\{1,\dots,n\}\ j=\{1,\dots,n\}\ j \neq i'}$$

$$< (v \cap u_{i'} \cap u_{i''}) - (\cup u_j) >$$

i'={1,...,n-1} i''={2,...,n} i'≠ i'' } j={1,...,n} j≠ i' j≠ i''

...

$$< (v \cap u_{i'} \cap u_{i''} \cap ... \cap u_{i^n}) >$$

Case B

Let us suppose that a direct descendants of the root node has a leaf descendant node, for example, the $< u_{i_1} >$ node is the leaf descendent of $< u_i >$.

In this case:

- Apply case a of the optimization algorithm to the conceptual sub-graph with root $< u_i >$.
- Replace the node $< u_i >$ with the resulting disjoint classes.
- Apply case a of the optimization algorithm to the obtained conceptual graph.

The approach can easily be further generalized to the case in which the descendant node $< u_{i_1} >$ is not a leaf descendent of node $< u_i >$.

The implementation of any partitioning algorithm/extension can be based on two tools, respectively called *class-name generator* and *class generator*. With the class-name generator, only the name labels of the object graph are computed; with the class generator, the object classes with their attributes/attributes and operations are generated. In real world situations, this number can be rather large, so the suggested idea is to create an object class in the database, only when at least one object belongs to it. The consistency property is very useful for the class generator. Moreover, it implicitly gives information about the class attributes/ attributes and operations to associate with a class name.

CONCLUSION AND FUTURE RESEARCH DIRECTIONS

Conceptual database design, which is essential in researches on information systems and software developments, is defined by approaches to mappings from conceptual to logical database models. New engineering requirements and current technologies favor the conceptual database design evolution. This chapter focuses on graphs of classes representing *conceptual/logical database models*, on methods for their construction and on algorithms of mapping from conceptual to logical database models. Specifically, starting from the formal approach exploited to design the model of a conceptual database methodology, an optimization algorithm of partitioning, based on the decomposition of objects and the inheritance of attributes, is proposed and extended. The extended algorithm, which defines a formal constructive mapping from conceptual to logical database models, aims to show how some updates reflecting modifications occurring in the real life can affect the conceptual design. The paper evidences the idea that model design which retains quality aspects, such as maintainability and re-usability over a long life time, suggests also appropriate implementations that can be characterized by innovation and productivity.

The following motivations justify the approach:

Semantic data models and object database systems have similar mechanisms of abstraction; however, while semantic data models have never been implemented efficiently, object database systems have reached a remarkable level of efficiency. On the contrary, while semantic data models are adequate for conceptual design, object database systems can display serious shortcomings in their ability to describe the dynamic nature of the real world entities. Semantic data models enhance *flexibility,* whereas object models enhance *efficiency*. The mapping from semantic data models to object systems is a means to achieve both the conflicting desiderata of *flexibility* and *efficiency.*

Model *correctness* is also desired for conceptual design. Correctness is preserved designing formal mappings based on the model equivalence.

The problem of changing the class of an object is not presented in semantic data models. This paper formalize the baseline for creations of methods with flexibility of semantic models and efficiency of object systems, developing mappings from semantic models to logical/object models. MDA techniques and tools can be applied to both enterprise information systems and software engineering systems. The conceptual graph proposed in this chapter is a minimal model which can be employed to support graphical formalisms of databases, database specification languages, UML and so on. An algorithm of partitioning based on the direct computation of the classes has been defined and extended. The optimization algorithm results in a minimal object model which is sufficiently abstract to be translated into specific relational/object/XML models. Future research is concerned with refinements/extensions of the proposed notions to enclose refined/extended concepts common to information systems and software development.

Algorithms of partitioning have been exploited within:

- ASSO, a formal methodology of conceptual Database Design for Quality (Locuratolo, 2005),
- Re-ASSO, a re-engineering method (Locuratolo & Loffredo & Signore, 1998),
- Partitioning transportation to the level of the concept theory (Locuratolo & Palomäki, 2012),
- Digital preservation (Locuratolo & Palomäki, 2013).

A formal relationship holds between ASSO and B (Locuratolo & Matthews, 1999 c; Locuratolo, 2009). The ASSO model can be translated systematically into B-machines; these define the semantics of the ASSO model at a lower abstraction level where more formal details must be stated explicitly with respect to the conceptual model. The B-toolkit has been used to prove the model consistency; however practical benefits can be achieved constructing an ASSO toolkit which exploits the introduced approach for defining the conceptual design of ASSO. Re-ASSO is a re-engineering method based on ASSO.

In concept theory, it is possible to make a distinction between the intensional/concept level, which is the level of human thinking and the extensional/set theoretical level which is the level of computer science. Algorithms of partitioning are defined at the set-theoretical level and cannot be directly applied to the intensional level. In (Locuratolo & Palomäki, 2012) an appropriate methodology has been defined to transport algorithms of partitioning at the concept level. In (Locuratolo & Palomäki, 2013) a structure of concepts, called *ontology for database preservation,* has been defined and mapped to the database models. The results presented in this chapter can be usefully employed also in this research.

ACKNOWLEDGMENT

Figure 5 has been reprinted from " Extensional and Intensional Aspects of Conceptual Design" by Elvira Locuratolo & Jari Palomäki in Information Modelling and knowledge Bases XIX, edited by Hannu Jaakkola, Yasushi Kiyoki & Takahiro Tokuda, pg. 168, copyright 2008, with kind permission from IOS Press.

REFERENCES

Abrial, J. R. (Ed.). (1996). *The B-Book: Assigning programs to meanings.* Cambridge, UK: Cambridge University Press. doi:10.1017/CBO9780511624162

Badia, A. (2005). From conceptual models to data models. In van Bommel, P. (Ed.), *Transformations of knowledge, information and data: Theory and applications* (pp. 283–302). Hershey, PA: Idea Group Inc. doi:10.4018/978-1-59140-527-6.ch007

Batini, C. Ceri, S., & Navathe, S. B. (1992). *Conceptual database design: An entity-relationship approach.* Redwood City, CA: Benjamin Cummings.

Bernard, E. V. (1993). *Essays on object-oriented software engineering.* Englewood Cliffs, NJ: Prentice-Hall.

Booch, G. (1994). *Object-oriented analysis and design with applications.* Benjamin Cummings.

Cardenas, A. F., & McLeod, D. (1990). *Research foundations in object-oriented and semantic database systems.* Englewood Cliffs, NJ: Prentice Hall.

Ceri, S., & Fraternali, P. (1997). *Database applications with objects and rules.* Essex, UK: Addison Wesley Longman.

Coad, P., & Yourdon, E. (1991). *Object-oriented design.* Yourdon Press.

Elmasri, R., & Navathe, S. B. (Eds.). (2003). *Fundamentals of database systems.* Addison-Wesley.

Krogstie, J., Terry, H., & Siau, K. (Eds.). (2005). *Information modeling methods and methodologies.* Hershey, PA: Idea Group Publishing.

Li, X., & Parsons, J. (2011). Assigning ontological semantics to unified modeling language for conceptual modeling. In Siau, K., Chiang, R., & Hardgrave, B. (Eds.), *Systems analysis and design: People, processes, and projects* (pp. 180–194). AMIS.

Locuratolo, E. (1998). *ASSO: Portability as a methodological goal.* (Technical Report, IEI:B4-05-02).

Locuratolo, E. (2005). Model transformations in designing the ASSO methodology. In van Bommel, P. (Ed.), *Transformations of knowledge, information and data: Theory and applications* (pp. 283–302). Hershey, PA: Idea Group Inc. doi:10.4018/978-1-59140-527-6.ch013

Locuratolo, E. (2009a). *An approach to the evolution of conceptual methods.* (ISTI-TR-007).

Locuratolo, E. (2009b). Database design based on B. In Erickson, J. (Ed.), *Database technologies: Concepts, methodologies, tools, and applications* (pp. 400–456). Hershey, PA: Information Science Reference. doi:10.4018/978-1-60566-058-5.ch028

Locuratolo, E. (2011). *Meta-modeling to design the structure database schema.* In K. Siau, R. H. L. Chiang, & B. C. Hardgrave (Eds.), *Systems analysis and design: People, processes, and projects,* Vol. 1 (pp. 195–215). (Advances in Management Information Systems, vol. 18). United States of America: M E. Sharpe.

Locuratolo, E., Loffredo, M., & Signore, O. (1998). Database reengineering for quality. In *Proceedings of the 6th Re-engineering Forum,* Firenze.

Locuratolo, E., & Matthews, B. (1999). On the relationship between ASSO and B. In Jaakkola, H., Kangassalo, H., & Kawaguchi, E. (Eds.), *Information modelling and knowledge bases X* (pp. 235–253). Amsterdam, The Netherlands: IOS Press.

Locuratolo, E., & Palomäki, J. (2008). Extensional and intensional aspects of conceptual design. In Jaakkola, H., Kiyoki, Y., & Tokuda, T. (Eds.), *Information modelling and knowledge bases XIX* (pp. 160–169). Amsterdam, The Netherlands: IOS Press.

Locuratolo, E., & Palomäki, J. (2012). *Construction of concepts and decomposition of objects.* (Technical report TR-02-2011, ISTI-TR-02-2011).

Locuratolo, E., & Palomäki, J. (2013 in press). Ontology for database preservation. In Nazir, M., Colomb, R. M., & Abdullah, M. S. (Eds.), *In Ontology-based applications for enterprise systems and knowledge management*. Hershey, PA: IGI Global.

Locuratolo, E., & Rabitti, F. (1998). Conceptual classes and system classes in object databases. *Acta Informatics, 35*(3), 181–210. doi:10.1007/s002360050118

Ma, Z. (2006). Database modeling of engineering information. In *Database modeling for industrial data management emerging technologies and applications* (pp. 35–61). Hershey, PA: Idea Group Publishing. doi:10.4018/978-1-59140-684-6.ch001

Matthews, B., & Locuratolo, E. (1999c). In Woodcock, J., & Davis, J. (Eds.), *Formal development of databases in ASSO and B* (pp. 388–410). Lecture Notes in Computer Science.

Rumbaughj, J., Jacobson, I., & Booch, G. (1999). *The unified modeling languages reference manuals*. New York, NY: Addison-Wesley.

Spagnolo, A. M. (2000). *Incrementare la qualità in ambito Basi di Dati*. Tesi di Laurea, Università degli studi di Pisa, Corso di laurea in Scienze dell'Informazione.

Yuan, J. (2006). Semantic-based dynamic enterprise information integration. In Ma, Z. (Ed.), *Database modeling for industrial data management emerging technologies and applications* (pp. 35–61). Hershey, PA: Idea Group Publishing. doi:10.4018/978-1-59140-684-6.ch006

ADDITIONAL READING

Aloia, N., Barneva, S., & Rabitti, F. (1992). Supporting physical independence in object databases. *Database Technology, 4*(4), 265–286.

Badia, A. (2005). From conceptual models to data models. In van Bommel, P. (Ed.), *Transformations of knowledge, information and data: Theory and applications* (pp. 283–302). Hershey, PA: Idea Group Inc. doi:10.4018/978-1-59140-527-6.ch007

Kangassalo, H. (1992/93). A system and methodology for conceptual modelling and information construction. *Data & Knowledge Engineering, 9*, 287–319. doi:10.1016/0169-023X(93)90011-D

Li, X., & Parsons, J. (2011). Assigning ontological semantics to unified modeling language for conceptual modeling. In Siau, K., Chiang, R., & Hardgrave, B. (Eds.), *Systems analysis and design: People, processes, and projects* (pp. 180–194). AMIS.

Petit, J. M., & Hacid, M. S. (Eds.). (2005). From conceptual database schemas to logical database tuning. In P. van Bommel (Ed.), *Transformations of knowledge, information and data: Theory and applications* (pp. 283-302). Hershey, PA: Idea Group Inc.

Soraya, K. M., Zakaria, M., Luis, F. P., Slimane, H., Stefanie, R. M., Shazia, S., & Karsten, S. (Eds.). (2008). *Joint Proceedings of 5th International Workshop on Ubiquitous Computing, 4th International Workshop on Model-Driven Enterprise Information Systems, 3rd International Workshop on Technologies for Context-Aware Business Process Management*. In conjunction with ICEIS 2008, Barcelona, Spain.

Spyratos, N. (2006). A functional model for data analysis. In Legind Larsen, H. (Eds.), *FQAS 2006, LNAI 4027* (pp. 51–64). Springer-Verlag.

Zicari, R. (1992). A framework for schema updates in an object-oriented database system. In Bancilhon, F. (Eds.), *Building an object-oriented database systems: The story of O$_2$* (pp. 146–182). Morgan Kaufmann Publishers.

KEY TERMS AND DEFINITIONS

Conceptual Graph: Acyclic graph/specialization hierarchy of classes in is-a relationships. Its Property: each object can belong to any class of the graph.

Extended Conceptual Graph: Conceptual graph of classes extended with elementary operations.

Extended Logical/Object Graph: Logical/object graph of classes extended with elementary operations.

Extended Partitioning: Set of properties characterizing the mapping algorithms from extended conceptual graph to extended logical/object graph.

Extended Specialized Conceptual Class: Specialized conceptual class of an extended conceptual graph.

Logical/Object Graph: Acyclic graph/specialization hierarchy of classes in is-aL relationships. Its property: each object belongs to one and only one class of the graph.

Partitioning: Set of properties that characterize the mapping algorithms from conceptual graphs to logical/object graphs.

Specialized Conceptual Class: Class of a conceptual graph having attributes inherited from its higher level classes as well as specific class attributes.

Chapter 3
A Survey on Secure Software Development Lifecycles

José Fonseca
DEI/CISUC, University of Coimbra/UDI, Polytechnic Institute of Guarda, Portugal

Marco Vieira
DEI/CISUC, University of Coimbra, Portugal

ABSTRACT

This chapter presents a survey on the most relevant software development practices that are used nowadays to build software products for the web, with security built in. It starts by presenting three of the most relevant Secure Software Development Lifecycles, which are complete solutions that can be adopted by development companies: the CLASP, the Microsoft Secure Development Lifecycle, and the Software Security Touchpoints. However it is not always feasible to change ongoing projects or replace the methodology in place. So, this chapter also discusses other relevant initiatives that can be integrated into existing development practices, which can be used to build and maintain safer software products: the OpenSAMM, the BSIMM, the SAFECode, and the Securosis. The main features of these security development proposals are also compared according to their highlights and the goals of the target software product.

INTRODUCTION

The Software Development Lifecycle (SDL) is a conceptual model used by software houses in the management of the process of analyzing, developing, controlling and maintaining software (Sommerville, 2010). Some of the most well-known models are the Waterfall (Royce, 1970),

the Rapid Application Development (Martin, 1991) and the Spiral (Boehm, 1986). At the time when these SDLSs were developed, the software security awareness was not as relevant as it is today, so it was not a big concern to take into account. In fact, the typical approach of dealing only with development best practices is not sufficient for current applications that have to face

DOI: 10.4018/978-1-4666-3679-8.ch003

the constant pressure of web attacks, although they can improve the overall quality and help mitigate some common issues.

These traditional SDLs are still in widespread use nowadays, but they are not effective when building secure systems that have to face the huge number of threats that can arise from anywhere, like those that come from the web and are so pervasive (Howard & LeBlanc, 2003). Both logic and coding bugs must be thoroughly addressed during all the phases of the development process, therefore reducing the cost of deploying unsecure application. This is of utmost importance for web applications that will be exposed to the growing number of hackers and organized crime that can strike at any time, from any place in the Globe. This is what an integrated Secure Software Development Lifecycles (SSDL) does from the start to the end of the life of an application. In fact, using a SSDL is one of the recommendations of the Verizon's 2009 data breach report in order to prevent the application layer type of attacks, including SQL Injection and XSS (Baker et al., 2009).

This chapter presents an overview of the most important SSDLs that are used nowadays to build software products that have to face the many threats that come from the web: the Open Web Application Security Project (OWASP) Comprehensive, Lightweight Application Security Process (CLASP), the Microsoft Secure Development Lifecycle, and the Software Security Touchpoints. Although there is a general consensus about the advantages of using a SSDL, this subject is still in its early adoption by the industry. It takes time to implement and execute, it costs money and it implies a change in the way organization works, which is usually difficult to achieve. The way a secure software should be developed is still generating a growing number of discussions and there is a considerable number of proposals trying to gain adopters and overcome the problems and technical difficulties of applying them in the real world (Higgins, 2009). This chapter also introduces other

relevant initiatives, which can be adapted to the existing SDL, devoted to building and maintaining a safer software product: the Open Software Assurance Maturity Model (OpenSAMM), the Building Security In Maturity Model (BSIMM), the Software Assurance Forum for Excellence in Code (SAFECode) and the Securosis building a web application security program.

This chapter also discusses the issue of selecting a software development lifecycle according to the reality of the software product being developed. This involves identifying the security issues that should be addressed from a development point-of-view and then map these issues with the features of existing lifecycles to make the right choice and tune any relevant aspects.

SOFTWARE DEVELOPMENT AND SECURITY

One important metric of software quality is assurance: "a level of confidence that software is free from vulnerabilities, either intentionally designed into the software or accidentally inserted at any time during its lifecycle, and that the software functions in the intended manner" (CNSS Secretariat, 2006). To achieve software assurance developers need to build assured software: "Software that has been designed, developed, analyzed and tested using processes, tools, and techniques that establish a level of confidence in its trustworthiness appropriate for its intended use" (CNSS Secretariat, 2006). To achieve this goal, developers must rethink the software development process and address all the phases of the SDL: design, code and documentation (Howard & LeBlanc, 2003). This is like applying the defense-in-depth strategy to the various phases of the software development lifecycle making it more security aware.

To understand the security measures that vendors use for software assurance, Jeremy Epstein analyzed eight software vendors with small to very large revenues (Epstein, 2009). The security measures analyzed were software developer training, software design review, execution of penetration testing using humans and tools during the SDL, and source code analysis. The study showed that almost every company is conscious of the risks of insecure software and performs all these activities, to some extent. However, although their clients do not ask explicitly for security, software vendors implement security assurance mechanisms because they are aware that in case something goes wrong it will bring them negative consequences. Other companies should follow this practice, given that the web application scenario is so prone to vulnerabilities and it is so common for an application to be probed by possible hackers. In fact, "If you do not perform security testing for your application, someone else not working for your company will" (Howard & LeBlanc, 2003). Customers do not ask for security but, if security fails, they will move to another solutions provider.

Software developers frequently see functionality as more important than quality or security. This is natural since the functionality is what represents the need for a given product. Without it there is even no need for security because there will be nothing to be secured. However, security should be seriously considered. A Gartner report says that 75% of attacks take place through the application level and predicts that, by 2009, around 80% of companies will have suffered a security incident due to application vulnerabilities (Lanowitz, 2005). The report also adverts for the need to build secure applications and test applications for security from the early start of the project during the application development lifecycle.

One major problem is that typical SDLs in use nowadays are not effective when building secure systems. Security is not integrated in the SDL and it is seen just as an additional process activity (Marmor-Squires & Rougeau, 1988). To obtain a secure product, the typical development approach needs to be extended. For example, the OWASP's Enterprise Security API Project (ESAPI) addresses this problem by providing a set of APIs to interface all security controls needed to build a secure application including input validation, output encoding, error logging and detection (Williams, 2008). These APIs include toolkits for the major programming languages and can be used by software developers during the SDL to increase security with minimum intrusion in their development process.

Some other researchers propose secure development guidelines (Auger, 2007), like the OWASP's "A Guide to Building Secure web Applications and web Services" (Wiesmann, Curphey, Stock, & Stirbei, 2005) and the "Complete web Application Security: Phase 1–Building web Application Security into Your Development Process" (SPI Dynamics, Inc., 2002). SANS series of working papers in Application Security describe a checklist of twelve methods to avoid two of the most important classes of mistakes done by developers: poor input validation and output filtering (Kim & Skoudis, 2009). These bugs affect the input and the output of web applications, protecting both the back-end mechanisms including the storage of malicious data, and the user through what is presented and executed by the web browser. In fact, solving these two problems would mitigate SQL Injection and XSS, as well as many other common web application problems. They propose a set of 10 best coding practices, and they also highlight the need to perform static analysis and penetration testing to secure the web application, which are common procedures among SSDLs.

Contrary to some beliefs, using a SSDL becomes profitable in the long term: "it is much cheaper to prevent than to repair" (McGraw, 2006). The use of a SSDL reduces the overall cost of development because it allows finding and eliminating vulnerabilities early in the process (Howard & Lipner, 2006; Microsoft Corporation, 2009a). A case study of client's data presented by Fortify suggests that the cost of fixing critical vulnerabilities later in the process, after releasing the software, is about 100 times more onerous than fixing vulnerabilities earlier in the requirements phase (Meftah, 2008). This trend was also observed in the data on software errors collected by Barry Boehm, although the benefit may be "only" 5 times higher (Boehm & Basili, 2001). Boehm's data covers the more general case of fixing all software errors, whereas the Fortify data is specific to critical vulnerabilities. Another report, this time prepared by RTI for the National Institute of Standards and Technology states that the cost of eliminating vulnerabilities increases all the way from design stage to post release (RTI, 2002). In the report, the cost at post release is double than at beta test and 30 times more than at design stage. The DIMACS Workshop on Software Security report refers to the following relative cost expenditures for lifecycle stages: design is 15%, implementation is 60% and testing is 25%. The same report also quotes an IBM study stating that the relative cost weightings are (Mead & McGraw, 2003): design = 1, implementation = 6.5, testing = 15 and maintenance = 100. According to a group of researchers from MIT, Stanford University and @Stake quoted by (Berinato, 2002) it is possible to have a Return Of Investment (ROI) of 21% at the design stage, 15% at the implementation stage and 12% at the testing stage. Although the values may vary, all these studies support that it is far less expensive to fix errors and vulnerabilities early in the start of the software development than after the software has become operational. It is, therefore, quite clear that the most effective security investment is the one spent in earlier phases of the lifecycle, although it must also be present through all the process till the end of the life of the software.

These requirements are present in development lifecycles with security built in. The following sections present an overview of important SSDLs in use nowadays and four initiatives aimed at providing security and control that can be integrated in existing SDLs with lesser effort.

OWASP COMPREHENSIVE, LIGHTWEIGHT APPLICATION SECURITY PROCESS (CLASP)

CLASP has been, since 2006, an OWASP project led by Pravir Chandra (who also developed OpenSAMM and BSIMM that will be discussed later). CLASP consists of a set of components with formalized security best practices that covers the entire SDL (not just development), so that security concerns can be adopted from the early stages of the SDL used by the organization (OWASP Foundation, 2006). This set of 24 security related activities that can be easily integrated into the SDL of the application allows systematically addressing security vulnerabilities. Eleven CLASP resources provide tools and other artifacts to help automate the process wherever possible. This SSDL heavily relies on the organization of the project team in roles where each one has a perfectly defined set of activities and responsibilities that they have to take care of. This is done in contrast with other SSDLs where these activities are part of a development step of the SSDL.

The CLASP is organized into high-level perspectives of the CLASP Process called CLASP Views (Figure 1):

1. **Concepts View:** Defines that the basic security services that must be satisfied for each resource are: authorization, confidentiality, authentication (identity establishment and integrity), availability, accountability, and non-repudiation. This is done following seven application security best practices:
    a. Institute awareness programs.
    b. Perform application assessments.
    c. Capture security requirements.
    d. Implement secure development practices.

Figure 1. The CLASP organization (adapted from OWASP Foundation, 2006)

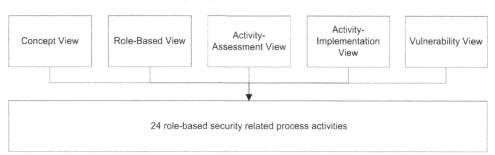

e. Build vulnerability remediation procedures.

f. Define and monitor metrics.

g. Publish operational security guidelines.

2. **Role-Based View:** Shows how a project team should execute security issues depending on the specific responsibilities of every role (project managers, security auditors, developers, architects, testers, and others). The designer, architect and project manager roles are the ones that need to be trained specifically for security, mainly logical bugs. Developers only need to code right, without bugs, following the policies, standards, and guidelines in place in the organization.

3. **Activity-Assessment View:** Maps the various roles with the specific security related process activities (there are 24 of them) they have to implement. These activities are: Institute security awareness program, Monitor security metrics, Specify operational environment, Identify global security policy, Identify resources and trust boundaries, Identify user roles and resource capabilities, Document security-relevant requirements, Detail misuse cases, Identify attack surface, Apply security principles to design, Research and assess security posture of technology solutions, Annotate class designs with security properties, Specify database security configuration, Perform security analysis of system requirements and design (threat modeling), Integrate security analysis into source management process, Implement interface contracts, Implement and elaborate resource policies and security technologies, Address reported security issues, Perform source-level security review, Identify, implement and perform security tests Verify security attributes of resources, Perform code signing, Build operational security guide, Manage security issue disclosure process.

4. **Activity-Implementation View:** Details each one of the 24 role-based security related process activities.

5. **Vulnerability View:** Detailing the consequences, problem types, exposure periods, avoidance and mitigation techniques of security vulnerabilities. It considers 104 vulnerability types, their categories, exposure periods, consequences, platforms affected, resources, risk assessment, avoidance and mitigation periods.

The set of 24 activities is detailed in the free to download book (OWASP Foundation, 2006). This book contains which activities are bound to each role, among all the information needed to implement this SSDL into an organization, like the taxonomy used, vulnerabilities, detailed actions, use cases, etc. It also has a section on CLASP resources explaining the most important concepts, which can be used as a starting point to improve security training and security awareness: basic principles, examples, core security services, worksheets covering sample coding guidelines and system assessment, sample roadmaps, etc. To help move from the current SLD to CLASP, the roadmap section provides a set of steps for organizations that want a minimum impact on their ongoing projects (containing only 12 activities) and for organizations that want to apply it holistically (containing 20 activities).

MICROSOFT SECURE DEVELOPMENT LIFECYCLE

The Microsoft SSDL is a mandatory methodology in use by Microsoft since 2004, used to deliver more reliable software with security and privacy built in (Howard & LeBlanc, 2003; Howard & Lipner, 2006; Microsoft Corporation, 2009a). Over 50% of Microsoft flaws were design flaws (Mead & McGraw, 2003), so it is not a surprise that their SDL is heavily based on threat modeling (also known as threat analysis or risk analysis) done in the early stages of development. Threat modeling is an application security auditing procedure consisting in formally identifying and mapping all the possible attack vectors of the application. It helps reduce the number and severity of vulnerabilities in the application code, including design

ones, according to results provided by Microsoft (Microsoft Corporation, 2009a).

The Microsoft SSDL is based on the following guiding principles (Microsoft Corporation, 2008):

1. **Secure by Design:** Secure architecture, design and structure; Threat modeling and mitigation; Elimination of vulnerabilities; Improvements in security.
2. **Secure by Default:** Least privilege; Defense in depth; Conservative default settings; Avoidance of risky default changes; Less commonly used services off by default.
3. **Secure in Deployment:** Deployment guides; Analysis and management tools; Patch deployment tools.
4. **Communications:** Security response; Community engagement.

The Microsoft SSDL is based on a set of activities for each phase and it can be applied incrementally into an existing ongoing development process (Figure 2).

One of the core aspects of this SSDL is the use of the threat modeling theory. Threat modeling focuses on a high level of the development, in the design and architecture of the product, and helps uncover design issues and point out which components are at risk, before implementation (Howard, 2009). Threat modeling describes the attack surface, the threats of the system and the assets that may be compromised from the point of view of the attacker. The potential attack vectors (threats) are added to the model and this

Figure 2. The Microsoft security development lifecycle (adapted from Microsoft Corporation, 2009a)

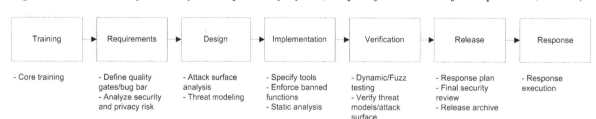

enables the fix of design flaws, therefore preventing such attacks. OWASP also uses this threat modeling process because it is easy to learn and adopt (Wiesmann et al., 2005). Other SSDLs also use threat modeling, although the actual implementation may differ from the Microsoft one.

The risk of each threat can be estimated using the DREAD (Damage potential, Reproducibility, Exploitability, Affected users, Discoverability) method, rating numbers from 1 to 10 for each DREAD item. The DREAD is rather subjective to apply, and needs a high degree of expertise. This is the main reason it was replaced by a heuristic model derived from Microsoft Security Response Center bulletin ratings. It contains four rankings: Critical, Important, Moderate and Low. These rankings are much easier to apply and are also more effective, since they are based on many years of experience. To help in the process of applying the Microsoft threat analysis and modeling and estimate the risk Microsoft provides a set of tools.

According to Rauscher and colleagues, threat modeling has limitations on the real ability to obtain the necessary data and the mitigation is based on previous known attacks, so a creative attacker may still be able to be successful (Rauscher, Krock, & Runyon, 2006). To cope with this, the authors propose a vulnerability analysis using the eight tenants already used by the communication industry: human, policy, hardware, software, networks, payload and power. This methodology allows the address of a finite number of general classes of vulnerabilities, instead of an infinite number of specific threats that can exercise those vulnerabilities. So, working together threat analysis and vulnerability analysis can produce better results.

To uncover design flaws the system is decomposed in components and each component is analyzed according to each one of the STRIDE approach where the effect of the bug is classified using the threat groups that have their related opposite security property (Table 1). When a threat is found, the bug enabling it is corrected in the code.

To make this SSDL easier to apply and to help check the phases of the process, it is integrated into the Microsoft's development tool VisualStudio.NET (Microsoft Corporation, 2009b).

SOFTWARE SECURITY TOUCHPOINTS

The Cigital's Software Security Touchpoints is a manageable set of seven best practices, proposed in 2004, that can be applied to the SDL being used by the organization (waterfall, spiral, etc.). In the book "Software Security" (McGraw, 2004), the author presents the best practices procedures (touchpoints) showing how they can easily be applied during the existing SDL in use in the organization (Figure 3).

For the touchpoints, two levels of software bugs are considered: source code level and architectural level (McGraw, 2004, 2006). The two most important touchpoints are source code analysis and architectural risk analysis, because they focus on bugs found in the code and in the design, respectively. The touchpoints, in order of effectiveness are the following:

1. **Code review:** Using static analysis tools.
2. **Risk analysis:** Based on attack patterns and threat models.

Table 1. STRIDE threat model

Threat	Security Property
Spoofing	Authentication
Tampering	Integrity
Repudiation	Non-repudiation
Information disclosure	Confidentiality
Denial of service	Availability
Elevation of privilege	Authorization

Figure 3. The software security touchpoints (adapted from McGraw, 2004)

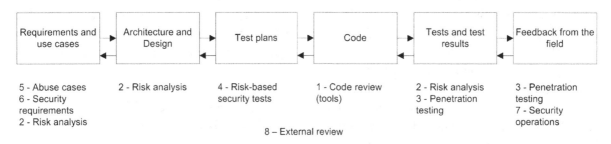

3. **Penetration testing:** Using the black-box approach that should also consider the architecture of the system.
4. **Risk-based security tests:** With traceability back to requirements.
5. **Abuse cases:** Describing the system behavior under attack.
6. **Security requirements:** Security must be present in the requirements, as well.
7. **Security operations:** Monitoring for security breaks during the use of the system.

Although External Review (the last, in the effectiveness order) is considered outside the design team, it is also necessary. Security training of each best practice is also a concern of this model.

An extensive set of articles themed Software Security Best Practices Building Security In for IEEE Security & Privacy were written by Gary McGraw, detailing the several best practices of the model (Arkin, Stender, & McGraw, 2005; Barnum & McGraw, 2005; B. Chess & McGraw, 2004; Hope, McGraw, & Anton, 2004; McGraw, 2004; Potter & McGraw, 2004; Taylor & McGraw, 2005; Verdon & McGraw, 2004).

INITIATIVES ON BUILDING AND MAINTAINING A SECURE SOFTWARE PRODUCT

For an organization, it is difficult and costly (at least in the short term) to change their development methodology from the ground up, even if

the objective is to deliver a higher quality product concerning security. To help with this migration process, several initiatives arouse aiming to integrate security in the SDL currently being used in the organization. Some of the most important initiatives are the OpenSAMM, the BSIMM, the SAFECode and the Securosis. One interesting concern among all of them is the lesson learned from the industry, so they are based on empirical data collected over the years from relevant software development houses. Some of these initiatives present not only an improvement in security, but also the means to measure or benchmark the current state of the evolution of the software development process inside the organization, concerning security. This helps verify and compare the current state of the development process and to specify goals for the future that can be measured.

Open Software Assurance Maturity Model (OpenSAMM)

The OpenSAMM was developed by software security consultant Pravir Chandra and it is intended to be easy to follow even by non-security experts. It includes a simple, well-defined and measurable maturity model for the organization (Pravir Chandra, 2009). It was originally founded by Fortify but it is now part of the OWASP. It was proposed in 2009, it is not tied to vendors but has a lot of industry participation, it is open and driven by the community.

The OpenSAMM model is based on four core Business Functions involved in the software development, each one with a set of three Security Practices (Figure 4). The Security Practices are activities related to security that build assurance for the related Business Function. Each Security Practice has three Maturity Levels (or objectives) with well-defined specific Objectives, Activities, Results, and increasingly stringent Success Metrics, Costs, Personnel and Related Levels.

The OpenSAMM model can be used as a benchmark to assess a security assurance program and create a scorecard showing its evolution. This ability to precisely score the security level of an organization and its evolution over time is a major advantage of the model. The assessment can simply be done for each Practice by scoring the answers, but a more detailed assessment can be done with additional auditory work. As an example, the interview template that helps determine the organization's current maturity level can be easily obtained from the web (Coblentz, 2009). This model is also prepared to ease the implementation of a software assurance program, by providing a roadmap that can be tailored for each organization need.

Building Security in Maturity Model (BSIMM)

The Building Security In Maturity Model (BSIMM) is a model developed in 2009 and derived from a beta version of the OpenSAMM (McGraw, Chess, & Migues, 2009). It is a practical approach based on empirical evidence and data

observation of nine software security initiatives from financial services, independent software vendors, and technology firms (Adobe, EMC, QUALCOMM, Google, Wells Fargo, Microsoft, DTCC and two other undisclosed companies). Unlike other SSDL methodologies, the BSIMM does not contain a theoretical compilation of best practices. It is a real-world collection of actual practices performed in the field. The nine underlying organizations follow different SSDLs and the best practices are derived from their experiences. So, regardless of methodology, most of the theoretical best practices proposed by other SSDLs are actually present in the BSIMM, and they all share a common ground. In fact, Cigital (that proposed the Software Security Touchpoints already discussed) is one of the partners of the BSIMM, along with Fortify (founder of the OpenSAMM). BSIMM is also considered the standard for financial firms by the Financial Services Technology Consortium and used by the U.S. Department of Homeland Security.

The BSIMM framework is called Software Security Framework (SSF) and consists of twelve normalized Practices each one with several activities associated to them (with objectives and activities) and grouped in four Domains (Figure 5).

Like the OpenSAMM, the BSIMM considers three levels of maturity with increasing security demanding and each one contains a set of activities within each practice, from an overall of 110 activities. This model can also be used to benchmark different organizations and prioritize

Figure 4. The software assurance maturity model (SAMM) (adapted from Pravir Chandra, 2009)

Figure 5. BSIMM's software security framework (adapted from McGraw et al., 2009)

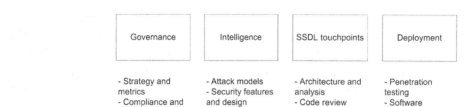

changes according to their score in the maturity level of each one of the twelve practices. Like the OpenSAMM, this ability to allow bechmarking the maturity of the security practices and its evolution is one of the advantages of this model. However, BSIMM is the result of the underlying field study showing the practices that are really used by some good referenced activities common to all of the leading software security initiatives in order to obtain a secure process of development.

Organizations can use the BSIMM skeleton to obtain a glance of the maturity model level during an assessment. It consists of the twelve Practices organized into the three maturity levels with their Objectives and Activities. This model is simpler to apply than the OpenSAMM but it necessarily lacks some information, like the guidance on how to measure and rank the Activities in order to obtain a comparable benchmark that can be used across the organizations.

Software Assurance Forum for Excellence in Code (SAFECode)

Like the BSIMM, the Software Assurance Forum for Excellence in Code (SAFECode) is an industry-led consortium formed in 2007, including the following members: EMC, Juniper Networks, Microsoft, Nokia, SAP, and Symantec. It is dedicated to increase trust in information and communication technology products and services. This consortium produced some publications focusing on secure development methods and practices (SAFECode,

2008a), an overview of industry best practices like the BSIMM model (SAFECode, 2008b) and principles of secure software development during training (SAFECode, 2009).

The SAFECode guide contains a list of SSDL best practices, actually being executed by the industry, which are proven to help deliver secure products (Figure 6). In the best practices for secure software programming, the SSDL focuses on the following aspects (SAFECode, 2008a):

1. **Requirements:** Including training in secure development and testing.
2. **Design:** With threat analysis before code commit.
3. **Programming:** Including static and dynamic code analysis tools and manual code review, input and output validation.
4. **Testing:** Consisting of fuzzing, penetration testing and external assessment.
5. **Code Integrity and Handling:** Focusing on access principles like the least privilege access, separation of duties and persistent protection.
6. **Documentation:** Defining software security best practices and how to configure the software for security.

The SAFECode also highlights the need for leaders to promote the use of these best practices to create a security aware conscience among everyone involved in the software process development.

Figure 6. SAFECode's best practices (adapted from SAFECode, 2008a)

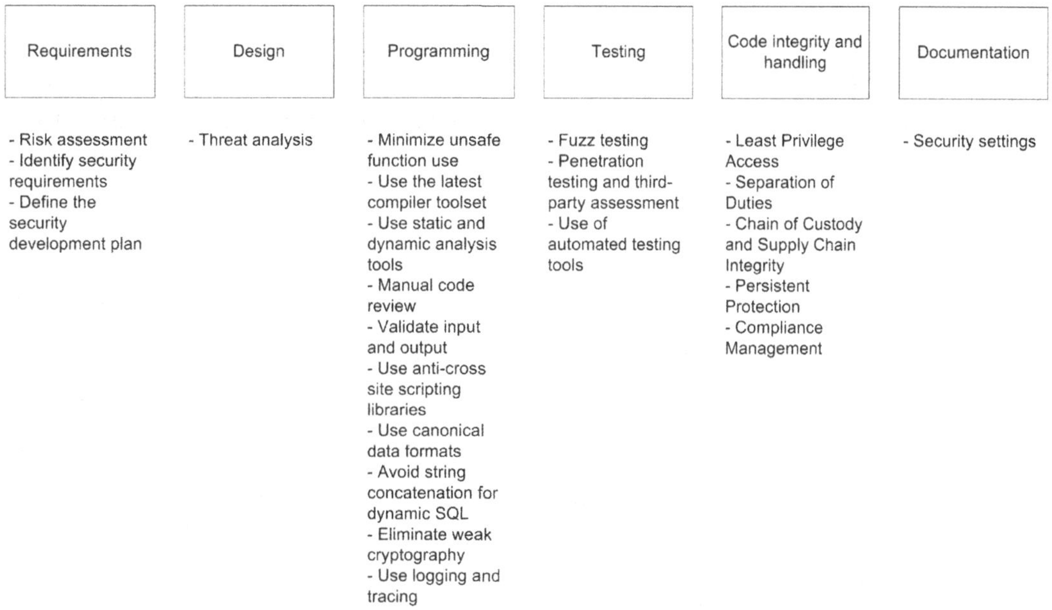

Requirements	Design	Programming	Testing	Code integrity and handling	Documentation
- Risk assessment - Identify security requirements - Define the security development plan	- Threat analysis	- Minimize unsafe function use - Use the latest compiler toolset - Use static and dynamic analysis tools - Manual code review - Validate input and output - Use anti-cross site scripting libraries - Use canonical data formats - Avoid string concatenation for dynamic SQL - Eliminate weak cryptography - Use logging and tracing	- Fuzz testing - Penetration testing and third-party assessment - Use of automated testing tools	- Least Privilege Access - Separation of Duties - Chain of Custody and Supply Chain Integrity - Persistent Protection - Compliance Management	- Security settings

Securosis Building a Web Application Security Program

Securosis released in 2009 a whitepaper sponsored by Core Security, Imperva and Qualys, about building a security program targeted specifically for web application development (Securosis, 2009). The paper proposes a SSDL with focus on the underfunding problem of web application security. The proposed SSDL is practical, inexpensive and presents the type of tools that should be used in the three stages of the proposed development cycle (Figure 7).

1. **Secure Development:** It focuses on initial procedures needed to develop the application like gathering the requirements, design, implementation and quality assurance. Static analysis and dynamic analysis tools are covered to partially help automate this stage.
2. **Secure Deployment:** It is at this stage where code complies with specifications and it is ready for vulnerability assessment (find security bugs) and penetration tests (classify and exploit security bugs).

3. **Secure Operation:** When the application is deployed, preventive tools must be used in order to monitor the operation. For this matter, web application firewalls, web application and database activity monitoring tools are used.

COMPARING THE SECURITY DEVELOPMENT PROPOSALS

Brook's Law on project management says (Brooks, 1995): "Adding manpower to a late software project makes it later". The same idea also applies to security: just adding security manpower to a late software project makes it later. And it still becomes unsecure, because patches do not always work very well (Arbaugh, Fithen, & McHugh, 2000).

A common expression among SSDL enthusiasts to highlight the differences between their thinking and current building methods is that software security is not the same as secure software (Gollmann, 1999). In fact, having security functions in a piece of software, like password authentication for example, does not make by itself

Figure 7. Securosis model (adapted from Securosis, 2009)

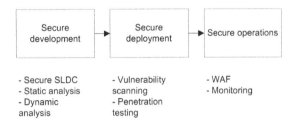

the application secure. It is also not sufficient to follow a single security procedure, because all of them have their benefits, but also their weaknesses. Developers need to coordinate together several tasks to be able to achieve a secure application (Barnett, 2008). It is this type of integration that a SSDL is supposed to provide.

Security concern must be present during all the phases of the software development lifecycle and security cannot be seen just as a minor issue. In fact, it must be a design goal (Jayaram & Aditya, 2005) and this is represented well in OWASP's (OWASP Foundation, 2006), Microsoft's (Howard & LeBlanc, 2003) and McGraw's (McGraw, 2006) software development lifecycles.

Security vulnerabilities must be mitigated during the development lifecycle, before the software is released. Code Inspection and Penetration Testing represent two key quality assurance procedures that must be used to detect security vulnerabilities. Code inspection is a white-box approach that consists in the formal review of the application code by an external team. Penetration testing is a black-box approach consisting in a set of tests made from the point of view of the users, where the external team tries to find all the possible vulnerable entry points of the application. Penetration testing can be performed manually or it can be done using automated tools, although even top commercial products have a high rate of false positive (non vulnerabilities that are tagged as vulnerabilities) and false negative (vulnerabilities

that are not identified) values (Ananta Security, 2009; Fonseca, Vieira, & Madeira, 2007; WhiteHat Security Inc., 2008).

Because of the novelty of the development approach using a SSDL it is still hard to find results derived from real data that can compare the improvement of the quality of the final product. However, as one of the first solid establishments in the area, Microsoft has published the results of the number of critical bugs found in some of the products they developed (Figure 8). Windows 2003 post-SDL had a decrease of over 60% of critical bugs compared to Windows 2000 pre-SDL, SQL Server 2000 had a decrease of over 80% compared to the releases pre-SDL and post-SDL and Exchange Server 2000 had a decrease of 75% compared to the releases pre-SDL and post-SDL. Taking into account the overall results, there is a 66% decrease of the number of critical bugs after applying the SSDL in their development.

The research area of SSDL process is still in its early stages with lots of new ideas flowing from one proposal to another. There is a mixture of organizations involved in more than a single SSDL project like Microsoft, Cigital, Fortify, OWASP, etc.; and some SSDLs share the same guru, like Gary McGraw, Pravir Chandra, and Michael Howard. Some SSDL methodologies derive from a fork of the early stages of other SSDL methodologies and share some of the others core ideas, like the Touchpoints, OpenSAMM and BSIMM.

This interest in better secure code practices and tools is shown by big investments in the security area and large acquisitions. In fact, according to Brian Chess, 2007 was a turning point because "It was the first year there was a bigger market for products that help you get code right than there was for products that help you demonstrate a problem exists" (Brian Chess, 2008). This is a good direction to follow: prevent the problem instead of chasing it in order to fix it after the damage.

Figure 8. Windows 2000, SQL Server 2000, Exchange Server 2000 pre- and post-SDL critical and important security bulletins (adapted from Lipner & Howard, 2005)

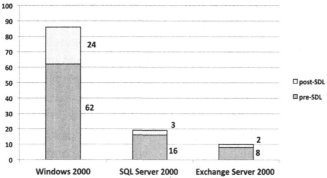

Table 2 presents an overview of the SSDLs described earlier in the chapter. The data shows that the focus on SSDLs is a new concern largely sparked after the 2002 Bill Gates trustworthy computing memo and the start of Microsoft security push. As time goes by, this subject is getting more interest from the industry: close to half of these major security development methodologies analyzed emerged in 2009.

Although there is still not enough data to make a detailed comparison among the various SSDLs presented, some remarks can be made. We can see that one of the constraints in applying a SSDL has to do with the cost that includes the need of changing processes, training and delaying the deliverable of the final product. Some SSDLs could be used in larger projects, whereas others are more suitable to smaller companies that cannot afford to make profound changes in the way the software is built.

The Microsoft SSDL can be applied to very large projects, like Operating Systems (OS) and big applications. They provide a set of tools to help in the process, integrated in their Visual Studio environment, but they must be run in the Windows OS. CLASP is lighter and can be adopted for smaller projects involving a fewer set of resources. It can be used as an SSDL or it can be easily integrated into an existing SDL with a reduced set of steps. The Touchpoints can be perfectly integrated into an existing SDL within the organization, helping to provide security to its software projects. The

Table 2. SDL security proposals comparison

	Name	Year	Highlights
SSDL	CLASP	2006	24 formalized security best practices that cover the entire SDL.
	Microsoft SDL	2004	Complete integrated SDL heavily based on risk analysis and based on a set of activities for each phase. Integrated in the Microsoft development suite. Suited for Operating System developers and large software houses.
	Touchpoints	2004	7 best practices that can be applied to the existing SDL.
Security Initiative	OpenSAMM	2009	Measurable maturity model with 3 maturity levels and 12 security practices. Can be used as a benchmark.
	BSIMM	2009	12 actual best practices used by the industry with 3 maturity levels. Can be used as a benchmark.
	SAFECode	2008	Overview of industry best practices with an emphasis on leadership.
	Securosis	2009	SSDL targeted specifically for web applications and focusing on automation by using tools.

Touchpoints present activities that should be applied to the various artifacts created during the development of software. They are independent of the target of the company, so they can be applied in all software development situations.

The other software initiatives focus on providing a set of best practices that are really being used by big references in the software development industry, which are proven to provide a good balance between the cost and the benefit they provide. OpenSAMM and BSIMM also provide means to benchmark the actual software development maturity concerning the adoption of the proposed practices. While SAFECode advises the need to have a leadership tailored for security and that this will drive the mentality change of the rest of the team in building a safer software product, Securosis focuses on existing tools that can help automate most of the processes required by implementing security in the SDL.

CONCLUSION

Every contribution towards building and maintaining a safer software product is welcomed, given the current state of insecurity, namely in web applications. All of the proposals analyzed in this chapter are worth mentioning and they all provide a step up in the level of security of the final product. Although they have different views on how to achieve their goals, in essence they have more in common than they have differences. This common ground constitutes the basic principles and best practices they all share, which can be seen as the core needed to increase security during software development:

1. Training for security
2. Architectural review
3. Source code review
4. Penetration testing
5. Documentation and security policies

Applications, especially on the web, are a constant target for hackers and are never safe given that new vulnerabilities and exploitation techniques are being discovered constantly in the technologies and components they use. This evolving environment quickly turns thought to be secure applications into undoubtedly unsecure applications. Even for applications developed with a SSDL, they may become vulnerable shortly after delivery. This is one of the reasons why the development process does not end with delivery and continues though the maintenance. Maintenance after deployment and during the entire working life of the application should be a mandatory requirement.

To build secure software, security must be present from the early stages of the software development taking into account both secure mechanisms and design for security. The use of a software development lifecycle considering security is of utmost importance if the objective is not only the prevention of security bugs, but also higher-level problems, like architectural, component interaction and broken access control over tiers. The security work should be applied since the early stages of development, during the definition of the requirements, architecture, design, coding, testing, validation, measurement, and maintenance of the software. This way of developing secure applications is not only cheaper in the long term, but also has already proven results from the industry.

REFERENCES

Arbaugh, W. A., Fithen, W. L., & McHugh, J. (2000). Windows of vulnerability: A case study analysis. *Computer*, *33*(12), 52–59. doi:10.1109/2.889093

Arkin, B., Stender, S., & McGraw, G. (2005). Software penetration testing. *IEEE Security & Privacy*, *3*(1), 84–87. doi:10.1109/MSP.2005.23

Auger, R. (2007). *Writing software security test cases.* Retrieved February 18, 2009, from http://www.qasec.com/cycle/securitytestcases.shtml

Baker, W. H., Hutton, A., Hylender, C. D., Novak, C., Porter, C., & Sartin, B. (2009). *The 2009 data breach investigations report.* Verizon Business RISK Team.

Barnett, R. (2008). *ModSecurity blog: Is your website secure? Prove it.* Retrieved May 16, 2009, from http://www.modsecurity.org/blog/archives/2008/01/is_your_website.html

Barnum, S., & McGraw, G. (2005). Knowledge for software security. *IEEE Security & Privacy, 3*(2), 74–78. doi:10.1109/MSP.2005.45

Berinato, S. (2002). *CIO - Return on security spending,* (pp. 43–52).

Boehm, B. (1986). A spiral model of software development and enhancement. *SIGSOFT Software Engineering Notes, 11*(4), 14–24. doi:10.1145/12944.12948

Boehm, B., & Basili, V. R. (2001). Software defect reduction top 10 list. *Computer, 34*(1), 135–137. doi:10.1109/2.962984

Brooks, F. P. (1995). *The mythical man-month: Essays on software engineering, anniversary edition* (2nd ed.). Addison-Wesley Professional.

Chess, B. (2008). Space race. *My Security Planet Fortify blog.* Retrieved May 12, 2009, from http://rgaucher.info/planet/Fortify_blog/2008/08/13/

Chess, B., & McGraw, G. (2004). Static analysis for security. *IEEE Security & Privacy, 2*(6), 76–79. doi:10.1109/MSP.2004.111

Coblentz, N. (2009). SAMM assessment interview template. *SAMM Assessment Interview Template.* Retrieved September 18, 2009, from http://spreadsheets.google.com/pub?key=rYpVqQR3026Zu4DNg8LBIwg&gid=3

Dynamics, S. P. I. Inc. (2002). *Complete web application security: Phase 1–Building web application security into your development process.* SPI Dynamics, Inc. Retrieved from http://cnscenter.future.co.kr/resource/rsc-center/vendor-wp/Spidynamics/Webapp_Dev_Process.pdf

Epstein, J. (2009). *What measures do vendors use for software assurance? Build security in.* Carnegie Mellon University. Retrieved from https://buildsecurityin.us-cert.gov/daisy/bsi/articles/knowledge/business/1093-BSI.html

Fonseca, J., Vieira, M., & Madeira, H. (2007). Testing and comparing web vulnerability scanning tools for SQL injection and XSS attacks. *13th Pacific Rim International Symposium on Dependable Computing, PRDC 2007* (pp. 365–372).

Gollmann, D. (1999). *Computer security* (1st ed.). New York, NY: John Wiley & Sons. Retrieved from http://www.wiley.com/legacy/compbooks/catalog/97844-2.htm

Higgins, K. J. (2009). The rocky road to more secure code. *DarkReading.* Retrieved September 18, 2009, from http://www.darkreading.com/security/app-security/showArticle.jhtml?articleID=216403548&pgno=1&queryText=&isPrev=

Hope, P., McGraw, G., & Anton, A. I. (2004). Misuse and abuse cases: Getting past the positive. *IEEE Security & Privacy, 2*(3), 90–92. doi:10.1109/MSP.2004.17

Howard, M. (2009). *A conversation about threat modeling.* Retrieved May 16, 2009, from http://msdn.microsoft.com/en-us/magazine/dd727503.aspx

Howard, M., & LeBlanc, D. (2003). *Writing secure code.* Redmond, WA: Microsoft Press.

Howard, M., & Lipner, S. (2006). *The security development lifecycle.* Redmond, WA: Microsoft Press.

Jayaram, K. R., & Aditya, P. M. (2005). *Software engineering for secure software - State of the art: A survey* (CERIAS TR 2005-67). Purdue University. Retrieved from https://www.cerias.purdue.edu/apps/reports_and_papers/view/2884

Kim, F., & Skoudis, E. (2009). *Protecting your web apps: Two big mistakes and 12 practical tips to avoid them*. SANS Institute.

Lanowitz, T. (2005). *Now is the time for security at the application level*. Gartner Group. Retrieved from http://www.sela.co.il/_Uploads/dbsAttachedFiles/GartnerNowIsTheTimeForSecurity.pdf

Lipner, S., & Howard, M. (2005). The trustworthy computing security development lifecycle. *Microsoft Developer Network*. Retrieved September 24, 2009, from http://msdn.microsoft.com/en-us/library/ms995349.aspx

Marmor-Squires, A. B., & Rougeau, P. A. (1988). Issues in process models and integrated environments for trusted systems development. *Proceedings of the 11th National Computer Security Conference* (pp. pp. 109–113). United States Government Printing Office.

Martin, J. (1991). *Rapid application development*. Indianapolis, IN: Macmillan Publishing Co., Inc.

McGraw, G. (2004). Software security. *IEEE Security & Privacy*, 2(2), 80–83. doi:10.1109/MSECP.2004.1281254

McGraw, G. (2006). *Software security: Building security in*. Addison-Wesley Professional.

McGraw, G., Chess, B., & Migues, S. (2009). *Building security in maturity model*. Fortify & Cigital.

Mead, N. R., & McGraw, G. (2003). *The DIMACS Workshop on Software Security*. DIMACS Center.

Meftah, B. (2008). *Business software assurance: Identifying and reducing software risk in the enterprise*. Presented at the 9th Semi-Annual Software Assurance Forum. Retrieved from https://buildsecurityin.us-cert.gov/swa/downloads/Meftah.pdf

Microsoft Corporation. (2008). *Microsoft security development lifecycle (SDL) version 3.2*. Microsoft Corporation.

Microsoft Corporation. (2009a). *The microsoft security development lifecycle* (SDL). Retrieved March 23, 2009, from http://msdn.microsoft.com/en-us/security/cc448177.aspx

Microsoft Corporation. (2009b). SDL process template. *MSDN*. Retrieved May 22, 2009, from http://msdn.microsoft.com/en-us/security/dd670265.aspx

OWASP Foundation. (2006). *OWASP - CLASP* (1.2 ed.). OWASP Foundation. Retrieved from http://www.owasp.org/index.php/Category:OWASP_CLASP_Project

Potter, B., & McGraw, G. (2004). Software security testing. *IEEE Security & Privacy*, 2(5), 81–85. doi:10.1109/MSP.2004.84

Pravir, C. (2009). *Software assurance maturity model: A guide to building security into software development* (1.0 ed.). OpenSAMM Project. Retrieved from http://www.opensamm.org/

Rauscher, K. F., Krock, R. E., & Runyon, J. P. (2006). Eight ingredients of communications infrastructure: A systematic and comprehensive framework for enhancing network reliability and security. *Bell Labs Technical Journal*, 11(3), 73–81. doi:10.1002/bltj.20179

Royce, W. (1970). Managing the development of large software systems. *Proceedings of IEEE Wescon* (pp. 1–9).

RTI. (2002). *Planning Report 02-3 The economic impacts of inadequate infrastructure for software testing*. NIST. Retrieved from http://www.nist.gov/director/prog-ofc/report02-3.pdf

SAFECode. (2008a). *Fundamental practices for secure software development*. SAFECode. Retrieved from http://www.safecode.org/publications.php

SAFECode. (2008b). *Software assurance: An overview of current industry best practices*. SAFECode. Retrieved from http://www.safecode.org/publications.php

SAFECode. (2009). *Security engineering training*. SAFECode. Retrieved from http://www.safecode.org/publications.php

CNSS Secretariat. (2006). *National information assurance (IA) glossary*. Committee on National Security Systems.

Security, A. (2009). *Web vulnerability scanners comparison*. Retrieved from http://anantasec.blogspot.com/2009/01/web-vulnerability-scanners-comparison.html

Securosis. (2009). *Building a web application security program*. Securosis. Retrieved from http://securosis.com/research/publication/building-a-web-application-security-program/

Sommerville, I. (2010). *Software engineering* (9th ed.). Addison Wesley.

Taylor, D., & McGraw, G. (2005). Adopting a software security improvement program. *IEEE Security & Privacy*, *3*(3), 88–91. doi:10.1109/MSP.2005.60

Verdon, D., & McGraw, G. (2004). Risk analysis in software design. *IEEE Security & Privacy*, *2*(4), 79–84. doi:10.1109/MSP.2004.55

WhiteHat Security Inc. (2008). *WhiteHat website security statistic reports* (No. 6th Edition). WhiteHat Security Inc. Retrieved from http://www.whitehatsec.com/home/resource/stats.html

Wiesmann, A., Curphey, M., van der Stock, A., & Stirbei, R. (2005). *A guide to building secure web applications and web services, V2.0.1*. OWASP Foundation. Retrieved from http://www.owasp.org/index.php/Developer_Guide

Williams, J. (2008). *Establishing a security API for your enterprise (ALPHA version)*. OWASP Foundation.

KEY TERMS AND DEFINITIONS

Attack: Malicious and intentional interaction with the system exploiting a vulnerability in order to take advantage from it.

Best Practices: Set of methodologies that should be followed during the software lifecycle in order to provide a better product.

Bug (in the Software): Error in the software code that makes the software provide a service that deviates from the correct service, as stated in the specification.

Hacker: In this context, an attacker, a person that exploits the vulnerabilities of the system or tries to use it in other ways that were not intended by the developer.

Secure Software Development Lifecycle (SSDL): Is a model to develop software with security embedded from the start to the end of the life of the software.

Security: Set of properties of the software (Confidentiality, Integrity and Availability) that should be preserved, even when the system is under attack.

Vulnerability: Weakness in the system that may be exploited by an attacker to jeopardize one or more security properties of the system.

Chapter 4
Quality Practices for Managing Software Development in Information System

Syeda Umema Hani

GSESIT, Hamdard University, Pakistan & Sir Syed University of Engineering & Technology, Pakistan

ABSTRACT

Information Systems are developed and acquired in business organization in order to achieve the competitive advantage. A good quality information system plays vital role in providing good product and service value to its customers. This study intends to discuss suitable quality practices which could not only support development of a good quality software product but also linked up well with the strategic needs of the organizational business. It first presents what industry recommends for quality practices of software development. Then a framework has been presented that links Information System's development process improvement with strategic needs of an organization. It also demonstrates development of a primarily process improvement activity i.e. "process improvement plan" depicting how business goals leads to an adaptation of process framework like Capability Maturity Model for Development (CMMI-DEV) while using multi-model PI approach and the benefits achieved with its adaptation targeting development of a Quality Information System.

INTRODUCTION

CMMI-DEV's relevant process areas have been highlighted where an organization could use Balance Score Card technique while setting its strategic goals and monitoring their performance related to Information System development. It also highlights the ability of framework through which benefits of achieving competitive advantage could also be monitored. The new version of Information System management framework "Control Objectives for Information and Related Technology" (COBIT) - 5 by Information Systems Audit and Control Association (ISACA)

DOI: 10.4018/978-1-4666-3679-8.ch004

has also been highlighted and its relevant process area mapping with Capability Maturity Model Integration (CMMI) for Development (DEV) has also been covered, so that users could easily make their choice of selecting both the suitable frameworks for managing quality development in Information System.

In last varying benefits are reported for using different software development methodologies in multimodal process improvement scenarios. It states agile methods are good for achieving goals quicker. Methods like Team Software Process (TSP), Rational Unified Process (RUP), and CMMI have also achieved their goals, and deliver very few defects.

In last conclusion has been made that the presented framework options are to fill in existing gaps in-between strategic management and Information System development fields and that it has been verified from the statistics that no single software engineering method appears to be perfect therefore multi model process Improvement approach is best to be used for the development of a quality information system.

The "Information Technology" based system depends intensely on "Software Development" activities due to the rapid changing advances in technological interfaces and also to cope up with the day to day business challenges in today's global business market. Therefore a quality development of software is unavoidable now days.

This chapter discusses important aspects related to current trends of using software development practices and their changing impacts on quality software development. These current trends comprise of possible Software Process Improvement (SPI) methods and the possible metrics used for the quantification of Software development quality benefits and the organizational performance improvement in order to achieve the competitive advantage in market.

It discusses how to cover up major gaps in between Information System development and business process that effect over all business system's quality. These gaps are related to the involvement of collaboration of Information System's related Strategic management, the performance monitoring of IT organization and finally with Software Development unit that exists in an IT setup.

BACKGROUND

Information Technology and an Information System

Information technology (IT) is a combination of computer technology including both hardware and software along with communication technology i.e. data and networks. IT is used to build an Information System (IS).

Definition: A collection of elements like people, data, processes, communications, and information technology works together to support business operations by solving problems and helps management and users in making decisions.

Types of IS and Roles in Decision Making

Day to day business operations in and organization generates data that an IS processes in to strategic or tactical information that helps the management in effective decision making. Its biggest advantage is that Information can flow up in the MIS information pyramid faster and more effectively.

Three Levels of Decision-Making of an Organization

There exist three levels of information management in any organization.

1. **Executive level:** It comes on the top level of management pyramid and at this level

of management long-term and unstructured decisions takes place.

2. **Managerial level:** It comes on the middle level of management pyramid and at this level of management semi-structured decisions takes place covering weeks and months.

3. **Operational level:** It lies at bottom of the management pyramid where structured decisions need to be taken on daily basis.

There are mainly two broad categories of IS which are utilized at afore mentioned three levels of "Information Management" in any organization. Let's take a quick look on different possible types of an IS that are used at different management levels of an organizations.

1. **Management Support System:** It supports managerial level strategic decision making for achieving competitive advantage and business level tactical decision making. It further comprises of Management Information System (MIS), Executive Information System (EIS) and Decision Support System (DSS).

   a. **MIS:** It facilitates mangers with pre-specified analysis and reporting tools.

   b. **EIS:** It facilitates executives with strategic as well as tactical information management.

   c. **DSS:** It facilitates executives with strategic as well as tactical information management. It provides interactive support for non-routine decisions what if analysis for End-users through text and graphs.

2. **Operation Support System:** It supports business processes and operations. It further comprises of Enterprise Communication System (ECS), Process Control Systems (PCS) and Transaction Processing Systems (TCS).

   a. **ECS:** It facilitates operations through team collaboration and communication.

   b. **PCS:** It supports operations, and monitor and control industrial and manufacturing process.

   c. **TPS:** It supports operations, and updates operational databases.

From above quick overview it is quite clear that IS are mainly software based solutions. Therefore it is important to understand what quality practices are required for the development and maintenance of an IS.

What is Quality?

Gerald Weinberg defines quality as "Something that values to some person. The tricky part is to find out who that person should be. It is value that makes a user's high quality system to low quality to someone else. Therefore it is also important to decide who is measuring quality and then find out how to assess it".

Roger Pressman defines it as "Conformance to explicitly defined functional and implicit characteristics that are expected of professionally developed software". Capers John adds in to it that "the professionally developed software should be either defect free or have tolerable level of defects".

Quality Challenges to Information Systems and its Targeted Benefits

Neil Potter defines the challenges which Information Systems are facing these days:

- Difficulty in developing Information Systems,
- Security breaches in an Information System,
- Maintenance of huge information,
- Employee's turnover and mistrust conditions,

- **Good Quality of Information:** Means the timely availability of updated information, accurate reliable and relevant content and the content presentation i.e. its detail and clarity.

Every above challenge has further details to deal with; if business overcomes above challenges as a result it adds value to the customer which could be measured as tangible i.e. quantifiable benefits as well as intangible unquantifiable benefits.

A study by Sherif Kamel mentions that through the quality development of information systems we could achieve primarily benefits like:

1. **Tangible goals:** These are quantifiable measurable goals and include for e.g. Improved Inventory Control, Increased production, and reduced administration cost as well as some intangible goals.
2. **Intangible goals:** These goals are usually difficult to measure for e.g. Enhanced customer service, Greater customer loyalty, and enhanced public image.

These tangible and intangible goals helps in to achieve benefits like enhanced competitiveness, confinement of market opportunities, improved products and services quality, increase in market share, support for corporate strategy, enhanced productivity of staff, increased revenue, reduced costs, increased customer service, good market exposure, and market visibility etc.

Realization from this section could be concluded as:

Since, The goal of information systems is to enable the organisation to achieve its business goals. Therefore, It is important to build (develop and acquire) information systems. Such that, The developing organization should target its goals related to the challenges it is facing and monitor their performance to guarantee successful completion of an information system's build process.

MAIN FOCUS OF THE CHAPTER

Issues, Controversies, and Problems

Current Quality Trends for Developing IS

Organizations who are involved in developing IS are already advised to use "Total Quality Management" approach to facilitate Quality Improvements with in a business using some well known quality standard for information system like ISO 9001 or SPI framework CMMI. Adaptation of these Quality standards leads to a Continuous Process Improvement (CPI) using which we could develop and maintain quality Information Systems. There is another term Business Process Redesign (BPR) which could also be managed well through achieving CPI.

Dependency of IS on Competitive Advantage

David Kroenke mentions that varying from industry to industry an organization's goals and objectives are determined through its competitive strategy. Competitive strategies could be achieved by the organization targeting following type of goals:

1. **Related to their products and services:** To create, enhance or distinguish its products and services from other competitors across its industry or across industry segment.
2. **Related to developing better business process:** To catch customer via high switching costs, to lock its suppliers through facilities and discouraging them from changing to another business, collaborate with other organizations and set standards, purchase costs could be reduced to provide benefits to everyone, and by reduce costs which in turn reduces prices and increases profitability to become a cost leader across its industry or across industry segment.

Competitive strategies require a business process that offers its customers benefits and value. Value to the customer means, his willingness in investing over product, service, or resource the system is offering.

The business process comprises of set of activities related to support (i.e. HR, Admin and management, Procurement, and Technology) and primary (i.e. logistics, operations, Sales and marketing, and services) that adds margin of value to organization's products and services through applying competitive strategies.

Conclusion is that once the business process has been defined, IS then be structured which can improve operational efficiency, and customer-supplier relationship through utilizing benchmarking and industry best practices i.e. adaptation of Process Improvement activities.

Desirable Goals for IS to Become a Competitive Advantage

Lê Ngọc Tiến suggests following goals which are used to make ground for current study:

1. Understand Information System for strategic organizational success. Strategic support includes doing the things in smarter way by setting direction i.e. vision, by creating standard i.e. setting performance goals and setting strategy for reaching goals.
2. Understand need for developing an Information System's business case.
3. Understand technological innovations to improve competitive advantage. It includes following:
    a. Organizational learning i.e. to improve organizational behavior by using acquired knowledge and insights.
    b. Using Total Quality Management (TQM) for monitoring the improving quality of operations, products and services.

c. Automation for performing operations faster and for doing things in better way using patters and trends.

Need of Quality Development and Acquisition for IS

ISACA is a body that formalizes different functions of information systems. These functions are related to its governance, audit, security and assurance professionals worldwide. ISACA has introduced the COBIT-5 framework. It focuses over the effective usage of IT for achieving the strategic objectives and the realization of business benefits achieved but its previous versions does not formalizes the software development activity of Information Systems.

Normally two approaches have been used for the development of IS i.e. Process oriented approach (proceeds trough GUI designing and approached towards data storage needs) and a Data oriented approach (data storage is first implemented then forms are designed to use the stored data).

No matter what approach the organization is using they usually adopt different software development methodologies as model or multi-model driven approach a for quality implementation of Information Systems without being known their benefits. These methodologies may include Agile, Xtreme Programming (XP), Team Software Process (TSP), CMMI with Spiral life cycle model, and RUP methodologies. These approaches have varying quality impacts which are covered in detail in last section.

At this point the Strategic Management field should get connected with Software Engineering field. Another type of Information Systems called ecosystems involve different industries working together for delivering value to the customer. For them IT also helps in establishing collaboration among participant firms and requires more advanced forms of software based solutions.

This chapter is about to understand standardization of Software Engineering and related practices, which could provide more value to the customers while interacting with Strategic Management field.

Different Process Improvement Approaches

To achieve the challenges highlighted in previous section there is a need to understand what Process Improvement (PI) is and what different approaches and combinations could be used to develop Information System as a competitive advantage.

Process Improvement could be categorized as per its usage approaches i.e. Classic Process-Centric approach and the Goal-Problem-Centric approach.

1. **Process Centric approach:** Improvement in which is started by following processes and progress towards business goals by looking into the business problems this approach has high risk of failure because before starting PI the organization has not targeted to bring solution of any specific problems therefore common result might be confusing and make the organization lost.

2. **Goal-Problem Centric approach:** This approach came in as a solution to the first approach, using it we could specify our goals first for resolving the problems which our current working process is facing. In order to resolve these problems we then define and specify PI efforts. Therefore our improvement actions will be in turn compliant with the goal actions. COBIT framework is developed for IT governance and is beneficial for IT audits but when software development quality is concerned at process side we could use PI standards like SEI CMMI, ISO9001 etc.

Here frameworks provide tailor-able PI suggestions to the organizations where as standards like ISO focuses more on documentation.

Rick Hefner gives another classification of PI as a Data Driven approach, Model Driven or Multi Model approach.

1. **Data-Driven:** In data driven approach one needs to charter team and clarify what its customer wants. Map process and specify critical to quality goals. Determine what your processes can do, apply Statistical Process Control for process performance measurement. Identify root causes of problems. Identify and prioritize improvement opportunities and implement improvement solutions. Apply causal analysis of data to control and assure mission success by identifying the customer's needs and reducing defects. Six Sigma and Lean comes under this category.

2. **Process or Model-Driven:** Such models determine the industry's best practices as (benchmarking and models) and comparing your current practices to the model. Appraisals and staff training is performed. Improvement opportunities are identified, prioritized and institutionalized. Finally the organizational process is optimized by going through continuous PI. CMMI framework or COBIT framework comes under this category.

3. **Multi Model Approach:** In multi model approach data driven models could be used in process based models to facilitate process improvement. For example "Six Sigma Processes" or "Balanced Score Card" approach could be used for supporting CMMI based process improvements.

For Information System development a Goal Centric approach with Multi Model approach would make right combination. As goal centric could link strategic goals with PI need and multi model could help us in reaching towards something that could be stated as perfect solution. For details check solution and recommendation section.

Solutions and Recommendations

This section first presents recommendations by industrial experts and then it discusses different possibilities of achieving quality development of an IS.

Recommendations by Industrial Experts

This section presents understanding of industrial experts what they think should be necessary for Quality Software Development.

Juan Lopez, CSM: Director of Software Development at TRX, Inc. and student of Linguistics at UT Arlington, Dallas, Fort Worth Area, www.trx.com

He presents following list of most important software development practices which are required for the quality software development:

1. An organizational commitment to excellence with a strong customer focus;
2. Data-based estimation, planning, budgeting, and program management including internal and external (e.g. ISBG) cost model comparisons; earned value management; risk management with value analysis; and dashboard monitoring;
3. Involved domain expertise in defining the concept of operation, use case scenarios, and system requirements with a strong focus on human-system integration;
4. Incremental and iterative engineering processes that are hybrids of CMM-I level 3 or above, Six Sigma, TSP/PSP, extreme programming, object-oriented methods, model-driven engineering; and employ formal change control and defect prevention

practices including pre certified components, formal specification with automated verification, joint application design, and quality function deployment;

5. Disciplined quality assurance and quality control with program and defect metrics, complexity analysis, static code analysis, coding standards, inspections, walk-through, integration and test planning, automated test coverage analysis, and test automation;
6. Data gathering and analysis is built in and makes it very easy to learn from personal mistakes, how to remove them, and how to prevent them.

Wayne Mack: Project Manager, PMP, Avaya Government Solutions, Washington D.C., http://www.avayagov.com

The majority of issues related to software quality tend to be acts of omission rather than acts of commission – issues tend to be things that the software development team did not do rather than things that they did wrong. This belief shapes my list as:

1. The development team must be actively involved in requirements gathering. The development team needs to have an inherent understanding of the issues to be addressed and this cannot be fully communicated through paper documents.
2. The development team must be given training in how to test. Although Test Driven Development (TDD) and "Do the simplest thing that could possibly work" address software that is developed from scratch, when using external components and libraries, the development team needs to understand how find inappropriate generic operation and restrict the capabilities to those needed for a particular design.
3. We need to bring back the concept of software reuse at an application or project level.

The focus needs to be on having a library of simple, common operations rather than complex generic algorithms. Wrap all GUI components into business data type specific components so that the data type is handled consistently throughout the application.

4. We need to have the development team focus on design for today rather than designing for future considerations. Focus needs to be on developing solutions to well-understood issues rather than attempting to solve poorly understood potential requirements. It is often these future capabilities that dramatically increase development time and test time, and when the future issue is actually realized, the design often turns out to be a poor fit. This results in wasted future effort in trying to save a poorly thought out approach when the future necessitates a change or addition.

5. Code refactoring needs to be embraced by management as a necessary step in ongoing software development efforts. The software structure needs to be continuously improved throughout the development and maintenance process. We need to change from believing "If it ain't broke, don't fix it" to "You probably don't know how broke it actually is." Lack of experience can lead to bad decisions; development teams need to be able to address these in the future. Schedule deadlines can lead to shortcuts; development teams need to be able to address these in the future. Refactoring needs to be explicitly recognized as a necessary step by management and not be relegated to a hidden activity by the development team. These steps lead to added responsibilities to the development team and require the development team to take on more tasks than simply programming all day. The senior level staff and team leads need to take on a broader range of skills and not be ever

more focused on intricate details of specific programming languages and environments.

Cor Lageweg: Project Manager at Molina Healthcare, Irvine, California http://www.molinahealthcare.com

Here is the list to produce the best possible software:

1. An organization-wide stated and active commitment to quality (allow quality to occur).
2. Promote quality at ALL levels; requirements, development, testing, configuration, implementation, support and mature team members (technical, functional and executive).
3. Clear, concise and transparent processes that promote and reward quality.
4. Verification of quality; static code analysis, code audits, automated testing, manual testing, etc. and metrics of some sort (# bugs, # missed features, etc).
5. Positive motivation; reward systems for individuals and projects that obtain a certain level of quality.

This section concludes that the major economic value of high quality Information System is to achieve shorter development schedules, lower development costs, lower maintenance costs, lower cost of quality, and lower total cost of ownership. Just concerning with the software defects is not enough for quality to drive benefits.

Misconceptions about CMMI Framework

Before selecting any specific approach for SPI we should also knows that, there exist few misconceptions about different SPI techniques. One thing to notify here is no matter which approach we are going to adapt, care should be taken for following realties as highlighted by Kent A. Johnson, which could help us in using good model combinations in a Multi Model approach:

1. CMMI encourages an organization to establish beneficial measures that relate to their "business" goals. (reality)
2. Agile methods do not need or use measurements. (misconception)
3. The seventh principle behind the Agile Manifesto says: "Working software is the primary measure of progress." Equally applicable over XP method. (reality)
4. Lean Software Development hates dysfunctional measures and local optimization, but promotes using cycle time (e.g., time to fix a reported defect) and customer satisfaction measures (e.g., net promoter score). (reality)
5. XP states that "working software is the primary measure of progress." (reality)

So no matter which Software Development approach an organization is following for the development of Information Systems, CMMI framework supports all classic as well as agile methodologies of software development and it could be easily adapted for the Quality development of Information System.

Option 1: CMMI Based Framework for Developing Quality IS

These days almost every business uses strategy maps to set and tract their business goals related to four viewpoints related to Financial, Customer, Internal Business Process, Learning and Growth. Balance Score Card approach is used to keep the performance track of Key Performance Indicators (KPI). These KPI are mapped with the goals defined in strategy map.

A framework is proposed that should link its business strategy map with benefits of achieving competitive advantage through Information System development, following quality framework like CMMI.

If an organization adapts process improvement practices like CMMI framework then it could link its goals with the KPI inside the balance score card tool. Through it they can keep track of overall organizational performance by tracking the performance of its KPIs.

The performance measurement is facilitated in BSC as each KPI is associated with some quantifiable metric value and KPI value predictions could also being made more accurately if empirically derived equations are set in same tool instead of just using target values for performance monitoring.

Figure 1 shows details of proposed framework. In other terms we could say the performance of CMMI benefits (interpreted as KPI) could be viewed and measured in to strategic management's four perspectives. Strategy map helps to maintain link in-between Strategic level and all the way long to project level process tracking.

Step 1: In-order to align CMMI framework with BSC, there is a need to make some strategy. The strategy for CMMI should not only focus over its constellation and later on dumped over business strategy but should be derived from business requirements.

Step 2: For the reason we could follow Goal Question Indicator Metric (GQIM) and ask Question what are the main problems faced in business and what role IS development will play in it?

Step 3: Here organization aligns process by answering issues. Prioritize the answers while focusing over initiatives with measurable results. Intention to finding measurable indicators should be about asking the right question.

Alignment of CMMI process areas with business goals using proper KPI provides value to organization as they make investments and improvements whereas BSC helps in checking effectiveness of adapted strategy. In an environment where one has to use multiple methods there is a need of alignment in between their relevant

Figure 1. Interaction of strategy map with CMMI process areas for developing IS with competitive advantage

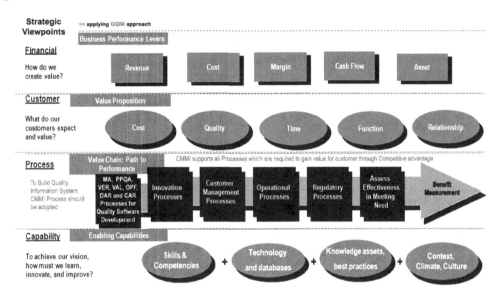

areas or steps. Table 1 presents different KPI considered to be used in BSC for Quality benefit measurement based on studies by Howard Rohm, Nancy R, and Julia H. Allen.

Mr. Chang, Richard Y and Mark W. Morgan in 2000 has proposed a Management cycle which is usually being follow in organizations for the implementation of BSC. Table 2 shows mapping of its different steps with CMMI process areas where alignment is necessarily needed.

Goal Question Indicator Metric Approach of Software Engineering

GQIM approach facilitates the process of driving business goals linked up with metrics and measurement needs for any process. This method could help setting up strategic goals in BSC tool which leads to the adaptation of CMMI like framework. Ikram Khan presents an example of GQIM approach in Figure 2.

CMMI Roadmap and Relevant Process Areas Used in Framework

For the proposed framework the most relevant CMMI roadmap which could be adapted is presented by Jan Jaap Cannegieter in technical report as the "Measurement roadmap". Its purpose is to identify and measure the quantitative improvements. It measures performance improvement, demonstrate process improvements results and identify and prioritize valuable KPIs of the organization. This roadmap could be used by the organizations who want to show the added value of process improvement quantitatively. Following CMMI Process Areas (PA) needs to be implemented:

Measurement and Analysis (MA) Maturity Level 2: Measurement and Analysis PA creates measurement capability and produces quantifiable results for all areas of Engineering, Project Management and Business thus it supports Management Information. Different process areas derive data based on its principles. Figure 3 highlights its major steps of MA PA.

Table 1. Possible performance goals and KPI for developing quality IS

Business Perspectives	Mission Objective or KPI or performance measures
FINANCIAL (Business Performance Levels)	
Questions to be asked: To create value for stakeholder, what financial objectives the organization must accomplish?	Revenue or Revenue Growth
	Cost invested on Software Development
	Margin or Operating Margin
	Cash Flow
	Assets
	Economic Value Added
	Maximize Shareholder Value
	Profitability
CUSTOMERS (Value Preposition)	
Questions to be asked: What do our customers expect and value? To achieve our financial objectives, what customer needs must we serve?	Cost or Price of Service
	Quality
	Time
	Function
	Relationship/Customer Satisfaction
	Customer Loyalty
	Image
	Service
Strategic competitiveness	Sustainable Competitive Advantage
	Inside Out market position
	Increase market share
INTERNAL PROCESS (INTERNAL BUSINESS PROCESS) (Value Chain: Path to performance)	
Questions to be asked: What processes are required for customer through competitive advantage? To satisfy our customer and stakeholders, in which internal business process must we excel?	Safety
	Innovation Process/process Enhancement
	Customer Management Process
	Operational Process or Operational Efficiency
	Regulatory Processes
	Access Effectiveness in meeting needs
	Productivity
	Business Efficiency
	Cycle Time
	Cost
	Quality

continued on following page

It states that for the alignment of measurement and analysis activities one has to establish measurement objectives first then specify measure and specify its related data collection and storage procedures, and the analysis procedure.

To provide measurement results one needs to collect measurement data then analyze it and finally store its results. By adapting Measurement and Analysis process area of CMMI we

Table 1. Continued

Business Perspectives	Mission Objective or KPI or performance measures
LEARNING AND GROWTH (Enabling capability)	
Questions to be asked: How must we learn to innovate and improve? To achieve organizational goal how must our organization learn and innovate?	Employee Satisfaction
	Skill and competitiveness or Employee personal development
	Technologies and Databases
	Knowledge assets and best practices
	Intellectual assets
	Context, Climate, Culture Or Organizational Enhancement
	Continuous Improvement
	Market Innovation

Table 2. Mapping CMMI process area alignment with the management cycle of performance score cards

Step Number	Management Cycle	Alignment with CMMI Process Areas
1. Collect/Plan or Revise Plan	Collect Information	OPF SP1.2, OPF SP3.4, IPM SP1.7, and generic practice GP3.2. discover flaws in current process and IS Products
2. Create/Do	Create the scorecard design	By gaining understanding of current process flaws from MA SG1 and OPF SG2. OPF SG2 Plans and implement required organizational process improvements through CMMI. DAR helps in decision making for selecting productive alternative as per added customer value criteria. BSC and cost benefit analysis could be performed here for evaluation purpose.
3. Cultivate	Cultivate acceptance and the measurement culture	MA (GQM) is properly applied and management is convinced by linking it with its goals and objectives.
4. Cascade	Cascade measures down through the organization	In OPM maintain BSC that sets a framework for MA SP1.1 i.e. what information do we need, and what are the measurement objectives associated with that need Then MA SP1.2 – MA SP1.4 establish the measurement infrastructure required to address that information need/measurement objectives.
5. Connect	Connects objectives and measures to employees	IPM process guarantees 1. Implementation of required organizational process improvements through OPF (Implementation of CMMI). 2. OPM SG1
6. Confirm/Check	Confirm effectiveness through evaluation leading to ongoing improvement	OPP gathers data from projects to measure and predict quality and business critical processes performance and quality product characteristics. In next cycles it could be termed as benefit measurement of deployed process improvement through OPM. OPM maintain analyze process performance using BSC.
7. Improvement/ ACT		From QPM and OPP it detects product and process deficiencies through applying root cause analysis in CAR.

could proceeds towards the fine adaptation of the proposed framework.

Process and Product Quality Assurance (PPQA) Maturity Level 2: It provides an objective insight into processes and products. It objectively evaluates process and product tasks, identify non compliance issues, provide feedback of QA to

Figure 2. GQIM approach example

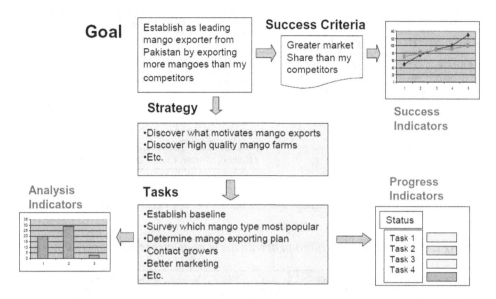

Figure 3. Measurement and analysis process area

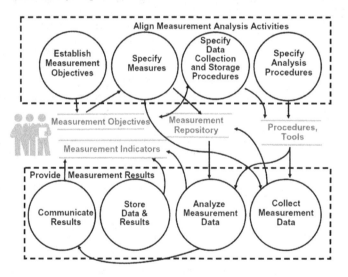

relevant staff and confirm that non conformance issues have been taken care off.

Organizational Process Focus (OPF) Maturity Level 3: Based on current organizational process strength and deficiencies it plans and implement required organizational process improvements. Interacting with integrated Product and process Planning PA it guarantees organizational commitment and availability of resources required

for process group for effective deployment of improvements.

Integrated Product and Process Development (IPPD) Maturity Level 3: It gives parallel development approach and integrates product development process with related processes for which product is being developed. These integrated processes accommodate information provided by the stakeholders related to all phases of product lifecycle from both business domain and technical software development functions and they also accommodate processes for teamwork.

Decision Analysis and Resolution (DAR) Maturity Level 4: It helps in decision making process. It analyzes multiple decisions and helps in identifying productive alternatives. Provides structured decision making process comparing alternatives against success criteria and selects the best. For developing IS to achieve competitive advantages, SWOT analysis method should be used for business planning, strategic planning, competitor evaluation, marketing, business and product development and research reports.

SWOT stands for to evaluate the strengths, weaknesses, opportunities, and threats. It can evaluate decisions like a company value, product or brand, business idea, a strategic option of entering into new market or introducing new product or service, a method for sales or an opportunity to make acquisition, a potential partnership, changing a supplier, outsourcing a service, activity or resource or an investment opportunity.

Organizational Performance Management (OPM) Maturity Level 5: The OPM process area enables the organization to manage its organizational performance in order to meet its business objectives by iteratively analyzing aggregated project level data to identify performance gaps against the business objectives, and then selecting and deploying improvements to bridge the indentified gaps. Business objectives may include improvement in all productivity related parameters. See last section for its details.

This PA is an extension of OPF practices by focusing on PI based on a quantitative understanding of the It interacts with MA PA to measures impact of deployed process and technology improvement by measuring related metrics as discussed in section "Standard Metrics for measuring benefits of SPI". Need of this PA has already been discussed in previous section "Quality challenges to Information Systems and its targeted benefits". These objectives or benefits stands as KPI's in balance score card system.

Organizational Process Performance (OPP) Maturity Level 5: This PA establishes measurements and gathers data from all projects. These measures are used to quantify process performance for the prediction of, quality and business critical processes and quality product characteristics. Once all necessary measurements have been established and models are constructed then it needs Quantitative Project Management to be implemented in parallel to realize process performance.

Quantitative Project Management (QPM) Maturity Level 4: It manages process using statistical measures for process control either using SPC or six sigma approach.

Execution of Framework for Developing a Process Improvement Plan

Neil Potter and Mary Sakry suggest following important steps to follow in-order to develop a Process Improvement Plan, these steps are also in compliant to the above proposed framework.

1. Scope the Improvement
   a. Identify Organizational Goals or the Business goals, achievement of which could be taken as the benefits achieved by Process Improvement activity (see Box 1 for examples).
   b. Identify problems or issues in current organizational process (see Box 1).
   c. Prioritize them and select the ones which are critical for business.
2. **Develop action plan:** List down actions following some process framework like CMMI and organize the actions according to their goals and problems.
3. Depending on action priority, perform actions, check their progress and take corrective actions (see Table 3). Now follow only those Process Improvement framework practices that could help you in gaining control on the identified problems which exists in your Organizational Process.

Box 1.

EXAMPLE 1
Goal 1: Successfully deliver product.
Group the identified problems that prevent each goal from being achieved and clarify goals.
EXAMPLE 2
Goal 1: Successfully deliver product A on dated: dd/mm/yy
Problem1: Need proper client requirements which should be track able and changes made into them should also be tracked as code is not traceable with their requirements at the time of testing.
Problem 2: Due to frequent changes in product goals it is hard to synchronize management's directions with the product version.

---

4. **Determine Risks and Plan to Mitigate, Implement the Plan and Check Progress:** By checking that is the organization making progress (the Goals or Our Improvement Plan or the Improvement Framework) depending on which process improvement approach we have adapted and conclude lessons learned.

Option 2: COBIT5 Framework for the Governance and Management of IT Enterprise

It defines value creation while realising the benefits utilizing optimal resource cost while optimising risk. It maps enterprise goals with IT-related goals and finally IT goals supported by critical processes. It also includes a capability model with objectives of process improvement and support in compliant to ISO/IEC 15504 Software Engineering process assessment standard.

CMMI Process Areas Support in COBIT-5

COBIT5 covers CMMI processes related to application building and acquisition processes in its Build Acquire Implement (BAI) track and some organizational and quality related processes from the Align Plan and Organize (APO) track.

Table 3.

Goals communicates the results we want to achieve	Purpose communicates why we want to achieve this goal	Actions	Priority * = compulsory
To reduce software development cycle time to some month range	To deliver earlier in order to get competitive advantage in market	Only allow changes at interface level. Enhancements will be entertained in next cycles on extra change.	1*
		Assign responsibility	2*
		Check progress and take corrective steps	
		Make Investigation for improvement in current functionality	3
		Track change requests	4
		Baseline changes	5

Table 4. Mapping of CMMI process areas with COBIT5 process areas

	COBIT5 Process Areas	CMMI-Dev Process Areas
Process for Governance of Enterprise IT		
Evaluate Direct and Monitor (EDM)		Out of Scope for this study
Processes for Management of Enterprise IT		
Align Plan Organize (APO)	01: Manage the IT management framework	OPD, OT
	02: Manage Strategy	OPF
	03: Manage Enterprise Architecture	
	04: Manage Innovation	
	05: Manage Portfolio	
	06: Manage Budget and Costs	
	07: Manage HR	
	08: Manage Relationships	APO081-5 - IPM SG2
	09: Manage Service Agreements	
	10: Manage Suppliers	SAM
	11: Manage Quality	OPD, OPF
	12: Manage Risks	RM
	13: Manage Security	
Build Acquire and Implement (BAI)	01: Manage Programs and Projects	OPD BAI01.9-OPM BAI01.8-PP, BAI01.11-PMC BAI01.3-IPM:
	02: Manage Requirements Definition	BAI02.01-RD, BAI02.01-DAR,
	03: Manage Solution Identification and Builds	BAI03.1- TS SG1 BAI03.2-TS SG2 BAI03.3-TS SG3 BAI03.5-PIntegration BAI03.6-PPQA perform QA BAI03.7-Validation BAI03.8-Validation BAI03.9-RM
	04: Manage Availability and Capacity	CMMI-SERVICES
	05: Manage Organizational Change Enablement	BAI05.1-7 – PMC SG3
	06: Manage Changes	CM
	07: Manage Change Acceptance and Transition-ing	CM
	08: Manage Knowledge	PP and PMC, MA
	09: Manage Assts	PP and PMC, MA
	10: Manage Configuration	CM
Deliver Service and Support (DSS)		Out of scope for this study

continued on following page

Table 4. Continued

	COBIT5 Process Areas	**CMMI-Dev Process Areas**
Monitor Evaluate and Assess (MEA)		For Assessment Purpose
	01: Monitor Evaluate and Assess performance and Conformance	PPQA and VER at project level
	02: Monitor Evaluate and Assess the System of Internal Control	
	03: Monitor Evaluate and Assess the System of External Control	

Table 4 shows CMMI to COBIT 5 process area mappings related to Software Development.

Measurement for Software Process Improvement

Tracy O'Rourke, CEO of Allen-Bradley - "Without the right information, you're just another person with an opinion".

Measurement is necessary to gain insight of organizational processes. If the processes are goal driven then its measures should also be derived thorough goals.

William A. Florac mentions that to help address business goals, software management functions could be fall into three categories: i.e. project management, process management, and product engineering. Each of which has its own objectives and issues. Project management is concerned with to meet planned commitments regarding cost, schedule, quality, and functionality while tracking product status. Table 5 shares sample product metrics communicating goals related to project and process issues.

Process management confirms that process is showing expected behavior and is under control. In case of any abnormal behavior it makes sure that improvement have been made to ensure it meets the business goals. Figure 4 depicts five perspectives of Process Management.

How Software Quality Standards or Quality Models Helps in Metrics Selection

Quality models comprises of a set of quality characteristics which specifies non functional quality requirements and criteria for quality assessment. In a study Vishal Sadana highlighted different types of Quality Models.

Models that could be used to establish measurements for assessing Quality include MacCall Model, Boehm Model, FURPS Model, ISO 9126, Dromey Model and Quality Factor Model. Table 6 shows different quality models and their supported quality characteristics.

If any organization follows any specific quality model for the measurement of quality practices adapted as part of its SPI program then that quality models contains some quality characteristics which should be accommodated while choosing measurement metrics. See next section for standard metrics that should be included in measurement program.

Standard Metrics for Measuring Benefits of SPI

For performing benefit measurement one needs to adapt following benefit measurement classes related to Project, Product and process:

Table 5. Mapping of business goals related to product and process issues with measureable attributes

Serial No	Business Goals	Measurable Product and Process Attributes
1	**Increase Function** Project Issue: Product Growth and stability Process Issue: Product Conformance	Number of Requirements Product Size Product Complexity Rates of Change Percent Non- Conformance
2	**Reduce Cost** Project Issue: Budgets expenditure rates Process Issue: Efficiency, Productivity, Rework	Product Size Product Complexity Effort Number of Changes Requirements Stability
3	**Reduce the Time to Market** Project Issue: Schedule Progress Process Issue: Production Rate Responsiveness	Elapsed time, Normalized for product characteristics
4	**Improved Produced Quality** Project Issue: Product Performance, Product Correctness, Product Reliability Process Issue: Predictability, Problem Recognition, Root Cause Analysis	Number of Defects introduced Effectiveness of defect detection activities

Figure 4. Process management and measurement perspectives

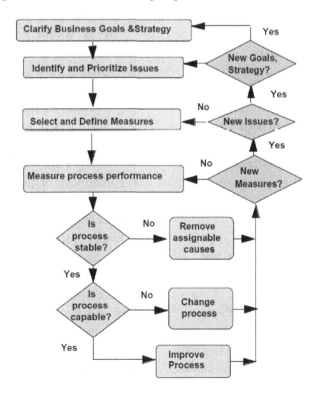

Table 6. Mapping of different quality models with their constituent quality characteristics

Quality Characteristics	Boehm	McCall	FURPS	ISO 9126	Dromey
Testability	x	x		x	
Correctness		x			
Efficiency	x	x	x	x	x
Understandability	x			x	
Reliability	x	x	x	x	x
Flexibility		x	x (extensibility, adaptability, maintainability)		
Functionality			x	x	x
Human Engineering	x				
Integrity		x		x(Security)	
Interoperability		x		x(Functionality)	
Process Maturity					x
Maintainability	x	x	x	x	x
Changeability	x				
Portability	x	x		x	x
Reusability		x			x

1. Effort
2. Schedule
3. Cost
4. Quality
5. Productivity
6. Customer Satisfaction
7. Return on Investment (ROI)

A doctorial research by the author proposes common measures of SPI benefit measurement which could be adapted across multiple organizations for the measurement and prediction of Quality and performance for IS development activities. For detailed measures under above classes check referred paper and thesis report.

Impact of Different Software Process Improvement Techniques on Software Quality

Many studies have been performed by different researchers and professionals for highlighting exact benefits of implementing different SPI techniques for example the study by Kent A. Johnson shows benefits of adapting CMMI PI framework in to five major PI classes:

- **Costs:** 10% decrease per maturity level (Northrop Grumman)
- **Schedules:** 50% reduction (General Motors, Boeing)
- **Productivity:** 25-30% increase in productivity within 3 years (Lockheed Martin, Harris, Siemens)
- **Quality:** 50% reduction of software defects (Lockheed Martin)
- **Customer Satisfaction:** 55% increase in award fees (Lockheed Martin)

Study by Capers Johan, shares benefit results of 10 software engineering methodologies and compares them in three major categories i.e. 1. Speed: Development schedules, effort, and costs. 2. Quality: Software quality in terms of delivered defects and 3. Economics: Total Cost of Ownership (TCO) and Cost of Quality (COQ).

Here speed based and Quality based comparisons have been presented which could help us in concluding priority of different software engineering methodologies to bring quality in software development process. The first comparison concerns with development speeds, costs, and

Table 7. Software engineering methodologies comparison speed wise (schedules, staff, effort, productivity)

	Methodologies	Schedule Months	Staff	Effort Months	FP Month	Development Cost
1	Extreme (XP)	11.78	7	84	11.89	$630,860
2	Agile/scrum	11.82	7	84	11.85	$633,043
3	TSP	12.02	7	86	11.64	$644,070
4	CMMI 5/ spiral	12.45	7	83	12.05	$622,257
5	OO	12.78	8	107	9.31	$805,156
6	RUP	13.11	8	101	9.58	$756,157
7	Pair/iterative	13.15	12	155	9.21	$1,160,492
8	CMMI 3/iterative	13.34	8	107	9.37	$800,113
9	Proofs/waterfall	13.71	12	161	6.21	$1,207,500
10	CMMI 1/waterfall	15.85	10	158	6.51	$1,188,870
	Average	13.00	8.6	112.6	9.762	$844,852

Table 8. Software engineering methodologies comparison defects wise (software defect potentials, removal, and delivery)

	Methodologies	Defect Potential	Defect Removal	Defects Delivered	High Severity Defects
1	TSP	2,700	96.79%	87	16
2	CMMI 5/ spiral	3,000	95.95%	122	22
3	Rational Unified Process (RUP)	3,900	95.07%	192	36
4	Extreme (XP)	4,500	93.36%	299	55
5	Object Oriented (OO)	4,950	93.74%	310	57
6	Pair Program /Iterative model	4,700	92.93%	332	61
7	Agile/scrum	4,800	92.30%	370	68
8	CMMI 3/ Itcr.	4,500	91.18%	397	73
9	CMMI 1/ Waterfall Model.	6,000	78.76%	1,274	236
	Average	4,370	92.23%	374	69

Table 9. Best software engineering methods in 10 benefit categories

Benefit Category	Methodology
Effort	CMMI ML 5
Cost	CMMI ML 5
Men Power	Agile
Schedule	XP
Quality (Defect potentials, Defect removal efficiency, Delivered defects, High-severity defects)	TSP
Total Cost of Ownership (TCO) and Cost of Quality (COQ)	TSP

short-term issues. Table 7 is sorted by the speed of development.

For applications of 1000 function points above data shows that the XP and Agile methods are the least time consuming methods, with TSP coming in third.

Second comparison is as per software quality, we have considered defect potentials, defect removal efficiency, delivered defects, and high-severity defects. The phrase "defect potential" refers to the sum of defects found in requirements, design, source code, documents, and "bad fixes." A bad fix is a new defect accidentally injected during an attempt to repair a previous defect (about 7% of attempts to fix bugs include new bugs). The phrase "defect removal efficiency" refers to the combined efficiency levels of inspections, static analysis, and testing.

When the focus of the evaluation turns to quality rather than speed, TSP, CMMI 5, and RUP are on top, followed by XP. Agile is not strong on quality so it is only on number 8 out of 10. The Agile lack of quality measures and failure to use inspections will also have an impact in the next comparison.

The phrase "be careful of what you wish for because you might get it" is appropriate for these methodology comparisons. Agile that focuses on speed are very quick. Methods such as TSP, RUP, and CMMI 5 that focus on quality have very few defects.

FUTURE RESEARCH DIRECTIONS

Currently companies are either using BSC framework for their performance improvement or improving their Software Development process in isolation. This chapter intensely highlights that both the practices are very important and should be used in right collaborative manner in order to turn your business success through Quality information system development and acquisition.

For upcoming research need organizations should explore the implementation of COBIT-5 and CMMI-SW or CMMI DEV along with CMMI SERVICES while using BSC technique for showing impact of BSC on facilitating value reporting and publicize their case studies and communicate the benefits achieved. Efforts should also be put on developing tools which could merge BSC with PI benefit predictions.

CONCLUSION

This chapter has discussed details of how to achieve competitive advantage for a business organization by developing it information System following Quality practices.

It has demonstrated how the adaptation of the proposed Process Improvement framework helps in achieving your business goals in-order to achieve the benefits related to organization's competitive advantage.

It has also demonstrated Process improvement elements like Process Improvement plan designing and details of CMMI's relevant process area where an organization could use BSC technique while setting its strategic goals related to IS development and how it could keep track of the benefits which will be achieved as a result of implementing PI for developing and acquiring an IS.

Benefits are also reported while comparing 10 different software development methods. Agile methods are good for achieving goals quicker. The methods that emphasize quality such as TSP, RUP, and CMMI 5 have also achieved their goals, and deliver very few defects. No single method appears to be perfect therefore multi model approach is best.

REFERENCES

Al-Fatah Karasneh, A. (2012). Impact of BSC on financial performance: An empirical study on Jordanian bank. *European Journal of Economics. Finance and Administrative Sciences*, *1*(46), 54–70.

Cannegieter, J. J., Heijstek, A., Linders, B., & van Solingen, R. (2008, November). *CMMI roadmaps: Software engineering process management*. Technical Note, CMUSEI.

Capers Jones. (2012, January). Evaluating ten software development methodologies. *Software Magazine*.

Chang, R. Y., & Morgan, M. W. (2000). *Performance scorecards*. San Francisco, CA: Jossey-Bass.

Florac, W. A. (1998). *Practical software measurement: Measuring for process management and improvement*. Paper presented at conference SEPG98.

Hani, S. U. (2009, December). *Impact of process improvement on software development predictions, for measuring software development project's performance benefits*. ACM Press. ISBM: 978-1-60558-642-7

Hani, S. U. (2012). *Impact of process improvement on software development predictions*. Unpublished doctorial research report, Graduate School of Engineering Science and Information Technology, Hamdard University, Pakistan.

Hefner, R. (2005, November). *Achieving the promised benefits of CMMI*. Presented at CMMI Technology Conference & User Group.

Johnson, K. A., & Kulpa, M. (2010, March). *Agile CMMI®: Obtaining real benefits from measurement and high maturity*. Presented at conference SEPG-2010.

Kamel, S. (2003). *Introduction to business information system: Internet marketing: Corporate and business unit strategy*. Lecture presented at the American University in Cairo.

Khan, I. (2006). *Software quality assurance through metrics*. Presented at training session, Business Beam, Pakistan.

Kroenke, D. (2009). Information systems for competitive advantage. In Laudon, K. C., Laudon, J. P., & Brabston, M. E. (Eds.), *Using management information systems: Managing a digital firm* (2nd ed.). London, UK: Prentice Hall.

Laudon, K. C., & Laudon, J. P. (2011). Information systems, organizations, and strategy. In *Using management information systems: Managing a digital firm* (2nd ed.). London, UK: Pearson Education Inc. Prentice Hall.

Mead, N. R., & Allen, J. H. (April 2009). *Making the business case for software assurance*. Special Report, Software Engineering Institute, Carnegie Mellon University.

Ng, K. (March 2008). *Framework to communicate the impact and benefits of software process initiative: The MSC Malaysia perspective*. SEPG 2008, Tampa Florida, USA.

Potter, N., & Sakry, M. (2011). *Making process improvement work: A concise action guide for software managers and practitioners*. Report by the process. *Group*.

Rohm, H., & Malinoski, M. (2012). *Strategy-based balanced scorecards for technology companies*. Retrieved from www.balancescorecard.org

Sadana, V. (n.d.). *A survey based software quality model*. Department of Computer Science. *University of Missouri-Rolla*.

Tiến, L. N. (2010). *Information systems analyses and design*. Retrieved through http://tienhuong.files.wordpress.com/2010/03/slides.ppt

ADDITIONAL READING

Burwick, D. M. (2008). *How to implement the CMMI, real process improvement using proven solutions*. Pittsburgh, PA: Business and Personal Solution Publishing.

Information Systems Audit and Control Association. (n.d.). *COBIT*. Retrieved from http://www.isaca.org/COBIT/Pages/default.aspx

Nashville. (2006, March). *Software measurement for beginners*. Presented at SEPG-2006 conference.

Rohloff, M. (2009). Lecture Notes in Computer Science: *Vol. 5701. Case study and maturity model for business process management implementation business process management* (pp. 128–142). doi:10.1007/978-3-642-03848-8_10

Statz, J. (2005). *Measurement of process improvement*. Technical Report.

Stevens, S. T. (2006, September). Applying CMMI and strategy to ATE development. *AutotestCon, Conference* Anaheim CA, (p. 813). ISBN: 1-4244-0051-1

Chapter 5
Project Management and Diagramming Software

Rizaldy Rapsing
King Faisal University, Kingdom of Saudi Arabia

ABSTRACT

There are numerous methods in managing project activities. Apart from it all, people involved in the project must carefully consider the project's objectives, timeline, cost, and roles of the participants. The complexity of the project challenges them in estimating, planning, scheduling, budget monitoring, resource management, and documentation. Many use word processors, presentations, or graphic software for some of these activities, but project management and diagramming software are offered now, supporting almost all of these tasks. This chapter aims to make readers aware of the different software that they can use in project management and diagramming. It lists the currently available commercial software, shareware, and freeware; and reviews four project management and two diagramming software.

INTRODUCTION

In reviewing the project management software, a simple project with 3 resources and 3 tasks has been applied to each tool. Later, the other features are briefly mentioned.

The 4 project management software or tools are:

1. 5pm by Quattre Group LLC,
2. Dolibarr by Dolibarrr Team,
3. Endeavour Software Project Management by Ezequiel Cuellar, and
4. GanttProject by The GanttProject Team.

In reviewing the diagramming software, the frequently used diagrams in software engineering are designed in both tools. Some of their features are also discussed.

The 2 diagramming software or tools are:

1. Dia by Dia Developers, and
2. yEd by yWorks GmbH.

DOI: 10.4018/978-1-4666-3679-8.ch005

This chapter intends for students and industry practitioners to be able to experience project management and realize the easy control and effectiveness of using any of these tools.

PROJECT MANAGEMENT SOFTWARE

Listed in Table 1 are some of the project management software available. They are obtainable as SaaS (software as a service), GPL (General Public License), proprietary, or open source.

To show the simplicity in using the 4 project management software selected, the succeeding sections demonstrate how to start a project using each of those 4 based on the beginning details of the sample project below:

- **Name of Project:** Library
- **Project Duration:** March 27, 2012 – September 26, 2012
- Resources
  - ○ Admin - System Administrator
  - ○ James - Project Leader
  - ○ John - Business Analyst
- **Initial Tasks:** See Table 2

5pm

Website: http://www.5pmweb.com/

Managing projects online comes easy with 5pm, a collaborative software offered as Software as a Service (SaaS). The look and feel of a windows file explorer is noticeable in its 2 major panels. The left panel contains the projects and tasks while the other contains relevant information (see Figure 1 with Label No. 1).

Looking at Label 1 of Figure 1, all projects and their tasks are shown in the left panel while the activities for the currently selected task/project are shown in the right panel. This is convenient since all information about a project or a task can be seen in one page only. As you select a project

or a task, its corresponding activities and other information are shown in the right panel. Same thing happens with a file explorer that contains drives and directories in the left and its contents on the right. Moreover, the layout can be customized and tasks can be collapsed.

See the Add drop down button on the upper left? Clicking it allows you to add a project, a task or multiple tasks.

Figure 1 with Label 2 shows the screen to add a project. Resources included in the project are assigned in Project Team and Clients. One important thing to note is the Notify by email field which identifies who should regularly receive mails about the project.

Figure 1 with Label 3 shows an example of adding a task. The Task Team contains the resources assigned to that task. There's still an option for Notify by email and the predecessor through Parent Task.

In Labels 1 and 4, visible on the side are 4 tabs for Projects, Timeline, Reports, and People. This part concentrated largely on Projects but the other 3 are of utmost importance too. Timeline, for instance (see Label 4) shows a Gantt chart that can be filtered by groups, projects, users, and duration. It's an interactive timeline that lets users modify a task by simply dragging or resizing its figure.

The Reports tab lets user generate report by group or project with specified duration. This reports can be directed to the printer or exported to CSV.

Remember the 3 resources: Admin, James and John? They were easily added through the People tab.

Other advanced features of 5pm includes:

- **Time tracking:** Allows you to set and compare the estimated time with the actual time spent in a task;
- **Sharing notes and files:** Enables users to see the logs/notes made by anyone and the files availed for partaking; and

Table 1. List of available project management software

5pm	Easy Projects .NET	Launchpad	phpGroupWare
24SevenOffice	eGroupWare	LibrePlan	PHProjekt
AceProject	enQuire - Grants Project & Contract Management	LiquidPlanner	Pivotal Tracker
Apollo	Exia Process	LisaProject	Planbox
Assembla	FastTrack Schedule	MacProject	Plandora
AtTask	Feng Office Community Ed.	MantisBT	Planisware 5
Basecamp	FinancialForce.com	MatchWareMindView 4 Business Edition	Planner Suite
Binfire	FIT Issue Management	Mavenlink	PLANTA Project
Bontq	FogBugz	Merlin	PPM Central/WorkLenz
BrightWork	Ganttic	MicroPlanner X-Pert	Primavera Project Planner
CA Clarity PPM	GanttProject	Microsoft Office Project Server	Principal Toolbox
Central Desktop	Gemini	Microsoft Project	Project KickStart
Cerebro	Genius Inside	Microsoft SharePoint Server	ProjectManager.com
Clarizen	Glasscubes	Microsoft Team Foundation Server	Project.net
CMiC	Goplan	Milestones Professional	Project-Open
codeBeamer	GroveSite	MindGenius	Projectplace
Collabtive	HP Project & Portfolio	Mingle	ProjectSpaces
Compuware Changepoint	Huddle	NetPoint	Projecturf
ConceptDraw Project	Hyperoffice	NetSuite	Projektron BCS
Contactizer	iManageProject	MyWorkPLAN	Proliance
Copper Project	InLoox	O3spaces	Prolog Manager
Deltek Open Plan	in-Step	OmniPlan	PSNext
DeltekWelcomHome	JIRA	OnePager Pro	QuickBase
DeskAway	Jonas Software	Onepoint Project	Rachota
Dolibarr ERP/CRM	Journyx	OnTime	Rally Software
Doolphy	Kayako helpdesk software	Open Workbench	Redmine
dotProject	KommandCore	OpenERP	Rplan
DynaRoad	KForge	OpenProj	SAP RPM
Endeavour Software Project Management	KPlato	Oracle Project Portfolio Management	SAP Business ByDesign

Table 2. Initial tasks for sample project

Task	Duration	Predecessor	Resources
Data Collection	3/27/12 – 4/2/12	None	James and John
Study Present System	4/3/12 – 4/9/12	Data Collection	Admin, James and John
Requirement Specification	4/3/12 – 4/16/12	Data Collection	James and John

Figure 1. Sample project using 5pm

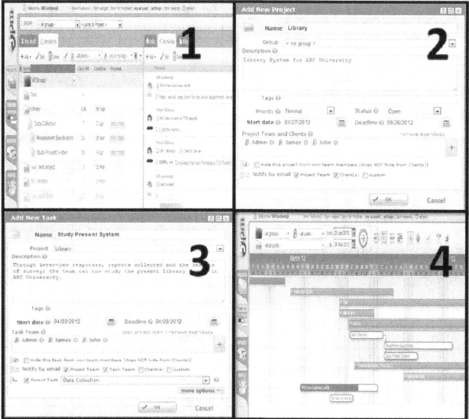

- **Email integration:** Lets the team and clients to automatically receive notifications, create tasks, or even assign teams.

Try to go to their website and enjoy the 5pm demo. You need not install anything to try it but you can already see for yourself the functions that it offers. You can lavish all its polished features with all information you need in just one page.

Dolibarr

Website: http://www.dolibarr.org/

Dolibarr ERP/CRM is an open source web-based software under GPL for Enterprise Resource Planning (ERP) and Customer Relationship Management (CRM) with other features including Project Management. Since it is an open source/

free software, users can access its codes, study and modify them without any kind of restriction. Its main modules include:

- System,
- Customer Relations Management (third parties, proposals, customer orders, contracts, interventions, shipments),
- Electronic Content Management,
- Financial Modules (accounting, invoices, taxes, social contributions and dividends, standing orders, donations, expenses and trip notes, and banks and cash),
- Human Resource Management,
- Products Management (suppliers, products, point of sales, stocks, services),
- Projects/Collaborative Work (agenda, projects), and

- Multi-Modules Tools (mass e-mailings, data exports, data imports).

The intention of this book is to focus only on one module of Dolibarr relating to Project Management. With this, only Projects/Collaborative Work is enabled.

Figure 2 shows 3 screenshots in using Dolibarr for our sample project. In Label 1, three tabs are visible, Home, Projects, and Agenda. Resources were added in the Home tab prior to adding a new project.

Seen on the left side of Figure 2 are options to create new project/task, list existing projects/tasks, and recording time spent. Adding a new project is shown in the figure's Label 1 with re-

cords on the project's reference no., label, third party, visibility, duration, and description.

Label 2 shows the dialog to add a new task. The field Child of project/task represents the predecessor, while the Allocated to field is the resource responsible or in-charge of the task. You can still add more resources in the task tab. This Tasks tab is visible in Label 3.

After input, Label 3 shows a Gantt chart that is automatically created by Dolibarr. The time interval can be shown as daily, weekly, monthly, or quarterly.

Other features of the Projects/Collaborative Work module of Dolibarr include:

Figure 2. Sample project using Dolibarr

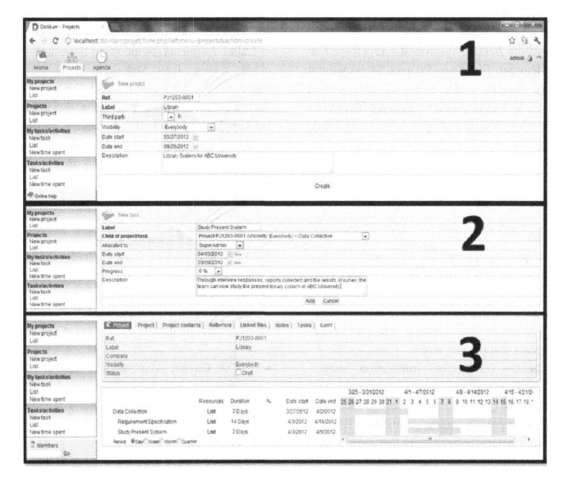

- Linked Files for sharing of files necessary in the project,
- Notes for users to see reports made by all of them, and
- Agenda which is a calendar of all incomplete and terminated events related to a certain project.

The power of Dolibarr as a collaborative software lies on the variety of modules that it comprise. Companies can study and utilize any of its modules at no expense. It has three auto-installers: DolliWamp for Windows, DoliBuntu for Debian or Ubuntu users, and DoliMamp for Mac users. Try downloading any of these installers and recognize the module-powered adeptness offered by Dolibarr.

Endeavour Software Project Management

Website: http://endeavour-mgmt.sourceforge.net/
Endeavour Software Project Management supports iterative and incremental development process which answers the weakness of the waterfall approach. It is also an open-source web-based tool under GPL for project management.

The main options of the tool include:

- Personal Space or Home,
- Planning (projects, iterations, and project plan),
- Requirements (actors, use cases, change requests, tasks, and project glossary),
- Defect Tracking,
- Test Management (test cases and test plan),
- Document Management (project documents and project wiki),
- Utilities (continuous integration, subversion browser, and forums),
- Reports (project member assignment, defects report, iteration cumulative flow, iteration defects by priority, iteration defects by status, and test plan execution), and

- Security (users, security groups, and logout).

Figure 3 in the next page shows 4 screenshots in using Endeavour Software Project Management for the sample project. The menu is located in the left panel as shown in Label 1, with the first three options visible: Personal Space, Planning and Requirements.

Resources can be added in the last option, Security.

By choosing Planning – Projects and the New button, a user will see the screen shown in Label 2. Take note that there are 2 tabs, Project and Project Members with the previous as active. Here, the project's name, duration, progress, status, and description are all entered. Resources are assigned in the Project Members tab.

By clicking the sub-option Tasks under the main option Requirements (shown in Label 1), and clicking the New button, the screen shown in Label 3 appears. Notice that there are 7 tabs in this screen: Task, Stakeholders, Documents, Attachments, Comments, and Dependencies. Task's information such as name, duration, etc. are supplied in the Task tab. Take note that the field Created by doesn't mean that he is part of the task. The resources for the task are assigned in Stakeholders tab. Files can be shared and attached using Attachments tab. Notes can be added using Comments tab. Lastly, predecessors are identified in the Dependencies tab.

After all tasks have been entered, clicking the Project Plan sub-option and the Project Schedule tab will show its Gantt chart.

Other features of Endeavour Software Project Management include:

- **Use Cases:** Also records actors, events, tasks, stakeholders, documents, attachments, and comments;
- **Iterations:** Also records use cases, defects, change requests, and tasks;

Figure 3. Sample project using Endeavour software project management

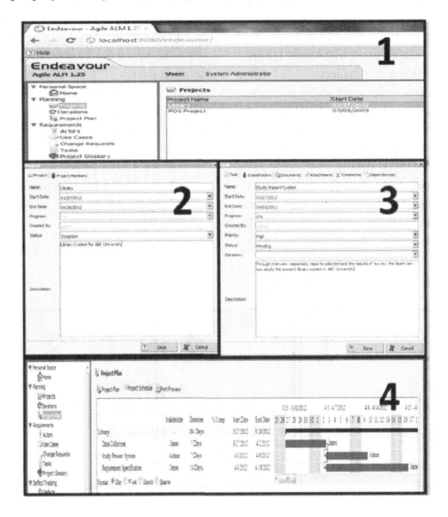

- **Change Request:** Also records stakeholders, documents, attachments, and comments;
- **Defect:** Also records stakeholders, documents, attachments, and comments;
- **Test Cases:** Also records steps and comments; and
- Reports of text, tables and charts on numerous information such as iteration, project members, defects, and test plan.

Endeavour comes as an easy way to organize a project's tasks, defects, tests, files, and comments. Its numerous significant features conspire to make it a formidable tool that should be included in college curriculum. The events included immerses students to the real world scenario of project management. Try downloading the tool and be amazed by what it can teach you.

GanttProject

Website: http://www.ganttproject.biz/

GanttProject is a free software for project management. The design simplifies project's outlook by immediately starting with a Gantt chart view. Even the main menu has been made so simple by limiting its options to Project, Edit, View, Tasks, Resources, and Help.

Add the resources first by clicking the Resource option in the main menu. Afterwards, create a new project by selecting Project and then New. The first 3 screenshots in Figure 4 with labels 1-3 are the steps for creating a new project.

Project information such as name, organization, web link, description, role sets, holidays, and weekend options are declared. Notice that the duration is not set since this information can be extracted from the tasks' details.

To create a new task, click the option Tasks in the main menu, then choose New Task. Press Alt-Enter or double click the newly created task to display its properties as shown in Figure 4 with Label 4. There are 4 tabs: General, Predecessors, Resources, and Custom Columns. The predecessor of the task is identified in Predecessors tab while the resources involve are assigned in the Resources tab.

Every time a task is added or modified, the Gantt chart automatically redraws itself as shown in Figure 4 with Label 5.

Other features of GanttProject include:

- **Resources Chart:** Shows the loads of every resource and identifies overloaded resources;

Figure 4. Sample project using GanttProject

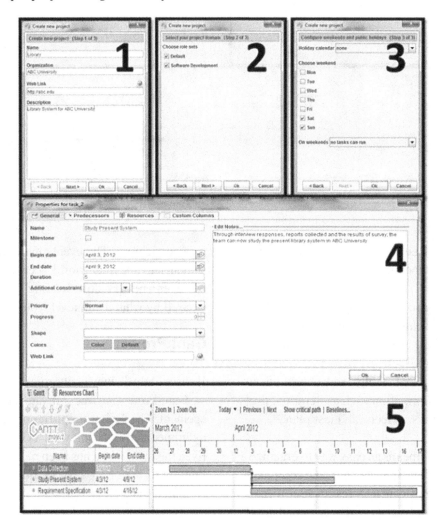

- **PERT chart:** Can be shown by choosing the View option in the main menu;
- Reports that can be directly sent to the printer or saved as PDF format; and
- Import/Export capability for MS Project.

GanttProject is a stand-alone Project Management tool that utilizes 3 charts: Gantt, PERT and Resource. GanttProject can be useful in projects that need no complex reports and details in the project. Its uncomplicated framework may be received by students and users as likable. Try to download it and find out for yourself its usefulness.

DIAGRAMMING SOFTWARE

Some diagramming software available are listed in Table 3.

These software are obtainable as proprietary, GPL (General Public License), EPL (Eclipse Public License), open source, or freeware.

In this part we will review Dia and yEd. Both tools are used in creating some of the most often used diagrams in Software Development such as

Entity Relationship Diagram, Data Flow Diagram, and Unified Modeling Language Diagram.

Dia

Developer: Dia Developers
Website: http://live.gnome.org/Dia

Dia is a free general-purpose diagramming software. It has a number of packaged shapes available and any of the objects can be combined together in one canvas. Its features are most similar to Microsoft Visio. It officially runs only on Windows platform.

Shown in Figure 5 are 4 examples of diagrams that were done in Dia. All these diagrams are drawn in separate canvas. Select File – New Diagram to start creating a diagram in a blank canvas. The toolbox on the left side shows standard objects, a pull-down button for the pre-defined set of objects, and the actual objects. Clicking an object and clicking an area in the canvas places an instance of that object.

In Figure 5 with Label 1, an example of an Entity Relationship diagram is shown with 2 entities having several attributes, a primary key, a relationship and its attributes, and an association

Table 3. List of available diagramming software

AgileJStructureViews	Enterprise Architect	Poseidon for UML
Altova UModel	Graphviz	PowerDesigner
ArgoUML	Inkscape	RISE
ARIS Express	Inspiration	Schematic
ATL	LucidChart	SmartDraw
Borland Together	MagicDraw UML	Software Ideas Modeler
BOUML	Microsoft Visio	StarOffice
Calligra Flow	Modelio	StarUML
ConceptDraw Office	Objecteering	Umbrello UML Modeller
Creately	objectiF	Visual Paradigm for UML
Dia	OmniGraffle	XCircuit
Diagram Designer	Open ModelSphere	yEd
DiamFC	OpenOffice.org Draw	
Eclipse UML2 Tools	Papyrus	

Figure 5. Sample diagrams using Dia

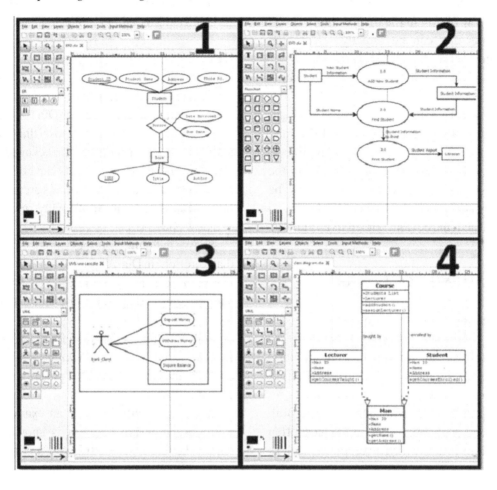

type. The shape package used is ER as shown in the label of the dropdown button on the left side.

In Label 2, an example of a Data Flow Diagram is shown with 2 entities, 3 processes, 1 data store, and 6 data flows. The shape package used is Flowchart.

In Label 3, an example of a Use-Case Diagram with an actor and 3 activities is displayed. The shape package used is UML.

In Label 4, an example of a Class Diagram with 4 classes is displayed. The shape package used is also UML.

Other shape packages or pre-defined objects in Dia are BPMN, ChemEng, Chronogram, Circuit, Cisco – Computer, Cisco – Misc, Cisco-Network, Cisco-Switch, Cisco-Telephony, Civil, Cybernet-ics, Database, Electric, FS, Gane and Sarson, GRAFCET, Jigsaw, Ladder, Lights, Logic, Map, Isometric, MSE, Network, Pneumatic/Hydrauli, RE-i*, RE-Jackson, RE-KAOS, SADT/IDEF0, SDL, and Sybase.

Using simple XML files, new shapes can be supported in Dia. Moreover, all diagrams can be exported to several formats including EPS, SVG, DXF, CGM, WMF, PNG, JPEG, and VDX.

Dia strikes as a convenient and powerful diagramming tool that offers wide array of objects for variety of diagrams. Students and software engineers can find Dia as an appropriate tool for their diagramming needs.

yEd

Developer: yWorks GmbH

Website: http://www.yworks.com/en/products_yed_about.html

yEd is a free general-purpose diagramming software that creates high quality diagrams such as flowcharts, network diagrams, UML diagrams, BPMN diagrams, mind maps, organization charts, and Entity Relationship diagrams. Platforms that support JVM such as Windows, Linux, and Mac OS can run yEd.

Figure 6 displays 3 diagrams made in yEd. All these diagrams are drawn in separate document.

Select File – New to start creating a diagram in a blank document. The palette on the right side shows its different categories that can be collapsed. The objects in the palette are of 2 kinds, the standard shape (circle, square, computer, person) and the line. They may be selected as a pair by double clicking each. Once chosen, click an area in the document and you will see an instance of the standard shape. Afterwards, drag from inside the standard shape and you will see a line drawn.

In Figure 6 with Label 1, shown are the different palettes available in yEd such as Shape Nodes, Modern Nodes, Edge Types, Group Nodes, Swimlane Nodes and Table Nodes, People, Com-

Figure 6. Sample diagrams using yEd

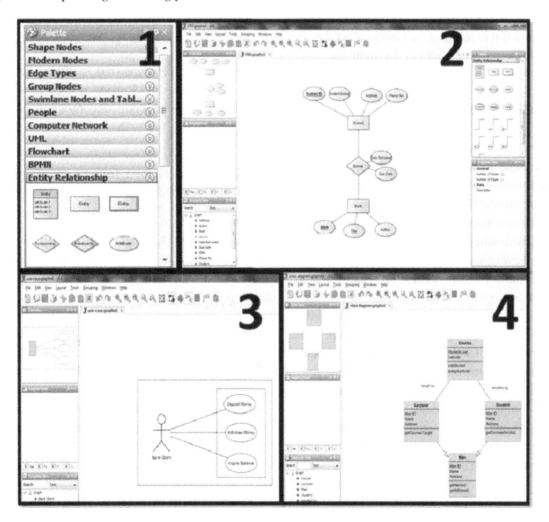

puter Network, UML, Flowchart, BPMN, and Entity Relationship.

In Label 2, shown is an Entity Relationship diagram with entities, relationship and attributes. The palette used here is Entity Relationship.

In Label 3, shown is a Use-Case diagram with actor and activities. The palette used here is UML. This same palette is used in the Class diagram shown in Label 4.

yEd has a feature that automatically layouts the objects in a diagram such as hierarchical, organic, orthogonal, circular, tree, etc. Its diagrams can also be exported in different formats including GIF, JPEG, PNG, EMF, BMP, PDF, EPS, SVG, and SWF.

yEd harbors as a trouble-free and serviceable diagramming software where numerous type of diagrams can be easily designed and printed in large and top notch quality. Users can certainly find yEd as a suitable tool in diagramming.

CONCLUSION

Project management and diagramming when carried out with the right software and tools can effect a systematize and laborsaving venture. Available now are several SaaS, shareware, freeware, commercial, and open source software that can aid participants and other stakeholders.

Endeavour Software Project Management and 5pm contain most of the features identified in project management such as scheduling, resource management, document management, tracking system, and reporting. Dolibarr prides itself with the modules for ERP, CRM, project management, and more. GanttProject, on the other hand, may come as a single-user application, but users from small companies where one or only a couple of people are involved in planning may benefit from it.

Meanwhile, both Dia and yEd show their respective clouts in diagramming. The palettes and shape packages in both software abound in the kind of charts and diagrams that they can produce.

Rather than insisting on software that are not directly related to project management and diagramming such as word processors and presentation software, users should submerge themselves in the numerous tools that are available after spending some cash or none at all.

REFERENCES

Comparison of project-management software. (n.d.) Wikipedia: The Free Encyclopedia. Retrieved December 31, 2011, from http://en.wikipedia.org/wiki/Comparison_of_project_management_software

Dia (Version 0.97.2) [Software]. (n.d.). Retrieved from from http://live.gnome.org/Dia/Download

Diagramming software (n.d.). Wikipedia: The Free Encyclopedia. Retrieved December 31, 2011, from http://en.wikipedia.org/wiki/Diagramming_software

Documentation for Dia. (December 2010). Retrieved March 24, 2012, from http://live.gnome.org/Dia/Documentation

Dolibarr ERP/CRM. (Version DoliWamp 3.1.1). [Software]. (n.d.). Retrieved from http://sourceforge.net/projects/dolibarr/files/Dolibarr%20 ERP-CRM/3.1.1/

Dolibarr User Documentation. (March 2012). Retrieved March 24, 2012, from http://wiki.dolibarr.org/index.php/User_documentation

Endeavour Agile, A. L. M. (2011). *Endeavour software project management* (Version 1.25) [Software]. Retrieved from http://sourceforge.net/projects/endeavour-mgmt/files/endeavour-mgmt/endeavour-mgmt-1.25/

GanttProject (Version 2.5) [Software]. (n.d.). Retrieved from http://www.ganttproject.biz/download

List of Unified Modeling Language tools. (n.d.). Wikipedia: The Free Encyclopedia. Retrieved December 31, 2011, from http://en.wikipedia.org/wiki/List_of_Unified_Modeling_Language_tools

Quatre Group LLC. (2009). *5pm* [Software]. Retrieved from https://demo.5pmweb.com/login.php

yWorks (2012). *yEd* (Version 3.9.1) [Software]. Retrieved from http://www.yworks.com/en/products_yed_download.html

Chapter 6
Software Development Methodologies for Cloud Computing

Izzat Alsmadi
Yarmouk University, Jordan

ABSTRACT

Cloud computing is recently taking a significant focus in the information technology fields as a possible future trend for how computer services and applications can be provided to users or businesses. Cloud computing is utilizing the recent large expansion of Internet and network technologies where the increase in the data size and transfer speed made it possible to make the Internet or the cloud a possible host for all or most users' applications and data. With this new technology, several changes are expected to occur in the information technology fields and systems to adapt to this field or technology. In this chapter, the author focuses on the possible impact on the way software companies will develop their software products. For example, the traditional client server system architecture is expected to be significantly impacted with cloud computing new framework. All software development concepts and activities will be revisited to discuss what things can be different in the cloud computing paradigm.

INTRODUCTION

Software development projects and process approaches are continuously evolving. They are affected by the type of the developed products, the nature of the project, and several other environmental factors. No software process development approach or model can work as the best for all types of projects. The time, budget and resources' constrains played also a significant role in deciding the best way to proceed in developing a particular software. In this chapter a focus will be on how software projects can be developed in the cloud computing projects. Focus will be on evaluating the different aspects of cloud computing projects from three dimensions. The first dimensions are related to software project concerns: project, product, process and people, and the second dimension is

DOI: 10.4018/978-1-4666-3679-8.ch006

related to the different types of cloud computing paradigms of service models: Infrastructure as a Service (IaaS), Platform as a Service (PaaS), Software as a Service (SaaS). The third dimension is related to cloud computing deployment models: Public cloud, Community cloud, Hybrid cloud, and Private cloud. After presenting an introduction section for each one of those three dimensions, we will discuss possible future development approaches that can be suitable for software projects' developments for cloud computing.

In terms of software product models, the widely known and popular object oriented model is currently competed by possible alternatives. For the web and cloud computing, service oriented model and architecture (SOA) is seen to many as a possible successor of the object oriented paradigm. In SOA, focus and the main design abstractions are built around the concept of services. Systems are decomposed based on the number and type of services they are offered to clients or users. Services are expected to be designed, implemented and deployed in very agile flexible manners that can allow different types of users to call and use such services with the least amount of possible efforts. Some of the popular object orientation (OO) concepts such as abstraction and encapsulation can still be used and applied to good SOA design. Such concepts are seen now as good software design principles rather than OO design principles. In abstraction, it is always important to decompose the system to the right level and number of services in the right granularity. Each service should have the right and relevant attributes, methods, associations, etc. that can help minimize its coupling with other services. Similarly, to apply encapsulation, services should be offered in ways that can relief the clients or users from any type of commitment or dependency in the implementation details of the service. This makes it easy to change the implementation details of such services with the least possible impact on clients. On the service side itself, encapsulation plays also an important role in separating the service representation or interface from its detail implementation. This can make it easy to update and change such service without impacting its interface or service clients. In an alternative opinion, some software designers see SOA as a complement to OO and not a replacement where SOA works in a higher level of details in comparison to OO. This means that both software product architectures can be implemented simultaneously.

In SOA, focus is on Web services rather than Web applications. The major difference is in isolating service provider from user and in providing generic services that are not intended for specific users and that are themselves unaware of the nature of use in the client side.

CLOUD COMPUTING

A recently growing trend and IT service platform is what is called cloud computing. In cloud computing, companies may outsource all their IT department functionalities to a cloud host company. The service level that cloud companies offer varies based on the previously mentioned classification based on what they offer for businesses and based on the business need and options. The cloud company can offer providing a particular software for individuals or companies (SaaS). It means that users will not get a downloadable copy of the software on their machine. Rather, they need to access the cloud every time they need the software and use it as a service. Users can still have any local generated files of the application. However, they may need the application in future for modifications. Charge of such service can be usually based on the usage period or time.

Users or businesses can also choose to outsource also their hardware or infrastructure. For example, a company may need several routers, IP addresses, bandwidth, etc. Such option maybe very useful for starters in high risk companies where owners hesitate to pay at front a large investment. Pay per use in this case is similar to the case of renting a car, apartment, etc, where it will be much less than the option of buying such hardware components. A company may also want to rent a data or database space in the cloud. Building and managing a database can be a complex task that requires a significant amount of resources. Database and data storage can be also rented through the options of cloud services. In a more comprehensive option, a company may choose to outsource all its platform to a cloud company. In that case, the company will be in charge and focus on their business roles. They will get rid of the local IT department and depend on the cloud company to provide all IT services that include: providing required software applications, network and infrastructure components, data and database management. Many companies, specially stable and large companies are hesitating to select this option and give up their data, core business, security, etc.

SOFTWARE DEVELOPMENT MODELS

Developing a software product can be an individual or a team project. It can be developed in a business for a particular customer or generic. It can be also developed by individuals either as students, amateurs, researchers, etc. Software products can be also small, medium or large. They can be simple or complex. They may vary based on all those characteristics and based on the domain or the users of the software. All those factors can decide the type or nature of the software development process or how software developers will develop the software. Nonetheless, there are some generic activities that occur in all software development processes. Those can vary in details and complexity. Major development stages include:

1. **Requirement gathering and analysis phase:** In this stage, analysts or developers are expected to analyze the problem domain

or where the project is triggered or initiated to find out what is the problem that this software is trying to solve. They may collect those requirements from documents, similar projects or users and candidate users of the current or the new system.

2. **Design stage:** In this stage, a solution is designed for the problem that was described in the requirement stage. The design is the model or the template that draws the guidelines for the actual implementation or the code. Any possible conflict that may arise in the code should be resolved looking at the software design. In most recent agile software development models, there is a little focus given to this stage and such models propose a light weight design without putting too much effort in it especially as in many cases such design may evolve and change in future.

3. **Implementation:** This is where the actual code of the project is developed. The code is the main deliverable in any software development project. In some cases where the project is about improving an existed software: some parts of the software maybe affected by this improving project while the rest of the code is not. For example, a refactoring process can be conducted to improve the user interface of a software or improve its quality trying to solve some of the problems in the existed software. In such cases, no new major functionalities are expected to be added.

4. **Testing:** Software products are testing for possible errors before their delivery to the users or the clients. They are tested first against the proposed requirements or functionality to make sure that the developed software satisfies the initial proposed requirements. Internal or white box testing activities are also conducted by developers to make sure that the internal structure of the code, the algorithms, methods, etc. will not cause

logical or semantic errors at the time of usage. Other testing activities include: black box testing to test the high level user visible system functionalities, system, integration, user, release, etc. testing in which each testing tries to expose possible problems in a specific area or concern of the software.

5. **Deployment:** After the testing stage, the software is prepared for release and deployment to users. Packaging and operating system or environment related issues are all considered at this stage to make sure that the system will be installed and work normally on users' machines or environment.

6. **Maintenance:** Any problems that may arise after releasing the software to the users are classified under a new stage called evolution or maintenance. Changed can occur for different reasons. They may occur due to new requirements that users requested. They may also occur due to errors or bugs found by users at the user environment. Other causes for changes can be due to response to environmental changes, software enhancements, etc.

SOFTWARE DEVELOPMENT PROJECTS: MODELS AND APPROACHES

The field of software development went through several evolutionary cycles. In early approaches of software development, previously mentioned activities or stages in software projects where clearly defined, and distinguished. For example, in the traditional waterfall model, those activities go through only one fixed cycle. Each stage has very well defined set of activities. Activities in each stage do not start until the completion of all activities in the previous stage(s). In addition and since the development stage goes only in one cycle, there is no return to any stage once it is completed.

Such project was only applicable when the project has fixed, known and stable requirements. Further, customer-company communication should be also stable or serious consequences may occur if improper products are developed at the end of the project.

Such development methodology is now only applicable in certain limited number of projects or cases. Several new software development methodologies are proposed and adopted despite the major type of activities in software developments (e.g. requirement, design, implementation, testing, etc.) stayed the same. For example, in methodologies such as: Rational Unified Process (RUP), incremental and spiral approaches, the project initial requirements are gathered and the project is divided into several modules or components. After that, cycles of development are applied where in each cycle, one module with several requirements is selected. Requirements gathering and analysis, design, coding, implementation and testing activities are then conducted on this specific module. Later cycles keep adding more requirements or modules and go through new cycles till completing the project. Such iteration approaches allow the software development team to adjust some issues that need to be adjusted based on new information from either the customers or from the development process itself.

More recent software development approaches such as Agile family (e.g. Scrum, Crystal and Extreme programming) proposed new ways of dealing with requirements, communicating with customers, progressing software activities to ensure that software projects are capable of handling the high agility and flexibility environment in which those project are developed. Software requirements tend to vary frequently even through the lifecycle of the software project development. Hence, software process models should be able to deal with such evolutionary nature. They should also acknowledge the need to continuously approach customers, provide them with incremental products and get their feedback. Further such feedback should be always welcome and changes should be always handled to keep the developed product up to the current need of its customers.

SOFTWARE DEVELOPMENT IN CLOUD COMPUTING PROJECTS

In addition to cloud computing, some new software project natures are different in terms of the developed product and settings of the software development companies. For example, in web services, class libraries and Application Peripheral Interfaces (APIs), software products are divided into two major components. Server side components (i.e. web services) that are developed to be generic and service a large number of possible users. On the other side, clients can develop their own interface or application to define how they are going to use such services to serve their own business goals. This may divided software projects into two major sections based on those developed on the server or the client side.

While many believe that cloud computing may have negative impact on small software development companies where giant cloud computing service providers will dominate and control the server side software, it is possible that some new opportunities may be expanded on the client side where small software companies can provide customized solutions.

Cloud computing may not only cause shifts to the nature of offered IT jobs, it may also case changes to the way software products are developed. Several software development models are discussed earlier. Agile development methodologies, as the most recent software development methodologies, came to respond to the need for continuous change embracement in software projects. By nature, software projects are evolutionary; requirements, environmental factors, and team members may change even through the life of the

software project. It is not clear yet whether such development models may also fit some of the new software project types such as: cloud computing and crowd sourcing. Initially, agile development maybe the best choice for such projects due to the fact that agile methodologies are iterative, focus more on communication between all project team members especially development team with customers, and also due to the fact that all agile methodologies accept and deal with changes through all the stages of the software development. However, in the case of cloud computing project, there are some unique characteristics in those projects that may affect the development model. Focus here will be on two aspects of cloud computing projects; First the development of generic or library style services and second, the fact that the software product will have two major components: library or server side component developed and hosted by the cloud company, and client side customized application hosted, and possibly developed in the client company or user.

For the first aspect, this service view was seen before cloud computing in web services and Service Oriented Architecture (SOA). Those are considered the triggers or the roots of cloud computing. Providing software products as services rather than applications implies new levels of encapsulation. In typical software design or object oriented view of encapsulation, the focus is in hiding implementation details for a specific class or piece of code from the class clients or users and show them only what they need in order to call or use the class services. This facilitates the ability for both the client and the server to change without impacting each other. At the whole software or application level, it is also important to shield the users from irrelevant details and only show them how to use the features or the services in the software without the need to know the details of how such services are implemented. However, in SOA or web services, there is a need to create web services that are generic to serve a large number of clients who may use the same service for different purposes. For example, examples of some of the freely available web services in the Web are services related to providing time, stocks and weather information to interested users. Clients can in frequent and agility manners, register and unregister to get the service. They may use the service for different purposes and both client and server can change without affecting each other. What kind of impact this may cause to the software development methodology? In typical software projects, the initial requirement stage focuses on collecting requirements from expected or targeted users to make sure that the software will provide the right services to its users. However, when software products are intended to a large section of users, possibly with known or unknown ways of using the specific product or service, the stage of requirement will be different. This does not mean that such important stage will or should be skipped. It will rather be implemented in a different way.

In the software industry, there are several examples of software products that are developed to be generic and not for a specific client or user, or even a specific section or category of users. Typical examples of such products include operating systems, databases, office products, etc.

Unlike typical software products, web services, or cloud computing services are real time services. This means that several new quality aspects of the developed software service should be continuously assessed to make that the service can always handle users' requests effectively. Examples of some of the important software quality attributes that will be high relevant in cloud computing include: performance, security, reliability, maintainability, and robustness. Those non functional requirements will be very important in judging the successfulness of a service possibly more than the actual functional requirements or services. This was not the case in typical software products or applications where the user is given the software to install

on their local machines. Failures related to the network and connectivity are then less important for majority of those products.

This may also cause a significant change on the software testing stage and its major activities. Current types of software testing activities include: unit, integration, user interface, functional and acceptance testing. Testing functions in real time specially to evaluate aspects related to the communication between clients and servers was only feasible in distributed systems. In this nature, all cloud computing classes of services are distributed systems where clients and servers are using the Internet as the network between them. Testing in such environment can be, in many cases, complex and unstable. Unlike before, in the cloud computing environment, the software components will be mixed with both network and possibly hardware components.

In the second previously described unique aspect in cloud computing software development is the division of all provided software products into server and client side portions. Each one of those two portions require different skills to learn and apply in order to successful develop and manage. While in some cases cloud computing companies may offer the choice to fully support a company for all its software requirements include customized components, in most cloud computing options, businesses or customers will have to build their own client side portion of the application. This is especially important to many businesses since their core unique business functions set in this application and hence it may be risky to outsource it. Nonetheless, security in general is one of the major barriers and challenges cloud computing providers need to handle proactively to ensure their clients that neither their software, data, or any type of information can be leaked.

Maintenance, evolution and customer service tasks and roles will be far more important in the cloud computing paradigm in comparison with earlier types of software projects. Those activities will not be optional or based on the contract in cloud computing. They will rather be a must specially as users are provided real time services and are charged based on that. Licensing can be easily managed and unlike traditional software products, fewer number of illegal users can use software services freely or without the consent knowledge of the service provider.

Contracting and cost issues are not yet clear enough in the different cloud computing services. Further, since the software product is divided into two parts where the cloud company is usually in charge of support of only the server side, conflicts may arise of the origin or source of problems and whether this should be investigated by the cloud computing company or not. In addition, in cases of network or external interrupts or failures, which side should be liable or compensated especially if some financially or technical damages occur based on this network failure or interruption?

CONCLUSION

Similar to many other new software projects' paradigms, cloud computing is expected to change several aspects in the software products and architecture. As a result, it is also expected that cloud computing will impact the way software products are developed in this specific area. Some of the distinguishable aspects of cloud computing include first the distribution of software elements between client or server or main specifically between service or software products' providers and consumers. In such paradigm, the Internet and distributed computing aspects are going to be very important. Several non functional aspects of the software products such as: performance, security, maintainability, etc. are going to play a major role in judging a good software product

or service or not. Software development models should be revisited to see the best way to develop software products in cloud computing paradigm. It is expected that such models will evolve from current existed new model such as agile or iterative approaches.

REFERENCES

Albert, L. (2010). What agile can do for government. *Agilex Technologies.* Retrieved March 1, 2012, from http://gcn.com/articles/2010/10/15/what-agile-can-do-for-government.aspx

Batchelder, B. (2008). *How we entered the cloud: Computing on the web.* First Annual Conference on Quality Software Development.

Chen, Y. (2011). *A dream of software engineers, service orientation and cloud computing.* Keynote presentation in the 13th IEEE Joint International Computer Science and Information Technology Conference, and in the IEEE Joint International Information Technology and Artificial Intelligence Conference, Chongqing, China, August 20-22, 2011.

Cohen, F. (2009). Load testing in the cloud with open source testing automation. *Beyond Testing Magazine, 1.*

Francis, L. (2009). *Cloud computing: Implications for enterprise software vendors.* ESV.

Greer, M., Rodriguez-Martinez, M., & Seguel, J. (2010). *Open source cloud computing tools: A case study with a weather application.* Florida: IEEE Open Source Cloud Computing.

Hogan, M. (2008). *Cloud computing and databases: How databases can meet the demands of cloud computing.* ScaleDB.

IBM Software Group. (2009). *The value of cloud computing to outsourcers and their clients*. IBM. Retrieved from ftp://ftp.software.ibm.com/software/uk/rational/cloud_computing_white_paper.pdf

IDC. (2012). *Software appliances ease cloud application deployment*. IDC Technology Spotlight.

Kettunen, P. (2011). *Rethinking software-intensive new product development: From product push to value evolution*. Retrieved from cloudsoftware-program.com

Koltai, B., Warnick, J., Agbaji, R., & Nilan, S. (2001). Test driven development. *ACM Transactions on Computational Logic*, *5*(50), 1–21.

Reed, J. (2011). *Cloud computing for law firms*. Advologix.com.

Rotibi, B., & Murphy, I. (2012). *Creative shorts: Twelve lifecycle management principles for world class cloud development*. Creative Intellect Consulting.

Sukumar, K., Vecchiola, C., & Buyya, R. (2004). The structure of the new IT frontier: Aneka platform for elastic cloud computing applications. *Computing*, *342*(1), 261–273. Retrieved from www.buyya.com/papers/AnekaMagazineArticle3.pdf

Wolf Frameworks. (2011). *Developing applications using platform-as-a-service: A paradigm shift in application development*. Retrieved from www.wolfframeworks.com

Yara, P., Ramachandran, R., Balasubramanian, G., Muthuswamy, K., & Chandrasekar, D. (2009). Global software development with cloud platforms: Software engineering approaches for offshore and outsourced development. *Proceedings of SEAFOOD 2009, Lecture Notes in business Information Processing*.

Zahedi, M. (2011). *Agile service networks for cloud computing*. Master thesis. Retrieved June 1, 2012, from http://www.idt.mdh.se/utbildning/exjobb/files/TR1191.pdf

Chapter 7
Information System and System Development Life Cycle

Monika Sethi
Panjab University, India

Anju Sharma
Thapar University, India

ABSTRACT

In the last decade, the role of monitoring information has become apparent. The availability of stead-fast information, offered in a suitable format is the basis for good decision making in an organisation. Organisations can use these information skills to solve practical problems as well. This chapter provide us knowledge of the features and purposes of information. It also discusses the role of information system for developing a new system using System Development Life Cycle (SDLC).

INTRODUCTION

The main objective of this chapter is to gain knowledge about the working of the information system and the role of System Development Life Cycle (SDLC). It will integrate various aspects of the input & output of the Information System into SDLC.

An information system is a combination of five elements like: human, data, software, hardware and network. All five elements are organized together to convert the given input into output by processing data into information. The system resources used for processing the information is hardware and software. Hardware refers to equipments used for transforming information as equipment resources and software refers to collection of programs, as material resources.

According to Silver et al. (1995) Information Systems can be defined as: "Information systems are implemented within an organization for the purpose of improving the effectiveness and efficiency of that organization. Capabilities of the information system and characteristics of the

DOI: 10.4018/978-1-4666-3679-8.ch007

organization, its work systems, its people, and its development and implementation methodologies together determine the extent to which that purpose is achieved."

To become skilled user of information and to know how organisations are achieving their aims and objectives, one should be very clear about the following factors of the information.

- **Information Source:** Information can be collected from various sources like: internal sources, external sources, primary sources, secondary sources etc.
- **Information Levels:** The information can also be classified based on its usage in any organization at different levels like strategic information, tactical information, operational information etc.
- **Information Quality:** Quality of information refers to reliability and its fitness for use. Attributes which affects the qualities are timelines, accuracy, adequacy, relevance, completeness, explicitness, exception base etc.
- **Information Perspective:** Information system plays very significant role in various perspectives of real world like end user perspective, organization perspective and global society perspective.

As in the above section various factors of information has been elaborated and next is the elements of information systems are as follows:

- **Human:** Consist of information specialist and end users.
- **Data:** Deals with transforming the data into information.
- **Software:** Includes procedures and programs for information management.
- **Hardware:** Are equipments and machines used for data processing.
- **Network:** Include communication media and support.

Components of Information System

In a broad sense two major categories of information system are CIS (Computer Information System) and BIS (Business Information System) these both collectively form a new idea that is CBIS (Computer Based Information System) for business.

According to O'Brien (2003): "Some make a clear distinction between information systems, computer systems, and business processes. Information systems typically include an ICT component but are not purely concerned with ICT, focusing in instead on the end use of information technology. Information systems are also different from business processes. Information systems help to control the performance of business processes"

CBIS (Computer Based Information System) incorporates following types of information and support systems at various levels of management. An information system is a form of information and communication technology (ICT) in which data is processed using human efforts.

Management Support Systems:

- Expert System (ES) /Executive Support System (ESS)
- Decision Support System (DSS)
- Management Information System (MIS)

Operation Support Systems:

- Transaction Processing System (TPS)
- Office Automation System (OAS)

Organisational levels and types of information system are shown in Table 1.

Expert Systems (ES)/Executive Support System (ESS)

An ES/ESS is designed to make strategic decisions by senior management. ES/ESS involve modeling

Table 1. Organisation levels and type of information system

Strategic Level	Expert System (ES) /Executive Support System (ESS)
Tactical Level	Decision support system Management information system
Operational Level	Transaction Processing System (TPS) Office Automation System (OAS)

tools such as "what-if" etc to analyze, that helps strategic decision-making.

According to Hoffer et al., (2003): "An expert system [ES] attempts to codify and manipulate knowledge rather than information. The focus on developing expert system is acquiring the knowledge of the expert in the particular problem domain."

Expert System is typically an interactive computer procedure/program that is used to imitate reckoning and heuristics by gaining the knowledge from human experts for decision making. An expert system works in two phases as shown in Figure 1.

- Knowledge base
- An inference engine

The knowledge base contains problem domain and stores information about the facts and rules. The inference engine is a control mechanism use to draw conclusions considering, facts and rules to apply on different problem domains when solving the user's query.

Decision Support System (DSS)

DSS is a computer-based information system that supports decision-making activities in an organization. It is an interactive and flexible tool of decision making used preferably at strategic and tactical level in an organization, which is of low frequency but high prospective consequences. DSS facilitate a manager to walk around a range of

alternatives to get best out of them. DSS consists of database for data management, data management models and user interface. A DSS database contains data, which is extracted before entering the database as it comes from several sources of information. Data management models are use to develop DSS applications. The user interface supports the interaction between user and DSS.

According to Keen & Morton (1978): "The concept of decision support has evolved from two main areas of research: The theoretical studies of organizational decision making and the technical work on interactive computer systems".

Various components of Decision support system (DSS) are shown in Table 2.

Management Information System (MIS)

MIS deals with the information that is needed to manage different organizational activities. It is the most efficient and effective information system to manage organizational resources like people, technology, information etc.

According to O'Brien (1999): "Management information systems involve three primary resources: people, technology, and information or decision making. Management information systems are distinct from other information systems in that they are used to analyze operational activities in the organization".

Initially, the concept of MIS was to process data and made required reports at regular intervals. The changes in the concept comes when a clear

Figure 1. Phases of expert system

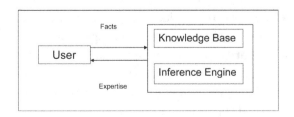

Table 2. Components of decision support system (DSS)

Hardware	A personal computer or computer network provide primary hardware resource for DSS
Software	it contains software modules and application packages to manage DSS databases
Data Resources	As DSS database contains all data and information, the purpose of data resource is to store data and information most needed by managers for a specific type of decision
Model Resources	This includes mathematical and analytical techniques as stored programs, subroutines and spread sheets etc
People Resource	Managers and DSS specialist can use DSS to get alternative decisions for a problem domain

distinction is made between data and information. The information is used for processed data.

The structure of MIS can be divided in two areas:

1. On the basis of management activities
2. On the basis of functional/processing activities

Management activities include:

- **Strategic planning:** Define goals, policies etc.
- **Tactical planning:** Define acquisition of resources, monitoring etc.
- **Operational planning:** Effective and efficient use of existing factors

Functional/Processing activities include:

- Processing transactions
- Generating reports
- Maintaining master files
- Processing support applications etc.

Transaction Processing System (TPS)

TPS is used to collects information about transactions, and control these transactions. This is a computerized system that process and records the daily transactions necessary for a business. It processes routine transactions efficiently and accurately, for example: billing systems, payroll systems, stock control systems, production & purchasing systems, etc. Four elements of Transaction processing systems are:

1. **Inputs:** Transactions or events.
2. **Processing:** Sorting, listing, merging, updating.
3. **Outputs:** Detailed reports, lists, summaries.
4. **Users:** Operational personnel, supervisors.

TPS processes transactions into two different ways like:

1. **Batch Processing:** Data is mounting up in some course of time and processed periodically in batches.
2. **Real Time Processing:** Data is instantaneously processed after a transaction occurs.

A TPS consists of Transaction Processing Monitor (TPM), databases, and transactions. Transaction Processing Monitor is used to control transaction execution. Main functions of TPS are: process data generated by transactions, maintain accuracy, ensure data integrity, timely delivery of documents and reports and increase efficiency.

Office Automation System (OAS)

OAS refers to computer system used to create, collect, store and manipulate office information which is needed to perform a specific task. Raw data storage, electronic information transfer, and digital management of information etc. OAS automate office system, enhance communications at every level and increases productivity. OAS help any individual to perform personal record keeping efficiently using simple computer based tools like: spreadsheet programs, text & image processing systems, database systems etc.

LAN is the backbone of office automation system which allows users to transmit data, image and voice across the network. All office functions like dictation, typing, copying, filing, fax, and recording etc comes under office automation. Some most common OAS is: text processors, electronic document management systems, electronic massage communication systems, teleconferencing and video conferencing systems.

To develop a good information system, we need to have a set of rules and models that gives us a framework for creating a planned and controlled information system. For this purpose it is mandatory to integrate information system into System Development Life Cycle (SDLC). Next section elaborate the concept of SDLC in detail.

SYSTEMS DEVELOPMENT LIFE-CYCLE

The system development life cycle (SDLC) is a process of developing an information system, or developing models that one can use to develop the information system. The aim of SDLC is a high quality system that matches the customer requirements, in terms of time, cost, effectiveness and efficiency. The SDLC provides a set of phases and activities for system development. The process of SDLC started from problem identification, after identification: analysis of the problem that, whether it really exists or not. Once the analysis part is over system analyst has to go through feasibility study. If the problem/need pass the feasibility phase then the development of the system starts. Once the system is ready, various testing techniques are applied to check the accu-

racy; only then the system is implemented. Result of each phase of SDLC act as an input data for the next phase.

According to Geoffrey Elliott & Josh Strachan (2004): "The traditional life cycle approaches to systems development have been increasingly replaced with alternative approaches and frameworks, which attempted to overcome some of the inherent deficiencies of the traditional SDLC."

Phases of SDLC are as follows:

1. Identification of a problem/need
2. Feasibility study
3. Analysis of the problem/need
4. System design
5. System testing
6. Implementation and maintenance

Different phases of SDLC are shown in Figure 2.

Identification of a Problem/Need

This is the first and phase of system development life cycle. This is the most crucial phase for the success of the project. The main question of this phase is:

What is the problem/need? This leads to an initial investigation that if the problem is solved by enhancing the existing system or organisation needs to replace it. This phase is further divided into two phases: The first phase investigates, identified, prioritized and arranged the problem domain. The second phase initiates the project for problem domain and a detailed work plan is made.

Feasibility Study

After initial investigation a feasibility study takes place in time constraints and written or oral report is made. By considering the economic, technical and behavioural factors the feasibility study respond. A feasibility study is carried out

Figure 2. System development life cycle (SDLC)

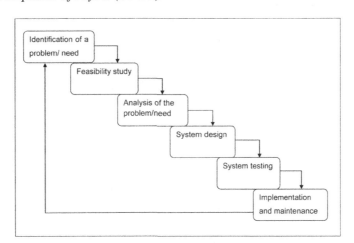

to select best system the meets all constraints and requirements. The main objective of this phase is to determine whether it is feasible to develop the new system. There are seven types of feasibilities:

1. **Technical Feasibility:** Whether the project can be carried out with existing system? Can existing staff work well with new system? Whether a new technology can be implemented at its best?
2. **Economic Feasibility:** Does organisation have enough funds for developing a new system? Whether there are sufficient benefits as compared to cost incurred?
3. **Operational Feasibility:** Whether it can be utilised at its best if implemented?
4. **Social/Behavioural Feasibility:** Whether the users easily adapt the changed system?
5. **Management Feasibility:** Whether the system be acceptable by the management?
6. **Legal Feasibility:** Whether a system passes all legal litigations?
7. **Time Feasibility:** Whether the system can be implemented within the given time constraints?

Analysis of the Problem/Need

System analysis is a process of collecting realistic data, understand the business requirement and create a logical model of the new required system. System analyst works on identified problem and feasible suggestions for convalescing the system functioning. System analysis is done to find answers for each of the following question: *What, How, Who, When, and Why.*

This phase is concerned with the thinking process of system analyst. It endeavors to make a new efficient system that satisfies the organizational needs, this phase results in a logical system design. Systems analysis is a repetitive process that continues until an ideal and suitable solution comes out. Some major activities of this phase is collect required information, define system requirements, build prototypes, scrutiny of existing hardware and software, evaluate alternatives and conceptual data modeling.

Different analysis tools are used to accomplish the above activities. Some of the tools are flowchart, data flow diagram (DFD), data dictionary, structured english, decision trees and decision tables. Most of these tools are graphical in nature, one of the most commonly used tools is

DFD. Symbols used for making DFD are shown in Figure 3.

System analysis phase ends up with a document that describes user requirements, plans, recommendations and a logical design in the form of above mentioned tools.

System Design Phase

This phase is totally based on the document produced by analysis phase about the required system. Keeping in view the recommendations of the analyst the designing of the system starts. It is the decisive phase in the development of a system. Till the time we are dealing with logical system designs but as resultant it will be converted into the physical system design. Normally, the designing of a system is done in two stages:

1.   **Basic Design stage:** In this stage, the specification and features of the new system are specified. The cost/benefit analysis of a new system is done for every proposed design. If the proposed design is considered to be feasible, then the whole process moves to the structured design stage.
2.   **Structured or Detailed Design stage:** In this stage, the basic design comes out with more structured details. It is the blue print of a

Figure 3. Symbols of data flow diagram

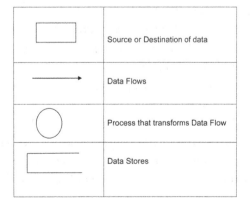

▭	Source or Destination of data
→	Data Flows
◯	Process that transforms Data Flow
▭	Data Stores

new system with components, compositions and inter-relationships required in analysis document. The design is then documented in the required specifications and offered to management and end users for their review and consent.

This phase involves the activities like detailed description of input and outputs, database models, design of forms and reports, hardware and software platforms, codification schemes (if needed), design application architecture, design of user interfaces, design of system interfaces and design of system controls.

System Testing Phase

Now the system is build and approved from management and user but still is not ready for implementation as it has to go through testing phase. A successful test ensures that the system is ready to use. It is an important phase for the actual success of a system.

According to IEEE Standard for Software Unit Testing (1986): "Software testing is the process of analyzing a software item to detect the differences between existing and required conditions (that is, bugs) and to evaluate the features of the software item".

In this phase verification and validation of the system/software is done for various testing techniques.

According to IEEE Standard Glossary of Software Engineering Terminology (1990): "Verification (the first V) is the process of evaluating a system or component to determine whether the products of a given development phase satisfy the conditions imposed at the start of that phase. Validation is the process of evaluating a system or component during or at the end of the development process to determine whether it satisfies specified requirements."

In this phase tester ensures that the system/software meets the organizational requirements, and works as expected by the user. This phase also make out defects and errors in the system that is to be fixed. In case of software systems, after codifying the whole programs, a test plan is developed and run on a given system.

If the output of the test run matches the required results only then the system is considered a part of implementation process. The best approach of testing is Pilot testing. In this testing a system is installed at only one location and then program and system testing is performed Both these tests clears all the bugs/errors and problems in the system. Once the system passes the test then it is installed in all required areas. There are various testing techniques used for this purpose. Two main types are: Black Box testing and White Box Testing.

According to IEEE Standard Glossary of Software Engineering Terminology (1990): "Black box testing (also called functional testing) is testing that ignores the internal mechanism of a system or component and focuses solely on the outputs generated in response to selected inputs and execution conditions." and "White box testing (also called structural testing and glass box testing) is testing that takes into account the internal mechanism of a system or component."

Six test strategies for black and white box testing are:

1. **Unit testing is based on white box testing:** According to Kolawa & Dorota (2007): "Unit testing is a method by which individual units of source code, sets of one or more computer program modules together with associated control data, usage procedures, and operating procedures, are tested to determine if they are fit for use."

2. **Integration testing is based on black and white box testing:** It is a testing strategy in which software and hardware components are tested individually and collectively to appraise the interaction between them.

3. **Functional and system testing is based on black box testing:** According to Kaner, Falk, & Nguyen (1999): "Functional testing is a type of black box testing that bases its test cases on the specifications of the software component under test. Functions are tested by feeding them input and examining the output, and internal program structure is rarely considered."

4. **System testing is based on black box testing:** It is performed on a complete incorporated system to evaluate: The component at or outside the limits of its requirement and this strategy is known as Stress testing. The compatibility of the components with the specified performance requirements and is also known as performance testing. How much a user can learn to prepare inputs and understands the outputs of a system this is also known as usability testing.

5. **Acceptance testing is based on black box testing:** Acceptance testing is conducted to determine whether the system satisfies the user as per the predefined criteria and made it acceptable to the user.

6. **Regression testing is based on black and white box testing:** This testing is done throughout all testing's, to verify whether any change or modification have not introduce new faults.

According to Savenkov (2008): "One of the main reasons for regression testing is to determine whether a change in one part of the software affects other parts of the software."

Implementation and Maintenance Phase

After the user acceptance of the new developed system, the implementation phase begins. It is the phase where assumption/requirements turn into practice. In this phase the users are trained about the system and starts using it. The developer of the system provides two types of documents about the system to the organisation. These are:

1. **Operator/user Document:** This document complete description of the system for the user is given like *how to operate, what error messages can occur and how to solve it.*
2. **System Document:** This document contains the details of system design, process flows etc, it makes organisation to understand the system and changes to be made in the system and permissions granted for changes, to satisfy new user needs.

Now maintenance means to tune the system for variation needed in the working flow environment. If any error occurs it must be noted carefully and corrected time to time. The review of the system is done for understanding the full capabilities of the system in this phase the required changes for the additional requirements are noticed and performance is checked in terms of quality and efficiency.

To manage all the phases of SDLC different models or methodologies are used, such as waterfall, spiral, cocomo, prototype, iterative process model etc.

According to Rajiv Mall (2008): "Software development organizations have realized that adherence to a suitable well defined life cycle model helps to produce good quality products and that too without time and cost overruns".

As we have discussed earlier the integration of information system into SDLC, now a person is needed who control and supervise the whole system development process. The system analyst is the person who analyses and supervises the whole process of system development life cycle. The coming section elaborate the role of system analyst:

SYSTEM ANALYST

The System Analyst is the person who is responsible for every activity in system development life cycle in an organization. During his job, the analyst must be clear about the requirements of the organization. System analyst must make sure that system be flexible to adapt the changing requirements of the organization.

According to Shelly, Cashman, & Misty (2008): "Because they often write user requests into technical specifications, the systems analysts are the liaisons between vendors and information technology professionals"

In any organization a system analyst is abide by responsibilities and accountabilities and designated with power of authority. Various responsibilities of System Analyst are as follows:

1. Assists current users in identification of problems by implementing a new system or by changing an existing system.
2. Investigates the real problem to determine the feasibility of the solution.
3. Assists the prospective users in proposing new or changed system.
4. Making estimates of the cost in developing a new system using appropriate tools.
5. Designs users' manuals and conduct training programs for the developed system.
6. Assists the users in the installation and use of new system being implemented.

Accountabilities of System Analyst are as follows:

1. Post implementation reviews to estimate cost/benefit ratio.
2. Making the users aware of the system before installation.
3. To verify all proposed functional specifications.

4. To handle users and management complaints about the working of the system.

In order to accomplish his responsibilities System Analyst is authorised for the following activities in an organization:

1. Communicate informally with the management, sponsors and affected people in the organization.
2. Assign tasks to subordinate members of the team.
3. Refuse to undertake activities which appear to be infeasible and unjustified.
4. Examine relevant supplies of material related to previous or current systems.
5. Supervising the testing phase before the system is implemented.

CONCLUSION

Information Systems are indispensable to the any organization to meet the future challenges. The five information systems described in this chapter illustrate the qualities required to make any organization best in the approach (Computer Based Information System) CBIS makes a new and updated contribution to the information system literature and will assist any organization in classifying a wide variety of systems.

As the interconnectivity and interdependency of information systems increases, it is gaining a huge amount of importance. In this chapter we have analyzed the concept of information quality to make a new system uses the different phases of SDLC. Therefore, this chapter propagates a subjective and user-centric approach to develop a new system.

REFERENCES

Elliott, G., & Strachan, J. (2004). *Global business information technology* (p. 87).

Hoffer, J. A., George, J. F., & Valacich, J. S. (2003). *Modern system analysis and design* (p. 23). Pearson Education Asia.

IEEE ANSI/IEEE Standard 1008-1987. (1986). *IEEE standard for software unit testing.*

IEEE Standard 610.12-1990. (1990). *IEEE standard glossary of software engineering terminology.*

Kaner, C., Falk, J., & Nguyen, H. Q. (1999). *Testing computer software* (p. 42). Wiley Computer Publishing.

Keen, P. G. W., & Morton, S. (1978). *Decision support systems: An organizational perspective* (p. 93). Reading, MA: Addison-Wesley, Inc.

Kolawa, A., & Huizinga, D. (2007). *Automated defect prevention: Best practices in software management* (p. 75). Wiley-IEEE Computer Society Press.

Mall, R. (2008). *Fundamentals of software engineering* (p. 32). PHI.

O'Brien, J. (1999). *Management information systems – Managing information technology in the internetworked enterprise.* Boston, MA: Irwin McGraw-Hill.

O'Brien, J. A. (2003). *Introduction to information systems: Essentials for the e-business enterprise.* Boston, MA: McGraw-Hill.

Savenkov, R. (2008). *How to become a software tester* (p. 386). Roman Savenkov Consulting.

Shelly, G. B., Cashman, T. J., & Vermaat, M. E. (2008). *Discovering computers.* Boston, MA: Thomson Course Technology. ISBN 10: 1-4239-1205-5

Silver, M. S., Markus, M. L., & Beath, C. M. (1995). The information technology interaction model: A foundation for the MBA core course. *Management Information Systems Quarterly, 19*(3), 361–390. doi:10.2307/249600

Chapter 8
Towards a Theoretical "Cybernetic" Framework:
Discovering the Pedagogical Value of the Virtual World "Second Life"

Pellas Nikolaos
University of the Aegean, Greece

ABSTRACT

In the last decade, there is a common conviction and connectedness for modern e-learning practices to use online virtual environments (or worlds) for arousing students' interesting in various experiential activities. In this perspective, this chapter creates and proposes a "Cybernetic Planning Framework" (CPF), which combines the diversity of educational theories and practices, yielding in a common basis for their inclusion. The present chapter focuses on Second Life's qualitative characteristics that can be utilized to construct a "teaching-organizational" framework, which is essential for planning effective and meaningful distance learning courses. This gain averred a "cybernetic model," in which users enhanced pedagogical authorities and principles of Contemporary Learning Theories that previous studies carried out in Second Life. This premise recapitulates the value-added of this chapter, which can successfully be adapted to any 3D "open" and "sustainable" education system, emphasizing on integration and innovation of teaching methods.

INTRODUCTION

The exponential growth and diffusion of new Information and Communication Technologies (ICT) in Higher Education have significantly changed over the form and manner of operation. With the adoption of new Web-based technologies are rapidly being developed and still developing, distance [electronic] learning (or otherwise named as "e-learning") acquired as a new dimension and its features that allows students searching and re-positioning the system's changes, particularly with the regard of web-learning environments. Beneath this light, the guiding axis integration in distance

DOI: 10.4018/978-1-4666-3679-8.ch008

education is to offer assistance as educational institutions and collaborative implementation of dynamic change of ideas, taking more account of adult users' needs and interests, thus helping them to form new relationships with knowledge.

Distance learning through the utilization of ICT can provide the educational research an important "context," in which students will work and discover knowledge. The components of the "frame-action," includes the possible correlations between knowledge, values and management practices that leads to social, cognitive and emotional development of the knowledge, which is widely emphasized by the theorists of Cognitive Psychology. The "framework" that we described earlier, requires the construction of new tools for analysis and modeling of interactions and includes four pillars:

1. The criteria that determine the status of an individual or collaborative activity (individual or corporate division of labor, etc.).

2. The interactions that occur between users (type, negotiation of cognitive resources, etc.).

3. Operations that are being performed, such as the constructing model of learning, the foundation of concepts etc.

4. The effect of the activity in the learning process-the cognitive outcome. The most important thing is to understand that the relationship between these axes, whereas a state that determines causes different patterns of individualism and cooperation, can trigger cognitive mechanisms and produce cognitive effects.

From the aforementioned reasons, it is crucial to identify these additional parameters (at least to be associated with past or current theories and principles formalities related to the cognitive process under certain conditions), which either have been ignored or not adequately been examined

so far and to see if they could and they have the potential to lead to positive learning outcomes. The effectiveness of the action-methods will become apparent when it becomes a "good guide" for the navigation of learning activities by encouraging the adult-learner and the other correspondents to interact with the environment. Therefore, it does not give weight in the instrument, but the design models and simulators of the "real" world in order to "build" itself, the student's knowledge, fulfilling the goal of learning more directly.

This "frame" (or "context-action") application of psychological, cognitive and social processes, in which they actively adapted, should be considered in advance. During the distance learning process, we must choose the means and methods that best suit to the context. A medium that is used to support a learning activity, which follows the theory of constructive learning approach to teaching, should be anyway as the primary purpose of encouraging students both to co-construction of knowledge, but also for effective collaborative action with the others, so that they persuade: (a) alone to assess the knowledge gained, and then (b) collectively understand the degree of realization of the goals set. But, in order for e-learning to be effective, it should thoroughly be studied in three dimensions that govern it (Strijbos et al., 2004): *pedagogical, technological* and *organizational*. The most important of the three considered dimensions is the *pedagogical*, which focuses on teaching and learning process, and how it can be used to enhance this process and the expected results. The *technological* dimension is providing the appropriate infrastructure to enable the implementation of e-learning. Last but not least the *organizational* dimension must be taken seriously in terms of roles and interactions between students, teachers and cognitive resources (see Figure 1).

As Dillenbourg (2008) mentioned, collaborative learning cannot any longer be limited, but it may include individual learning activities (work or pilot studies, etc.) and activities for the whole

Figure 1. The multidirectional cycle of three e-learning dimensions

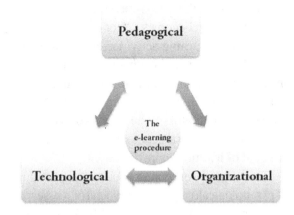

class (class-wide) with the participation of professor (introductory lectures, concluding sessions etc), obviously referring to the latest techniques of [D-]CSCL (Computer Supported Collaborative Learning between distributed users). [D-]CSCL is a bonding terminology that is used for a variety of approaches to education, which include a common mental effort for students or pupils and teachers that require the use of computer technology and communications. The research on collaborative learning with computer support ([D-]CSCL) can be organized into three categories (Bruckman & Bandlow, 2002): a) distance learning, b) retrieval, and c) sharing information. Therefore, within the context of [D-] CSCL from a distance, in the next sections, this paper will assess the technical ability to perform collaborative learning in a virtual three-dimensional environment from a distance, and consider the affordances that can strengthen this collaborative learning process. Within a three-dimensional virtual environment, evidences' are defined as active properties between an object and a user (in other words, the alternative ways in which the user can interact with an object).

In the last decade, it has been observed a growing interest in the commission of distance learning courses in networked virtual environments (or worlds). The interactivity of computing environments and the social form of modeling, allows the design of learning activities in accordance with contemporary Learning Theories. The rich social features, offer to participants the option of digital multi-users' communication and sharing of experiences, within a 3D "natural" space or place, where with the help of rich graphics causes a sense of coexistence in a global digital community. During designing a virtual world, it is almost always necessary to apply the main process of organization, management and implementation of educational practice, which includes one or more pedagogical theories and practices (Sebok & Nystad, 2004).

The technological infrastructure that virtual environments support, can transform the existing distributed networks, into habitable and navigable three-dimensional locations. These collaborative works and simulated sharing experiences can be supported by participants with the age average, showing the new emerging relationship between human and computer communications. The pedagogical value in recent years became even more useful for distance learning, were segregated spatially and temporally trainee's users engage in cooperative and collaborative types of action, group-based learning, and coexisting in common virtual spaces and interact via synchronous or asynchronous communication formats, which are often offered (bulletin board, written text, dialing voice, etc.). Previous studies on the cognitive performance of students using virtual worlds, showed that during the teaching process, they are achieving a more easily reorganization of prior knowledge, to revise old beliefs and new representations of learning (Pellas, 2010; Bailenson & Yee, 2007; Miao et al., 2007; Maher & Bilda, 2006). Even though, most recent findings have showed the need of using new teaching methods that are applied in any "innovative" learning environment (Yamashita, 2006; Sorensen, 2006; Oliveira et al, 2003). However, the abundance that is delighted, is difficult to derive a common pedagogical model, which implement and incorporate the designing process. In this view, it is necessary to present a methodological framework that we can use as a basis to establish an evaluation framework with educational terms for each virtual environment (Heiner et al., 2001).

This paper focuses on collaborative learning in distributed users, who are synchronized in time and space in a public place and work effectively together to achieve a common goal with the support of a computer. Its roots are a general term, which combines an understanding of how people learn in groups, with the permitted technology ("technological literacy"), computer networks and associated hardware, software, services and techniques. In this case, the creation of the "framework" was made to assist of a "cybernetic model" and for the implementation; we have chosen the virtual world of Second Life.

THEORETICAL UNDERPINNINGS

It is crucial to observe that there is no clear and strict definition of the term *"virtual world"* or *"virtual environment,"* and so we try to give below, some of the most prevalent. The term itself is controversial and of course leads to misunderstandings and hours of philosophical discussions. On this occasion, we truly believe that we must construct a definition about virtual environments and finally re-thinking the applications that can be in these. With the average *"Virtual Environment"* (VE or 3DVE) we mean a computer system based on newer three-dimensional applications' of VR technology, which simulates in the PC (Personal Computer) screen a "physical" space or place, like this in real life and aims to present a visually interactive and multi-sensory "world," which is exclusively for users and influence their actions in a positive way. On the other side, a *"Virtual World"* (VW) is the result of a virtual environment's operational structure, which includes the representation of a natural environment and "variants" in conjunction with a fantastic placement, where users' "virtual rooms" are freely without restrictions and commitments. This distinction very clearly indicates that virtual world's rules

for building and interpreting data is supporting the operation of the "physical" environment as a computer system. A 3D environment is hosted on a server or even in a form of software, which is stored on the PC's hard disk, giving users the impression that is to be established on a "solid state," where everything looks and move normally. The absolute connection between them is the users' capacity for the upcoming changes and developments that are promoted by the time and place. Moreover, the most important contribution that 3D VR lays is the ease managing for one or more subjects, even when it involves hazardous or inadequate processes, which could not be performed in a real environment. In this context, the students learn from their mistakes, without dangerous effects on their actions, and as a result they "produce" their own feedback and reuse it (debugging).

As we were previously mentioned, the dynamic view of three-dimensional virtual reality (3D VR) can provide a highly intuitive contact between human and computer, as it incorporates the features to interact with real and virtual world. We thus described all the components and processes that make up a "system" three-dimensional reality, i.e. a virtual environment (or world), which allows geographically dispersed users; to interact collectively in real-time. Besides, common characteristics of these technologically upgraded environments can be exploited by modern pedagogy, which includes the primarily cognitive and collaborative tools, different types of supportive education - "supporting frameworks" (conceptual, procedural, meta-cognition) and access to sources of knowledge and teaching models.

The key points - for supporting e-learning applications in virtual environments - is to provide opportunities for interaction between users and the distributed networked virtual reality system (Ott, 1999; Johnson et al., 1996). Users' adaptation requires a mutual modification of learning "transforms" the 1-D dimensional selection and presentation of informative tissue, in a 3D multiuser environment that let users discover, research or communicate freely, in order to avoid the static mapping of the overall construction of knowledge. The upgrading quality of the "immersing experience" is presented by the three-dimensional virtual world to a PC screen and the absolute connection of these can gives a new dimension in terms of key learning areas, such as:

1. "Experimenting," this includes student's reflection experience, knowledge and individual skills for problem-solving activities,
2. "Constructive-Experiential," which illustrates from a student to conquer the processing of primary data sources and knowledge and last but not least,
3. "Social engagement," which develops a dialectical relationship between users (teachers and students), for shaping a common framework for activity and learning, which will eventually lead to collective responsibility and co-construction of the team-based knowledge field.

An equally important issue that is being discussed at this stage is the smooth functioning and efficiency of innovative e-learning methods. Through this research process, the basic issue of finding common ground perspectives for the organization and the adaptation of courses within a dynamically changing virtual environment that meets the needs and requirements of its users, cannot be missed from the related virtual worlds' researches. Our teaching strategy requires a "cybernetic model" which is related to a structured learning environment (Jackson, 2000; Beer, 1981). Primarily, this should be supported in managing the complexity of interactions among participants, which determines the role of everyone individual user and although which communication channels are available for use. This distinction very clearly indicates also on how effective the organizational interactions can be managing crucial circumstances in the environment (Britain & Liber, 1999; Liber, 1998).

The construction of our model follows Stafford Beer's "Viable System Model" (VSM) (Beer, 1972), which is a speculative model of the organizational structure of any "viable" or "autonomous" system. This participation would be structured in such a way as to allow separate meetings of users to take place in an "adaptable" changing environment, which has capable requirements that right owners want. VSM is a system that is alleged cybernetics description for applying to each body system and can provide autonomy (Beer, 1979).

Similarly, a key issue that must be explored by users who involved in the teaching-process vector (teacher and students) is the managing of "action groups" that is used for delivering courses. So at this point, if the purpose of education is to provide a more effective teaching method, compared with the traditional, reinforcing the provided quality of education, then advance called alone to examine or remove the methods, techniques and tools that will help him to accomplish his work rationally. Companions in this effort are adult learners who are directly involved to find the final pedagogical value-added of this virtual environment. Therefore, we can consider as an appropriate organizational structure for teaching elements in a virtual world, providing an easier management of complex interactions and communication channels (synchronous and asynchronous) between members, keeping intact the specificity and behavior which was as presumably the same as the real.

CONSTRUCTIVE DIMENSIONS FOR AN EFFECTIVE COLLABORATIVE LEARNING PROCESS

Collaborative learning can be defined as the "working together framework" on a specific issue and in such a way it can promote individual learning through collaborative processes. This means that both the trainers and the students are active participants in the learning process. Although, knowledge is not something that is delivered to learners, but something resulting from active dialogue between those who seek to understand and use concepts and techniques. The collaboration learning process has resulted in a level of knowledge of learning community that is greater than the sum of knowledge of individual members'. Cooperative activities lead to the emerging learning, which is the result of interaction between (no assembly) of knowledge and views of all those who are involved in the formation (Whipple, 1987). This means two things:

1. Firstly that educational environment provides the appropriate stimuli, and
2. Secondly, that knowledge is gained. Every person is different, since this depends strongly on the temper, the previous experiences and learning styles. Particular importance is the premise that knowledge is not given from the beginning, but it will unveil from students in the environment.

The idea that active knowledge is from human's constructions has also influenced and interacts with existing conceptions and experiences, which seems to be common core theories of Constructivism. Driver (1988) considers the following six characteristics determine the constructive approach to the learning process that:

- Students are not passive recipients, but individuals who are actively involved the learning process.
- The student involved in an active learning process, which involves the construction of meaning (and importance) of things through interpersonal discussion and collaboration with other learners.
- Knowledge is not entirely objective, but individually and socially constructed and the nature is controversial. It can be assessed by the person under extent to match the

experience and it's consistent with other aspects of knowledge.

- Learning is not about imparting knowledge, but includes the organization's specific activities that promote learning.
- Learners participate in authentic learning activities, i.e. activities have always existed in reality and not just prefabricated for the purposes of teaching. The authenticity of an incentive can engage participants in the learning process, and prepare to deal with such activities.
- The curriculum is not only a "syllabus", but a project plan learning materials, resources and related cases on the subject of learning, through to learners constructing knowledge.

The highly important is trying to incorporate these features into an online 3D VR system that should provide information, such:

- **The problem-space project (manipulation space):** It presents for learners an interesting problem to solve or project to completion. The problem has been original and interesting enough to cause jam trainee. So, the system should provide tools for viewing multimedia the material.
- **Related cases (case studies):** It access to a set of similar related experiences, where learners draw information to substitute insufficient experience with this problem. These cases also help the representation of complexity in a learning environment, offering and considered multiple perspectives or approaches to learners' problems.
- **Resources (information resources):** Accessing to data resources (documents, graphics, audio, video and animation) relating to the matter, which support the analysis of the problem.

- **Cognitive tools (cognitive artifacts):** The new technological tools through which students can simulate the original functions and operations should be done to tackle problems such as stress and microcosms.
- **Dialogue via communication tools (3D VoIP or chat text):** Supporting communication between all participates in the educational process. So, the online 3D VR system should use email, chat, forum, video conference etc.

McConnell (1994), also, argues that cooperative learning is a source of valuable results that is increasing the ability to teamwork, confidence, etc. Also, Sharan (1980) agrees that collaborative learning can provide better understanding of the learning process. In addition to academic arguments, the use of collaborative learning has several important advantages. The main ones are as follows:

- **Promote users' interactions:** like intercultural relations and contact with different cultures, ideologies, etc.
- **Increase self-esteem:** in the learning community members working with common goals and agreed rules. This helps develop a sense shared responsibility, mutual support and fostering a friendly climate encourages learning. Such a framework is conducive to the socialization of individuals and may be particularly beneficial to those members who for various reasons (e.g. low self-esteem) are reluctant to express their views.
- **Extraordinary motivation:** as it is known that people feel the need to live in social groups. Therefore, the organization of students is being depicted through learning communities.

Learning in collaborative ways, can achieve common goals that are cognitive and perfectly

suited to the nature of needs, while isolation that violate the innate tendencies for communication and interaction. The interaction of individuals within a community learning can be a powerful motivational tool for learning to promote skills that are related to organization and communication in within groups (Hand & Treagust, 1995). An online 3D VR system which supports collaborative learning procedures should be offered tools such as: email, discussion groups, chat, whiteboard (Brainstorming), screen sharing, under responses (response pads), audio- (audio-conference), or video-conference. The study of how people work together using computer technology, addressing issues involving the use of email, the subject that includes an awareness of the actions of other users, video conferencing, chat systems and common real-time applications, as collaborative writing or planning. In this case, the interdisciplinary field includes computer science, economics, sociology and psychology. The researches' way is based on developing new theories and technologies to coordinate groups working together.

The meaning of all this is that integrated assessment represents complex interactions across spatial and temporal scales, processes and activities. It can involve one or more mathematical models, but may also represent an integrated process of assessment, linking different disciplines and groups of people. Managing uncertainty in integrated assessments can utilize models ranging from simple models linking large-scale processes, through models of intermediate complexity, to the physically explicit representation of Earth systems. This structure is characterized by trade-offs between realism and flexibility, where simple models are more flexible but less detailed, and complex models offer more detail and a greater range of output. Neither single theory describes and explains the dynamic behavior across scales in social-economic and ecological systems (Rotmans & Rothman, 2003), nor a single model can represent all the interactions within a single entity, or provide responses to questions in a rapid turnaround time (Schellnhuber et al., 2004). This functional integration of different scales and across scales is required in order to comprehensively assess 3D VR systems.

THE POLYMORPHIC DIMENSION OF CONTEMPORARY LEARNING THEORIES

Nowadays, we recognize more and more the need to introduce social-cultural teaching methods, which emphasize on the social role of the teacher and learners. Collaborative learning in association with Web-based technologies is seen today as an active process that facilitates the interaction and direct contact between users in learning the material. The change of the theoretical background and a shift to a more "constructivist" method has dictated the move from teacher-centered (or "instructive") in an exploratory, independent and collaborative way of learning. Many of the teaching procedures have been taken for granted in traditional education, merit review and adjustment to new technological and communication data. Among to the factors that are impressing to be effective, the various educational applications of computers should be based explicitly or implicitly on Contemporary Learning Theories and psycho-pedagogical aspects that reflect into the real needs of the educational community.

Especially in the case of distance learning, the main problems and needs of implementation and identify are not only the existing infrastructure, but also the pedagogical methods that were used in the past. This has led researchers and even the development of "innovative" teaching models, since it was found that there has developed a new technology quite correct, documented and adapted in pedagogical design. Besides, after these findings, e-learning could not replace traditional teaching methods that are launched in the "mixed" mode of learning or "Blended learning," which combines traditional teaching methods and use

new technological tools such as Web 2.0. The efforts of e-learning program implementation through the use of collaborative environments should be based primarily in the field of cognitive human-computer communication area and the collaborative work by introducing an important social dimension to the experience. Supporting online collaborative learning is characterized by a high rate of interaction between users with an interface, which brings as results produce a large amount of information, describing their actions in the system.

The characteristics of these approaches, according to the former authors (Piaget, 1985; Vygotky, 1978) and proponents (Sajadi & Khan, 2011; Hamat & Amin-Embi, 2010; Earl, 2005; Jonassen & Rohrer-Murphy, 1999; Kozulin, 1999; Salomon, 1995; Cole & Engestrom, 1993; Sierpinska, 1993; Lave & Wenger, 1991; Leontiev, 1978) are summarized for:

1. The need of creating equal opportunities for excluded social groups, ensuring lifelong learning and the exemption from space-time commitments that is imposed by the traditional way. In this case, it's pretty remarkable to believe that Open and Distance learning can be an equivalent and equally effective framework for education with much more opportunities unlike of "conventional,"

2. The team knowledge building is available to learners allocated in a shared learning environment, coupled with the possibility of centralized planning and management courses with emphasis on collectivity, which leads users to co-creation and co-construction of knowledge,

3. The interactive and social form of modeling, allow designing learning activities in accordance with modern pedagogical approaches,

4. Active-cognitive construction that contributes to the depth of understanding,

5. The learning process that takes place in context with independent activity, social and

mental support in authentic places (situated cognition),

6. The community, through which learning takes place, helps to disseminate the culture and practices, and

7. The conversation (discourse) which is enabled for participation and negotiation in the community.

In conclusion, from the overwhelmingly of the juxtapose researching principles, we need to say that a wide range - during the cognitive performance of students by using virtual environments – have showed that the teaching process is achieved more easily with the re-organization of prior knowledge, the revision of old beliefs and new representations which can depict at the same time in their visual field (Okada et al., 2003; Johnson et al., 1999; Johnson et al., 1998).

THE REFORMATIVE ROLE OF [D-] CSCL IN REORGANIZATION AND STRENGTHENING OF KNOWLEDGE

According to Slavin (1983), learning-based teamwork, refers to instructional techniques, in which participants' work and learn together as members of a small group to achieve a common goal. In group-based activities it can be varied depending on the number of members, composition (homogeneous or heterogeneous in their ability), gender (same or opposite sex) and type of cooperation. In this section it is important and should be noted that an effective collaborative activity must primarily distinguish the key features and principles that govern it. Thus, the main characteristics that should be careful are:

- The nature of the collaboration work or learning
- The nature of collaborators
- The number of co-responders
- Previous relationship between teammates

- Time-period of [D-] CSCL scripts

Also, our main authorities for a "meaningful" collaborative learning are:

- Focus on real-work tasks.
- Structure tasks so as to emphasize in interpreting preview of learning (e.g. it's necessary to draw on the diverse skills in the group).
- Create mechanisms for social and task-oriented interaction.
- Create mechanisms for linking the groups' work of other individuals and groups-including groups outside formal educational circles.
- Teacher's function as co-worker and facilitator rather than instructor.
- Constructing of interpersonal computing management into a synchronous groupware method.
- Flexible interactive applications for multiperson tasks.

Also, Dillenbourg (1999) stresses to work out the deeper sense of teamwork highlights the distinction of collaboration the term of "partnership" (cooperation), observing that a collaborative group activity is when it associates with members that have:

- An equal (or symmetric) relationship that performs to the same activity range.
- **A common goal:** In part the objectives externally identified as common, but it really is a matter for negotiation process that contributes to a common understanding about what those goals.
- **A similar view of working together on the project:** We recommend cooperation (collaboration), but the partnership (cooperation) to have independent targets (vertical division of labor). Instead, the cooperation division of labor based on differ-

entiation of roles, but is not fixed and immutable, but team members can be rotated (horizontal division of labor).

- Basic observation, which converge several researchers, is that symbolic tools used to structure and expression meanings to shape both the cognitive skills of the individuals (Kaput & Roschelle, 2000; Vygotsky, 1997a), and the learning environment (context) (Papert & Resnick, 1995).

With all these things that are given above, we clearly understand that as a "collaborative learning process" is defined as any group in which learning takes place at least some of the important learning interactions between students ("horizontal interaction"). The organization, therefore, students and/or professional learning communities to collaborate to achieve common cognitive goals, it is perfectly adapted and harmonized with nature and needs. Unlike, the isolation violates the innate tendencies for communication and interaction. For these reasons the work within a community learning may itself be a powerful motivation for learning.

Completing our thoughts, we could point out that teaching a design-based process with students' relationships with the "other" classmate-is, in essence, the plan upon which it could build the universal human "co-experiencing" in terms of solidarity and understanding. In this sense, and as far as all the innovative actions will continue to coexist with school education and to integrate within the new teachers, teaching-organizational design of the curriculum will enrich the arsenal of the education community towards the project of vague as to the subject is or its terms, "sustainability" promoted by the late "sensitized" state-transnational entities to defend their development plans. An absolute processing is that [D-] CSCL emphasizes in social reorganization and subsequent repositioning of research and learning fields. This essentially means that learning is not treated as a phenomenon that just happens "inside the head of each person," but instead is formed in a social context, and involves the interaction of the learner with other people, with symbolic tools and instruments, and the environment. This approach of learning is even more interesting when contrasted with the label that first found the evidence of intelligence in social contexts and then is internalized by individuals. It seems that the social context is a formative factor in learning, especially if learning described as a process of participation (participation metaphor) in communities of practice (Lesser & Prusak, 1999; Hildreth et al., 1998). In this case, learning process becomes a matter of communication in the language of the community, and object of action according to the "norms" of the community. These are practical "norms" of social interaction, which are shaped by the community (e.g. what is an acceptable explanation, one that has criticized what and what can be challenged, etc.) (Yackel et al, 2000).

In conclusion, the dimension of collaborative tools that a [D-] CSCL script provides is an integral part of the learning process. This usage is determined by the experience of individuals, particularly the practices and actions of the community attended by the user of the tool (Nemirovsky et al 1998; Meira 1998). Consequently, we cannot see in depth the role of computing in collaborative learning, if not reserve a human activity which embraces and transforms, and if you do not take into account the broader context (e.g. classroom's characteristics), in which humans' activities took place. These dimensions are not only important to investigate the learning process, but also for designing and evaluating learning environments based on the use of collaborative technology.

VIRTUAL ENVIRONMENTS AND COLLABORATIVE E-LEARNING

Unlike, most of two-dimensional "systems" are designed exclusively for learning (see LMS: Learning Management Systems, as Blackboard or Moodle), but in virtual environments there is no difference as regards the final learning product that should be submitted by students' experiences, particularly through:

1. Creating online communities, both in initial training, and the subsequent, namely of "Lifelong Learning" (Bull & Kajder, 2004),
2. Engaging in action's scientific issues, enhancing their social behavior (Kafai, 2006),
3. Promoting and enriching the social-cultural development, the transformation of social relations into mental functions (Barab et al., 2005),
4. Providing an environment for programming and coordination (Read et al., 2006),
5. Exploring new mathematical concepts, and promote scientific research (Clarke et al., 2006),
6. Connecting learning materials and enchanting of psycho-pedagogical frameworks, which defined the modern theories of learning to better study, observation and understanding of the cognitive users (Dieterle & Clarke, 2005).

Therefore, the added contribution to education could be classified:

1. Under a wide range of situations where the student can proceed to remove (deductively) or generalized knowledge (inductive), and
2. It can be verified if the "abstract" knowledge is gained to be applied in this particular case.

The expanded use of PCs and Internet in Higher Education, in conjunction with modern pedagogical theories that emphasize on inquiry-based learning, problem-solving and decision-making processes are influenced most strongly across the range of teaching and learning process and tend to change the traditional way (e-) educational practice. Still, it's necessary to be mentioned that "transferring" virtual environments in a modern practical-teaching framework for collaborative e-learning, suggesting primarily the jointly carried out work between distributed users. They are usually employed in a learning activity or a project, giving a more social dimension to their experience. The advantages of cooperation in this effort focused on conducting an effective training, acquiring new social skills and intercultural relations, and finally increasing their self-esteem. However, here we should note that in any collective interaction and involvement of users' cognitive mechanisms' and the whole cycle that is spent, there is always some sort of "warranty," so to produce the required knowledge, and achieve the final learning outcome (see Figure 2).

In the view of this reasoning, the creation of a "cybernetic" evaluation framework should establish an "open" environment for learning that supports modern considerations for learning, did not need to refer to "Neo-behavioral approaches" of knowledge (see Pavlov, Skinner), as this could (theoretically) supporting learning activities in modern (cooperative) learning environments. Contrast of established theories as (Social-) Constructivism, Activity Theory, Situated or Distributed Learning, can be used as a "substrate" for the implementation of training courses and it depicts between the dipole of humanity and society.

In addition, an important point which should be of particular importance for e-learning with modern social-cultural theories of learning, is the core of the empirical-experiential data, in which learning occurs in modern environments. The parameters' convergences of theoretical social-constructive approaches to learning (through the experience) are better understood when are (Lave & Wenger, 1991; Vygotsky, 1987; Piaget, 1971c; Piaget, 1970b):

1. Understandable as a process and not as a result,
2. Occur as an ongoing effort through activity experiences,

Figure 2. The representation of collaborative e-learning

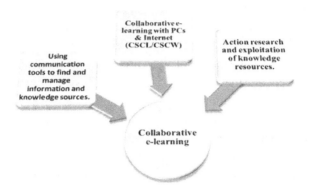

3. Relate directly to resolve potential conflicts and ways to adjust to a specific environment,

4. Elaborate the structural learning dimension as a "holistic" process that includes both the cross-thematic integrated communication between people and demonstrates the "relational synchronization" (or relational concept) for:

   a. Adapting in the learning environment, and

   b. Creating individual knowledge, based on teammate's experience.

In general, these theories define that the construction of knowledge takes place in collaborative environments through discussions that include the creation and understanding the communication (between individual using and groups) of performing activities. In a socio-cultural approach to understand the basic assumption, we can imagine a person who participates in a social "system." The culture of this system and the tools that can be used for communication (especially the tongue) form, cognitive construction and a source of teaching and evolution indicate his learning place.

Thusly, Human-Computer Interaction (HCI) in the learning process constitutes a "philosophical" (conceptual) framework, whereby the most appropriate unit of analysis is human's activity, consists of several components that interact with each other (subject, humanity, division work, etc.)

with emphasis on creating tools that mediate relationships for human and object. This new "system" represents the broader context and practice field, in which learning ability can be accomplished with underlying *conciliators' tools*. These *tools* can be classified into two categories: a) "natural" & b) "psychological". But this relatively distinction between "natural" and "psychological" tools is not always clear. This can be seen on Web-based technologies, which are "natural" tools, but the interactivity that is included, making them like "communication" tool. The "symbolic" (technical) properties for the main system include several items such as text, audio, video, etc. These "psychological" tools are fostering a rich understanding of messages and interactive communication between people based on experience, knowledge and culture (Bates & Poole, 2003).

CATEGORIES OF 3D VR SYSTEMS

Virtual reality can be applied to a wide range of applications. The utility of 3D VR in the educational process creates all the necessary conditions for more appropriate and effective learning. The general use of virtual environments in education related to the possibility of first-person experiences with the use of physical behavior (national presence) and providing as much freedom as possible to navigate and interact with objects in virtual environments, and encouraging participation users, who are deemed to have a lower profile in real life.

Taking into account this proof, 3D VR is considered as a very powerful visualization tool that can be integrated effectively into the learning process. The absolute connection of this combines all the features of audiovisual interaction with infinite possibilities. The "visualization" is a recognized tool for data representation and concepts that help in understanding and assimilating the content of teaching. Virtual environments are utilized system's interface, where users acquire a more mental experience, than its interaction with an ordinary environment. The above factors contribute that it can successfully be used in education, specifically with:

- The use of 3D VR is especially the case of *visualization*, in which the experience of creating a simulated environment or model is very important for knowledge.
- The educational process is carried out under *realistic conditions* for worlds (microworld, macro-worlds), which are not visible to humans without the aid of special instruments.
- Through *interaction* with the virtual environment provides a better opportunity to consider an object or a process, in a manner which includes multi-sensory manipulative skills and physical movement.
- The *sense of presence* in virtual environments through to a particular strengthen student's interest (Peachey & Herman, 2011; Bronack et al., 2008), offering in learning process more "edutainment" aspects.

From these perspectives, three-dimensional virtual reality can be described as a very powerful tool in education. Considering this figure, the educational applications that are provided, users can explore and learn thematic areas which are inaccessible in the real world. At this conceptual approach the raft - importance and develop a system for virtual reality training application - focuses on cognitive, spiritual, social and emotional processes of students. Apart from these facts, a 3D VR system can exploit and highlight the characteristics of productive teaching principles and of course the theory of "Social Constructivism," which paves the way for development of new teaching approaches and theories (Bricken, 1990). A virtual environment can be defined and changed the location, scale, density of information, interaction, response system and the timing and level of involvement of the user. These two approached kinds of learning environments can be defined as:

1. *Multiuser Virtual Environments* (MUVEs), is a popular form of multimedia environments that was initially aimed for entertainment. MUVEs (like River City, Croquet) can be designed for the educational community incorporating learning objects or problems in a virtual environment or context. Users explore the environment and examine digital objects. In such an environment there are modern means of communication between users. Educational MUVEs are being designed to support research into learning and conceptual understanding. Usually there is no one right way of completion of work or solving a problem. Various solutions are justified, as in real life, some solutions may be better than others. Great importance is placed on cooperation of the students. Unlike MUVEs are designed solely for entertainment, but educational MUVEs are usually an end product that must be submitted by the students according to their experience. We can use them in educating for:

   a. Creating online communities and initial teacher training and after the training in their professional development (Bull et al., 2004),

b. Engaging in actions on scientific issues, promoting social behavior (Kafai, 2006),

c. Promoting social development through enrichment cultures (Barab, 2005),

d. Providing an environment for collaboration and planning-based learning (Bruckman, 1997),

e. Creating and exploring new mathematical concepts (Elliott, 2005), and

f. Promoting the scientific research (Clarke et al., 2006).

2. *[Distributed-] Collaborative Virtual Environments* ([D-] CVEs) are collaborative learning environments, where students work in teams from distributed areas with great multi-user communication applies. A [D-] CVE consists a set of virtual worlds or a "standalone" world, which offers educational service to its users. Developments in modern knowledge about human cognitive performance leading to improved teaching plans and educational applications (Vosniadou, 1996). Furthermore, cognitive performance suggests that learning requires the reorganization of prior knowledge, the revision of old beliefs and new representations. The additional investigations lead to the development of computer visualization learning environments, intelligent virtual reality micro worlds. Additionally, data is instrumental in teaching effectiveness and completeness of the interaction, configuration, and the realism of these open-access virtual environments.

A more general description of the type of [D-] CVEs is a composition of simple models of virtual environments and CVEs (Steed & Tromp, 1998) models with interaction in the classroom (Bigge & Shermis, 1992). A [D-] CVE as a visual – interactive environment can be considered to consist of three main elements:

1. **The cyber entities:** Participants (avatars) or groups of participants.
2. **The actions between virtual actors:** Interactions with the environment and interactions with objects.
3. **The status of cooperation:** The environment, the objects within it, the activity that is the subject of cooperation and pedagogy (the style of teaching/learning that is used).

COMMON FEATURES

The dynamic view of three-dimensional virtual reality can provide a highly intuitive contact between man and computer, as it incorporates the features of the interaction of real and virtual world. In this way all the descriptive elements and processes that make up a virtual reality system, which would allow all users in geographically dispersed collective interaction in real time. Distributed Collaborative VE-systems, are also extensions of MUVEs and aimed at collaborative work. The [D-] CVEs are designed to provide complete, clear and stable framework for cooperation that combines both the participants and their information in a public space presence. These goals create the ability to support a wide range of collaboration applications, such as education (Koleva et al., 2005).

On this occasion, these types of 3D VR systems are not aimed only at a group practice and additional training in tasks such as synchronous and asynchronous learning. A [D-] CVE is a virtual world, offering educational opportunities to its users. Several ways of user interaction such as chat, voice and gestures through graphical representation of users are taking place on it. This type of interaction is supported by the management of shared 3D objects. It also supports the users-system interaction since users navigate or execute commands for introducing objects and making changes in the 3D world. The main characteristics of a [D-] CVE are (de Freitas, 2008):

1. **Shared place:** The virtual world allows multiple users to participate.
2. **Interface (Graphical User Interface-GUI):** The virtual world depicts a 3D space visually.
3. **Immediacy:** Interaction takes place in real time.
4. **Interactivity:** The virtual world allows users to modify, develop, and construct content.
5. **Duration:** It still exists regardless of whether individual users are online or not.
6. **Socialization:** The virtual world allows and encourages the formation of the world through social groups.

Processes that occur during learning in the [D-] CVEs are the following:

1. Interaction with the environment to construct a contemporary knowledge field.
2. Interaction between team members to create new dimensional forms of learning.
3. Engagement in the learning process.
4. Active involvement of participants in the construction of knowledge.
5. Active cooperation and collaboration.
6. Dissemination of knowledge among team members and groups together.
7. "Transferring the knowledge" between groups.

Similar noteworthy is that students are asked to solve problems, arising from everyday experience. In addition, a collaborative environment that can support from a VR technology, the [D-] CVE is designed to provide flexibility and many possibilities of representation. In the face of this image of globalization, the best understanding of science concepts is difficult and time consuming; students can explore only a few basic concepts. The strategy focuses on depth rather than covering all materials in depth. The [D-] CVE facilitates a meta-cognitive awareness by allowing students to express their comments and representations of knowledge about an object and then compare it with others. Students are made aware of what they know and what they must learn. Moreover, the variety and type of information that it can offer may resolve complex problems from different angles.

ENVIRONMENTAL FACTORS INFLUENCING THE CHOICE

Today we recognize more and more the need to introduce social-cultural teaching methods, which emphasize the social role of teacher (instructor) and learners. Modern computing environments like VW can be an area of convergence and implementing learning theories, cognitive psychology and developments in educational technology. The assessment of their abilities in the learning process manifested both through social interactions that occur between disparate users within the "action-based framework" and beyond its limits. Therefore everyone might meet the needs of modern electronic forms (e-) learning, and from creating innovative educational environments to explore objects and environments, yet intuitive and natural way.

Collaborative learning by using PCs is treated and continues to be seen today as an active process that facilitates the interaction and direct contact between users' learning materials. The transfer of the definition in practical-teaching framework for collaborative distance learning (or collaborative e-learning) in virtual environments, suggests mainly the work carried out jointly between distributed users, who are usually "employed" in a learning activity or a project, giving a more social dimension to their experience. The advantages of cooperation in this context, efforts are focused on conducting an effective training, learning new social skills and intercultural relations, and finally to increase self esteem. As a part of departure we should mention here that in any collective interaction and involvement of users *"cognitive mechanisms"* and the whole *"knowledge cycle"* that is spent, there is always some sort of "warranty," so to produce the required knowledge, and achieve the final learning outcome.

The world's training is specifically designed for education, such as military, operational and medical education makes use of these tools. World's mirrors are the main developments concerning the use of mash-up. The field of applications such trainees could provide some real innovation in the processes of learning and sharing content on a global scale. This approach could lead to the formation of global self-organizing communities of interest centered on an object and to support specific goals or as part of any experimental work. The Mash-ups applications have benefits of education and training, allowing data to be organized in levels, increasing the learning experience. Google Earth is the best known of these worlds. More and more mash-ups can be embedded in other applications. The concentration of the various applications is facilitated by interoperability and this presents interesting options for education and training, particularly a mixture of real and virtual space. Factors influencing the choice platform in virtual worlds (Michael et al., 2008):

- Focus on social interaction, formal and informal,
- Review by the user,
- Ability to co-ordination,
- Sentimentality,
- Strong sense of social presence,
- Spontaneous, unplanned interactions, develop socialization,
- Improving communication during formal interaction,
- 3D interaction and experience,
- Exchange of documents,
- Unlimited scalability and portability,
- Freedom to developer – teach,
- Modern applications exchange,

- Internal or external growth (from very large to very small),
- Equal Java or C++ application formats (for designers),
- "Open-source" software (in some cases),
- Use - multimedia development tools,
- Multiple communication channels (group wave of asynchronous or synchronous communication tools),
- Flexible interactive technologies for multi-person tasks.

A NEW REVELATION FOR KNOWLEDGE TRANSFORMATION

The technology support aims to transform today's networks and/or shared PCs, habitable and navigable in three-dimensional locations where the collaborative work it supported and shared participants' experiences of all ages. The pedagogical use of multi-user virtual worlds in recent years became even more useful for distance learning. Virtual worlds are separated spatially and temporally trainee users, working in teams, co-construct knowledge, coexisting in a common virtual space and interact through modern or an asynchronous form of "multiple uses" contact, which often offered (bulletin board, written text, voice dialing etc.).

Moreover, various kinds of applications of virtual environments are grouped into the following five categories: *role-playing game worlds, social worlds, work-based worlds, training worlds and the world's mirrors*. These different types of virtual worlds offer a wide range of social interactions, collaborations and innovations in learning and teaching. The social worlds are extremely popular and successful. The social aspect of these worlds is clearly related to the processes of learning, and thus ideal for use in educational contexts (de Freitas et al., 2006). The most interesting aspects of this type of virtual worlds are primarily the work that is achieved through them, but rather uses as a social or socializing tool. With these data emerged five key issues for any research activity in educational collaborative virtual environments are:

- **The educational community:** It contains an updated view of how students learn. Naturally, scientific groups are sharing these beliefs and teachings that provide support through discussion and deposit the knowledge about virtual worlds in education. These groups can be targeted for transferring experiences and practices of the inner world (in-world) by the creation of virtual schools in the external world.

- **The social commitment:** It's inherent in pedagogy and refers to learning experiences, in which social engagement is important for the creation of knowledge. There is a wealth of empirical evidence supports these approaches. These are emphasized on the friendship and social relationships in the classroom as important in themselves, and there are signs that can help to achieve significant academic results (Howe & Mercer, 2007). The mediator's avatar interaction in virtual worlds can facilitate verbal and nonverbal communication skills and believes that this global social pedagogical approach may be accepted as useful pedagogical methods of the virtual world. Virtual worlds allow for collection of student data more efficiently than is possible in a traditional classroom and this could be exploited by the teacher in the context of social constructivism. Under this approach, the student should be able to review and reflect on internal interactions that occur in problem solving and the same knowledge in a curriculum with a social context.

- **Flexible ways of expression activities:** The modes of expressive activities are activities and interactions that occur in differ-

ent ways, text-based, verbal or sensory-motor. This means that there can be through a variety of learning tools best approaches to a wide range of learners (autistic children, blind students, etc.) (Sheehy et al., 2008).

- **Progressive support for classroom activities:** In these lines, scaffolding research in the learning process is noted as the fundamental role of social interaction in the knowledge's development.

- **Authenticity of classroom activities:** This issue depicts in situations where an activity or skill has meaning for the student, which could reflect real life. Virtual activities can be evaluated as authentic in terms of knowledge from the Educational Community. The virtual environment facilitates the development of authentic activities without which they could grow.

SECOND LIFE

The evolution of technological power of PCs and Internet has given the opportunity to create innovative electronic environments for both entertainment and learning. The premise of ICTs' rapid growing cultural and digital literacy, made many users ("digital natives") more receptive to networked virtual environments, due to the potential "dip" and interaction that are provide. The new technological infrastructure to accompany the rapid spread of broadband networks and additional developments, such as Web 2.0 applications and creating distributed 3D virtual environments (3DVEs), have changed far beyond traditional methods of distance education (Sivan, 2009; Spence, 2005). Moreover, the rapid development of electronic social networks has changed the "cyberspace" in a rapidly growing communication system, bringing to the front many facets of *"networked collectivity."*

Second Life (SL, http://secondlife.com/), has many similarities with Web 2.0 modern applications, such as Facebook, YouTube, Wikipedia, and Flickr. The open-ended architecture, the "persistence" (i.e. a virtual world that continues to exist even after a user exits from the world and that user-made changes to its state are, to some extent, permanent) (Koster, 2004) and the collaborative nature with emphasis on creating communities, integrate in the Web 2.0 phenomenon and also the evolution of this technology, which hoping to support a new grow things about 3D applications, Web 3.0 (or Web 3D). Web 3D was initially the idea to be fully demonstrated and used to navigate websites with the three-dimensional way. By extension, the term now refers to all "interactive" three-dimensional content, embedded web pages that can be seen through a web browser. Web-based technologies in accordance with 3D applications usually require the installation of a three-dimensional web viewer (like SL's Viewer) to identify the users with their personal content.

Second Life, as an interactive three-dimensional virtual world allows a wide range of creativity, since users can create 3D objects. It's crucial remarkable that it allows easy, versatile modern communication, direct connectivity to external Internet site and it is enabled for exploration and innovation. The big advantage of SL in relation to blogs and wikis is that relationships are between people who do not belong to the same group of interests and therefore, may have greater wealth and variety of applies. Moreover, it's considered a forerunner of the next phase of Internet evolution, which is the three-dimensional Internet, where the interaction of humans will evolve from a "flat"to an "immersive" networked experience, integrating and completing the two-dimensional web. The three-dimensional vision of the internet is not only a virtual world, but many, interlinked virtual spaces, to which the user can navigate with a unique virtual self (avatar or virtual entities) and a common interface, such as a Web browser, in which it provides access in many other websites (see Figure 3).

USING SECOND LIFE FOR E-LEARNING ACTIVITIES

The culture of digital culture and studying made many users ("digital immigrants") more receptive to virtual environments, because of the possibility of "immersing" into them. The inspiration for the creation of virtual worlds was the literature of cyberpunk as it was depicted on Neal's book Snow Cash, in 1992. The main aim of Linden's Lab founder, Rosedale Philip (the creator of SL), was to create a world such as the "Metaverse" that Neal describes as a world where users can interact, play, work and communicate with other users distributed from around the world. This was one of the most important reasons that SL was chosen for our research, as we try to investigate the functional characteristics of this virtual world and as a result to understand and interpret the factual teaching statements. It is one of the most famous three-dimensional imaging emulators of the global 3D virtual reality and therefore, it considered to be one of the most functional platforms in terms of scenarios and technical collaborative e-learning ([D-] CSCL) (Pellas, 2012; 2011; Fox et al., 2009; Poole, 2008; Alvarez, 2006).

For more than six years, SL is being used as a creative *"canvas"* of knowledge that can be considered as a supplement (or not) for the traditional environment of a classroom, providing new opportunities even for an existing curriculum. Almost daily, new educational institutions are active on it and exploiting or developing exclusive e-learning programs to deliver high-quality services to a global audience at low cost (Broaddribb & Carter, 2009). Educational institutions can use this "canvas" to create secure geographical areas (Grid's) and enhance experiential or empirical e- learning activities.

Second Life (SL), with the passage of time, is one of the well-linked virtual worlds that attract the interest of both social-networking friends and educational institutions from all around the world. The technical infrastructure completes on our

Figure 3. First page for downloading Second Life client viewer (http://secondlife.com/)

personal computer screen, a three-dimensional virtual reality network system for supporting communication and collaboration with geographically distributed users, over 18 years old. The first creative conception of SL was not planned for any particular scientific research program, as almost all three-dimensional virtual reality "systems" was opposed from, but clearly for entertainment. Among the factors of impressing it doesn't prevent some universities to use it as "educational tool" for organizing, managing and transferring their "knowledge field" (Zaid et al., 2011; Macedo & Marcado, 2010; Wang & Hsu, 2009; Gazzard, 2009; Smith & Berge, 2009; Arreguin, 2007; Prasolova-Førland et al., 2006; Cohen, 2006).

Even a small-scale literature review, can convince us to a large extent on adult users experience level in educational activities. The specificity of these activities is being associated with conducting research in SL and general support services for students. More specifically, some of the areas in which e-training was attended by online courses related to:

1. Information & Communications Technology (Esteves et al., 2009; Jarmon et al., 2008),

2. Economics and Entrepreneurship seminars (Gajendra et al., 2010; De Lucia et al., 2009),

3. Physics (Vrellis et al., 2010),

4. Education for adults with special needs (Ziekle et al., 2009; Nicosia, 2008),

5. Fine Arts (Nie et al., 2010; Ritter-Guth et al., 2008),

6. Ethnography research (Boellstorff, 2008),

7. Librarians researches (Mon, 2009; Nicosia, 2008),

8. Language learning (Ibáñez et al., 2011; Peña et al., 2009 Sanchez, 2008),

9. Teachers' Continuing Professional Development (Kallonis & Sampson, 2010; Vasileiou & Paraskeva, 2010),

10. Assessment of empirical studies (Pellas, 2011),

11. Engineering though "Sloodle" (Simulation Linked Object Oriented Dynamic Learning Environment) (Callaghan et al., 2009).

Numerous potential advantages of these studies shows that SL may be an alternative future promise to traditional academic approaches of e-learning. In this new perspective, we found the term *"e-learning 2.0,"* which gives more emphasis on social learning and social media, like blogs, wikis and even virtual worlds, like Second Life. The multimedia - interactive applications can be regarded as a relatively new teaching tool that allows the application of modern teaching methods and strategies for e-learning (Dunn, 2010; Pellas, 2010; Vosinakis, et al., 2010; Boulos et al., 2007; Hobbs et al., 2006; Childress & Braswell, 2006; Hughes & Moshell, 1997). Students are discovering new areas of interest and become practically *"seekers of knowledge"* and not mere recipients of directives and regulations (see Figure 4).

QUALITATIVE AND FUNCTIONAL TECHNICAL CHARACTERISTICS

The use of SL as a *"canvas"* of knowledge creation can be considered a supplement (or not), even the traditional environment of a classroom, providing new opportunities even for an existing curriculum. Almost daily new educational institutions, operating in SL and develop exclusive e-learning programs by exploiting the platform to deliver high quality services to a global audience. However, prior to entering students and planning activities on the environment of the SL, teachers should be concerned to regard with:

1. **Identifying the purpose and gains of the course:** It is important from the beginning of the learning process for learners to be informed of the purpose and objectives of the course to be achieved by using the SL or equivalent activities.
2. **Implementing systems requirements and technical equipments:** Without addressing the minimum requirements that SL's program "run," students will have difficulty for slowing down and "buddy" their computers. So, at the outset of each strip it should provide users with the appropriate infrastructure.
3. **Exploiting interactive connection between course content and activities:** It is imperative the need to explain gradually to the teacher online course content and activities because students want to understand the contribution of Second Life and as a result upgrade the quality of each lesson.
4. **Using "adaptively" the virtual space or place:** Second Life as a "globalized" environment can be useful for creating specific learning areas or exploring virtual sites to promote various types of interaction and the formation of a "learning community."
5. **"Supporting a technocratic framework" for learning activities:** Even though, SL can help in e-skills learning because of the complexity of the interface should be placed in the design of these activities.

Consequently, the learning process will be taking place within a social context of 3D virtual reality, which will provide the necessary cognitive tools and the appropriate supportive environment, which helps the individual "community of inquiry" that the students gradually learn, explore and to exploit their technical characteristics. Of course if it is rich in features, it does not automatically make it ideal for educational use. At this time, however, it's deemed necessary to quantify the degree of usability and quality characteristics that are combined with the possibilities that can be offered as a tool for learning support (see Table 1).

PROBLEM STRUCTURING

Contemporary Learning Theories by the use of ICT in the learning process comes as a continuation of the effort to find the right balance of systemic approaches and practices that are included in the problems of ambitious plans to major upheavals in education. Experience in a virtual environment can lead to the acquisition of general skills (such as cognitive, emotional motor) on the solution of problems that can be transferred to other cognitive areas of real life. The environments of this kind are

Figure 4. Collaborative activities in Second Life

an ideal place for learning basic concepts of learning, such as angles, variables, retroactivity etc.

Such an application collects all the studies of basic and applied research, whose objectives are the "formulation" of human learning processes and as a result the model captures or knowledge spaces that are both cognitive and computer. Obviously, it is placed in the field of cognitive science at the crossroads of the meeting of information technology in the teaching of science, cognitive psychology and educational sciences. It is clear that in modern problems of this approach is not restricted to modeling procedures that are capable of solving them in a specific site. This modeling must also take into account the level of the learner, including, to the extent possible, a generation of knowledge. So, we see a clear change in the problematic relationship with the classical principles of programmed instruction. This context is referring to the use of 3D virtual practicality interactive learning environments, supporting remote collaborative activities.

The main questions that can be raised by all these, then, are:

1. Can contemporary learning methods and the organization of complexity that is being provided from Second Life deals with the "cybernetic" model and even more increasing users' needs?

2. Does the pedagogical "cybernetic" model that is being developed, addressing with the current challenges that education facing today?

Ultimately, we must be stressed in the imminent reflection that is incorporated into the educational environment and the teacher and the student can take on some forms of reflection. It can be defined as, "an active, constant and careful consideration of any kind of perception or knowledge alleged in the light of the background behind it and the further conclusions to which it tends" (Dewey 1933, p. 118). From this perspective, we should take seriously into account issues such as specific activities that have enabled students to achieve the required goals, and have understood the specified activities. From the perspective of the student, it would like to have feedback prompt on how activities are compromised and if they could be implemented differently.

Our main ambition and concern is to formulate a problem and its solutions imply that uncertainty, ambiguity and disagreement need to be reduced. The developers of stakeholders' and knowledge perceptions are central elements to create a joint problem formulation. Ideally, the outcome of

Table 1. Technical features of Second Life enhancing the growth of the learning process

Supporting a variety of e-learning scenarios	With SL, students can support interactive activities in conjunction with collaborative learning techniques (brainstorming, Jigsaw), carrying out various scenarios ([D] -CSCL) and case studies. Apart from these, SL offers tools, such as private and public chat via text, voice or video and audio interaction with objects and the formation of groups, giving the user a *"sense of social presence"*.
Strengthening users' representation and awareness	Through the combined conjunction of gestures, imitations, virtual existence and communication with conversations (chat text, notes) or voice dialing (IM), users can exchange views, while explaining their actions.
Providing artifacts and tools that help users' to reduce the "cognitive overload" from the introduction	A standard option of user's "interface" is available to support both in the form of graphical representation and the variety of multimedia tools for fine organization and coordination of learning activities.
Configuring a virtual multimedia educational area of design	SL is an environment with emphasis on multimedia and virtual interactive objects. Users can communicate by using hypermedia applications such as voice and text, upload images or make broadcast audio and video in the virtual space.
Implementing an open-access and user-oriented virtual space in which participation is free	The vast majority of people that registering in SL are over 18 years old. However, apart from previous, there is a world for teenagers (13-17 years - Teen SL) and the virtual content is generated solely by underage users (Rufer-Bach, 2009)
Spatial flexibility in exploring a virtual environment	Spatial parameters such as size, architecture, infrastructure and physical environment affect the way students shape their social contacts (Ponti & Ryberg, 2004). To promote the educational value in virtual environments it should "meet" teacher's and students' expectations spatial and temporal flexibility, exploiting the inherent social stimuli that they receive in their spatial organization. Inasmuch, SL provides a unique and flexible environment for educators who are interested in implementing [D-] CSCL scenarios and explore the application of new media.
Accessible & ergonomic design of a virtual space for different categories of users	Designers should take into account that the virtual space will be utilized by users with different e-skill levels in communication technologies and information. Despite the fact that everyone have different level of "technological literacy," although SL is easily accessible because it provides guidelines for users during the first contact with the environment (e.g. Help Island).
Designing a space for users who can assume different and distinct roles	Approximately, a virtual learning system should support distinct roles and different rights access. In this direction, a very important function of SL is to create "action groups." This feature allows the creator of the group to assign different roles and set permissions for members.
Developing and implementing mix-method pilot programs	Develop and implement mix-method pilot programs on distance-education is targeted at Europeans serving teachers of primary and lower secondary Education and is based on modern-teaching methodologies with the assistance of Contemporary Learning Theories.
Creating a variety of teaching models	Developing a variety of teaching Models for Distance Learning, which will provide recommendations on the appropriate teaching models, approaches and ways of using available ICT. This notion will be assessable, in order to provide high quality professional development teachers in global Education.
Teaching interference	Teaching interference in the ranks of participants in the pilot training program to evaluate the effectiveness content of the program and make revisions and by further impulses.
Constructing of a multilingual Knowledge Base	Design and development of multilingual Knowledge Base in e-Education, which will produce a variety of educational materials and tools to support teaching roles and whose development is an ongoing process. Whereby, that will allow feedback and registration of educational content; created from end users.
Maintain an e-Learning community in Education for teachers	In the first stage, it is crucial to establish a network of communication among participants in the pilot implementation of teacher training program, but long-term goal will be the network to preserve and extended to a pan European communication channel that allows sharing expertise and experiences among teachers and contribute to the upgrading of e-Education.

problem structuring is 'negotiated knowledge'; which is agreed upon and valid. The content that is being developed during a participatory process should not be seen as final or permanent.

OUTLINE SCOPE AND MAIN PURPOSE

The outline scope of this work within the scope of analytical presentation and "reading" the quality and functional features of Second Life that focuses on:

1. Providing the opportunity for improvement of service quality and a variety of teaching and learning methods, when this is not be distinguished from the "traditional,"
2. Reducing the administrative burden of organizing and distributing knowledge resources assumed by teachers, and to help support the memory/cognitive background of each student, allowing them to manage first hand time and their tasks more creatively and second to show more willingness and understanding of their subject knowledge and finally,
3. Contributing through 3D virtual imaging to explore scientific concepts, principles and rules that govern the real world, by using three-dimensional simulations and integration models in learning environments for better imaging effects, so that students can better understand their "cognitive level."

Similarly noteworthy to this position, is the wide acceptance of the fostering needs for a more holistic approach to virtual sustainability. Constantly, the vast majority of practical solutions remains elusive and tends to exhibit underlying conflicts between different paradigms and their accounted methods. This chapter argues the need to wield multiple (social-) cognitive pedagogical tools that embody the principles of a systemic-

cybernetic thinking framework for the organizational complexity of the learning process through virtual worlds. The objective of our research integrates both to emergencies and innovative teaching methods in the multi-interactive virtual world of Second Life and also creates a supporting "cybernetic" framework, which assesses the features that governing the pedagogical value-added.

CYBERNETIC E-EDUCATION

The increasing demands of modern society have also led some countries to implement "national levels of learning" to ensure the acquisition of "basic knowledge". The strong support of the "national level" to find a "panacea" for all problems facing modern education, but these, as illustrated by the experience of countries, like USA, should be treated with extreme caution; as such moves appear to undermine the educational process, diversity and essence of some problems of education. As a part of an ongoing effort to determine the "national level" or pressures for increased efficiency and productivity improvement of schools, teachers are losing their autonomy and incentives for program design with imagination and creativity and turn into brutal applicators predetermined by other analytical the program. Unfortunately, such an approach is aligned with the traditional factory model of learning, teaching and school organization (Vrasidas, 2000; Callahan, 1962).

It should also be stressed here, that the educational systems and pedagogical approaches vary according to the philosophy and resources of the state that creates them. Based on the current literature, it is important that educational systems are open, flexible and guided by a student-centered philosophy (Lin & Hseih, 2001; O' Loughlin, 1992; Burton et al., 1986; Bovy, 1981). Students are placed in the center of the learning environment and surrounded by trainers from other students from learning materials and technological tools that facilitate learning and manage the learning process.

Within the context of increasing demands of the teachers presented a modern global trend for "lifelong learning". It is important for teachers continue to learn and be trained continuously. The creation of open universities and the proliferation of online learning (online learning or e-learning) will fill a gap in the needs of modern learners for continuous learning. The open universities (e.g. Open University of England or the Open University of Greece), are a breakthrough in the field of higher education and applied with great success. Such institutions substantiate the democratic ideals of a culture which need to be accessible to all. The open and distance education is based on the simple principle that an effective learning is not necessary that teachers and students be in the same physical space, at the same time.

On the other hand, a thing that should be taken into account is that the conceptual definition of the "Cybernetics" theory, until now, is understanding through the study of communication and organization-factor control of any system, whether it refers to computers or humans (Wiener, 1948). The use of both in teaching and learning process requires the interpretive approach is used by such conditions, leading to the emergence of dynamic and functional elements of a "system" (Bertrand, 1994). The basis of the cybernetic "system" is expressed through a set of components, whose properties are intertwined so as to form a "whole", which is in constant communication and action (or reaction) with the external environment (Ashby, 1956). The value-added of this theory lies in the connection of the operation and study of the effect of human action. Thus, this individually single "system" complex is self-adjusting and interacts in an ever changing-adaptable environment (Cannon, 1932). This means that the behavior occurs will be evaluated as an action within the environment. If the actual behavior that is expected is based on initial information then it received by the achievement of communication and the positive response

of the environment will lead him to "remember" it (feedback) for the future reuse (Jarvilehto, 1999; Tomas, 1995).

The acceptance of actors' autonomy in the teaching process is particularly the student refers to the pedagogical-psychological condition of "self-evaluation." In conclusion, the "Cybernetics" is reduced to a theory of documentation and the enrichment of a servant to the Practice Teaching Science, as *"Cybernetic e-Education"*. This theory deals with the "outline" relationship under a new "meeting" dimension between teacher and students. With the selection and supportive organization to learning materials, methodology and offer the means (supervisory) that will facilitate the learning and teaching process from a distance. The importance of the "other" users in the process of creating knowledge makes virtual platforms or even more the modern learning environments in "places" of humans' interactions i.e. "places" where these human expectations are in dialogue and create a small collective. In this collective, the distance learning program is familiar with students' needs with respect and understanding. According to this point, we realize that in addition to their own expectations that there also needs and expectations of others', cannot be ignored or negate their personal options. Given that, the structure and operation of such programs and the observed abnormalities can be taught in school, we would say that the teaching design for distance education programs in the systemic approach allows us to:

1. Shift our focus to the "who" is talking about our world, "how" and "why."

2. Form conscious "interlocutors" to our world, starting the conversation in democratic dialogue and consultation.

3. Create in the field of teaching-learning transaction the relationship of the student with the "other" classmate-and through all these.

4. Build solidarity as a principle of our coexistence with each "other."

Based on the interpretive reading of the particular field of Systemic Thinking and Practice which we presented, it appears that is yielding the following conclusions about their position in the Educational System and the role they could play. The first conclusion is related to the same school care and education. If we accept that the education system as a social observer-system co-exists and co-evolve back to the other social systems-observers (legal entities of public or not), we could conclude that it cannot accept changes that will seriously disrupt the terms of co-evolution coexistence: the rationality, efficiency and competitiveness. Thus, focusing on knowledge of the social context and the "institutional partners" consider necessary: the instrumental, fungible market knowledge. All, therefore, the attempted reforms of curricula, can make academia more attractive (in the words of the reformers) that can be owned by the students a wealth of information, but it stops there. To go below preconditions of radical social-political transformation and concurrent radical changes in thinking and world-view our data within the scope must be depend in our socio-political expectations and demands.

After this first conclusion is obvious, the second regards the position of Universities' Programs from a distance, as autonomous and independent activities. We think that it was glad the momentum, creating by this "free" and "autonomous" field of thought within the university setting. If we perceive it as all about trying-both in research and in terms of practice, to open the horizons of our pedagogical reflection, then the program of distance education (and other) habitats, will become free and democratic consciousness. The solidarity of people and the creative thinking that respects human nature and the "measure" in this situation will be become more effective. The third and final conclusion is derived from an action-research with students in the way it works for the same systemic approach. Considering that, the environmental group of students with whom we tested the artifacts educational value, with the program that was spent in their free time and in a period of school life that was extremely difficult, we would say that systemic thinking can serve as a strong internal motivation for young adolescents. With this last conclusion, we need to take seriously into account, as one of the problems that are often faced by teachers, the difficulty of raising students after a full curriculum spectrum.

PEDAGOGICAL DESIGN IMPLEMENTATION IN ACCORDANCE WITH THE SYSTEMIC APPROACH

Theories of educational action-planning within learning environments are similar to the functional description of teaching with a more detailed technocratic look, which varies depending on the model of learning ([social-] Cognitivism or [social-] Constructivist). Romiszowski's book (1974) also contains a number of tables that describe systematically the periods of the systems approach, systems development of hypermedia generation and levels of educational planning. In general, we can say that the following procedures, which could coordinate the educational process, are:

- Teacher's interest in the organizational structure of the teaching process. Initial attempts are establishing the goals and classifying to them in a legitimate context for students.
- Identification of long and short term goals.
- Identify the necessary elements including a teaching process (i.e. students, material for learning, through transmission of knowledge).
- Data collection based on the social characteristics of learners (non-profile, knowledge and motivation).
- Modify and change the form of education according to the procedure.
- Analysis of potential teaching which owns and limitations are presented.

- Constructs an operating system of teaching and learning.
- Provision of mechanisms that allow it to assess.

The design of teaching is a detailed application of this model base. We refer of course to the organization and design, which are inspired by "systems" theory that we described above. This should ensure that we are often interested in changing the behavior of the student and the choice of using media sources (Stolovitch & La Roque, 1983). Rather, what we said above, now we must note that the systemic organization of knowledge on the part of the teacher is an important event. With a second reader review, we would say that the description of this work focuses on the type of work, which will be paid by students to gain their objectives. This of course could not be differentiated from the assembled materials (kits), which are a subset of a more integrated learning system specified in the training of students (Rothwell & Katanas, 1998; Edmonds, 1994; Dick & Carey, 1990; Briggs, 1979; Wong & Raulenson, 1975).

The design, also according to Gagne et al. (1988), is founded to their theory on 5 principles:

- Individualization of instruction.
- Short and long term planning.
- Need for leveraging and organize applications.
- Use of the systemic approach to configuring knowledge.
- Calculation of learning conditions.

The pedagogical material that is developed in this case leads to some interesting conclusions, which include theories, simulations, and databases (e.g. monitoring activities for the student). The pedagogical strategy is aimed at the development of psycho-physical entity of the student to become a knowledge society considered as good as the real life. But through a variety of processes, simulations and experiments, we could draw the

basic features of a framework of action-that would include possible benefits or advantages and potential disadvantages or limitations, so to better understand the field of research in which learning processes are performed. So, according to what we said above, the benefits that are concentrating on:

- Easy integration of new information to existing system.
- Ability to create modeling and simulating conditions of reality, through an imaginary grid of action for the acquisition of knowledge.
- Choose and greater use of all or a subset of information or properties, resulting from the processing ergonomic system.
- Total and collective classification of information generated through research activities.
- Presented in a common area or location (i.e. same screen), multiple representations of the same phenomenon.
- Synthesis of interactive practical reality, which will be used and in fact.
- Adapting the system to varying levels of knowledge of students, according to ability.
- Display of structured knowledge in selected sections of students to become more easy and regular information in a database which will process their data.
- Revealing references to any system or reasoning processes that are not explicitly explains the process of learning.

In contrast, modern computer systems for education and opposites have some potential limitations that hinder their learning development path, including:

- Lack of processing power to further investigate the possibility of general and specialized knowledge in which the facts are presented and poorly fragmented by specific modes.

- Encourage the "mono-thematic" approach of cognitive areas and as a result we have to substantiate the data by using additional fields of study to achieve a result.
- Limited potential questions and display the screen of knowledge, which can confuse either the student or the misinformation.

Frequently it recapitulates the findings and ideas that we developed, we conclude in options for the new training and implementation of additional educational needs of modern science, including those of [D-] CSCL (see Figure 5).

It is understood, that modern multi-user virtual environments (or worlds), provide a wealth of tools for cooperation and communication that obviously making them a good choice for collaborative activities between different types of students, according to the new visual learning already mentioned. In summary, the 3D virtual desktop reality technology, used by virtual worlds, can be used in:

- **Educational issues:** Education is the main sector where collaborative virtual environments are finding wider acceptance. The positive effect of using virtual was analyzed above.

- **Collaborative structures:** Collaborative digital architecture designing, in which students construct and evaluate their structures. The positive effects of such an approach were achieved through email or IM, structured "brainstorming" chat interfaces, task awareness, flood control.
- **Cooperation in working conditions:** They can use simulation of work, which was costly in. Actually, they are testing the ability of a group to cooperatively solve a problem. Such virtual worlds used (for example, where training or aircraft engineering evaluation).
- **Educational tour in museums or ancient places:** As we mentioned, virtual environments contain advanced tools for modeling allow users to browse or even create a composite structure. In this way can simulate a digital museum or an ancient city.
- **Observation and evaluation of human behavior in the dynamic groups:** Using virtual environments under competitive conditions, such as electronic games in virtual places for example, grouping students' training strategies, and enable observers to record team behavior.

Figure 5. Blueprints definitions of workgroup computing through cybernetics

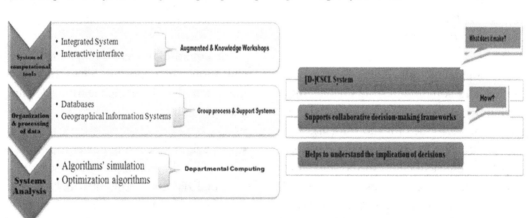

Apart from the above approaches to examine the usefulness of a collaborative organizational framework for their implementation, with the empirical level of the students shows further future investigations that should implement innovative ways in which:

- Students will enjoy and understand largely learning in an organized environment while improving their performance.
- They can more easily play a positive role in upgrading their personality traits, which are very useful and beneficial for both group cooperative meetings in real life and to achieve personal goals and ambitions.

Finally, according to what we said above we can support our position that the repositioned within organizational complexity and diffusion of knowledge systems and in particular that of virtual environments. So, we can better understand the importance of the knowledge available provided the pupil, which cannot be independent of the social contours in which they live and grow. Meanwhile the services and knowledge should be repositioned to connect with the cultural characteristics of situations in the birth of such knowledge with the help of authentic activities, which as we saw in the teaching-organizational context, can be a reliable source of practical application in everyday life.

EFFICIENT OPERATION FACTORS TO SUPPORT SUSTAINABLE [D]-CSCL AUTHENTIC SCENARIOS THROUGH VIRTUAL WORLDS

From all above we can understand that virtual worlds can provide original activities that have usability and reporting on real life. They depict the complexity of everyday situations and provide a choice of different levels of difficulty or involvement of the learner. These problems should be investigated by apprentices after posing their own questions and relate it to their daily lives. The original work is generated, because their solution may cause the recognition and resolution of other adjacent problems. In addition, learners can look authentic work from different angles, using different sources, collaborate and reflect on, to distinguish those who have interdisciplinary work and arriving at different solutions or learning outcomes (Herrington et al., 2003).

This objective can be achieved by creating authentic learning environments, with the participation of all stakeholders will gradually lead to similar changes in the classroom. 3D virtual learning environments, such as virtual worlds can support authentic activities, which may have the educational value that can be studied intensively. Learning researchers have distilled the essence of the authentic learning experience down to 14 design elements, providing educators with a useful checklist that can be adapted to any subject matter domain. The satisfaction of the above issues with these advanced collaborative multi-user virtual environments, look forward to a more direct and dynamic contact with the student's educational materials. This is visible through the key factors undoubtedly can provide the CVEs for a more effective learning of distributed users by using PCs and Internet ([D]-CSCL). Such functions are:

1. **The 3D place as a "real-world" place:** A VW provides many authentic activities that match with the real-world tasks of professionals in practice as nearly as possible. Learning rises to the level of authenticity when it's relevant students to work actively with abstract concepts, facts, and formulae inside a realistic—and highly social—context mimicking "the ordinary practices of the [disciplinary] culture.

2. **Interactive collaborative applications:** Success is not achieved by an individual learner working alone. Authentic activities

make collaboration integral to the task, both within the course and in the real world.

3. **Metacognitive reflections:** Authentic activities enable learners to make choices and reflect on their learning, both individually and as a team or community. In a well-designed and organized virtual learning place, students use as a basic source of information on the Internet. However, due to the inherent problems of disorientation and "cognitive overload" that is often faced by users in a hypermedia environment, whether the free navigation and searching is enough to lead a learning procedure (Jonassen, 1991; Hammond & Allison, 1989), and the achievement of a lesson objective is currently doubtful (Romiszowski, 1990).

4. **Interdisciplinary perspective of learning contents:** One of the most that we must take seriously in this case is virtually content's relevance which is not confined to a single domain or subject matter specialization. Instead, authentic activities have consequences that extend beyond a particular discipline, encouraging students to adopt diverse roles and think in interdisciplinary terms. Appropriately, the search information from students initially limited to specific sources such sites have been identified and assessed by the teacher and then depending on the student's skills and goals activity seeking to expand to other sources on the Internet.

5. **Integrated assessment:** It is not merely summative in authentic activities but is woven seamlessly into the major task in a manner that reflects real-world evaluation processes. In any occasion assessment represents complex interactions across spatial and temporal scales, processes and activities. Managing uncertainty in integrated assessments can utilize models ranging from simple models linking large-scale processes, through models of intermediate complexity, to the complex, physically explicit representation of "Earth systems."

6. **Multiple sources and perspectives:** Obviously, authentic activities provide more opportunities for students to examine sources from a variety of theoretical and practical perspectives. Using a variety of resources, students require distinguishing relevant from irrelevant information in the process.

7. **Multiple interpretations and outcomes:** Rather than yielding a single correct answer obtained by the application of rules and procedures, authentic activities allow for diverse interpretations and competing solutions.

8. **Sharing frameworks and contexts:** The environment and its artifacts are shared by users, and the common knowledge of current and previous activities enhance user participation in organized activities.

9. **Providing clear means for situational awareness:** The awareness of a situation is a knowledge that is promoted through perceptual information gathered from the environment a specific place and time. For the awareness of a situation must be constantly updated on changes in the environment, therefore, knowledge is being generated from the exploration and interaction with the environment. Just briefly, users must know what is happening around them.

10. **Supporting negotiation and communication:** The transfer of necessary information is essential factor in fostering cooperation has to do with a specific goal achievement and cooperative with strengthening of social activities that support the current collaborative work.

11. **Providing flexibility and support multiple views:** This factor refers to the provision different aspects of a target or secondary target, or views tailored to serve user needs in different roles.

12. **Flexible interactive technologies for multiperson tasks:** The study of how people

work together using computer technology, addressing issues involving the use of email, the subject that includes an awareness of the actions of other users, video conferencing, chat systems and common real-time applications, as collaborative writing or planning.

13. **Augmented knowledge workshops:** An interdisciplinary field that includes computer science, economics, sociology and psychology. The survey is based on developing new theories and technologies to coordinate groups working together.

14. **Motivation and engagement:** As we report earlier, SL can be used as an innovative open-source authoring system scenarios based learning problem solving (problem-based) and decision-making possible, while controlling the impact they may have. 3D learning environments features make the learning procedure a greater extent than in corresponded 2D environments. The faithful representation of the reality and the enhance representation of spatial knowledge, the opportunities for experiential learning, the enhance motivation or teammates engagement in authentic activities and the facilitation of an effective collaborative-learning process are only some of them.

DESIGNING A "CYBERNETIC" MODEL (THEORETICAL-ACADEMIC PART)

The use of collaborative virtual environments can enhance the quality of education and achieving a more effective teaching in comparison with the traditional (Schutte, 1997). This development is particularly important when the learning environment can support different pedagogical approaches to issues concerning: (a) the following methods of teaching (especially in teamwork), (b) technical learning (Jigsaw, brain flowing etc.), and (c) multimedia resources (video, audio, text) to be used by students (with the teacher's association) to acquire knowledge. To be able more understanding of how can this be achieved through a didactic approach, it is required the adoption of an appropriate "teaching" model.

For virtual environment integration in education should be conducted several studies on pedagogical processes both to investigate the proper method of teaching, and the way out, to create a conceptual design framework combining theories of learning and pedagogical practices and forms the basis for application in such environments. A model that could be used as a basis for establishing the framework for evaluation of pedagogical view is the "cybernetic model" (Britain & Liber, 2004; Michailidou & Economides, 2003; Liber, 1999).

According to Britain & Liber (2004), an evaluation method of a virtual learning environment based on "cybernetic model", is reflected through the key features that "Viable System Model" (VSM) governs. This "model" contains the control and management of operational and organizational structures of systems, as it is suggested by the British theoretical Anthony Stafford Beer (1926-2002), who first got to the effective organization and governmental systems management (Beer, 1959). The main features of VSM permit effective action against the organizational complexity of natural and technical interactions that govern each system making it practicable (Kutsikos, 2007). The axes of VSM's structure, can interpret an "educational" approach, which determines specific key characteristics of our model and corresponding effectiveness of "cybernetic administration" development of teaching and learning components.

Practically, this "systemic" approach can provide the basis for practical implementation of the "cybernetic model", but with the essentials that VSM offers (Dickover, 1994). Still, is important to mention that VSM, which be used in this study, describes the mechanisms that must have held by any complex system as to remain "viable" (Achterbergh, et al., 2003). It is crucial to characterize a system as "sustainable," when it can maintain its original identification and simultaneously performing for the purpose, in which it was created in the dynamically changing environment in which it operates (Donalson, 1992). Additionally, it's pretty remarkable the concept of "sustainability" that is being achieved through two fundamental characteristics (Hull & Lio, 2006; Kaplan & Herring, 2000): a) *autonomy,* which refers to the degree of freedom in decision making and b) *adaptation,* which refers the ability of the system to assume new "ingredients" and release them. The basic key feature of the VSM is the modeling of a system, as a recurrent form of the same system (feedback), while the same is a subsystem of a larger (see Figure 6).

Therefore, issues of VSM's integration in virtual worlds should be involved with (Britain & Liber, 1999):

Negotiation: Firstly an e-learning program management unit (usually at the department level) needs to negotiate the available resources to the modules it is constructed from. The act of verbal and non-realized with broadcasters, in which people negotiate relationships, acts, agreements, etc. are part of each communication activity defined by the intentions of speakers/three-and achieve results. Among this prominent position it is held by the possibility of establishing cooperative frameworks and constructive properties where each student can express both its particularities in learning through the negotiation of knowledge with the knowledge of others. Virtual communities offer learning opportunities in the place and time as the student theoretically unlimited communication.

Coordination: The coordination and proper communication of a group condition are keys to success, namely high performance and long-term

Figure 6. The elaborated VSM, module level (source: Espejo & Harnden, 1989)

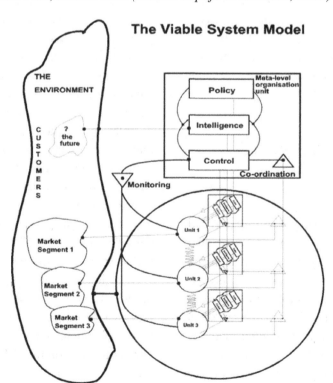

survival. It is offering support, information and knowledge in order to complete the mission (task) group, and the need for coordination comes from the interdependence of its members.

Monitoring: Monitoring is the regular observation and recording of activities taking place in a project or program. This is a routine procedure for collecting information on all aspects of the project and an easy way to check on how project activities are progressing. It is a systematic and deliberate observation which provides feedback prompt on the progress of a project program. Teachers will ensure that every moment you have the necessary information, the tools and resources in order work successfully in a productive environment.

Self-organization: In many institutions teachers talk continuously about their teaching, and learn from each other's experience as it takes place – they can help each other by teaching sessions, or through peer-observation, or by sharing resources with virtual tools to support this sort of self-organization between courses or modules.

Adaptation and balancing the needs of the present and the future: Any distance learning program must be constantly examining its set of modules, and considering whether and when new modules may be needed, based on changes in the knowledge domain, the needs of society, and the new resource capabilities (e.g. funding sources). In this situation, technology can and does play a large part in this, but usually not integrated with the VLE, where the needs for adaptation are expressed.

The above reason led us to identify an active effort to determine the development and presentation of a methodological framework that could be used as a basis for establishing a framework for evaluation of a pedagogical-organizational-technological point of view (Kolas & Stampe, 2004; Heiner et al., 2001; Clark & Maher, 2001) in this case would achieve with "Viable System Model" assistance.

CONSTRUCTING THE FRAMEWORK (PRACTICAL-TEACHING PART)

At this stage it is necessary to establish that formal teaching establishment of distributed users on Web-based technologies, requires participation and an organization of the student population and also "cybernetic" management. This kind of "management," looks first for activation of the "wholeness" of members (psychosomatic entity of each student) and also to better dimension of the communication (sensory-motor alarm, cognitive and verbal abilities/skills of each student), through discussions with the teacher and the other (Landon, 1999). Therefore, integration issues, such as the trading of knowledge resources, coordination, monitoring (by the teacher), individualized activity, self-organization of "nomads" of knowledge and their adaptation to the virtual environment, will be selected by training activities and hence valuation provided the educational value of each collaborative environment, which may be used for teaching.

In addition to various methodological approaches (Mason, 1998), we can say that "cybernetic model" - as a methodology for the evaluation of collaborative virtual learning environments - may be raising some questions. Some of them result from the successful integration of this method in the SL, i.e. a form of teaching that includes the acting subject (teacher and learners). Such an evaluation process can "produce" the acquiring educational values of a more complete form, in which users are asked to identify the tools provided by the virtual platform and allow dialogue, communication, interaction and action learning between users by principal purpose of knowledge acquisition (Crawley, 1999).

It's noteworthy that teacher's main objective during the e-learning process by using a virtual environment "converted" to "space-action" applications, should primarily be for student organization and knowledge acquisition by themselves. Even during drawing a lesson from a distance, within Second Life, it is almost always necessary in the organization process, management and implementation of educational practice, which may include one or more pedagogical principles and Learning Theories. Besides, the multiplication of cognitive research has fundamentally changed the "default" view on using of PCs, bringing forth the idea of "cybernetic approach of open environments" and the question that arises is: *"how can we construct a learning environment that takes into account student's unpredictable operation?"* (Bertrand, 1995, p. 103-104).

The teaching strategy that is proposed with the "cybernetic model," is related to the organizational structure of a learning environment, in accordance with VSM principles that is prescribed (Jackson, 2000; Forrester, 1994). This should primarily be based on managing the interactions among participants ("Law of the necessary diversity": *Ashby's law requisite variety*), as each team determines available channels of communication and interacts with the organizational structure and the available knowledge resources that are required for managing ("Managing Diversity": *Variety of Management*) (Ashby, 1956).

In our case, the "system's model," i.e. the virtual interface (data frame), is directly related to the actual user's environment (physical context). Hence the expressed relationship gives the ability for dynamically change of behavior in the "adaptable" operating environment through the interactions of sub-systems (human and technical resources) in different levels of feedback. A key issue that must be explored is the proper management of "action groups" that are generated during the delivery of courses.

The most appropriate organizational structure of teaching in a virtual world is to provide an easier management of interactions and communication channels between team members at the same levels as with their physical presence. With these data we believe that VSM can provide a support base for exploring a "training" framework, which would adjust SL's environment. This contribution can be used pedagogically, and contributes the

organizational management of the educational framework for action-based activities and interactions with the system, especially when the number of students is large (up to 30).

PROJECT DESIGN

The interaction that 3D VR offered, in general involves the coordination of knowledge, the psycho-motor and effective domain of students who articulate the relationship between "student-project." The data are instrumented in teaching completeness and efficiencies of learning are interactions, customization, the realism and the "open" learning environment. Investigations in the learning field are placed on the acquisition of knowledge within a system of interactions among individuals, social and material context. The acquisition of knowledge does not depend on the stimuli or the individual mental processes, but by a set of factors consistent with human and environment interaction (Steinkuehler & Williams, 2006; Koleva et al., 2000).

Indeed, the development that has brought the humans' cognitive performance, leading to improve the teaching plans and educational applications. Thus, we conclude that the use of such environments could support the "modern" Learning Theories, in which participants can create, edit and manipulate almost any form of digital information. Objects, processes and "residents" (avatars) of the virtual world are "elements" of an active and ready to manipulate their project. Actually, teamwork and creative learning that offered in virtual worlds, allowing teachers and students using computer technology in a productive collaborative state.

Taking into account the mention that occurs as a core of creating an institution-teaching framework, it should primarily be in the research field that involves:

1. Using potentially SL's functional characteristics (channels of communication between users, text editing tools, etc.), and also
2. Processing the e-learning "system," namely form:
   a. Strengthening the quality improvement of courses by using innovative methods, concept aiding the development course of instruction, when this involved a large number of students, and
   b. Understanding the organizational and operational structure of e-courses, with a parallel and efficient "action-group" management. We also know that from the outset designed, primarily Second Life targeted for users over 18 years old.

Therefore, it is natural for Higher Education to meet students and teachers need of that grade. Furthermore, the educational use of SL, "invite" trainee's users and teachers to cooperate in a coherent "open-access" world, with virtual objects, multiple options and approaches with a more constructive attitude. The use of computational interactive tools and applications that SL offers, contributes students to build individual or social knowledge in situations that are functional and purposeful, while developing and meta-cognitive consciousness.

The design, development and implementation of educational scenarios and activities by using this virtual environment is currently based on general pedagogical principles framework that are the result of concepts and are developed in recent years in the field of cognitive and social-cultural theories of learning. The main teaching/instructional activities to design learning scenarios and activities proposed to be related to the construction of exploratory roles (Soloway, 1990), supporting processes active construction of knowledge, developing a rich conceptual network (Genovese, 2003), take advantage of students prior knowledge, experience and intuitions (diSessa, 1995), devel-

oping a new strong relationship between student-teacher (Hoyles, 1999), and creating collaborative learning environments (Vergnaud, 1987).

REQUIREMENTS ANALYSIS

The claims and the description of the teaching approach with the assistance of VSM, co-shaped and renovated through to a theoretical framework, assessed the added functionality offered by the SL, along with those proposed by Pereira et al. (2000):

General requirements: (a) identify the outline and objective gain, (b) determinate actions and interactions between teacher and students to receive feedback, (c) review the activities of the student depending on the feedback received.

Special requirements: (a) *from student's part*: a sense of social space, increasing the interaction between teacher and students, (b) *from virtual communities part*: conversion-transformation of SL's environment on a social world, which will inhabit knowledge's field and its members will have the sense of "coexistence" for a reasonable period of time and gradually develop emotional bonds, thus forming "networks of human relationships" (c) *from Professor's part*: possibility of defining groups and modes of interaction, (d) *side of the transmission*: using meta data, simple and functional user interface, (e) *the part of the pedagogical-didactic*: creating a virtual learning place, which follows constructive principles of a social-educational approach and inter-changeable roles teacher-student, (f) *side of technology*: open source software, broadband connection (ADSL).

A "CYBERNETIC" PEDAGOGICAL APPROACH FOR MANAGING LEARNING ACTIVITIES IN SECOND LIFE

The Viable System Model (VSM) is a management tool for assessing the viability of an organization or business, namely the ability to meet its objectives and to adapt in constantly changing external environment. The VSM can highlight problematic areas in managing the organization and suggest actions to address them. The use of this model can, in an era where the increasing complexity and speed of the crisis makes known management theories increasingly obsolete, the VSM is an effective tool to directly improve the overall performance, objectives and adaptation organizations and people in the rapidly changing business environment. It combines international, successful implementation to organizations of all types and sizes, with the holistic scientific theory of Systemic Science and Cybernetics. The application and thus the contribution of the VSM can help an organization to:

- Recognize the signs which depend on the survival.
- Separate the functions by their management information of an organism.
- Optimize the control and coordination processes within the organization.
- Maximize the autonomy of the departments/parties without losing total control.
- Create a competitive advantage through a more efficient structure.

The benefits of adaptation in a virtual environment will help us to discover a large extent:

- Increase capacity of each virtual world to successfully meet the demands of users, who will over time be looking more and more effective applications for the understanding of learning (especially when distance).
- Eliminate any bureaucratic failures observed occasionally in person to learn.
- Discover opportunities to reduce costs through simpler, more effective management.

- Operating ranges to maximize effectiveness.
- Smooth internal procedures.
- More effective management of customers/suppliers.
- Developing resilience.

Our methodology is being developed and based on the Viable System Model, using the principles of the cybernetics science, which studied the human body as a perfect example of the organization that is able to adapt, to be autonomous and to survive. He concluded that all organizations irrespective of size (e.g. a man or machine) different types (e.g. private or public) must perform the following 5 key processes to survive:

1. Policy (Purpose, Values, Direction, Identity)
2. Intelligence (Research, Development and Custom)
3. Control (Cohesion, Synergy)
4. Coordination (Stability, Harmony functions)
5. Operation (Application, Implementation Outer Purpose)

The character of our methodology is both pedagogical and researching. Cybernetic e-Education, as they develop pedagogical thinking of teachers who will set up and back, thinking of their students. Research, since each step of evolution will take place, and there will be the subject of reflection to improve the design of the next. After, say, the total project will acquire the form of a "critical self-exploratory process" or a "research-action", with subjects acting teachers and students who will join the network.

The creation of such a network is necessary for two reasons.

1. First, because both the Distance Education and its use of [D-] CSCL projects in virtual worlds, animated by common pedagogical-didactic principles as:

a. Addressed issues that arise in the field of everyday life of students of a university community where our students experience events or situations that puzzle as to deeper causes, which are physical, biological, social, political and cultural,

b. Adopted, as shown by their key texts, the "collaborative team-teaching," active learning and an "interactive style" cognitive process and,

c. Oriented values in the sense of fulfillment of the terms and conditions from which the student will emerge as a free and a self-aware personality, able to express their expectations and to share with others in a context of mutual understanding and respect. In other words, geared to how it develops, the scope of the teaching act, the transition from the "I" in "me and the other ', i.e.' we 'and the' we 'in' us and others ", i.e. "all together."

2. Second, because, in our opinion, the common pedagogical principles discussed can be expressed, to test and mature in the Systemic Thinking and Systemic Methodologies created critically,

3. The aim of this work is to create a "cybernctic" methodology because in this way teachers and students are initially, then:

4. Be familiar with the tools Systemic thinking critically based methodologies, the educational artifacts (pedagogical models, e.g. scripts and textures),

5. Test their ability to utilize the new independent thinking-based tools of the dealing subject-matter,

6. Approach the subject-matter without analyzing the classical categories, nature and society but in social systems and conscience,

7. Highlight the curriculum of the University and describes in detail the alternative educational areas away from human interaction, where we learn to plan methodically, deliberately, freely, and, above all to have interactive expectations.

The type and use of the model depend on the approach to reality, which is adopted by the researcher. Thus, the models can be regarded as artifacts that can capture an existing "real" system, in order to explain and predict the likelihood of its development or direct it to them. However, they are regarded as artifacts that depict an aspect of our everyday reality in order to organize their thinking critically about it. In our case the models have a pedagogical character, are designed by the stakeholders in a situation, a phenomenon or an event that can take symbolic forms recognizable by participants in the process and form their own *"mutual visa-generated shapes of reality."*

Any formal establishment of a teaching process for distributed users ([D] -CSCL case), requires the participation and the "cybernetic" management plan of the student population. Learning management should be looking forward first to the activation of all current members (including the psycho-physical entity of students) and also the best communication aspect (sensory-motor, cognitive and verbal abilities/skills of each student), through the conversations with the teacher and other members. With this highly important meaning, we want to illustrate how the VSM could be adapted as an organizational-educational framework and as a result we suggest some processes that Second Life can perform, which will use as a pedagogical framework for evaluating functionality.

Meanwhile, this search will build on the adaptation that VSM offers, which consists the requirements and pedagogical principles governing on each "open" virtual learning environment. Through this process sought the evaluation of the collaborative virtual environment, which is a tedious task and should take account of modern Learning Theories, but also the variety of educational issues such as interactivity, adaptability, interaction and collaborative learning (Redfern & Naughton, 2002).

For this attempt we try to build a framework evaluation for SLs' pedagogical value, that takes into account: (a) the organizational context of teaching-based model of Beer (VSM: Viable System Model), which includes "cybernetic management" of the e-learning process between users and "medium" (SL), (b) the "support-ive" environment which governs activities and educational principles, including data from the theoretical framework, in accordance with earlier studies, which were based on assessment of SL as an alternative "tool" for e-learning courses. Through this process, we will try and assess the provided pedagogical value of SL. Thus the core of the *Methodological Framework* includes the procedure in Table 2.

CONCLUDING REMARKS

The modern covering difficulty in the field of educational research with the use of virtual worlds is definitely the future direction of distance learning. In this perspective, any 3D VR system must give us serious outcomes and also it should be defined as an ideal practical-teaching implementation framework. We should not forget that the challenge was not revealed by previous studies that are presented in the theoretical part, as the weight in these cases had fallen to the form and features acquired by the learning process in virtual environments, without reference to the organizational plan that should be followed.

In this work, we tried to highlight this observed research gap through the creation of a "cybernetic model" which has basic management principles of VSM and our definitely believe that it regards not only SL, but all three-dimensional learning "systems" which should assist teachers to remove the existing "technocratic" methodological concerns of producing "substantial" knowledge. The main

contribution of this act will make us understand whether the organizational structure of a virtual world, like SL, would be an important learning platform, which will offer support to:

1. Educational efforts for implementing innovative e-courses in a psycho-educational background that supports contemporary learning theories (see Constructivism, and Distributed or Situated Learning theories),
2. Fully aware of the beneficial functional characteristics of an "open" environment for action-based learning process is an "institution"-an organization- and "social"-a knowledge framework to underpin and implemented innovative teaching interventions,
3. Effective ways where students learn over their thoughts and actions through the management of "action groups."

In SL's case, the advantages that offer are located in "different" ways where:

1. Students can identify more easily through interactive tools (voice call, textual specifications, etc.) that is offered by the virtual platform, with other users,
2. Each student is able to contribute its own knowledge resources in the group, while monitored by the teacher, creating the same learning content (active/experiential learning),
3. Leads to easy customization and personalization of learning structure material which interact harmoniously and learning activities carried out during the evolution of the teaching act, and finally
4. The "open-access" virtual world of Second Life can become an *"incubator"* of knowledge for trainee's users where they collect and organize the appropriate informational material for their courses. This particular show that the virtual platform can accept

Table 2. Methodological framework procedure

Methodological framework valuation of pedagogic value of Second Life (Professor)	Teaching and learning field for activities in the virtual environment Second Life (Medium)
A. Negotiation Includes processes that concern the negotiation of knowledge resources among students and teacher. With this dialogue development, students may understand the value of using SL and as a result activating them "totality." **Use of tools:** Voice call, IM, chat text, note cards **Teaching principles** *A. Principle of interactivity* The ability to build a dialogue through the exchange of views of students must be respected by teachers and vice versa. The teacher should inform students of: (a) their activity part, (b) how to achieve educational goals on a particular issue and (c) what tasks must be performed. According to Gagné's reasoning, in the teaching process is necessary to set goals, which will be on par with students' capabilities that acquire after the teaching process (product of learning). The learning process can be achieved with various methods such as discovery, guided teaching, practice, repetition (or summary). *B. Supervisory Authority* The use of images, videos and audio that SL offers, enhance the multiple representation of information, while increasing the energy of "cognitive presence". *C. Principle of supply systematic knowledge* One of the key goals in education that offers a structured and systematic way for searching most important sources of knowledge. In this way students are introduced to the course content.	**Improving teaching action based on Social Constructivism** *Inform trainees for teaching scopes, methods and learning materials:* There should be an opportunity for dialogue and negotiation among members of the school community and also the available choice of knowledge resources within SL. The availability can be determined through group discussions and suggestions of the teacher. Students should be able to enroll in group's course grades, or design their own, so they can chat and exchange views within the framework that teacher set (Rappa et al., 2009). *Cognitive development through social interaction:* To become more effective the way of learning it should be linked to the concept of Vygotsky's ZEA (Zone of Proximal Development), i.e. there is a mediating function of the environment and people between them (progressive facilitation) for achieving the expected result, both academic and social life (support frame) (Weusijana et al., 2007).
B. Coordination Includes processes of coordination, teamwork, learning activities and sharing ideas ("brainstorming") through to all available tools that SL provides. **Teaching principles** *A. Principle of reference & interaction* The cooperation and interaction of social and material framework in line with the theory of *Distributed Learning,* includes the concept of "reference". This concept focuses on building personal dialogue and coordination of users' sharing knowledge resources. To achieve interactivity and complementary of these two concepts, according to Hollan et al. (2000), should become apparent three types of distribution: (a) the distribution of learning processes among members, (b) coordinating environmental or material structures and (c) the breakdown of the social and material framework should stress the inter-subjective shaping of meaning, which focuses on the interactions, mutual participation and mediation tools and resources dynamically changing on the SL's environment. *B. The principle of synergy and complementary* The principles of synergy and complementary of techno-social world and creative adaptation, actually can offer a "dynamic networked" collaborative learning context between users and environments. This is bound by the adults' willingness and ability of the continuous knowledge flow. The (original) integration of this knowledge, performances and experiences in the process of distance learning is in fact the acceptance of the mechanisms and tools involved in the cognitive process and acquisition of knowledge (Dabbagh, 2005).	**Improving teaching action based on Distributed Learning** *Designing collaborative learning conditions in the virtual environment:* The potential uses of SL lies in the possibility of developing cooperation mechanisms for the team. Essentially there must be social and material distribution of intelligence. The material may be based on: (a) use the environment for the execution of activities and (b) use of tools and artifacts (notes, prims). *Creation of a collaborative learning context:* Throughout the course process, the teacher should monitor students and encourage them to cooperate. Certainly in the course, there is the possibility of incorporating elements of SL inside in LMS (Learning Management System) for greater flexibility in applications (e.g. Moodle). Professors should support that process will connect students' feedback about their actions to achieve the objectives at each level of the learning structure (Kemp & Livingstone, 2009). *Ability for building exploratory roles:* Increased (cognitive or mental type) interaction with the user and not to promote the sense of autonomy may him in understanding the creation and construction of scientific knowledge. Nonetheless, the creation of a panel discussion among the members, through chat text (i.e. That is cognitive tools) that SL offers, will help members discover their real needs for better distribution of the organizational structure of the course through direct communication teacher-trainees (feedback prompt) (Jeffery & Collins, 2008).

continued on following page

Table 2. Continued

Methodological framework valuation of pedagogic value of Second Life (Professor)	Teaching and learning field for activities in the virtual environment Second Life (Medium)
C. Monitoring One of the most important pedagogical parameters is monitoring student progress from the teacher and as a result receiving the appropriate feedback to self-assess. Teacher role in this section will be facilitating and prescriptive (mediator). According to Vygotsky's thoughts, learning process leads directly to the development and teacher acts like "mediator" (Welk, 2006: para. 3). **Teaching principles** *A. The principle of incentives for active participation* Each student must be encouraged continuously during the learning process, to coordinate with others. Although the exploring concepts of self-support and self-evaluation of students will be informed for teachers. *B. The principle of using feedback* In any improper attempt by the students, for every "wrong" function, they must receive feedback. The student is informed of the unexpected occurrence of the reaction, noted the "where" and "why" of error, and guided by the directives, the accepted response. *C. Expression and support of complex and multi-level structure of cognitive schemas* The representations that students may build conceptually are formed into shapes and affect different parts. The conceptual schemas, which are complex cognitive constructions of each human being, should somehow emerge. Under this perspective, the interest will not be focused on building a representation of the concept, but in the way that different representations that can be linked together by setting up so more complex conceptual structures.	**Instructional activities based on: (a) of C. Rogers views & (b) Social-Constructivism theory** *Growing new dimension roles between students and teacher:* As it refers to the processing they must: (a) focus on direct control of the activities of the student by the teacher, (b) lead to a more effective communication and (c) in this case to better address problems that may arise, based on the cognitive needs instructional use of users (Macedo & Morgado, 2009). *Guiding lines of participatory learning:* The potential way that SL offers, for tele-transporting to places (universities, libraries, museums), may help both ineffective organizational structure and to develop the learning process. Each student, should be able to seek ways of solving a variety problems (e.g., multimedia content creation or restructuring of materials according to outline framework set by each team, etc.), under the supervision of professor. At this point likely to be the principle of gradual reduction in assistance from more experienced people, is called "assisted discovery" or use vouchers frameworks "decreasing guidance" (fading scaffolding). The role of the teacher in the "vygotskian" thinking field, attaches the great importance of the new dimension communication and mediation training as a "driver" of growth and learning (De Lucia, et al., 2009).
D. Personalization (Independent Learning) The system should enable permitting students to seek either databases or other sources, i.e. Learning by doing (J. Dewey). **Teaching principles** *A. Principle of individualized instruction* Based on individual characteristics and interests of students, the virtual system should perform simultaneous interactions between themselves and thus fine efforts of cooperation and socialization. *B. Principle of active learning and participation in learning* Within the context of teaching instrument should be designed activities that build on existing experience and knowledge of the student. *C. Principle of ownership* A primary factor in student participation is active prominent role in learning, in order to process and correlate alone elements.	**Instructional activities based on: (a) Gagne's views & (b) Constructivism theory** *Utilization students' prior knowledge and empirical experiences:* The default students' view, was formed during the prior experience and learning and it might affect their observations and interpretation (Gagne's "additive model") (Wang et al., 2009). Learners can through the search engine system equipment, looking for other members, and understanding the self-assess of their knowledge (learning material). *Supporting processes of knowledge in an active construction way:* A variety of cognitive processes can be used for the learning progress, including (Kim & Beak, 2010; Coksel-Canbek et al, 2009): (a) the focus of students with information relevant from the learning material, (b) the organization of information in conjunction with existing thoughts and finally (c) the "denaturation" of new representations, concepts and ideas into knowledge. In this case principles of constructive perception of learning, i.e. the active individual construction of thought, are formed in SL's interactive environment (Can, 2009).

continued on following page

recreational to offer a lot of in distance education. The possibility of even giving to save the file learning activities ("Database"), it can even feedback for future reuse, which demonstrates its pedagogical usefulness.

The overall conclusion can help us to qualitatively transform a virtual space in an innovative learning platform, which supports key factors for enhancing the maximum degree of "immersion experience" for users, such as engagement, inter-

Table 2. Continued

Methodological framework valuation of pedagogic value of Second Life (Professor)	Teaching and learning field for activities in the virtual environment Second Life (Medium)
E. Self-organization The "architecture" structure of the virtual environment should allow students to organize activities and interact with the system in the simulate world. This could be achieved through specific tools for organizing and managing various information channels. **Teaching principles** *A. Principle of interaction* Students should be able to interact with almost all applications or virtual objects. Also, they should be planning a careful action that is associated with their actions and serve the general purposes of learning. Considered important and the ability to "reconstruct" virtual materials or add their own. *B. Principle to provide a support framework for developing representations* The framework is necessary for the emergence of mental representations. This is naturally recognized as individual cognitive structures, are neither easily understood nor generally aware of those who have them. *C. Principle of interaction* Students may have opportunities for using system's tools that are provided to respond and interact with other members for better organizing and coordinating. Teachers' involvement - as a further factor - can broaden the action framework for learners and take advantages of the interactive environment.	**Improving teaching action based on Situated Learning** *Organize and enforcement actions by the trainee's users:* When students complete the process, they may be grouped to separate communication and interact with each other (construction and hospitality learning activities) to reach on the center – *"learning goal"* (Eliens et al., 2010). Key elements here are: (a) the importance of the framework that is linked to cognitive activities and (b) learning is the product of interaction that takes place through a process of cognitive apprenticeship, which is embedded in "communities of practice". The concept is based on the process of *"Legitimate Peripheral Participation"* (Esteves et al, 2008). *Develop framework for implementing learning activities:* The strategies of the framework that supports SL, concerning the possibility of building new representations based on already existing thoughts in multiple forms of representation with concrete and abstract objects and the existence of integrated tools (communication or creating multimedia objects) that can be used for learning. The construction of knowledge occurs through negotiation of meaning and consensus building, allowing and testing the validity of such knowledge. All members of the learning community are expected to learn, ready to engage in activities required and must be interested in the success of other members. The fact of organizing around a particular subject area and the practice of giving members a sense of common action and common identity. The interior of the community of practice allows interaction and negotiation of information through the acquisition of experience of its members from participating in the community and jump into a different regime from the periphery of the community toward the center (Vasileiou & Paraskeva, 2010).
F. Adjustment (Adaption) The "adaptive quantity" of the system, depending on teacher's requirements and learners' needs is the key selection criteria for creating distance learning programs. The components of "adaptation" that constitute the educational context of the activity (activity-centered approach), is a measure of guidance, and the creation of a learning community consists as well as an important reason for choosing SL's environment. **Teaching principles** *A. Modification of teaching materials* The ability to modify the teaching material can be offered by SL, through 3D modeling and multimedia tools. This may be an easier way to add or remove the learning material or meet adult users' needs and interests. The "exploratory nature" that's displayed through SL, gives an autonomous tendency, freedom of movement and discovery of knowledge, can end the process to assess progress by the teacher. *B. Authorities investigating the expression through multiple external representations direct manipulation* SL with so many available multimedia tools, allowing student expression, exploration of their ideas and perceptions through the use of multiple simultaneous proportional representation (virtual) and symbolic form (vision-acoustic mix). In this context, it provides users the ability to handle and connect external representations (images and symbols representing concepts), by adding and integrating new images or symbols.	**Improving teaching action based on Activity theory** *Implementation:* The ability of displaying multiple representations of concepts and phenomena, is considered as one of the most special advantages of three-dimensional systems. The notion of simulation phenomena and processes that are difficult to place in the school environment and the creation and study of "alternative worlds", is imperative. The use of multiple representations that SL offers may help adult users to illustrate concepts depending on each subject that they need (Robbins, 2007). *Developing a rich conceptual network of knowledge:* The construction of scientific knowledge requires creating representations at three levels: the macro-pilot, the individual-microscopic & symbolic-mathematical level and the connection of these representations (Mennecke et al., 2008). The assembly of an efficient lesson organizational structure, by feeding the database with deemed information it's necessary for students to understand: (a) the visual understanding of objects and (b) the optical-audible combination of data and information. The contribution of such an action would help other users (avatars) to "tele-transport" quickly and easily accessible for the educational process areas. This new figure represents the context and practice in which learning is accomplished, and includes, besides student population and teacher, mediation tools (multimedia tools in SL), the object of activity (possibly creating a database data), a community, rules and division of roles between the subject and the other members of the community. The unit of analysis is the whole context in which acts the subject and thus the framework is consolidated as an activity system (Schmeil & Eppler, 2008).

est, motivation, imagination and interaction with learning materials. Finally, we reached the main goal of our research in which we enrich the prior literature that deals with the "position" of virtual environments in education. Indeed, we bring up some very interesting data which give the usefulness of 3D environments for supporting learning communities and it should become an apt choice for learning via Internet (e-learning).

STRUCTURAL ELEMENTS FOR FUNCTIONAL FEATURES TO TEST DRIVEN-DEVELOPMENT WORKS IN THE FUTURE

The last decade of 21th century has undoubtedly watershed in the evolution of the Web 2.0. This development has allowed millions of people around the world to access, share, exchange and information. At the same time both public and private organizations have implemented electronic applications with high functionality and interaction, accessible to any user with the appropriate infrastructure to display. These changes significantly affected the daily lives of citizens. Thousands of websites run daily, providing electronic services and leading to the elimination of bureaucratic procedures. The advantages that could be offered by VSM in Public Management and e-Government, in particular states that are divided into two major categories: (a) increase productivity of the Public Administration and (b) produces better services for citizens and businesses. As for the first, it is achieved by reducing the cost of providing services, reducing the need to communicate with the public, with better coordination among agencies and use common standards, by making better use of information technologies and communications leads to reorganization of procedures and the possibility of new services and methods of operation, such as tele-working, tele-education and forums. The second is ensuring by reducing the time of service, costs for citizens and businesses, increase

security and data integrity services and the ability to provide services not discriminate on gender, color and age.

Moreover, an online service user need not know the function, structure and responsibilities of organizational units of the Administration involved with the service. Another important advantage of e-Government is the use of ICT to make government and services more accessible, more effective and more accountable to their citizens. This is achieved by:

- Providing a greater access to government information, development opportunities in rural and traditionally deprived areas;
- Promoting the public involvement in the interaction with public governmental bodies;
- Reducing the likelihood of corruption and profiteering by making all procedures more accessible and understandable to ordinary citizens.

On the other hand, more future works on the use of virtual worlds in e-Education are constantly multiplied exponentially and is expressed through the interest of many organizations to implement their action plans. Considering the fact that multinational companies and organizations use virtual environments for collaborative activities and facilitation of meetings in a multi-user (versatile) space, we can then easily understand their vital importance for the future and even the future of computing. We could not mention the effort made by IBM for the creation of its own virtual platform for the conference members of the company, called *Virtual Collaboration for Lotus Same Time (VCS)*, which allows simultaneous audio or textual communication and sharing slides and text writing into 3D objects. With these data, therefore the future research could focus its interest in:

1. What applications can be considered effective and appropriate for students not only of

Higher Education and other levels (K-12 & Secondary)?

2. Could virtual worlds to work in conjunction with applications that support social networks and Web 2.0, in order to meet the requirements of the new generation of users?
3. To continue the virtual environments seem to be the "Wild West" of cyberspace, as regards the younger and how we could penetrate such a "taboo"?

REFERENCES

Achterbergh, J., Beeres, R., & Vriens, D. (2003). Does the balanced score-card support organizational viability. *Kybernetes: The International Journal of Systems & Cybernetics*, *32*(9/10), 1387–1404. doi:10.1108/03684920310493314

Alvarez, M. (2006). *Second Life and school: The use of virtual world worlds in high education*. Trinity University, San Antonio, TX. Retrieved June 12, 2011, from http://www.trinity.edu/adelwich/worlds/articles/trinity.manny.alvarez.pdf

Arreguin, C. (2007). *Reports from the field: Second Life community convention 2007 education track summary*. Retrieved December 2, 2007, from http://www.holymeatballs.org/pdfs/VirtualWorldsforLearningRoadmap_012008.pdf

Ashby, W. R. (1956). *Introduction to cybernetics*. London, UK: Methuen.

Bailenson, J., & Yee, N. (2007). Virtual interpersonal touch: Haptic interaction and co-presence in collaborative virtual environments. *International Journal of Multimedia tools and Applications, 37*(5), 5-14.

Barab, S., & Duffy, T. (2000). From practice fields to communities of practice. In Jonassen, D., & Land, S. (Eds.), *Theoretical foundations of learning environments* (pp. 25–55). New Jersey: Lawrence Erlbaum Associates.

Barab, S., Thomas, M., Dodge, T., Carteaux, R., & Tuzun, H. (2005). Making learning fun: Quest Atlantis, a game without guns. *Educational Technology Research and Development*, *53*(1), 86–107. doi:10.1007/BF02504859

Bates, A., & Poole, G. (2003). *Effective teaching with technology in higher education*. San Francisco, CA: Jossey Bass.

Beer, S. (1959). *Cybernetic and management*. London, UK: English Universities Press.

Beer, S. (1972). *Brain of the firm*. London, UK: Allen Lane, The Penguin Press.

Beer, S. (1979). *The heart of enterprise*. London, UK: John Wiley.

Bertrand, Y. (2005). *Contemporary theories and practice in education* (2nd ed.). Madison, WI: Atwood Publishing.

Bigge, M., & Shermis, S. (1992). *Learning theories for teachers*. Harper Collins.

Bignell, S., & Parson, V. (2010). *Best practicing in virtual worlds: A guide using problem-based learning in Second Life*. Universities Derky & Aston and Higher Education Academy Psychology Network.

Boellstorff, T. (2008). *Coming of age in Second Life*. Princeton, NJ: Princeton University Press.

Boulos, M., Hetherington, L., & Wheeler, S. (2007). Second Life: An overview of the potential of 3-D virtual worlds in medical and health education. *Health Information and Libraries Journal*, *24*(4), 233–245. doi:10.1111/j.1471-1842.2007.00733.x

Bovy, R. C. (1981). Successful instructional methods: A cognitive information processing approach. *Educational Communications and Technology Journal*, *29*(4), 203–217.

Bricken, W. (1990). *Learning in virtual reality.* Technical report No. HITL-M-90-5, University of Washington.

Briggs, J. (1977). *Instructional design: Principles and applications.* Educational Technologies Publications.

Britain, S., & Liber, O. (1999). *A framework for pedagogical evaluation of virtual learning environments.* JTAP, JISC Technology Applications, Report 41. Retrieved from http://www.leeds.ac.uk/educol/documents/00001237.html

Broaddribb, S., & Carter, C. (2009). Using Second Life in human resource development. *British Journal of Educational Technology, 40*(3), 547–550. doi:10.1111/j.1467-8535.2009.00950.x

Bronack, S., Sanders, R., Cheney, A., Riedl, R., Tashner, J., & Matzen, N. (2008). Presence pedagogy: Teaching and learning in 3D virtual immersive world. *International Journal of Teaching and Learning in Higher Education, 20*(1), 59–69.

Bruckman, A., & Bandlow, A. (2002). HCI for kids. In Jacko, J., & Sears, A. (Eds.), *The human-computer interaction handbook: Fundamentals, evolving technologies, and emerging applications.* Lawrence Erlbaum and Associates.

Bruckman, A. S. (1997). *MOOSE Crossing: Construction, community, and learning in a networked virtual world for kids.* Unpublished Doctoral Dissertation, Massachusetts.

Bull, G., & Kajder, S. (2004). Tapped in. *Learning and Leading with Technology, 31*(5), 34–37.

Burton, J. K., Niles, J. A., Lalik, R. M., & Reed, M. W. (1986). Cognitive capacity engagement during and following interspersed mathernagenic questions. *Journal of Educational Psychology, 78*(2), 147–152. doi:10.1037/0022-0663.78.2.147

Callaghan, M. J., McCusker, K., Lopez Losada, J., Harkin, J. G., & Wilson, S. (2009). Engineering education island: Teaching engineering in virtual worlds. *ITALICS, 8*(3). Retrieved June, 2011, from http://www.ics.hearacademy.ac.uk/italics/download_php?file=italics/vol8iss3/pdf/italicsVol8Iss3Nov2009Paper01.pdf

Callahan, R. E. (1962). *Education and the cult of efficiency.* Chicago, IL: University of Chicago Press.

Can, T. (2009). Learning & teaching languages online: A constructivist approach. *Novitas Royal, 3*(1), 60–74.

Cannon, W. (1932). *The wisdom and the body.* New York, NY: Nerton.

Churchill, E., Snowdon, D., & Munro, A. (2001). Collaborative virtual environments: Digital places and spaces for interaction. In Churchill, E. F., Snowdon, D. N., & Munro, A. J. (Eds.), *Collaborative virtual environments digital places and spaces for interaction* (pp. 3–17). London, UK: Springer-Verlag Publisher.

Clarke, J., Dede, C., Ketelhut, D. J., & Nelson, B. (2006). A design-based research strategy to promote scalability for educational innovations. *Educational Technology, 46*(3), 27–36.

Clarke, J., Dede, C., Ketelhut, D. J., & Nelson, B. (2006). A design-based research strategy to promote scalability for educational innovations. *Educational Technology, 46*(3), 27–36.

Clarke, S., & Maher, M. (2001). *The role of place in designining a learner centered virtual learning enviroment.* Presentation from Computer Aided Architectural Design (CAAD). Retrieved April 20, 2008, from http://web.arch.usyd.edu.au/-mary/Pubs/2001pdf/CF2001.pdf

Cohen, K. (2006). *Second Life offers students a virtually real education.* The Phoenix Media/Communications Group. Retrieved April 20, 2008, from http://thephoenix.com/Article.aspx?id=20561&page=1

Coksel-Canbek, N., Mauromati, M., Makridou-Bousiou, D., & Demiray, U. (2009). *Lifelong learning through Second Life: Current trends, potentials and limitations.* Retrieved 12, June, 2011, from http://academia.edu.documents.s3.amazonaws.com/847924/Lifelong_learning_through_Second_Life.pdf

Cole, M., & Engestrom, Y. (1993). A cultural-historical approach to distributed cognition. In Salomon, G. (Ed.), *Distributed cognitions: Psychological and educational considerations.* New York, NY: Cambridge University Press.

Crawley, F. (1999). *16.882J: Systems architecture.* (Class notes). Cambridge, MA: MIT graduate course.

Crawley, J. N. (1999). Behavioural phenotyping of transgenic and knockout mice: Experimental design and evaluation of general health, sensory functions, motor abilities, and specific behavioural tests. *Brain Research, 835,* 18–26. doi:10.1016/S0006-8993(98)01258-X

dc Freitas, S. (2008). *Serious virtual worlds: A scoping study.* Bristol, UK: Joint Information Systems Committee. Retrieved May 24, 2010, from www.jisc.ac.uk/publications/publications/seriousvirtualworldsreport.aspx.

de Freitas, S., Harrison, I., Magoulas, G., Mee, A., Mohamad, F., & Oliver, M. (2006). The development of a system for supporting the lifelong learner. *British Journal of Educational Technology, Special Issue, Collaborative E-Support for Lifelong Learning, 37*(6), 867-880.

De Lucia, A., Francese, R., Passero, A., & Tortora, G. (2009). Development & evaluation of a virtual campus on Second life: The case of second DMI. *Computers & Education, 52,* 220–233.

De Lucia, F. R., Passero, I., & Tortora, G. (2009). Second Life technological transfer to companies: The case study of the CC ICT sub centre. *Journal of E-Learning & Knowledge Society, 5*(3), 23–32.

Dede, C. (2002). *No cliché left behind: Why education policy is not like the movies.* NCREL National Educational Technology Conference.

Dewey, J. (1933). *How we think: A restatement of the relation of reflective thinking to the educative process.* Boston, MA: D. C. Heath. Brilliant.

Di Sessa, A. (1995). Epistemology and systems design. In diSessa, A., & Hoyles, C. (Eds.), *Computers and Exploratory Learning* (pp. 15–29). Springer Verlag. doi:10.1007/978-3-642-57799-4_2

Dick, W., & Cary, L. (1990). *The systematic design of instruction.* Harper Collins.

Dickover, N. (1994). Reflection-in-action: Modeling a specific organization through the viable system model. *Journal of Systemic Practice & Action Research, 7*(1), 43–62.

Dieterle, E., & Clark, J. (2006). *Multi-user environments for teaching and learning.* Retrieved June 12, 2011, from http://64.94.241.248/rivercityproject/documents/MUVE-for-TandL-Dieterle-Clarke.pdf

Dillenbourg, P. (1999). What do you mean by collaborative learning? In Dillenbourg, P. (Ed.), *Collaborative-learning: Cognitive and computational approaches.* Oxford, UK: Elsevier.

Dillenbourg, P. (2008). Integrating technologies into educational ecosystems. *Distance Education, 29*(2), 127–140. doi:10.1080/01587910802154939

Donaldson, R. E. (1992). Cybernetics and human knowing: One possible prolegomenon. *Cybernetics & Human Knowing, 1*(2/3), 11–13.

Driver, R. (1988). Theory into practice II: A constructivist approach to curriculum development. In Fensham, P. (Ed.), *Development and dilemmas in science education* (pp. 133–149). London, UK: The Falmer Press.

Dunn, R., Szapkiw, A., Holder, D., & Hodgson, D. (2010). Of student teachers and avatars: Working towards an effective model for geographically distributed learning communities of pre-service educators using virtual worlds. In D. Gibson & B. Dodge (Eds.), *Proceedings of Society for Information Technology & Teacher Education International Conference 2010* (pp. 423-427). Chesapeake, VA: AACE.

Earl, C.-M. (2005). Peace building and human security: A constructivist perspective. *International Journal of Peace Studies, 10*(1), 69–86.

Edmonds, G. S., Branch, R. C., & Mukherjee, P. (1994). A conceptual framework for comparing instructional design models. *Educational Research and Technology, 42*(2), 55–72. doi:10.1007/BF02298055

Elliott, J. L. (2005). *AquaMOOSE 3D: A constructionist approach to math learning motivated by artistic expression.* Unpublished Doctoral Dissertation, Georgia Institute of Technology, Atlanta, GA.

Espejo, R., & Harnden, R. (1989). *The viable system model.* New York, NY: John Wiley & Sons.

Esteves, M., Antunes, R., Fonceca, B., Morgado, L., & Martins, P. (2008). Lecture Notes in Computer Science: *Vol. 5411. Using Second Life in programming's communities of practice. Groupware: Design, Implementation, and Use* (pp. 99–106).

Esteves, M., Fonsecaa, B., Morgado, L., & Martins, P. (2009). Using Second Life for problem-based learning in computer science programming. *Journal of Virtual Worlds Research, 2*(1).

Forrester, J. (1994). Policies, decisions and information sources for modeling. In Morecroft, J., & Sterman, J. (Eds.), *Modeling for learning organizations.* Portland, OR: Productivity.

Fox, J., Bailenson, J., & Binney, J. (2009). Virtual experiences, physical behaviors: The effect of presence on imitation of an eating avatar. *Presence (Cambridge, Mass.), 18*(4), 294–303. doi:10.1162/pres.18.4.294

Gagné, R. M., Briggs, L. J., & Wager, W. W. (1988). *Principles of instructional design.* New York, NY: Holt, Rinehart and Winston.

Gajendra, S., Sun, W., & Ye, Q. (2010). Second Life: A story of communication tool in social networking and business. *Information Teaching Journal, 9*(3), 524–534. doi:10.3923/itj.2010.524.534

Gardiner, M., Scott, J., & Horan, B. (2008). Reflections on the use of Project Wonderland as a mixed-reality environment for teaching and learning. *Researching Learning in Virtual Environments International Conference Proceedings,* The Open University, UK.

Gazzard, A. (2009). Teleporters, tunnels & time: Understanding warp devices in videogames. *Proceedings of the Digital Games Research Association* (DiGRA).

Gee, J. P. (2003). *What video games have to teach us about learning and literacy.* New York, NY: Palgrave Macmillan. doi:10.1145/950566.950595

Genovese, J. (2003). *Piaget, pedagogy & evolutionary psychology.* Retrieved May 24, 2010, from http://www.epjournal.net/filestore/ep01127137.pdf.

Hamat, A., & Amin-Embi, M. (2010). Constructivism in the design of online learning tools. *European Journal of Educational Studies*, *2*(3), 237–246.

Hammond, N., & Allison, L. (1989). Extending hypertext for learning: An investigation of access and guidance tools. In Sutcliffe, A., & Macaulay, L. (Eds.), *People and Computers V* (pp. 293–304). Cambridge, UK: Cambridge University Press.

Hand, B., & Treagust, D. (1995). Development of a constructivist model for teacher inservice. *Australian Journal of Teacher Education*, *20*(2), 28–29.

Haycock, K., & Kemp, J. (2008). Immersive learning environments in parallel universes: Learning through Second Life. *School Libraries Worldwide*, *14*(2), 89–97.

Heiner, M., Schneckenberg, D., & Wilt, J. (2001). *Online pedagogy – Innovative teaching and learning strategies in ICT-environments*. Workpackage 1, Working group 7/8 Pedagogy, 3453/ 001-001 EDU-ELEARN. Retrieved May 2, 2011, from http://www.cevu.org/reports/docs/WP1_WG7_8BP.pdf

Henri, F. (1994). Distance learning and computer-mediated communication: Interactive, quasi- interactive or monologue? In O'Malley, C. (Ed.), *Computer supported collaborative learning*. Berlin, Germany: Springer-Verlag.

Herring, C., & Kaplan, S. (2000). Viable systems: The control paradigm for software architecture revisited. *ASWEC '00: Proceedings of the 2000 Australian Software Engineering Conference*, (p. 97). IEEE Computer Society.

Herrington, J., Oliver, R., & Reeves, T. C. (2003). Patterns of engagement in authentic online learning environments. *Australian Journal of Educational Technology*, *19*(1), 59–71.

Hildreth, P., Kimble, C., & Wright, P. (1998). Computer mediated communications and international communities of practice. [The Netherlands: Erasmus.]. *Proceedings of Ethicomp*, *98*, 275–286.

Howe, C., & Mercer, N. (2007). *The primary review: Research survey 2/1b, children's social development, peer interaction and classroom learning*. Cambridge University.

Hughes, C., & Moshell, J. (1997). Shared virtual worlds for education: The ExploreNet experiment. *Multimedia Systems*, *5*(2), 145–154. doi:10.1007/s005300050050

Hull, C. E., & Lio, B. H. (2006). Innovation in non-profit and for-profit organizations: Visionary, strategic, and financial considerations. *Journal of Change Management*, *6*(1), 53–65. doi:10.1080/14697010500523418

Ibáñez, M. B., García, J. J., Galán, S., Maroto, D., Morillo, D., & Kloos, C. D. (2011). Design and implementation of a 3D multi-user virtual world for language learning. *Journal of Educational Technology & Society*, *14*(4), 2–10.

Jackson, M. (2000). *Systems approaches to management* (pp. 69-71, 272-279). New York, NY: Kluwer Academic.

Jarmon, L., Keating, E., & Toprac, P. (2008). Examining the societal impacts of nanotechnology through simulation: Nano scenario. *Simulation & Gaming*, *39*(2), 168–181. doi:10.1177/1046878107305610

Jarmon, L., Traphagan, T., & Mayrath, M. (2008). Understanding project-based learning in Second Life with a pedagogy, training, and assessment trio. *Educational Media International*, *45*(3), 157–176. doi:10.1080/09523980802283889

Jarvilehto, T. (1999). The theory of the organism environment system III: Role of effect influences on receptors in the formation of knowledge. *Integrative Psychological & Behavioral Science*, *34*(2), 90–100. doi:10.1007/BF02688715

Johnson, A., Moher, T., Ohlsson, S., & Gillingham, M. (1999). The Round Earth Project – Collaborative VR for conceptual learning. *IEEE Computer Graphics and Applications, 19*(6), 60–69. doi:10.1109/38.799741

Johnson, A., Roussos, M., Leigh, J., Barnes, C., Vasilakis, C., & Moher, T. (1998). The NICE project: Learning together in a virtual world. In *Proceedings of IEEE Virtual Reality Annual International Symposium* (pp. 176-183). Albuquerque, USA.

Johnson, D. W., & Johnson, R. T. (1996). Cooperation and the use of technology. In Jonassen, D. (Ed.), *Handbook of research for educational communications and technology* (pp. 1017–1044). New York, NY: Macmillan.

Jonassen, D., & Rohrer-Murphy, L. (1999). Activity theory as a framework for designing constructivist learning environments. *Educational Technology Research and Development, 47*(1), 61–79. doi:10.1007/BF02299477

Jonassen, D. H. (1991). Objectivism versus constructivism: Do we need a new philosophical paradigm? *Educational Technology Research and Development, 39*(3), 5–14. doi:10.1007/BF02296434

Kafai, Y. B. (2006). Playing and making games for learning: Instructionist and constructionist perspectives for game studies. *Games and Culture, 1*(1), 36–40. doi:10.1177/1555412005281767

Kallonis, P., & Sampson, D. (2010). Implementing 3D virtual classroom simulation for teachers' continuing professional development. *Proceedings of the 18th International Conference on Computers in Education*. Putrajaya, Malaysia: Asia-Pacific Society for Computers in Education.

Kaput, J., & Roschelle, J. (2000, October). *Shifting representational infrastructures and reconstituting content to democratize access to the math of change & variation: Impacts on cognition, curriculum, learning and teaching.* Paper presented at the workshop to Integrate Computer-based Modeling & Scientific Visualization into K-12 Teacher Education Programs, Ballston, VA.

Kemp, J., & Livingstone, D. (2009). *Putting a Second Life "metaverse" skin on learning management systems.* Retrieved 12, June, 2011, from: http://www.sloodle.com/whitpaper.pdf

Kim, B. K., & Beak, Y. (2010). Exploring ideas and possibilities of second life as an advanced elearning environment. In Hao Yang, H., & Yen Yuen, S. C. (Eds.), *Handbook of research on practices and outcomes in e-learning: Issues and trends* (pp. 165–181). Hershey, PA: Information Science Reference.

Knowles, M. (1984b). *Andragogy in action. Applying modern principles of adult education.* San Francisco, CA: Jossey-Bass.

Kolas, L., & Stampe, A. (2004). *Implementing delivery methods by using pedagogical design patterns.* Retrieved 29 May, 2011, from www2.tisip.no/E-LEN/papers/EDMEDIA/Symposia-NTNU.pdf

Koleva, B. N., Schnadelbach, H. M., Benford, S. D., & Greenhalgh, C. M. (2000). Developing mixed reality boundaries. In *Proceedings of Designing Augmented Reality Environments* (DARE 2000) (pp.155–157). Elsinore, Denmark.

Koster, R. (2004). *A virtual world by any other name?* [Msg 21]. Message posted to http://terranova.blogs.com/terra_nova/2004/06/a_virtual_world.html

Kozulin, A. (1999). The concept of activity in Soviet psychology: Vygotsky, his disciples and critics. In Lloyd, P., & Fernyhough, C. (Eds.), *Lev Vygotsky- Critical assessments: Vygotsky's theory* (*Vol. I*, pp. 179–202). New York, NY: Routledge.

Kutsikos, K., & Makropoulos, D. (2006). Distribution-collaboration networks (DCN): A network-based infrastructure for e-government services. *International Journal of Applied Systemic Studies, 1*, 1.

Land, S., & Hannafin, M. (2000). Student-centered learning environments. In Jonassen, D., & Land, S. (Eds.), *Theoretical foundations of learning environments* (pp. 1–23). Lawrence Erebaum Associates.

Landon, B. (1999). *Online educational delivery applications: A web tool for comparative analysis.* Retrieved June 12, 2011, from http://www.ctt.bc.ca/landonline/index.html

Lave, J., & Wenger, E. (1991). *Situated leaning: Legitimate peripheral participation.* Cambridge, UK: Cambridge University Press. doi:10.1017/CBO9780511815355

Leontiev, A. N. (1978). *Activity, consciousness and personality.* Prentice-Hall.

Lesser, E., & Prusak, L. (1999). *Communities of practice, social capital and organizational knowledge.* Retrieved January 15, 2010, from http://www.providersedge.com/docs/km_articles/Cop_-_Social_Capital_-_Org_K.pdf

Liber, O. (1998). Structuring institutions to exploit learning technologies: A cybernetic model. *Association for Learning Technology Journal, 6*(1), 13–18. doi:10.1080/0968776980060103

Liber, O. (1999). *A pedagogical framework for the evaluation of virtual learning environments.* Bangor, University of Wales. Retrieved January 15, 2010, from http://www.jtap.ac.uk

Liber, O. (2004). *A framework for the pedagogical evaluation of e-learning environment.* Retrieved January 15, 2010, from http://www.pgce.seton.ac.uk/IT/School_ICT/VLEusage/VLEpedagogy.pdf

Lin, B., & Hsieh, C. (2001). Web-based teaching and learner control: a research view. *Computers & Education, 37*, 377–386.Macedo, A., & Morgado, L. (2009). *Learning to teach in Second Life.* Retrieved 15 January, 2010, from http://www.eden-online.org/contents/conferences/OCRC's/Porto/AM_LM.pdf

Maher, M., & Bilda, G. (2006). Studying design behavior in collaborative virtual environments. In R. N. Pikaar, A. P. Komihgsreld, & J. M. Settels (Eds.), *Proceedings of 16th World Congress on Ergonomics* (IEA 2006 Congress). Maastricht, The Netherlands: Elsevier. Retrieved 15 January, 2010, from http://www.web.arch.usyd.edu.au/-mary/Pubs/2006pdf/Maher-1248.pdf

Manninen, T. (2000). Interaction in networked virtual environments as communicative action - social theory and multi-player games. In *Proceedings of CRIWG2000 Workshop*, October 18-20, Madeira, Portugal, IEEE Computer Society Press.

Mason, R., & Rennie, F. (2008). *E-learning and social networking handbook: Recourses for higher education.* New York, NY: Routledge.

Mayrath, M., Sanchez, J., Traphagan, T., Heikes, J., & Trivedi, A. (2007). Using Second Life in an English course: Designing class activities to address learning objectives. In C. Montgomerie & J. Seale (Eds.), *Proceedings of World Conference on Educational Multimedia, Hypermedia and Telecommunications 2007* (pp. 4219-4224). Chesapeake, VA: AACE.

McConnell, D. (1994). *Implementing computer supported cooperative learning*. London, UK: Kogan Page.

McGrenere, J. L. (1996). *Design: Educational electronic multi-player games. A Literature Review*. Department of Computer Science, The University of British Columbia.

Meira, L. (1998). Making sense of instructional devices: The emergence of transparency in mathematical activity. *Journal for Research in Mathematics Education*, *29*(2), 121–142. doi:10.2307/749895

Mennecke, B., Triplett, J., Hassall, L., Heer, R., & Jordan-Conde, Z. (2008). *Embodied social presence theory*. Retrieved January 15, 2010, from http://www.papers.ssrn.com/abstract=1286281

Metrick, S., & Epstein, A. (1999). *Emerging technologies for active learning, part 1: Multi- user virtual environments*. LNT Perspectives. Retrieved 12, June, 2011, from http://www2.edc.org/LNT/news/Issue10/feature3a.htm

Miao, Y., Pinkwart, N., & Hoppe, H. U. (2007). A collaborative virtual environment for situated learning of car driving. *International Journal on Advanced Technology for Learning*, *3*(4), 233–240.

Michailidou, A., & Economides, A. A. (2003). E learn: Towards a collaborative educational virtual environment. *Journal of Information Technology Education*, *2*, 131–152.

Mon, L. (2009). Questions and answers in a virtual world: Educators and librarians as information providers in Second Life. *Journal of Virtual Worlds Research*, *2*(1).

Nemirovsky, R., Tierney, C., & Wright, T. (1998). Body motion and graphing. *Cognition and Instruction*, *16*(2), 119–172. doi:10.1207/s1532690xci1602_1

Nicosia, L. (2008). *Adolescent literature and Second Life: Teaching young adult texts in the digital world. New literacies: A professional development wiki for educators. Improving Teacher Quality Project (ITQP)*. Federally Funded Grant.

Nie, M., Roush, P., & Wheeler, M. (2010). Second Life for digital photography: An exploratory study. *Contemporary Educational Technology*, *1*(3), 267-280.

Okada, M., Yamada, A., Tarumi, H., Yoshida, M., & Moriya, K. (2003). DigitalEE II: RV-augmented interface design for networked collaborative environmental learning. In *Proceedings of the International Conference on Computer Support for Collaborative Learning* (pp. 265-274). Illinois, Chicago.

O'Loughlin, M. (1992). Rethinking science education: Beyond Piagetian constructivism toward a socio-cultural model of teaching and learning. *Journal of Research in Science Teaching*, *29*, 791–820. doi:10.1002/tea.3660290805

Oliveira, M., Mortensen, J., Jordan, J., Steed, A., & Slater, M. (2003). Considerations in the design of virtual environment systems: A case study. *Proceedings 2nd International Conference on Application and Development of Computer Games*, Hong Kong, January 2003. Retrieved 15 January, 2010, from http://www.cs.ucl.ac.uk/research/w/Dive

Ott, D. (1999). *Collaboration dans un environnement virtuel 3D: Influence de la distance à l'objet référencé et du "view awareness" sur la résolution d'une tâche de "grounding". Travail de mémoire pour l'obtention du Diplôme "Sciences et Technologie de l'Apprentissage et de la Formation".* Université de Genève Faculté de Psychologie et des Sciences de l'Education.

Papert, S., & Resnick, M. (1995). *Technological fluency and the representation of knowledge. Proposal to the National Science Foundation.* MIT Media Laboratory.

Peachey, A., & Herman, C. (2011). Presence for professional development: Students in the virtual world. *Learning Technology, 13*(4), 11–14.

Pellas, N. (2010). *Using CVEs (collaborative virtual environments) in K-12 education.* Virtual Worlds - Best Practices in Education. 1ˢᵗ International Conference in Second Life.

Pellas, N. (2011). *Distance learning in the virtual world of Second Life.* Athens, Greece: Free Publishing. (In Greek)

Pellas, N. (2012). Towards a beneficial formalization of cyber entities' interactions during the e-learning process in the virtual world of "Second Life". In Renna, P. (Ed.), *Production and manufacturing system management: Coordination approaches and multi-site planning.* Hershey, PA: IGI Global.

Peña, J., McGlone, M., Jarmon, L., & Sanchez, J. (2009, November). *The influence of visual stereotypes and rules on language use in virtual environments.* Paper to be presented at the annual meeting of the National Communication Association.

Pereira, M., Harris, A., Duncan Davidson, R., & Niven, J. (2000). *Building a virtual learning space for C&IT staff development.* Centre for Open and Distance Learning. The Robert Gordon University. Paper presented at the European Conference on Educational Research, Edinburgh. Retrieved 15 January, 2010, from http://www.leeds.ac.uk/educol/documents/00001651.html

Piaget, J. (1970b). *Structuralism.* New York, NY: Basic Books.

Piaget, J. (1971c). *Genetic epistemology.* New York, NY: Harper & Row.

Piaget, J. (1985). *The equilibration of cognitive structures: The central problem of intellectual development.* Chicago, IL: University of Chicago Press.

Poole, M. (2008). Blue skies: Education in Second Life. *Christian Perspectives in Education, 1*(2). Retrieved 15 January, 2010, from http://digitalcommons.liberty.edu/cpe/vol1/iss2/4

Prasolova-Førland, E., Sourin, A., & Sourina, O. (2006). Cyber campuses: Design issues and future directions. *The Visual Computer, 22*(12), 1015–1028. doi:10.1007/s00371-006-0042-2

Rappa, N., Yip, D., & Baey, S. (2009). The role of teacher, student & ICT in enhancing student engagement in multi-user environments. *British Journal of Educational Technology, 40*(1), 61–69. doi:10.1111/j.1467-8535.2007.00798.x

Read, S., Miller, L., Appleby, P., Nwosu, M., Reynaldo, S., Lauren, A., & Putcha, A. (2006). Socially optimized learning in a virtual environment: Reducing risky sexual behavior among men who have sex with men. *Journal of Human Communication Research, 32*(1), 1–34. doi:10.1111/j.1468-2958.2006.00001.x

Redfern, S., & Naughton, N. (2002). Collaborative virtual environments to support communication and community in internet-based distance education. *Journal of Information Technology Education*, *1*(3), 201–211.

Ritter-Guth, B., & Nicosia, L. Pasteur, E. (2008). Literature alive! *EDUCAUSE Review, 43*(5). Retrieved 3 December, 2010, from http://www.educause.edu/educause+review/educausereviewmagazinevolume43/literaturealive/163184

Robbins, S. (2007). A futurist's view of Second Life education: A developing taxonomy of dynamic spaces *Second Life Education Workshop 2007: Part of the Second Life Community Conversation* (pp. 27-33). Chicago, IL: Hilton.

Romiszowski, A. (1974). *Selection and use of instructional media*. London, UK: Kogan Page.

Romiszowski, A. J. (1990). The hypertext/hypermedia solution—But what is exactly the problem? In Jonassen, D. H., & Mandl, H. (Eds.), *Designing hypermedia for learning* (pp. 321–354). Heidelberg, Germany: Springer. doi:10.1007/978-3-642-75945-1_19

Rothwell, W., & Katanas, C. (1998). *Mastering the instructional design process: A systemic approach*. San Francisco, CA: Jossey Bass Publishers.

Rotmans, J., & Rothman, D. (Eds.). (2003). *Scaling issues in integrated assessment*. Lisse, The Netherlands: Swets & Zeitlinger.

Rufer-Bach, K. (2009). *The Second Life grid*. Canada: Wiley Publishing, Inc.

Sajadi, S., & Khan, T. (2011). An evaluation of constructivist approaches to eLearning for learners with ADHD: Development of a constructivist pedagogy for special needs. *European, Mediterranean & Middle Eastern Conference on Information Systems* (pp. 656-671). Athens, Greece.

Salomon, G. (1995). No distribution without individual's cognition: A dynamic interactional view. In *Distributed cognitions: Psychological and educational considerations* (pp. 111–137). New York, NY: Cambridge University Press.

Sanchez, J. (2007a). A socio-technical analysis of second life in an undergraduate English course. In C. Montgomerie & J. Seale (Eds.), *Proceedings of World Conference on Educational Multimedia, Hypermedia and Telecommunications 2007* (pp. 4254-4258). Chesapeake, VA: AACE

Schellnhuber, H. J., Crutzen, P. J., Clark, W. C., Claussen, M., & Held, H. (Eds.), *Earth system analysis for sustainability: Dahlem Workshop report 91*. Cambridge, MA: MIT Press.

Schmeil, A., & Eppler, M. (2008). Knowledge sharing & collaborative learning in Second Life: A classification of Virtual 3D group interaction scripts. *Journal of Universal Campus Sciences*, *14*(3), 665–677.

Schutte, G. (1997). *Virtual teaching in higher education: The new intellectual superhighway or just another traffic jam?* Retrieved 15 January, 2010, from http://www.csun.edu/sociology/virexp.html

Sebok, A., & Nystad, E. (2004). Design and evaluation of virtual reality systems: A process to ensure usability. *Proceedings of 'Virtual Reality Design and Evaluation Workshop 2004*. University of Nottingham. Retrieved 15 January, 2010, from http://www.view.iao.fraunhofer.de/Proceedings/papers/sebok.PDF

Sharan, S. (1980). Cooperative learning in small groups: Recent methods and effects on achievement, attitudes and ethnic relations. *Review of Educational Research*, *50*(2), 241–271.

Sheehy, K., Ferguson, R., & Clough, G. (2008). Learning in the panopticon: Ethical and social issues in building a virtual educational environment. *International Journal of Social Science, Special Edition: Virtual Reality in Distance Education, 2*(2), 89-97.

Sierpinska, A. (1993). The development of concepts according to Vygotsky. *Focus on Learning Problems in Mathematics, 15*(2 & 3), 87–107.

Sivan, Y. (2009). Overview: State of virtual worlds standards in 2009. *Technology, Economy, and Standards, 2*(3). Retrieved 15 January, 2010, from https://journals.tdl.org/jvwr/article/view/671/539

Slavin, R. E. (1983). *Cooperative learning.* New York, NY: Longman.

Smith, M. A., Farnham, S. D., & Drucker, S. M. (2000). The social life of small graphical chat spaces. *Proceedings of the Conference on Human Factors in Computing Systems* (CHI'00) (pp. 462-469). Hague, The Netherlands: ACM Press.

Soloway, E. (1990). Quick, where do the computers go? *Communications of the ACM, 34*(2), 29–33. doi:10.1145/102792.102797

Sorensen, E. (2006). Learning to learn: A meta-learning perspective on pedagogical design of e-learning. In Center of Research on Lifelong Learning (Eds.). *Learning to learn network meeting report* (pp.48-53). Isra, Italy: European Commission.

Spence, J. (2008). Demographics of virtual worlds. *Virtual Worlds Research: Consumer Behavior in Virtual Worlds, 1*(2). Retrieved 15 January, 2010, from http://journals.tdl.org/jvwr/article/download/360/272

Steed, A., & Tromp, J. (1998). Experiences with the evaluation of CVE applications. [University of Manchester, UK.]. *Proceedings of Collaborative Virtual Environments CVE, 98*, 123–130.

Steinkuehler, A., & Williams, D. (2006). Where everybody knows your (screen) name: Online games as "third places.". *Journal of Computer-Mediated Communication, 11*, 885–909. doi:10.1111/j.1083-6101.2006.00300.x

Stolovitch, D., & La Rocque, G. (1983). *Introduction a la technique de l' instruction.* Prefontaine Editions: St. Jean sur Richelieu.

Strijbos, J. W., Martens, R. L., & Jochems, W. (2004). Designing for interaction: Six steps to designing computer-supported group-based learning. *Computers & Education, 42*, 403–424.

Tomas, D. (1995). Feedback and cybernetics: Reimagining the body in the age of cyborg. In M. Featherstone & R. Burrows (Eds.), *Cyberspace/cyberbodies/cyberpunk: Cultures of technological embodiment* (pp. 21-43). London, UK: Sage.

Vasileiou, V., & Paraskeva, F. (2010). Teaching role-playing instruction in Second Life: An exploratory study. *Journal of Information Technology & Organizations, 5*, 25–50.

Vidgen, R. (1998). Cybernetics & business processes: Using the viable system model to develop entire process architecture. *Knowledge & Process Management: The Journal of Corporate Transformation, 5*, 118–131. doi:10.1002/(SICI)1099-1441(199806)5:2<118::AID-KPM19>3.0.CO;2-3

Vosinakis, S., Koutsabasis, P., Zaharias, P., & Belk, M. (2010). *Problem-based learning in virtual worlds: A case study in user interface design.* Experiential Learning in Virtual Worlds - Exploring the Complexities, Interdisciplinary Press. Retrieved 12 June, 2011, from http://www.inter-disciplinary.net/wp-content/uploads/2011/02/vosinakisepaper.pdf

Vosniadou, S. (1996). Learning environments for representational growth and cognitive flexibility. In Vosniadou, S., DeCorte, E., Glaser, R., & Mandl, H. (Eds.), *International perspectives on the design of technology supported learning environments* (pp. 13–24). Hillsdale, NJ: Lawrence Erlbaum Associates, Inc.

Vrasidas, C. (2000). Constructivism versus objectivism: Implications for interaction, course design, and evaluation in distance education. *International Journal of Educational Telecommunications, 6*(4), 339–362.

Vrellis, I., Papachristos, N. M., Natsis, A., & Mikropoulos, T. A. (2010). *Measuring presence in a collaborative physics learning activity in Second Life.* 7th Pan-Hellenic Conference with International Participation "ICT in Education", September 23-26, Korinthos, Greece.

Vygotsky, L. (1935/1978). *Mind in society: The development of higher psychological processes.* Cambridge, MA: Harvard University Press.

Vygotsky, L. (1987). *The collected works of L.S. Vygotsky, 1. Problems of general psychology (including Thinking and Speech- Minick N., transl.).* New York: Plenum.

Vygotsky, L. S. (1997a). *The collected works of L.S. Vygotsky (Vol. 3).* (Rieber, R. W., & Wollock, J., Trans.). New York, NY: Plenum Press.

Wang, S., & Hsu, H. (2009). Using the ADDIE model to design Second Life activities for online learners. *TechTrends, 53*(6), 76–81. doi:10.1007/s11528-009-0347-x

Welk, D. (2006). The trainer's application of Vygotsky's "zone of proximal development" to asynchronous, online training of faculty facilitators. *Online Journal of Distance Learning Administration, 9*(4). Retrieved 15 January, 2010, from http://www.westga.edu/~distance/ojdla/winter94/welk94.htm

Wertsch, J., & Stone, A. (1985). The concept of internalization in Vygotsky's account of the genesis of higher mental functions. In Wertsch, J. (Ed.), *Culture, communication, and cognition: Vygotskian perspectives* (pp. 162–179). New York, NY: Cambridge University Press.

Weusijana, B., Svihla, V., Gawel, D., & Bransford, J. (2007). Learning about adaptive experience in multi-user virtual environments. *Second Life Education Workshop 2007 Part of the Second Life Community Convention* (pp. 34-39). Chicago, IL: Hilton.

Weusijana, B., Svihla, V., Gawel, D., & Bransford, J. (2009). MUVE's and experimental learning: Some examples. *Innovate: Journal of Online Education, 5*(5). Retrieved 12 June, 2011, from http://www.edutek.net/Kofi/MUVEs_and_Experiential_Learning-Some_Examples.pdf

Whipple, W. R. (1987). Collaborative learning. *AAHE Bulletin, 40*(2), 3–7.

Wiener, N. (1948). *Cybernetics or control and communication in the animal and the machine.* Cambridge, MA: MIT Press.

Wong, M., & Raulenson, P. (1974). *A guide to systematic instructional design.* NJ: Educational Technology Publications.

Yackel, E., Rasmussen, C., & King, K. (2000). Social and socio-mathematical norms in advanced undergraduate mathematics course. *The Journal of Mathematical Behavior, 19,* 275–287. doi:10.1016/S0732-3123(00)00051-1

Zaid, B., Jamaludin, R., & Hosam, A. (2011). Perceived satisfaction levels and student learning performance towards Second Life virtual environment for learning the Islamic concepts. *Australian Journal of Basic and Applied Sciences, 5*(9), 1860–1864.

Zielke, M. A., Roome, T. C., & Krueger, A. B. (2009). A composite adult learning model for virtual world residents with disabilities: A case study of virtual ability Second Life Island. *Journal of Virtual Worlds Research, 2*(1), 4–20.

KEY TERMS AND DEFINITIONS

Digital Natives and Digital Immigrants: Virtual worlds such as Second Life are highly effective and efficient for learners who have grown up with technological developments such as the Internet, mobile phones, etc. Very often uses the terms "digital natives" to describe this generation and this contrasts with the "digital immigrants", who had to learn how to adopt and adapt to these technologies. These then, are "digital natives" more fond of the social dimension of learning. They prefer cooperative and communicative learning activities and also seek the immediacy offered by on-line communities.

Sim (Host/Node): Physical server (server) of the Second Life (SL), which simulates one or more areas (regions). It is the software supporting the virtual representation of land area (256x256 regions) in the host of SL. The Sims can be either isolated "islands", or united. These areas typically used by universities called "standard prims" and have an area of 15.000 prims.

Sloodle (Simulation Linked Object Oriented Dynamic Learning Environment): It is an open source project, which integrates multiuser environment to that of SL Moodle, especially for the management of learning. It provides a set of tools that are embedded in web-based learning management system and can be used by teachers. The Sloodle integrates multi-user environment in the Second Life environment Moodle. Through its commitment to an active community of developers and users, the Sloodle project hopes to develop valid and workable pedagogy for teaching Web-based 3D virtual learning environments.

SL Viewer Client: The viewer must be downloaded from the homepage of Linden Lab (http://secondlife.com/). The client, which resembles like a web-browser to open the "window" environment of SL.

Web 2.0: Web 2.0 goes beyond the limited platform, and the user can act on the Web, as it did with his computer. Most experts talk about a new way of web design which is based on user interaction, allowing the user to change the environment so the page and its contents. Typical applications of Wcb 2.0 are social networking media, such as wikis and weblogs. Many of the commands of interactions that characterize the operation of Web 2.0 are already known from various social networking sites like Facebook or YouTube.

Web 3D: The Web3D was the original idea to be fully demonstrated and used to navigate websites with the three-dimensional way. By extension, the term now refers to all "interactive" three-dimensional content, embedded web pages that can be seen through a web browser. The Web3D technologies usually require to install a 2D (two-dimensional) web viewer (or client viewer), to identify the user with this kind of 3D content. The inspiration for the creation of virtual worlds, was the literature of the "cyberpunk" and especially by Stephenson Neal's book in 1992, named as *"Snow Crash."*

ZEA (Zone Proximal Development): The position of Vygotsky, that social intercommunication generates cognitive development of each individual, evidenced through the endorsement of ZEA, which is defined as "the distance between the occupied level of development, as determined by an independent problem solving and the level of potential development as it determined by the ability to solve it under the guidance of an adult or more capable peers in cooperation.

Chapter 9
Information Systems and Software Development

Arshad Siddiqi
Institute of Business Administration, Pakistan

ABSTRACT

Information Systems are complex systems; the development of the Information Systems according to the business needs is a very tedious and time consuming task. These business applications, whether designed to be performed as a single task or intended to be used company-wide, integrated system, must be designed specifically for the company's unique culture, needs, objectives, and goals. Thus, the developing team must be very clear about the users, user needs, corporation goals, time frame, and financial resources allocated to the to the development project. While the Information Systems are to be using the most advanced development tools and methodology, it must be simple for the users to understand, comprehend, and use they should be capable of performing all the functions necessary to perform a tasks efficiently. While the software should be comprehensive and state of the art, it should not be unduly cumbersome. Careful attention must be given during the development process that the software system should be both functional and efficient; one must remember that an Information System is actually a combination of various software systems which are self-contained top perform specific activities on one hand and to be able to interact and perform effectively with the other software systems. Combined, these software systems become the Information System.

DOI: 10.4018/978-1-4666-3679-8.ch009

INTRODUCTION

Information Systems Development Life Cycle is the basic essence of the successful, timely and cost effective development of an information system. The development process goes through a number of distinctive steps from the conception of information system till the implementation; thus it's called ISDLC or Information Systems Development Life Cycle.

BACKGROUND

The operational computers came into being in 1940s which were very slow and had very limited memory capacity, thus the programs were written in the Assembly Language. Assembly language was very tedious, error prone and took a lot of time and effort. Some initial languages were developed like Plankakul, ENIAC Coding System, BINAC for UNIVAC. This was the time when each instruction set was developed specifically for a manufactures and could not be used on any machines of other manufactures.

The first three modern programming languages were developed in 1950s and 1960s interestingly enough are still in use today in more advanced shape and with additional features.

These languages are:

- **FORTRAN (1955):** the "FORmula TRANslator," invented by John Backus *et al.*;
- **LISP (1958):** the "LISt Processor," invented by John McCarthy *et al.*;
- **COBOL (1959):** the COmmon Business Oriented Language, created by the Short Range Committee, heavily influenced by Grace Hopper;
- **ALGOL 60 and ALGOL 68:** "ALGOrithmic Language" for Burroughs large systems.

See Appendix A, for the list of Language development after these initial languages.

Information System Development Process

There are various Development Processes which can be followed and deployed effectively to develop the Software Systems. We will explore some of them in this chapter.

Software Development Life Cycle: SDLC Model

Every software development process includes the phases of Planning, Designing, coding and testing before it can be implemented for operation (see Figure 1). Thus all SDLC goes through several initial phases:

- Requirement gathering Phase
- Designing Phase
- Development and Implementation Phase
- Testing/Modification Phase

Requirements Gathering Phase

During the Requirements Gather Phase, the needs of the organization are outlines by the developer; this includes extensive interviewing of the organization's stake-holders, managers and other users and in Marketing Organizations even the clients

Figure 1. Software development life cycle: SDLC model

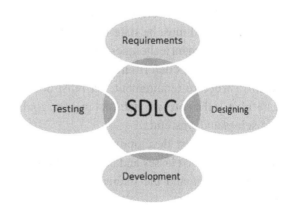

are considered and stake-holders. The wish-lists are gathered and tabulated into; far-fetched, must-have, good-to- have and future-needs. These are converted into the features of the software and it is expected to do, what type of date is to be processes, how the data would be accessed and handled; what type of reports are needed, in what frequency. How many auto generated reports, on-demand reports and occasional reports?

Software Development Phase

I this phase the Development Team goes through determining the listing of the feature and functions of the system. The wish-list is converted into the operational design. The emphasis of the design and development is on the Goals of the system rather than the methodologies used in getting the end results. The designers must consider many different criteria of hardware to be used, Operating Systems Platform, User Ease, Three Click user ease and other subsystems which need to be connected and interact with each other.

This is the phase where the wish list is converted into reality. The designers must make sure on making a realistic, practical and operational design which conforms to the requirements outlined and agreed in the Requirement gathering Phase.

Implementation Phase

This is the most cumbersome phase; here the results of the Design Phase are converted into the systems code. The developers have to conscientious of fact that on one hand the software being developed and implemented must be state-of-the-art, using modern development techniques, providing for all user requirements, conforming to the Hardware and Infrastructure requirement, yet must not be wasteful as if the software does not met the goals it is useless and wasteful.

Using the latest developmental concept, to make sure that the classes and class-interactions are very explicit and the interactions with the data-base are direct.

Testing

In depth series of tests are performed to make sure that the results of the implementation phase meets the requirement goals and the functions are verified. Usually the test plan is composed of Unit Tests and Systems Test. Unit tests are performed to check the individual components of the software whereas the Systems Tests are performed to check the validity and operability of the entire system. The Integration process combines the various sub-systems into a whole and complete system.

Water Fall Software Development Life Cycle Model

The Waterfall life Software Development Life cycle model, also known as the classic or linear-sequential life cycle model, is one of the simplest to understand and use (see Figure 2). The Waterfall model is characterized by a series of steps which must be completed in a linear, sequential order. Each phase is completed and verified before development progresses to the next phase.

However, there is also the mechanism built into the system which constantly monitors the system's development as per the user requirements. As you can see that on the ride side of the above diagram, the arrows are pushing the systems to the next levels like the water flowing from the upper activity to the next lower activity. This is why this model is called the Water Fall Software Development Model.

However, there are three arrows on the left side, that are in the upward direction which signifies that the reverse movement is also possible under certain circumstances, this is why the model is known as Water Fall Software Development Life Cycle.

Systems Design to Requirement Analysis

This is the first place where during Systems Design phase a requirement may be felt to be missing or required for the proper completion of operation of

Figure 2. Water fall software development life cycle model

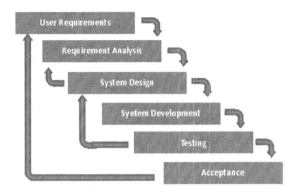

the system, thus the process take a reverse turn and goes back to requirement Analysis. The requirements are critically analyzed with the help of the user and modified accordingly. Once the user and the development team are satisfied the system goes back to the Development Phase. The Developer must be cautious not to over use this facility other the system development will not proceed according to the schedule and the main characteristic of the systems may be changed too drastically that the systems output might become totally divergent to the initial objective of the system.

Testing to Systems Design

The Testing Phase is very crucial in any ISDLC. Thus if during the Testing some critical errors might be detected, the Systems development takes another reverse action and goes back to Systems Design to evaluate the design critically and make required changes accordingly. This is an expensive exercise in terms of time and cost. However it is essential to stop the project totally derailing from its original objective.

Acceptance to User Requirements

This basically means that either the Systems Development Team totally failed to understand the User Requirements or the User has become smart and understands the requirements much better. This could result in drastic loss of time and resources. It may be so severe that the project may be totally abandoned.

Thus to save the embarrassment, loss of resources and time, it is absolutely essential the ample time must be spent of the first phase of understanding, documenting, discussing and User Requirements and getting the user's approval.

It is also very important to keep the user involved throughout the ISDLC to avoid any pitfalls and deliver the system to the user on time and as per his requirements.

Systems Development Life Cycle (SDLC)

Another simple development process is simply called the Systems Development Life Cycle as shown in Figure 3. The SDLC is totally cyclical, it moves perpetually. There are six phases:

1. Planning
2. Analysis
3. Design
4. Coding
5. Testing
6. Maintenance

Figure 3. Systems development life cycle (SDLC)

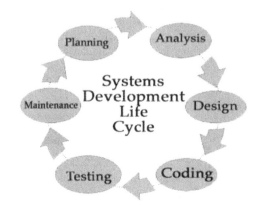

Once the system is in Maintenance, the next planning phase starts either to:

- Upgrade the system with new technology.
- Redesign the system for new requirements.
- Get rid of Operation bugs.
- Enhance the systems with new features.
- Expand the system with new routines.
- Redesign the system to connect to other systems, etc.

Flexible Approach to Information System Development Life Cycle

The Information System Development Life Cycle (ISDLC), has become integral part of a systems development process (see Figure 4). This concept was put forward by Blumenthal during the late sixties. Now it is the backbone of any systems development and ISDLC methodology, procedures, methods and practices are the required practice for the proper development. Without the application of ISDLC it is next to impossible to develop, test and implement any system successfully or within the stipulated time frame.

There are several steps that must be adhered to; these are:

1. Definition Phase
   a. Preliminary Investigation
   b. Feasibility Analysis
   c. Information Gathering
   d. System designing
2. Development Phase
   a. Designing and Development
   b. Procedures
3. Implementation Phase
   a. Implementation
   b. Testing and Evaluation
4. Operation Phase
   a. UAT (User Acceptance Testing)
   b. FAT (Final Acceptance Testing)
   c. Operationalization

Systems Development from scratch is not as simple and straight forward as one might think in the beginning. There is a lot involved. The four phases shown above are four distinct phases, however they are totally interdependent. The success of the next phase depends on the successful completion of the previous phase.

There are many factors directly affecting the speed and success of the systems implementation like:

- The complexity of the system
- Users understanding of his needs
- Designers expertise to understand these needs to convert into features of the system
- Users behavior towards the system
- Critical nature of the systems to satisfy the user
- Developers ability to convert the features into programs and routines
- Developers expertise to test the systems for 'all' possibilities

Figure 4. Flexible approach to information system development life cycle

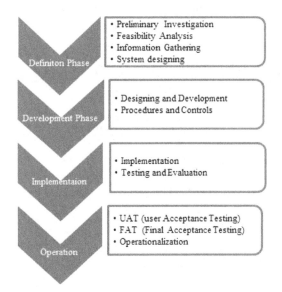

- Users ability to test the system, evaluate its usage and accept it or call for modifications
- Designers willingness and ability to redesign and redevelop the missing aspects of the system
- The design of the system must be volatile enough to meet the challenges of the time and increasing requirements.
- The design should be so robust as to minimize the possibilities of last minute changes.
- The system design must be flexible and time tested.

The Traditional Approach

The traditional approach of ISDLC had been rather rigid in the order of the various steps of the development process to assure the control over the design and development process. However, it was recognized very quickly that rigidity does not work in practice.

The development process must be flexible enough to vary throughout the entire process varying with the complexity and the nature of the systems which is under development. It is of immense importance that the user should be involved in every step the entire development processes.

At times, depending on the complexity of the systems under development the traditional development procedures may have to be modifies to meet the demands. According to Gremillion and Pyburn [7] the systems managers may have to abandon traditional approach and evaluate projects by varying criteria of commonality, impact, and structure to choose the right development approach.

While McFarlan [9] has noted that various projects of different nature would require significantly different management approaches to mitigate the risks and time constraints including other risks such as cost overruns, tight time schedules and the technical abilities of the development team to avoid outright failure.

McFarlan identifies three dimensions that influence the risk inherent in a project:

1. Project size (dollar expense, staff, number of departments affected),
2. Experience with the technology,
3. Project structure.

Consequently, he proposes that a risk profile should be built from the offset through intensive interviews with the users, team members to choose a specific development process. This means that the various phases of the ISDLC will be dependent on the nature of each specific project. A success of the process in one project cannot be expected from every subsequent project.

Thus various attributes and requirements of the systems to be developed dictates the emphasis on various phases of the ISDLC phases and the scope of each systems development would be much greater than what McFarlan's classification and every step of in ISDLC could have several distinct dimension with varying emphasis.

Various Factors Affecting the ISDLC

No ISDLC can be developed in isolation. There are numerous factors that the methodology and success of the development. The factors differ from culture of the organization and the technical expertise of the development team. There are two main factors which effects directly:

- Organizational Structure is a major factor as this shows:
  - Which departments are directly connected to the project,
  - Which departments are the primary users,
  - Which departments are the secondary users,
  - How many departments are involved in the project,
  - Who are the decision makers,

- ○ Who are the principle users.
- What is the Technical expertise level?
  - ○ Is there a strong technical expertise amongst the users?
  - ○ Are the top decision makers technically oriented?
  - ○ Will the ICT department be the prime owner of the system?
  - ○ Who will be responsible for the operation or data entry of the system?
- Maturity of the Organization:
  - ○ Are the users experienced enough to be part of the development team?
  - ○ Will they be part of the operation team?
  - ○ Will they own and operate the system independently?
  - ○ How many application have been developed by the organization?
  - ○ How many of-the-shelf packages are being used?
- Information Systems Policy:
  - ○ Is there specific IS policy?
  - ○ Is there a strong Data Processing Department?
  - ○ Are the DP functions distributed amongst the departments?
  - ○ Is there a distributive processing culture of central processing?
  - ○ Who own the data; DP department or the users departments?
- Technological Maturity of the organization:
  - ○ Are there any projects developed used advanced technology?
  - ○ How many systems are still being batch processed?
  - ○ If they have a centralized DP Center, how long ago was it established?
  - ○ How savvy are the employees with the data services?
- Technical Awareness of the Organization:

- ○ Is there a Structured Transaction Processing System?
- ○ How high up the organization level is Information Processing Department?
- ○ Is the reporting system highly structured?

The above mentioned analysis would reveal the nature of the organization like:

- What should be the complexity of the systems design?
- What Development tools should be used?
- How much user interaction to be expected?
- How much training would be required for the IT staff and users?
- How extensive should be the design of the system?
- What should be the data entry methodology?
- What testing methodologies should be used?
  - ○ How would the system be tested?
  - ○ Who will do the User Acceptance Test and Final Acceptance Test?
  - ○ Who will certify the system design?
  - ○ Who will certify the final tests?
  - ○ Who will approve the overall process and final completion?

Types of Systems Development

Once an organization has decided to go into systems development, may it be a highly structure centralized large organization or a decentralized small organization, the following types of projects will be required to be developed:

1. Design and development of a new system
2. Enhancement or Modification of an existing system
3. Major redesign of an existing system due to technology or business changes

4. Installation of new pre-developed systems
5. Installation of new features to an existing system
6. Error eradication or correction of an existing system

The ISDLC as described earlier, differ for the types of the system being developed. The degree of involvement of any stage will correspond to the requirements of the type, for example; the design and development of a new system will naturally go through the all levels of ISDLC, where as an enhancement or modification will not require the extensive designing efforts. The installation of new pre-developed systems by passes the initial stages of ISDLC and goes directly to installation. To calculate the time and efforts required to install a system depends on the Dimensions of the System.

Sequencing of ISDLC Phases

ISDLC is a very systematic systems development technique. There is a definite correlation amongst its various steps. There must be a logical sequence of these well-defined steps (see Figure 5). Generally and logically the development precedes top-to-bottom, from a overall prospective of the systems to technical details to actual programming and finally testing and implementation.

Of course depending on the complexity of the system design the duration of these will differ amongst various systems. However the basic concept remains the same. Additionally, there are various dimension of an ISDLC. These dimensions further categorize the systems development process.

Various Dimensions of an ISDLC

There are various dimensions which must be considered controlled effectively for a system to be developed in a proper and efficient manner. These Dimensions are:

1. The Vertical Dimension
2. The Horizontal Dimension
3. Time Frame Dimension
4. Human Aspects Dimension
5. Non-Human related Dimension
6. Systems Control Dimension

The Vertical Dimension

This is the sequence and number of the step in the development process; from Definition Phase to Operation Phase as shown and discussed earlier. Various unforeseen factors directly affect the progress of the development and the cost of the system. Specific cost evaluation must be done to see if there might be some steps that may be combined, reduced or eliminated. Specialized software could be used instead of in-house development; this could be faster and even cheaper. Another good point of this approach is that this "plug-in" software keeps on improving by newer versions, and can easily and inexpensively upgraded.

There should be flexibility in the development process, thus each step must be flexible enough to utilize the latest software packages as and when needed. Making the process very rigid and carved in stone is an unacceptable approach in the modern systems development approach. The beauty of this flexible approach is that elements within

Figure 5. Sequencing of ISDLC phases

the modules being developed can be modified for better performance or cost effect.

The Horizontal Dimension

Information systems are developed in a formal process with gradual progress toward the ultimate goal of Operationalization of the system. Each step in the development process is considered as a sub-project with its own goals, task lists, deliverables, time lines with interactions and dependencies of other sub-projects. These sub-projects have their own check points and mile stones which are checked and audited accordingly.

As the development proceeds, these milestones, checkpoints or features may be increased or decrease due to external factors like, time or funds constraints, change of the final deliverables of the overall system, change of the basic requirements, etc.

In my view the following elements of the development process can be place in the list of the Horizontal Dimension:

1. Initial evaluation of the organization and it culture,
2. ICT maturity of the organization,
3. As-is analysis of the organization,
4. To-be analysis, including wish list and realistic requirements,
5. Information need analysis,
6. Systems logical and physical design analysis,
7. Hardware systems requirements analysis,
8. System Development,
9. SOP Development,
10. Implementation,
11. User Training,
12. User Acceptance Testing,
13. Final Acceptance Testing,
14. Parallel Run (In case there exists an old system),
15. Go Live.

Time Frame Dimension

Each Project has its own time frame. There is no specific or accurate formula or gauge that could be applied to every project. Time varies due to the following reasons:

1. Complexity of the system
2. Availability of resources
   a. Technical
   b. Financial
   c. Previous experience of the team
   d. Previous experience of the users
3. Interest of the upper management
4. Commitment of the upper management

However there are a number of methods that can be applied to make sure that the ISDLC take the most time effective route and the system development proceeds most effectively; some of the following committees could be formed and they should meet on regular intervals:

- Formation of Project Steering Committee
- Weekly Progress Evaluation Committee
- Procedures Evaluation Committee
- Quality Control and Inspection Committee
- Mile stone and Goals Control Committee
- Procedures Formation and Implementation Committee
- Quality Control Audit and Inspection Committee
- Technical Walkthrough Committee

Human Aspects Dimension

There are two aspects of this dimension:

- Systems Developers; such as Analysts, Designers, Developers, Programmers, Data Base Administrators, Procedure Writers, Trainers, Auditors, Quality Assurance Personnel, Activities Controllers, etc. Some or all of these may be required in large sophisticated systems but may not be required in simple straight forward short duration systems.

- Users; such as Administration, Financers, Primary and Secondary Users etc.

Non-Human Related Dimension

Other resources like office space, computer resources like systems, operation times, storage devices, etc.; capital investment and any other resources required for the successful implementation of the system fall into this category.

Systems Control Dimension

This is one of the most unforgotten dimensions yet it has the same over even more importance that the other dimensions. This dimension, if utilized properly guarantees the successful implementation of the system. Even though there are numerous methods that can be deployed to guarantee the ISDLC progress in the desired direction, time frame and cost estimates, however the selection of appropriate Systems Control Tools is essential for the successful culmination of an ISDLC.

Segregation of Dimensions

It is not possible to segregate these dimensions very clearly. Usually, these dimensions are associated with the Vertical Dimension, but the ISDLC is not a segregated system, each activity is inter-dependent with other activities. Sometimes out of sequence activities have to be performed depending on the nature of the system. In complex systems prototype routines may be deployed to see the behaviours of the system. Sometime pilot programs may even be developed. A good technique is to deploy Controlled Databases to make sure that if there is a bug detected it is not due to the data.

Sometime organizational changes or even the objective of the system may be redefined during the ISDLC; this can affect the system with devastating results and may even totally breakdown the fabric of the system. Thus the Information System designers and developer must pay close attention to the changing factors and should not try to segregate the Dimensions.

ISDLC Planning and Reviewing

Each ISDLC is different as each Information System is different from each other, thus there is no definite methodology that could be applied to every system development process. The designers and developers, who have developed a system earlier, must be careful not to apply the same process to the new systems without actually doing complete analysis of the requirements and features of the new system.

It is worth noting that the principles of systems development remain the same however the methodologies change according to the nuances of each system. Experiences of previous development endeavors should be wisely applied in the new scenario and only those portions which directly apply to the new system should be adopted.

Proper planning for the ISDLC is like putting the first brick of the building perfectly. It is this very brick that would guide the further progress of the system, thus very careful understanding of the requirement and corresponding planning would guarantee the success in the rest of the development.

Traditional Development

The traditional development approach was very structured top to bottom (see Figure 6). It started from the Planning stage and ended at deployment after passing through Analysis, Design, Development, Testing and Deployment, as shown on the left side of the diagram below.

However, the major problem with this straight line development was that if any thong goes wrong in between there was no turning back. Actually

Figure 6. Traditional development

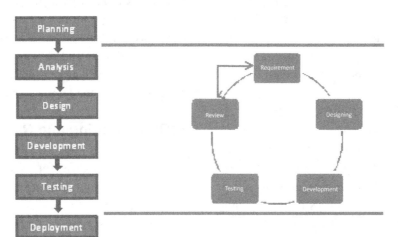

this system was to atrociously bad that the developer would not even know about the problem till he reaches the end that that had made a serious error, after investing huge amount of cost and time.

This was usually created very embarrassing circumstances for the developer and most annoying situation for the user. The whole system had to be scraped to start over but again without any guarantees the systems would actually wok this time.

A definite development was the creation of the Iterative process of development. This is shown in the right side of the diagram above.

Between Planning and Deployment five steps were added in circular process; these were Requirement followed by Design to Development to Testing and Review. If the project passed the review it was set for the deployments. If the project fails in any of the step before Review or in the review the project was bumped back as many step as required. Let say if the Project failed in the Review due to the poor Designing, the project was thrown back to the Designer for rework and project would restart from there.

This was good but still far from perfect; something much better was required like RAD!

Rapid Application Development (RAD)

In 1980s, at Dupont, Barry Boehm and Tom Gilb developed a methodology called Rapid Iterative Production Prototyping (RIPP). James Martin then further developed the RIPP to be more formalized process known as Rapid Application Development (RAD). RAD compresses the step-by-step development of conventional methods into an iterative process. The RAD approach thus includes developing and refining the data models, process models, and prototype in parallel using an iterative process. User requirements are refined, a solution is designed, the solution is prototyped, the prototype is reviewed, user input is provided, and the process begins again.

James Martin, in his book first coining the term, wrote, "Rapid Application Development (RAD) is a development lifecycle designed to give much faster development and higher-quality results than those achieved with the traditional lifecycle. It is designed to take the maximum advantage of powerful development software that has evolved recently."

Professor Clifford Kettemborough of Whitehead College, University of Redlands, defines Rapid Application Development as "an approach to building computer systems which combines Computer-Assisted Software Engineering (CASE) tools and techniques, user-driven prototyping, and stringent project delivery time limits into a potent, tested, reliable formula for top-notch quality and productivity. RAD drastically raises the quality of finished systems while reducing the time it takes to build them."

Online Knowledge defines Rapid Application Development as "a methodology that enables organizations to develop strategically important systems faster while reducing development costs and maintaining quality. This is achieved by using a series of proven application development techniques, within a well-defined methodology."

Looking at the above three definitions of Rapid Application Development, it becomes clear that RAD is the technique for quicker development of a System or an Application. This expedites the whole application development process along with keeping the quality of the development at the expected high level. Since the two main things that must be controlled in any system development are Time and Quality, can be addressed effectively and efficiently, RAD is of great interest to all Systems Developers as by saving the Time and keep the quality high, great savings could be attained.

The Need of RAD

Traditional SDLC from Seventies are still in use mainly due to:

- Traditional SDLC
- Traditional Systems Developers
- Lack of knowledge RAD
- Lack of knowledge of modern tools like CASE
- Fear of the unknown

Still the highly structured step-by-step SDLC from the seventies are used widely, as these SDLC are very rigid in nature and structured sequentially, these are not easy to modify. Strangely the feature of them being structured and sequential was a great quality of SDLC, now this is considered a draw back in faster and economic development.

This very rigid and cumbersome process required user's approval before the development could proceed to next step. Once the user requirements and design was "frozen" the system coding, testing and implementing was proceeded.

The History of RAD

The Gartner Group writes, "Many of the business processes devised after World War II, have remained essentially the same. Corporations are now finding that work organized stepwise incurs unavoidable delays and errors as paper is handed off from person to person and unit to unit...IT is the single most powerful tool for breaking traditional assumptions and rules about business, and it is the tool that makes new ways of operation possible." This comment by Gartner Group clearly enunciates the importance of RAD how it revolutionizes systems development process by using modern tools for reducing development time, increasing quality and saving over all development cost.

As mentioned earlier, RAD uses the modern automated techniques and development tools to essentially restructure Information Systems development process. These tools convert the menial stepwise development process to automatic transformation into Information Systems Development. The following activities are replaced by RAD:

- Manual designing of charts and requirement sheets,
- Manual Software Coding process – this depended on the developers expertise,
- No manual designing,
- Replacing volatile systems development to more stable development,
- Error detection and rectification is quick and inexpensive,
- Provide stable systems,
- Development becomes more capable,

- Chances of errors are lesser,
- Much faster than manual development.

The typical systems development is expensive and time consuming, which creates tension and backlog for the organizations. Similarly the maintenance of the production systems is very expensive consuming 60% - 70% of the Information Systems Departmental budget. This delay and cost is associated with the following reasons:

- Different systems are developed by different teams, thus there is no specific development philosophy used.
- Either there is not much documentation available or it is obsolete.
- The record for modifications to the system is not kept properly.
- Quick fixes are made and forgotten to be recorded.
- Databases are changed at per the need but not documented properly.
- Short cut subroutines are created using different techniques not compatible with each other.

When the organization needs to upgrade the old system, it becomes a nightmare. They developer usually grope in the dark to figure out where to start and what to do! Even when the new systems are to be developed, the traditional systems development techniques are usually too slow and too expensive to be economical, they are designed using fixed formats and have very little flexibility.

Due to the conventional methods, it took very long for the systems to be delivered to the user, and then it was a long and hard battle to train the user to see the results of his toil and expenses. Sometime this process took so long that due to the long development process the user's needs would fundamentally change, rendering the system to be useless.

Sometimes it is even better, quicker and economical to simply get a new system developed and dump the old system. This however, is not that simple and it is easier to say but very cumbersome and time consuming getting it done, thus most organizations keep using the old system and suffer, then slowly start using manual system.

RAD is the solution! It is the new methodology and technology for faster, better, cheaper and quicker systems development and deployment. The availability of CASE - Computer Aided Software Engineering tools propels the case of RAD.

CASE: COMPUTER AIDED SOFTWARE ENGINEERING

The CASE tools make the life of the developers so much simpler and wholesome. They can develop and implement systems with ease and many times faster than before. Due or these new integrated CASE tools the traditional software development processes have become obsoleted and so has changed the thought process.

These CASE tools provide previously generated and tested code to the developer to simply apply appropriately. These tools are not depended to any programming language or plate form. This is a far cry from the old methodology of SDLC.

Great thing about CASE Tools is that it supports the Rapid Application development; once again, irrespective of the programming language or plate form, for example CASEMaker's Totem 5.0 supports RAD for COBOL Development.

Stanley Marcus of Neiman Marcus said, "There are only two things of importance. One is the customer, and the other is the product. If you take care of customers, they come back. If you take care of the product, it doesn't come back. It's just that simple. And it's just that difficult."

RAD provides:

- Rapid Application Development

- Provides better quality products
- Consumes substantially less development time
- Ensures greater customer satisfaction
- Reducing the elapsed time between User Design and Implementation
- Increases prospects of User's satisfaction.
- Substantially cheaper that the traditional SDLC
- Provides integration of the end-users in the development of the application

Operation of RAD

Due to the Interactive prototyping feature of RAD lets development teams to deliver fully operational prototypes to the Users. They would test the routines return to the users if any reworking was required. This goes on back and forth till the users are satisfied with the operation. By this time without knowing the users would have helped in developing the entire system for implementation in a very short time.

Rapid Iterative Production Prototyping (RIPP)

The work of Barry Boehm and Tom Gilb paved the way for the formulation of the methodology called Rapid Iterative Production Prototyping (RIPP) at DuPont in the mid-to-late 1980s. James Martin then extended the work done at DuPont and elsewhere into a larger, more formalized process, which has become known as Rapid Application Development (RAD). RAD compresses the step-by-step development of conventional methods into an iterative process. The RAD approach thus includes developing and refining the data models, process models, and prototype in parallel using an iterative process. User requirements are refined, a solution is designed, the solution is prototyped, the prototype is reviewed, user input is provided, and the process begins again.

CONCLUSION

ISDLC is very difficult or it can be easy; it depend on the collaboration of the Know-how of Development Team, Active Participation Users and the proper selection and utilization of the Development Methodology. The better these three facets of development are applied the faster, better and cheaper will be the final product.

REFERENCES

Ahituv, N., & Neumann, S. (1982). *Principles of information systems for management. Dubuque, IO: William C.* Brown.

Blumenthal, S. C. (1969). *Management information systems: A framework for planning and development.* Englewood Cliffs, NJ: Prentice-Hall.

Buchanan, J. R., & Linowes, R. G. (1980). Understanding distributed data processing. *Harvard Business Review, 8*(4), 43–153.

Buchanan, J. R., & Linowes, R. G. (1980). Making distributed data processing work. *Harvard Business Review, 58*(5), 143–161.

Ein-Dor, P., & Segev, E. (1978). *Managing management information systems.* Lexington, MA: Lexington Books, D.C. Heath and Company.

Gibson, C. F., & Nolan, R. L. (1974). Managing the four stages of EPP growth. *Harvard Business Review, 52*(1), 76–88.

Gremillion, L. L., & Pyburn, P. (1983). Breaking the systems development bottleneck. *Harvard Business Review, 61*(2), 130–137.

Lucas, H. C. (1975). *Why information systems fail.* New York, NY: Columbia University Press.

McFarlan, F. W. (1981). Portfolio approach to information systems. *Harvard Business Review, 59*(5), 142–150.

McFarlan, F. W., McKinney, J. L., & Pyburn, P. (1983). The information archipelago Plotting a course. *Harvard Business Review*, *61*(1), 145–156.

McKenney, J. L., & McFarlan, F. W. (1982). The information archipelago-Maps and bridges. *Harvard Business Review*, *60*(5), 109–119.

1982*Principles of information systems for management*. Dubuque, IO: William C. Brown.

Sprague, R. H., & Carlson, E. D. (1982). *Building effective decision support systems*. Englewood Cliffs, NJ: Prentice-Hall.

KEY TERMS AND DEFINITIONS

Computer Aided Software Engineering (CASE) Tools: Make the life of the developers so much simpler and wholesome. They can develop and implement systems with ease and many times faster than before. Due or these new integrated CASE tools the traditional software development processes have become obsoleted and so has changed the thought process.

Information Systems Development Life Cycle (ISDLC): The basic essence of the successful, timely and cost effective development of an information system. The development process goes through a number of distinctive steps from the conception of information system till the implementation; thus it's called ISDLC or Information Systems Development Life Cycle.

Rapid Application Development (RAD): Compresses the step-by-step development of conventional methods into an iterative process.

Software Development Life Cycle (SDLC): Includes the phases of Planning, Designing, coding and testing before it can be implemented for operation. Thus all SDLC goes through several initial phases such as Requirement gathering Phase, Designing Phase, Development and Implementation Phase and Testing/Modification Phase.

Waterfall Software Development Life Cycle (WF Model): The Waterfall life Software Development Life cycle model, also known as the classic or linear-sequential life cycle model, is one of the simplest to understand and use. The Waterfall model is characterized by a series of steps which must be completed in a linear, sequential order. Each phase is completed and verified before development progresses to the next phase.

APPENDIX

Chorography of Languages Development

Some important languages that were developed in this period include: (Source Wikipedia)

- 1951 - Regional Assembly Language
- 1952 - Autocode
- 1954 - IPL (forerunner to LISP)
- 1955 - FLOW-MATIC (forerunner to COBOL)
- 1957 - FORTRAN (First compiler)
- 1957 - COMTRAN (forerunner to COBOL)
- 1958 - LISP
- 1958 - ALGOL 58
- 1959 - FACT (forerunner to COBOL)
- 1959 - COBOL
- 1959 - RPG
- 1962 - APL
- 1962 - Simula
- 1962 - SNOBOL
- 1963 - CPL (forerunner to C)
- 1964 - BASIC
- 1964 - PL/I
- 1967 - BCPL (forerunner to C)
- 1968 - Logo
- 1969 - B (forerunner to C)
- 1970 - Pascal
- 1970 - Forth
- 1972 - C
- 1972 - Smalltalk
- 1972 - Prolog
- 1973 - ML
- 1975 - Scheme
- 1978 - SQL (initially only a query language, later extended with programming

Then From 1980 other languages were developed like:

- 1980 - C++ (as C with classes, name changed in July 1983)
- 1983 - Ada
- 1984 - Common Lisp
- 1984 - MATLAB
- 1985 - Eiffel
- 1986 - Objective-C

- 1986 - Erlang
- 1987 - Perl
- 1988 - Tcl
- 1988 - Mathematica
- 1989 - FL (Backus)
- 1990 - Haskell
- 1991 - Python
- 1991 - Visual Basic
- 1991 - HTML
- 1993 - Ruby
- 1993 - Lua
- 1994 - CLOS (part of ANSI Common Lisp)
- 1995 - Java
- 1995 - Delphi (Object Pascal)
- 1995 - JavaScript
- 1995 - PHP
- 1996 - WebDNA
- 1997 - Rebol
- 1999 - D
- 2000 - ActionScript
- 2001 - C#
- 2001 - Visual Basic .NET
- 2002 - F#
- 2003 - Groovy
- 2003 - Scala
- 2003 - Factor
- 2007 - Clojure
- 2009 - Go
- 2011 - Dart

Chapter 10
Toward Agile Interactive Software Development Process Models for Crowd Source Projects

Izzat Alsmadi
Yarmouk University, Jordan

Saqib Saeed
Bahria University, Pakistan

ABSTRACT

Typical traditional software development models are initially designed for company-style software project teams. They also assume a typical software project that has somewhat clear goals, scope, budget, and plan. Even Agile development models that are very flexible in considering previous project parameters assume somewhat stable team and project structures. However, in recent years, the authors have noticed expansion in software projects that are developed in a very illusive flexible team, scope, budget, and plan structures. Examples of such projects are those projects offered in open competition (also called crowd sourcing) structure for software developers to be part of. In typical open competition projects, initial, high level project ideas are submitted to the public through the Internet. The project initiators give their initial requirements, constraints, and conditions for successful products or submissions. Teams can be organized before or through the competition. Submission and evaluation of deliverables from teams are subjected to project initiator evaluation along with evaluation teams organized through the open competition host. This chapter investigates all traditional project characteristics. The authors elaborate on all those elements that should be modified to fit the open competition agile structure. They use several case studies to demonstrate management issues related to managing software projects in open competitions.

DOI: 10.4018/978-1-4666-3679-8.ch010

INTRODUCTION

The evolution and expansion of the Web makes it easy and convenient to move many human activities to this venue that connects humans around the world together. Even governments are making use of some websites to get feedback from the citizens as a whole (i.e. the crowd). For example, websites such as: http://www.ideastorm.com, http://ideascale.com, and http://www.uservoice.com/ to encourage citizens to submit their opinions and ideas to their government to be assessed and evaluated. In this scope of software projects, our focus in this chapter is in the software projects styles aside from the traditional business style companies. In this chapter, we will discuss issues related to challenges of managing software development projects in untraditional styles where all project major elements (i.e. team, scope, budget, success factors, software development model) are not clear. In the first section, we will summarize current software development models taking those major elements into consideration. The second section will discuss software open competition projects. We will list some of the known websites who offer open competition software projects. We will elaborate on their marketing strategies. Using the same major project attributes mentioned earlier (i.e. team, scope, budget, success factors, software development model, etc). In comparison with traditional software development projects and using case studies, we will demonstrate how traditional software development models will fail short in conducting successful open competition projects. The last section will include a proposal for a new open competition model or at least possible enhancements for traditional software development models. Case studies will be also used here to demonstrate the proposed models. Below are initial possible references that will be used in the chapter.

Software process is a set of complex activities required to develop software systems. There are many known software process models such as water fall, spiral, incremental, Rational Unified Process (RUP) and agile models. All those process models carry out same mandatory activities e.g. requirements elicitation, software design, coding, testing, evolution and project management. However, they are different from each other based on the way they perform such tasks. For example, a water fall model follows a straightforward process that starts from requirement. Once requirement stage is finished, design stage is started and so on until finishing all software activities. Such traditional model does not allow back links from a stage to the previous stages. Furthermore development stages are distinctly divided and separated and it does not allow overlapping of stages. On the other hand, most of the other development methodologies are flexible in this manner and allow incremental cyclic process where in each cycle a small part of the project is developed and all process activities are executed in a cyclic manner.

Figure 1 describes typical software process activities. Project initiation and planning are the early tasks in a software development lifecycle where the project boundaries and feasibilities are generated. After the approval of customer and developers, detailed level planning is carried out by development team, focusing on estimation of cost, resources and scheduling. In the next phase system and user requirements are gathered, documented, prioritized and finalized. The major deliverable of this initial stage is software requirement specification (SRS), which highlights system and user requirements. In this initial stage, problem domain is analyzed looking for why we are developing this software, who asked for this solution, what were the problems in the domain or in the existing system (if a system exists). Software and system analysts are the people who usually perform activities in this task or stage. They meet with domain users and stake holders in trying to analyse the current system and specifying requirements for the sought solution.

Figure 1. Software process activities (SWEBOK 2008)

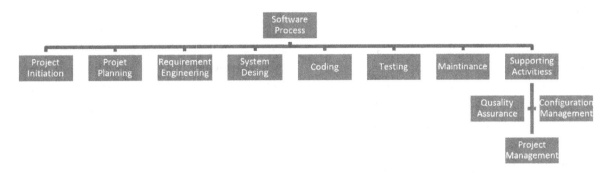

In the next stage a design is proposed (i.e. documents, graphs, pseudo code, etc.) that fulfils all requirements in the SRS. Traceability (i.e. clear link between SRS and design) should be examined to make sure that all requirements specified in the SRS are handled and at the same time no unnecessary elements exist in design. After the design, implementation stage starts to translate the theoretical solution from design into code. Testing occurs in each stage to make sure that every deliverable is developed as expected. Nonetheless, there is a separate testing stage after coding to test the major deliverable of the software project (i.e. the code or the program). Once the software is handed over to customer it may also require further changes, this phase is termed as maintenance stage. Along with these core activities different supporting activities are carried out in software development process. These include quality assurance, configuration management and project management activities.

There are several factors that affect the decision of selecting the right process model. This include: the flexibility/stability of the requirements, nature of the software project, time to market, amount of testing, documentation and quality required, the level of competition and several other factors that can be related to the software, the users, the domain or the environment.

The remaining of the chapter is structured as follows. Section 2 describes software process models in the context of the subject of the chapter and section 3 describes some of the related work. Section 4 introduces open source projects and e-coding projects and websites in the scope of software development. Section 5 introduces the elements that should be modified in traditional models to fit the view of open source and e-coding projects and is followed by a conclusion.

1. SOFTWARE PROCESS AND PROJECT MODELS

In a previous paper we described teaching software engineering based on four concerns: software processes, projects, people and products (Alsmadi and Dieri, 2009). We will use a similar approach to describe software project models.

1.1. Process: Software Process Oriented Models

Most software development models described in software engineering literature are process oriented. This means that each model is specified and distinguished from other models based on the way activities are performed. In one classification, process models can be divided into forward process models such as waterfall model that have all process activities in a straightforward manner in comparison with cyclic process models such as agile, incremental, RUP, etc [Alsmadi and Dieri 2009] which advocate multiple cycles of developmental activities.

Every software model is a process model, which means that they focus only on one element of the software project and ignore the impact of the other factors on the software project. For example, based on the nature of the software project, an agile development process for building safety critical software can be different from an agile process for enhancing existing Human Resource Management (HRM) software. We will focus on some of the aspects that can be used to distinguish models based on project, people or product types.

1.2. Product: Software Product Oriented Models

Software product models can be divided based on several perspectives. In one classification approach, software products can be classified based on the nature of the software into: system, support and application software. In some other naming convention, system and support software are called upstream software while application software are termed as downstream software. Based on the platform, software products can be also classified into: Web, OS and mobile applications. Several software vendors are trying to offer the same product in those three different platforms. While major functionalities can be the same, however, each application environment has its constraints on the user interface, input and output interactions.

The programming language used to realize software systems is also another variable used for classification. Software products are either written by high level programming languages (e.g. Java, C#, C++, etc). Scripting languages (e.g. Java script, VB script, PHP, ASP, etc) and in some cases assembly or machine level could be used to realize software applications. From software project management perspective software products can be classified based on size or

complexity. E.g. Constructive Cost Estimation model, COCOMO divided software products into: organic, semidetached and embedded based on size or complexity. On the basis of based model software products can be classified into commercial, open source and free software. Software products can also be classified into generic (for the general market) and custom (for a specific company or sector) products. Finally based on the product domain software applications can be classified into several types such as: multimedia and graphics, business, enterprise, communication, educational, games, utilities, science and engineering, database, APIs, and several other types. A software development model that works well for revenue oriented commercial software should be totally different from a software project built in the open source community. In section 4 of this chapter, we elaborate on the distinguished elements for two types of software products: open source and open competition projects. We analyze those types based on the factors that affect the software development process and that should be considered when managing the development of such products.

1.3. People, Software People Oriented Models

A software people model is a software development methodology that is centered on the people and their roles. In people models, we list individuals or roles e.g. Analyst, GUI designer, architect, software developer, tester, etc. and elaborate on activities that each one of those should perform. In the following cases we highlight the scenarios to demonstrate when a development model should be better people oriented rather than process oriented.

Case 1: Company A is a small startup software development company. The owner/general manager is expected to manage all activities of different types e.g. website, testing and improving a product, product debugging and support, etc. The company has few employees. The main goal for the manager at this stage is to: first survive this company in terms of revenue, and second to find a specific day-day task for employees. In such scenario, a software process model may not work well as projects are scattered and different in size, type, nature, revenue, etc Secondly both waterfall and cyclic models may fail to give the manager the ability to handle all projects having different level of progress, required employee skills, etc.

A software people or project oriented model works better in helping managers in allocating the right people in the right time for each project. For example, if the company is handling a small project of building a website, one employee maybe able to handle all the project from the start to the end alone. Such employee will collect requirements and build the design, develop and test the website. In another small project of evaluating another application for another company, test and improve such legacy software, it is possible also that only one or two people (skilled in largely testing and development) may also be assigned such project. This does not mean that those two individuals can't seek help from other individuals in the company, if other skills are required. It just simply means that this project will largely be handled by them. In many software companies around the world, such cases are real and may then never use or apply any of the development process models that are widely known in software engineering literature.

Case 2: In an open source project two software developer friends decided to build specific software for a defined purpose. The company and the development team in this case are those two friends. They are expected to handle all tasks in an unstructured manner. They may spend an initial stage collecting and writing requirements. They may decide to work in parallel while each individual will try to solve the same problem in isolation from the other, before combining their thoughts and ideas together. Once they put their product online and open a discussion board for it, all users can work as evaluators and testers. Requirements themselves may continuously evolve based on users' feedbacks. The development cycles can be very short. They can be also different in time and size based on the number of new, modified or corrected requirements that will be included in the new release. Many tasks that are typically performed in typical projects e.g. feasibility study, cost estimation, user evaluation or testing, etc. may not be necessary for such projects.

Case 3: In research and development/student projects, the nature of the software development process can be different from traditional software development projects. Such projects may continuously evolve in their requirements, design, etc. In such projects, users usually only have generic simple requirements description. Those projects may also be performed by one or a single team of projects. These individuals may have very good skills in specific areas of the software development process while lacking many other skills. They may need to learn those new skills, ask for help from friends, professional individuals, etc. Such decisions may not be answered in early development stages which may make management decisions difficult.

All those examples or cases are listed to justify the need for new software development models that are not process oriented. Such models may not be completely different from traditional software development process models. They can have different versions or solution elements to deal with the people or project oriented cases.

1.4. Project, Software Project Oriented Models

Similar to people oriented models, in software project development models, the project type and nature should be important factors to affect project management decision making. Similar to software products, software projects can be classified based on different perspectives. In one view, they can be classified according to product classification. They can also be simply classified based on size and complexity Software projects can be also classified into new/reengineering/maintenance projects. Each one of those projects has its different expectations of success, revenue, resources, testing, etc. Each one also requires different type of roles or skills. Generic software development models may not be applicable to all those types of projects as such generic models are meant largely for new software products. Based on the amount of work from externals, software projects can be classified to in-house, partial out sourcing or completely buy/hire a company to develop the product. The company may have the right to own and modify the code permanently or may have only the right to use the software (temporary or permanently). Based on risk and criticality software projects can also be classified into critical and uncritical systems. Such criticality maybe defined by the company or the user and based on different aspects such as: money, health, level of accuracy or testing, importance, etc. Similar to products, software projects can be also classified in generic software projects to develop custom products.

2. EVOLUTION OF SOFTWARE PROCESS ORIENTED MODELS

Initially computers were mainly used for solving mathematical and scientific problems where algorithms were well defined and human involvement was minimal in selecting the work flow of the programs. Programmers employed computers to solve their own problems, writing their instructions in machine readable programs. Later assembly language was used as programming environment followed by structured and object oriented paradigms. Furthermore evolution of mini and personal computers meant that software systems were required in other domains especially for office automation and educational purposes. This resulted in complex software internals, thereby increasing the complexity of its development activity too. As a result now software applications were not only transforming mathematical algorithms into computer instructions but also supporting human practices in carrying their work in efficient manner. There was no standard development methodology employed to carry out software development and as a result most of the software projects turned failure, leading to the software crisis. As a result the concept of software process emerged. Software process simply could be defined as the methodology to realize a software product. Humphrey (1989) described software process as a set of tools, methods and practices used to produce a software product. Pressman (1996) defined software process as a three phase activity i.e. definition, development and maintenance. The definition phase focuses on extending requirements, whereas development phase transforms those requirements into software system and finally maintenance phase aims at corrective actions and enhancements in software system after release.

The oldest software process model is waterfall model, which advocates for carrying out developmental activities in sequential way (cf. Royce, 1970; Pressman, 1996). This model works well when requirements are well known and fixed, which is very rare in real world projects. In order to improve its limitations prototyping (cf. Bischofberger. and Pomberger, 1992), spiral (cf. Boehm, 1988), incremental model (cf. Larman and Basili, 2003), V model (cf. Pressman, 1996), Rapid application development (cf. McConnell, 1995) and object oriented paradigm (cf. Booch et al., 2007). Rational Unified Process (RUP) is an object oriented model proposed and used by IBM, which stresses on using the Unified Modelling Language (UML) design elements and tools development by IBM. The model divides the process activities into micro and macro levels based on the division of the whole project into several modules (cf. Kruchten, 2003). In order to reduce the development time, and increase flexibility the notion of agile development emerged. These approaches accommodate changing requirements throughout the development process. The claim is that software projects are evolutionary by nature and the life time or the feasibility of the requirements for a software project may themselves be changed through the software development process. Agile development itself is not a software development process, but it is an approach advocating short iterative cycles, active user involvement and limited documentation (cf. Boehm and Turner, 2003; Schuh, 2005). Some of the software process methodologies which adhere to agile principles are following.

- Scrum (cf. Schwaber and Beedle, 2002)
- Feature driven development (cf. Palmer and Felsing, 2002)
- Crystal methodologies (cf. Cockburn, 2008)
- Adaptive software development (cf. Highsmith, 2000)
- Dynamic system development methodology
- Extreme programming (cf. Beck, 2000; Paulk, 2001)
- Lean software development (cf. Poppendieck, 2001)

Open source and global software development approaches, where work is carried out by different distributed teams has posed new challenges for software engineers, as traditional software development approaches are not optimal in this scenario. The major highlight of these development methodologies is computer based communication in contrast to face to face meetings (Raymond, 1998; Wayner, 2000).

There are several examples of development models proposed for free or open source projects. Cathedral and the Bazzar is one of the models which is usually mentioned as a typical example in open source development models or methodologies. The model appeared for the first time in 1996-1997 by Eric Raymond. The two words represent a combination of two models: Cathedral from the commercial world, and Bazaar from the Linux world. Rather than having specific activities and tasks, this model focused on some guidelines on open source development process. (Sharma et al, 2002) proposed a framework for open source development. They suggested that such framework should be able to systematically guide the creation and management of such communities within an organization. Such approach can be accomplished through three steps: community building, governance and infrastructure. The main idea is to have a light framework for communication to facilitate the flow of information among source code development community. A similar idea is discussed by (Madey et al, 2002) to enforce utilizing social networks in the open source development projects. It will be very important to extend source code version controls such as: subversion, source safe, etc to an Internet version (i.e. Distributed revision control systems). Such extension is expected to occur in the open source community in the near future. Despite these research efforts there is a need for a process model which could support open source and outsourced software development processes.

3. UNTRADITIONAL SOFTWARE DEVELOPMENT PROCESSES

Traditional software development process such as the waterfall process model is initially proposed for a typical project and software company style. Those are developed in established companies based on requirements that are, to a large extent, defined and known and agreed upon before the start of the development process. In such environment, the software development process is relatively easy to manage and run. However, in the current environment, perhaps it is unlikely for a company to have or win a project with all such stable criteria. Based on the software projects concerns we described earlier (i.e. project, people, product and process), at least one of those elements can be unstable or fixed in a particular project. There are some new untraditional software development process models (e.g. Agile methodologies) that are tried to handle and deal with such instability. The majority of recent software development process models focus on the instability in the requirements. However, there are some cases, where the requirements or at least the initial requirements are are fixed, yet the process, people or the project is unstable. In this section, we will discuss open source and open competition projects as examples of those agile projects.

3.1. Open Source and Open-Competition Projects

The Internet has opened the opportunity for expanding software projects coordinations across the globe. Team members, software project client and development team members can be all distant from each other and yet be able to communicate and run a successful project. Internet communication and social networking tools facililitate the ability to bridge or handle location and communication based problems between all stakeholders. In the software industry, software products are developed and available through different alternatives. Software products can be commercial. A company can buy a software or ask a software company to develop a software for a specific cost. This is the generic business model that is typical to any other type of business. In such model, all business, sale, and marketting strategies can be applicable.

Through the Internet, several software applications can be found free. This means that owners or developers of those software provide the executable of those software online without cost to be used permanently. If the free usage is limited for a specific time, such software can be called: trial version, shareware, etc. For marketting purpose, commercial companies may offer shareware versions of their. They may offer their software either in full versions, temporary, or in small or demo versions permenantly. Nonetheless, some software companies or individuals may offer their software completely free premanantly.

Software as a Service (SaaS) is another method of providing software products. Those products are provided as services which means that an Internet or network connection is always neede between service consumer and provider. Service consumers are given user names and password to access service and are usually charged based on the period or level of service.

Their is also another method to acquire software products. This is called "open source". Open source software products are not only free, the product source code is also available for users to study, use, modify, improve, and possibly redistribute under the open source license. There are several benefits of using open source products. Those include cost, flexibility, quality and reliability.

Acquisition cycles and associated entry costs are minimal for open source software. Total Cost of Ownership (TCO) is usually used to diffenertiate between free and open source software products where open source projects have no limits on number of users, licenses, period of usage, upgrade or support cost, etc. Flexibility means also that users escaped vendors lock-in as they have the freedom to switch from one product to another without liable consequences. The flexibility that open source projects offer is based on the fact that users are free to select or stop selecting a particular open source product. If a particular business requirements are changed, users can select to customize/change the open source project or they can decided to select another open source project without serious liable comitments for the earlier open source product. While initial thoughts assume that commercial products have higher quality as they have dedicated company with professional testing and evaluation unlike open source products. However, due to the large number of users and due to the fact that source code is available to users, bugs in open source projects are public. This give them the opportunity to be publically assessed, discussed and fixed. A large amount of developers globally contribute and analyze the code making it constantly increasing the quality. The life of an open source product is usually longer than the life of a commercial product. Open source products do not depend on a single company or entity where its faiulre may lead to a product end.

3.2. Open Source Projects Development Models

Open source projects are getting more and more popular in the software industry. There are also several models for building an open source software. Such models can be divided based on several charachtaristics. For example, based on revenue, some open source projects are completely free and open source. Developers of such projects offer such software for users to use, and extend without any cost. However, such users may not be comitted to solve bugs or maintain their products for users or customers. Anyone can write closed source versions or updates of such software and sell the

resulting software, as these permissive licenses allow such modification and redistribution. Many large open source products start in such model and then several companies exist to extend, support and maintain such software projects. Another form of revenue based models depend on offering certain features for free and extended, premium, or advanced features at cost (e.g. freemeium). Many open source projects started in individual efforts by a single developer or possibly a team of individuals (i.e. before forming a company). Upon initial signs of success, such indivudual or team may decide later on to form a company.

In such open source project the software developers act as: system analysists, designers, testers and users in addition for their software development tasks.

As many open source projects were initially based on personal or individual efforts, it is possibly difficult to predict whether such in such models a specific software development model has been used or adapted. More stable larger projects in terms of team size however may have a more clear development methodology. In addition, the teams who work on open source projects are usually distant based and with agile evolutionaly teams that contoninously change. New developers join and some may leave.

3.3. Open Competition Projects Development Models

By open competition projects we mean those sofwtare projects that use the Internet for communication between project stake holders without having an actual company for software development. This include several types and we discuss four types.

The first version of open competition projects are those websites which offer software development projects (such as: www.codeproject. com, www.devarticles.com, www.devshed.com, www.programmersheaven.com, www.codeguru. com, www.dreamincode.net). In those websites, software developers or programmers themselves usually describe requirements and develop the program based on those requirements. They usually try to solve a problem they faced through their study, work, etc. Similar to open source projects, users can download the executable and the source code of those projects.

In the second case websites offer code jobs for money. These websites work as mediators between projects' oferrers and developers. Projects' requestors submit their project requirements. Developers register their names as professionals and then bid for those submitted projects. Bids can include time and cost estimations. Those time and cost esttimations can be either submitted as constraints by projects' oferrers or by freelance coders. Exmples of such websites are www.freelancer.com, http://www.ifreelance.com, http://www.elance.com www.scriptlance.com, www.odesk.com, www.rentacoder.com, www.project4hire.com, www.guru.com, www.crowdspring, www.designcrowd, www.99designs, etc.

In the third category websites are usually not revenue oriented and they offer projects among students as competition. Moral rather than monitory rewards are usually offered in such competitions. Examples of such websites are www.tunedit.org, http://www.imaginecup.com.

In those three types of projects, there are some common attributes firstly, as mentioned earlier, the Internet is the main outlet of communication between code requestors and providers. Secondly typical business profile does not apply for software developers in those projects. While there are some small size companies who utilze those websites for revenue generation, nonetheless, the majority of software developers in those websites act on individual basis. There are some cases of open competitions (e.g. Netflix Prize, http://www.netflixprize.com) that turns to a successful commercial product.

The open competition or crowd source models are recently getting more popularity as many companies think that their are some programming

tasks that may not justify to hire one or more employees for. Such tasks can be outsourced in some way or another. In this sense crowd source can be considered as an extension to outcoursing rather than open source (where open source is a product model), while crowd and out source are process or project development models. Perhaps, with the expansion of crowd source websites and the accessibility of the Internet, crwod sourcing is expected to expand at the cost of out sourcing as crowd sourcing gives the ofering company to see different alternatives with the best or cheapest price for them with the fastest possible time searching for the best candidates. Crowd source websites are visited by a large number of experienced developers of all categroies and majors where it is always likely to find several possible cancidate indivduals or teams who are ready to offer solutions for your software or business problems. Examples of some of the generic tasks that can be crowd or outsourced include: some selected quanity repeitive tasks (e.g. those offered in Amazon Mechnical Turk: http://www.mturk.com). Other examples include: translation, graphic, database and website design and implementation.

The fourth type of open competition or crowd source projects are offered by some companies or entities on unplanned, or unperiodic bases. For example, in 2008, Cisco systems Inc. held an I-Prize contest in which teams using collaborative technologies created innovative business plans for a grand prize of US$250,000 (Dave 2008).

Many expert and senior software develpers may decide to work from home in the crowd course arena. Following are some reasons why crowd sourcing options can be seductive to many senior or expert software developers.

- **The leverage of working from home or any where:** Working in crowd source projects gives the developer the freedom to work from home or from any other place, work on their own and based on their own schedule. They can choose when to work and when to take a holiday. In the current Internet globally connected world and with the advance of telecommunication technologies, an expert developer can be in a rural island or a town competing in major projects and working in software project.

- **The leverage of working as independent and be their own boss:** For many senior software developers, working in a stressful environment with possibly bosses that they dont feel comfortable to work with can be a major problem. The nature of the software development and the expnasion of crowd source arenas enable software developers to gain a significant amount of continous and steady salary working on crowd source projects.

- **The ability to make their own brand or name:** Many software developers beleive that they can be underestimated or appreciated working in a large software company. Working as individuals and through many successful projects can help them make their own name popular and well known.

4. SOFTWARE EVOLUTIONARY MODELS

Applying a software development process model such as: waterfall, agile, Rational Unified Process (RUP), etc to an open source project is not practical. Open source development project should be people, project oriented or a hybrid model based project nature, resources, level of experience for people developing the project. Based on the classifications described earlier for people and project types, we can divide people and project models based on those classifications. For example, it is possible to divide project models into: small, medium and large size project development models. This size can be specified based on the size of the team working on the project or based on the prod-

uct size (e.g. Lines of Code LOC, requirements, components, etc).Based on information from management principles, we describe expectations from people or project oriented models.

- **Shared effective leadership:** In Open Source Projects (OSP), there is a need for a shared form of decision making that promote all individuals participation in making decisions. Leader effectiveness is measured in terms of contribution quality. Traditional systems are heavily centralized. Relatively few senior professionals are involved in taking decisions. In a shared leadership, conflict may arise. Nonetheless, in worst cases, redundant solutions can be offered. Users can then decide for best alternative.

- **Collective tasks and parallel programming:** While requirement and components may not be always separable, it is possible in several cases to work on parallel programming approaches, looking for the best possible solution for a particular problem.

- **Incremental errors corrections:** Errors are used as a basis for learning. If activities fail to achieve goals in one release, the implementation of the activities is examined to determine whether changes can be made to improve a given situation or whether something entirely different needs to be done. This analytical approach allows code community to openly examine shortcomings and discuss ways of overcoming them.

- Get help from others. A people oriented development model divides tasks based on people or roles. If a particular skill is not available, developer or team of developers should be open to seek help from externals. Open source project culture should be based on communication and collaboration.

- Provide people with the right tools. One of the major factors in development acceleration is the usage of Computer Aided Software Engineering (CASE) tools in all software development stages. Knowledge and training on using those tools should be shared and communicated among team members.

All in One Project Team: In many cases, software developers or designers working in crowd source projects may end up working alone on some projects. They may have then to do all kinds of tasks and activities starting from acting as users to collect and clarify all requirements. They also need to work as system analysts, designers, developers and testers. Such all in one type of job descriptions can be annoying to many software developers where they can be good developers and/or designers while they may have limitations to work in the other roles. In reality, their project may fail in some cases due to cosmetic reasons. Many software developers may underestimate the marketing and communication skills that they should have to be able to present themselves and their products in the right presentation and be able to properly "sell" themselves and their products.

The Challenge of Evaluation: The majority of the software projects in the crowd source competitions are evaluated through customers. For the best, fair and balance evaluation, especially in some cases where there is a strong competition on a project and many candidate projects are submitted, evaluation can be critical and sensitive. In most cases, clients are expected to reward and take only one project from all those submitted. Another serious challenge in such evaluation is that users can't take a long time to test and evaluate the different systems. They are expected to announce winners within a relatively short time. In addition, it is widely known that many good aspects of software design may need a significant amount of time to be evaluated. Evaluators are at

a high risk in lacking the ability to evaluate a good design. They are unintentionally encouraging the development of somewhat low quality software products. Evaluators usually evaluate products based on the specified requirements and based on some quality attributes that can be evaluated quickly.

4.1. People Based Project Decomposition

In traditional software development projects, requirements are gathered, a design is built, and then components are divided among software development team. In a large team, it is possible that each task is accomplished by a different individual (e.g. analyst, designer, developer, tester, etc). In open source and open competition projects it is possible that one individual may have to do all kinds of tasks. In other cases, where two or more software developers will be part of the project, nonetheless, especially when team members are distant from each other, project will be divided into components where each team member will be: analyst, designer, developer and tester for his/her own part. Figure 2 shows an example of a project divided based on people. This simple diagram indicates three basic things: Division is based on only initial, no through requirements, divisions must not be equal, and each division includes all types of tasks. An important indication from Figure 2 is that a people oriented model is not divided based on typical software development people roles (e.g. analyst, designer, developer, and tester) as such setting may occur in traditional business environments. However, in open source and open competition projects people models are divided based on the people who are part of the project no matter of their type of skills.

In some cases, division can be even based on releases. People and release based decompositions are not unpopular in such projects. In many of

Figure 2. People oriented project decomposition

First Developer	Second Developer	Third Developer
Part 1	Part 2	Part 3
Construction: Design Coding, & Testing	Construction: Design Coding, & Testing	Construction: Design Coding, & Testing
Construction: Design Coding, & Testing	Construction: Design Coding, & Testing	Construction: Design Coding, & Testing
Construction: Design Coding, & Testing	Construction: Design Coding & Testing	Construction: Design Coding, & Testing

those projects, individuals can frequently join or quit a particular team.

In Figure 3, it is proposed that after requirement and initial design stage, the project should be decomposed across the different teams. In traditional software process development models, decomposition occur based on the product. For example, in an iterative model, a product will be decomposed into 3 components (each will have a certain number of requirements) and then the project will go in 3 iterations to develop one component in every iteration. In each iteration, design, coding and testing for the component at hand will be performed. A final stage of integration and testing will occur at the end of the three iterations. A people model will divide requirements into people such as X, Y, Z. Everyone will have a certain number of requirements to develop and hence each developer has their own component. Each one will decide on the number

of iterations, or even the traditional software model to follow. While initial requirements' decomposition is considered product based, hence in such people oriented decomposition, product is further decomposed based on individuals and each individual component goes in a construction cycle independent from other individual components. The nature of the decomposition can depend on people, project and product classifications we mentioned earlier.

4.2. Team Distribution

The cooperation between software developers in the new forms of software project can take several different alternatives. In agile development models, pair programming is sometime used to enhance accuracy through having two developers working together. On the other hand, parallel programming can be used in open source and open competition

Figure 3. The proposed model for open source and competition projects

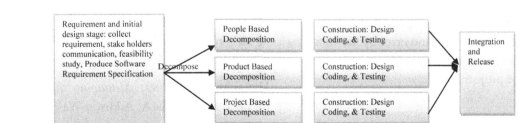

projects in several options. As mentioned earlier, in some cases of leadership conflict, parallel programming can be used to develop two alternatives and then select the best option or even broadcast them and let users decide. Team members can develop their own project sub component and test and evaluate the sub components of other team members. With no clear centralized leadership, shared evaluation is critical to avoid developing a disproportionate product. Different team members can frequently switch the roles (e.g. analyst, designers, developers, testers, users) among the different software projects.

CONCLUSION

In software engineering, software development projects are expanded on several scales and levels. The evolution of the internet, telecommunication and communication technologies made it possible to develop or acquire software products in more flexible and agile alternatives in comparison to traditional software development. In this chapter, several ideas are explored to discuss new development approaches for open source and open competition projects. There are several distinguished characteristics for those projects that make applying traditional software development process models impractical. We proposed people and project model approaches as an alternative for the traditional process model approaches. Software projects can be classified into several classifications, based on the project size, platform, domain, etc and each one of those classifications will have a distinguished development model that can be best used for. Shared leadership, effective communication channels and error cyclic fixing should be major common principles among all open source projects' models.

ACKNOWLEDGMENT

This chapter is an extended version of a paper "A software development process for open source and open competition projects" published in International Journal of Business Information Systems.

REFERENCES

Alsmadi, I., & Dieri, M. (2009). Separation of concerns in teaching software engineering. In *Proceedings of CISSE 2009,* USA. Retrieved from http://conference.cisse2009.org/proceedings.aspx

Bischofberger, W. R., & Pomberger, G. (1992). *Prototyping- oriented software development–Concepts and tools.* New York, NY: Springer-Verlag. doi:10.1007/978-3-642-84760-8

Boehm, B., & Turner, R. (2003). *Balancing agility and discipline: A guide for the perplexed.* Boston, MA: Addison-Wesley.

Boehm, B. W. (1988). A spiral model of software development and enhancement. *IEEE Computer,* *21*(5), 61–72. doi:10.1109/2.59

Booch, G., Maksimchuk, R., Engle, M., Young, B., Conallen, J., & Houston, K. (2007). *Object-oriented analysis and design with applications* (3rd ed.). Reading, MA: Addison-Wesley Professional.

Guélat, J.-C. (2009). *Integration of user generated content into national databases – Revision workflow at swisstopo.* 1st EuroSDR Workshop on Crowd Sourcing for Updating National Databases, Wabern, Switzerland.

Howe, J. (2008). *Crowdsourcing: Why the power of the crowd is driving the future of business.* Crown Business.

Humphrey, W. (1989). *Managing the software process. Reading.* MA: Addison-Wesley.

Kruchten, P. (2003). *The rational unified process: An introduction* (3rd ed.). Boston, MA: Addison-Wesley Longman Publishing Co., Inc.

Larman, C., & Basili, R. V. (2003). Iterative and incremental development: A brief history. *IEEE Computer*, *36*(6), 47–56. doi:10.1109/MC.2003.1204375

Madey, G., Freeh, V., & Tynan, R. (2002). *The open source software development phenomenon: An analysis based on social network theory*. AMCIS.

McConnell, S. (1995). *Rapid development*. Redmond, WA: Microsoft Press.

Palmer, S. R., & Felsing, J. M. (2002). *A practical guide to feature-driven development*. Prentice Hall International.

Paulk, M. (2001). Extreme programming from a CMM perspective. *IEEE Software*, (November-December): 19–26. doi:10.1109/52.965798

Pressman, R. S. (1996). *A manager's guide to software engineering*. New York, NY: McGraw-Hill.

Raymond, E. S. (1998). The cathedral and the bazaar. *First Monday*, *3*(3).

Royce, W. (1970). Managing the development of large software systems. *Proceedings of IEEE WESCON*, Vol. 26, (pp. 1–9. 25).

Schuh, P. (2005). *Integrating agile development in the real world*. Hingham, MA: Charles River Media.

Schwaber, K., & Beedle, M. (2002). *Agile software development with Scrum*. Upper Saddle River, NJ: Prentice-Hall.

Sharma, S., Sugumaram, V., & Rajagopalan, B. (2002). A framework for creating hybrid-open source software communities. *Information Systems Journal*, *12*(1), 7. doi:10.1046/j.1365-2575.2002.00116.x

Software Engineering Research Laboratory. (2008). Institute of Electrical and Electronics Engineers, Inc. Retrieved from www.swebok.org

Wayner, P. (2000). *Free for all*. New York, NY: HarperCollins.

Webb, D. (2008). *Why the Cisco i-Prize is so powerful*. ComputerWorld Canada. Retrieved from http://www.itworldcanada.com/a/Daily-News/563ea3a9-deab-4536-8b24-819f8de1c3d4.html

Chapter 11
Software Development Techniques for Constructive Information Systems

Runa Jesmin
Imperial College London, UK & Harefield Hospital, UK

ABSTRACT

This chapter discusses the software engineering lifecycle, history, and software architecture as well as the foundation of Information Engineering and Information Systems. The first part of this chapter discusses the software lifecycle phases and how to make effective use of various technical methods by applying effective technical and other efficient methods at the right time. This chapter also shows the technical similarities between software database design and Information System's database design. In the second part of this chapter, the author introduces the information engineering life cycle and discusses the key phrases for information engineering as well as Information System. In fact, this part is a good dictionary of information and software engineering. This chapter provides guidance for decision-makers in selecting an appropriate Information System strategy that contributes to the achievement of information engineering sustainability targets and leverages competitiveness.

1. INTRODUCTION

The term 'life cycle' means the changes that happen in the life of an animal or plant. In software engineering, this term is usually applied to artificial software systems to mean the changes that happen in the 'life' of a software product. Various identifiable phases between the product's 'birth' and its eventual 'death' are known as lifecycle phases.

Typical software lifecycle phases are (Leszek, 2005):

1. Requirement Analysis
2. System Design
3. Implementation
4. Integration and Development
5. Operation and Maintenance

DOI: 10.4018/978-1-4666-3679-8.ch011

There are a number of life cycle models – each for a different way of organising software development activities.

2. BACKGROUND

In software engineering, life cycle models representing different software engineering methodologies, aim to centralise developers efforts around critical issues such as usability, efficiency, reliability and customer satisfaction.

There are numerous books in software modelling but comparatively Information Engineering fields could improve with more research in this area (Ivar et al,1999). On the contrary, Information Engineering is certainly well developed in providing successful system for overall profit and success (Sidney et al. review of 1974).

There are many Information Engineering dictionaries available in the market (e.g. business-dictionary.com) but this chapter will provide the reader a good simple groundwork of Information Engineering.

3. SOFTWARE DEVELOPMENT

John Tukey has used the term "software" the first time in the American Mathematical Monthly journal in January 1958. However, the purpose of software remains the same today as it was in the 1940s – at the very beginning of computing.

Today software development is often used to enhance a company's enterprise information capabilities by building new functions into an already existing infrastructure, or by gluing together existing systems to carry out new services (Kevin et al. 2005).

In general, the emphasis in software development is increasingly on systems as components in larger systems, components, which interact and combine with each other, perhaps in ways that were not envisaged by their original developers.

The true process of software development is usually based on an irrational process (Pauline, 2004). A rational approach to software development is believed to lead to better software development. In addition, measurements of project progress are made simpler if an initial agreement on how a project is to be carried out exists, based on such guidance.

(Parnas & Clements, 86) Faking the design process allows ease of readability and understanding of the development process by outsiders.

3.1 Software Architecture

Software architecture is a coherent set of abstract patterns guiding the design of each aspect of a larger software system.

A Dutch computer scientist first used the concept 'Software architecture' in 1960s but has increased in popularity since the early 1990s, largely due to activity within Rational Software Corporation and within Microsoft.

Mary Shaw and David Garlan's book on Software Architecture perspective on an emerging discipline in 1996 brought forward the concepts in Software Architecture, such as components, connectors, styles and so on.

The software architect develops concepts and plans for software modularity, module interaction methods, user interface dialog style, interface methods with external systems, innovative design features, and high-level business object operations, logic, and flow.

Software architecture describes the coarse grain components (usually describes the computation) of the system. The connectors between these components describe the communication, which are explicit and pictured in a relatively detailed way. In the implementation phase, the coarse components are refined into "actual components," e.g, classes and objects. In the object-oriented field, the connectors are usually implemented as interfaces.

For example, partitioning a system into a GUI, functional core, and data repository. The GUI depends on the core because it invokes operations of the core, and the core may depend on the GUI (if it invokes GUI operations to display the result of computations, for example). The core depends on the repository. There may be no other connections – this kind of architecture is termed as a three-tier architecture.

4. PARTICIPANTS IN SYSTEMS DEVELOPMENT PROCESS

See Figure 1 for a diagram.

4.1 The Information System Engineering

There are many methods for developing Information Systems. The method is chosen to specify various characteristics of the development projects, some examples are:

- Size, scope, and constraints - time, budget etc.
- User requirements

One of the most common methods is the Systems Development Lifecycle (SDLC) methodology is based on the waterfall model. Waterfall model is a logical step-by-step approach to systems development (see Figure 2).

Figure 1. Participants in information systems development process

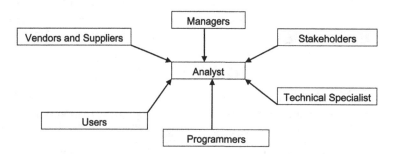

Figure 2. Information system development lifecycle

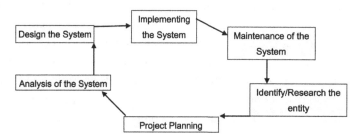

4.2 Information Engineering

Information Engineering is a method to create and maintain Information Systems.

4.2.0 Planning

4.2.0.1 Strategic Planning

Steps of Strategic Planning:

1. Identify Strategic Planning Factors
    a. Goals
    b. Critical Success Factors
    c. Problem Areas

Goals: Strategic plan depends on the nature of the project, members' culture, size and complexity of the project's environment and above all knowledge and expertise of the creators or planners.

Critical Success Factors: (Sidney et al. review of 1974) Studied over 56 corporations, with 619 diverse businesses and concluded that strategic planning establishes relationship between strategic planning and profit performance.

Problem Areas: Whilst identifying the strategic planning factors, one would have difficulty to see 'the forest for the trees'. This is due to too many factors affecting the main goal of the project and individual set of strategies needs careful selection to achieve the goal.

'Weakness could be identified' as problem areas and careful planning is the key to overcome the above.

4.2.0.2 Corporate Planning

Steps of Corporate Planning:

1. Objects
    a. Organizational Units
    b. Locations
    c. Business Functions
    d. Entity types

The Corporate Planning Objects defines the business scale.

The scale limits subsequent system analysis and where subsequent system changes could occur.

Organizational Units and Locations: Organizational units are the various organizational departments. Places where the business operations occur are Organizational locations.

Business Functions: The related groups of business processes to support the mission of the organization are called Business functions.

Entity types: An entity is a distinct, self-existence and independent. Organization (business) manages different categories of data. Major categories of data including people, places, corporations, limited liability companies, and sole proprietorships are types of common entities of business.

4.2.0.3 Develop Enterprise

Enterprise Model: Information and resources of an identifiable business, functions, processes and definition of the business structure is the Enterprise Model of Business. Enterprise Model is the core model of all other models.

How to Develop Enterprise Model:

1. **Function decomposition:** Makes complex business process simple by showing its individual element. Function decomposition is very useful to facilitate large business and to solve complicated business process. It is a top down approach planning.
2. **Entity-Relationship Diagram or ERD:** Entity is a person, object, place or event for which data is collected.
3. Within an information system, entity relationship diagram graphically represents the entity and the relationship between the entities. Relation between the entities could be one to one, one to many, many to one and many to many.

Attribute is the collected data about the entities (see Figure 3).

Planning Matrices: Planning matrix represent the relationships between data entities and other organizational planning objects. Planning matrix can be manipulated to understand the patterns of relationships.

For example: A series of matrices can be developed to cross-reference various elements of the organization such as:

1. **Function-To-Data:** Identifies the data that are captured, used, updated, deleted within each function.
2. **Data-to-Function:** Identifies the relationship between data entities and business functions within the enterprise.
3. **Function-to-Objective:** Identifies the functions within the Business Objective.
4. **Unit-to-Function:** Identifies the relationships between organizational entities and each business function.
5. **Location-to-Unit:** Identifies the organizational units that are located in or interact with a specific function.
6. **Location-to-Function:** Identifies business functions that are being performed at different organizational locations.

7. **Process-to-Information System:** Identifies the Business Processes that supports information Systems.
8. **Information System-to-process:** Identifies the information systems that support each business process.
9. **Information Systems application to business objective:** Identifies the information systems that support each business objective.
10. **Business Objective to Information Systems application:** Identifies the Business Objectives that supports the Information Systems.

4.2.1 Analysis

1. **Develop Conceptual Model (detailed E-R Diagram):** Conceptual Model describes a system based on qualitative assumptions about its elements, their interrelationships, and system boundaries.
2. **Develop Process Models (data flow diagrams):** A data flow diagram representing sequence of activities is a business process model.

4.2.2 Design

1. **Design Databases (normalized relations):** Normalization eliminates unreliable functional dependencies within the existing attributes of existing relations.
2. Design Processes
   a. **Action Diagrams:** In design process, action diagrams provide graphical overview of the system/business. To build an action diagram you need to identify data components and their relationship.
   b. **User Interfaces:** Menus, screens, reports: The content that makes user interfaces includes menus, screens, reports and user interaction with the content of the user interface.

Figure 3. Figures shape-description for ER Diagram

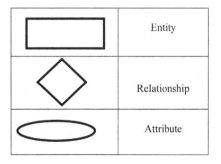

[rectangle]	Entity
[diamond]	Relationship
[ellipse]	Attribute

4.2.3 Implementation

1. **Build database definitions (tables, indexes, etc.):** The aim to build a database is to manage, edit and upgrade the content that has been built (with data) for a business or organization.
2. **Generate Applications (program code, control blocks, etc.):** Control blocks do not hold memories. In fact, program code can create the format control block will hold. Control Block usually has Application Programming Interface calls for the programmer.

CONCLUSION

In this chapter, we have discussed the definition of different areas of Information Engineering and given some hints in software engineering.

In next edition of this book, we will discuss the relevant development processes, keeping in mind that learners get a more complex, broad and in depth understanding of the Information Engineering.

FUTURE RESEARCH DIRECTIONS

At present, we have sound research direction for Information Engineering, for Software Engineering and for other similar research areas.

It would be interesting to direct the future research towards the trend and transition of Information Engineering research areas and how certain areas (e.g. database modelling, system development) have been developed due to the well-developed research in Information Engineering and vice-versa.

REFERENCES

Jacobson, I., Booch, G., & Rumbaugh, J. (1999). *The unified software development process*. Addison Wesley Publication.

Kan, P. (2004). *Structuring specifications of reactive systems using B*. PhD Thesis, Kings College, University of London.

Lano, K. (2005). *Advanced system design in Java*. London, UK: Butterworth-Heinman.

Maciaszek, L. A., & Liong, B. L. (2005). *Practical software engineering*. Addison Wesley Publications.

Parnas, D., & Clements, P. C. (1986). A rational design process: How and why to fake it. *IEEE Transactions on Software Engineering, 12*(2), 251-256. ISSN: 098-5589

PhD Thesis. (2007). *Accessible and Usable Internet System*. Kings College, University of London.

Schoeffler, S., Buzzell, R. D., & Heany, D. F. (1974). Review: Impact of strategic planning on profit performance. *Harvard Business Review*, (March-April): 137–145.

Section 2
Advanced Topics in Software Engineering

Chapter 12
Software Security Engineering – Part I:
Security Requirements and Risk Analysis

Issa Traore
University of Victoria, Canada

Isaac Woungang
Ryerson University, Canada

ABSTRACT

It has been reported in the literature that about twenty new software vulnerabilities are reported weekly. This situation has increased the security awareness in the software community. Nowadays, software services are expected not only to satisfy functional requirements but also to resist malicious attacks. As demand for more trustworthy systems is increasing, the software industry is adjusting itself to security standards and practices by increasing security assessment and testing effort. Even though there is a consensus that better software engineering is to improve software quality in the early stage of software development, so far, various approaches that have been proposed to analyze and quantitatively measure the software security target, primarily show the finished software products in their operational life. There are few achievements on how to reduce or effectively mitigate the security risks faced by software products during the development process. In this chapter, the authors introduce a novel model-driven perspective on secure software engineering, which integrates seamlessly software security analysis with traditional software development activities. A systematic security engineering process that starts in the early stages of the software development process and spans the entire software lifecycle is presented. Fundamental software security concepts and analysis techniques are also introduced, and several illustrative examples are presented, with focus on security requirements and risk analysis.

DOI: 10.4018/978-1-4666-3679-8.ch012

INTRODUCTION

Over the last decades, software quality attributes such as maintainability, reliability, and performance have been widely studied. In contrast, less attention has been paid to the field of software security, sometime due to the complex and multifaceted nature of the notion of security or for economical reasons such as the need to shorten "time to market". As of today, the study of software security still remains immature. Current approaches to software security engineering referred to as *"penetrate and patch"* consist mostly of fixing security flaws after they have been exploited. *"Penetrate and patch"* is a fictitious solution which deals only with the symptoms and not the deep causes of the problem. This can be worrisome because software applications are often deployed in malicious environments in which security attacks and intrusions happen all the time. The computer security technology business is a fast growing sector, with increasing marketing opportunities. The CSI/FBI annual survey is an insightful reference of how often computer crimes occur and how expensive they can be. In their survey for the year 2003, it was reported that the total annual financial losses were $201,797,340 (Richardson, 2003).

This observation could actually be worse since only 251 out of the 530 participants (47%) reported their losses. The survey also shows other compelling statistics: 92% of the respondents detected attacks during the last 12 months while 75% of the respondents acknowledged financial losses due to security breaches. As mentioned above, only 47% reported their losses though. Therefore, the question is: how do organizations cope with such attacks?

Many organizations address security from three different perspectives: prevention, detection, and reaction. According to the 2003 CSI/FBI survey (Richardson, 2003), 99% of the respondents use a mixture of various technologies pertaining to those perspectives. For example, more than 90% use prevention technologies such as firewall, access control, and physical security.

Firewall technology has been used so far to protect and isolate segments of networks against untrusted networks, by filtering out harmful traffic. However, there are several limitations on firewall technologies, which make them insufficient to achieve strong network protection. There are several widely publicized exploits that allow hackers to access sensitive data by tunneling through authorized protocols. In order to provide a stronger level of security, most organizations combine firewalls with a range of security monitoring tools named intrusion detection systems (IDS); 73% of the company surveyed by CSI/FBI use intrusion detection systems. The role of IDS is to monitor and detect computer and network intrusions, in order to take appropriate measures that would prevent or avoid the consequences. Intrusion detection systems, however, are severely limited by their ineffectiveness in detecting new forms of attacks. This is unfortunate, since the Internet is a wild zone, where new forms of security attacks are developed and executed daily.

A large number of these attacks succeed because of the existence of software flaws such as buffer overflow, Trojan horse, or race conditions. These flaws may be directly related to the security mechanisms themselves, which in a large number of cases are implemented as software (e.g. firewall, IDS, encryption scheme etc.). They may also be related to other software applications whose primary purpose is not security related.

As a matter of fact, it is commonly agreed (Mc Graw, 1998) that software carries the biggest security challenge of today's systems: about 20 new software vulnerabilities are reported weekly. Unfortunately software security engineering is still in its infancy. Current approaches to software security engineering referred to as *"penetrate and patch"* (Mc Graw, 1998) consists mostly of fixing security flaws after they have been exploited. *"Penetrate and patch"* is a fictitious solution which deals only with the symptoms and not the deep causes of the problem.

A more effective approach to software security consists of treating it from a quality assurance perspective and integrating security concerns in the entire software life cycle from the requirements definition to the production stage. Following a well-defined process allows us to clearly define the actual security issues faced by the system, to select and implement appropriate protection mechanisms, and to make sure that these mechanisms work when they are needed. Our focus in this Chapter is on security requirements and risk analysis. A new model-driven perspective on secure software engineering is described, which integrates seamlessly software security analysis with traditional software development activities, resulting in a systematic security engineering process.

The rest of the Chapter is organized as follows. Firstly, several aspects of software security are discussed. Secondly, the software security engineering lifecycle is described, along with security requirements. Thirdly, a discussion on the security risk analysis is presented as related to the notions of threat, vulnerability, and attacks. A medical record keeping system example is used to illustrate the studied concepts.

ASPECTS OF SOFTWARE SECURITY

Software Aspects

Our society is critically dependent on a wide range of software systems, tools, and applications. Almost every software system deployed today must be accompanied by some defense mechanisms against malicious adversaries. These mechanisms cannot be well understood without a-prior and comprehensive knowledge of software aspects. Of course, the development and deployment of software security mechanisms is dependent of both the software aspects and the chosen software

security engineering method (such as the one proposed in this work). Key software aspects (see Figure 1) include:

- **Software type:** Typically, a software can be classified either as customized (i.e. developed for specific purpose), generic, embedded into a hardware, real-time based, processing-based, or a combination of these types (Lethbridge and Laganière, 2001).
- **Software development life cycle:** A conceptual framework that describes the activities performed at each stage of a software development project. As an example, the Waterfall model and its variants (Lethbridge and Laganière, 2001).
- Software deployment and maintainability.
- **Software usability:** Which captures the degree of user friendliness of a software system (Lethbridge and Laganière, 2001). In this capacity, security should have minimal impact on the system's usability - this can be realized for instance by balancing the security features with the usability factors.
- Software privacy and security.

Aspects of Software Security

Technically, software security can be defined as a combination of *confidentiality*, *integrity*, and

Figure 1. Software aspects

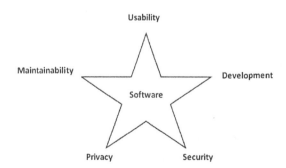

availability (CIA) aspects (ITSEC, 1991). Of course, the interpretation of these aspects and the contexts in which they occur or can be achieved are variable, depending on the needs of the system, software actors, and of the organizations policies.

In general, *confidentiality* refers to keeping the data and resources secret or concealing the existence of data. The key related questions that should be addressed are: who needs which data (data/resource access)? How do we know a user is who he/she claims to be (user's authentication, i.e., identity and verification). Typically, breaching confidentiality will result in unauthorized disclosure of data (FIPS, 2004).

Integrity can be viewed as referring to the correctness and trustworthiness of data and resources, ensuring that only authorized modification on these data and resources are permitted (integrity may refer to data integrity or origin integrity, both relying on trust management and authorization). However, the interpretation of integrity is context-dependent, i.e. the integrity of an asset (data or resource) could mean its precision, accuracy, consistency, currency, usefulness, meaningfulness, to name a few, or any combination of asset's properties.

Finally, *availability* refers to ensuring that the data and resources can be accessed by authorized entities when needed. Its interpretation is also context-dependent, i.e. the availability of an asset could mean that it is useful, or it has sufficient capacity, or it can be completed in an acceptable period of time, or any combination of asset's properties. When considering the aforementioned CIA aspects, the policies, processes and software must be viewed and analyzed under the same security perspective.

The CIA objective should be balanced in order to fulfill the security goals. For instance, in a network environment, disconnecting a computer from the Internet will increase the data confidentiality, but the price is that the data availability and data integrity will suffer due to lack of updates. Having extensive checks of the data by many different software actors/systems will increase the data integrity while making the data confidentiality worse since more people will access the data. Data availability will suffer as well due to locks on the data under verification.

An analysis of the potential impacts of CIA on organizational resources, operations, and software actors is presented in (FIPS, 2004) in terms of security objectives, defined as low, moderate, and high. The interdependency between confidentiality, availability, and integrity is discussed in (Bishop, 2004).

It should be pointed out that accountability and security assurance are added as additional aspects (NIST, 2004). Accountability refers to making sure that an entity's action can only be traceable to that entity, i.e. one can tell who did what and when. Accountability can be achieved through audit (weak form of accountability) - this consists of examining the audit logs for evidence of the deed and the identity of the perpetrator, as well as through non-repudiation (strong form of accountability) – this is used to detect a false denial of an act, for instance, through using a method which requires the users to sign some requests for the system's actions. Assurance can be interpreted as a mean for enforcing or validating the correctness of software/system protection mechanisms. It can also be used to indicate how much to trust a system, by designing assurance arguments capable of convincing or ensuring that: (1) The required functionality is present and correctly implemented; (2) There is sufficient protection against unintentional errors, and sufficient resistance to intentional penetration and by-pass. Three kinds of assurance (Traore, 2009) contribute to a strong assurance argument:

- **Design assurance:** This type of assurance consists of using security engineering practices to identify important threats and choose appropriate countermeasures.
- **Development assurance:** This type of assurance consists of using disciplined pro-

cesses to implement the design correctly and deliver the final system securely and reliably.

- **Operational assurance:** This type of assurance mandates a secure installation, configuration and a day-to-day operation of the system.

Software Security Goals

The above mentioned software security goals can be realized by using an iterative secure software development life cycle model such as the one proposed in this Chapter (see Figure 2), coupled with a threat modeling technique (Howard and Le Blanc, 2002), (Graff and Van, 2003), (Curphey, 2006).

As part of a software security process (Howard and Lipner, 2006), threat modeling is an essential step. It helps defining the design goals from a security perspective. It also helps integrating these goals into the software architecture, design, and configuration.

Threat modeling can be considered as a methodological process that complements the software risk analysis and mitigation processes (see Figure 2), with the goal to: (1) determine the level of risks at various views of the software system, (2) identify those areas of the software with most exposure to attacks that are needed to be tested, and (3) test these areas. Typically, two approaches are employed: (1) Adversarial-based threat modeling - this approach consists of identifying holes and vulnerabilities in the software system, then, investigate them with the goal of gaining access to their objectives, and (2) Defensive-based threat modeling - this approach focuses on identifying existing and probable vulnerabilities, then determine how to remove the most possible ones and use countermeasures to reduce further potential attack risks.

SOFTWARE SECURITY ENGINEERING

Software Security Lifecycle

As mentioned above software security engineering is a field that is still immature. Little work exists on the topic in the research literature. This Chapter proposes a global approach to building secure software that covers the main aspects of traditional software life cycle. Figure 2 describes the main activities involved in this approach:

- During the *planning phase*, the system requirements are expressed along with the expectations in terms of security. This involves defining the services expected from the system and the resources involved. By identifying resources and services, protection goals can be formulated accordingly.

- The planning phase is followed by the *analysis phase*. The system requirements augmented with the security aspects are analyzed as usual by identifying the key functionality. This consists of determining and specifying the use cases. The use cases identified at this level correspond to expected system functionalities. A lot of security issues, however, are based on unexpected system behaviors. So in addition of regular use case analysis, it is essential to study the system response to unexpected events or circumstances. This is carried during misuse analysis, where *misuse cases* are identified (Sindre and Opdahl, 2001). Misuse cases are negative use cases, which capture unexpected usage scenarios. Misuse analysis triggers the construction of the threat model underlying the system. It is the initial step of security risk analysis process during which potential attack targets are formulated at a higher level.

Figure 2. Software security life cycle

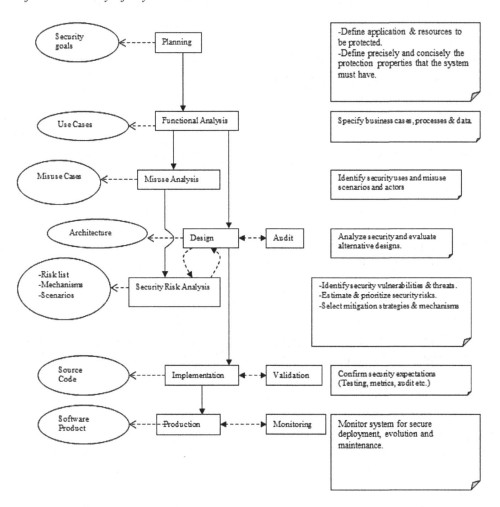

- The outcome of the analysis phase is fed into the *design phase*. Further refining the use cases identified earlier carries out the design. The outcome of the design is the software architecture description.
- The initial software architecture obtained serves as basis for *security risk analysis phase*. At this stage, the risk analysis consists of further refining the misuse cases identified earlier into a more complete and detailed threat model. Misuse cases typically represent target of security compromise, which can be refined using analysis

techniques such as attack trees (Moore et al., 2001) presented later. Security risk analysis mainly consists of 'what if' analysis, during which the system is investigated for potential vulnerabilities and threats. The outcome of this phase is a list of potential risks. Identified risks should be categorized and prioritized using either some qualitative or quantitative scheme. Identifying the risks allows selecting appropriate protection mechanisms; there is no need to protect a system against some unlikely threat. Prioritizing the risks allows conducting some costs analysis and deciding the level of protection worth implementing. There is no need for investing more efforts and money in protecting a system, which worth less. For instance, it doesn't make sense to spend $20,000 in securing a resource which worth only $10,000.

Adopted risk mitigation strategies and mechanisms are then integrated in the design, giving rise to a secure software architecture, which serves as blueprint for the implementation. But before proceeding to the implementation, it is more appropriate to evaluate the design against the security requirements, which may lead to alternative (more secure) architectures.

Evaluation methods vary from informal to formal. Informal methods consist of 'what if' analysis during, which various scenarios are weighed. Evaluation techniques based on metrics provides more systematic way for predicting the level of security based on the design. Evaluation techniques based on formal methods are more rigorous but more difficult and thereby more expensive to use.

- During the *implementation phase*, the software code obtained is audited or tested for security. Security auditing can be done manually by inspecting the source code based on security guidelines, or automatically using auditing tools. The main goal is to validate the final application with respect to the original security requirements.
- The *production phase* comes after the *implementation* and consists of deploying, operating, and maintaining the software product. During this phase the application must be continuously monitored for security. First, we need to ensure that the application is securely deployed. Initial security configuration is a prerequisite for the operation of any secure system. The operation

and maintenance of the system must conform to security practices and standards. The evolution of the system must also be carried out securely.

For all these activities it is essential to ensure that the security policy is never violated. The security policy is a document that defines precisely and concisely the protection mechanisms that the system must provide. The security policy serves as basis for the elaboration of the system security requirements. It is important to mention that the security policy is a more abstract and general document. The system security requirements should be refined, adapted, and integrated into the general system requirements.

Security Requirements

Fundamental Computer Security Requirements

The Trusted Computer Security Evaluation Criteria (TCSEC) (Thompson, 2003) requires that a secure system be composed of six required parts as shown in Figure 3.

These parts, referred to as fundamental Computer Security Requirements (see Figure 3) include:

- **Security Policy:** There must be an explicit and well-defined security policy enforced by the system.
- **Marking/Labeling:** Access control marking/labeling must be associated with objects.
- **Identification:** Individual subjects must be identified.
- **Accountability:** Audit information must be selectively kept and protected so that actions affecting security can be traced to the party responsible for a particular event.
- **Assurance:** The computer system must contain hardware/software mechanisms

Figure 3. Fundamental computer security requirements

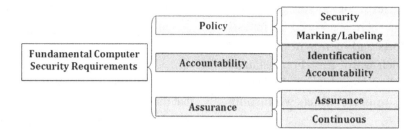

that can be independently evaluated to provide sufficient assurance that the system enforces security requirements.

- **Continuous Protection:** The trusted mechanisms that enforce these basic requirements must be continuously protected against tampering and/or unauthorized modifications.

Software Security Requirements

Traditionally, security used to be built into software systems as an after-thought, mostly after the core functionalities have been implemented. Sound and effective security engineering, however, require integrating security concerns in the entire software life cycle. In this regard, security requirements must be formulated as early as possible, preferably at the time of software requirements elicitation. Security requirements must be expressed at the time when expected system functionalities are decided. At this early stage, security requirements typically consist of high-level goals, which may be drawn on fundamental security requirements as expressed above for TCSEC. A software security requirements document typically involves little product-specific knowledge, since the application is not built yet. Like any kind of requirements document, it should focus on defining what level of security should be provided rather than how security should be implemented.

It should include at minimum the following types of information:

- Identify potential users and associated security requirements.
- Define security management policy and actors.
- Define the target environment, network, hardware and software infrastructure.
- Identify existing security infrastructure that can be leveraged.
- Define resources and services, their required protection level, and their level of criticality.

As the development goes on, these high-level security requirements should be refined into a more specific policy that expresses concisely the protection goals for the system. This typically may take place after thorough security risk analysis for the system as shown in Figure 4. During the risk analysis process, a threat model identifying the specific threats faced by the system is established. Based on the threat model, a security policy that characterizes the specific protection mechanisms required for the system is defined.

The early version of a security policy can be an abstract document drawn from the organization's global security policy or an existing generic security policy model. But for the policy to be useful, it should be refined and instantiated by integrating the particular security concerns of the application, and the specific resources and services provided or used by the application.

The initial architecture obtained after functional design is revised for security by integrating

Figure 4. Functional and security requirements analysis

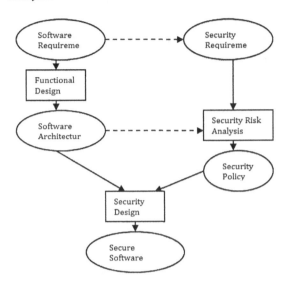

the protection rules and mechanisms specified in the security policy. The outcome of this revision is a security-aware architecture, which should in principle provide the protection level required for the application.

Example: A Medical Record Keeping System

In order to illustrate the concepts introduced in this Chapter, we take as running example the requirements of a medical record keeping adapted from (Traore and Aredo, 2004). The functional and security requirements for the system are summarized here. An initial set of use cases from the functional requirements are also derived; which will serve later for security risk analysis purpose.

Functional Requirements

The purpose of this system is to maintain electronic records for patients' medical information at a hospital. The medical records are kept in a central database (perhaps attached to a departmental mainframe computer). These medical records

are accessible remotely from the Internet as well as from various terminals operated by authorized medical personnel (e.g. doctors, nurses etc), and by patients.

Security Requirements

Security is an essential characteristic of the record keeping system. The system must provide special protection features dealing with suspicious users, disclosure of private information, and unauthorized modification of protected information.

The actors involved in this system are the patients, doctors, authorized health workers (e.g.: nurses, accountants, secretaries, etc.) and site administrators. The main resources to be secured are medical records of patients. A patient may choose a unique family doctor who is automatically granted the right to read and modify medical records of the patient. The family doctor may refer a patient to a specialist, who should be granted access to his record. Only authorized doctors can read or update a medical record. An authorized doctor is a registered doctor that a patient has chosen either as his family doctor or as "guest" doctor, e.g. a specialist, or for travel reasons or unavailability of family doctor etc. The patient is the only person that is allowed to choose his/her own doctor.

A patient may have read access to his own medical record, but he cannot modify it. The site administrator is the only person who can create, delete, read, or modify a patient record. Every access to the patients' records must be audited. Only Auditors can read the audit log. To avoid conflict of interest, auditors should be third parties not involve in the regular operation of the system. The system is required to be secure, i.e. it must ensure that integrity, confidentiality, and availability are always preserved.

Architecture

In order to conduct thorough security risk analysis, a clear understanding of the environment in which the software system will be deployed should be established. Figure 5 shows an example of physical and networked architectures for a theoretical hospital. Knowing this, a potential attacker could attempt to gain access at any point. In such a hospital configuration, some level of physical security at building access points can be expected. Hospitals are essentially a public service, and as such, are accessed by everyone. This raises security concerns that also need to be addressed.

Use Case Analysis

The analysis of the functional requirements starts by expressing the use cases. We start with an initial list of use cases and actors (as shown in Figure 6). At this stage, the focus is mainly on eliciting

the functionalities as indicated in the functional requirements. Non-functional requirements such as security will be taken into account later.

Our initial list consists of the following actors and use cases.

Use Cases:

- **Maintain:** Collection of functions related to the administration and maintenance of the record keeping system. This use case will typically need to be further refined.
- **Create record:** Record creation operation.
- **View record:** Record searching, opening and reading operations.
- **Update record:** Edition of the record in order to update existing information. This

Figure 5. Physical network architecture for the medical record system

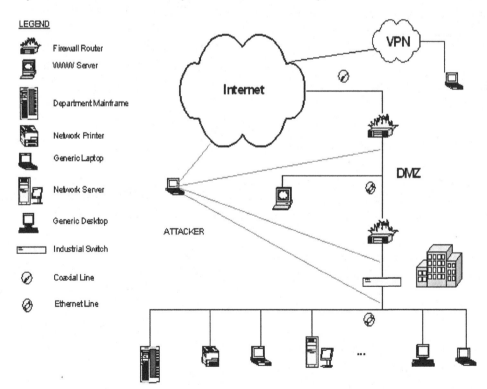

Figure 6. Initial use cases for the medical record system

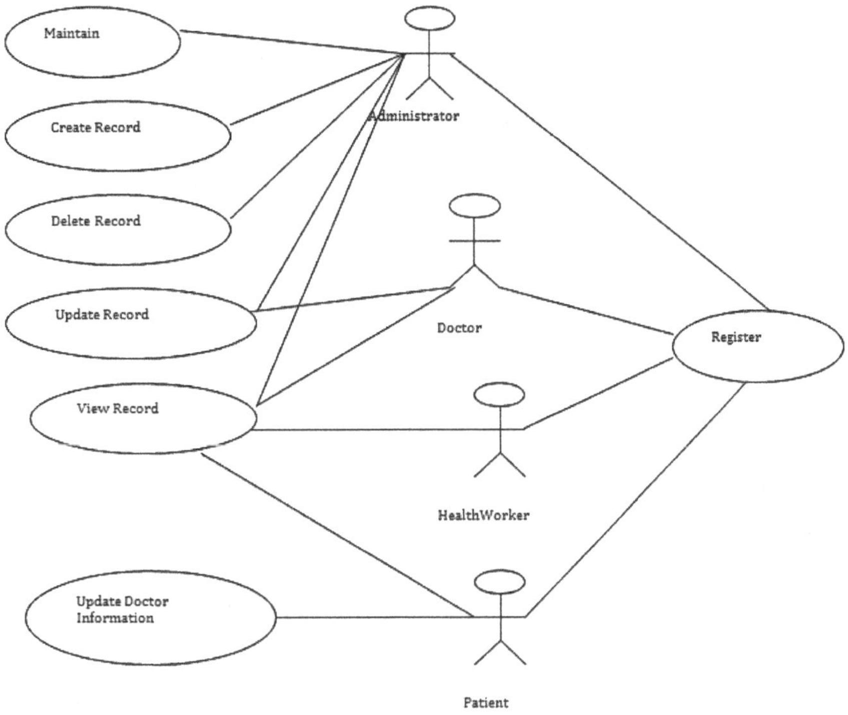

operation must not allow deletion of existing information.

- **Delete record:** Deletion of partial or full content of the record.
- **Register:** Provides a collection of features and functions for user registration.
- **Update doctor information:** Allow patients to add or remove doctors from their list of authorized doctors.

Actors:

- **Administrator:** In charge of the administration of the system.
- **Doctor:** Registered doctor chosen by a patient or referred to by a family doctor.
- Patient
- **Health Worker:** Encompasses various categories of health workers (e.g. nurses, management, billing, pharmacists etc.)

who may access patients' records for various purposes.

SECURITY RISK ANALYSIS

Overview of Security Risk Analysis

The key concepts that come in play when dealing with security risk issues include the notions of threat, vulnerability, and attack:

- A *threat* corresponds to any potential situation that can have an undesirable impact on the computer system resources or services.
- A *vulnerability* corresponds to some weakness in the system that makes the occurrence of a threat possible.
- An *attack* corresponds to some action taken by a malicious user to exploit a system

vulnerability, leading to the effective occurrence of a threat.

- A *security risk* is a related concept that corresponds to the chance or possibility for a threat to materialize. It can also be defined as the possibility or chance that an attack succeeds.

Security risk analysis is a process through which the system's vulnerabilities and cor-
responding threats to its security are identified and evaluated. The risk created by the threats are evaluated quantitatively or qualitatively and prioritized. Based on risks prioritization, appropriate mitigation strategies and mechanisms cab be selected. The main goal of a successful risk analysis is to significantly reduce the likelihood of successful attacks.

Software Vulnerabilities

A variety of computer security vulnerabilities have been identified and are being discovered on a regular basis. Specialized organizations such as CERT or BugTraq (US-CERT, 2012) maintain a list of vulnerabilities reported by organizations and individuals.

There are several sources of software vulnera-
bilities. Some of the most popular ones include race conditions exploit, access control mishandling, poor cryptographic choices and implementations, misplaced trust, database protection, and input validation issues (Bishop, 2004). In the sequel, a taxonomy of common software vulnerabilities (Jiwani and Zelkowitz, 2004) is presented, then two of those kinds of vulnerabilities, namely input validation and race conditions, are discussed. The specialized literature on other categories of software vulnerabilities can be found in (Howard and Le Blanc, 2002), (Viega and McGraw, 2001).

A Taxonomy of Software Security Vulnerabilities

A taxonomy represents a good basis for under-
standing and analyzing potential vulnerabilities in a software system. Several taxonomies have been proposed in the literature for security flaws. One of the most famous one is attributed to Landwher et al. (Landwher et al.,1994). A recent taxonomy dedicated for software security flaws (Jiwani and Zelkowitz, 2004) was derived from the taxonomy proposed by Landwher et al. (Landwher et al., 1994).

This taxonomy (shown in Table 1) is a good help in understanding software security vulner-
abilities. It is a three-axis taxonomy specifying what are the cause, location and impact for each category of vulnerability. The cause corresponds to the genesis or origin of the vulnerability. The location corresponds to the functionality or service that contains the flaw. The impact refers to the potential consequence of the vulnerability on the system in case of successful exploit, i.e. it corresponds typically to the threat created by the vulnerability.

Input Validation Attacks

Input Validation attacks is a general class of at-
tacks, in which the attacker invokes some functions with malicious input leading to some unwanted consequence. In general, these forms of attacks succeed simply because inputs to corresponding functions have not been properly validated. Popu-
lar examples of input validation attacks include: buffer overflow attacks and unexpected operator attacks. Unexpected operator attacks consist of passing some unexpected operator to a program as input causing some malicious action to take place. On the other hand, buffer overflow attacks exploit program vulnerabilities to excessively long input values.

Table 1. Taxonomy of security vulnerabilities (Jiwani & Zelkowitz, 2004)

Cause	Location	Impact
Validation errors	System initialization	Unauthorized access
Domain errors	Memory management	Root or system access
Serialization or aliasing errors	Process management or Scheduling	Denial of service
Errors due to inadequate Identification or authentication	Device management	Integrity failure
Boundary and condition errors	File management	Crash, hang or exit
Covert channel	Identification or authentication	Failure
Exploitable logic errors		Invalid state File manipulation Errors due to clock changes

Buffer Overflow

Buffer overflow vulnerability is a recurring security problem that has been around for some time. The cost of a successful buffer overflow attack can be extremely high simply because it may give an administrative control of the system to the attacker. The anatomy of a buffer overflow is quite simple (Pfleeger and Pfleeger, 2003). When a program is invoked, an activation record is added to the activation stack, which contains the return address, the addresses of local variables and buffers. An attacker can cause the internal buffer to overflow by copying excessively large input to it. This may overwrite the local variables, the return address, to name a few. The return address may for instance be replaced by an address chosen by the attacker where an attack code is located. The attack code will then run with the privilege of the original program. Since most programs in this case run with administrative privileges, this gives complete control of the system to the attack code.

Buffer overflow happens mainly in unsafe programming languages such as C and C++, in which there are several functions that are vulnerable to mishandling of long input values. Examples of such functions include string manipulation functions such as strcpy or sprintf.

Race Conditions Vulnerabilities

Race conditions are mostly known for robustness problems that they create in concurrent programs. However, some race conditions represent the sources of serious security bugs. A security attack based on race conditions consists of exploiting a window of vulnerability between events execution in order to force the system to behave in unanticipated ways.

Illustrative Example

Let's consider the aforementioned medical record keeping software system. Figure 7 depicts a UML sequence diagram that demonstrates a "View Record" interaction between a doctor and the record keeping software system.

It is assumed that the medical records are stored in their encrypted form as a second layer of defense. This is not unusual with highly sensitive documents (e.g. password files etc.).

Any useful read scenario involves obtaining a key from the key server and decrypting the record. The record is then re-encrypted before storing.

Figure 8 shows a state chart diagram describing the dynamic behavior of the *Record* object shown in Figure 7. The record is either in ciphertext or in cleartext format.

Considering that the medical records are stored in their encrypted form, an intruder who is able to break into the system using for instance a password-cracking tool would also have to decrypt the record before being able to do any kind of useful job with it. Let's assume that an intruder can access the server (file or database) storing the records but not the keys server. Hence, he/she may be able to access the encrypted records but he/she cannot decrypt them. The intruder, however, can still run an attack tool concurrently with the record-keeping tool that repeatedly tries to access the records. Figure 9 shows a sequence diagram describing such interaction from the Intruder's perspective whereas Figure 7 describes the doctor's perspective.

If there is no concurrency control mechanism in place, two possible schedules among others, that may occur, are as follows:

Schedule 1: *<decrypt( ), view( ), read( ), encrypt( )>*
Schedule 2: *<decrypt( ), read( ), encrypt( ), view( )>*

Schedule 2 is acceptable whereas Schedule 1 is not. Indeed, in Schedule 1, the attacker takes advantage of a window of vulnerability to access the record in cleartext. An alternative design, which is more secure, may consist of introducing a concurrency control mechanism that will prevent unauthorized access to the cleartext file.

Figure 11 and Figure 12 depict the sequence diagrams describing the doctor's perspective and intruder's perspective respectively, under this

Figure 7. Sequence diagram for the View Record interaction

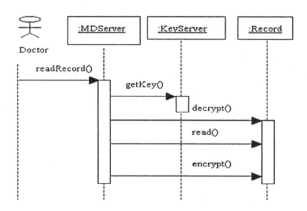

Figure 8. UML state chart diagram for record object

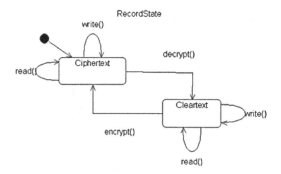

Figure 9. Concurrent read record interaction by an intruder

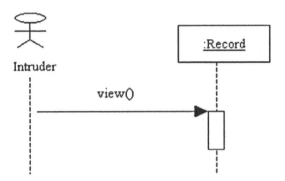

scenario. Also, under the same scenario, the dynamic behavior of the *Record* object is described by a concurrent statechart as shown in Figure 10. The concurrency control mechanism represented by the object *CController* grants exclusive access to only authorized users during the window of vulnerability where the record is in cleartext format. Any read attempt by a non-authorized user will be blocked.

Actually, standard concurrency control mechanisms are not always efficient in handling such kind of problems because they are primarily geared towards consistency issues. For instance, security anomalies may occur in concurrent read, which is not considered anomalous by the traditional locking mechanism.

THREATS MODELING

As previously stated, threat modeling spans several phases of the software life cycle. It is initiated during misuse analysis, where security compromise targets are defined at a higher level as misuse cases. The misuse cases are further refined during the design phase using security analysis techniques such as attack trees or the Operationally Critical Threat, Asset, and Vulnerability Evaluation (OCTAVE) method (Vacca, 2009). OCTAVE is a security threat analysis technique that was developed by the Software Engineering Institute at

Carnegie Mellon University (CMU-SEI). Attack trees will be discussed in the sequel.

Threats Categories

Having a generic catalogue of threat represents a good aid for threat identification for a given system. Table 2 proposes a classification of security threats in eight categories. This categorization is consistent with the STRIDE threat model (Howard and Le Blanc, 2002).

The threats categories listed in Table 2 are briefly described as follows.

- **Masquerade:** This occurs when a malicious user impersonates a different (legitimate) user. The malicious user pretends in such case to be a different user, by for instance using his authentication information such as username or password. Masquerade attacks often originate from dictionary attacks targeting weak authentication data.
- **Privilege escalation:** This occurs when some intruder gains more privileges, including administrative ones, than legally authorized. This typically allows the intruder to perform some actions out of his legal operational capabilities.
- **Concealment:** This consists for an intruder of successfully hiding his identity or trace of activity.

Figure 10. Read record with concurrency control: statechart diagram

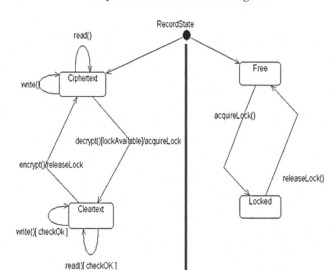

Figure 11. Sequence diagrams for read record with concurrency control: intruder's perspective

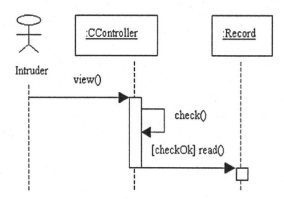

Figure 12. Sequence diagrams for read record with concurrency control: doctor's perspective

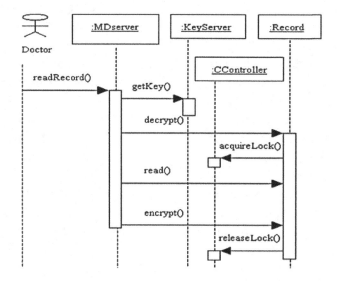

Table 2. Threats categories and corresponding security countermeasures and mechanisms

Threats	Countermeasures	Examples of Security Mechanisms
Masquerade	Authentication	Password Biometrics Certificate
Privilege escalation	Authorization	Access control Intrusion detection
Repudiation	Accountability	Digital signatures Timestamps Audit
Information leakage	Authorization, Confidentiality	Access control Encryption
Data Tampering	Authorization, Integrity	Access control Digital signatures Digest functions Message Authentication Codes (MAC)
Deduction of information	Confidentiality	Inference control
Denial of service	Availability	Filtering Throttling
Antagonism	Privacy Protection	Filtering Privacy-enhanced protocols

- **Repudiation:** This occurs when some user falsely denies participation in an action.

- **Information leakage:** This consists of dissemination of information to unauthorized individuals, resulting to This typically leads to loss of confidentiality, or anonymity, or misappropriation of sensitive data by an intruder.

- **Data Tampering:** This consists of unauthorized modification or deletion of sensitive data.

The data may be located in a storage facility or in transit over the network.

- **Deduction of information:** This consists of statistical or analytical deduction of sensitive information based on publicly available summaries.

- **Denial of service:** This occurs when an authorized user is denied a requested service within a specified maximum waiting time. Denial of service threat typically material-izes by blocking a legitimate user access to some computer resource due to some malicious actions taken by another user.

- **Antagonism:** This consists of a range of threats that merely antagonize or annoy a user such as sending unsolicited images (e.g. pornographic) or emails (e.g. spams) to users.

Stealing or cracking a legitimate password, and then login in the system using the identity of the victim conducts a *masquerade* attack typically. If the attacker logs in as an ordinary user, he/she may try to *escalate* his privileges by gaining for instance the root control of the system using a buffer overflow attack. Without the root control, there is little that he/she can do within the system. Having the root control of the system, his/her next move may consist of *concealing* his/her presence by replacing for instance the appropriate system files or programs (e.g. *ps, du, netstat*) by the corresponding trojaned versions.

A Trojan horse is a program that performs both covert and overt actions. The *overt* action is the advertised purpose of the program. The *covert* action is typically a malicious action, which is executed as a back-end thread. For instance, a Trojan version of the *ls* program will perform its regular function, which consists of listing the files available under the current directory. Simultaneously, it may conduct in the back-end some malicious actions such as sending by ftp copies of the same files to the intruder, who owns it.

Misuse Case Analysis

In software security engineering, it is essential to start incorporating security early in the development stage. To achieve this objective, one needs to gather not only functional requirements, but also security requirements in order to assess the risks and threats associated with the system that the developer is trying to build.

One way of analyzing security threats is through Misuse Cases (Sindre and Opdahl, 2001). Misuse cases are based upon the popular ideology of studying negative scenarios to overcome hurdles in the overall goal. As in the war, the strategy consists in analyzing every possible scenario, whether it is expected or unexpected, that can happen. This allows the soldiers to be better prepared and increases the chances of winning. It is the same inspiration that is behind the notion of Misuse Cases.

Misuse cases are a form of use cases that have hostile intent. Where use cases depict the functions required by a normal user to successfully operate the system; misuse cases depict the functions required by a hostile user (e.g. a hacker) to attack or misuse a system. This may seem insignificant, but in fact, it is extremely useful in identifying vulnerabilities in the system that can be protected and patched up, before they are exploited in a way that may lead to the breakdown of the system.

By combining use cases with misuse cases, software developers can:

- Get a better understanding of the hazards associated with the system.
- Easily deduce security requirements.
- Generate comprehensible test cases to check for security holes in the system.

Definition and Motivation

Misuse case is a new concept that came in light only recently; hence so far not much work has been done in this area. Early work on the topic was due to Sindre and Opdahl (Sindre and Opdahl, 2001); further effort was on this same topic was made by Alexander (Alexander, 2003). According to Alexander, misuse cases are an indispensable tool that can help software developers elicit a number of aspects about a system including security requirements, safety requirements, functional as well as non-functional requirements, exceptions and test cases.

It seems obvious from their name that misuse cases are related to use cases. The purpose of use cases is well known. The question that arises is: what are misuses cases used for? To put it simply, misuses cases are the inverse of use cases. In general, use cases describe the interaction between a user and a system through a set of functions that the user can perform on the system. In essence, use cases look at the *happy scenarios*, i.e. typical events flows of a system for all the identified functions. There are occasional exceptions that need to be taken care of, but these are not due to security threats but rather from unexpected input or undesired behavior. The interesting thing is that the entire design process is based upon the use cases that are recognized during the requirements phase. And if use cases are examined, one can realize that they do not point out any security hazards at all. Thus, in effect, the system is actually designed without having security in mind from the beginning.

Most designers do not think about security threats until very late in the development phase or even until after the system is deployed. This leads to careless design and holes that can easily be exploited by hackers. A solution to this problem is that negative scenarios should be taught as well, i.e. potential security threats or attacks beforehand. Misuse cases provide a way to accomplish this. Being the opposite of use cases, misuse cases describe the interaction between the system and a rogue user, who wishes to harm the system by exploiting the functions that the system provides. Thus, instead of looking at what the system does, misuse cases focus on what shouldn't be done to the system. In (Sindre and Opdahl, 2001), Sindre and Opdahl describe misuse case a more formally as follows:

A misuse case might be defined as a completed sequence of actions which results in loss for the organization or some specific stakeholder (Sindre and Opdahl, 2001).

They also define a mis-actor as follows:

A mis-actor is the inverse of an actor, someone who intentionally or accidentally initiates misuse cases and whom the system should not support in doing so (Sindre and Opdahl, 2001).

In short, misuse cases can help identify potential *misusers*, potential threats, and ways of mitigating those threats to stop the misusers from abusing the system and/or the normal users.

Illustrative Example

In (Sindre and Opdahl, 2001), Sindre and Opdahl describe a nice template that can be followed for documenting misuse cases. The following example depicted in Figure 13 illustrates their idea. In Figure 13, the misuse cases are drawn with black ovals and a mis-actor is represented by a black stickman. Everything else is pretty much the same as in a normal use case diagram. What is interesting to note here is the relationship between use cases and misuses cases. For example, in the above diagram, if the hacker obtains the password, he/she can log on to the system. But, if we have a variable password, then, it will prevent the hacker from logging on. In general terms, what is happening here is kind of Newton' third law; which states that for every action there is an equal and opposite reaction. Thus, this zigzag pattern actually pushes the designer to think of adding security features ahead of time and to diffuse as many threats as possible. Of course, some threats are a bit tricky

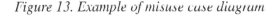

Figure 13. Example of misuse case diagram

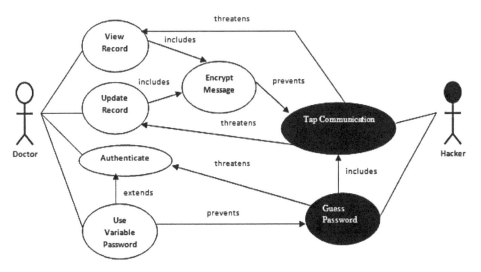

to prevent. But, the solution to such threats can later be discovered when the diagram is refined. At least, the first version of the diagram creates an awareness of potential threats that could be used to break into the system.

Like use cases, the misuse cases in the above diagram can also be fully dressed. This is illustrated for the "Guess Password" misuse case as follows.

As shown in Figure 14, a fully dressed misuse case looks very similar to a normal use case; except there's just one difference. At the end, there is something called *Capture Points*. Sindre and Opdahl (Sindre G. and Opdahl, 2001) describe these as "options for how the misuse may be prevented and/or detected at particular steps." Notice, how in the *basic path*, a step may have a capture point associated with it. This is extremely useful because it means that the hacker's footsteps cannot only be followed, but the hacker can be stopped from getting to his goal. Hence, by drawing use case diagrams in a way that combines use cases and misuse cases, the designers can identify com-

prehensible functional requirements, and more importantly security requirements. When these requirements get translated to design (use case diagram to class diagram for example), the security aspects of the system would also be developed alongside other functional aspects. In economic terms, this would lower the cost of the system since it would lower the chances of upgrading the system against threats.

Notation and Template

The example in the previous section has been tailored just to present the idea behind misuse cases as well as their relationship to use cases. A more generic template is provided in (Sindre G. and Opdahl, 2001) which formalizes the notation used for writing and drawing misuse cases. This template can be used as is or it can be customized according to specific design issues. However, it serves as a good basis for describing misuse cases. Below is a summary of the main elements

Figure 14. Fully dressed misuse case

Name:

Guess Password

Summary:

A hacker obtains and later misuses doctor's password for viewing or editing records by tapping messages sent through a compromised network host during log on

Basic Path:

1. A hacker has hacked a network host computer and installed an IP packet sniffer. (A1)
2. All sequence of messages sent through the compromised host are intercepted. (C3)
3. The hacker collects user names and passwords. (C3)
4. The hacker uses the usernames and passwords to gain illegal access. (C1) (C2)

Alternate Paths:

A1. The crook/hacker has operator privileges on the network host; no hacking is necessary.

Capture Points:

C1. The password does not work because it has been changed.

C2. The password does not work because it is time-dependant.

C3. Tapping is not possible because the messages are encrypted.

Figure 15. Guess password misuse case

Figure 16. Mis-actor (hacker)

presented in that template from (Sindre G. and Opdahl, 2001).

Drawing Template

When drawing a misuse case in a use case diagram, it is represented by a black oval. For example, in Figure 13, the "Guess Password" misuse case is drawn (see Figure 15).

Similarly, a mis-actor (hacker/crook) trying to harm the system is drawn as a black stickman. A caption for the mis-actor is also drawn underneath the stickman. For instance, as shown in Figure 16, the hacker is represented as:

Relations Template

According to (Sindre G. and Opdahl, 2001), there are four main relations that can be formed for misuse cases.

- **Includes:** This can be from a misuse case to another misuse case, or it could be from a misuse case to a use case. An includes relation represents that a misuse case utilizes some functionality from another use/misuse case. To illustrate this, if we look at Figure 13, the "Guess Password" misuse case includes the "Tap Communication."
- **Extends:** An extends relation is used to show that a misuse case expands/extends the functionality of another use/misuse case. For example, a "Denial of Service"

attack doesn't necessarily have to include illegal actions, it could simply flood the system with a large number of requests.

- **Prevents:** This is drawn from a use case to a misuse case to indicate functions that prevent misuse. As in Figure 13, the "Use Variable Password" use case prevents the "Guess Password" misuse case. An alternative to "Prevents" which is often used is "Mitigates".
- **Detects:** This is the same as "prevents", except it is used to indicate functions that may detect misuse of a system. Again, this is drawn from a use case to a misuse case.
- Two other relations that could be used, that are not discussed in (Sindre G. and Opdahl, 2001) are "Threatens" and "Aggravates."
  - **Threatens:** A threatens relation is drawn from a misuse case to a use case indicating that the misuse case threatens the use case and could be employed to harm that use case.
  - **Aggravates:** This relation is drawn from a use case to a misuse case when a use case increases the success rate of that misuse case and makes things even worse.

An illustration of these two relations is depicted in the example of a web portal security system shown in Figure 17.

Figure 17. Threatens and aggravates

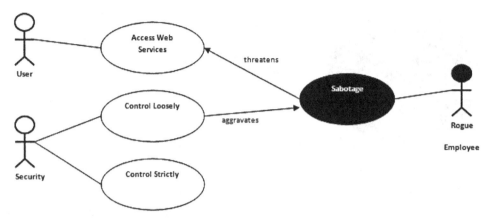

Writing Template

In (Sindre G. and Opdahl, 2001), Sindre and Opdahl presented a general template for writing a fully dressed misuse case. The items belonging to this template are defined below, in order:

- **Name:** The name of the misuse case.
- **Summary:** A brief description of the overall goal of the misuse case.
- **Author:** Person who wrote the misuse case.
- **Date:** The date when it was written.
- **Basic Path:** The normal path of action taken, ending with success for the mis-user, or failure for the system. The path is written in point format, where each point is numbered (as shown in Figure 14).
- **Alternative Path:** Various ways or alternate routes the mis-user could take to accompish his goal. These are also written in point format, where each point is numbered along with the prefix A (as shown in Figure 14).
- **Capture Points:** This item is the main difference between a use case and a misuse case. The capture points represent the options for how the misuse may be prevented and/or detected at particular steps. Again, these are written in point format, where each point is numbered along with the prefix C (as shown in Figure 14).
- **Extension Points:** These are optional paths that may be included in the misuse case in some situations. These are options taken by the mis-user, for instance to hack aronud obstacles, whereas capture points work against the mis-user. Extension points are also written in point format, where each point is numbered along with the prefix E.

Note that the advantage of using point format to represent the above-mentioned items is thay can be associated to the Basic Path. For example, in Figure 14, the Capture Points and Alternate Points are linked to certain steps in the Basic Path, indicating when a mis-user could take an alternate path or when he can be stopped.

Illustrative Example

In order to illustrate misuse case analysis, we consider once again our medical record keeping system example.

As mentioned previously, the initial list of use cases given above focuses primarily on specifying the functionality, security is not taken into account. It is, however, essential to address security concerns as early as possible. In order to do so, we need to analyze how a potential hacker can misuse the functionality specified by the use cases. Misuse case analysis consists of identifying interactions scenarios that are illegal from the perspective of the system security requirements. For instance a security requirement for the record keeping system specified above says, "Only authorized doctors can read or update a medical record. An authorized doctor is a registered doctor that a patient has chosen." So to be secure the system must ensure that only doctors authorized by a patient can access his record.

An initial list of misuse cases based on our initial list of use cases is depicted in Figure 18. The misuse cases represented in black can be described as follows:

- **Repudiation:** An authorized user denying participation in some actions in the system. For instance, a doctor may deny that he has modified a patient record at some time in the past.
- **Denial of service:** Consists of preventing a legitimate user from effectively using the system.
- **Tampering:** Illegitimate modification or deletion of medical records.
- **Disclosure:** Unauthorized disclosure or reading of patient health information.
- **Masquerade:** A user pretending to be a different user when using the system.

The *Repudiation misuse* case "threatens" all the legitimate use cases; so to avoid clutters we didn't link it directly to any of the use cases. The same applies for the *Denial of service* misuse case as well.

Our initial list of misuse cases is based directly on the generic list of threats given earlier. The threats which are relevant to the system functionality were selected. However, to make them more specific, more explicit names for the misuse cases

could be used. For instance, instead of *tampering,* one can use *Record tampering.*

Specifying the mitigation strategies can further refine the collection of use cases and misuse cases. This consists of defining some new use cases, which mitigates the threats carried by the misuse cases. The goal of these new use cases is to ensure that illegal scenarios carried by misuse cases are not allowed.

The refined use case diagram is shown in Figure 19. The following new use cases are specified:

- **Audit:** Mitigates repudiation threat and consists of logging all the sensitive operations that may take place on patients' records.
- **Authorization:** Mitigates tampering and disclosure, and consists of ensuring that every access to patients' records is allowed by the security policy.
- **Authenticate:** Consists of verifying the identity of users by ensuring that they are really who they claim to be.
- **Throttling:** Consists of limiting the number of requests to the system. The limitation typically concerns anonymous connections, which represent a major source of DoS attacks. Authenticated connections are in general not restricted.

The use cases identified during the use case analysis drive the design of the software architecture, which will be used as basis for subsequent security risk analysis activities. The initial software architecture can be designed by analyzing the scenarios involved in the different use cases. For the record keeping system, one can propose the initial class diagram depicted by Figure 20. This class diagram consists of the following elements:

- **Interface RecordManager:** Provides a collection of function for medical record creation, edition and deletion.

Figure 18. Misuse cases-Initial threats

Figure 19. Misuse cases-mitigation

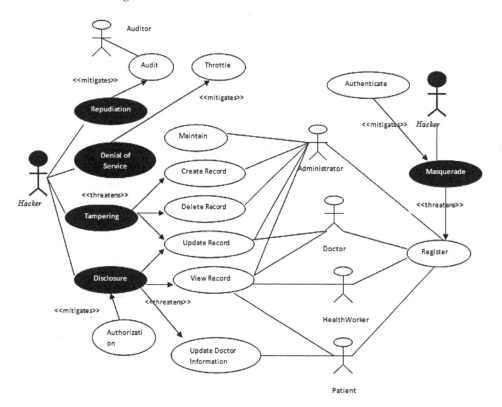

- **Interface UserManager:** Provides a collection of functions for user registration, logon, and management.
- **Interface AuditManager:** Provides a collection of functions for updating, viewing, and deleting audit data.
- **Record, AuditLog, and User:** Represent corresponding persistent data. A User object may be one of the following: patient, doctor, health worker, administrator, or auditor.

A high-level perspective of the software architecture for the record keeping system is depicted in Figure 21. Clients submit their requests using a web browser, which sends them to the web server for processing. Web components hosted by the Web server may consist of HTML forms, JSP, Servlets or ASP components. The web server forwards if necessary the requests to the application server, which hosts the business logic. The business logic may be implemented using technologies such as CORBA, EJB (OMG, 2012) or DotNet (DotNet, 2012). The business components in their turn may access or store persistent data in the database.

The Directory Server, which is in this case an LDAP server, provides user authentication data and service.

Figure 20. Initial class diagram for record keeping system

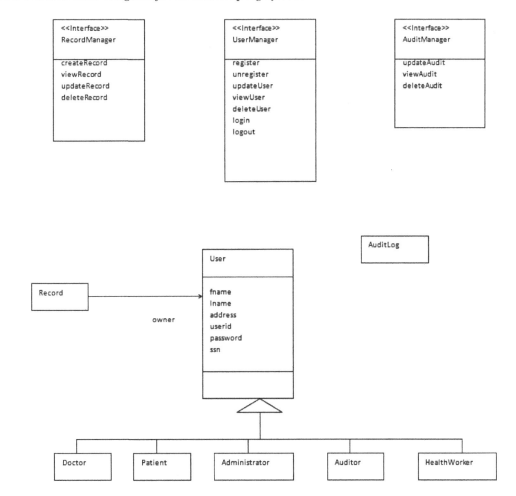

Table 3 summarizes how the software components depicted in Figure 21 are allocated between the different components layers.

Attack Trees

Overview of Attack Trees

Attack trees consist of a security threat derivation and modeling technique that is inspired from the fault tree technique used fault tolerant computing (NCSC, 1987). This technique can be used to derive security threat at the network, system, or application level. In this Chapter, our main interest is on threat modeling at the application level. Attack tree technique ensures that the threat model for a system being developed is completed, justifiable, and well documented.

Risk Analysis

Security risk analysis may be conducted by examining how the different threats categories impact the architectural components and connectors. For instance, by considering the interconnection between the web browser and server, a possible threat consists of a hacker reading or modifying the patient medical information by intercepting them during a web session. Another example of threat may consist of a hacker intercepting the medical information en route from the web server to the application server. Another interesting example may consist of a hacker intercepting and misusing the authentication data in route from the web server to the authentication server (see Table 4).

Conducting risk analysis may help identifying several kinds of threats; this is similar to the STRIDE approach (Howard and LeBlanc, 2002). A more systematic approach consists of combining this strategy with attack tree technique. In that case, the targets (or goals) of the attack trees will correspond to the misuse cases identified earlier. An attack tree may typically be provided for each misuse case. The attack scenarios described by the attack trees will be derived from the analysis of the architectural components and connectors as done in the STRIDE approach (Howard and LeBlanc, 2002).

Figure 21. Initial software architecture for record keeping system

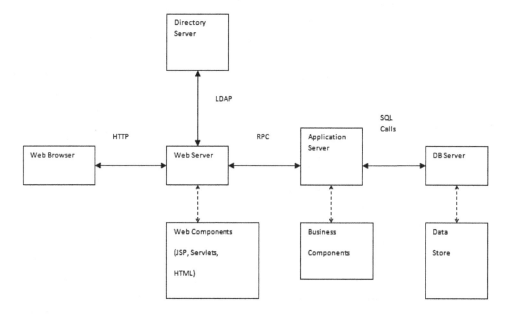

Table 3. Components types

Components Types	Components
Web components	HTML Forms, JSP, Servlet
Business components	RecordManager, AuditManager
Data store	Record, AuditLog
Authentication components	UserManager, User

Notation

The core model of the attack tree technique is, as the name indicates, a collection of trees. The root of an attack tree represents an event, which itself represents a security compromise for the system. The nonleaf nodes of the tree refine incrementally and iteratively the compromise by describing underlying steps and conditions. Different levels of abstractions can be used. So the level of details provided depends on the amount of information available and the purpose of the modeling. A nonleaf node of a tree can be decomposed either as a conjunction or a disjunction of sub-nodes as follows:

- **AND-decomposition:** Conjunction of a set of attack sub-goals.
- **OR-decomposition:** Disjunction of a set of attack sub-goals.

Table 4. Components and connectors

Components and Connectors Types	Components and Connectors Instances
Core Processes	Executables, Business logic, web services
Persistent Data	SQL data, XML data, registry data, authentication data, authorization data, logs.
Communication Channels	Sockets, pipes, RPC, SOAP, HTTP, TCP/IP
Non-persistent data	Cookies, authentication data, credit card numbers, order information

Figure 22. AND-decomposition

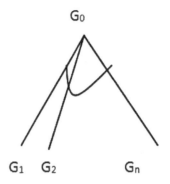

Attack trees can be represented either graphically or textually.

AND-decomposition are described graphically by joining the arcs incident to the AND-node by a single arc (see Figure 22).

The corresponding textual representation is given as follows:

```
Goal G₀
    AND G₁
        G₂
        ...
        Gₙ
```

OR-decomposition are described graphically by joining the arcs incident to the OR-node by a double arc (see Figure 23).

The corresponding textual representation is given as follows:

Figure 23. OR-decomposition

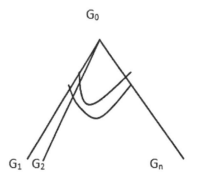

Figure 24. Example of attack tree

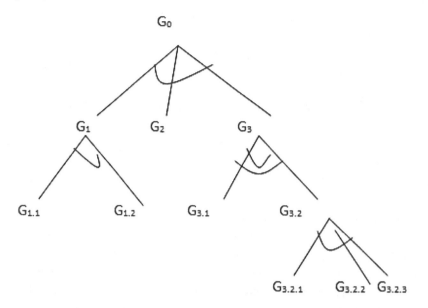

```
Goal G₀
   OR G₁
      G₂
      ...
      Gₙ
```

A typical attack tree consists of the combination of several AND and OR decompositions

For instance, Figure 24 shows an attack tree consisting of three AND-nodes and one OR-node.

The textual representation corresponding to this tree is as follows:

```
Goal G₀
   AND G₁
         AND G₁.₁
             G₁.₂
      G₂
      G₃
         OR  G₃.₁
             G₃.₂
                AND G₃.₂.₁
                    G₃.₂.₂
                    G₃.₂.₃
```

Graphical representations are appropriate only for small trees. For large trees, they tend to become unmanageable, in which case it is preferable to use textual representations.

Illustrative Example

Here, an example of attack tree that targets medical record disclosure for our aforementioned record keeping system is given. As recommended by Moore et al. (Moore et al., 2001), the attack tree in a textual fashion (high level view only) is shown below since the size of the attack tree is large. The root node of the attack tree is the disclosure/compromise of the patient information.

System Compromise: Disclosure of Patient Information

OR 1. Physically scavenge discarded items from Hospital
2. Monitor emanations from Hospital machines
3. Recruit help of trusted clinician insider
4. Physically access hospital networks or machines

5. Attack hospital intranet using its connections with Internet

6. Attack hospital intranet using its connections with public telephone Network (PTN)/VPN

7. Attack Application server using its connections with Web server

8. Attack DB server using its connections with Application server.

9. Directly access patient information in DB server

Disclosure of the patient information may happen in various ways, including physical access to dumpsters, emanations monitoring, social engineering, to name a few. Disclosure of the patient information at the software architecture level can happen in several locations including the following:

- Browser-Web server connections.
- Web server-Application server connections.
- Application server-DB server connections.
- Direct attack on the DB server.

Each of the nodes of the above-mentioned high-level view depicts one of the multiple ways through which the disclosure of the patient information can be achieved. Each of these nodes must be further refined as a sub-tree of the global tree describing patient information disclosure. In Box 1, the refined sub-tree corresponding to node 5 is depicted.

Further refinement to the above sub-tree may be achieved using attack patterns, which are introduced later in this section.

Usage

An important use of attack trees consists of determining intrusion scenarios, which can be used later as basis for security testing of the final implementation. Intrusion scenarios are derived from an attack tree by traversing the tree in a depth-first manner. For instance, the attack tree shown in Figure 24 involves exactly the following two intrusion scenarios:

$$s_1 = <G_{1.1}, G_{1.2}, G_2, G_{3.1}>$$

$$s_2 = <G_{1.1}, G_{1.2}, G_2, G_{3.2.1}, G_{3.2.2}, G_{3.2.3}>$$

Another important use of attack trees is for the estimation of the risks posed by the corresponding threats. Risks evaluation requires that for each node of the tree, the estimation of the *effort* and *criticality* of the corresponding threat be determined.

- **Effort:** This parameter captures the amount or level of skills, knowledge, or resources needed by an intruder to enact a given threat. The effort can also be viewed in terms of likelihood or chance of occurrence of a given threat.
- **Criticality:** This captures the value, cost or importance of the assets exposed when the threat materializes.

The estimates of criticality or effort may be obtained by combining expert consensus with available field and test evidence, or based on experience from past projects or historical databases. These estimates may be recorded during a brainstorming session, where the potential list of threats for the system is established.

Criticality and *effort* can be estimated qualitatively. In this case, criticality can be estimated by using a ranking scheme that spans from high to moderate or low. In this case, the *effort* can be measured by estimating the likelihood of the attack to succeed (e.g. highly likely, likely, less likely, unlikely).

Alternatively, a quantitative approach for estimating the *criticality* and *effort* may be used. In this case, a common approach consists of estimating the *criticality* and the *effort* on a scale from 1 to 10, where 1 represents lowest effort

Box 1.

5. Attack hospital intranet using its connections with Internet
    OR 1. Monitor communications over Internet for leakage
        AND 1. Obtain connection shared with hospital
             2. Install/execute/record network communication using scanner
      2. Get trusted process to send sensitive information to attacker over Internet
        OR 1. Replace trusted process with modified version
             AND 1. Located trusted process that attacker has access to
                  2. Supplant trusted process with modified (maliciously) version
             2. Use trusted process (unaltered) to send sensitive information
             3. Gain privileged access to Web server
    AND 1. Indentify hospital domain name
        2. Identify hospital firewall IP address
          OR 1. Interrogate hospital Domain Name Server
             2. Scan for firewall identification
             3. Trace route through firewall to Web server
        3. Determine hospital firewall access control
          OR 1. Search for default listening ports
             2. Scan ports broadly for any listening ports
             3. Scan ports stealthily for listening ports
                OR 1. Randomize target of scan
                    2. Randomize source of scan
                    3. Scan without toughing target host
        4. Identify hospital Web server operating system and type
          OR 1. Scan operating system services' banners for OS signature
             2. Probe TCP/IP stack for OS characteristic information
        5. Exploit hospital Web server vulnerabilities
          OR 1. Access sensitive shared Intranet resources directly
             2. Access sensitive data from privileged account on Web server
                AND 1. Get access to privileged account on hospital Web Server
                    OR 1. Exploit buffer overflow vulnerability to Access privileged account
                        2. Exploit unexpected operator vulnerability to Access privileged account
                2. Scan files for sensitive data

(respectively least critical), and 10 represents highest effort (respectively highly critical). On this ground, risk can be calculated by dividing the criticality by the effort:

$$\text{Risk} = \frac{\text{Criticality}}{\text{Effort}}$$

Estimates may be provided only for the leaf nodes in the attack tree. Using estimates at the nonleaf nodes and their logical connections can derive risk estimate at a parent node.

Risk at an OR-node can be estimated as the highest risk factor among the children nodes. This is based on a security design principle referred to as the "weakest link", which states that an intruder is more likely to penetrate in the system by the weakest link, or is more likely to go after the highest value target. Hence, in the example shown in Figure 25, the risk factor at node G_0 is equal to the risk at G_2, which carries the maximum risk factor.

The risk factor at an AND-node is a combination of the risk factors at its sub-nodes.

Various mathematical combination operations may be used. A simplest operation may consist of averaging the risk. This approach is applied in the example given in Figure 26.

Example: Calculate the risk factor at node G_0 for the attack tree given in Figure 24, considering the estimates at the leaf nodes given in Table 5.

We start by assigning the risk values to the leaf nodes as shown in Figure 27. By combining and propagating the risk values, the aggregate risk at G_0 is obtained as 5.66.

Figure 25. Example of risk estimation for an OR-node

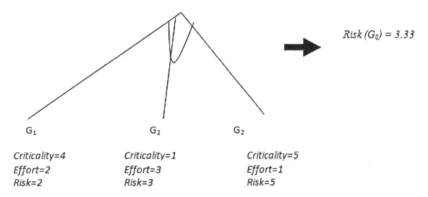

Figure 26. Example of risk estimation for an AND-node

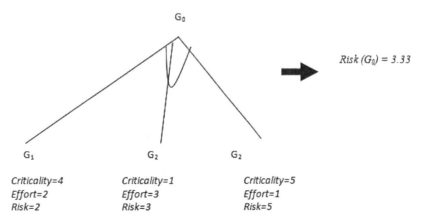

Figure 27. Example of risk estimation

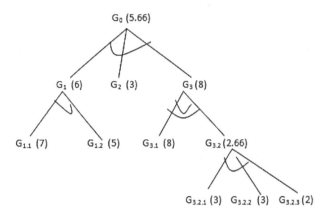

Attack scenarios are derived from attack trees. They are used to prioritize security threats using for instance the aforementioned quantitative approach. The prioritized threats list is then used to select appropriate security mechanisms, which must be integrated into a more secure architecture.

Attack Patterns

The idiosyncrasies of popular attacks methods can be captured in a structured way in attack patterns that can be reused in the design of attack trees (Moore et al., 2001). An attack pattern is a generic representation of an attack that commonly occurs in specific contexts. An attack pattern can be defined by specifying the following characteristics:

- **Goal:** Objective of the attack specified by the pattern.
- **Preconditions:** A list of preconditions for the attack to occur.

- **Steps:** Main steps for conducting the attack.
- **Post-conditions:** A list of post-conditions, which become true if the attack succeeds.

Figure 28 shows an example of an attack patterns suggested by Moore et al. (Moore et al., 2001) which exploits buffer overflow vulnerability.

Attack patterns are often used to refine attack trees. Typically, this is achieved by identifying and instantiating patterns whose goals match the goal specified at specific nodes of the attack tree.

Example: For instance, the non leaf node 5.3.5.2.1.1 in attack tree given previously for the medical record keeping system (see Figure 24) can be refined using buffer overflow attack pattern. The sub-tree given in Box 2 depicts this in italic.

CONCLUSION

Computer security has been the purpose of intensive research activities for more than three decades. In spite of the fundamental results obtained in those works, research in software security is still in its infancy. As a consequence, in contrast with other software quality aspects, there is little guidance about how to build and deliver secure software

Table 5. Example of risk assignment

Nodes	Risk
G_{11}	7
G_{12}	5
$G_{3.1}$	8
$G_{3.2.1}$	3
$G_{3.2.2}$	3
$G_{3.2.3}$	2

Figure 28. Example of an attack patterns (Moore et al., 2001)

> **Goal:** Exploit buffer overflow vulnerability to perform malicious function on target system
>
> **Precondition:** Attacker can execute certain programs on target system.
>
> **Attack:**
>
> **AND** 1. Identify executable program on target system susceptible to buffer overflow vulnerability.
>
>   2. Identify code that will perform malicious function when it executes with program's privilege.
>
>   3. Construct input value that will force code to be in program's address space
>
>   4. Execute program in a way that makes it jump to address at which code resides
>
> **Postcondition:** Target system performs malicious function.

Box 2.

```
5. Exploit hospital Web server vulnerabilities
   OR 1. Access sensitive shared Intranet resources directly
      2. Access sensitive data from privileged account on Web server
         AND 1. Get access to privileged account on hospital Web server
               OR 1. Exploit buffer overflow vulnerability to access
                     privileged account
                     AND 1. Identify executable program on Web server
                           susceptible to buffer overflow vulnerability
                        2. Identify code that would provide access to
                           privileged account when executed with program's
                           privilege
                        3. Construct input value that will force code to be
                           in program's address space
                        4. Execute program in a way that makes it jump to
                           address at which code resides
                  2. Exploit unexpected operator vulnerability to access
                     privileged account
            2. Scan files for sensitive data
```

systems. In this chapter, we have attempted to introduce fundamental computer security results that can be applied to enhance software security, with focus on security requirements and risk analysis. Details on these results can be found in the literature, for instance, the books by Howard et al. (Howard and Le Blanc, 2002) and Viega and McGraw, 20010 provide interesting insights on secure software design and implementation.

REFERENCES

Alexander, I. (2003). Misuse cases: Use cases with hostile intent. *IEEE Computer Society, Focus Magazine*.

Bishop, M. (2004). *Introduction to computer security* (1st ed.). Addison-Wesley Professional.

Curphey, A. (2006). Web application security assessment tools. *IEEE Security and Privacy Archive, 4*(4).

DotNet. (2012). *Dot net framework 3.5*. Retrieved March 5, 2012, from http://msdn.microsoft.com/enus/library/w0x 726c2.aspx

FIPS - Federal Information Processing Standard (FIPS-PUB199) 199. (2004). *Standards for security categorization of federal information and information systems*. Retrieved March 2, 2012, from http://csrc.nist.gov/publications/ fips/fips199/FIPS-PUB-199-final.pdf

Graff, M. G., & Van Wyk, K. R. (2003). *Secure coding: Principles & practices*. O'ReillyPub.

Howard, M., & LeBlanc, D. (2002). *Writing secure code*. Redmond, WA: Microsoft Press.

Howard, M., & Lipner, S. (2006). *The security development lifecycle*. Redmond, WA: Microsoft Press.

ITSEC. (1991). *Information technology security evaluation criteria*. European Commission Communities. Retrieved March 2, 2012, from http://www.is- frankfurt.de/publikationenNeu/Recent-DevelopmentinInformation.pdf

Jiwani, K., & Zelkowitz, M. (2004). Susceptibility matrix: A new aid to software auditing. *IEEE Security and Privacy, 2*(2), 16–21. doi:10.1109/MSECP.2004.1281240

Landwher, C. E., Bull, A. R., McDermott, J. P., & Choi, W. S. (1994). A taxonomy of computer program security flaws, with examples. *ACM Computing Surveys, 3*(26).

Lethbridge, T. C., & Laganière, R. (2001). *Object oriented software engineering: Practical software development using UML and Java* (1st ed.). Maidenhead, UK: McGraw Hill.

McGraw, G. (1998). Testing for security during development: Why we should scrap penetrate-and patch. *IEEE Aerospace and Electronic Systems, 13*(4), 13–15. doi:10.1109/62.666831

McGraw G. (2004). Software security. *IEEE Security & Privacy*, Feb.

Moore, A. P., Ellison, R. J., & Linger, R. C. (2001). *Attack modeling for information security and survivability*. (Technical Note CMU/SEI-2001-TN-001).

NCSC. (1987). *A guide to understanding discretionary access control in trusted systems*. National Computer Security Center (NCSC). *NCSC-TG, 003*(Sept), 30.

NIST. (2004). *Security considerations in the information SDLC*. (NIST Special Publication SP 800-64 Rev. 1). Retrieved March 2, 2012, from http://www.iwar.org.uk/comsec/resources/security- life-cycle/index.htm

OMG. (2012). *The Object Management Group*. Needham, MA: Author. Retrieved March 5, 2012, from http://www.omg.org/

Pfleeger, C. P., & Pfleeger, S. L. (2003). *Security in computing* (3rd ed.). Prentice Hall.

Richardson, R. (2003). *CSI/FBI computer crime and security survey. Technical Report.* CSI.

Sindre, G., & Opdahl, A. L. (2001). Templates for misuse case description. In *Proceedings of the 7th International Workshop on Requirements Engineering, Foundation for Software Quality (REFSQ'2001)*, Interlaken, Switzerland, June 4-5.

Thompson, H. H. (2003). Why security testing is hard. *IEEE Security and Privacy*, *1*(4), 83–86. doi:10.1109/MSECP.2003.1219078

Traore, I. (2009). *Course notes: ELEC 567 advanced network security and forensics*. Graduate course offered at the Department of Electrical and Computer Engineering, University of Victoria, B.C. Canada, Spring.

Traore, I., & Aredo, D. B. (2004). Enhancing structured review using model-based verification. *IEEE Transactions on Software Engineering*, *30*(11). doi:10.1109/TSE.2004.86

US-CERT. (2012). *United States Computer Emergency Readiness Team*. Retrieved March 3, 2012, from http://www.kb.cert.org/vuls

Vacca, J. R. (2009). *Computer and information security handbook*. Elsevier.

Viega, J., & McGraw, G. (2001). *Building secure software*. USA: Addison-Wesley.

Chapter 13
Software Security Engineering – Part II:
Security Policy, Analysis, and Design

Issa Traore
University of Victoria, Canada

Isaac Woungang
Ryerson University, Canada

ABSTRACT

This chapter explains the major objectives of a security policy, with focus on how applications that can protect data at all access points can be developed. Access control models and their known issues are discussed. From a security policy prospective, the security design principles and modeling using the UML are also discussed. In addition, an informal discussion on potential software security metrics that can be used for security measurement, and that are currently the purpose of active research, is conducted. Finally, a discussion on security testing involving the use of these metrics, are discussed. Several examples are used to illustrate the studied concepts.

INTRODUCTION

More often, security is compromised not only by breaking the mechanisms such as encryption or security protocols that have been put in place in organizations, but by actually identifying and making use of the weaknesses by following the way that they are being utilized. Integrating the security requirements analysis into the standard requirements process has been proved to be the right direction to pursue. In our Chapter entitled "Software Security Engineering – Part I: Security Requirements and Risk Analysis," a novel model-driven perspective on secure software engineering was proposed, which integrates seamlessly software security analysis with traditional software development activities, resulting to a systematic security engineering process. A discussion on the

DOI: 10.4018/978-1-4666-3679-8.ch013

security risk analysis was also presented as related to the notions of threat, vulnerability, and attacks. These steps are not a one-time deal in the sense that they should be complemented with the development of a security policy for the organization (as well as its updates) in order to realize a complete and effective security protection framework. A security policy can be characterized as driven by the different methods used for performing the risk analysis in conjunction with the support of the organization's management in developing a plan to deal with security, in addition to the actual security protocols in place in the organization.

There is a common consensus among computer security actors and professionals that ensuring the security of the software for an organization is a continuous process that relies on the improvements made on the formulation of the security policy, with the goal to efficiently asses the security risks. Typically, this process involves formulating a statement that spells out the types of defenses that are needed to be configured so that unauthorized access to the system is blocked (access control), the methods to be used by the organization to respond to attacks (attack models and countermeasures), the manner in which the organization's resources should be safely handled so as to avoid or reduce the loss/damage of data and resources.

Different types of risk analysis can be used to design a security policy as well as to update and improve it. Two benchmark approaches that are often used.

The first one is the Survivable Network Analysis (SNA) developed by the CERT (US-CERT, 2012). The SNA approach comprises four steps: (1) *System definition* – where the system's organizational requirements are defined, and the system architecture is analyzed; (2) *Essential capability definition* – where the essential assets and services of the system are identified and marked as critical to the organization; (3) *Compromise capability definition* – where scenarios of intrusion to the system are defined and the types of damage result-

ing from these intrusions can be identified and traced within the targeted system architecture; (4) *Survivability analysis* – where potential point of failure in the system are identified and methods for addressing them are presented, along with recommendations on improving the system's capability to survive the above intrusions and related attacks.

The second benchmark approach is Threat and Risk Assessment (TRA) approach discussed in (ACSI, 2012). The TRA approach is composed of four steps as well: (1) Asset definition – where the information/data need to be defended (such as software, hardware, etc) are identified; (2) Threat assessment – where the types of threats affecting the asset are identified; (3) Risk assessment – where each asset is evaluated for existing safeguards and risks to other assets; (4) Recommendations – where recommendations on methods each risk identified in Step 3 are provided (as part of a security policy).

Any of the above risk analysis frameworks can be used as a starting point towards designing and developing a security policy process. To this purpose, several systematic approaches (so-called security policy roadmaps) have been proposed in the literature (ITSEC,1991), (ISO17799, 2012), (ISS, 2001), (Sun, 2001), (SANS, 2007), (Security Classification: PUBLIC, 2011). each of which reflects in its own fashion the way that safeguards and controls that protect information from security threats can be identified, the issues and factors that should be considered when setting up the policies, and how these policies can been developed and their compliancy can be measured (Krishni, 2001). The goal of these guidelines and controls is to ensure that the developed security policy reflects the organization's security needs as much as possible.

Typically, the approach used in designing a security policy roadmap consists of: (1) identifying the assets to be protected; (2) identifying the vulnerabilities and threats and their likeliness to occur; (3) Determine a cost effective measures to be used to protect the asset; (5) Release the findings to the appropriate parties; (6) Monitor and update the process in a continuous manner in order to improve it.

In this Chapter, our attention is on introducing the major objectives of a security policy, with focus on access control models and their known issues are discussed. From a security policy prospective, the security design principles and modeling using the UML are also discussed. In addition, an informal discussion on potential software security metrics that can be used for security measurement, and that are currently the purpose of active research, is conducted. Finally, a discussion on security testing involving the use of these metrics, are discussed. Several examples are used to illustrate the studied concepts.

The rest of the Chapter is organized as follows. First, the concept of security policy is introduced, along with an illustrative example: the British Medical Association (BMA) policy. Second, access control models and related known issues are discussed. Third, a great deal of wisdom regarding security analysis and design is presented. Fourth, a discussion on how to construct secure software is presented. Finally, some discussions related to software security validation, verification and testing are presented. Examples are given to illustrate the above-mentioned concepts.

INTRODUCTION TO SECURITY POLICY

Definition

A security policy is a document that describes precisely and concisely the protection properties that a system must have. It is built on a threat model, which itself drives the system design. The precise information security policy for computerized information systems has been defined by ITSEC (ITSEC,1991) as "the set of laws, rules,

and practices regulating the processing of sensitive information and the use of resources by the hardware and software of an IT (information technology) system or product."

Typically, an organization will have many policies governing all aspects of its operations.

An information security policy focuses primarily on information control and dissemination, particularly for automatic information systems. It addresses many issues such as disclosure, integrity, and availability concerns; how and what information is to be handled by the organization; access decisions, just to name a few. The information security policy can exist at any level of the system development, from top-level decision to hardware or software implementation choice, and may be refined at any of these phases.

Security Policy Objectives

A typical security policy has three major objectives, namely, the preservation of the information's confidentiality, integrity and availability. In many cases, the process and refinement of the written security policies are concerned with those three objectives.

Confidentiality, or the prevention of unauthorized disclosure of information, is one the primary objectives of most security efforts. Unauthorized disclosure may occur during the course of data transmission by wiretapping or eavesdropping, through access to information by unauthorized users (e.g. hackers) or by other means.

Integrity pertains to ensuring that data continues to be a proper representation of the information, and that the information processes continue to perform the correct processing operations, and also that the information retains its original level of accuracy (Bishop, 2004).

The *Availability* objective is generally achieved by ensuring that the system is accessible to authorized users when needed.

Example of the British Medical Association Policy

The British Medical Association (BMA) policy is a security policy proposed by Anderson for medical record keeping in British Health Organizations (Anderson, 1996). The BMA Security Policy includes the following nine key components as described in Figure 1.

The BMA policy attempts to address most of the fundamental goals of security: prevention, detection, and recovery. It is centered on two principle ideas: all access to patient data must be authenticated and permitted, and customer notification and consent is required for several key operations. Prevention is addressed by the *access control*, *control*, *consent and notification* and the *trusted computing base* items. The *consent and notification* and *aggregation control* items address detection.

While this is potentially enough to secure the patients data in a computer storage system with protected access points, it does not deal with several other issues. For instance, the policy does little, in general, towards defending against social engineering attacks and "dumpster diving." Furthermore, Anderson (Anderson, 1996) pointed out that the main threat to most modern-day systems comes from insiders. As such, the definition of secure computing base comes into question. He also points out that through the corruption of insiders, third parties may obtain private information.

As a mitigating factor, Anderson (Anderson, 1996) raised the possibility of using encryption to secure the patient data that is consumed in the hospital environment. This can help achieving a realistic secure computing base. With this in mind, the BMA policy can be used as the foundation for a patient medical record system.

It must be ensured that the definition of secure computing base is thoroughly evaluated in order to assure the security of the entire system. As such, consideration must be given to how applications that can protect data at all access points can be developed not only on the system, but also within the physical and networked architectures.

Figure 1. The BMA security policy

1. *Access control:* each identifiable clinical record shall be marked with an access control list naming the people or groups of people who may read it and append data to it. The system shall prevent anyone not on the access control list from accessing the record in any way.
2. *Record opening:* a clinician may open a record with herself and the patient on the access control list. Where a patient has been referred, she may open a record with herself, the patient and the referring clinician(s) on the access control list.
3. *Control:* One of the clinicians on the access control list must be marked as being responsible. Only she may alter the access control list, and she may only add other health care professionals to it.
4. *Consent and notification:* the responsible clinicians must notify the patient of the names on his record's access control list when it is opened, of all subsequent additions, and whenever responsibility is transferred. His consent must also be obtained, except in emergency case or in the case of statutory exemptions.
5. *Persistence:* no one shall have the ability to delete clinical information until the appropriate time period has expired.
6. *Attribution:* all accesses to clinical records shall be marked on the record with the subject's name, as well as the date and time. An audit trail must also be kept of all deletions.
7. *Information flow:* information derived from record A may be appended to record B if and only if B's access control list is contained in A's.
8. *Aggregation control:* there shall be effective measures to prevent the aggregation of personal health information. In particular, patients must receive special notification if any person whom it is proposed to add their access control list already has access to personal health information on a large number of people.
9. *Trusted computing base:* computer systems that handle personal health information shall have a subsystem that enforces the above principles in an effective way. Its effectiveness shall be subject to evaluation by independent experts.

ACCESS CONTROL

Overview of Access Control

In this section we give an overview of access control policies and mechanisms.

Access is a specific type of interaction between an *object* and a *subject* that results in the flow of information between the two entities. Access controls place constraints on this flow of information where the subject can be a user or process acting on behalf of the user. Access control has evolved to become what it is looks like today through the efforts initiated by military and national security arenas, as well as, the academic and commercial research laboratories. It has been an active area of research since the 1960's and 1970's.

The purpose of Access Control is to fulfill, in part, the security policy of a given entity. As stated in (NCSC, 1987), "access control is part of the control objective that refers to a statement of intent with respect to control over some aspects of an organization's resources or processes." This statement usually comes in the form of a security policy. A security policy is a statement of intent that defines control over access to, dissemination of, and modification of information. The security policy has to accurately reflect the laws, regulations, and general policies from which it is derived.

Using access control, the authenticated user access to resources can be restricted. However, access control cannot secure a system alone. In fact, it should be used in conjunction with other required components of a secure system (as shown in the high-level diagram depicted in Figure 2) to help create a secure system. These additional components of a secure system are explored in some details in (DoD, 1985), (Sandhu and Samarati, 1994).

In summary, access control is primarily concerned with the restriction of access to resources for legitimate subjects/users. A security program named *reference monitor* tracks legitimate subject access to resources. This reference monitor consults an authorization database to check the validity of a user request. A security administrator maintains this database. Depending on the security model and policy, some access control entries in the database may be modified by the users.

Figure 2. Example of secure system

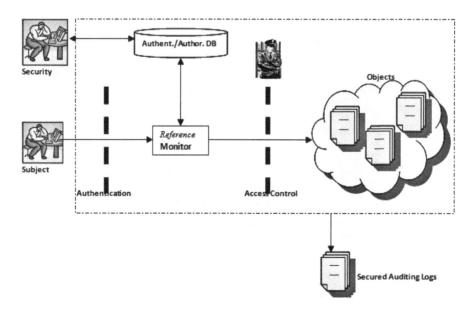

Types of Access Control

There are two main types of access control, *discretionary* and *mandatory*, which can be used alone or in combination:

- **Discretionary Access Control (DAC):** This type of access control is also referred to as identity-based access control (IBAC) or division C in TCSEC is a model applied when the user has the ability to allow or deny access to a particular object. Thus, access control is left to the *discretion* of the owner of the user. For instance, in UNIX systems, the user can grant/deny access to his files to other users. As defined in The Trusted Computer Security Evaluation Criteria - TCSEC (Thompson, 2003), the DAC is:

A means of restricting access to objects based on the identity of subjects and/or groups to which they belong. The controls are discretionary in the sense that a subject with a certain access permission is capable of passing that permission (perhaps indirectly) on to any other subject (unless restrained by mandatory access control).

The DAC is based on user identity and is the most widely known form of access control. The DAC is a means of placing access restrictions on objects based on the identity of subjects and/or the groups to which the subject belongs (Thompson, 2003). These controls are referred to as discretionary because a user or process given discretionary access to information is able to pass that information along to another subject. The key to the DAC is the identity of the user. Access control matrices (studied further in this Chapter) are used to determine whether to grant or deny a particular access request.

- **Mandatory Access Control (MAC):** This type of access control is occasionally referred to as rule-based access control or division B in TCSEC, is a model that goes beyond the DAC model since it adds sensitivity labels to subjects and data objects that are used to enforce a set of mandatory access control rules (Thompson, 2003). In this case, the operating system controls the access, and the user cannot override the controls. It is based on fiat and the identity is irrelevant; i.e. the access is determined by the operating system and an individual user cannot alter the access permissions for an object. Mandatory access controls are based on the results of a comparison between the user's trust level and the sensitivity designation of the information (Thompson, 2003). The operating system or the trusted computing base (TCB) authorizes access to a given object if the security level of the subject label is greater than or equal to the object label. As defined in TCSEC (Thompson, 2003), MAC is:

A means of restricting access to objects based on the sensitivity (as represented by a label) of the information contained in the objects and the formal authorization (i.e., clearance) of subjects to access information of such sensitivity.

The DAC model differs from MAC model in that it implements the access controls of the user. It is important to stress that the DAC model is not a replacement for mandatory controls, rather, the DAC model allows one to place finer-grained access controls on resources within a mandatory access policy model.

Access Control Models

Early works on access matrix models were authored independently by Lampson (Lampson, 1974) and Harrison et al. (Harrison, 1976) who proposed their so-called HRU model. A key contribution of the HRU model consisted of the formalization of the notion of *safety* in access control models. Given an authorization scheme, the safety problem consists of identifying reachable states that violates the security constraints. In spite of its expressiveness, it was pointed out (Harrison, 1976) that the HRU model fails in handling the safety problem in the general case.

Harison et al. (Harrison, 1976) established that the safety problem was nondecidable in the general case. Other models were later proposed that addressed the safety problem but at the price of reduced expressiveness. Examples of such models include the take-and-grant models (Jones et al., 1976) and the Schematic Protection Model (SPM) (Sandhu, 1992a). A more general model, referred to as Typed Access Matrix (TAM) model, was further introduced by Sandhu (Sandhu, 1992b), which addresses the safety problem with acceptable expressive power.

Another model, which has gained a widespread acceptance in the last decades is the role-based access control (RBAC) model proposed by Ferraiolo and Kuhn (Ferraiolo and Kuhn, 1992). The RBAC model is based on the activities that the subjects execute on the system. As such, it fits well with the structure of many organizations.

In order to illustrate some basic notions of access control, the access matrix model is examined in the sequel, followed by the TAM model and RBAC model. Finally, a brief overview of other examples of popular access models is presented.

Access Control Matrix

An access control matrix is used to determine whether to grant or deny a particular access request. It provides a framework for describing the protection systems. It is based on the notion of states and state transitions, where a matrix represents the state of a protection system, and the state transitions are described by *commands*.

An access matrix can be viewed as a snapshot of the protection system specifying at a given time which access should be granted or denied.

More formally the state of a protection system can be defined as a triple *(S, O, M)* where:

- O is a set of *objects*, which are the protected entities of the system. Each object is uniquely identified by a name.
- S is a set of *subjects*, which are active entities of the model (it is assumed that $S \subseteq O$).
- M is an *access matrix*, with rows corresponding to subjects and columns corresponding to objects. An entry M[s, o] in the access matrix lists the *access rights* of the subject *s* for the object *o*.

An access control matrix is a two dimensional structure where, for example, in a row-based representation, one might have an entry that states: "ALICE can access ALICESFILE and JIMSFILE." In a column-based format, one could have equivalently the following entry "JIMSFILE can be accessed by JIM, ALICE, and SUE."

It is common to have the subjects represented on the rows and the objects represented on the columns, with each position in the matrix representing the access type held by that subject for that object. Now, let's look at a basic matrix example depicted by Figure 3.

A graphical view of a set of users and their associated access permissions related to a set of protected objects is shown in Figure 4. The permissions can be read as follows: *r = read, w = write, c = control, p = passing ability*.

Given that a system may often support a significantly large number of users, implementing an access control matrix as a true matrix may not be practical at all.

In practice, the access control matrix model is most commonly implemented by the current operating systems using the following assets: capabilities, profiles, access control lists (ACLs), protection bits, and passwords. For instance, with ACLs, each object maintains a list of access rights of subjects that want to access the object.

Figure 3. Example of access control matrix

	ALICESFILE	JIMSFILE	SUESFILE	BOBSFILE	REPORT1	REPORT2
ALICE	Rw	r			r	
JIM		rw				
SUE		r	Rw	R		r
BOB				Rw		
Mgr Ann	Cp	rp	Cp	Cp	c	c
MIKE					r	r

Figure 4. Role relationships in the RBAC model

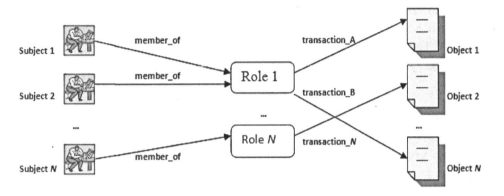

With capability, each subject maintains a list of capabilities it has for each object.

Typed Access Matrix Model

The Typed Access Matrix Model (TAM) was proposed by Sandhu (Sandhu, 1992b) as a refinement of the HRU model (Harrison, 1976) that provides strong typing. The TAM model has arisen out of the need to have stronger safety properties. It is formally defined as a triple $(\mathfrak{R},T,T_s)$ (Sandhu, 1992b), where:

- $\mathfrak{R}$ is a finite set of rights.
- T is a finite set of objects types.
- T_s is a finite set of subjects types, with $T_s \subseteq T$.

The TAM model introduces strong typing into the access matrix model as formalized by Harrison et al. (Harrison, 1976). The protection state is defined as a typed access matrix. The commands through which transitions between states are executed are specified by a sequence of primitive operations that change the access matrix. The TAM model commands are expressed using the following format (Sandhu, 1992b):

```
command c(x_1:t_1,...,x_k:t_k)
            if r_1 ∈ M[x_s1,x_o2] ∧
...∧ r_m ∈ M[x_sm,x_om]
            then op_1; op_2;
...;op_n;
    end
```

There are six primitive operations defined as follows where $z \in \mathfrak{R}$ and s and o are integers between 1 and k. enter z into $[x_s,x_o]$ create subject x_s of type t_s

Sandhu (Sandhu, 1992b) established that the safety issue could be made tractable without loss of expressive power in the TAM model. An algorithm is provided, which can be used to compute the maximal state (after successive application of commands), where no rule can be applied any more. This typically corresponds to the maximal amount of rights that the subjects can gain under this authorization scheme.

Example Using a Medical Record Keeping System

In order to illustrate the concepts of access control matrix introduced in this Chapter, we consider as example the requirements of a medical record keeping system (MRKS) adapted from (Traore and Aredo, 2004). The functional and security requirements for the system are summarized as follows.

Functional Requirements of the MRKS

The purpose of the MRKS is to maintain electronic records for patients' medical information at a hospital. These records are stored in a central database and can be accessed remotely from the Internet and internally through a number of servers controlled by authorized medical personnel and patients.

Security Requirements of the MRKS

Security is an essential characteristic of the MRKS system in the sense that the system should be able to provide the special protection features against suspicious users who want to fraudulently access the private information of authorized users.

The actors of MRKS are patients, doctors, authorized health workers and site administrators. The main resources to be secured are medical records of patients. A patient may choose a unique family doctor who is automatically granted the right to read and modify medical records of his/her patient. In case a patient is referred to a specialist by his/her doctor, that specialist will have full access to the patient's record. Accessing and updating the medical reports of patients is a task dedicated only to authorized doctors, i.e. registered

doctors chosen by a patient or guest doctor (specialist recommended by the patient's doctor). The patient is the only person that is allowed to choose his/her own doctor. A patient can have read access to his/her record, but has no permission to modify it. The site administrator is the only person who can create, delete, read or modify a patient record. Access to the patients' records should be audited and auditors are the only people authorize to read and analyze the audit log. Auditors are considered as third parties and should not be involved in the regular operation of the system. The system should preserve the integrity, confidentiality, and availability of all its entities.

Architecture of the MRKS

In our Chapter entitled "Software Security Engineering – Part I: Security Requirements and Risk Analysis," a security risk analysis was conducted based on the system architecture depicted in Figure 5. The analysis of the functional requirements of such system was also discussed by means of a use case analysis.

Using the TAM Model to Design an Access Control Model for the MRKS

According to the TAM model (Sandhu, 1992b), it is required to define a triple $(\mathfrak{R}, T, T_s)$, where $\mathfrak{R}$ is a finite set of rights, T is a finite set of objects types, and T_s is a finite set of subjects types, with $T_s \subseteq T$.

Based on the class diagram depicted in Figure 6, one can define for each actor a subject type, as well as an object type for each protected resource. Subjects are of course considered as part of objects types. The following definitions are introduced:

- T_s = *{Patient, Doctor, Administrator, Auditor, HealthWorker, User}*
- $T = T_s \cup$ *{Record, AuditLog}* = *{Patient, Doctor, Administrator, Auditor, HealthWorker, User, Record, AuditLog}*

Figure 5. Physical network architecture of the MRKS

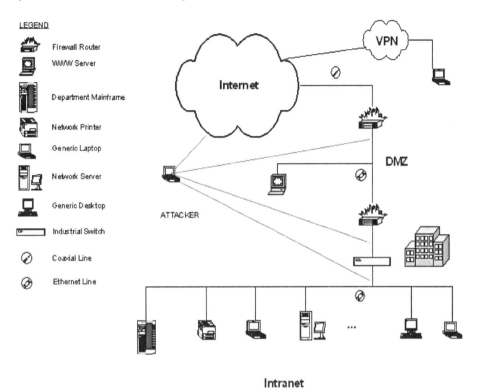

Intranet

The following set of basic rights can be assumed for $\mathfrak{R}$:

- $\mathfrak{R}=$ *{read, write, delete, own, create, execute}*

Now, one needs to define the sensitive operations specified and restricted by the security requirements. For each of these requirements, the access rules should be defined. These access rules represent the core of the access control model. It is also required to identify the operations that can modify the protection state. Here, a command is associated with each of those operations. These commands are defined using the above given template which uses a combination of primitive operations. They define the dynamics of the system, by which the secure states transitions take place.

For the MRKS example, the sensitive operations are first identified from the list of operations specified in the initial class diagram depicted in

Figure 6. In Figure 6, it is obvious that all the operations provided by interfaces *RecordManager* and *AuditManager* should be restricted. The situation, however, is different for the interface *UserManager*: On one hand, the operations *register*, *login*, and *logout* could be unrestricted; they should be available to any user. On the other hand, the operations *unregister*, *updateUser*, *viewUser*, and *deleteUser* for a given user should be restricted to only the administrator and corresponding users.

The following operations may lead to a protection state modification:

- $\Gamma=$ *{register, unregister, updateUser, destroyUser, createRecord, destroyRecord}*

It is assumed that the operations *destroyXXX* remove entirely the corresponding objects (e.g. User, Record). In contrast, the operations *deleteXXX* simply erase their contents.

Figure 6. Initial class diagram for the MRKS

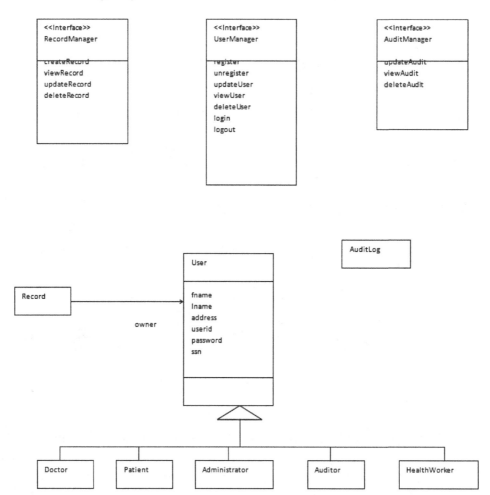

For each of these operations, a command is defined using the same name. In the sequel, two examples of commands are given, which specify (as their names indicate) a record creation by an administrator and a doctor selection by a patient. Based on the security requirements, the following two examples of commands are given, in which M represent the access control matrix.

The first command is for record creation for a patient by an administrator:

```
command createRecord (a: Ad-
ministrator, p: Patient, r: Record)
              create object r of
type Record; enter Own into M[p,r];
```

```
enter read into M[p,r]
      end
```

As a result of this command, an empty record is created, and the patient is granted ownership and readership privileges on the record. This is an example of unconditional command.

The second example is a conditional command. It is related to a sub-operation of *updateUser* operation, which does not appear in the class diagram in Figure 6 (note that in this class diagram, will need to be refined to include such information). This command deals with the choice of a doctor by a patient:

```
          command addDoctor(p: Pa-
tient, d: Doctor, r: Record)
                    if own ∈ M[p,r]
                    then enter own into
[d,p]; enter read into M[d,r]; enter
write into M[d,r]
          end
```

In this case, the patient needs to own the record as precondition. As a result of this choice, the patient is "owned" by the doctor. In addition, the doctor is granted read and write rights on the patient's record.

Role Based Access Control

Role Based Access Control (RBAC) has been called the dominant access-control model of the 1990s, replacing the MAC and DAC models, which were dominant in the 1970s and 1980s. The RBAC model first was introduced by Ferraiolo and Kuhn (Ferraiolo and Kuhn, 1992). It is an access control mechanism that is policy neutral, yet policy oriented. Ferraiolo and Kuhn (Ferraiolo and Kuhn, 1992) credited the need for a model that can efficiently address the security issues related to processing unclassified sensitive information. This was justified by the fact that TCSEC and other policies that focused on the US Department of Defense (DOD, 1985) were also needed for the protection of access to classified information. Civilian governments and corporations who have unique security needs and policies that cannot easily be met using traditional DAC and MAC models could use the RBAC model. While the DAC and MAC models are recognized by official government documents, researchers and practitioners have found that they do not cover many practical requirements (Ferraiolo and Kuhn, 1992), (DOD, 1985).

RBAC policies are based on the activities that the subjects execute on the system. In order for this policy to be used, roles must be identified on the system and have to be assigned to subjects. The roles (occasionally referred to as groups) can be defined as a set of responsibilities and actions related to a particular working activity (Sandhu and Samarati, 1994). In the RBAC model, users cannot pass access permissions onto other subjects at their discretion, something which they can do in DAC-based systems.

In Figure 4, the basics of the RBAC model are illustrated. Subjects are assigned roles independently of the assignment of roles to transactions on objects. Within the RBAC model, it is possible for a subject to play different roles at different times, or in some implementations, more than one role at the same time. When a subject assumes a role, he/she has permission to perform all accesses for which the role is authorized. The formal mathematical descriptions of the RBAC model was introduced in (Ferraiolo and Kuhn, 1992), (Ferraiolo, 2001).

Now, let's summarize the formal notational work of Ferraiolo and Kuhn (Ferraiolo, 2001). Without any implementation specific information, the RBAC model can be defined in terms of sets and relations:

- For each subject, the active role is the one that the subject is currently using:
  - $AR(s: subject) = \{$the active role for subject $s\}$
- Each subject may be authorized to perform one or more roles:
  - $RA(s: subject) = \{$authorized roles for subject $s\}$
- Each role may be authorized to perform one or more transactions:
  - $TA(\{r: role\}) = \{$transactions authorized for role $r\}$
- Subjects may execute transactions. The predicate exec(s,t) is defined as:
  - $exec(s: subject, t: trans) = $ true iff subject s can execute transaction t.

Transactions are all user activities conducted on the system, with the exception of identification and authorization (e.g.: login).

The model requires three basic rules:

1. **Role assignment:** A subject s, can execute a transaction t, only if the subject has selected or been assigned a role:

"s: subject, t: trans (exec(s,t) Þ AR(s) [1] Æ)   (1)

2. **Role authorization:** A subject's active role must be authorized for the subject:

"s: subject(AR(s) Í RA(s))   (2)

3. **Transaction authorization:** A subject can execute a transaction only if the transaction is authorized for the subject's active role:

"s: subject, t: trans (exec(s, t) Þ t $\in$ TA(RA(s)))
(3)

The combination of rules (1) and (2) ensures that the users can play only roles for which they are authorized. With the addition of rule (3), one can ensure that users can only execute transactions that they are authorized for. Since, in rule (3), the conditional is true "only if" the transaction is authorized for the subject's active role, there is no restriction from creating additional rules on the transaction execution.

Ferraiolo and Kuhn (Ferraiolo, 2001) also stressed that it is possible to redefine "transaction" to refer only to the transformation procedure, rather than including a binding to objects. These authors provided an example in the form of a fourth possible rule to refer to the object access:

4. **Transaction to object access:** A subject can access an object if it is permissible for a subject s, in role r, to access object o in

mode x using transaction t. Where x is taken from some set of modes (e.g., read, write, append, etc):

"s: subject, t: trans, o: object(exec(s, t) Þ access(AR(s), t, o, x)   (4)

Since a given subject may play several roles, privileges abuse may happen in case of conflict of interest. For instance, a bank manager who is at the same time a customer may take advantage of his position to grant himself some unlawful loans. To prevent such abuse, the RBAC model introduces a fifth rule named *principle of separation of duties* defined as follows:

5. **Principle of Separation of Duty:** Predicate meauth(r) (for mutually exclusive authorizations) defines the set of roles r that subject s cannot assume because of the separation of duty requirement.

(" r_1,r_2 role) [r_2 $\in$ meauth(r_1) Þ [("s: subject) [r_1 $\in$ RA(s) Þ r_2 $\notin$RA(s)]]]   (5)

The RBAC model also includes the notion of *role hierarchy*, which typically expresses an inheritance relationship between roles. A role r_1 inherits from r_2 means that all permissions of role r_2 are inherited by role r_1.

To further our understanding of the RBAC model, let's consider the following multi-role relationship example. Within most organization, there is an object-oriented hierarchical structure to which employees belong to. This is commonly referred to as the "*is-a*" relationship. For example, let's consider the following people:

- Bob is an employee of an accounting firm, who is also a senior partner; Sue is also a partner with the accounting firm; Alice is an accountant working for the firm; Tom is also an accountant at the firm; Ed is an intern working for the firm for the summer; Eve is an employee of the firm who does not perform any accounting duties; and Mike is an office assistant. Mike and Eve may only access "Object 7" and "Object 8." Sue and Bob, however, due to the nature of hierarchical roles, can access any object.

This relationship can be visualized as shown in Figure 7.

With this understanding, several advantages of the RBAC model have been identified (Ferraiolo and Kuhn, 1992), (Ferraiolo, 2001), (Sandhu and Samarati, 1994) as follows:

- **Authorization management:** This is due to the logical independence in specifying subject authorizations in two parts: (1) assigning access rights for objects to roles, and (2) assigning subjects to roles.

- **Hierarchical roles:** These are due to the nature of roles in everyday life. It is natural to generalize and specify these relationships into a hierarchical structure. In doing so, a role inheritance hierarchy can be built, thus simplifying the authorization management.

- **Least privilege:** Allowing a subject to sign on with the minimum privilege necessary to perform a given task reduces the danger of unintended errors or attacks.

- **Separation of duties:** Allowing a task to be separated among different subjects. Based on the principal that no single subject should be given enough privileges to misuse the system on their own.

- **Object classes:** These allow objects to be classified into groups, similar to how sub-

Figure 7. Hierarchical roles

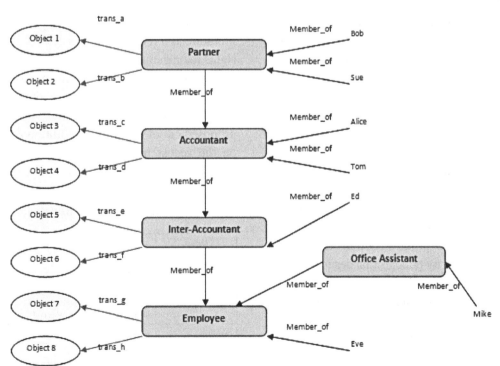

jects are grouped into roles. Access authorization of roles can then be based on object classes rather than on individual objects, thus simplifying the authorization management.

Illustrating the RBAC Model Using the Medical Record Keeping System (MRKS)

Using the RBAC model on the above-mentioned MRKS example, one needs to define the roles, the transactions, the relations between transactions and roles, and the subjects and their authorized roles, mutually exclusive roles if any.

The following definitions can be given for the MRKS:

- **Set of roles:** *R = {Doctor, Patient, Administrator, Auditor, HealthWorker}*
- The relations between transactions and roles are defined in Table 1.

According to the security requirements, the role *Auditor* is mutually exclusive with any other role. One may also decide that the same characteristic should apply for the *Administrator* role.

Other Access Control Models

In the sequel, we will briefly discuss other forms of access control models, starting with the more historical one and moving forward to some of the more recent developments.

Bell-LaPadula: D. E. Bell and L. J. LaPadula of the MITRE Corporation (Bell and LaPadulla, 1973) developed a formal state transition model of computer security policies that describes a set of access control rules. The model deals with how information flows within a computer system and is primarily concerned with confidentiality. The Bell-LaPadula model takes the entities of the computer system and divides them into an abstract

set of subjects and objects. Within the model, a system state is defined to be secure if the only permitted access modes of subjects to objects are in accordance with a specific security policy.

Chinese Wall: The Chinese Wall policy (Brewer and Nash, 1989) merges commercial discretion with legally enforceable mandatory controls. It is reportedly as important to the financial world as the Bell-LaPadula model is to the military organizations, and cannot be correctly implemented by a Bell-LaPadula model. The basis of this policy is that subjects are only allowed access to information that is not in conflict with any other information that they already possess.

Document Dissemination Control: Keeping in mind that the original electronic access controls arose out of a need to have an equivalent means of securing electronic data to what was already used in the dissemination of printed data, military and government systems have many such people-paper systems in use that typically involves an authentication scheme combined with a mandatory access control mechanism based on labeling (Graubart, 1989), (McCollum, et al., 1990). Dissemination control was further investigated in the research literature as it relates to access control and digital rights management (Thomas and Sandhu, 2004).

Usage control (UCON): This model is a generalization of access control to cover obligations, conditions, continuity, and mutability. It was proposed out of the need for additional revisions on the access matrix model and was formally

Table 1. Example of roles assignment

Roles	Authorized transactions
Patient	ViewRecord
Doctor	ViewRecord, updateRecord
Administrator	createRecord, viewRecord, updateRecord, deleteRecord
Auditor	updateAudit, viewAudit, deleteAudit
HealthWorker	ViewRecord

defined in (Sandhu and J. Park, 2003), (Zhang et al., 2004). Several systems have been proposed to deal with issues from dissemination controls including PAC, ORAC and ORGCON.

Known Issues with Access Control

Discretionary access control mechanisms are vulnerable to Trojan horse attacks since the mechanism only restricts access to objects based on the subject identity that is attempting access (NCSC, 1987). Other problems were also raised (NCSC, 1987) based on how the DAC model is implemented. These problems are as follows:

- Protection bits lack the ability to easily control access to each object to the granularity of a single user.
- Capabilities and profiles may encounter design problems with revocation of access and group access to objects.
- Passwords are subject to Trojan horses and therefore should not be used unless they are combined with another mechanism.
- The deletion of subjects and objects is a potential problem for any DAC mechanism.

It has been noted, however, that lattice security models can effectively deal with Trojan horse attacks.

The MAC and DAC models are also inadequate for efficiently addressing issues such as the NOFORN and ORCON labeling found in people-paper systems (Graubart, 1989). Other forms of access control have been recommended to solve this issue. Few of these are: the Propagated Access Control (PAC) (Graubart, 1989), the Owner-Retained Access Control (ORAC) (McCollum et al., 1990), and the Organization Controlled (ORGCON) (Abrams et al., 1991). The ORAC model has interesting attributes since it allows the owner to retain control over their objects

indefinitely through the attachment of mandatory access control lists (ACLs) to individual objects.

Using ACLs to implement the access matrix model has some disadvantages for access review and revocation on a per-subject basis (Sandhu and Samarati, 1994). However, on a per-object basis, they perform well. Authorization tables, or a combination of capabilities and ACLs, are a recommended alternative. All the access control mechanisms also have to deal with the issue of controlling administration and auditing in order to achieve the status of a secure system.

Security Analysis and Design

Security Design Principles

A great deal of wisdom regarding secure system development has been collected in the past decades. This has led to the definition of several security design principles, which are currently used for the design and implementation of secure systems (Saltzer and Schroeder, 1975). Table 2 gives a list of the most popular of these principles. Our goal is to derive from these principles a collection of properties that can be used to guide the definition of software security metrics.

The main characteristics of these principles are *simplicity* and *restriction*. Simplicity is essential in secure systems engineering for obvious reasons: complex mechanisms are difficult to build, maintain, and use, and thereby tend to increase risks. Simplicity is highlighted by the principles of "economy of mechanism" and "psychological acceptability," and also in a certain way by the principle of "*open design*" which states that complexity does not add to security.

The *restriction* characteristic is based on the rationale that no one deserves unlimited trusts; people can always misuse the privileges granted to them. The most secure system is the one that doesn't grant any privilege, however this is unusable. For the system to be usable, it has to grant some privileges. These privileges must be limited to the strict minimum required to fulfill the system's functionality. The *restriction* characteristic is highlighted by principles such as "least privilege," "separation of privilege," "least common mechanism," "complete mediation," and "fail-safe defaults." "Complete mediation" requires that every element be protected by at least one mechanism, which mediates with the requesters. "Separation of privilege" requires using diverse defensive strategies so that if one strategy turns out to be inadequate, another hopefully would counter an attack. The goal of the "least common mechanism" principle is to minimize sharing because shared mechanisms increases the risk for information leakage between elements.

Besides restriction and simplicity, the security design principles also emphasize further aspects such as security composition and the relation between security and fault-tolerance. The "Weakest link" principle refers specifically to the security composition. According to this principle, the security of a collection of elements is at best equal to that of the least secure element in that collection. The "*Secure failure*" principle highlights the link between security, reliability and fault tolerance. The goal of this principle is to ensure that the system remains secure in case of failure. This can be achieved by adopting redundancy techniques used to achieve fault tolerance.

Security Modeling Using the UML

Several interesting research works are ongoing on security modeling using the UML. SecureUML (Lodderstedt et al., 2002) is one such proposal that is relevant and interesting for illustrating some of the concepts introduced in this Chapter. It is a method for modeling the access control policies and how they can be integrated into a model-driven software development process (such as the one introduced in our Chapter entitled "Software Security Engineering – Part I: Security Requirements and Risk Analysis"). In fact, SecureUML is an extension of UML for expressing authorization constraints and access control requirements, with a particular focus on RBAC models.

SecureUML is based on an extended RBAC model. The extension mainly covers the dynamic aspects. The above introduced traditional RBAC

Table 2. Security design principles

Principles	Definitions
Least privilege	A subject should be granted only the minimum number of privileges that it needs in order to accomplish its job.
Fail-Safe Defaults	The default access to an object is none.
Economy of Mechanism	Security mechanisms or systems should be kept as simple as possible.
Complete Mediation	All accesses to objects must be checked beforehand.
Open Design	Security of a mechanism must neither depend on the secrecy of design nor the ignorance of others.
Separation of Privilege	Permission must not be granted based on a single condition.
Least Common Mechanism	Mechanisms used to protect resources must not be shared.
Psychological Acceptability	The introduction of a security mechanism should not make the system more complex than it is without it.
Weakest link	A system is only as secure as its weakest element.
Secure Failure	When a system fails its behavior becomes more insecure. So it is important to ensure that the system fails securely.

model does not support system dynamics such as the notion of state, the evolution of the system parameters over time, to name a few. SecureUML uses the concept of *authorization constraints* to capture such notions. Authorization constraints are typically used to express various forms of access rules, which is an important aspect of the implementation of any access control policy.

Standard for RBAC

The RBAC model underlying the SecureUML is based on the standard for RBAC (Ferraiolo et al., 2001), which is a refinement of the original RBAC model (Ferraiolo and Kuhn, 1992). The model consists of five components described as follows:

1. **USERS:** The set of users. A user corresponds to a person or a software agent.
2. **ROLES:** The set of roles. A role corresponds to a job or function in an organization.
3. **OBS:** The set of objects. An object corresponds to a resource that may be protected by the security rules or mechanisms.
4. **OPS:** The set of operations. An operation corresponds to an action that can be conducted on an object.
5. **PRMS:** The set of permissions. A permission corresponds to the right to execute an operation on one or several objects.

Compared to the original RBAC model (Ferraiolo and Kuhn, 1992), the concepts of users and operations are introduced on the RBAC underlying the SecureUML. Users correspond to subjects, the combination of operations and permissions correspond to transactions. Permissions and users are assigned to roles through a permission assignment relation (PA) and a user assignment relation (UA) respectively.

UML Profile for SecureUML

The SecureUML metamodel defines metamodel types *User, Role, Permission*, to represent the corresponding elements. In a UML model, instances of these metamodel types are naturally represented using corresponding stereotypes (e.g.: user, permission, role). A permission is defined as a relation object linking a role to a model element (e.g.: protected) or resource set. A resource set represented by *ResourceSet* type corresponds to a set of model elements used to define some permission. The semantics of permission is defined by specifying an action type, which represents a class of operations on a particular type of protected object. Action types are defined using *ResourceType* elements. A resource type defines all action types available to a metamodel type. An *AuthorizationConstraint* expresses one or several access rules as specified by the access control policy. It can be expressed as a UML constraint using the Object Constraint Language (OCL).

Illustrating the SecureUML Using the Medical Record Keeping System (MRKS) Example

The SecureUML profile suggested in (Lodderstedt et al., 2002) is platform-dependent. This profile is used to generate a security language named the *host language*, which is specific to the intended execution platform. In the rest of this section, we use the notation proposed for EJB in order to illustrate the design of our medical record keeping system access policy.

In the host language for Enterprise JavaBeans (EJB) (Sun, 2001), model elements which correspond to EJB components are expressed using the stereotype <<ejb>>. In the example class-diagram, EJB default methods such as finder methods will be omitted in order to avoid clutters. These methods are generated automatically even though they still need to be secured. The resource type for EJB suggested in (Lodderstedt et al., 2002) (as shown in Figure 8) partially matches the needs of our example system; thus, we will extend and reuse it in the sequel.

The resource type is defined as a class with stereotype <<resourceType>>. The action types

Figure 8. Resource type for EJB

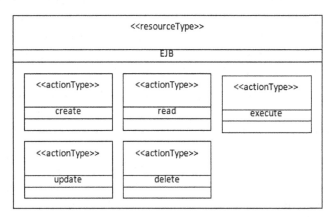

are defined as nested classes within the resource type class, with stereotype <<actionType>>.

In order to avoid clutters, the example class diagram is decomposed into two partial diagrams:

- The first diagram depicted in Figure 9 shows the roles' permissions for protected resources. In Figure 9, roles are labeled using the stereotype <<role>>. Permissions are shown as association classes defining corresponding action types and labeled using the stereotype <<permission>>. The diagram in Figure 9 involves some authorization constraints that are represented as UML constraints using stereotype <<AuthorizationConstraint>>. An authorization constraint may be bound to a permission, in which case it defines additional restriction (e.g. precondition) on the permission. It may also be bound to a class or resource view using a UML dependency, in which case it restricts all the involved methods.

Two examples of authorization named *Readership* and *RecordPersistence* are defined in the diagram shown in Figure 9. *RecordPersistence* is an example of class bound constraint, which ensures that the deletion of record entries can happen only after a specified delay set hereto 100 years. This restricts accordingly access to all attributes and methods of the EJB component Record. *Readership* is an example of permission bound constraint. It restricts access to all read methods on Record objects to their respective owners, authorized doctors and health workers, and system administrators in the MRKS.

- The second partial class diagram depicted in Figure 10 emphasizes on the resource views. A *resource view* represents a subset of the features (e.g.: attributes, methods) provided by a given type. Typically, a resource view is used to express permissions or authorization constraints on either a single feature or a subset of features provided by a resource type. It is modeled as a UML class labeled with stereotype <<resourceView>> and linked to the referenced type using a UML dependency labeled with stereotype <<context>>.

CONSTRUCTION OF SECURE SOFTWARE

To ease the design and development of secure software systems and related applications, one option is to make use of security frameworks that already embodied security functions, and require-

Figure 9. SecureUML partial class diagram

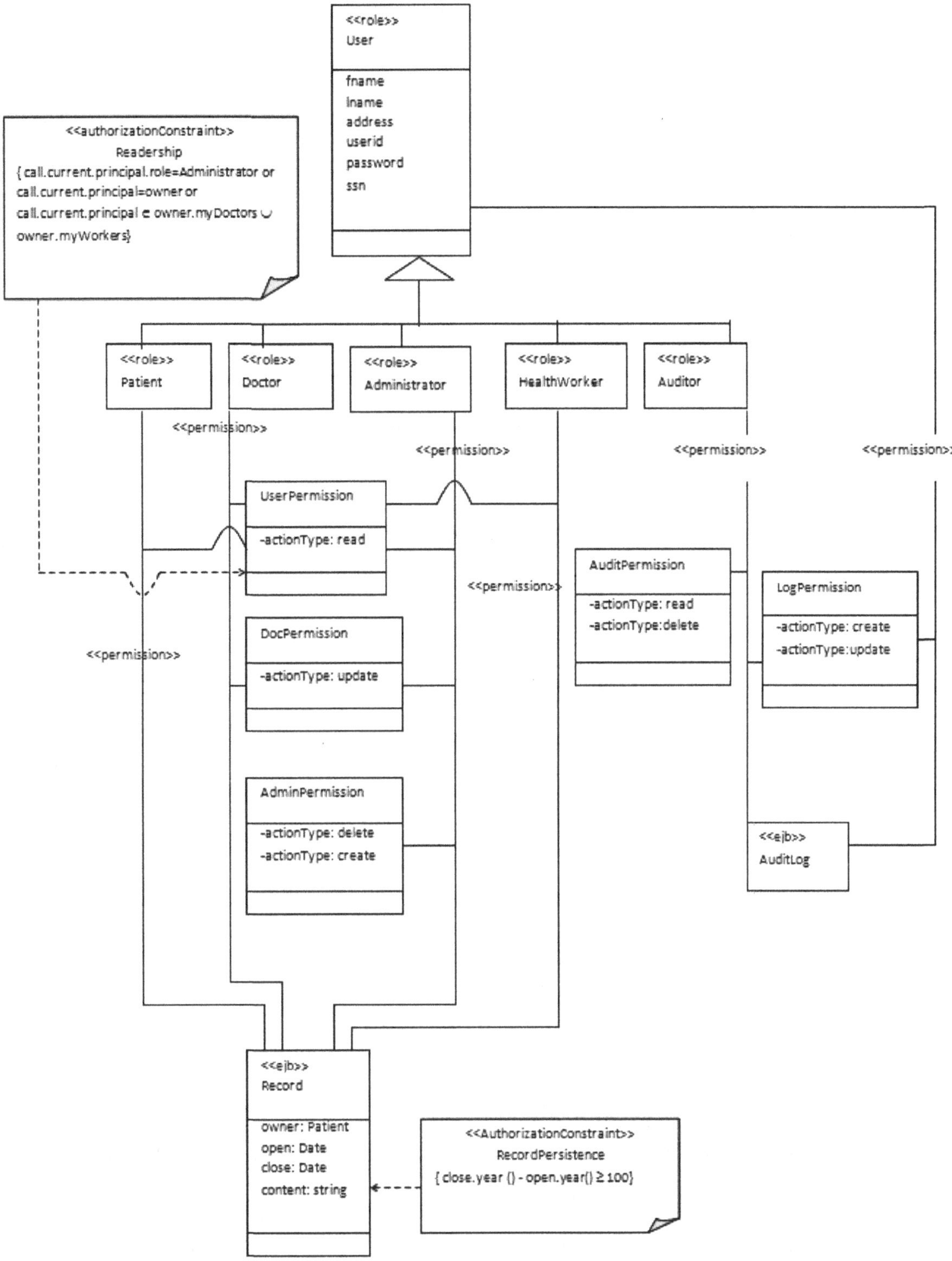

Figure 10. SecureUML partial class diagram emphasizing the resource view

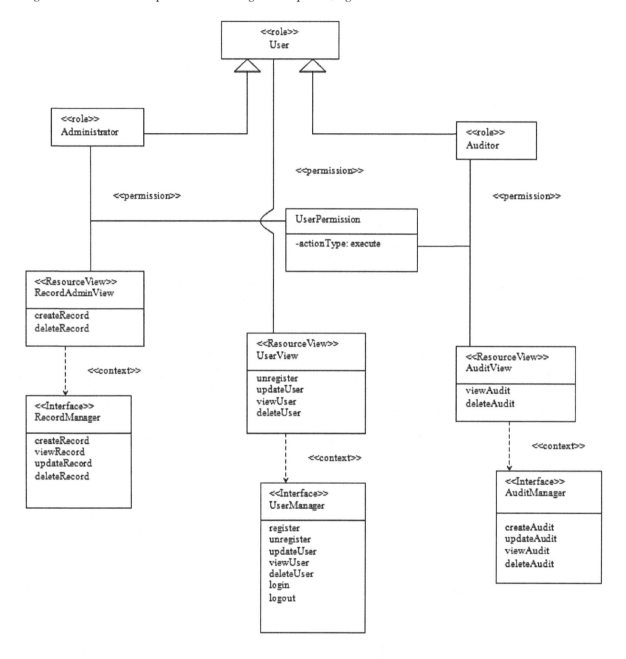

ments such as authentication, authorization, data validation, encryption, to name a few.

Representative security frameworks include: the Generalized Framework for Access Control (GFAC) (Abrams et al., 1991), the Software Security TouchPoints (McGraw, 2004), ISO/IEC 15408 (also known as Common Criteria for Information Technology Security Evaluation v2.3)

(CC, 2007), SAFECode (Simpson, 2008), the Open Web Application Security Project (OWASP) and Java OWASP (OWASP, 2009), the Integrated Security Development Framework (ISDF) (Alkussayer and Allen, 2010). In the sequel, two of the above-mentioned frameworks in which there are important access control requirements, are briefly highlighted.

Generalized Framework for Access Control (GFAC)

The main idea underlying the GFAC framework (Abrams et al., 1991) is that all access control requirements can be viewed as rules expressed in terms of attributes by authorities. Access control requirements involve three kinds of elements:

- **Authority:** Who is responsible for elaborating security policies.
- **Attributes:** These correspond to the characteristics and properties of the subjects and objects involved in the secure system.
- **Rules:** These formalize the access control decisions.

Considering the attributes of the subjects and objects, access control decisions are made based on the rules defined in the security policy.

The GFAC model separates the access control procedure in two parts: adjudication and enforcement:

- **Adjudication:** This is performed by the Access Decision Facility (ADF).
- **Enforcement:** The Access Enforcement Facility (AEF) makes the enforcement of the decision. The ADF carries the rules underlying the access control policies of the system. The access operations performed by the system are provided and made available by the ADF.

The other components involved in the GFAC framework are as follows:

- Subject
- Object
- **Access Control Information (ACI):** Information used by the ADF to make access control decisions.
- **Access Control Rules (ACR):** These are embodies access control rules.

The modus operandi of the GFAC model is described in Figure 11.

In practice, in the GFAC model, when a subject wants to access to an object, it sends a request to the AEF. The AEF then forwards the request to the ADF with additional information (related to the subject) encapsulated in the ACI. Basing itself on the rules defined in the ACR, the ADF makes decision about whether access shall be granted or not, and notifies the AEF about that decision. Then accordingly, the AEF will or will not grant access to the resource.

Integrated Security Development Framework (ISDF)

The design of the ISDF model (Alkussayer and Allen, 2010) comprises two modules: the secure software development life cycle (SSDLC) and the Security Patterns Utilization Process (SPUP), which seamlessly interact together to incorporate the security patterns into the traditional software development life cycle. The activities included in each phase of the ISDF model are described in (Howard and S. Lipner, 2006), (McGraw, 2006).

SECURITY ASSESSMENT

Security Metrics

According to the systems security engineering capability maturity model (SSE-CMM) metrics Committee, "security metrics focus on the actions (and results of those actions) that organizations take to reduce and manage the risks of loss of reputation, theft of information or money, and business discontinuities that arise when security defenses are breached" (Nielsen, 2000). Security metrics are needed to evaluate the current level of security, to identify resources for improvements and to implement those improvements. In (Alger, 2001), Alger outlines the difference between measurements and metrics. Measurement gives

Figure 11. GFAC: Generic architecture and scenario

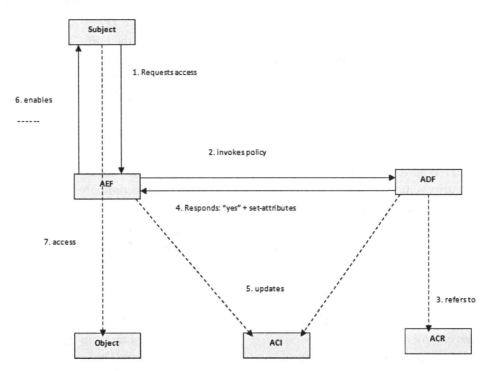

a snapshot of specific parameters represented by numbers, weights or binary statements. Taking measurements over time and comparing them with specific baseline generate metrics.

Metrics have been successfully developed for a broad range of quality attributes including reliability, performance, and maintainability. Notable exception remains the field of software security, which is still immature. The software security metrics available are still in the research stage. However, according to Vaughn (Vaughn, 2001), there are various different measures and metrics that may be useful in predicting systems security characteristics including: penetration success rates, coupling and cohesion of security relevant software, testing defect rates, process quality, to name a few.

Security metrics are difficult to generate because system security key building blocks such as asset value, threat, and vulnerability are difficult to evaluate and measure objectively. In spite of the efforts being made to provide objective measures

of vulnerabilities through the development of tools and benchmarks, the evaluation of important facets of vulnerabilities remains largely subjective. Hence, few concrete security metrics have been proposed so far. In the sequel, an informal discussion is conducted on potential software security metrics which are currently the purpose of active research.

Obvious targets of measurement are common security attributes, which include confidentiality, integrity, availability, non-repudiation, and authentication. Besides these attributes, there are several other characteristics of software systems that can be used for security measurement (Liu and Traore, 2004). Some of these metrics are described a s follows.

- **Reliability:** This metric refers to the probability that a system delivers a given service during a specified time interval. Reliability gives an indirect measure of security. It provides a necessary but not sufficient condition for security.

- **Availability:** This represents the fraction of time during which the system delivers its intended service in a specified time interval. Availability is often related to denial of service (DoS) attacks, but it can be used to measure the impact of any successful security attack on the system.
- **Performability:** This metric measures the system performance in the presence of failure.
- **Safety:** This metric quantifies the probability that the system functions safely during a specified time period. A breach in safety typically leads to catastrophic damage such as loss human lives or significant monetary loss. Safety as a security related measure targets the consequences of security breach for sensitive data.
- **Vulnerability:** This metric quantifies the amount of security flaws that can be potentially exploited to break into the system.
- **Attackability:** This metric quantifies the ability of the system to resist security attacks.

Security Testing

Security testing is a required activity for systems seeking the Trusted Computer System Evaluation Criteria (TCSEC) certification at classes C1 through A1 (DOD, 1985). The main purpose is to establish whether the security functions of a system are implemented and can be trusted to exhibit the level of specified security.

Security testing is different from functional testing (Thompson, 2003). While functional testing checks for proper functioning of the expected system services, security testing looks for unexpected behavior of the system. The focus of security testing is more on checking defensive mechanisms rather than checking the system's functionality. To achieve this objective, security-testing process typically consists of exercising the system on its edges and analyzing how it behaves.

Like in functional testing, security testing techniques can be divided in black-box and white-box techniques. White-box techniques require knowledge of the source code. Black-box approaches involve testing the software without access to the source code and possibly with little documentation on the internal of the system. A good approach to testing should adequately combine both kinds of techniques.

Effective security testing involves the combination of one or several techniques including regular security testing approach driven by security risk analysis and security fault injection, source code auditing, testing based on known vulnerabilities, and red teaming. Each of these techniques is briefly discussed in the sequel.

Regular Testing

Standard security testing uses as inputs a requirements document describing the key functionalities and a software architecture document describing the software components and modules along with their interfaces and interconnections. The requirement document allows one to identify the *use cases* and *misuse cases*. Providing an *attack tree* allows one to refine each misuse case.

As seen previously, an attack tree typically describes in detail the sequence of actions taken by the intruder in order to achieve a security compromise as specified by a misuse case (Alexander, 2003). Attack trees are used to generate attack scenarios, which in turn serve as basis for the security test case generation. Testing in this setting consists of trying risky attack scenarios and evaluating the response of the software system to these attacks.

Test Planning

Test planning starts by identifying the components of the system and their interconnections. A monolithic application with no connection or interaction with the environment is less likely to be subject to security problems. Security issues arise because the application interact or exchange some data with the environment. Hence, security testing will typically consists of ascertaining how these interactions affect the system. This involves identifying the system's interfaces, their inputs and outputs. According to (Mc Graw, 1998), (Viega, and McGraw, 2001), security test planning involves the following activities:

1. Identify the system components and their interfaces.
2. Prioritize the interfaces based on their level of vulnerability.
3. Determine and characterize the data used by each interface.
4. Conduct security testing activities.

From the testing perspective, only security-relevant components are considered. For each component, the testing assumptions as well as the interfaces should be defined. Interfaces also need to be ranked according to their level of potential vulnerability. The goal of the ranking is to establish a testing priority by deciding in which order components and their interfaces will be tested. Naturally, the most vulnerable components or interfaces must be tested first.

Test Case Generation

A good guide for generating test cases is to use as basis the attack scenarios identified during the risks analysis process. The system should be exercised by trying each attack scenario. Attack scenarios consist of sequences of actions or functions executions that may lead to security compromise. For each interface, the data accessed must be specified. At least one or more test cases should be developed for each interface.

In order to generate the actual test cases instances, appropriately input data should be chosen to be fed to the functions involved. These can be

achieved by using a combination of fault injection techniques and standard test coverage techniques. Fault injection consists of exercising the software under extreme or unexpected conditions and observing how it behaves. The primary objective of fault injection is to make the system behaves insecurely and ascertain whether the defensive mechanisms work properly under these scenarios. Fault injection techniques consist of perturbing the application by injecting faulty data. This may consist of perturbing the container (e.g.: file) or the content, i.e. the data itself. Perturbing the container may consist of changing its name, denying access to it, or granting partial or restricted access to it (e.g.: granting for instance read-only permission instead of read and write access to a file).

Perturbing the data may consist of changing the format of the data or its nature. The format may consist of canonical representations such as size. The nature of the data is related to the kind or meaning of the data.

For instance, a function expecting as input data a file name, say of 20 characters maximum, may be tested by sending it a 1000 characters file name. A 1000 characters file name is unusual but if the function does not check properly the input size, this may lead to a successful buffer-overflow or denial of service.

Source Code Auditing

The choice of a programming language is one of the most important technological decisions faced by a project team. The main concerns taken into account by many projects are efficiency, representational power, or convenience. For instance, people tend to choose C or C++ when efficiency is in line. A typical reason for choosing a language by convenience is the need for reusing an existing open source. Unfortunately, security is rarely a concern when choosing an implementation language. As a consequence, a large number of programs are released with an overwhelming number of security vulnerabilities. For instance C or C++

languages are unreliable because of unrestricted pointers and a lack of reasonable error-handling facilities. Hence, they can easily serve as target for buffer overflow or denial of service attacks. This doesn't mean that languages such as Java are totally safe. For instance, an improper error handling in Java can be used to conduct denial of service attacks.

Overall, the more error checking a language can do statically, the more reliable the program written in this language is from a security perspective. This can be ascertained by auditing the source code.

Source code auditing involves looking for implementation-specific vulnerabilities by thoroughly reviewing the program source code. This starts by identifying all the system inputs. these include inputs from local or remote users, inputs from any other programs trusted or untrusted, inputs from API's and GUI's files or networks, to name a few.

With a clear understanding of these inputs, the auditing proceeds by examining vulnerabilities patterns such as race conditions, buffer overflows, unexpected operators attacks, covert channels, to name a few.

Auditing large and complex software systems can be time consuming and difficult. Fortunately, there are tools (Jiwani and Zelkowitz, 2004) that statically scan source code for function calls and constructs that are known to be unsafe or prone to security flaws such as buffer overflows. These tools help focusing the security analysis by spotting problems and suggesting potential remedies. They also help the auditor in prioritizing the vulnerabilities by giving relative assessments of their severity. These tools, however, have some limitations including the following:

- They generate a large amount of data, which can overwhelm the auditor.

- They are not 100% reliable: they still carry a significant amount of false positives.
- They still require a significant level of expert knowledge.

Overall, these can represent very effective tools in the hands of security experts who can quickly interpret their findings and decide the proper course of actions to be taken.

Checking for Known Vulnerabilities

Source code auditing tools heavily rely on known security vulnerabilities databases in order to identify security bugs in programs. Besides these general-purpose databases, it is also a good practice to compile a list of known vulnerabilities specific to the program under testing based on previous releases. Often these vulnerabilities might be absent from the databases implemented by auditing tools. Several studies (Landwher et al., 1994), (Mell et al., 2005) have shown that the same vulnerabilities can be carried over across several versions or releases of the same software product. Identifying and testing these vulnerabilities is an important step in the software security testing process.

Red Teaming

Red teaming consists of simulating the hackers' behaviors in order to locate and exploit security bugs in a software system. Even though read teaming can sometimes uncover some serious bugs, the approach is severely limited by the fact that they start with little information about the system. The main assumption being that red teams should not have more information than a potential hacker could obtain. This constraint limits the effectiveness of the approach.

CONCLUSION

This chapter presented the major objectives of a security policy, with focus on how applications that protect data at all access points can be developed. Major access control models and their known issues were discussed. In addition, security modeling using the UML has also been discussed, along with a view on how this concept can be used in conjunction with security frameworks that deal with important access control requirements, to design and develop secure software systems. The Medical Record Keeping System (MRKS) was taken as an example to illustrate the above concepts. Finally, from a software verification and validation perspective, potential software security metrics that could be used for the security measurement and testing of software systems built upon the above concepts were discussed. In the future, it would be interesting to consider the benefit of the studied concepts when building secure software systems and applications.

REFERENCES

Abrams, M. D., Heaney, J. E., King, O., LaPadula, L. J., Lazear, M. B., & Olson, I. M. (1991). Generalized framework for access control: Towards prototyping the ORGCON Policy. *Proceedings of the 14ʰ National Computer Security* Conference, Baltimore, MD, USA.

ACSI - Australian Communications – Electronic Security Instruction 33. (2012). *The Information Security Group of the Australian Government's Defense Signals Directorate*. Retrieved March 18, 2012, from www.dsd.gov.au/_lib/pdf_doc/acsi33/acsi33_u_0904.pdf

Alexander, I. (2003). Misuse cases: Use cases with hostile intent. *IEEE Computer Society, Focus Magazine*.

Alger, J. I. (2001). *On assurance, measures, and metrics: Definitions and approaches*. Workshop on Information-Security-System Rating and Ranking, Williamsburg, Virginia, May 21-23.

Alkussayer, A., & Allen, W. (2009). The ISDF framework: Integrating security patterns and best practice. *Journal of Information Processing Systems*, 6(1).

Anderson, R. J. (1996). A security policy for clinical information systems. *Proceedings of the IEEE Symposium on Security and Privacy*. ISBN: 0-8186-7417-2

Bell, D., & LaPadulla, L. (1973). *Secure computer systems: Mathematical foundations*, Vol. 1. Technical Report MTR-2547. Bedford, MA: MITRE Corporation.

Bishop, M. (2004). *Introduction to computer security* (1st ed.). Addison-Wesley Professional.

Brewer, D. F. C., & Nash, M. J. (1989). The Chinese Wall security policy. In *Proceedings of the 1989 IEEE Symposium on Security and Privacy*, (pp. 206-214).

CC - Common Criteria for Information Technology Security Evaluation v2.3. (2007). Retrieved from http://www.commoncriteriaportal.org/public/developer/index.php?menu=2

DOD - Department of Defense Standard. (1985). *Department of Defense trusted computer system evaluation criteria*. (DOD 5200.28-STD, GPO 1986-623-963, 643 0, Dec. 26).

Ferraiolo, D. F., & Kuhn, R. (1992). *Role-based access controls*. 15ʰ National Computer Security Conference.

Ferraiolo, D. F., Sandhu, R., Gavrila, S., Kuhn, R., & Chandramouli, R. (2001). Proposed NIST standard for role-based access control. *ACM Transactions on Information and System Security*, 4(3). doi:10.1145/501978.501980

Graubart, R. (1989). On the need for a third form of access control. In *Proceedings of the 12th National Computer Security Conference*, Baltimore, MD, USA, 10-13 Oct.

Harrison, M., Ruzzo, W., & Ullman, J. (1976). Protection in Operating Systems [Aug.]. *Communications of the ACM, 19*(8), 461–471. doi:10.1145/360303.360333

Howard, M., & Lipner, S. (2006). *The security development lifecycle SDL: A process for developing demonstrably more secure software.* Redmond, WA: Microsoft Press. Retrieved March 18, 2012, from http://csrc.nist.gov/rbac/ferraiolo-kuhn-92.pdf

ISO. IEC 17799 - International Organization for Standardization, BS ISO/IEC 17799:2000 - Information technology. (2012). *Code of practice for information security management,* 1st Edition, 2000-12-01.

ITSEC - Information Technology Security Evaluation Criteria. (1991). *Commission European Communities.*

Jiwani, K., & Zelkowitz, M. (2004). Susceptibility matrix: A new aid to software auditing. *IEEE Security & Privacy, 2*(2), 16–21. doi:10.1109/MSECP.2004.1281240

Jones, A., Lipton, R., & Snyder, L. (1976). A linear-time algorithm for deciding security. In *Proceedings of the 17th Symposium on the Foundations of Computer Science*, (pp. 33-41).

Krishni, N. (2001). *How to check compliance with your security policy.* Retrieved from http://www.sans.org/infosecFAQ/policy/compliance.htm

Lampson, B. (1974). Protection. *ACM Operating Systems Review, 8*(1), 18–24. doi:10.1145/775265.775268

Landwher, C. E., Bull, A. R., McDermott, J. P., & Choi, W. S. (1994). A taxonomy of computer program security flaws, with examples. *ACM Computing Surveys, 3*(26).

Liu, M. Y., & Traore, I. (2004). UML-based security measures of software products. In *Proceedings of the 4th International Conference on Application of Concurrency to System Design (ACSD-04)*, Hamilton, Ontario, Canada, June.

Lodderstedt, T., Basin, D. A., & Doser, J. (2002). SecureUML: A UML-Based Modeling Language for Model-Driven Security. *In Proc. of the 5th International Conference on the Unified Modeling Language (UML '02),* Springer-Verlag London, UK, ISBN:3-540-44254-5.

McCollum, C. J., Messing, J. R., & Notargiacomo, L. (1990). Beyond the Pale of MAC and DAC - Defining New Forms of Access Control. *In Proc. of the Symposium on Security and Privacy*, Oakland, CA, USA.

McGraw, G. (1998). Testing for Security during Development: Why we should scrap penetrate-and-patch. *IEEE Aerospace and Electronic Systems, 13*(4), 13–15. doi:10.1109/62.666831

McGraw, G. (2004). Software security. *IEEE Security & Privacy, 2*(2), 80–83. doi:10.1109/MSECP.2004.1281254

McGraw, G. (2006). *Software Security: Building Security.* Addison-Wesley.

Mell, P., Bergeron, T., & Henning, D. (2005). Creating a Patch and Vulnerability Management Program. *Computer Security Division, National Institute of Standards and Technology (NIST) Special Publication 800-40 Version 2.0*, Gaithersburg, MD, USA, 75 pages.

NCSC - National Computer Security Center. (1987). A Guide to Understanding Discretionary Access Control in Trusted Systems. *NCSC-TG, 003*(Sept), 30.

Nielsen, F. (2000). *Approaches to security metrics.* NIST and CSSPAB Workshop, Washington, DC, June 13-14.

OWASP - The Open Web Application Security Project. (2009). Retrieved March 18, 2012, from https://www.owasp.org/index.php/Category:OWASP_Project

Saltzer, J., & Schroeder, M. (1975). The protection of information in computer systems. *Proceedings of the IEEE, 63*(9), 1278–1308. doi:10.1109/PROC.1975.9939

Sandhu, R. J., & Samarati, P. (1994). Access control: Principles and practice. *IEEE Communications, 32*(9).

Sandhu, R. S. (1992a). Expressive power of the schematic protection model. *Journal of Computer Security, 1*(1), 59–98.

Sandhu, R. S. (1992b). The typed access matrix model. In *Proceedings of the 1992 IEEE Computer Society Symposium on Research in Security and Privacy*, Oakland, CA, USA, (pp. 4-6).

Sandhu, R. S., & Park, J. (2003). *Usage control: A vision for next generation access control.* MMM-ACNS. doi:10.1007/978-3-540-45215-7_2

SANS Institute. (2007). *Information security policy - A development guide for large and small companies.* SANS Institute, InfoSec Reading Room.

Security Classification. PUBLIC. (2011). *Information security policy*, Version 2.1. Ministry of Labour, Citizens' Services and Open Government, British Columbia, Canada. Retrieved from http://www.cio.gov.bc.ca/local/cio/informationsecurity/policy/isp.pdf

Simpson, S. (2008). *Fundamental practices for secure software development: A guide to the most effective secure development practices in use today.* Retrieved March 18, 2012, from http://www.safecode.org

Sun Microsystems, Inc. (2001). *How to develop a network security policy: An overview of internetworking site security.* Retrieved March 18, 2012, from http://www.sun.com/software/whitepapers/wp-security-devsecpolicy

Sun Microsystems, Inc. (2001). *Enterprise Java-Beans specification*, Version 2.0. Retrieved March 18, 2012, from http://java.sun.com/ejb/docs.html

Thomas, R., & Sandhu, R. S. (2004). Towards a multi-dimensional characterization of dissemination control. *Proceedings of the IEEE International Conference on Policies for Distributed Networks and Systems.*

Thompson, H. H. (2003). Why security testing is hard. *IEEE Security & Privacy, 1*(4), 83–86. doi:10.1109/MSECP.2003.1219078

Traore, I., & Aredo, D. B. (2004). Enhancing structured review using model-based verification. *IEEE Transactions on Software Engineering, 30*(11). doi:10.1109/TSE.2004.86

US-CERT - United States Computer Emergency Readiness Team. (2012). Retrieved March 18, 2012, from http://www.kb.cert.org/vuls

Vaughn, R. B. (2001). *Are measures and metrics for trusted information systems possible?* Workshop on Information-Security-System Rating and Ranking, Williamsburg, Virginia, May 21-23.

Viega, J., & McGraw, G. (2001). *Building secure software.* Addison-Wesley.

Zhang, X., Park, J., Parisi-Presicce, F., & Sandhu, R. (2004). A logical specification for usage control. *Proceedings of the 9th ACM Symposium on Access Control Modules and Technologies.*

Chapter 14
A Comparative Analysis of Software Engineering Approaches for Sequence Analysis

Muneer Ahmad
King Faisal University, Saudi Arabia

Low Tang Jung
University Technology PETRONAS, Malaysia

Noor Zaman
King Faisal University, Saudi Arabia

ABSTRACT

DNA is considered the building block of living species. DNA sequence alignment and analysis have been big challenges for the scientists for many years. This research presents a comparative analysis of state of the art software engineering approaches for sequence analysis, i.e. genome sequences in particular. Sequence analysis problems are NP hard and need optimal solutions. The underlying problems stated are duplicate sequence detection, sequence matching by relevance, and sequence analysis by approximate comparison in general and by using tools, i.e. Matlab and multi-lingual sequence analysis. The usefulness of these operations is also highlighted, and future expectations are described. The proposal describes the concepts, tools, methodologies, and algorithms being used for sequence analysis. The sequences contain the precious information that needs to be mined for useful purposes. There is high concentration required to model the optimal solution. The similarity and alignments concepts cannot be addressed directly with one technique or algorithm; a better performance is achieved by the comprehension of different concepts.

DOI: 10.4018/978-1-4666-3679-8.ch014

INTRODUCTION

Sequences are logical units that contain vital information, for instance consider biological sequences that compose of nucleotide base pairs in the form of A (Adenine), T (Thymine), G(Guanine) and C (cytosine). The structure and position of these pairs in sequence determine the personality, habits and inheritance characteristics of species.

The mining of useful information from the vast repositories of sequence data brings interesting results related to genes and their functional properties, the main attention and focus of biologists is to differentiate species on behalf of these functional characteristics, many different solutions have been proposed that claim to bring optimal results. It is worth knowing that direct matching in sequence repository data is not efficient and may bring inaccurate and slow results, so going beyond the exact match is necessary for optimality.

Modern computational technology and good devices has made the job of scientists relatively easy in bringing accurate results, this reflection is quite positive in micro-array DNA technology and image data-sets comparison techniques where huge bulky genetic data is approximately compared promptly.

The data is spread over chips and relevancy is determined. The other tools like MATLAB, TRADOES and EBMT are now broadly used for sequence manipulation. FASTA and BLAST are also very popular in biological researchers for sequence comparisons, different people have developed many tools for analysis of not only the genetic sequences but corpora sequences, the lexical analysis explores the hidden resources in these structures, global alignment tools have replaced local one and multiple alignment techniques have given way to know more about diversity in functional properties of species in sequences.

People are interested in mining some kind of association rules in genetic and lexical data, these rules will better help to understand the patterns in data and further exploration may lead to more

knowledgeable and interesting results that could not be available by query application phenomenon. The query application only generates views that are provided through datasets within a confined domain and redefined rules in the form of queries, later solutions present the query enhancement techniques but that are not as optimal as direct rule generation from datasets.

Scientists now use latest systems in biotechnology for storage of genetic data, employing data ware housing techniques and analyzing the DNA sequences, it is not limited to computations but can solve many different complex biological problems.

A BRIEF DISCUSSION OF RESEARCH OVER SEQUENCE ANALYSIS

We have presented a brief summary of research done for sequence analysis, Bansal (1995) has presented a sophisticated way for the presentation of information in the form of a frame work which helps understanding multiple sequences as ADT (abstract tool to integrate information achieved from proposed idea). The authors tried to develop a library that could contain generic high level language for generation of useful phylo-genetic tree. Complex analysis at multiple sequences had been performed by derived groups of amino acids in homologous protein (sharing some common properties along with identification of constrained columns. A help from PROLOG TOOL was taken to apply proposed frame work.

Kappen and Salbaum (2003) had presented a sequence comparison approach that could annotate a comparison between a mouse chromosome 9 and a human chromosome 15, the data draft sequences had been obtained from genetic databases and a complex map containing 14 genes has been presented as a genome map, the framework described in the paper for data interpretation and demonstration can be quite helpful for generation of more complex maps provided time constrained is kept in mind, the ideas may lead towards implementation of automated genome annotation techniques. Another added benefit of this approach was the extraction of common properties between species.

Nahar, Hamel, Popstova and Gogarten (2007) had proposed an interactive tool which was web based and provided comparative genome sequence analysis. The authors have taken help from self adjusting maps for depiction of possible evolutionary concepts in to achieve certain results. The visual identification of horizontally transferred genes was not available in other techniques/tools.

Chang et al., (2005) proposed a framework for efficient gene identification and functional annotations. The package helps in comparative analysis for different genomes. It plots numerous measures for all positions in a long DNA sequence and could perform whole genome comparison. The framework proposes a cross-species pathway comparison on customized starting and ending points of pathways.

Cornell et al., (2001) has presented Genome Information Management System GIMS) that served as a data-ware house. It helped in incorporating genomic sequence and functional data. This ware house had been explained by giving an example of yeast genome data. It could answer many useful queries and serves as a basis for future exploration by creating a large data-ware house with genomic and functional features. The authors observed that framework would provide better effective analysis of genome with functional properties.

Ahmed, Pan and Vandenberg (2005) have proposed an algorithm that is experimentally evaluated in a distributed grid environment that provides very scalable and low computational cost. As multiple sequence alignment and comparison problem falls in a domain of length so parallel approach focusing on the parts of sequences and then integrated can lead to better approximate results, so main focus remains on utilization of grid computing for large biological data. The algorithm was studies in three different distributed environments including a single cluster environment, a single cluster grid environment and a multi cluster grid environment.

Agrawal and Khaitan (2008) proposed a heuristic approach for multiple sequence alignment. It was observed that dynamic programming algorithm involved computational complexity. It could bring slow and inefficient results. The proposed algorithm was compared with CLUSTALW which took $O(N2n2)$ time complexity against $O(N \log2(Nn2))$ for modified technique. The proposed approach also made the alignment process more dynamic as the order of sequences added to the multiple sequence alignment also depended on the already computed multiple sequence alignment.

Cai Juedes and Liakhovitch (2000) had described a comprehensive evolutionary computational approach for multiple sequence alignment by representing a set of 17 clusters of orthologous groups of proteins and compared the results with the standard results from CLUSTALW and found the proposed results better than the standard approach.

Liu Weiguo Schmidt, Voss and Muller-Wittig (2007) proposed a streaming approach for multiple sequence alignment. This approach is based on PC graphics hardware, using modern graphics processing units for high performance computing with low cost make it possible to depict more sophisticated results. The authors have reformulated dynamic programming algorithm bases alignment as streaming algorithm in terms of computer graphics hardware boundaries.

Zhao et al., (2008) presents an improved Ant Colony algorithm that is more sophisticated form of previous technique, the authors claim that their modified approach can operate genomic sequences of any length while traditional Ant Colony approach uses fixed length sequences, the modified approach can avoid local optimum problem, so proposed technique brings robust and efficient results

Arslan and He (2006) described an improved algorithm for multiple sequence alignment problem, this approach considers two layers each of which corresponds to part of the dynamic programming matrix for the alignment of the given sequences and computes each layer differently using dynamic programming technique, in this way the proposed approach is much more efficient than traditional approach that uses weighted automata and performance is claimed to be much better than other approaches.

Davidson (2001) depicts an approach that is basically an integration of dynamic programming and heuristic approach with minimal amount of additional overhead, the idea is that dynamic matrix is traversed along anti-diagonals, bounding the computation to exclude partitions of the matrix that can't contain optimal paths, so the heuristic approach will prune the unnecessary paths from this matrix and present an optimal solution to the problem.

Rashid, Abdullah, Talib and Ali (2006) shows a fast dynamic programming based sequence alignment algorithm uses the reduced amino acids alphabet to transform the protein sequences into a sequence of integers and uses n-gram to reduce the length of the sequence, and then traditional approach is used to get the similarity measure between two sequences.

Agrawal Ankit, Huang and Xiaoqiu (2008) claimed a better performance by presenting a modification to the iterative approach by incorporating in it the use of multiple parameter sets. Preliminary experiments indicate that using multiple parameter sets gives significantly better performance than using a single parameter set, and than using a simple match/mismatch scoring scheme. The authors generate a family of matrices at various distances and multiple matrices for different conservation rates have been used for bringing an optimal alignment.

Chen, Pan, Juan Chen and Wei Liu (2006) have described partitioned optimization algorithms for multiple sequence alignment that significantly improves solution time and quality by utilizing the locality factor of the problem. The algorithm solves the multiple sequence problems in three phases;

first, an automated and suboptimal partitioning strategy is used to divide the set of sequences into several subsections. Then a multiple sequence alignment algorithm based on ant colony optimization is used to align the sequences of each subsection. Finally, the alignment of original sequences can be obtained by assembling the result of each subsection. The ant colony algorithm is highly optimized in order to avoid local optimal traps and converge to global optimal efficiently.

Rajko and Aluru (2004) presents an algorithm that achieves both space and time optimality, the proposed approach solves the sequence alignment problem sequentially in O(mn) time and O(m+n) for space where m, n being lengths of sequences, the authors claim that proposed approach is also applicable to many other sequence problems including local and global alignments and is equally useful for range of techniques available for parallel dynamic programming. This approach is equally beneficial for small and large sequences but internal calculations are complex and computational stuff is there.

Zne-Jung and Chou-Yuan Lee (2005) depicted an intelligent system for multiple sequence alignment, a fuzzy genetic algorithm with local search is proposed, it enhances the performance of genetic algorithm by incorporating local search and fuzzy logic theory, in this approach, genetic algorithm performs a multiple directional search by maintaining a set of solutions and designed fuzzy theory to dynamically adjust the probability of cross over, mutation and local search during evolutionary process, achieves better performance in both low similarity and high diversity.

Nasser, Nicolescu and Murray (2007) presented a fuzzy logic for approximate matching of subsequences. Fuzzy characteristic functions are derived for parameters that influence a match. The authors developed a prototype for a fuzzy assembler. The assembler was designed to work with low quality data which was generally rejected by most of the existing techniques. The assembler was tested on sequences from two genome projects namely, Drosophila melanogaster and Arabidopsis thaliana. The results were compared with other assemblers. The fuzzy assembler successfully assembled sequences and performed similar and in some cases better than existing techniques.

Ahmad and Mathkour (2009) devised an algorithm that is recursive based and brings better solutions at multiple alignment levels, and can be modified a little to be used for Local Alignment and Global Alignment also. The Internal functionality of the algorithm is competent enough to deal with all kinds of alignments with small changes. Recursion brings fast and accurate results that are why this algorithm can be considered to be at high level of efficiency and reliability. The Algorithm uses a recursive procedure for its operation. It inputs any no. of Strands and divides them into equal length blocks. The individual blocks are made responsible to provide information about matching, miss matching pairs, gaps and percentage match of all Strands. The iterations are performed recursively to move into all blocks. The final information is obtained by integrating the information got from individual blocks.

Ahmad and Mathkour (2009) presented an entirely different idea for sequence analysis by using Matlab histogram comparison techniques between multiple genetic data sets formed from the raw nucleotide base pair structure (e.g A-adenine, T-Thymine, G-guanine, C-cytosine). The proposed technique involves a sequence of steps from extraction to final comparison. The raw data is extracted from a heap of sequence sets containing GAPS, this data is then passed through a filter that transform the genetic data into image pixel data (image pixels represent nucleotide base pair structure), these pixels are fed into Matlab by using command library, this library first converts the RGB format to Gray-level and then generates the histogram graphs of data sets, the comparison leads to desired analysis of genetic data from a different prospective that is equally beneficial for multiple sequences.

Ahmad (2009) presented an algorithm (called DSDR) that operates on a set of Bi-Lingual and Mono-Lingual Corpora and iterates in the same set to find all possible duplications present in the set. Once the duplications are found, the DSDR removes duplicated Chains and refreshes the databases resulting in remarkable reductions in the sizes of the databases. In addition, the speed of searches of certain Chains from Bi-Lingual and Mono-Lingual Corpora becomes quite fast and accurate.

SEQUENCE ANALYSIS TOOLS

Following are a few tools developed for sequence analysis.

Emboss

EMBOSS is used to compare two sequences based on nature of compression and desired result. The tool can be used two way, one section of it is called Needle which is used when comparison is required at whole length of both sequences and other is called Water which provides region wise similarity in strands.

ClustalW2

This tool depicts the relevance of similarity and difference in sequence comparison visually. It provides good meaningful sequence match for both DNA and protein sequences and to some extent, demonstrate the evolutionary relationship in sequences.

Kalign

It is supposed to be a fast and accurate multi sequence alignment tool. It requires a supported format for input data strands and can also input data by user command lines, it can provide interactive sequence results for both protein and DNA strands.

MAFFT Tool

MAFFT is a tool designed for alignment of sequences using Fast Fourier Transforms, it is claimed to be high level multi alignment tool with prompt and quick results. The beauty of this tool is the GAP extension feature provided and also requires a specific format for input data strands.

MUSCLE Tool

MUSCLE is a multi sequence alignment tool and compares the sequence by LOG EXPECTATION; it is supposed to provide better performance than CLUSTALW2 or T-COFEE, it also requires strands to be in specific format and can generate output data tree that fan help better understand the alignment.

T-COFFEE Program

It is also a multi sequence alignment program that has the capability to combine the alignment being derived from some other alignment programs, so it provides a kind of refinement from other tools, it can produce the alignment in a sequence of two by two resulting in global and local alignment. This section-wise alignment can be then combined in an integrated final refined multi alignment structure.

BASIC METHODOLOGIES

Some of the basic methodologies used for sequence comparisons are described below:

- Dynamic Programming Method as an extension.
- Progressive Methods.
- Iterative Methods.

Dynamic Programming Methods as an Extension

The Dynamic Programming Method used for Global Alignment of a pair of sequences can be extended for Multiple Sequence Alignment with a limitation that that it becomes computationally expensive with increasing input size of data resulting in degrading performance.

Progressive Methods

Progressive Methods use the Dynamic Programming Method to built the MSA (Multiple Sequence Alignment) starting with most related sequences and then progressively adding less related sequences to initial alignment. It relies over CLUSTALW and PILEUP methods.

The limitations of these methods start with nature of sequences. In case, the sequences are relevant, better results can be achieved. In worst cases, when the sequences are closely related, the computational cost is high with increased degradation of performance.

Iterative Methods of MSA

Iterative Methods attempt to correct for the problem raised by Progressive Methods by repeatedly realigning subgroups of sequences and then by aligning these subgroups into Global Alignment. The programs MultiAlin(1988) and DIALIGN align multiple sequences using these methods (see Table 1).

PROTEIN STRUCTURAL AND FUNCTIONAL RESEARCH

There are 64 possible codon types in prediction of protein. These codons comprise of tri-nucleotide bases like TTT, TTC, TTA, TTG, TCT, TCC, TCA, TCG, TAT, TAC, TAA, TAG, TGT, TGC, TGA,

Table 1. Performance comparison of methods

Method	Approach	Applicability	Suitability	Non Suitability	Performance
Dynamic Programming	Based on a scoring scheme	Sequence Alignment	Local and Global Alignment	Multi alignment	May involve computational overhead
An Extension of DPA	Global alignment	Sequence Alignment	All kinds	Degrades with increasing input size	Restricted to small and medium strands
Progressive Methods	Align most relevant sequences	Sequence Alignment	Multiple Sequence Alignment	Sequences with dissimilarity	Suitable for initial similarity and degrades with diverse chains
Iterative methods	Based on progressive methods	Sequence Alignment	Multiple Sequence Alignment	Lengthy and initial dissimilar chains	Involves computational overhead in increasing sequence length

TGG, CTT, CTC, CTA, CTG, CCT, CCC, CCA, CCG, CAT, CAC, CAA, CAG, CGT, CGC, CGA, CGG, ATT, ATC, ATA, ATG, ACT, ACC, ACA, ACG, AAT, AAC, AAA, AAG, AGT, AGC, AGA, AGG, GTT, GTC, GTA, GTG, GCT, GCC, GCA, GCG, GAT, GAC, GAA, GAG, GGT, GGC, GGA, GGG. Out of these 64 patterns, 20 are required as there is more than one pattern associated with one protein type.

Table 2 shows the protein values against trinucleotide bases of codons. First column represent the Codon triplet and second column represents the protein type.

RESEACH FOCUS FOR SEQUENCE ANALYSIS

Researchers are familiar and been using certain tolls for analysis, for instance, Matlab is widely used to analyze the DNA sequences. It can address the following issues related with sequences:

- Sequence comparison with formal methods
- Sequence alignment with formal methods
- Denoising DNA sequences
- Analysis of DNA signal
- Codon composition and analysis

- Spectral density estimation
- Histogram comparison
- Transforms for sequence analysis

As a case study, we compared two sequences taken from NCBI and generated the histograms of both sequences described by Ahmad and Mathkour (2009). The results showed a variation ranges from zero to fifty horizontal axes and almost similar for the remaining, so all the sequence data that falls in this category will generate the likely histogram, the differences at multiple points depict that sequences were much different or alike.

Similarly as another case study done by Muneer and Mathkour (2009). We took formal datasets Chimaera Monstrosa that contained 18580 nucleotides of Adenine, Guanine, Thymine and Cytosine. Cumulative size of data becomes 37160 bytes arranged in the form of a uni-vector.

Poly Odontidae contained 16512 nucleotides of Adenine, Guanine, Thymine and Cytosine. Cumulative size of data becomes 33024 bytes arranged in the form of a uni-vector.

It is worth noting that comparative analysis between both species is being done at translation level, so this level is vital in analysis. We split this layer into three more layers to get a better benefit of this layered analysis.

Table 2. Protein symbols versus tri-nucleotide patterns

TTT	P	TCT	S	TAT	T	TGT	C
TTC	P	TCC	S	TAC	T	TGC	C
TTA	L	TCA	S	TAA	S	TGA	S
TTG	L	TCG	S	TAG	S	TGG	T
CTT	L	CCT	P	CAT	H	CGT	A
CTC	L	CCC	P	CAC	H	CGC	A
CTA	L	CCA	P	CAA	G	CGA	A
CTG	L	CCG	P	CAG	G	CGG	A
ATT	I	ACT	T	AAT	A	AGT	S
ATC	I	ACC	T	AAC	A	AGC	S
ATA	I	ACA	T	AAA	L	AGA	A
ATG	M	ACG	T	AAG	L	AGG	A
GTT	V	GCT	A	GAT	A	GGT	G
GTC	V	GCC	A	GAC	A	GGC	G
GTA	V	GCA	A	GAA	G	GGA	G
GTG	V	GCG	A	GAG	G	GGG	G

In each phase, our interest lies in determining the accurate start and stop position of codons that perform the relative analysis. We get the ORF in the second data set of Poly Odontidae. By entering the start positions we can get stop codons. The start positions of the second dataset Frame 1 are 10798 to 11395, 14641 to 15559. It is clear that there is an evident difference in codon regions for both frames of these species. The corresponding translated regions are so entirely different that we cannot guess even the idea of sub-channels similarity.

At second level, we intend to find the codon positions for Frame 2 of both species, we found a series of other regions occupied between first and second frame that don't contribute the peptide translation regions.

Similarly the frame 2 of Poly Odontidae describes its codon position from 11120 to 11465 and 12464 to 12887. This shows a massive difference in datasets at this level as we move with increasing nucleotide subsequences, we may get larger differences but this case does not seem to be true for all genetic datasets. This is the reason

that phenomenon has been given importance in selection these particular sets.

Discussing the last frame set in this sequence, we first find the codon composition for these frames, for instance consider frame 3 of Chimaera Monstrosa. It shows that major ORF starts from 4019, 11948 and 14328. This massive difference in codon compositions also provide an evidence that first translated region lies some four thousand while second and third regions have jump gaps. This is the variation in translated regions in species. Third frame for Poly Odontidae goes from 2796 to 3242, 6315 to 6722 and 12753 to 13217. It shows that first 2 codon positions are relative similar while third position again describe a jump gap. Performing comparative analysis this level, reveals the facts that both genetic data finds a kind of extremity in behavior which make them relevant at certain codon composition and different at others.

The codon count describes the tri-nucleotide behavior of sequences. We need to find the degree of relevancy in terms of strengths of nucleotide bases. For instance, we have selected frame 1 from codon composition of both species and compare the strength.

Our aim focuses on comparative analysis of codon strength at this stage. For the purpose, we need to calculate the codon count for Poly Odontidae.

The tri-nucleotide composition of these molecules represents the amino acids. By calculating these combinations, we can get the volume of the specific amino acids. Some of the amino acids for these codons ATA, CTA, ACC and ATC are as follows respectively:

- Ile Isoleucine
- Leu Leucine
- Thr Threonine
- Ile Isoleucine

WHY SEQUENCE ANALYSIS?

The Genome Sequence Analysis will help biologist to devise genetic therapy and solutions for genetic disorders. It will also open ways to explore genetic diversity in species; a very challenging goal of this study will be to uncover the wealth of biological information hidden in genetic data. A good generalization of these concepts will better help in areas of molecular medicines that would provide more generic sophisticated medicines for curing diseases. It is definitely a genomic revolution and next decade will reveal the real work and achievement for biologists.

CONCLUSION

Bioinformatics is a very rapidly emerging field of research. The genome sequence analysis is an interesting and challenging task that needs great attention. The analysis brings very promising relevance between species. We are now able to find certain genetic similarity and differences in apparently different and diverse creatures, the micro-array technology, phylo-genetic tree creation and many other alignment/analysis tools have helped biologist greatly.

This article describes some of the aspects of software engineering approaches and tools for the sequence analysis. We also presented some comparative analysis in the form of different case studies to reveal the significance of results achieved by employing certain bioinformatics techniques. Although a comprehensive research has been done in various areas of this field, still optimal solutions are lacking. It was also observed that different solutions can be integrated and generalized to describe solutions of many other related problems.

REFERENCES

Agrawal, A., & Huang, X. (2008). Pairwise DNA alignment with sequence specific transition-transversion ratio using multiple parameter sets. *International Conference on Information Technology,* (pp. 89–93).

Agrawal, A., & Khaitan, S. K. (2008). A new heuristic for multiple sequence alignment. *IEEE International Conference on Electro/Information Technology,* (pp. 215–217).

Ahmad, M., Khan, H. M., & Mathkour, H. (2009). An integrated statistical comparative analysis between variant genetic datasets of Mus musculus. *International Journal of Computational Intelligence in Bioinformatics and System Biology*, 1(2), 163-176. ISSN: 1755-8042

Ahmad, M., & Mathkour, H. (2009). *A pattern matching approach for redundancy detection in bilingual and mono-lingual corpora.* IAENG 2009.

Ahmad, M., & Mathkour, H. (2009). Genome sequence analysis: A survey. *Journal of Computer Science, 5*(9), 651-660. ISSN 1549-3636

Ahmad, M., & Mathkour, H. (2009). *Genome sequence analysis by Matlab histogram comparison between image-sets of genetic data*. Hong Kong: WCSET.

Ahmad, M., & Mathkour, H. (2009). *Multiple sequence alignment with GAP consideration by pattern matching technique*. International Conference on Signal Acquisition and Processing, Malaysia.

Ahmed, N. Y. P., & Vandenberg, A. (2005). Parallel algorithm for multiple genome alignment on the Grid environment. *Proceedings of 19th IEEE International Symposium on Parallel and Distributed Processing*, (p. 7).

Arslan, A. N., & He, D. (2006). An improved algorithm for the regular expression constrained multiple sequence alignment problems. *Sixth IEEE Symposium on Bioinformatics and Bioengineering*, (pp. 121–126).

Bansal, A. K. (1995). Establishing a framework for comparative analysis of genome sequences. *First International Symposium on Intelligence in Neural and Biological Systems*, (pp. 84–91).

Cai, L. D. J., & Liakhovitch, E. (2000). Evolutionary computation techniques for multiple sequence alignment. *Proceedings of the 2000 Congress on Evolutionary Computation*, Vol. 2, (pp. 829-835).

Chang, Y. F., Chen, C. Y., Chen, H. W., Lin, I. H., Luo, W. X., & Yang, C. H. ... Chang, C. H. (2005). Bioinformatics analysis for genome design and synthetic biology. *Proceedings of Emerging Information Technology Conference*.

Chen, Y., Pan, Y., Chen, J., & Liu, W. (2006). Partitioned optimization algorithms for multiple sequence alignment. *20th International Conference on Advanced Information Networking and Applications*, (Vol. 2, p. 5).

Cornell, M. N. W., Paton, W. S., Goble, C. A., Miller, C. J., Kirby, P., & Eilbeck, K. ... Oliver, S. G. (2001). GIMS-A data warehouse for storage and analysis of genome sequence and functional data. *Proceedings of the IEEE 2nd International Symposium on Bioinformatics and Bioengineering Conference*, (pp. 15–22).

Davidson, A. (2001). A fast pruning algorithm for optimal sequence alignment, bioinformatics and bioengineering conference. *Proceedings of the IEEE 2nd International Symposium*, (pp. 49–56).

Kappen, C., & Salbaum, J. M. (2003). Comparative genome annotation for mapping, prediction and discovery of genes. *Proceedings of the 36th Annual Hawaii International Conference on System Sciences*.

Lee, Z.-J., & Lee, C.-Y. (2005). An intelligent system for multiple sequences alignment. *IEEE International Conference on Systems, Man and Cybernetics*, Vol. 2, (pp. 1042–1047).

Liu, W., Schmidt, B., Voss, G., & Muller-Wittig, W. (2007). Streaming algorithms for biological sequence alignment on GPUs. *IEEE Transactions on Parallel and Distributed Systems*, *18*(9), 1270–1281. doi:10.1109/TPDS.2007.1069

Nahar, N., Hamel, L., Popstova, M. S., & Gogarten, J. P. (2007). GPX: A tool for the exploration and visualization of genome evolution. *Proceedings of the 7th IEEE International Conference on Bioinformatics and Bioengineering*, (pp. 1338–1342).

Nasser, S., Vert, G. L., Nicolescu, M., & Murray, A. (2007). Multiple sequence alignment using fuzzy logic. *IEEE Symposium on Computational Intelligence and Bioinformatics and Computational Biology*, (pp. 304–311).

Rajko, S., & Aluru, S. (2004). Space and time optimal parallel sequence alignments. *IEEE Transactions on Parallel and Distributed Systems*, *15*(12), 6. doi:10.1109/TPDS.2004.86

Rashid, N. A. A., Abdullah, R., Talib, A. Z. H., & Ali, Z. (2006). Fast dynamic programming based sequence alignment algorithm. *The 2nd International Conference on Distributed Frameworks for Multimedia Applications*, (pp. 1–7).

Zhao, Y., Ma, P., Lan, J., Liang, C., & Guoli, J. (2008). An improved ant colony algorithm for DNA sequence alignment. *International Symposium on Information Science and Engineering,* Vol. 2, (pp. 683–688).

Chapter 15
Development of Enterprise Content Management Systems:
A Procurement–Centric Approach

Jaffar Ahmad Alalwan
Institute of Public Administration, Dammam, Saudi Arabia

ABSTRACT

Enterprise systems development approaches can be classified into development-centric and procurement centric approaches. Based on the component-based system development methodology (CBSD), this chapter proposes a procurement-centric framework to develop enterprise content management (ECM) system. Adopting CBSD to develop ECM system avoids the drawbacks of the development-centric approaches, and remedies the ECM field lacks where there is no system development method that helps in selecting and implementing the ECM system. To validate the proposed framework, the author applies it to a case study from a large research institution with more than 30,000 students.

INTRODUCTION

Enterprise systems are one of the major IT investments in many organizations (Fan et al., 2000), and the development of these systems is considered important not only by researchers but also by practitioners. The development approaches of the enterprise systems can be classified into development-centric (i.e. waterfall, spiral models) and procurement-centric approaches (Tran and Liu, 1997). Component-based software development (CBSD) (Fan et al., 2000; Brereton and Budgen, 2000; Sugumaran and Storey, 2003) is one of the procurement-centric approaches that is widely used to develop enterprise systems. Many researchers believe that CBSD is capable of reducing several challenges that are faced by the traditional development approaches (Sprott, 2000; Sugumaran and Storey, 2003; Brereton and Bugden, 2000). Other researchers believe that CBSD will lead the shift from having large and difficult to modify systems into having smaller

DOI: 10.4018/978-1-4666-3679-8.ch015

and flexible systems (Due, 2000; Fan et al., 2000; Fichman and Kemerer, 2002).

As one current example of enterprise systems, enterprise content management (ECM) systems are implemented by many organizations to deal with the increasing information overload and with the structured and unstructured data complexity. Smith and McKeen (2003) defined ECM as "the strategies, tools, processes and skills an organization needs to manage all its information assets regardless of type over their lifecycle." According to Gartner, ECM includes the following core components: document management, web content management, records management, document imaging, document centric collaboration, and workflow (Woolley and Fletcher, 2007).

From financial point of view, the market of ECM is appealing for many vendors. Dunwoodie (2004) mentioned that the ECM market is estimated to be $1.54 billion; Meta Group estimated the ECM market to be $2.3 billion in software and $7 billion in services (Content Manager, 2004). Gartner estimates the ECM software revenue to exceed $5.1 billion by 2013 (EMC Corporation, 2009). Although there is a difference in the estimated market figures, the numbers indicate that the ECM market is growing. The numbers also explain the reason of the great interest that newer competitors to the market (i.e. Oracle, IBM, Microsoft) have. The senior director of Oracle noted, "Content management is entering a period of significant change and potentially explosive growth" (Buchheim, 2006). The market of ECM can be categorized as commercial (i.e. IBM, EMC, Interwoven, Vignette, Microsoft and Open Text), open-source (i.e. Plone and Mambo), and hosted systems (i.e. SpringCM and Document Commander) (Kemp, 2007). Commercial ECMs are more popular than the other two categories; Gartner has ranked EMC Documentum as the leader of ECM 2009 (EMC Corporation, 2009).

Although ECM can be viewed as an evolutionary phase of information management and its importance is escalating (Tyrväinen et al.,

2006; Boiko, 2002), ECM field lacks a system development method that helps in selecting and implementing the system, and avoid the drawbacks of traditional development approaches. By adopting Sharp and Ryan's (2010) CBSD framework, the purpose of this paper is to remedy that lack by proposing a development framework for ECM systems based on CBSD approach and ECM literature. To validate the proposed framework, we will apply it to a case study from a large research institution with more than 30,000 students.

We believe this research idea has dual contribution: academic as well as practical. The main theoretical contribution is extending the CBSD approach to ECM literature. To the best of our knowledge, this extension is a new idea that has not been discussed before. Also, the suggested framework provides the practitioners with a roadmap that facilitates developing ECM systems by applying the proposed CBSD framework.

The rest of the paper is arranged as follows. The related literature review of ECM and literature review of systems development approaches are discussed in sections 2 and 3 respectively. The proposed framework is presented in section 4. Then the proposed framework is applied to a case study in section 5. Finally, we conclude in section 6.

RELATED ECM LITERATURE REVIEW

ECM Association (AIIM) defines ECM as "the strategies, methods and tools used to capture, manage, store, preserve, and deliver content and documents related to organizational processes. ECM tools and strategies allow the management of an organization's unstructured information, wherever that information exists". (www.aiim. org). According to Meta Group, ECM is defined as "...the technology that provides the means to create/capture, manage/secure, store/retain/destroy, publish/distribute, search, personalize and present/view/print any digital content (i.e. picture/ images/text, reports, video, audio, transactional data, catalog, code). These systems primarily focus on the capture, storage, retrieval, and dissemination of digital files for enterprise use" (Munkvold et al., 2006, p.71).

Despite the definitions differences, there is consensus on ECM processes (activities). ECM allows organizations to simplify heterogeneous data and process structured and unstructured information (O'Callaghan and Smits, 2005). There is a consistency among researchers that ECM is not only a practical set of technologies but also organizational concepts that involve many business perspectives (Blair, 2004; Munkvold et al., 2006; Tyrväinen et al., 2006; Brocke et al., 2009). Rockley (2006) reported that one of the main goals of ECM implementation is to have transparent content sharing by making different and disparate applications (i.e. web content management, records management) interoperable. By having shared transparent content that facilitated cross department collaboration, capturing of knowledge and content can be easier (Jenkins, 2004). In the same vein, many researchers believe that ECM overlaps with knowledge management (KM); Duffy (2001) and Carvalho et al. (2001) suggested ECM as one type of KM. ECM can be considered a subfield of knowledge management (Nordheim and Paivarinta, 2006). Specifically, some researchers believe that ECM is one tool of KM tools. Tyndale (2002) defined Knowledge management tools as the tools that "promote and enable the knowledge process in order to improve decision-making"; he mentioned the following as some examples of KM tools: intranet, content management, document management, and web portals.

Based on a recent comprehensive review of ECM literature (Alalwan and Weistroffer, 2012), we have noticed that there is scarcity in research that discusses the development of ECM systems. From the 91 papers that we reviewed, we have found only two papers that discuss the topic of

selecting and evaluating ECM systems. Vitari et al. (2006) argue that choosing the most suitable CMS for organizations needs is complicated task. The authors claim that there are difficulties in pre-purchasing evaluation of CMS because there is no analysis framework. They proposed two tools based on the analysis of 23 CMS; one tool is for analyzing CMS and the second is for understanding the strategy of CMS vendors; the applications of analyzing CMS framework, and the applications of identifying strategies framework are also discussed in Vitari et al. (2006). Boateng and Boateng (2007) discuss the selection of open source content management systems (CMS). The discussion is based on evaluating the following four open source CMS: Moodle, Drupal, Xoops, and Mambo. The main drawback of these two papers is focusing only on "selection" of the ECM systems rather than the whole development cycle.

Based on ECM literature review, we conclude the following. First, ECM systems are viewed as an evolutionary phase of information management and its importance is becoming more evident (Tyrväinen et al., 2006; Boiko, 2002). Second, ECM field lacks a system development method that helps in selecting and implementing the systems. Therefore, the objective of this paper is to propose a development framework for ECM systems based on CBSD approach and ECM literature.

RELATED LITERATURE REVIEW OF SYSTEMS DEVELOPMENT APPROACHES

Traditional development-centric approaches, including structured approach, and object-Oriented approach, have the premise of developing systems through planning, analysis (what the system will do), design (how the system addresses the problems), and implementation (programming and building the system). These approaches are effective in providing a systematic method for systems development. However, some researchers argue that the traditional approaches have several drawbacks that lead to eliminating the dynamic nature of the systems (Brereton and Bugden, 2000; Fan et al., 2000). Hoffer et al. (2005), for example, argue that the system development lifecycle approach (SDLC) face several challenges in gathering requirements from users, facilitating changes, and maintaining the systems. Although modularity idea is adopted in development-centric approaches, modularity is not asserted enough since change in one code may affect the functionality of another code, which leads to serious problems (Hopkins, 2000; Waguespack and Schiano, 2004).

Taking the object-oriented approach as a foundation, content-based system development (CBSD) is considered the emerging paradigm that can handle the previous challenges (Fan et al., 2000; Sharp and Ryan, 2010). Tran and Liu (1997) classify CBSD as a procurement-centric approach because it can handle the identification, evaluation, selection, procurement, and integration of the determined software package. Waguespack and Schiano (2004) argue that the main focus of CBSD is on component awareness, which aims for the appropriate software selection to meet system requirements. The goal of CBSD is to build software systems rather than software programs (Fan et al., 2000). To be more specific, the goal of CBSD is "development of software from pre-fabricated parts, reuse of those parts across applications and contexts, and easily maintainable and customizable parts to develop new functions and features" (Sharp and Ryan, 2010, p. 61). This goal is accomplished by designing applications consist of pre-fabricated software components that are platform independent and distributed across the network (Vitharana et al., 2003; Fujii and Suda, 2006). Sharp and Ryan (2010) argue that CBSD comprises of the following phases: intelligence, design, choice, and implementation. The details of these phases will be discussed in section 4.

CBSD is discussed in several IS domains such as multi-agent systems (Shepherdson et al., 2007), global development of distributed systems (Kotlarsky et al., 2007), and composition of components (Kim et al., 2007). In addition, CBSD is also investigated in the development of commercial-off-the-shelf (COTS) domain (Li et al., 2008). Enterprise systems, such as ERP, CRM, and ECM, are considered touchstones of COTS (Rosemann et al., 2004). For instance, He et al. (2009) propose component library-based software development methodology that is useful in developing ERP software. Marjanovic (2005) propose a process-oriented customer relationship management system based on component-based technology.

Based on this literature review, we conclude that CBSD is an emerging development methodology that can handle system development challenges, which cannot be handled by the traditional development approaches. In addition, CBSD is already utilized to develop COTS systems (i.e. ERP, CRM). Therefore, CBSD can be used to develop other enterprise systems such as ECM systems.

THE PROPOSED FRAMEWORK

Sharp and Ryan (2010) propose a component based system development framework that consists of the following four phases: intelligence, design, choice, and implementation. Intelligence refers to the requirement analysis. Design refers to the systems architecture, and cataloging and retrieval. Choice touches on the selection of the system. Implementation is related to the assimilation and installation of the system and the training of the employees. The proposed model in this paper focuses on three phases: intelligence, choice, and implementation phases (see Figure 1). The design phase is disregarded because ECM component model is considered as a function-based model rather than an architecture-based model (Chowdhury, 2008; Kampffmeyer, 2006). The proposed model can capture the requirement analysis, best modules selection, assimilation and installation, and training. Therefore, the long-term success of ECM systems can be gained by adopting the suggested model.

Intelligence Phase

In the intelligence phase, the ECM requirements are determined. Many systems, which are adopted by traditional approaches, failed because requirements are not determined accurately (Hoffer et al., 2005). It is argued that requirements determination is better with CBSD than with the development-centric approaches since active stakeholders involvement is emphasized in all the development phases, and the discovery of new requirements is also encouraged (Jain et al., 2003). Stakeholders work together to identify the ECM systems that satisfy the given requirements.

Table 1 shows some examples of the involved stakeholders and their roles in each of the ECM development phases.

Defining the stakeholders and understanding their roles in requirements determination is essential. Stakeholders can be defined as any individual who affects or affected by the requirements of the ECM systems, and should be involved in the development process. Brownsword et al. (1998) suggest that stakeholders should include acquisition manager, system designer, system integrator, and policy maker to help determining the organizational and the technical requirements of the system. Fowler (2008) includes staff, partners, and suppliers as examples of stakeholders. According to Sharp and Ryan (2010), the role of the stakeholders in requirements determination is to help identifying, prioritizing, and evaluating the requirements that satisfy the works' needs. Stakeholders are also encouraged to discover new requirements that may accomplish the work tasks more efficiently.

The major ECM functional requirements can be categorized around the following components: capturing (i.e. collecting the content), managing (also called processing), storing and preserving (also called maintaining), and delivery (Vitari et al., 2006; Smith and McKeen, 2003; Tyrväinen et al., 2006; Kampffmeyer, 2006). Each component can have several subcomponents. Capturing com-

Figure 1. CBSD framework for ECM development

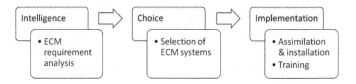

Table 1. Examples of involved stakeholders and their roles in ECM development phases

Involved stakeholders	Stakeholders' roles	ECM development phase
System managers Policy makers Acquisition Managers Department Heads System designers Records & document staff Web content staff	Designating the organizational and technical requirements of the system to accomplish business tasks efficiently	Intelligence
	Aligning the business objectives to the ECM requirements, and selecting the system based on objectives' priority	Choice
	Testing the ECM systems in the pilot phase, and continue evaluating the system and sending their feedback for continues improvement	Implementation

ponent can have the following subcomponents: recognition (i.e. intelligent character recognition), document imaging, forms processing, indexing (i.e. categorization). The subcomponent of management component can be: document management (i.e. versioning management), e-mail management, digital asset management (i.e. multimedia content management), collaboration (i.e. collaborative authoring), web content management (i.e. website visualization), records management (i.e. retention management), workflow/business process management (i.e. process organization). Storing and preserving component can have the following subcomponents: repositories (i.e. file system, data warehouses), archival (i.e. network attached storage/storage area network (NAS/SAN)), backup (i.e. recovery), and migration. The subcomponents of delivery component can include: content integration, search and retrieval, personalization, and publishing. Figure 2 summarizes the main functional components and their subcomponents.

The non-functional ECM requirements can include different features such as interoperability and security (Boateng and Boateng, 2007; Waquespack and Schiano, 2004). Kemp (2007) argues that interoperability is one of the barriers to ECM adoption. Interoperability ensures that content from different vendors of hardware and software is supported. Many vendors of ECM systems adhere to industry standards such as XML web services in order to have the interoperability feature (Kemp, 2007).

The security features are essential for all ECM components to forbid unauthorized access to the ECM application, and to ensure credibility and integrity by controlling the organizational content (Boateng and Boateng, 2007). Private Key Infrastructure (PKI) technology is used to test the authenticity of electronic signature, which has different security levels (i.e. in Europe electronic signature has three security levels: simple, advance, and qualified); digital rights management is another ECM security technology that is

used to secure the copyrights and property rights (Kampffmeyer, 2006).

Choice Phase

In the choice phase, the appropriate components that fulfill both functional and non-functional requirements are selected. Organizations need to select the right combination of the previous components and subcomponents that matches their needs based on stakeholders' feedback and business process analysis. At the same time, aligning the organizational objectives with the features of the system requirements helps in selecting the most effective components. Vitharana et al. (2004) suggest that managerial goals help in identifying the most efficient components. Organizational objectives include: cost savings in information processing (Rockley, 2006; Päivärinta, and Munkvold, 2005), satisfy governmental regulations and standards (compliance), having professional representation of the enterprise in the eyes of its stakeholders

Figure 2. ECM functional components and subcomponents

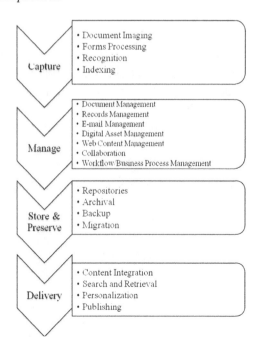

(Päivärinta, and Munkvold, 2005), and increase the efficiency and the flexibility of business processes (Reimer, 2002). The choice phase should be based on aligning and balancing the managerial goals and the ECM systems requirements as shown in Figure 3.

Implementation Phase

Finally, the implementation phase is to integrate and assemble the selected components of ECM systems. Implementation phase is the "process of integrating a set of components to build a component application system" (Jain et al., 2003, p. 297). Implementation of ECM should be aligned with the organization business processes (Brocke et al., 2008) that are defined in the previous phases. Training should also be conducted in this phase to familiarize the final users with the new system. Smith and McKeen (2003) emphasize the importance of training people with analytic skills (technology skills, statistical modeling and analytic skills, knowledge of the data, knowledge of the business, communication and partnering).

CASE STUDY

In this section, we analyze the development of the ECM systems in the Graduate Admissions (GA) department of a large research institution with more than 30,000 students. GA department, which traditionally uses software with

limited ECM capabilities (i.e. Lotus Notes and SCT Banner) in its routine processes, receives extensive amount of document (8 documents for each of 6000 applications in 2008) during the admission application time. The director of recruitment and admissions mentions, "For each graduate application, we typically receive two or more college transcripts, at least one test score, three reference letters, and a personal statement. We plan on imaging transcripts and any other of these materials we receive." Therefore, an ECM system is needed to handle this extensive amount of documents.

The first phase in the framework is the intelligence phase. In that phase system requirements need to be determined based on workflow/business process analysis and stakeholders involvement. Figure 4 shows the main stages (queues) of the workflow in the department of GA. The figure shows that the workflow consists of the following queues: linking queue where web and paper applications are received, counsellor queue, program director queue, and admit/or reject queue.

The ECM systems in GA are accessed by two business functions: recruiting and graduate admission programs. The manager of business application services emphasizes that the stakeholders should be involved in the planning process, and their exact needs should be well understood. Stakeholders of GA department, which include staff, different program directors, and students, need accessible, collaborative, and secured information resources to support excellence and in-

Figure 3. Alignment between ECM systems requirement and organizational objectives in the choice phase

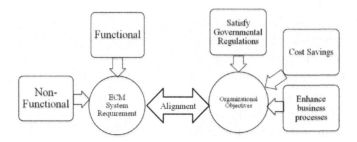

Figure 4. Business process analysis in the GA

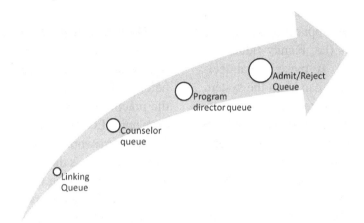

novation. They need an easier and an advanced method to search, find, use, share, store, and keep high quality information among different departments. The employees' time and efforts in doing the routine activities, for instance, need to be reduced. It is also necessary to ensure that right authority matches with the right employee's role. In order to understand the stakeholder needs, a comprehensive stakeholder consultation, that includes surveys, interviews, and contextual observation, is conducted by the implementation team.

Based on business process analysis and stakeholders involvement, the functional and non-functional requirements are identified. The functional requirements, which are represented by the combination of the required components of ECM systems, are determined. In the capture component, document imaging and indexing are essential to capture, route, and view the internally generated documents. Capture component is also required to be able to import and export the needed documents, and to be able to have tracking feature. In the manage component, collaboration is necessary to make the application documents available electronically for more than 80 program directors, and to allow multiple users access the system simultaneously. Workflow management is also important to enhance the workflow of the

GA activities, and to maintain an effective content lifecycle among different users. In the store and preserve component, repositories and backup are the necessary subcomponents. In the delivery component, content integration and search and retrieval are the required subcomponents.

Furthermore, four non-functional requirements are also specified. Accessibility is identified to provide continuing access to content. Integration is determined to be compatible with existing architecture, and to be able to integrate with the current software applications (i.e. Lotus Notes, SCT Banner). Customization is determined to have customizable tools that help in simplifying the workflow of GA activities. Finally, security is crucial to have secure access to documents, and to provide the security level that matches with different groups of users.

The second phase of the framework is the choice phase. In this phase, the organizational objectives of the research institution are highlighted and aligned with the functional and non-functional requirements. The research institution would like develop an ECM systems to improve quality of the admission activates, diversify revenue streams and undertake efficiency reforms resulting in financial viability and sustainability, reduce the storage of paper files by having a long term storage of electronic documents, improve and protect reputation of the research institution. Also, the ECM system provides the GA with the required compliance support by meeting the legislative requirements (i.e. Family Education Rights and Privacy Act). To make a final decision about the system that can align the system requirements to the organizational objectives, several ECM systems have been analyzed. The research institution selects ImageNow system, which is manufactured by Perceptive Software Inc. In the implementation phase, ImageNow system is integrated with other components such as records management system. Training, in addition to integration with other applications, are ranked first to that research institution in term of the importance to the system adoption decision. Perceptive Software trains users by applying the approach of "train the trainer" in order to ensure the training of large number of staff.

CONCLUSION

ECM systems can be viewed as an evolutionary phase of information management and its importance is escalating (Tyrväinen et al., 2006; Boiko, 2002). The development of these systems is considered important not only by researchers but also by practitioners. ECM field lacks a system development method that helps in selecting and implementing the system, and avoid the drawbacks of the traditional development approaches. We have proposed a development framework for ECM systems based on CBSD approach and ECM literature. The framework consists of three phases: intelligence, selection, and implementation. After describing the framework, we have applied it to a case study from a large research institution. We conclude that in order to develop ECM systems by adopting CBSD, business processes need to be analyzed and the stakeholders need to be involved not only in the intelligence phase, but also in the choice and implementation phase. Thus, develop-

ing ECM systems by adopting CBSD can lead to having successful ECM systems.

The main academic contribution of this paper is introducing CBSD approach to ECM literature, which is a novel idea that is not discussed before. Also, the suggested framework provides the practitioners with a roadmap that facilitates developing ECM systems by applying the proposed CBSD framework. However, the main drawback of this research is that it cannot be generalized to another setting since it is evaluated only in one case study. Therefore, more research is needed to ensure the validity of the framework. Finally, there several important research questions that we did not consider in this paper, and can be investigated in future such as: what is the long-term influence of developing ECM systems based on CBSD approach? What are the barriers in that development process? Is developing ECM systems by CBSD more effective than developing ECM systems by traditional approaches?

REFERENCES

Alalwan, J. A., & Weistroffer, H. R. (2012). Enterprise content management research: A comprehensive review. *Journal of Enterprise Information Management*, 25(4).

Boateng, B. A., & Boateng, K. (2007). Issues to consider when choosing open source content management systems (CMSs). In St.Amant, K., & Still, B. (Eds.), *Handbook of research on open source software: Technological economic and social perspectives* (pp. 255–268). doi:10.4018/978-1-59140-999-1.ch020

Boiko, B. (2002). *Content management bible*. New York, NY: Hungry Minds.

Brereton, P., & Budgen, D. (2000). Component-based systems: A classification of issues. *IEEE Computers*, 33(11), 54–62. doi:10.1109/2.881695

Brocke, J., Simons, A., & Cleven, A. (2008). A business process perspective on enterprise content management: towards a framework for organisational change. *Proceedings of the 16th European Conference on Information Systems*, Galway, Ireland, (pp. 1680-1691).

Brocke, J., Simons, A., & Cleven, A. (2009). Towards a business process-oriented approach to enterprise content management: The ECM-blueprinting framework. *Information Systems and E-Business Management*, *9*(4), 1–22.

Brownsword, L., Carney, D., & Oberndorf, T. (1998). *The opportunities and complexities of applying commercial-off-the-shelf components*. SEI Interactive. Retrieved from http://www.sei.cmu.edu/interactive/Features/1998/June/Applying_COTS/Applying_COTS.htm

Buchheim, R. (2006). The future of ECM. In R. Stalters (Ed.), *AIIM Expo, Conference and Exposition*, (pp. 3-9).

Carvalho, B. de R., & Ferreira, M. T. (2001). Using information technology to support knowledge conversion processes. *Information Research, 7*(1).

Chowdhury, J. (2008). Enterprise content management system-revolution for data ware housing. Retrieved from http://www.karmayog.org/it/upload/During%20the%20era%20of%201980_1.doc

Content Manager. (2004). *ECM market to reach $9B in software and service*. Retrieved from http://www.contentmanager.net/magazine/article_445_ecm_market_software_services.html

Corporation, E. M. C. (2009). *EMC ranked leader in Gartner 2009 ECM magic quadrant*. Retrieved from https://community.emc.com/docs/DOC-5189

Due, R. T. (2000). The economics of component-based development. *Information Systems Management*, *17*(1), 92–95.

Duffy, J. (2001). The tools and technologies needed for knowledge management. *Information Management Journal*, *35*(1), 64–67.

Dunwoodie, B. (2004). Global ECM market still likely to consolidate. *CMS Wire*. Retrieved from http://www.cmswire.com/cms/enterprise-cms/global-ecm-market-still-likely-to- consolidate-000301.php

Fan, M., Stallaert, J., & Whinston, A. B. (2000). The adoption and design methodologies of component-based enterprise systems. *European Journal of Information Systems*, *9*(1), 25–35. doi:10.1057/palgrave.ejis.3000343

Fichman, R. G., & Kemerer, C. F. (2002). Activity based costing for component-based software development. *Information Technology Management*, *3*(1-2), 137–160. doi:10.1023/A:1013121011308

Fowler, D. (2008). *Implementing enterprise content management using Microsoft SharePoint. Capstone Report*. University of Oregon.

Fujii, K., & Suda, T. (2006). Semantics-based dynamic Web service composition. *International Journal of Cooperative Information Systems*, *15*(3), 293–324. doi:10.1142/S0218843006001372

He, S., Chang, H., & Wang, Q. (2009). Component library-based ERP software development methodology. *International Conference on Interoperability for Enterprise Software and Applications China*, (pp. 34-38).

Hoffer, J. A., George, J. F., & Valacich, J. S. (2005). *Modern systems analysis* (4th ed.). Upper Saddle, NJ: Prentice Hall.

Hopkins, J. (2000). Component primer. *Communications of the ACM*, *43*(10), 27–30. doi:10.1145/352183.352198

Jain, H., Vitharana, P., & Zahedi, F. M. (2003). An assessment model for requirements identification in component-based software development. *The Data Base for Advances in Information Systems, 34*(4), 48–63. doi:10.1145/957758.957765

Jenkins, T. (2004). *Enterprise content management: What you need to know.* Open Text Corporation.

Kampffmeyer, U. (2006). Enterprise content management. DMS EXPO 2006 in Köln.

Kemp, J. (2007). A critical analysis into the use of enterprise content management systems in the IT industry. Retrieved from www.aiimhost.com/whitepapers/JamesKemp_ECMReport.pdf

Kim, I., Bae, D., & Hong, J. (2007). A component composition model providing dynamic, flexible, and hierarchical composition of components for supporting software evolution. *Journal of Systems and Software, 80*(11), 1797–1816. doi:10.1016/j.jss.2007.02.047

Kotlarsky, J. I., Oshri, J., van Hillegersberg, K., & Kumar, K. (2007). Globally distributed component-based software development: An exploratory study of knowledge management and work division. *Journal of Information Technology, 22*(2), 161–173. doi:10.1057/palgrave.jit.2000084

Li, J., Conradi, R., Slyngstad, O. P., Torchiano, M., Maurizio, M., & Bunse, C. (2008). A state-of-the- practice survey of risk management in development with off-the-shelf, software components. *IEEE Transactions on Software Engineering, 34*(2), 271–286. doi:10.1109/TSE.2008.14

Marjanovic, O. (2005). Process-oriented CRM enabled by component-based workflow technology. *Proceedings of the 18th Bled eConference,* Bled, Slovenia, June 6-8.

Munkvold, B. E., Päivärinta, T., Hodne, A. K., & Stangeland, E. (2006). Contemporary issues of enterprise content management: The case of Statoil. *Scandinavian Journal of Information Systems, 18,* 69–100.

Nordheim, S., & Paivarinta, T. (2006). Implementing enterprise content management: From evolution through strategy to contradictions out-of-the-box. *European Journal of Information Systems, 15*(6), 648–662. doi:10.1057/palgrave.ejis.3000647

O'Callaghan, R., & Smits, M. A. (2005). Strategy development process for enterprise content management. *Proceedings of the 13th European Conference on Information Systems,* Regensburg, Germany, (pp. 1271-1282).

Rockley, A. (2006). *Content management 2006: Market directions and trends.* The Rockley Bulletin.

Rosemann, M., Vessey, I., Weber, R., & Wyssusek, B. (2004). On the applicability of the Bunge–Wand–Weber ontology to enterprise systems requirements. *Proceedings of the 15th Australasian Conference on Information Systems.*

Sharp, J., & Ryan, S. (2010). A theoretical framework of component-based software development phases. *SGMIS Database, 41*(1), 56–75. doi:10.1145/1719051.1719055

Shepherdson, J. W., Lee, H., & Mihailescu, P. (2007). mPower -- A component-based development framework for multi-agent systems to support business processes. *BT Technology Journal, 25*(3-4), 260–271. doi:10.1007/s10550-007-0083-8

Smith, H. A., & McKeen, J. D. (2003). Developments in practice VIII: Enterprise content management. *Communications of the Association for Information Systems, 11*(33), 647–659.

Sprott, D. (2000). Componentizing the enterprise application packages. *Communications of the ACM, 43*(3), 63–69. doi:10.1145/332051.332074

Sugumaran, V., & Storey, V. C. (2003). A semantic-based approach to component retrieval. *The Data Base for Advances in Information Systems, 34*(3), 8–24. doi:10.1145/937742.937745

Tran, V., & Liu, D. (1997). A procurement-centric model for engineering component-based software systems. *Proceedings of the 5th International Symposium on Assessment of Software Tools and Technologies*, (pp. 70-80).

Tyndale, P. (2002). A taxonomy of knowledge management software tools: Origins and applications. *Evaluation and Program Planning, 25*(2), 183–190. doi:10.1016/S0149-7189(02)00012-5

Tyrväinen, P., Päivärinta, T., Salminen, A., & Iivari, J. (2006). Characterizing the evolving research on enterprise content management. *European Journal of Information Systems, 15*(6), 627–634. doi:10.1057/palgrave.ejis.3000648

Vitari, C., Ravarini, A., & Rodhain, F. (2006). An analysis framework for the evaluation of content management systems. *Communications of the Association for Information Systems, 18*(37), 782–803.

Vitharana, P., Jain, H., & Zahedi, F. (2004). Strategy-based design of reusable business components. *IEEE Transactions on Systems, Man and Cybernetics. Part C, Applications and Reviews, 34*(4), 460–474. doi:10.1109/TSMCC.2004.829258

Vitharana, P., Zahedi, F. M., & Jain, H. (2003). Design, retrieval, and assembly in component-based software development. *Communications of the ACM, 46*(11), 97–102. doi:10.1145/948383.948387

Waguespack, L., & Schiano, W. T. (2004). Component- based IS architecture. *Information Systems Management, 21*(3), 53–60. doi:10.1201/1078/44432.21.3.20040601/82477.8

Woolley, R., & Fletcher, D. (2007). *Research summary: Enterprise content management.* White paper, Department of Technology Services.

Chapter 16
Fault Tree Analysis (FTA) via Binary Diagram Decision (BDD) for Information Systems Design

Fausto Pedro García Márquez
University of Castilla-La Mancha, Spain

Alberto Pliego Mangurán
University of Castilla-La Mancha, Spain

Noor Zaman
King Faisal University, Saudi Arabia

ABSTRACT

A fault tree analysis (FTA) is presented as a qualitative method for studying the state of the WT as a system considering to its different sub-systems. The quantitative analysis of the FTA is done by Binary Diagram Decision (BDD). The size of the BDD generated by the transformation from FTA to BDD will depend of the ordering of the FTA events. This work employed the top-down-left-right, the level, and the "and" methods for listing the events. Finally, a classification of the events is done based on their importance measures. The importance measures has been calculated by the Birnbaum (1969), Critically and Structural heuristic methods. A comparative analysis is done, and the main results are presented.

INTRODUCTION

An FTA model is a graphical representation of logical relations between events (usually failure or fault events). Complex systems analysis may produce thousands of combinations of events (cut-sets) that can cause the system failure. The determination of these cut-sets can be a large and time-consuming process even on modern high speed digital computers. The determination of the exact top event probability also requires lengthy calculations if the fault tree has a great number of cut-sets.

DOI: 10.4018/978-1-4666-3679-8.ch016

Example

Figure 1 shows an example of a pumping station from the A reservoir to B reservoir. The system has three valves and two pump motors. The FTA associated to the system given in Figure 1 is shown in Figure 2.

Figure 1. Pumping station

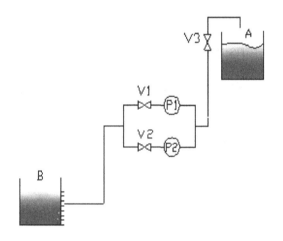

Figure 2. FTA associated to the system shown in Figure 1

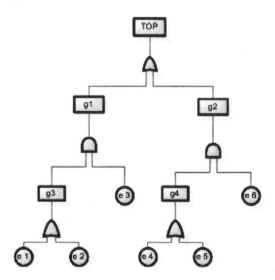

Nomenclature:

- **V:** Valve
- **P:** Pump
- **Top:** Reservoir A does not received water.
- **g1:** V3 does not receive wáter
- **g2:** V1 and P1 do not receive wáter
- **g3:** V2 and P2 do not receive wáter
- **e1:** Level in B is not enough
- **e2:** Fault in V3. Closed
- **e3:** Fault in P1
- **e4:** Fault in V1. Closed
- **e5:** Fault in P2
- **e6:** Fault in V2. Closed

For many complex fault trees this requirement may be beyond the capability of the available computers. As a consequence, approximation techniques have been introduced with a loss of accuracy. BDD provides a new alternative to the traditional cut-set based approach for FTA that leads to the determination of the output value of the function through the examination of the values of the inputs.

BINARY DIAGRAM DECISIONS

Binary Decision Diagrams (BDDs), as a data structure that represents the Boolean functions, were introduced by Lee (1959) and further popularised by Akers (1978), Moret (1982), and Bryant (1986).

A BDD is a directed acyclic graph (V, N), with vertex set V and index set N. Vertex set contains two types of vertices. On the one hand, a terminal vertex has as attribute a value: value(v) ∈ {0,1}, where a 1 state, that corresponds to system failure, or a 0 state which corresponds to a system success. All the paths that have 1 state provide the cut-sets of the fault tree. On the other hand, a non terminal vertex v has as attributes an argument index(v) ∈ N {0,1,…,n} and two descendants, low(v) and high(v) ∈ V, that are connected by a branch. Each vertex has a vertex 0 branch that represents a non occurrence basic event, or 1 branch that represents an occurrence basic event. For any non-terminal vertex v, if low(v) is also non-terminal, then index(v) < index(low(v)), and if high(v) is non-terminal, then index(v) < index(high(v)).

A BDD has a root vertex v that leads to denote a function f_v which is defined recursively as: Firstly, if v is a terminal vertex and value(v) = 1, then f_v = 1. In other case, when value(v) = 0 then f_v = 0; Secondly, if v is a non terminal vertex with index(v) = 1, then f_v will be:

$$f_v(x_1,...,x_n) = x_i \cdot _{\text{flow}(v)}(x_1,...,x_n) + x_i \cdot _{\text{high}(v)}(x_1,...,x_n)$$

Conversion from FTA to BDD

The following template conversion method is used for obtaining the BDD from the FTA (Jinglun & Quan, 1998). Then the level of unreliability can be determined from the BDD easily.

Let A be a vertex set as A = $A(A_1, ..., A_n)$. If $A_1, ..., A_m$ are the A descendant vertices, then:

index($A(A_1, ..., A_n)$) = min(index(G_i)), where $1 \leq i \leq n$.

Let $x_1, ..., x_m$ be Boolean variables, then the following expressions can be obtained:

1. If $R(x_1, ..., x_m) = S(x_1, ..., x_m) \cup T(x_1, ..., x_m)$, using "binary OR template", then BDD of $R(x_1, ..., x_m)$ is denoted as:
    R = ite(S, 1, ite(T, 1, 0)) = ite (S, 1, T), where "ite" means If-Then-Else.
2. If $R(x_1, ..., x_m) = S(x_1, ..., x_m) \cap T(x_1, ..., x_m)$, employing "binary AND template", then BDD of $R(x_1, ..., x_m)$ is obtained as:
    R = ite(S, 1, ite(S, 1, 0)) = ite(S, 1, T).

According to the previous equations it is possible to get the next rules: Let $G_1, G_2, ..., G_n$ be a BDD, then:

Get-rid-of formula

$$\text{ite}(1, G_1, G_2) = 1 \cdot G_1 + 1 \cdot G_2 = 1 \cdot G_1 + 0 \cdot G_2 = G_1$$

$$\text{ite}(0, G_1, G_2) = 0 \cdot G_1 + 0 \cdot G_2 = 0 \cdot G_1 + 1 \cdot G_2 = G_2$$

$$\text{ite}(G_1, G_1, 0) = G_1 \cdot G_1 + G_1 \cdot 0 = G_1 \cdot G_1 = G_1$$

$$\text{ite}(G_1, 1, 0) = G_1 \cdot 1 + G_1 \cdot 0 = G_1$$

$$\text{ite}(G_1, G_2, G_2) = G_1 \cdot G_2 + G_1 \cdot G_2 = (G_1 + G_1) \cdot G_2 = G_2$$

Expansion Formula

$$\text{ite}(\text{ite}(G_1, G_2, G_3), G_4, G_5) = \text{ite}(G_1, \text{ite}(G_2, G_4, G_5), \text{ite}(G_3, G_4, G_5))$$

Absorption Formula

$$\text{ite}(G_1, \text{ite}(G_1, G_2, G_3), = \text{ite}(G_1, G_2, G_4) \quad G4$$

$$\text{ite}(G_1, G_2, \text{ite}(G_1, G_3)) = \text{ite}(G_1, G_2, G_4) \quad G4$$

- Changed-order formula
- If index(G_2) < index(G_1) $\leq$ index(G_3), then

$$\text{ite}(G_1, G_2, G_3) = \text{ite}(G_2, \text{ite}(G_1, 1, G_3), \text{ite}(G_1, 0, G_3))$$

If index(G_3) < index(G_1) $\leq$ index(G_2), then

$$\text{ite}(G_1, G_2, G_3) = \text{ite}(G_3, \text{ite}(G_1, G_2, 1), \text{ite}(G_1, G_2, 0))$$

If index(G_2) $\leq$ index(G_3) < index(G_1), then

$$\text{ite}(G_1, G_2, G_3) = \text{ite}(G_2, \text{ite}(G_3, 1, G_1), \text{ite}(G_3, \text{ite}(G_1, 0, 1), 0))$$

If index(G_3) < index(G_2) < index(G_1), then

$$\text{ite}(G_1, G_2, G_3) = \text{ite}(G_3, \text{ite}(G_2, 1, \text{ite}(G_1, 0, 1)), \text{ite}(G_2, G_1, 0))$$

Example of Conversion from FTA to BDD

The rules defined in previous section will be applied to the fault tree (FT) shown in Figure 2 considering the following ranking of the events:

$$e_1 < e_2 < e_3 < e_4 < e_5 < e_6$$

The previous FT can be denoted as:

$$\text{Top} := (g_1 \backslash g_2)$$

$$g_1 := (g_3 \& e_3)$$

$$g_3 := (e_1 \backslash e_2)$$

$$g_2 := (g_4 \& e_6)$$

$$g_4 := (e_4 \backslash e_5)$$

The basics events, applying the 'ite' rules, can be expressed as:

$$e_1 = \text{ite}(e_1, 1, 0)$$

$$e_2 = \text{ite}(e_2, 1, 0)$$

$$e_3 = \text{ite}(e_3, 1, 0)$$

$$e_4 = \text{ite}(e_4, 1, 0)$$

$$e_5 = \text{ite}(e_5, 1, 0)$$

$$e_6 = \text{ite}(e_6, 1, 0)$$

where

$$g_3 := (e_1 \backslash e_2) = (\text{ite}(e_1, 1, 0) + \text{ite}(e_2, 1, 0))$$

In the cases that present an OR door, will be:

$$g_3 := (e_1 \backslash e_2) = (\text{ite}(e_1, 1, e_2))$$

$$g_4 := (e_4 \backslash e_5) = \text{ite}(e_4, 1, e_5)$$

and when an AND door is presented:

$$g_1 := (g_3 \& e_3) = (\text{ite}(e_1, 1, e_2)) \cdot (\text{ite}(e_3, 1, 0))$$

where

$$g_1 := (g_3 \& e_3) = (\text{ite}(e_1, 1, \cdot \text{ite}(e_3, 1, 0), e_2 \cdot (\text{ite}(e_3, 1, 0)))$$

$$= \text{ite}(e_1, 1 \cdot \text{ite}(e_3, 1, 0), \text{ite}(e_2, 1, 0) \cdot (\text{ite}(e_3, 1, 0))$$

$$= \text{ite}(e_1, e_3, \text{ite}(e_2, e_3, 0))$$

and

$$g_2 := (g_4 \& e_6) = (\text{ite}(e_4, 1, e_5)) \cdot \text{ite}(e_6, 1, 0) = \text{ite}(e_4, e_6, \text{ite}(e_5, e_6, 0))$$

Finally,

$$\text{Top} := (g_1 \backslash g_2) = \text{ite}(e_1, e_3, \text{ite}(e_2, e_3, 0)) + \text{ite}(e_4, e_6, \text{ite}(e_5, e_6, 0))$$

being:

$$\text{Top} := (g_1 \backslash g_2) =$$

$$\text{ite}(e_1, e_{3+} \text{ite}(e_4, e_6, \text{ite}(e_5, e_6, 0)), \text{ite}(e_2, e_3, 0) + \text{ite}(e_4, e_6, \text{ite}(e_5, e_6, 0))) =$$

$$\text{ite}(e_1, \text{ite}(e_3, 1, + \text{ite}(e_4, e_6, \text{ite}(e_5, e_6, 0))), \text{ite}(e_2, \text{ite}(e_3, 1, \text{ite}(e_4, e_6, 0)), \text{ite}(e_4, e_6, \text{ite}(e_5, e_6, 0))))$$

This expression is plotted in Figure 3.
The cut-sets obtained from Figure 3 are:

$$GC_1 = e_3 \cdot e_1$$

$$GC_2 = e_6 \cdot e_4 \cdot (1 - e_3) \cdot e_1$$

$$GC_3 = e_6 \cdot e_5 \cdot (1 - e_4) \cdot (1 - e_3) \cdot e_1$$

Figure 3. BDD of the FT shown in Figure 2 considering $e_1 < e_2 < e_3 < e_4 < e_5 < e_6$

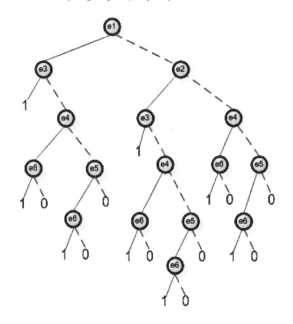

$GC_4 = e_3 \cdot e_2 \cdot (1 - e_1)$

$GC_5 = e_6 \cdot e_4 \cdot (1 - e_3) \cdot e_2 \cdot (1 - e_1)$

$GC_6 = e_6 \cdot e_5 \cdot (1 - e_4) \cdot (1 - e_3) \cdot e_2 \cdot (1 - e_1)$

$GC_7 = e_6 \cdot e_4 \cdot (1 - e_2) \cdot (1 - e_1)$

$GC_8 = e_6 \cdot e_5 \cdot (1 - e_4) \cdot (1 - e_2) \cdot (1 - e_1)$

The fault probability of the top event can be calculated as:

$P(Top) =$

$[P(e_3) \cdot P(e_1) +$

$[P(e_6) \cdot P(e_4) \cdot (1 - P(e_3)) \cdot (P(e_1)] +$

$[P(e_6) \cdot P(e_5) \cdot (1 - P(e_4)) \cdot (1 - P(e_3)) \cdot (P(e_1)] +$

$[P(e_3) \cdot P(e_2) \cdot (1 - P(e_1)] +$

$[P(e_6) \cdot P(e_4) \cdot (1 - P(e_3)) \cdot (P(e_2) \cdot (1 - P(e_1))] +$

$[P(e_6) \cdot P(e_4) \cdot (1 - P(e_2)) \cdot (1 - P(e_1))] +$

$[P(e_6) \cdot P(e_5) \cdot (1 - P(e_4)) \cdot (1 - P(e_2)) \cdot (1 - P(e_1))] +$

$[P(e_6) \cdot P(e_5) \cdot (1 - P(e_4)) \cdot (1 - P(e_3)) \cdot P(e_2) \cdot (1 - P(e_1))]$

In case that:

$P(e_1), P(e_2), P(e_3), P(e_4), P(e_5), P(e_6) = 0.01$

The fault probability of the top event will be:

$P(Top) = 3{,}9796.10^{-4}$

RANKING FOR THE EVENTS

The BDD method does not analyse the FTA directly, but converts the tree to the Boolean equations that will provide the fault probability of the top event. This conversion presents several problems, where the variable ordering scheme chosen for the construction of the BDD has a crucial effect on its resulting size.

In order to show it the previous FTA transformation to the BDD will be considering the following ranking of the events:

$e_3 < e_1 < e_2 < e_6 < e_4 < e_5$

Then:

$g_3 := (e_1 \backslash e_2) = ite(e_1, 1, e_2)$

$g_4 := (e_4 \backslash e_5) = ite(e_4, 1, e_5)$

In this case $e_3 < e_1$ and $e_6 < e_4$, therefore g_1 y g_2 will be:

$g_1 := (g_3 \& e_3) = ite(e_1, 1, e_2) \cdot ite(e_3, 1, 0) = ite(e_3, ite(e_1, 1, e_2), 0)$

$g_2:= (g_4 \& e_6) = ite\,(e_4, 1, e_5) \cdot ite\,(e_6, 1, 0) = ite\,(e_6, ite\,(e_4, 1, e_5), 0)$

and,

$Top:= (g_1 \backslash g_2) = ite\,(e_3, ite\,(e_1, 1, e_2), 0) + ite\,(e_6, ite\,(e_4, 1, e_5), 0)$

$= ite\,(e_3, ite\,(e_1, 1, ite\,(e_2, 1, ite\,(e_6, ite\,(e_4, 1, e_5), 0))), ite\,(e_6, ite\,(e_4, 1, e_5), 0))$

The BDD is shown in Figure 3.
The cut-set will be:

$GC_1 = e_1 \cdot e_3$

$GC_2 = e_2 \cdot (1 - e_1) \cdot e_3$

$GC_3 = e_4 \cdot e_6 \cdot (1 - e_2) \cdot (1 - e_1) \cdot e_3$

$GC_4 = e_5 \cdot (1 - e_4) \cdot e_6 \cdot (1 - e_2) \cdot (1 - e_1) \cdot e_3$

$GC_5 = e_4 \cdot e_6 \cdot (1 - e_3)$

$GC_6 = e_5 \cdot (1 - e_4) \cdot e_6 \cdot (1 - e_3)$

Considering $P(e_1)$, $P(e_2)$, $P(e_3)$, $P(e_4)$, $P(e_5)$, $P(e_6)=0.01$, the probability of the top event will be:

$P(Top) = 3{,}9796.10^{-4}$

It has been demonstrated that the BDD associated to the FT given in Figure 2 can be reduced with a best ordering of the events. It can be seen in Figure 5. The probability of the top event is the shame employing any of the BDDs associated to the FT (see Figure 2).

Ranking Criteria for the Events

The level in any event is understood as the number the gates that has higher up the tree until the top event. The "level" method creates the ranking of the events regarding to the level of them. In case

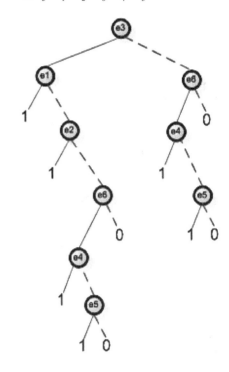

Figure 4. BDD of the FT shown in Figure 2 considering $e_3 < e_1 < e_2 < e_6 < e_4 < e_5$

that two or more events have the same level, the event will have highest priority if it appear early in the tree (Malik et al., 1988). Employing the Level method to the FT given in Figure 2, the ranking of the events is shown in Table 1.

Top-down-left-right (TDLM) method generates a ranking of the events by ordering them from the original fault tree structure in a top-down and then left-right manner (Bartlett, 2003; Bartlett & Andrews, 2001). In other words, the listing of the events is initialized, at each level, in a left to right path and basic events that are found are added to the ordering list (see Figure 1). In case that any event is encountered and it is already located higher up the tree and has therefore already been incorporated in the list, then it is ignored. The TDLM is shown in Figure 6.

Xie *et al.* (2000) suggest by the AND criterion that the importance of the basic element is based on the "and" gates that there are between the *k* element and the top element, because in FTA

Figure 5. Comparison of the BDDs given in Figures 3 and 4

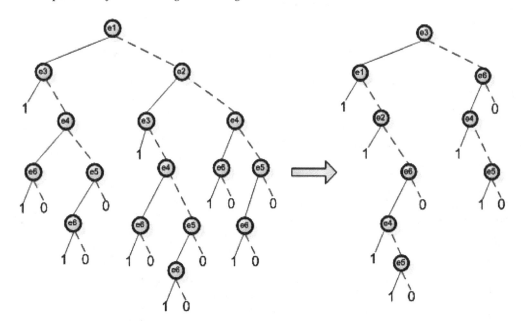

Table 1. Ranking of the events (see Figure 2) by the Level method: $e_3 < e_6 < e_1 < e_2 < e_3 < e_4$

Events	N° Levels
e1	3
e2	3
e3	2
e4	3
e5	3
e6	2
g1	1
g2	1
g3	2
g4	2

Figure 6. TDLR method for FT from Figure 2: $e_3 < e_6 < e_1 < e_2 < e_3 < e_{4<} e_5$

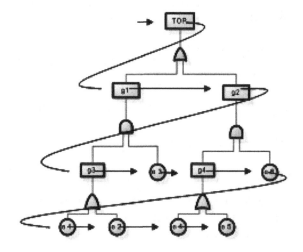

the "and" gates imply that there are redundancies in the system. Consequently, basic events under an "and" gate can be viewed as less important because it is independent to other basic events occurring for the intermediate events (Xie et al., 2000).

The depth first search (DFS) method goes from top to down of the tree and each sub-tree on the left. It is a non-recursive implementation and all freshly expanded nodes are added as last-input last-output process (Cormen et al., 2001). Figure 7 shows the DFS method applied to the FT from Figure 2.

Figure 7. DFS approach for the FT shown in Figure 2: $e_3 < e_1 < e_2 < e_6 < e_4 < e_5$

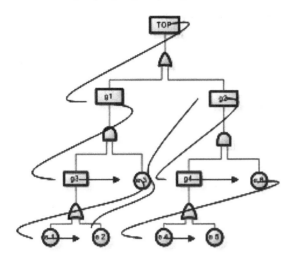

Figure 8. BFS method applied to the FT given in Figure 2: $e_1 < e_2 < e_3 < e_4 < e_5 < e_6$

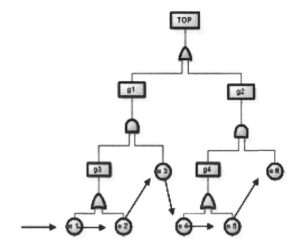

The breadth-first search (BFS) algorithm begins ordering all the child events obtained expanding from the standpoint by the first-input first-output procedure (FIFO) (see Figure 8). The events do not considered are added in a queue list named "open". It is recalled "closed" list when it is studied (Jensen & Veloso, 2000; Jensen, Bryant, & Veloso, 2002).

CASE STUDY

The FTA showed in Figure 1 has been taken as an example case study, where is explain in detail how are obtained the associated BDD and the fault probability. It has two multiple occurring events that occurs more than one place in the FTA, B and C, also known as a redundant or repeated event.

The ranking obtained has been done by the methods of DFS, TDLR, BFS and AND, and the lists are shown in Table 2.

The logic equations of the gate outputs are given by:

G5=C+E

Table 2. Rankings obtained for the case study

Success	DFS	TDLR	LEVEL	BFS	AND
A	4	4	3	4	4
B	1	2	3,2	2	1
C	2	3	3,4	3	3
D	3	1	2	1	2
E	5	5	4	5	5

G4=A+G5

G3= B+ C

G2= B+ G4

G1= D+G3

The BDD associated to the FTA (see Figure 9) is shown in Figure 10.

From BDD showed in Figure 1.2 can be obtained the probability of the top event, Q, as:

$$Q = q_D q_B + q_D (1 - q_B) q_C q_A q_E$$

The probabilities q of successes A, B, C, D and E, and the probability of the system, Q, are

315

Figure 9. FTA with some repeat events

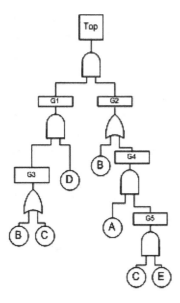

Figure 10. BDD of the case study

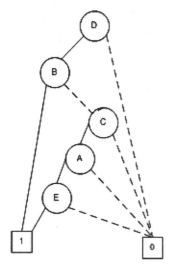

shown in Table 3. The second row considers the same fault probability of each success. The fault probability of each success has been multiplied by two in following rows, where the last column shows the success that its probability has been modified.

The most important events for the failure probability of the system are B and D. B is a multiple occurring event, but D is a simple occurring event. As it is shown in Table 2, the TDLR and BFS and AND methods find these events in the firsts two positions of the rankings, but only the AND provided D as first in the raking, where the other methods, that find the same solutions for every events, find B first in the ranking.

A set of fault trees has been considered in order to test the ranking obtained by the methods aforementioned. They are presented in Table 4. Different size of the events and structures, considering structures as number of "and" and "or" gates, and levels, has been considered.

Results

The effectiveness of the Level, TDLR, AND, DFS and BFS methods has been done regarding to the cut sets number obtained by the BDD. If the size of cut sets increases, then the computational time required for calculating the Q probability of the top event will rise.

The numbers of cut sets of the fault trees, described in Table 4, obtained by the AND, Level, BFS, DFS and TDLR methods are shown in Figure 11. BFS provides generally bad results in most of the cases, especially when the fault tree has a high number of events, levels and "or" and "and" gates. Otherwise the Level and AND methods generate the ordering of the events with a minimal cut-sets. The conclusions regarding to Level, DFS and TDLR methods should be studied for each fault tree.

Table 5 illustrates the computational time required for solving the problem. The results are proportional to the number of cut sets showed in Figure 11, and therefore the conclusions aforementioned.

Table 3. Probabilities for A, B, C, D and E events

q_A	q_B	q_C	q_D	q_E	Q	Event
0,001	0,001	0,001	0,001	0,001	0,000001	
0,002	0,001	0,001	0,001	0,001	0,000001	A
0,001	**0,002**	0,001	0,001	0,001	0,000002	B
0,001	0,001	**0,002**	0,001	0,001	0,000001	C
0,001	0,001	0,001	**0,002**	0,001	0,000002	D
0,001	0,001	0,001	0,001	**0,002**	0,000001	E

Table 4. Fault tree case studies

FAULT TREE	Size	AND	OR	LEVELS
a	4	2	2	2
b	5	3	3	3
c	6	3	3	3
d	7	3	3	2
e	8	3	3	2
f	11	5	5	4
g	12	2	10	7
h	12	3	10	3
i	19	6	8	3
k	25	6	16	12
l	17	8	9	5

Table 5. Computational time to solve the fault trees

FAULT TREE	TDLR	DFS	BFS	LEVEL	AND
a	0,2562	0,1978	0,2405	0,2631	0,3069
b	0,2043	0,1778	0,2129	0,2367	0,2479
c	0,2803	0,2460	0,2708	0,3443	0,3518
e	0,6710	1,1247	1,3357	0,9155	0,7441
g	1,1204	0,9909	1,1514	1,5979	1,1212
h	1,6582	2,3293	2,6790	1,6373	1,6831
i	1,6323	1,9792	2,6346	1,9134	1,7061
k	1,7258	3,9333	5,5591	2,0434	0,9315
l	14,1120	9,7190	19,8986	6,7753	6,3727

Figure 11. Numbers of cut-sets given by AND, Level, BFS, DFS and TDLR methods

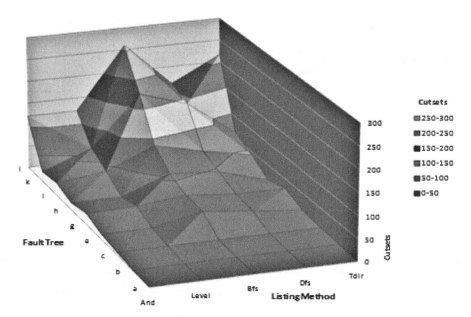

CONCLUSION

In this work is proposed a Fault Tree Analysis (FTA) in order to study qualitatively the state of a system according to the condition of each event.

The FTA has been analysed quantitatively employing Binary Diagram Decisions (BDD). The size of the BDD will depend of the events ordering, which has been done employing the top-down-left-right, the level, the depth first search, the breadth-first search, and the AND methods. For this case study the "and" method presents the best results, where the cut-sets for the fault tree is reduced considerably, and therefore the computational cost for solving the fault probability of the top event.

REFERENCES

Akers, S. B. (1978). Binary decision diagrams. *IEEE Transactions on Computers*, *27*, 509–516. doi:10.1109/TC.1978.1675141

Bartlett, L. M. (2003). Progression of the binary decision diagram conversion methods. *Proceedings of the 21st International System Safety Conference,* August 4-8, 2003, Ottawa, (pp. 116-125).

Bartlett, L. M., & Andrews, J. D. (2001). Comparison of two new approaches to variable ordering for binary decision diagrams. *Quality and Reliability Engineering International*, *17*(3), 151–158. doi:10.1002/qre.406

Birnbaum, Z. W. (1969). On the importance of different components in a multicomponent system. In Korishnaiah, P. R. (Ed.), *Multivariate analysis* (pp. 581–592).

Bryant, R. E. (1986). Graph-based algorithms for Boolean functions using a graphical representation. *IEEE Transactions on Computers*, *35*(8), 677–691. doi:10.1109/TC.1986.1676819

Cormen, T. H., Leiserson, C. E., Rivest, R. L., & Stein, C. (2001). *Introduction to algorithms* (2nd ed., pp. 540–549). MIT Press and McGraw-Hill.

Jensen, R., & Veloso, M. M. (2000). OBDD-based universal planning for synchronized agents in non-deterministic domains. *Journal of Artificial Intelligence Research*, *13*, 189–226.

Jinglun, Z., & Quan, S. (1998). Reliability analysis based on binary decision diagrams. *Journal of Quality in Maintenance Engineering*, *4*(2), 150–161. doi:10.1108/13552519810213707

Lee, C. Y. (1959). Representation of switching circuits by binary decision diagrams. *Bell System Technology*, *38*, 985–999.

Malik, S., Wang, A. R., Brayton, R. K., & Vincentelli, A. S. (1988). Logic verification using binary decision diagrams in logic synthesis environment. In *Proceedings of the IEEE International Conference on Computer Aided Design*, ICCAD'88. Santa Clara CA, USA, (pp. 6–9).

Moret, B. M. E. (1982). Decision trees and diagrams. *Computing Surveys*, *14*, 413–416. doi:10.1145/356893.356898

Rune, J., Jensen, M., Bryant, R. E., & Veloso, M. M. (2002). SetA*: an Efficient BDD-based heuristic search algorithm. In *Proceedings of AAAI-2002*, Edmonton, Canada.

Xie, M., Tan, K. C., Goh, K. H., & Huang, X. R. (2000). Optimum prioritisation and resource allocation based on fault tree analysis. *International Journal of Quality & Reliability Management*, *17*(2), 189–199. doi:10.1108/02656710010304591

ADDITIONAL READING

Andrews, J. D., & Moss, T. R. (1993). *Reliability and risk assessment*. Longmans.

Burrus, C. S., McClellan, J. H., Oppenheim, A. V., Parks, T. W., Schafer, R. W., & Schuessler, H. W. (1994). *Computer-based exercises for signal processing using MATLAB* (pp. 43–59). Englewood Cliffs, NJ: Prentice-Hall.

Cozens, N. J., & Watson, S. J. (2003). *State of the art condition monitoring techniques suitable for wind turbines and wind farm applications*. Report for CONMOW project.

Garcia Marquez, F. P., Vaibhav, S., & Mayorkinos, P. (2011). A review of wind turbine maintenance management procedure. *Proceedings of the Eighth International Conference on Condition Monitoring and Machinery Failure Prevention Technologies*.

Giebel, G., Oliver, G., Malcolm, M., & Kaj, B. (2006). Common access to wind turbines data for condition monitoring. Riso National Laboratory. In *Proceedings of the 27th Riso International Symposium on Material Science*, Denmark, (pp. 157-164).

Lambert, H. E. (1975). Measures of importance of events and cut sets. *SIAM, Reliability and Fault Tree Analysis*, (pp. 77-100).

Watson, S. J., Infield, D. G., & Xiang, J. (2008). *Condition monitoring of wind turbines – Measurements and methods*. IET Renewable Power Generation.

Chapter 17
Developing Semantic Web Applications

Qazi Mudassar Ilyas
King Faisal University, Saudi Arabia

ABSTRACT

Semantic Web promises to make the content on World Wide Web machine understandable, thus enabling creation of an agent based web where automated programs can accomplish a variety of tasks that involve interpretation of the content and are not possible with existing web technologies. As Semantic Web technologies are being adopted by the industry at a rapid place, there is the need to develop awareness among developer community about components of typical Semantic Web applications and principles driving the design of these components. This chapter gives a brief introduction to the Semantic Web and components common to all Semantic Web applications. The common components include ontology development, content annotation, and information extraction using reasoning. Basic design principles and available alternative choices are highlighted for ontology construction and content annotation. Reasoning component is not discussed because stable reasoners are available such as RACER, FaCT++ and Pallet and any Semantic Web application can make use of them without having to reinvent the wheel. A running example is used to enhance understandability of the concepts described.

INTRODUCTION

Semantic web was proposed by Tim Berners Lee about a decade ago with the objective of making content on World Wide Web machine understandable. According to W3C (World Wide Web Consortium):

The Semantic Web provides a common framework that allows data to be shared and reused across application, enterprise, and community boundaries.

As the semantic web technologies can help to formally describe any content, these tools and techniques have been widely used in a number

DOI: 10.4018/978-1-4666-3679-8.ch017

of domains to support description and automatic discovery of the content. Semantic search is one of the key applications of these technologies that can help in knowledge discovery, extraction, and management (Ilyas 2004(a), (b)). Some of other interesting applications of semantic web include e-government (Magoutas 2010), healthcare (Thuay 2012), e-learning (Barros 2011), contextual advertising (Khan 2009), business process reengineering (Damjanović 2010), web service description and discovery (Talib 2006) and disaster management (Ilyas 2010, Ahmed 2012).

The first section of the chapter gives a brief introduction to semantic web technologies by highlighting shortcomings of existing web technologies and how semantic web promises to overcome them. Architecture of a typical semantic web application is presented and key components of a typical semantic web application are described. Ontologies are backbone of all semantic web applications that provide common understanding of a domain of interest. The most common approaches for ontology development include manual ontology construction and semi-automatic development. Both approaches are discussed with basic design principles and methods/technologies used for each choice. Content annotation is the next phase in ontology development that involves creating link between the text and domain description in the form of ontologies. Both manual and semi-automatic content annotation methodologies are discussed. Finally, a typical application is shown to describe how an application can make use of these technologies for better information extraction. The chapter is closed with further readings and conclusions.

BACKGROUND

Almost a decade ago, Sir Tim Berners Lee clarified to the whole world that existing World Wide Web is not an implementation of what he had actually conceived about this giant source of information and communication. A significant component of this huge network of networks was relationships among resources on this network but somehow they were completely missed and replaced with simple hyperlinks. These hyperlinks connect these resources but they do not possess/express the relationship between these resources. These relationships could play a vital role in expressing the contextual information about these resources and this contextual information could be used in many ways for machine understandability of content. Consider web pages shown in Figure 1 that display information about a faculty member Dr Qazi Mudasar Ilyas who works at King Faisal University and teaches System Analysis and Design. The web page of Dr Ilyas (http://www.mudassar-ilyas.info) contains links to the university homepage (http://www.kfu.edu.sa) and the course homepage (http://www.kfu.edu.sa/ccsit/courses/sad.html) but these links are merely a way to point to these resources without any hint of giving the following description and relationship between the resources:

- Dr Ilyas is an *assistant professor*
- King Faisal University is an *educational institute*
- Dr Ilyas *works at* King Faisal University
- System Analysis and Design is a *course*
- King Faisal University *offers* System Analysis and Design
- Dr Ilyas *teaches* System Analysis and Design

What impact this missing information has and what could be possible if we had this background information available on the Web? Consider information searching, a very common task performed by every user of the Web. We use search engines for this task. If someone is looking for information about academic staff in King Faisal University and gives "academic staff" and "King Faisal Uni-

Figure 1. Conventional World Wide Web where web pages are connected together simply by hyperlinks

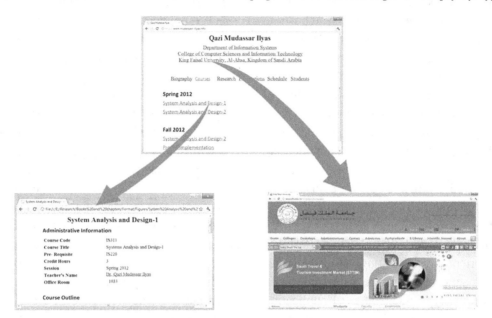

versity" as keywords then she will not find this webpage because a search engine does not know that every assistant professor is an academic staff member too. Information searching is one small use case scenario. Other exciting and useful cases where semantic web can prove helpful include but are not limited to information extraction, information synthesis to generate knowledge, maintaining information, and even supporting decision making on the Web which is not thinkable with the existing model of World Wide Web.

Tim Berners Lee re-iterated his original vision of web – which he calls Semantic Web now – to propose a model to incorporate these concepts and relationship in World Wide Web (Lee 2001). He proposed to add a new layer in the Web – ontologies – to capture domain specific knowledge. Ontologies are machine-understandable descriptions of domain that capture consensual knowledge (Gruber 1993). These descriptions when attached with any content in the form of annotations can lead to explicit meanings of the annotated content. This explicit knowledge coupled with rules and

inference engine can lead to generation of implicit knowledge.

Consider the example given above. An ontology could be used to describe the domain of university. This description may contain the following: (Please note that from this forward bold and italic *font* is used to represent a source, concept, attribute or relationship in an ontology).

- A set of concepts in the domain of university such as *students, faculty, courses, books, examination* and *grade*
- Hierarchical relationship between these concepts such as every *student* is a subconcept of *person* and every *faculty member is a person*
- A set of attributes to describe these concepts such as a *course* can be described by *course title, course number and credit hours* etc.
- Other associative relationships between concepts such as faculty member teaches a course (*teaching* is association between the concept of *faculty member* and *course*)

- Constraints or conditions such as a *course* must have exactly one *course number* (cardinality constraint)
- Lexical or grammatical relationships between concepts including synonyms, homonyms, and antonyms etc such as *faculty member, teacher* and *academic staff member* are synonyms. It may also include terms for a concepts in different languages
- Finally, an ontology may consist of instance data in the form of annotations of content

Figure 2 presents an example ontology for the domain of university.

If this background knowledge is attached with the web pages of Dr Ilyas, King Faisal University and System Analysis and Design, then a semantic web enabled search engine will be in a much better position to find/extract the relevant information required by the user.

Figure 2. An excerpt from university ontology

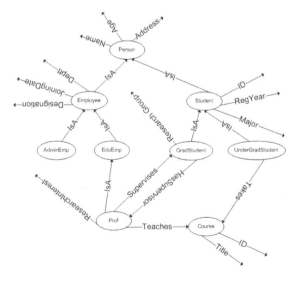

ENGINEERING SEMANTIC WEB APPLICATIONS

This section presents architecture of a typical semantic web application. This generalized architecture can be used in an application making use of the power of semantic web technologies.

A semantic web page looks exactly similar to a human being as a conventional web page but for machines, the background knowledge linked with this content in the form of annotation makes it understandable. This background knowledge (read ontologies), annotated content and inference engine can be used to reason about this knowledge. This reasoning process can lead to generation of new knowledge and unambiguous understanding of the content. Let us briefly explain this whole process.

Engineering Ontologies

As mentioned above, ontologies are backbone of semantic web application as they provide the foundation in the form of domain knowledge. Several ontologies may exist for one domain with different levels of exhaustivity, specificity and granularity.

Exhaustivity is the breadth of coverage of ontology, i.e., the extent to which concepts and relations are covered. Consider running example of domain of university. An ontology having only two concepts *student* and *course* would have very low exhaustivity while an ontology covering *students, courses, faculty, degree programs, library, learning resources, examination* and *schedule* has a high granularity.

Specificity is the depth of coverage i.e, the extent to which the specific concepts are covered and how deep the concept sub-concept hierarchy is built. An ontology having only once concept of *learning resources* has a low specificity. An ontology can be constructed having a deep concept sub-concept hierarchy for learning resources in which case it would have high specificity. Figure 3 shows an example of learning resources with relatively higher specificity.

Granularity is level of detail in the ontology i.e., the extent to which concepts and relation types are precisely defined. In the domain of university, a concept *student* can be defined with low granularity having only three attributes *ID*, *name* and *degree program*. This concept can also be defined with high granularity using more attributes such as *age*, *gender*, *cell number*, *address* and *courses registered*.

After deciding these basic requirements of ontology, an ontology construction can be started. Various approaches exist for construction of ontologies. The most popular approaches consist of manual and semi-automatic ontology construction.

Manual Ontology Construction

Most of manual ontology construction methodologies use a variant of the methodology suggested by Natalya F. Noy (Noy 2001). This approach suggests the following phases for ontology construction:

- **Determine Domain and Scope of Ontology:** The domain, coverage, possible uses and questions to be answered by the ontology are decided.
- **Consider Reusing Existing Ontologies:** Existing ontologies can give a starting point to the new ontology to be developed. A number of ontology libraries are available that contain thousands of ontologies and they can be considered in construction of a new ontology.

Figure 3. A relatively richer taxonomy of learning resources

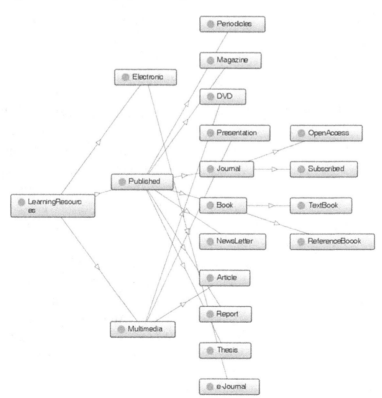

- **Enumerate Important Terms in the Ontology:** In this phase, all important terms are collected. This phase is closely related with the next two phases of defining the concept hierarchy and defining properties of these concept.
- **Define Concepts and Concepts Hierarchy:** A top-down or a bottom-up approach can be used to define most general or most specific concepts respectively. With more iterations, more concepts can be added to completely cover the semantics of the target domain. Generally, a combination of these approaches is a more common practice, in which the most important concepts are identified first and more general and specific concepts are built around them.
- **Defines properties of Concepts:** There are two types of properties of concepts. The first are attributes of the concepts such as *name, age, gender*, and *degree program* for a concept of *student*. Second, there is an association or relationship between two concepts such as *teaches* is a relationship between the concepts of *teacher* and *course*.
- **Define Constraints on the Concepts:** Constraints or restrictions are applied to the concepts to describe them unambiguously and they serve to infer implicit knowledge based on this explicit knowledge. There are various types of restrictions. Some of them are given below:
  - A value type restriction restricts a property to have a specific type of value such as the *age* of *person* must always be non-negative integer.
  - A cardinality constraint restrict a property to have a defined number of values. This restriction can be used to express that an instructor must teach at least one course or a person must have exactly one last name.
  - A domain restriction restricts the concepts to which a relational property can be applied such as the domain of *teaches* property must be *teacher* to express that only *teachers* can teach *courses*.
  - A range restriction restricts the types of values a relational property can have such as we can define range of *teaches* property to restrict that only *courses* can be taught.
- **Create Instances:** The last step in the ontology is the generation of class instances. Please note that it can be a part of ontology process but generally instances are generated in annotation process after ontology has been developed. By an analogy with Object Oriented Paradigm, an ontology can be thought of a blue print of classes and the instances are objects that use these classes. In the running examples, we can define an instance *of Dr Ilyas* belonging to the concept teacher and *System Analysis and Design* as an instance of the concept *course*.

Semi-Automatic Ontology Construction

Ontology construction is a laborious process and needs domain knowledge as well as knowledge of ontology construction. In certain cases, it may involve digging information from large databases that contain hundreds of concepts, relationships and properties. In such cases it becomes extremely difficult to find concepts, arrange them in concept hierarchy and establish relationships. A number of approaches have been proposed to help ontology construction (Houa 2011 and Wei 2012). The aspects in which these approaches can prove to be useful include:

- Identifying concepts from large data sets.

- Establishing concept-hierarchy from concepts identified or provided by an ontology engineer.
- Establishing relationships between concepts.
- Identifying attributes for the concepts.
- Populating ontology with instance data.
- Merging ontology with similar scope and coverage in a domain.
- Mapping concepts between various ontologies.
- Ontology evaluation.
- Ontology refinement based on ontology usage patterns.

Although a detailed discussion is out of scope of this book chapter but some of techniques used to perform the tasks mentioned above are briefly described below:

- **Data Visualization:** Can be used to get an overview of a set of documents or other resources that can help in early phasing of ontology construction such as domain and data understanding.
- **Document Clustering:** Can be used to extract concepts from a set of document. A number of variation exist but the most basic technique for document clustering consists of representing a document as a word-vector and using Term Frequency/Inverse Document Frequency (TF/IDF) to measure significance of a term in this set of documents.
- **Cosine Similarity Measure:** Can be used to measure similarity between documents that can help in document categorization to help ontology population task.
- **Latent Semantic Indexing:** Can be used to extract hidden semantic concepts or topics from a set of documents. This can be used to identify properties of concept.
- **Propositional Rule Learning Algorithms:** Can be used to form attri-

bute value rules. These rules can be used to populate ontologies.

- **Stream Mining:** Can be used to learn from a stream of data without actually storing it. It can be used to update the ontologies quickly.

More information about semi-automatic ontology construction can be found in Buitelaar et al. (Buitelaar 2005).

Content Annotation/ Ontology Population

Once the ontologies are in place, the next step is to create instance data by linking content with these ontologies. A number of tools are available to annotate the content manually but manual annotation cannot scale to the huge size of World Wide Web. A number of tools exist to help in this annotation process by extracting entities and suggesting concept such as TopBraid (TopBraid 2012), Annotea (Annotea 2012), Annozilla (Annozilla 2012) and Knoodl (Knoodl 2012). Reeve et al. (Reeve 2005) present a survey of current text-based annotation tools and Dasiopoulou et al. (Dasiopoulou 2011) present survey of semantic image and video annotation tools.

In the running example of this chapter, the following instances could be created and relationships established:

- Dr Ilyas is annotated as a *faculty* instance.
- King Faisal University is annotated as a *university* instance.
- System Analysis and Design is annotated as a *course* instance.

Some attribute-value pairs could be defined as shown in Table 1.

While attributes are assigned simple string values, resources are also linked together in annotation process. Some of relationships between the resources are shown in Table 2.

Table 1. Instances with some attributes and their values

Instance	Attribute	Value
Dr_Ilyas#	Full name	Qazi Mudassar Ilyas
	Designation	Assistant Professor
	EmailSHA1Sum	044088723846f920d4ae457238cd4b36eab22010
KFU#	FullName	King Faisal University
	Type	Public University
	Established	1975
	Location	Al-Ahsa
SAD#	CourseTitle	System Analysis and Design
	Credits	3
	Type	Core

Table 2. Relationships between a few resources

Resource 1	Relationship	Resource 2
Dr_Ilyas#	WorksAt	KFU#
Dr_Ilyas#	Teaches	SAD#
KFU#	WebSite	http://www.kfu.edu.sa
SAD#	PreRequisite	DBF#
SAD#	IsTaughtBy	Dr_Ilyas#

Figure 4. Using TopBraid Composer to manually annotate content

Figure 5. Using knowledge and information management (KIM) platform to annotate content semi-automatically

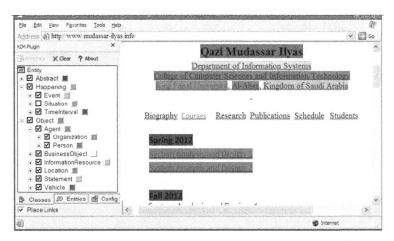

Figure 6. A complete Semantic Web application

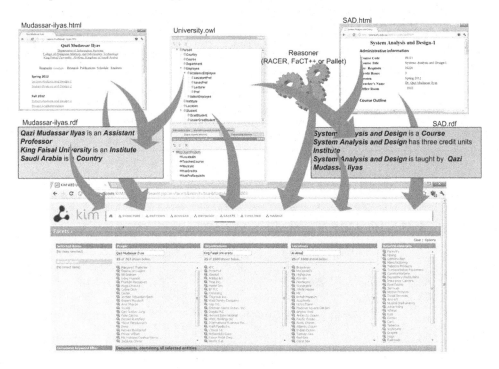

Figure 4 presents Topbraid Composer, a tool that can be used to generate content annotations manually. Figure 5 shows an example web page annotation using KIM (Knowledge and Information Management), an Internet Explorer plugin that uses GATE (General Architecture for Text Engineering) to help annotation process by automatically extracting entities and mentions.

Connecting the Dots: A Complete Semantic Web Application

Figure 6 presents architecture of a typical semantic web application using the example of university. The ontology provides the backbone for this application and they are linked with the conventional content through annotations. When a human being visits a web page of instructor, university or course, she sees the same site as if it would be a conventional web page. But when an automated software agent "visits" these pages, it can "understand" the content because of explicit description of concepts and content annotations. In addition to conventional html content, we also have ontologies in place that describe the domain of university. Figure shows how the plain text in these pages (and possibly any multimedia content too) is linked in the form of annotations. For a webpage *Mudassar-ilyas.html*, we *have mudassar-ilyas.rdf* that describes the content in the html file. Similarly content on webpage of the course System Analysis and Design is described through *sad.rdf* that creates link between the plain text and machine understandable description of concepts used in this text. It is worth noting that when a human visitor visits these pages, they look exactly same as conventional pages as ontologies and rdf content (annotations) is not visible to them. However, when an intelligent agents visits html pages, it can also see files with same name but with rdf extension for annotations of this content (e.g., sad.rdf for webpage sad.html). These annotations lead the software agent to descriptions of these concepts in the form of ontologies e.g., university. owl in this case. Now consider a software agent is asked to fetch information about all "academic staff members", the webpage of Dr Ilyas would be a valid result because of the following trace:

- The web page of Dr Ilyas mentions him as an Assistant Professor.
- This is annotated with the *assistant professor* concept from university ontology.
- The concept *assistant professor* is derived from *academic staff member* concept which means that every *assistant professor* is also an *academic staff member*.

As shown in Figure 6, a semantic web agent will not see only html content but the results returned by it will also make use of ontologies and content annotations. A reasoner is also used by these applications to perform reasoning on this explicit knowledge to derive implicit knowledge and this, in fact, is the real power of semantic web.

FUTURE RESEARCH DIRECTIONS

After spending the last decade in laboratories, Semantic Web applications have now started springing up in real life applications. Software metrics are used to measure quality of software. As semantic web is a new paradigm in software development, evaluation techniques need to be developed to evaluate quality of these applications. Software quality metrics also need to be defined in this regard. These metrics will measure true potential and impact of these technologies.

CONCLUSION

The design components of a typical semantic web application described in the chapter can give a starting point to a developer interested in semantic web application design.

REFERENCES

Ahmed, I., & Ilyas, Q. M. (2012). Gleaning disaster related information from World Wide Web. *Journal of Theoretical and Applied Information Technology*, 40(2).

Annotea. (2012). Retrieved from http://source-forge.net/projects/metadata-net/files/

Annozilla. (2012). Retrieved from http://annozilla.mozdev.org/

Barros, H., Silva, A., Costa, E., Bittencourt, I. I., Holanda, O., & Sales, L. (2011). Steps, techniques, and technologies for the development of intelligent applications based on Semantic Web Services: A case study in e-learning systems. *Engineering Applications of Artificial Intelligence*, 24(8), 1355–1367. doi:10.1016/j.engappai.2011.05.007

Buitelaar, P., Cimiano, P., & Magnini, B. (2005). *Ontology learning from text: Methods, applications and evaluation. Frontiers in Artificial Intelligence and Applications.* IOS Press.

Damjanović, V. (2010). Semantic reengineering of business processes. *Information Systems, 35*(4), 496–504. doi:10.1016/j.is.2009.06.003

Dasiopoulou, S., Giannakidou, E., Litos, G., Malasioti, P., & Kompatsiaris, Y. (2011). A survey of semantic image and video annotation tools. In Paliouras, G., Spyropoulos, C. D., & Tsatsaronis, G. (Eds.), *Knowledge-driven multimedia information extraction and ontology evolution.* Springer Verlag. doi:10.1007/978-3-642-20795-2_8

Gruber, T. R. (1993). A translation approach to portable ontology specifications. *Knowledge Acquisition, 5*(2), 199–220. doi:10.1006/knac.1993.1008

Houa, X., Ong, S. K., Nee, A. Y. C., Zhang, X. T., & Liu, W. J. (2011). GRAONTO: A graph-based approach for automatic construction of domain ontology. *Expert Systems with Applications, 38*(9), 11958–11975. doi:10.1016/j.eswa.2011.03.090

Ilyas, Q. M., & Ahmad, I. (2010). A conceptual architecture of SAHARA - A semantic disaster management system. *World Applied Sciences Journal, 10*(8), 980–985.

Ilyas, Q. M., Kai, Y. Z., & Talib, M. A. (2004). A journey from information to knowledge: Knowledge representation and reasoning on the web. *Information Technology Journal, 3*(2), 163–167. doi:10.3923/itj.2004.163.167

Ilyas, Q. M., Kai, Y. Z., & Talib, M. A. (2004). A conceptual architecture for semantic search engine. In *8th IEEE International Multi-topic Conference* (INMIC2004), Lahore, Pakistan (pp. 606-610).

Khan, S., Ilyas, W. M., & Anwar, W. (2009). *Contextual advertising using Semantic Web approach.* International Conference on Frontiers of Information Technology, Abbottabad, Pakistan.

Knoodl. (2012). Retrieved from http://www.knoodl.com/ui/home.html;jsessionid=0129154041003C2F75412AD22293E146

Lee, T. B., Hendler, J., & Lassila, O. (2001). The Semantic Web, a new form of web content that is meaningful to computers will unleash a revolution of new possibilities. *Scientific American.*

Magoutas, B., & Mentzas, G. (2010). SALT: A semantic adaptive framework for monitoring citizen satisfaction from e-government services. *Expert Systems with Applications, 37*(6), 4292–4300. doi:10.1016/j.eswa.2009.11.071

Noy, N. F., & McGuinness, D. L. (2001). *Ontology development 101: A guide to creating your first ontology.* Stanford Knowledge Systems Laboratory Technical Report KSL-01-05 and Stanford Medical Informatics Technical Report SMI-2001-0880.

Reeve, L., & Han, H. (2005). *Survey of semantic annotation platforms.* ACM SAC 2005, Santa Fe, New Mexico.

Talib, M. A., Kai, Y. Z., & Ilyas, Q. M. (2006). A framework towards web services composition modeling & execution. *International Journal of Web and Grid Services, 2*(1), 25–49. doi:10.1504/IJWGS.2006.008878

Thuy, P. T. T., Lee, Y. K., & Lee, S. (2012). (in press). S-trans: Semantic transformation of XML healthcare data into OWL ontology. [Corrected Proof]. *Knowledge-Based Systems.* doi:10.1016/j.knosys.2012.04.009

Topbraid. (2012). Retrieved from http://www.topquadrant.com/products/TB_Composer.html

Wei, Y., Wang, R., Hu, Y., & Wang, X. (2012). From web resources to agricultural ontology: A method for semi-automatic construction. *Journal of Integrative Agriculture, 11*(5), 775–783. doi:10.1016/S2095-3119(12)60067-7

ADDITIONAL READING

Allemang, D., & Hendler, J. (2011). *Semantic Web for the working ontologist, Second Edition: Effective modeling in RDFS and OWL*. Morgan Kaufmann.

Antoniou, G., & Harmelen, F. V. (2008). *A Semantic Web primer*. The MIT Press.

Davies, J. (2006). *Semantic Web technologies: Trends and research in ontology-based systems*. Wiley. doi:10.1002/047003033X

Gerber, A., Merwe, V. A., & Andries, B. (2008). *A functional Semantic Web architecture*. European Semantic Web Conference 2008, ESWC'08.

Passin, T. B. (2004). *Explorer's guide to the Semantic Web*. Manning Publications.

Pollock, J. T. (2009). *Semantic Web for dummies*. Wiley.

Yu, L. (2011). *A developer's guide to the Semantic Web*. Springer. doi:10.1007/978-3-642-15970-1

KEY TERMS AND DEFINITIONS

Annotation: Annotation, or tagging, is about attaching names, attributes, comments, descriptions, etc. to a document or to a selected part in a text.

Machine Understandability: The process whereby a software agent can understand the meaning of certain concepts to accomplish a task or take decision.

Ontology: A formal and explicit specification of a shared conceptualization.

RDF: Resource Description Framework is the basic framework to describe resources on World Wide Web.

Semantic Web: It is not a separate Web but an extension of the current one, in which information is given well-defined meaning, better enabling computers and people to work in cooperation.

Software Agent: A software program that acts for a user or other program in a relationship of agency.

Software Metrics: A measure of some property of a piece of software or its specifications.

Chapter 18
Knowledge Management

Arshad Siddiqi
Institute of Business Administration, Pakistan

ABSTRACT

Knowledge is the essence of life, and Knowledge Management (KM) is the methodological formulation of strategies and practices deployed by the businesses and organization identify, define, develop, and utilize the tacit and explicit information within the organization for better use of developing and marketing new products and ideas. Knowledge is a knowing and understanding of facts, figures in form, or data or information about something or some entity. Knowledge can be acquired by various sources which could include facts and figures from books, news media, discussions, or books. It is a familiarity with what is happening around one and how does it affect. It can be acquired from any media; books, magazines, television, radio, or Internet. It can be in the form of raw data, or structured information, facts and figures, or description, depiction, or sketched.

INTRODUCTION

There are various types of knowledge available to us. Some knowledge is gained from the day we are born e.g. knowledge of our parents, surroundings and belongingness. This type of basic knowledge, which one gains, is inherited from mother, and this basic knowledge serves as the building block of all future knowledge; to live a successful life.

In this chapter, we will look at the various types of knowledge; how do we gain them and use them effectively for successful life.

DOI: 10.4018/978-1-4666-3679-8.ch018

BACKGROUND

Knowledge is a familiarity with facts, information, descriptions or skills acquired through experience or education. It can refer to the theoretical or practical understanding of a subject. It can be implicit or explicit; and it can be more or less formal or systematic.

MAIN FOCUS OF THE CHAPTER

The main focus of this chapter is to define "knowledge" and its importance in our everyday life. The word Knowledge is usually used for the meaning of 'knowing," like "I have no knowledge of that" where the speaker is saying that I do not know of it or about it. Whereas we are looking at it in much more depth, in various definitions, usages and its importance in today's fast moving world.

DEFINITION OF KNOWLEDGE

The following quote from Bertrand Russell's "Theory of Knowledge" illustrates the difficulty in defining knowledge:

The question how knowledge should be defined is perhaps the most important and difficult of the three with which we shall deal. This may seem surprising: at first sight it might be thought that knowledge might be defined as belief which is in agreement with the facts. The trouble is that no one knows what a belief is, no one knows what a fact is, and no one knows what sort of agreement between them would make a belief true. Let us begin with belief.

Philosophically the study of knowledge is called "epistemology," which was defined by the philosopher Plato as "justified true belief." Plato 424-348 BC was a mathematician and a philosopher. He was the student of Socrates, writer of philosophical dialogues, and founder of the Academy in Athens, the first institution of higher learning in the Western world. Along with his mentor, Socrates, and his student, Aristotle, Plato helped to lay the foundations of Western philosophy and science.

Epistemology meaning "knowledge, science" It addresses the questions:

- What is knowledge?
- How is knowledge acquired?
- To what extent is it possible for a given subject or entity to be known?
- How do we know what we know?

Knowledge acquisition is not simple and straight forward; it involves complex cognitive processes involving:

- **Perception:** How well one perceives a situation.
- **Communication:** How accurately does one communicate it others.
- **Association:** How is the situation associated with concerned entities.
- **Reasoning:** What are reasoning of the occurrence of the situation?

Scientifically, *cognition* refers to mental processes including understanding, remembering, producing and giving attention to problem solving and decision making decisions.

Cognition is such a concept that it is part of the various studied with different names like:

- **Information Technology:** Information processing.
- **Psychology and Cognitive Science:** Individual's psychological functions.
- **Social Psychology called Social Cognition:** Attitudes, attribution and group's dynamics.

TACIT AND EXPLICIT KNOWLEDGE

While knowledge is said to be related to the capacity of understanding in human beings, basically the two types of knowledge Tacit and Explicit make up the knowledge (See Figure 1).

Figure 1. Tacit and explicit knowledge

Tacit knowledge is knowledge which is difficult to transfer from one person to another by means of writing it down or explaining it. This is a learned, acquired, experienced and experimented knowledge that is gained over years of hard work and dedication. Since it is not written down, it cannot be taught using a classroom environment or the white board. It is transferred slowly and gradually forms the teacher to pupil.

For example: a carpenter of class and years of experience learns his trade over years of hard labor, experimentation and perseverance. If he wants to transfer his Tacit Knowledge to his apprentice, he will have to go through the same process; however, it will take him lesser time if he is intelligent, observant and a quick learner.

Now, this Tacit Knowledge can be classified as Explicit Knowledge as it is not residing in the brain of the old carpenter, it has been transferred to his pupil especially, however it remain Tacit if it is still not written down and not available for other to learn easily.

Learning a language is a good example of tacit knowledge; it is not possible to learn a language just by reading a book. A native speaker starts learning it from birth and continues so without knowing the rules, grammar or other nuances of the language. These are learned slowly by daily interaction with the parents, siblings, friends and neighbors. Strangely he can speak the language using the correct grammar mostly, even though it is formally taught in the schools much later.

People often take the Tacit Knowledge, as normal knowhow! Some people are not often aware of the Tacit Knowledge they possess or how valuable it is to them or to the others. Since these people usually do not understand the value of this Tacit Knowledge, its effective transfer is not easy as it is not written down nor easily explainable, it generally requires extensive trust between the teacher and pupil and personal contact.

There cannot be a time frame associated with this knowledge transfer and it cannot be accel-erated. Usually, the pupil has to observe every move the teacher, understand every word uttered by the teacher and comprehend every action. An example is that of a master craftsman. He has gained his Tacit Knowledge over many years of experimentation, toile and hardship. All the mastery has accumulated is not written on any media, it all resides in his head, eyes and hands. His pupil – apprentice has to have confidence in his teacher, must have patience to learn slowly, bearing the wrath of the teacher at times and must have a lot of determination.

When a child tries to learn riding a bike, he can get the initial instruction from his elder brother, father or uncle, but he has to learn by repeated tries of how to ride a bicycle, how to balance, if the bike falls to the left, he must steers to the left and vice versa, however, since this information is not written in any manuals it provides no help to the rider in riding a bicycle; riders become aware of this fact by scrapping their knees and elbows. Understanding this is the Tacit Knowledge and the application of this gives him the expertise to ride the bike safely and flawlessly.

Tacit Knowledge cannot be easily shared. It involves personal learning and developing skills, but not in a way that can be written down. Tacit Knowledge often consists of attributes related to their culture, up-bringing and habits that we do not even recognize in ourselves.

In Knowledge Management, Tacit Knowledge is an inherent knowledge possessed by an individual, which is difficult to be communicated to the others using words, diagrams or demonstrations, whereas on the other hand Explicit Knowledge is easy to communicate, demonstrate and transfer.

Another way to view the two knowledge is that the Tacit Knowledge is Hidden and difficult to explore whereas the Explicit Knowledge is available to anyone who wish to acquire it, in a most systematic, dynamic and convenient manner.

Explicit Knowledge is that which has been in existence for some time and is being used commonly and is available easily. It has been tried and tested and finally classified and stored in a physical media like books and literature or may even be available in form of information available on the hyperspace.

Explicit Knowledge is easily understood, used and is available, however Tacit (Implicit) Knowledge is not written down, is not easily available and not widely understood thus could have far reaching outcomes and consequences.

THE FOUR KNOWS CONCEPT

The Four Knows concept (Figure 2) broadly categorizes the knowledge as:

1. **Know – How:** Tacit Knowledge (Skills)
2. **Know – What:** Explicit Knowledge (Facts and Figures)
3. **Know – Why:** Science (Investigative)
4. **Know – Who:** Network (Social)

Figure 2. The four knows concept

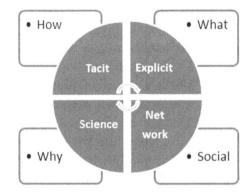

TRANSFORMATION OF TACIT KNOWLEDGE INTO EXPLICIT KNOWLEDGE

The transformation is not easy and involves lot of perseverance, desire for learning and acquiring of the skills. However since Tacit knowing is not written on any readable media, as it resides in someone's head and skilled hands!

The learning and skills have to be transferred from teacher to pupil in a very practical and demonstrative way. This process of transformation from Tacit to Explicit (Figure 3) can be termed either of the following.

1. Codification

It is the standardization process and development of norms, principles and methodologies of a language or course etc. If there is a Programming Language is being codified, it depends on the stage of standardization and the following points are to be considered:

- Is it a new language or an off shoot of an existing language?
- Is it a basic programming language or intelligent?
- Is it a self-code generating language?
- Is it specialized language like Artificial Intelligence?
- Is it specific to an industry?
- Does it have special syntax or vocabulary, etc?

In a well-known model of language planning by Einar Haugen, codification is only the second step. Step one is the selection process, step three is the elaboration of vocabulary (especially technical terms) and step four the implementation of the changes in society.

According to Heinz Kloss there are four following steps involved in Codification:

Figure 3. Transformation of tacit knowledge into explicit knowledge

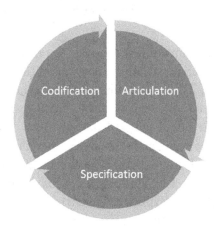

Step 1: Status Planning – Selection of Language
Step 2: Corpus Planning – Codification of a Language
Step 3: Elaboration of Vocabulary
Step 4: Securing its Acceptance

2. Articulation

Course articulation, in our case as we are talking about teaching, deals with the process of comparing the course contents which are transferred between various level of learning institutions like Schools, Colleges or Universities.

This process compares the courses being taught in similar level institutions so that students once completed a course may not have to repeat is again in another institution where they are transferring to. Their earned credits are also transferred. This process could be done under an Articulation agreement or on course basis.

3. Specification

A *specification or specs* in short is a defined set of requirements which are to be met to the dot to may any system work according to the requirements and needs of the user. If the results or the outcome of a programming language fails to meet the specs, it is termed as OOS or being Out of Specification. The Technical Standards are driven from the initial Specifications. These Specs are used to create the Data Sheets, which describes the technical characteristics of a system, item or product.

NEED FOR TRANSFORMATION OF TACIT KNOWLEDGE INTO EXPLICIT KNOWLEDGE

The basic need for this transformation is to make available the tacit knowledge of the previous employees to the new employees. As this knowledge is gained by the previous employees over decades of learning, experimentation and failures at a huge cost invested by the employers, it must be transferred to keep the continuity of the quality of the operation, greater efficiency and at a lower cost.

These codifications provide:

- Automatic Replication of the Performance by the New Employees
- Continuation of Process
- Cost Saving
- No Down Time or Delays
- Maintenance of Quality
- Increased Confidence of the New Employee

Ikujiro Nonaka's model of organizational knowledge creation, in which he proposes that tacit knowledge, can be converted to explicit knowledge. In that model tacit knowledge is presented variously as uncodifiable ("tacit aspects of knowledge are those that cannot be codified") and codifiable ("transforming tacit knowledge into explicit knowledge is known as codification"). This ambiguity is common in the knowledge management literature.

Figure 4. Knowledge and technology

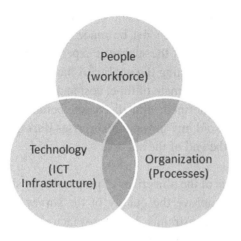

KNOWLEDGE MANAGEMENT IN ICT PERSPECTIVE

What is Knowledge? We have already defined that there are two types of Knowledge, Tacit and Explicit. Now we will look at the Management part of Knowledge.

There are three over-Lapping components of Knowledge as shown in Figure 4.

Knowledge and Technology

There is no globally agreed definition of Knowledge; however each definition has the following common integral part (Knowledge Management by Elias M. Awad, Hassan M, Ghaziri 2004):

- Using accessible knowledge from outside sources.
- Embedding and storing knowledge in business processes, products and services.
- Representing knowledge in databases and documents.
- Promoting knowledge growth through the organization's culture and incentives.
- Transferring and sharing knowledge throughout the organization.
- Assessing the value of knowledge assets and impact on a regular basis.

KNOWLEDGE MANAGEMENT

According to Parsaye, there are three major approaches to the capture of tacit knowledge from groups and individuals. They are:

- Interviewing experts.
- Learning by being told.
- Learning by observation.

Interviewing experts can be done in the form of Structured Interviewing or by recording organizational stories.

Structured Interviewing

The basic purpose of Structured Interview is the collection if data for creating a database for various needs, like; Statistical Surveys, Promotion of candidates, Job allocations; etc. Usually a questionnaire, which could be answered by the interviewee or by the interviewer, is used as the basic tool for information gathering, and then various statistical packages like SPSS are used to display the data into the required fields converting it into usable information and showing various statistical trends. Statistical Tends are integral part of the discipline of Statistic, which deals with the data collection, the organizing it in usable tables and using analytical tools to analyze the data for interpretation to make sense to the researcher.

There is a marked difference between DATA and INFORMATION, even though the base of the two is the same but they should not be used interchangeably.

Data

Data is actually the plural of *Datum* meaning "something given." In the ICT world the data is raw gathering of facts and figures which are often represented by a combination of items organized in rows and columns, basically in a tabular form. Data can also be represented in Images or Graphs.

These images can be two of more dimensional matrix or in form of a photograph, or a hologram. In graphical form it could be Pie chart or a Bar diagram etc.

Data is usually unstructured and usually does not make much sense, as it could be a sequence of numbers of Alphabets that is why it is converted into Information.

Information

Information on the other hand is data formatted in sequence that provide a message, which is the basic means of communication of facts. Information paints a picture in the mind of the researcher about event or a concept clearly thus giving him the means to understand the situation and use it statistically.

Statistics is study of data after it has been collected through surveys, then organization of this data in more understandable form. This helps in the analysis and interpretation of the data to make useful and desirable sense out it. One has to be very clear and should not confuse Statistic with Static.

Since conducting Survey is of great importance we have to make sure that:

1. The objective of the Survey is very clearly defined.
2. We understand what do we expect to achieve from the survey.
3. The parameters are defined properly.
4. The methodology used is clearly understood.
5. How the data will be displayed and used.

We must have clear idea of the Survey methodology and it should clearly identify the principles about the:

1. Design of the survey to encompass all the factors required to get the desired results.
2. The data collection methodologies must be well defined, clear to understand and execute.
3. The processing procedures would be clearly understood and be executable.

4. The analytical tools for the data analysis must be defined and diligently used.
5. All efforts must be made to maintain the quality of the survey at expected levels, yet maintaining the quality of the survey.
6. The estimate of time, cost and quality must be defined, and discussed beforehand to avoid any unwanted surprises during or at the end of the survey.

One of the objectives of proper survey should be to improve the quality of the survey within the cost constraints. If the cost factor is a major constraints than cost may be reduced keeping the fixed level of quality.

Survey Sample

The survey sample must be fairly large, covering over thousands of responses to make sure to keep out all the biases and irregularities. This is why a very important challenge is to have a survey methodology to make intelligent decisions on:

- How to decide on the sample size and it validity.
- How to identify the sample members.
- How to contact the potential sample members and how to get info from the:
  - Reluctant responders.
  - Hard to reach or contact.
  - How to make sure that they are responding honestly.
- How to make and evaluate the questions.
- How to test the validity of the questions.
- How to test evaluate the question of the test sample.
- How to get the potential surveyors.
- What should be the mode of questioning.
- Would the questions be sect, religion or sex based.
- How to collect the response and evaluate their validity.

- How to train the interviewers and how to supervise them.
- How to check the data files for consistency, completeness and accuracy.
- How to detect and correct errors.
- Who would decide on the completion so the survey sampling process?

Types of Surveys

There are various types of survey, even though the intent of them all is to gather the data for a specific purpose. There are four types of survey that are used most often; Written, Three Step Written Survey, Telephonic, Internet and Face to face. Each of them have their own advantages and disadvantages, and are used for different purposes.

1. Written Survey

Written survey is formatted with specific questions and choices. Open ended questions are not given as the responses are too varied and open ended which are difficult to interpret in a specific format. These are cheapest to conduct and can be sent to a large audience, however since they can remain anonymous it is difficult to realize the validity of the responses. Usually the response rate is very low as the respondents have no interest or spare time to sit down and fill out the response form and then mail it back. Another disadvantage is that

if the questions are not intelligently worded the responses would be highly inaccurate. Most of the time sending written questionnaires to cold and uninterested prospective respondents is nothing more than the waste of time. The written survey can be sent to office or residences. Both have advantages and disadvantages, as shown in Table 1.

2. Three Step Written Survey

This provides better responses as it comprises of three steps.

- Firstly a qualified sample is selected, and then simple letter sent to them telling them about the survey and the importance of their response.
- Secondly a Survey Form is sent to them again with the letter of importance of their response.
- Thirdly a follow-up letter is sent to remind them. Sometime a small memento is promised for the response.

3. Telephonic Survey

The Telephonic survey are conducted in form of an interview, these are quicker, but denial rate is usually very high as people are too busy at the time and do not want to spend 10-15 minutes of their time. The advantage is that the interviewer could explain the

Table 1. Types of surveys

Type of Survey	Advantages	Disadvantages	Cost	Usability
Written Survey	Easy to conduct, not too expressive	Biased and low response rate	Cheapest to conduct	Very little
Three Step Written Survey	Much more qualified response	Long process	Little costly	High
Telephonic Survey	Qualified responses	Longer process	Cheap	Some
Internet survey	Quicker	Nonqualified	Cheap	Marginal
Face-to-Face Interviews	Explain questions, make observations, better responses	Need interviewer training, time consuming	Very expensive	High

question clearly to get a more qualified response. Sometime this can be construed as invasion of the privacy, thus no interview would be conducted, or the responder would simple answer without putting any thought to them to get over with the interview.

4. Internet Survey

Internet surveys could be e-mail or web based. These are considered as the invasion of the net privacy and most of the browsers are equipped to block them. These require greater IT expertise to conduct and mostly ignored by the recipients.

5. Face to Face

These are very expensive and time consuming to conduct, however the good point is that the interview could be more complex and detailed. If the interviewer is well-versed, large, relevant and substantiated usable data can be gathered in smaller sample size.

Similarly *Hypertext* refers to WWW or the World Wide Web and *Hypertext Link* refers to a link which connects two or more Information Resources, but goes beyond simple connections, it makes connections with other words that might define the concept or term, like *Allah* could have a hyperlink to *Islam* or *The Quran* in a book of religions or any other link dealing with Modern religions.

PROCEDURAL KNOWLEDGE

Procedural knowledge is also known as *How-to-do Knowledge,* is the knowledge applied in the performance of any task. It is also known as the *Implicit Knowledge* is different from various other categories of Knowledge as it is directly applied in performing a task or assignment.

If we look at it from the legal perspective, the Procedural Knowledge can be considered as the Intellectual Property; as under intellectual property law, owners are granted certain exclusive rights to a variety of intangible assets; defined by Wikipedia as:

Identifiable non-monetary assets that cannot be seen, touched or physically measured, which are created through time and/or effort and that are identifiable as a separate asset. There are two primary forms of intangibles - legal intangibles (such as trade secrets (e.g., customer lists), copyrights, patents, and trademarks) and competitive intangibles (such as knowledge activities (know-how, knowledge), collaboration activities, leverage activities, and structural activities)." Examples are; Artists work, Musicians Compositions or Authors literary works; similarly various Inventions and discoveries.

Procedural knowledge is its trade-dependent; thus it is not easily available and certainly much less easily available than the Declarative Knowledge.

Declarative Knowledge is also known as the Descriptive Knowledge of the Propositional Knowledge is a commonly known knowledge; like the knowledge of reading, writing, driving a car or performing a simple procedure like cooking or cleaning a room. Thus it can be expressed in simple language without any ambiguity or chance of misunderstanding. The Descriptive Knowledge is also known as the "Know-how Knowledge." In simple term the knowledge of doing regular daily mundane routine tasks.

However Procedural Knowledge involves more senses; like sight, hearing, smell, touch and taste, which is certainly one great advantage as it provides hands-on experience providing great help in solving problems and understanding of the limitations of a specific solution, etc.

PROCEDURAL KNOWLEDGE IN CLASSROOM

Procedural Knowledge is not learn in the class, it is learned outside the class through hit-and-trial process using hands and learning as one proceeds along. This is a goal oriented activity. One has to have a goal then then start working towards it, inventing tools and processes, procedures, learning models and performing activities to reach that specific goal. Of course one fails many times, gets derailed often and gets frustrated to the extent of abandoning the goal all together! Only the most persistent and stubborn find the way to reach the goal and success is attained.

The Procedural Knowledge sometimes comes close to the Tacit Knowledge. Some of the Procedures to succeed are learned over long durations and they are not written or even practice anywhere. It needs persistence, patience and lots of perseverance.

According to Cauley, 1986, "It can be tasks of specific rules, skills, actions, and sequences of actions employed to reach goals" a student uses in the classroom (Cauley, 1986). Cauley give the example for procedural knowledge as how a child learns to count on their hand/fingers when first learning math.

DECLARATIVE KNOWLEDGE

The static or factual data or information which is stored in some sort of storage, like human memory, computer storage or literature, which remains unchanged overtime, is called the Declarative Knowledge. The Declarative knowledge is also known as the Propositional Knowledge or the Description Knowledge.

Since it is a knowledge based on facts of life; how things work, what are their attributes and what are the relationships between them and other things, processes or events formulate the area of Declarative Knowledge. In short the Declarative Knowledge is the manual of understanding and getting things done.

We have already seen that the Procedural Knowledge is the understanding of how to work and operate a machine, let's say to perform! It is also termed as the know-how knowledge. Thus one can become more skilled in operation or solving a problem solving by depending on the Procedural Knowledge than Declarative Knowledge.

ARTIFICIAL INTELLIGENCE

As the term implies it is not the real intelligence or real knowledge, it is actually provided to a machine by embedding the Procedural Knowledge to its memory and then let it perform accordingly. Procedural Reasoning System or PRS is such an example. The Procedural Reasoning System or PRS is a framework of creating a real-time reasoning system (RTRS) to tackle the complex problems in a real time environment. To make use of PRS a set of knowledge set is defined and then PRS uses that to attain its goal, like navigating a robot through a complex maze. There is a device with in the RTRS called the Interpreter which is actually the data bank holding the set of procedures to operate a given algorithm or solve the complex problem.

The Interpreter is also tasked to maintain the attributes of the real world and how the various tasks are performed or achieved. Depending on this the interpreter sequences the tasks or goals to be attempted and at the same time it matches the Procedural Knowledge area which is to be applied to this problem solving challenge.

If AI Systems were to use the Declarative Knowledge, the set of instruction or operational information would mainly be about the basic actions that the robot might be able to perform like going ahead, stopping or turning etc. Thus the performance of the robot would be very restrictive is solving the problems or achieving any tasks.

DISPERSED KNOWLEDGE

The Dispersed Knowledge is the information which is not deposited into a specific set or repository; it is dispersed in the Universe. It is not controlled by an entity or organization. In other words it is the General Knowledge. As in the case of the General Knowledge, the Dispersed Knowledge is neither consistent nor is it trust worthy. It differs depends on the knowledge, understanding and motives of the knowledge holder. Thus as it differs variedly, one cannot be certain of its validity, completeness or accuracy. This might even be changed intentionally depend on the situations.

SITUATED KNOWLEDGE

The Situated Knowledge uses the characteristics features of the area to use the tools for finding the solutions; it is not principled thus it has no context or background. It is situation based thus the rules and modus operandi is different for each situation. The teams working research in different areas must recognize and adjust to the local conditions, specific practices and idiosyncrasies of the population of that area. Interestingly, these conditions changes from area to area and even locality to locality within a town let alone with in a country.

CONCLUSION

There is no life without Knowledge. There can be no systems operational without the Knowledge and the proper Knowledge Management. It is up to the individuals to look at the knowledge using the wholesome approach. The following must be considered and used when dealing with the Knowledge Management:

1. What is the problem at hand?
2. What is the problem universe?
3. What are the parameters?
4. What are the key actuators?
5. What are the constraints?
6. What is the Knowledge set available?
7. How is the knowledge classified?
8. What is the are the expected results?
9. What is the research teams mix of expetiese?
10. What type of knowledge is required to solve the problem?
11. Is the knowledge easily available or is it obscured?
12. Would the IT modeling required?
13. What are the expertise of the team?
14. Is time a constraint?
15. Is funding a constraint?
16. Any possible pitfalls?

REFERENCES

Bicycle and motorcycle dynamics. (n.d.). Wikipedia: The Free Encyclopedia. Retrieved from http://en.wikipedia.org/wiki/Bicycle_and_motorcycle_dynamics

Collins, H. M. (2001). Tacit knowledge, trust and the Q of sapphire. *Social Studies of Science*, *31*(1), 71–85. doi:10.1177/030631201031001004

Gordon, J. E. (2006). *The new science of strong materials*. Penguin Books.

Nonaka, I., & Takeuchi, H. (1995). *The knowledge creating company: how Japanese companies create the dynamics of innovation* (p. 284). New York, NY: Oxford University Press.

Nonaka, I., & von Krogh, G. (2009). Perspective-tacit knowledge and knowledge conversion: Controversy and advancement in organizational knowledge creation theory. *Organization Science*, *20*(3), 635–652. doi:10.1287/orsc.1080.0412

Parsaye, K., & Chignell, M. (1988). *Expert systems for experts* (p. 365). Hoboken, NJ: Wiley.

ADDITIONAL READING

Bao, Y., & Zhao, S. (2004). MICRO contracting for tacit knowledge - A study of contractual arrangements in international technology transfer. *Problems and Perspectives of Management*, *2*, 279–303.

Brohm, R. (1999). Bringing Polanyi onto the theatre stage: A study on Polanyi applied to knowledge management. In *Proceedings of the ISMICK Conference*, Erasmus University, Rotterdam, The Netherlands, 1999, (pp. 57–69).

Brohm, R. (2005). *Polycentric order in organizations*. Erasmus University Rotterdam: Published dissertation ERIM, hdl:1765/6911.

Dalkir, K. (2005). *Knowledge management in theory and practice* (pp. 82–90).

Gourlay, S. (2007). An activity centered framework for knowledge management . In McInerney, C. R., & Day, R. E. (Eds.), *Rethinking knowledge management*. Springer. doi:10.1007/3-540-71011-6_2

Patriotta, G. (2004). Studying organizational knowledge. *Knowledge Management Research and Practice*, *2*(1).

Ploszajski, P., Saquet, A., & Segalla, M. (2004). *Le savoir tacite dans un contexte culturel* (z:). Les Echos, Le Quotidien de L'Economie, 18 Novembre 2004, Paris 2004.

Polanyi, M. (1983). *The tacit dimension*. Doubleday & Co.

Sanders, A. F. (1988). *Michael Polanyi's post critical epistemology, a reconstruction of some aspects of 'tacit knowing*. Amsterdam, The Netherlands: Rodopi.

Smith, M. K. (2003). Michael Polanyi and tacit knowledge. In *The encyclopedia of informal education*. Retrieved from www.infed.org/thinkers/polanyi.htm

Tsoukas, H. (2003). Do we really understand tacit knowledge? In Easterby-Smith, M., & Lyles, M. A. (Eds.), *The Blackwell handbook of organizational learning and knowledge management* (pp. 411–427). Cambridge, MA: Blackwell Publishing.

KEY TERMS AND DEFINITIONS

Declarative Knowledge: The static or factual data or information which is stored in some sort of storage, like human memory, computer storage or literature, which remains unchanged overtime, is called the Declarative Knowledge. The Declarative knowledge is also known as the Propositional Knowledge or the Description Knowledge.

Implicit Knowledge: Is that which has been in existence for some time and is being used commonly and is available easily. It has been tried and tested and finally classified and stored in a physical media like books and literature or may even be available in form of information available on the hyperspace.

Knowledge: It is a knowing and understanding of facts, figures in form or Data or Information about something or some entity. Knowledge can be acquired by various sources which could include facts and figures from books, news media, discussions or books.

Knowledge Tagging: Is described, classified, categorized and referenced for easy access and understanding in some form of storage devices or containers. These containers are called the knowledge Tags.

Procedural Knowledge: Is also known as How-to-do Knowledge, is the knowledge applied in the performance of any task. It is also known as the Implicit Knowledge is different from various other categories of Knowledge as it is directly applied in performing a task or assignment.

Tacit Knowledge: Is knowledge which is difficult to transfer from one person to another by means of writing it down or explaining it. This is a learned, acquired, experienced and experimented knowledge that is gained over years of hard work and dedication.

Chapter 19
A Software Engineering Approach for Access Control to Multi-Level-Security Documents

Muneer Ahmad
King Faisal University, Saudi Arabia

Low Tang Jung
University Technology PETRONAS, Malaysia

Noor Zaman
King Faisal University, Saudi Arabia

Fausto Pedro García Márquez
University of Castilla-La Mancha, Spain

ABSTRACT

Access control to multi level security documents is very important and challenging issue. Millions of organizations around the globe intend to apply security levels over their confidential documents to protect from unauthorized use. Some numbered access control approaches have been proposed and an optimal solution is the need of the time. This chapter presents an overview of a robust software engineering approach for access control to multi-level security documents. The access control system incorporates stages including data refinement, text comprehension, and understanding of multi-stage protection and application levels. It will scan the document, tag the sections of certain text, understand the meaning of various levels, group-up the text using bottom-up approach, and then classify the levels as per protection norms (set as organization wise) defined. This approach will be very helpful for multi-level protection of precious information. Only authorized users would be able to access the information relevant to them as defined by the authorities.

INTRODUCTION

The information which is tagged can be termed as sensitive information (restricted by a group of people or government, agencies as per rules defined for its protection). The defined system must provide the check and balance to deal with tagged documents (identified as secure), e.g. the demands to secure particular information set under prescribed norms (to make it protected by unlawful use). It is worth mentioning that classified information passes through a series of steps to make it in a form that is secure.

DOI: 10.4018/978-1-4666-3679-8.ch019

The institutions may take benefits by relying over usefulness of precious document handling that include the way to share, collect, functionalize, feedback, associate and provide the fair and secure means for its protection. Gupta (1996) narrated that such multi level processing leads us to a fact that relevant information should be provided to relevant authority at specified time employing secure means. The only possibility that provide the state of the art methodology is to adopt certain criteria's that govern the security classification. All these efforts to protect the documents from unauthorized use are to judge the importance of documents travelling from one hand to another hand passing through different unsecure levels. The classification phenomenon reflects that all documents can't be treated with one norm of security. Different documents must possess different security levels. As an analogy, in an office environment, the documents arriving and departing the top management have different security requirements against the normal documents.

The series of channels that may describe the said phenomenon is to look for potential contributors that claim the ownership of this information, one the ownership is identified, the documents can be assigned different labels (as per policies defied to protect the information). The labeled information is further passed through security checks (security controls) as per some defined criteria. Finally the security controls can be listed against each classification as explained by Murata (2003).

Another very important aspect to protect this information depends over the factors that relevant institute demands the importance under which the information should be handled. So before implementing the security policies, the organization should review the levels of security tags set for protecting specified information. It is also mandatory that information in how much old? In the case, protection levels are rarely used, some latest information important for the organization should

be made protected (Wikipedia, 2012). Legislation and development of security norms also vary from organization to organization.

Some Common protection levels that could be used by organizations are termed as public, trusty, confidential and private. The government institutes may incorporate classification labels as Sensitive and Unclassified, confidential, Normal Secret and Top Secret. It is mandatory to mention the relationship between these tags for confirming the best product.

Secondly, once the security levels are implemented under organization policies and norms, the people working in such institutes must be given some basic and advanced training to get a clear picture for securing information. They must also understand and focus the need to protect their information. Likewise, different places may incorporate different security levels as per need (WikiPedia (Wiki), 2012).

A very little work has been done and being researched in the area of documents protection from unauthorized use. Current, state of the art research done by Alhammouri (2008) depicts piece wise security classification (may incorporate some approaches like TOP-BOTTOM approach).

Another current approach proposed by Damiani (2000) for document protection is utilization of access control model (using XML). This model has been implemented with a restriction to process it up to DTD (Data type definition) level only. It makes each data type definition to be pertained with specified information wrapped in the document (deciding which part can be accessed by user and which can't be).

The document protection can also be made by fragmenting the security levels into different security classes, as an analogy, the University of Auckland (New Zeeland) developed a tool for security protection of local documents. The tool implemented the security level as described the norms set by the institute. Another institute NIST

(National Institute of standards and Technology) developed a tool for its organization to protect official documents. Major focus was made for documents traffic coming in and going out from their institute (mother and children institutes). Microsoft Office Document Classifier also helps in classification and provides certain protection labels for securing Office documents. The tools Applies document to be marked between the security levels confidential, secret and normal etc. It also helps to protect the hidden information, avoids the leakage of precious information from unsecure use. The tool also makes it sure that information kept in the document can only be handled by concerned people. Another tool developed by Microsoft is Titus Labs Document Classification that is considered as a premier classification tool for Microsoft Office. It manages to protect the high level important information passing between specified institutions such as government and military offices (potential customers are made able to manage the classification, spread and get awareness for information protection vitally). The tool forces the user to select the suitable classification labels from the interactive menu of program, generates spreadsheet and can help in making presentations). Another very important tool called ArticSof (Cryptographic tool) is being employed for email classification, encryption and digital signature. Finally SECLORE is considered as a right management tool for securing information that employs dynamic rights to distribute the information among users for access control).

Zhao et al., (2008) proposed an algorithm that achieves more significant results over existing traditional approaches. The robustness of this approach is independence to align any sequence (any number) either local or global. It could further address the local optima problems associated with sequence alignments. The overall significance in results had been depicted as comparative analysis in gene sequences.

Arslan and He (2006) proposed another approach for MSA alignment. The solution has been given in the form of an approach incorporating 2 sections (layers) consisting of one section as DPA matrix (alignment). The algorithm analyzes each sequence using DPA approach section-wise. It was observed that depicted solution is more significant against common prevailing algorithms.

Davidson (2001) proposed a solution combining the flavors of DPA and another traditional algorithm reducing the overall computational complexity for sequence analysis. The addressed solution relates dynamic matrix at reverse diagonals. Significant set of mini solutions were combined to generate a resultant sophisticated solution claimed as an optimal one over existing traditional solutions.

Rashid, Abdullah, Talib and Ali (2006) presented a moderate DPA based approach for alignment of sequences employing reduction of quantity of nucleotide characters resulting in a transformation to RNA sequences reducing the lengthy sequences (differences and similarities have been identified to bring optimal results).

Agrawal, Ankit, Huang and Xiaoqiu (2008) has proposed an approach that is a modification of traditional iterative approach for increasing the performance measure (introduced multiple parameter sets). Results obtained through different experiments presented a significance of proposed approach over existing common approaches. It incorporated a generation of different related matrices (diverse distances between them). Optimal results were achieved by adjusting the weights.

Chen, Pan, Juan and Liu (2006) proposed an algorithm that was based on segmenting for improving the results (MSA alignment). The local optimization greatly helped in reducing the time complexity and achieving the significance. The proposed algorithm was layered into three stages, starting from partitioning of sequences to sub sequences and then combining / integrating the results to obtain a final score. The middle section is dependant over MSA taken from traditional Ant colony approach. The benefit of employing this traditional approach was to reduce the local traps for finding a good approximate solution.

Rajko and Aluru (2004) proposed a solution that determines a good approximation of both time and space complexities. The algorithm was found complex O (mn) for time and O (m+n) for space (m, n can be termed as sequence lengths). It was observed that proposed technique is beneficial equally for all sequence alignment problems that commonly take long time and provide inefficient results using traditional DPA and sequence alignment approaches.

Zne-Jung Lee and Chou-Yuan Lee (2005) provided a solution for MSA aided with a computational approach (fuzzy algorithm for genes addressing local optimization). The performance of common traditional algorithm has been rectified by addressing fuzzy approach with local search. For this solution, the algorithm for genes was used for multiple directional searches within a range of sub-solutions. It also incorporated fuzzy theory for auto adjustment of GA features like cross-over and mutation. It was observed that proposed solution was equally applicable for all existing systems related with MSA.

Nasser, Vert, Nicolescu and Murray (2007) proposed a solution in the form of a fuzzy logic (denying the notions of exact matching of sequences). Some special parameters that could intact with Fuzzy logic were obtained for best possible match. The research resulted in an establishment of a robust assembler. The proposed solution worked well for either low latency data that was inacceptable for existing approaches. The suggested assembler was examined from set of sequences from some projects (Drosophila and Arabidopsis). The proposed solution was analyzed over different datasets and significance was observed over existing solutions.

Ahmad and Mathkour (2009) proposed a recursive solution for MSA. The solution was found beneficial for all kinds of alignments. The algorithm performed local and global analysis by operating over a set of diverse genetic sequences. A scoring scheme was employed to calculate the relevance between different sections of sequences. Individual scores for sub section in sequences were accumulated to produce a final score for global calculations. The results achieved were found significant as compared with other traditional approaches.

Ahmad and Mathkour (2009) employed Matlab histograms as sequence comparison in a range of different sequences. The genetic data was transformed to image data. The algorithm read the image pixels by Matlab and generated section wise histograms. Finally, the histograms were compared to reveal the similarity and differences in sequences. The proposed solution was found equally useful for all kinds of alignments.

Ahmad proposed another recursive algorithm for text sequences (mono, bi and multi lingual). The algorithm was designed to remove all possible redundancies in a set of sequences. It was beneficial for large repositories of genetic sequences that carry duplication of genetic data resulting in a raw mass storage without benefits.

TEXT COMPARASION METHODOLOGIES

Some of the basic methodologies used for sequence comparisons are described as follows:

- An extension to DPA (Dynamic Programming Algorithm).
- Methods employing Progressive techniques.
- Methods employing Iterative techniques.

An Extension to DPA (Dynamic Programming Algorithm)

It was observed that traditional DPA Method that was basically used for GA (Global Alignment) over a set of data sequences could be refined to use for MSA (Multiple Sequence Alignment) with some certain limitations (can involve computational overheads by adding more weights as input data) which ultimately could reduce its performance.

Methods Employing Progressive Techniques

These methods are based on DPA (Dynamic Programming Method) that could build an alignment firstly aligning some similar sequences. It then adds progressively some unrelated sequences (the phase is called initial alignment). The basic components of this approach are CLUSTALW and PILEUP approaches.

The major drawbacks of such methods are relying over similar sequences. The significance is guaranteed for similar sequence data. On contrary, if sequence data are found dissimilar then degradation of performance is observed.

Methods Employing Iterative Techniques

These methods are found suitable when progressive techniques generate faulty results. Those faulty results can be rectified and improved employing these methods. Local alignment results are integrated to serve as global alignment that is rectified by iterative method (See Table 1). Some examples of such methods are MultiAlin(1988) and DIALIGN.

THE PROPOSED APPROACH

We have classified the proposed approach into three phases as follows:

1. Tagging and Analysis (Phase-1)

- Tagging Mechanism (Tag Editor)
- Tagging Memory (e.g. database or XML file)

Table 1. A comparative analysis of alignment methods

Method	Approach	Applicability	Suitability	Non Suitability	Performance
Dynamic Programming	Based on a scoring scheme	Sequence Alignment	Local and Global Alignment	Multi alignment	May involve computational overhead
An Extension of DPA	Global alignment	Sequence Alignment	All kinds	Degrades with increasing input size	Restricted to small and medium strands
Progressive Methods	Align most relevant sequences	Sequence Alignment	Multiple Sequence Alignment	Sequences with dissimilarity	Suitable for initial similarity and degrades with diverse chains
Iterative methods	Based on progressive methods	Sequence Alignment	Multiple Sequence Alignment	Lengthy and initial dissimilar chains	Involves computational overhead in increasing sequence length

2. Analysis of Un-Tagged Phrases (Phase-2)

- Analysis of un-tagged clauses
- Broken into words

3. Application of Security Policies (Phase-III)

- Placement of tagged and un-tagged clauses in order for application of security policies

Figure 1 describes the generic working model of this software engineering approach. The text document is passed through a series of filters that scan the document, generate and analyze the tokens based on memory models already attached with the

approach. The memory models depict the defined sets of phrases and their hierarchal relationship. It then tags the phrases in the following order,

- Reading Source Document
- Cutting Clauses into Specific Cutting Points
- Tagging Clauses
- Handling with Un-Tagged Clauses

In first phase, the proposed approach performs analysis over words in the documents by generating the tokens in some hierarchical steps in reading the source document. The document is scanned and analyzed based on the thresholds for separating points namely,

Figure 1. Generic working model of proposed system

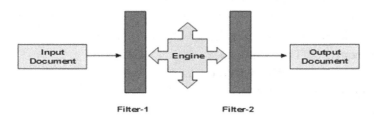

Figure 2. Filter-1 is a collection of classes responsible for fragment generation and analysis

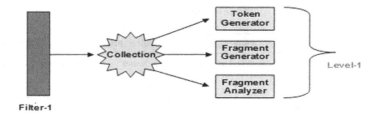

Figure 3. Text checker, clause checker and phrase checker

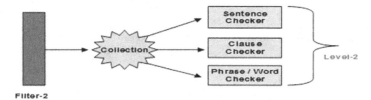

"a", "above", "after", "am", "an", "and", "any", "are", "as", "at", "because", "beyond", "by", "did", "do", "does", "except", "for", "from", "has", "if", "in", "is", "may", "nor", "nor", "of", "on", "or", "over", "shall", "since", "so", "such", "than", "that", "them", "then", "those", "till", "to", "under", "until", "up to", "was", "were", "what", "when". "where", "whereas", "who", "whom", "whose", "will", "with", "within"

We have also introduced the sentence break points for this particular analysis include Full Stop (.), Comma (,), Semi Colon (;), Colon (:)

The scanned document is partitioned in clauses with specific cutting points described previously.

Figure 2 describes the collection of classes that perform fragments and analysis. The clauses are tagged according to natural language processing rules. The tagged clauses are compared with the systems memory models for approximate comparisons. The untagged clauses are retagged based on certain predefined options (nature of clauses). The retagged clauses become the part of memory that helps to promptly relocate the phrases encounter in later scan of same or different documents.

In phase 2, all untagged clauses are processed. These clauses couldn't approximately map with the tagged memory.

Figure 3 depicts the sections of phase 2. Filter 2 parses the document by sentence analysis, clause checking and phrase / word checking. The untagged clauses are further analyzed by breaking them into words (granular level). The words are analyzed and fed into the translation memory after retagging.

In phase 3, the tagged and un-tagged text is marked according to security policies defined, e.g. top secret, secret, confidential, restricted, unclassified etc. Once the document is passed through the filters, it becomes protected from unauthorized use.

CONCLUSION

It has been observed that a very little work has been done and being researched in the area of security classification of documents, the proposed software engineering will classify the documents based on their security levels. It is engineered in the following by presenting a novel software engineering paradigm, analysis of text using bottom up approach, implementations of security at even granular levels, defining multi-level security authorities and channels. The proposed approach specifies the security classification of text document from un-authorized users. The mechanism is broken down into three phases. Phase 1 parses the document, filters it for tagged and un-tagged clauses. Phase-II works for fragmenting the clauses into sub clauses, comprehend, analyze and phase-III performs the application of security policies to the document. This approach is both good in single level and multi-level classification of information and will be considered as an enhancement towards the multi-level section wise security classification applications.

REFERENCES

Agrawal, A., & Huang, X. (2008). Pairwise DNA alignment with sequence specific transition-transversion ratio using multiple parameter sets. *International Conference on Information Technology, 17-20,* 89–93.

Ahmad, M., Khan, H. M., & Mathkour, H. (2009). An integrated statistical comparative analysis between variant genetic datasets of Mus musculus. *International Journal of Computational Intelligence in Bioinformatics and System Biology, 1*(2), 163-176. ISSN: 1755-8042

Ahmad, M., & Mathkour, H. (2009). *Genome sequence analysis by Matlab histogram comparison between Image-sets of genetic data*. Hong Kong: WCSET.

Alhammouri, M. (2007). Lecture Notes in Computer Science: *Vol. 4680. Management of groups and group keys in multi-level security environments* (pp. 75–80). Berlin, Germany: Springer. doi:10.1007/978-3-540-75101-4_7

Alhammouri, M. (2008). A design of an access control model for multilevel-security documents. *Advanced Communication Technology, 2*(17-20), 1476–1481.

Armstrong, C. J. (2007). Mapping information security curricula to professional accreditation standards. *Information Assurance and Security Workshop*, (pp. 30–35).

Arslan, A. N., & He, D. (2006). An improved algorithm for the regular expression constrained multiple sequence alignment problems. *Sixth IEEE Symposium on Bioinformatics and Bioengineering*, (pp. 121–126).

Baker, W. H. (2007). Is information security under control? *Investigating Quality in Information Security Management . Security & Privacy, 5*(1), 36–44. doi:10.1109/MSP.2007.11

Chen, Y., Pan, Y., Chen, Y., & Liu, W. (2006). Partitioned optimization algorithms for multiple sequence alignment. *20th International Conference on Advanced Information Networking and Applications,* Volume 2, (p. 5).

Damiani, E. (2000). Design and implementation of an access processor for XML documents. *Proceeding of the 9th International WWW Conference,* Amsterdam.

Davidson, A. (2001). A fast pruning algorithm for optimal sequence alignment, bioinformatics and bioengineering conference. *Proceedings of the IEEE 2nd International Symposium*, (pp. 49–56).

Desai, L. (2003). *Oracle collaboration suite: An Oracle Technical White Paper*. July 2003.

Gupta, M. (1996, November). Security classification for documents. *Computers & Security, 15*(1), 55–71. doi:10.1016/0167-4048(95)00023-2

Information Security. (n.d.). Wikipedia: The Free Encyclopedia. Retrieved from http://en.wikipedia.org/wiki/Information_security

Kajava, J. (2006). Information security standards and global business. *IEEE International Conference on Industrial Technology (ICIT),* (pp. 2091–2095).

Lee, Z.-J., & Lee, C.-Y. (2005). An intelligent system for multiple sequences alignment. *IEEE International Conference on Systems, Man and Cybernetics, 2,* 1042–1047.

Liu, R.-L. (2008). Interactive high-quality text classification. *Information Processing & Management, 44*(3), 1062–1075. doi:10.1016/j.ipm.2007.11.002

Murata, M. (2003). XML access control using static analysis. *Proceedings of the 10th ACM Conference on Computer and Communications Security,* Washington DC, USA.

Nasser, S., Vert, G. L., Nicolescu, M., & Murray, A. (2007). Multiple sequence alignment using fuzzy logic. *IEEE Symposium on Computational Intelligence and Bioinformatics and Computational Biology,* (pp. 304–311).

Rajko, S., & Aluru, S. (2004). Space and time optimal parallel sequence alignments. *IEEE Transactions on Parallel and Distributed Systems, 15*(12), 6. doi:10.1109/TPDS.2004.86

Rashid, N. A. A., Abdullah, R., Talib, A. Z. H., & Ali, Z. (2006). Fast dynamic programming based sequence alignment algorithm. *The 2nd International Conference on Distributed Frameworks for Multimedia Applications,* (pp. 1–7).

Saraçoğlu, R. (2008). A new approach on search for similar documents with multiple categories using fuzzy clustering. *Expert Systems with Applications*, *34*(4), 2545–2554. doi:10.1016/j.eswa.2007.04.003

Tan, S. (2008). An empirical study of sentiment analysis for Chinese documents. *Expert Systems with Applications*, *34*(4), 2622–2629. doi:10.1016/j.eswa.2007.05.028

Zhao, Y., Ma, P., Lan, J., Liang, C., & Ji, G. (2008). An improved ant colony algorithm for DNA sequence alignment. *International Symposium on Information Science and Engineering, Vol. 2*, (pp. 683–688).

Chapter 20
Trends in Information Security

Partha Chakraborty
Cognizant Technology Solutions, India

Krishnamurthy Raghuraman
Cognizant Technology Solutions, India

ABSTRACT

Information systems have transitioned from being designed for sophisticated users to systems for general populace. Have information security thoughts evolved likewise? The traditional understanding of security gravitated towards physical/network/platform/security and audit logging mechanisms. This chapter looks into evolution of information security, with the current impetus towards boundary-less enterprises, federated identities, the contemporary standards, and the need for federal governments to be involved in information security, ethics, and privacy concerns. With such a gamut of influencing forces, information security needs to be inbuilt with SDLC as a natural process rather than as an afterthought. This chapter covers information security trends in relation to cloud, mobile devices, and Bring Your Own Device. Convergence of information security with risk management and business process continuity is discussed. The authors indicate a few emerging research topics in the field of information security and outline the trends for future.

INTRODUCTION

Internet has enabled quick access of information transcending the limitations of time and geography. However, along with such convenience come grave risks: information on computers is more vulnerable to unauthorized access than information on printed papers. With physical papers, one can secure under lock and key. The ways of unauthorized access was limited. This is not true with information on computers. The silver lining is that the situation is not intractable: with the right application of techniques, tools and processes effective securing can be accomplished.

DOI: 10.4018/978-1-4666-3679-8.ch020

Though information security may mean different things to different people, one of the most succinct definitions is by the US Department of Defense (freedictionary.com, 2012):

The protection of information and information systems against unauthorized access or modification of information, whether in storage, processing, or transit, and against denial of service to authorized users.

An often repeated theme in any definition of information security is 'protection' (Whitman & Mattord, 2012). Well established core principles of information security are: *C*onfidentiality, *I*ntegrity and *A*vailability (*CIA* triad). Authentication enforces Confidentiality; Authorization enforces Integrity; Non-repudiation help enforce Availability. Deep appreciation of the information security principles coupled with insights on changing social and technical landscape and the business drivers will help in formulating the most appropriate way to accomplish information security.

Due to widespread access of electronic information for a variety of purposes, *information security has emerged as an interdisciplinary subject* covering technology to sociology to political science. This is fueled by reliable and cheap internet connectivity for a significant portion of world's population. According to a statistic published by The World Bank in 2010, a little more than 30% of the world population is using internet. The channels of access and ways of offering information services are going through significant changes with the arrival of mobile devices, cloud computing and social media. Such novel ways introduce new challenges for information security: more users, different channels of access, possibility for abuse. One can imagine that the most secure system is the one to which no one connects. The business realities are just the opposite: enterprises of today are characterized hyper connections.

The aim of this chapter is to equip the reader with a reasonable sense of appreciation of current trends in the area of information security and the approaches to deal with the challenges emerging from the recent trends. The focus of the chapter will be on information security as applicable to the realm of applications and data. This chapter will analyze how information security is influenced by federal governments and will briefly look at the landscape of standards and regulations. The chapter ends with an outline of some of the research topics in the field of information security.

BACKGROUND

Computers, internet and information systems trace their origins to defense and research organizations. The seed thoughts about the usage possibilities were remotely related to business and mass populace. Systems were meant for highly educated computer geeks doing scientific or military tasks. This is not quite so now. Information systems permeate all aspects of life of an average person. However, information security thoughts remained rigid and did not evolve sufficiently fast to accommodate the new arrival of users who had no knowledge on the workings of a computer.

Computers and information systems have proved themselves to be a reliable part in our unending quest for efficient ways of accomplishing a task. Now our lives are inseparably bonded with information systems and it is no longer an option for us whether to have a digital identity or not. With such pervasiveness and reliance of information systems in our everyday lives, the concerns of privacy and national security have risen to such a magnitude that federal governments promulgate regulations on how to deal with digital information.

While, on one hand we see increasing reliance on information systems by the citizen, the businesses are continuously faced with pressures to innovate. Businesses are increasingly collaborating. Fresh ways to secure information – one that allows and encourages flow of ideas yet not compromise on security is required. Access to information is a prerequisite for creative thinking.

An interesting evolutionary force is the technological innovations in the computing marketplace. Cloud computing, social media, mobile applications, bring your device to work all have varying – at times conflicting - information security needs. Often lost sight of, is the fact that information security is influenced and guided by enterprise business strategy. Business needs are the foundational influence that is not easily discerned in information security strategy. Ways of making it more explicit is highly desirable to bring the much needed business blessings for information security initiatives.

Information security is at the intersection of formidable forces: technological advances, increasing user base that is not computer savvy, fading of enterprise 'perimeterized' security fence, growing government regulations. This has made information security acquire a flavor and context that is very unique, intellectually challenging and actively researched. We will sample some of the pressing challenges and solutions in the coming sections.

INFORMATION SECURITY AND COLLABORATION ACROSS BOUNDARIES

The traditional success of enterprise was almost completely influenced by access to capital, raw materials and resources. Enterprises would create value and offer to consumers. Consumers had no choice but to accept what was offered by enterprises. The enterprises were built to operate all within: vertically integrated handling all functions themselves. Enterprises believed in 'owning' the resources and conditioned by this thought, information security evolved with a perimeter demarcating 'in' or 'out'. Such a view is anachronistic.

With globalization and easy access to information through the internet, means of collaboration have taken new but welcome hues. Talent can be accessed practically anywhere in the world and effectively collaborated. Consumers have themselves been part of value creation: one needs to look no further than an Amazon or an eBay. Tremendous value is created by consumers in the forms of ratings, suggestions, etc. Thus, the unidirectional value creation has undergone a metamorphosis: value today is co-created by consumers and no enterprise is big enough to have all resources and operate as a silo. Such overwhelming transformational realities have a telling influence in the discipline of enterprise security. Access to enterprises information can no longer be restricted to the employees: in areas where collaboration is required, access must be granted to partners as well. This calls for federated access to information resources. *Information security is emerging as a shared responsibility* within the federated ecosystem.

We will illustrate with a fictitious scenario. Get Well Medicines Inc is a global pharmaceutical company. The company has several research labs across the world for discovering new medicines. Its research spending has come under increasing board scrutiny due to the poor results in advancing new drug compounds. The situation is further exacerbated by spiraling costs in getting the right talent and the purchase of expensive research equipment. Get Well Medicines management met and discussed ways to partner with smaller companies providing specific research services. The management identified that some of the assays can be conducted by partnering with Elysium Clinical Services located in a cost effective destination. The management thought that the best way to do is to request Elysium Clinical Services to run the assays and send the results in agreed data format for upload to the Get Well Medicines data systems.

In the initial few months, all worked fine. Elysium Clinical Services wanted to provide value added services in terms of interpretations of assay results and it was much welcomed by Get Well Medicines. However, a crucial problem remains to be solved. In order to meaningfully analyze the assay results, Elysium Clinical Services needs visibility to a lot more surrounding data around the assays which exists in Get Well Medicines enterprise systems. Now, Get Well Medicines is faced with the dilemma: it cannot provide unfettered access to the partner as critical information is maintained in its systems nor can it deny the value added service as it will help the company to get the full benefit of collaboration.

Enterprises today are faced with this painful reality: enable collaboration yet protect information assets. From technology and process perspectives, the following are essential:

- **Identification:** The user should be able to use his/her existing login credentials and transparently access all the resources required. In the above case, Elysium Clinical Services employee should not be required to login with different sets of user id and password to Get Well Medicines. Creating additional identification mechanisms will act as a barrier to collaboration as the user will be forced to remember multiple user ids and password.
- **Tag Information Assets:** Get Well Medicines needs to segregate its information assets by various levels and assign collaboration possibilities. Examples: 'Critical' information is not available for any partner; 'Sensitive' information can be shared provided trust is established.
- **Policies and Contracts:** Information assets must be wrapped by policies that implement business requirements on the allowable access.
- **Active Monitoring:** Due to increased collaboration, the access of information must be monitored continuously against the

business contracts to ensure appropriate usage.

Federated Identity

Federation operates by a group of willing entities coming together and explicitly agreeing on ways of determining the authorized access (Bertino & Takahashi, 2011). In our scenario, Get Well Medicines needs to establish trust (See Figure 1) with Elysium Clinical Systems; when Elysium Clinical Services user logs in to Get Well Medicines information system (Step 1, in Figure 1), they will be transparently redirected to Elysium Clinical Services for authentication (Step 2 and 3, in Figure 1). After that, Get Well Medicines will allow access to the Elysium Clinical Services user.

Security tokens play the critical interplay between the parties of federation. SAML (Security Assertion Markup Language) and WS-Federation are the two common federated single-sign on (SSO) standards. SAML is an open standard developed by the OASIS (Organization for the Advancement of Structured Information Standards). WS-Federation (part of Web Services Security Framework) was developed by a group of companies led by Microsoft and it offers equivalent federated SSO functionality to SAML.

In the area of federated security, two other relevant protocol/standards are:

- **OAuth:** Open protocol for allowing access to resources. Attempts to provide a standard way for developers to offer their services via an API without forcing their users to expose their passwords. The concept is similar to that of valet key of luxury cars – allow access but limit possibilities.
- **OpenId:** Open Standards for how users can be authenticated in a decentralized way. Typically used in web sites.

Figure 1. Establishing trust across domains

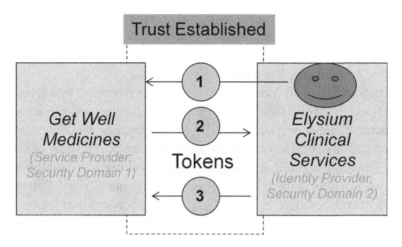

Figure 2. Information assets tagging & access policies

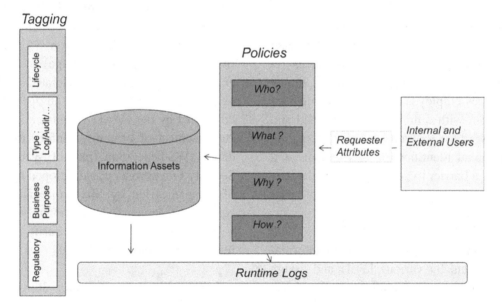

Information assets need to be tagged to determine the sensitive of information (See Figure 2). First of all, identification of assets that need to be exposed for collaboration must be done. Policies must be created to determine the level of access as depicted in Figure 2.

The access policies will interrogate at runtime and make such determinations as:

- **Who:** Who is seeking this information? Is it internal user or a partner? If so, what partner and what channel of access?
- **What:** What is the information sought? Is it very sensitive or can be shared?
- **Why:** What part of the business process does this information asset belong to? Is there a need for accessing this information?

- **How:** How is the information accessed (direct SQL, web services, APIs)? Is it for reading purposes (query) or transactional?

Policies should be implemented based on the information asset tagging and the requester attributes. All access requests should be actively monitored. With enterprises demanding seamless collaboration, the underlying software and infrastructure must be made inherently capable for meeting such business needs. This requires different thinking in how software development needs to be approached (Kelley Holland (2008)). *Information security has to be well thought out and inbuilt in the SDLC process itself.*

SDLC and Information Security

Information systems must be able to operate without compromising on security in collaboration scenario and in different deployment models (cloud computing) and ways of access (mobility). *Information security has to be intrinsic in systems* – not built as an afterthought. This begs for a fundamental rethink on how SDLC can incorporate security angle in all of its phases:

- Requirements Analysis Phase
    - Identify Information Types
    - Categorize Information Systems
    - Access Business Impact
- Design Phase
    - Risk Assessment, Threat Modeling
    - Select and Document Security Controls
    - Design Security Architecture – Defense in Depth, Fail Securely, etc.
- Development Phase
    - Develop Security Documentation
    - Develop System Security Plan
- Testing Phase
    - Conduct security testing

During requirement analysis, a clear understanding of the security requirements and the forces of influence must be carried out (Michael Howard and Steve Lipner (2006)). Abuse use cases can be developed which will feed to threat modeling activity. Threat modeling is an extremely critical step that forces the development teams to think about how the application that they are building can be compromised. Other design principles include fail economy, defense in depth, safe default, least privilege, etc. Developers need to be trained to write secure code. Automated tools need to be used to test for security defects in design. Figure 3 illustrates some components in secure SDLC.

Risks will be inherent in the software development if carried out without specific security focus. It is important to keep unrelenting focus on the understanding of the user base, data classifications, technology choices and security threats. Regulatory mandates great influence the extent and intensity for information security. Where privacy laws are well developed, the information security must be designed to comply with them.

Even though we discuss about information security during the software development process, the actual origin of information security stems right from business strategy itself.

INFORMATION SECURITY – BUSINESS ORIENTATION

Information security is often viewed as a technical domain. Words like firewalls, IP, digital signatures, encryption add further deterrence in attempts to give non IT perspective. Nonetheless, *information security has deep business significance* (LeVeque, 2006). Business risks influence information security principles; business continuity (Merkow & Breithaupt, 2006) is affected by how securely information assets are managed. At its core, information security is about preservation of confidentiality, integrity and availability of

Figure 3. Secure SDLC components

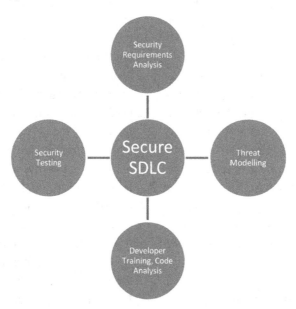

information. Let us briefly discuss how all these have deep business significance.

- **Confidentiality:** How will we ensure the privacy of sensitive customer information like social security number, credit card number,bank account number? Any breach of sensitive information like this will impact the business continuity and exposes the enterprise to not only bad publicity but also to legal penalties. What processes and technology can help ensure required confidentiality for running the business?
- **Integrity:** As much as confidentiality and availability is important, how will we ensure that the information is not tampered with? What policies and systems we have in place to ensure information integrity? Most decisions are taken based on information and hence it is extremely critical that the integrity of information is preserved at all times.
- **Availability:** How will we ensure that the information is available for authorized use whenever required? As lives are increasingly digital, it is extremely critical to ensure availability of systems and informa-

tion to carry out even mundane operations like withdrawing money, buying groceries, paying utility bills. The risk of lack of availability will, in most cases, influence the very existence of enterprise in competitive business environment.

Information security plays a pivotal role in risk management and business continuity. *Information security is closely linked with the business strategy.* Cognizing the central role of business in information security, 'Information Systems Audit and Control Association', better known as ISACA has come up with Business Model for Information Security (BMIS) (See Table 1).

BMIS ("An Introduction to Business Model of Information Security" www.isaca.org, 2012) proposes four legs each interconnected to one another. The legs are:

- Organization Design and Strategy
- **People:** Who implements which part of the strategy
- **Technology:** All tools, infrastructure and applications that enable to get things done, to realize the processes

Table 1. Dynamic interconnections of BMIS

Dynamic Interconnections	Brief
Emergence	How new ways and ideas that arise from people can be channelized through a process?
Human Factors	Connects Tehcnology and People
Enabling and Support	Connects Technology with Process
Culture	How the organization relates to its people? How empowered are they?
Governing	Sets limits on what the organization can do, how it will be monitored. Enabled by process.
Architecture	How technology helps organization achieves its strategy?

- **Process:** All formal and informal ways of getting things done

The four legs have Dynamic Interconnections (DI) with one another.

The model can be put to practical use by the following suggested steps:

Step 1: Analyze the business by business processes. For example, an insurance claims process may consist of claim filing, fraud detection, analysis of claims, handling inquiry, payment, dispute resolution. For each major constituent of business process such as – say 'analysis of claims' analyze possible business impact for information security threat.

Step 2: Risk Analysis. Figure out the possibility of occurrence of security threats. Prioritize the high risks.

Step 3: Risk Management. For the prioritized high risks, identify possible security measures. The security measures must be credible and should have all elements required (people, process, tools) for implementation.

Step 4: Map to BMIS: Understand where the strengths and weakness of the enterprise are. For instance, the organizational strategy may have a disconnect with technology and it will be revealed by 'Architecture DI'. This will help in implementation of well thought out response plan.

For instance, an organization may wish to benefit from the new advances in technology like cloud computing, mobile applications, social media and work force opting to use their computing devices of choice. Information security must enable – not restrict – such opportunities.

Information Security and Social Media

Social media has changed the possibilities of communication and collaboration as it addresses the basic human need to relate to one another. That social media is popular is eloquently illustrated by the fact that Facebook is perhaps the most visited website in the world. With more than a billion people using various forms of social media, enterprises can no longer afford to ignore it (See Box 1).

Getting closer to the customer is the mantra for any enterprise and that appears tantalizingly possible by tapping to the social media. Efforts like Social CRM aimed at integrating voices from social media with internal data sources are gaining foothold in enterprises. Obviously, such initiatives have a direct bearing on information security. Table 2 illustrates this.

Paradoxically, in the very origin of social media is sown the seed for information security challenge: assumed trust. In the individual centric social media, since the interactions are within the trusted groups, the security was assumed. However, when social media gets integrated with enterprises, there is a need for a more solemn outlook. Figure 4 illustrates components of a possible social media information security policy.

Box 1.

The Benign Power of Social Media *http://www.govtech.com/pcio/CIOs-Social-Media-Security-Risks-021111.html* *When a deadly tornado touched down in Cincinnati, Ark., last New Year's Eve, state officials could have relied on typical channels like TV and radio to warn citizens of dangerous road conditions and weather patterns. Instead, the Arkansas Homeland Security and Preparedness Agency chose to tweet up-to-the-minute storm reports. The result: "We were overwhelmed by the level of volunteers who came in to support our citizens in their time of need," said Arkansas CTO Claire Bailey. "We had to turn people away."*

Table 2. Social media and information security

Use Case	Examples	Information Security Challenges
Grass Root Information Source	Engage with customers directly and hear about product or service complaint	• Identifying where to hear and what to hear • Whether to feed data back to enterprise
Sentiment Analysis	Understanding brand perception about a product	• Accessing and analyzing unstructured data • Categorization, encryption
Viral Marketing	Stimulate sales by word of mouth and promotions	• Sharing sensitive information • Regulatory Compliance • Ensuring authenticity of purchase requests
Form Communities	Grouping like minded people and targeting specific messages	• Privacy and Ethics • Compliant with Regulations

Figure 4. Components of social media information security policy

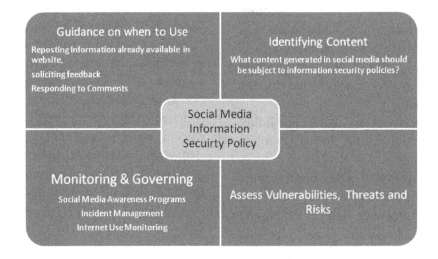

The below are some tips on dealing with social media from information security perspective:

- Establish a response system. Actively monitor and respond.
- Use to further engage with regulators. Report suspicious activity to regulatory authorities.
- Have specific guidelines for employees and partners.
- Continuously educate and engage with your employees.

INFORMATION SECURITY AND CLOUD COMPUTING

Ease of access to resources through internet coupled with advances in hardware technology has created fertile soil for revolutionary and awesome possibilities in computing. Due to years of successful offshore initiatives, location independence (that work can happen elsewhere) has gained credibility in enterprises. At this opportune mix of evolutionary forces, were sown the seeds for transformation of traditional hardware and software market to IT services market. How can computing be achieved as operating costs as opposed to capital costs? To look at this, one needs to see how computing has evolved historically.

Broadly, the computing evolution can be considered as having four stages: Mainframes, Client-Server, Web Applications and Cloud Computing.

Stage 1: Arrival of Mainframe – created the power of processing beyond manual capabilities.
Stage 2: Client Server – gave business users access to computing capabilities.
Stage 3: Web Applications – gave greater ability to collaborate across organizations and boundaries.
Stage 4: Cloud Computing – IT capabilities itself provided as services therefore removing the need for on premise infrastructure.

National Institute of Standards and Technology (NIST) defines cloud computing as '*a model for enabling ubiquitous, convenient, on-demand network access to a shared pool of configurable computing resources (e.g., networks, servers, storage, applications, and services) that can be rapidly provisioned and released with minimal management effort or service provider interaction*'.

Pregnant definition, indeed! Fundamental implication of this is that control of IT assets will no longer be possible by enterprise IT teams alone. Cloud provider will manage parts of the IT estate. *Thus information security has transformed to be a shared responsibility* – between enterprise IT and the cloud provider. This calls for great deal of clarity on who does what and how information security is approached (See Box 2).

Such tectonic shifts alter the fundamental contours of information security domain. As computing evolved over the years, the attendant information security challenges concomitantly kept its pace of change: from bothering itself about how to securely feed data to mainframe machines to how to protect information assets residing in an alien environment. In fact, according to most surveys, 60-80% of enterprises cite security concerns as the number one inhibitor to cloud adoption.

To understand the true import for information security arising out of cloud computing (Vic (J.R.) Winkler (2011)), a closer study of the model of cloud computing is warranted. The cloud model has some essential characteristics, delivered via a fix set of service models, in predetermined deployment methods. Table 3 illustrates this.

Private cloud is infrastructure that will be used only by the enterprise (not shared) and shows the essential characteristics listed above. Public cloud is shared infrastructure. Hybrid cloud is combination of private and public clouds: parts may reside in private (See Table 4). Community cloud is for a group of people/enterprises for specific business objectives.

Box 2.

> *Faux Pas in Cloud!*
>
> http://money.cnn.com/2011/06/22/technology/dropbox_passwords/index.htm
>
> *It's the security nightmare scenario: A website stuffed with sensitive documents leaves all of its customer data unprotected and exposed. It happened this week to Dropbox, a cloud storage site used by 25 million customers to store documents, videos, photos and other files. For four hours on Sunday, a site glitch let visitors use any password to log in to customers' accounts.*
>
> *"This should never have happened," Dropbox wrote in its blog.*
>
> *But it did -- and as individuals and corporations move to storing sensitive information in online lockers, they could get burned.*
>
> *"Any trust in the cloud is too much trust in the cloud -- it's as simple as that," says Dave Aitel, president and CEO of security firm Immunity Inc. "It's pretty much the standard among security professionals that you should put on the cloud only what you would be willing to give away."*

Table 3. Cloud computing model

	Essential Characteristics	*Service Model*	*Deployment Methods*
CLOUD COMPUTING MODEL	• On Demand, Self Service • Network Access • Resource Pooling • Rapid Elasticity • Measured Service	• Software as a Service (SaaS) • Platform as a Service (PaaS) • Infrastructure as a Service (IaaS)	• Private Cloud • Public Cloud • Community Cloud • Hybrid Cloud

Table 4. Cloud computing and information security

Delivery Model and Deployment Methods	*Examples*	*Impact on Information Security*
SaaS	• Billing • Document Management • Human Resources Management	*Only application will be accessed. Hence, security related to web browser and the application are the focus.*
PaaS	• Database • Dev and Testing Environments • Business Intelligence	*Platform components and how the platform is created will be important to understand and test.*
IaaS	• Compute Resources • Storage	*Virtualization Security is important. The infrastructure is simply exposed and the impact is around how it is made as a service.*
Private Cloud	• Cloud exclusive for enterprise • Could be on premise or bought from a cloud provider	*If on premise, no different than how we will approach any other application.* *If procured from outside, access concerns (to the cloud) need to be looked into.*
Public Cloud	• Amazon Electronic Compute Cloud, • Windows Azure Platform Services, • IBM Blue Cloud, • Sun Cloud	*Concerns around sharing of infrastructure*
Hybrid Cloud	• Enterprises having production data infrastructure in house and dev/test infrastructure on cloud	*How are private and public clouds linked? What goes where? How is it secured?*
Commodity Cloud	• Microsoft Government Community Cloud	*Concerns around sharing data, ensuring privacy and monitoring access*

The service model and deployment methods determine the type of information security challenges enterprises will have to confront with.

Cloud Security Alliance (CSA) (Cloud Security Alliance, https://cloudsecurityalliance.org/) the umbrella body on cloud security has suggested the following approach for information security:

- Determine exactly what data or function is being moved to cloud.
- How important is the data or function for your organization?
- Analysis of data flow in and out of cloud.
- What service and deployment models are being considered? Are the risks commensurate with the criticality of information assets?

Ultimately, the cost of providing satisfactory control should not overweigh the benefits for moving to cloud. Cloud providers may not provide the level of transparency desired for enterprises to fully comprehend the security risks. The security architects are responsible for the security and integrity of data, even when it is held by a service provider. The below are some tips for information security architects working on cloud solutions:

- Understand how the provider has architected the cloud infrastructure and how the services are managed from process and personnel perspective. Evaluate if this poses any threat.
- How are the logs maintained? Can the cloud provider commit to sharing logs and help investing inappropriate or illegal activity should it occur?
- Data Import: How to import data from cloud back to enterprise?
- What are the contractual obligations that can be put in the service agreement?

Information Security in the Age of Mobility

Ubiquitous, affordable, easy to use mobile device is probably the most significant technology innovation in the past few years. Mobile applications have gone beyond gaming to transforming ways of doing business. The initial wave was on how to increase workforce productivity – a typical work flow approval process that was mobile enabled for shortening of approval cycle. The current themes of mobile application are far grave: inventing of new business processes that take advantage of innate mobile capabilities like GPS, camera, etc. Businesses are hoping to find new, immersive and more natural ways of interaction. With advances in communication, mobile phones are set to emerge as the preferred and primary platform for information access.

Before we discuss about the information security challenges and approaches, a good appreciation of some underlying technical aspects of mobile devices will be helpful. Devices are memory constrained. The application footprint should be as small as possible. Keeping power consumption at the minimum is important. The apps are single user apps. Due to the compactness, the risk of losing the device is high.

Mobile devices are more vulnerable than desktop computers to viruses and spam attacks (See Box 3). At run time, more than identity, the context of an action plays a prominent role in determining what needs to happen. The challenge to the enterprise rises from how to provide access to enterprise information assets without compromising on enterprise security. Fundamental concerns are around (Himanshu Dwivedi, Chris Clark, David Thiel (2010)):

- Securing Data
  - Transmission: Data in motion
  - Storage: Data in rest
  - Protecting Data Integrity

Box 3.

How secure are mobile applications?

http://www.cnbc.com/id/38415911/Citigroup_iPhone_Banking_App_Had_Security_Flaw

Citigroup customers were told to upgrade to a newer Apple iPhone personal banking application after a security glitch was discovered during a routine security review.

The flawed mobile banking app may have saved personal account information such as account numbers, bill payments and security access codes in a hidden file on users' iPhones the report said. Information may have also been saved on users' computers according to the report.

The report indicated there is growing concern about security challenges with wireless apps with potential leakages of confidential information.

- Securing Access
  ◦ Distribution of Application
  ◦ Application & Data Access Levels
- Device
  ◦ Physical Security
  ◦ How Different Apps in the Device Coexist?

The worksheet in Table 5 will help give an excellent overall view of the risk profile.

An important point to bear in mind is that depending on the device, the threat varies. For instance, buffer overflows are not critical for Blackberry due to J2ME usage. Mobile apps typically communicate through web services. This mix of technology creates challenges for information security.

An interesting development for information security on mobile device is 'Security-by-Contract (SxC)' (See Figure 5). The key idea of the SxC is that a digital signature should not just certify the origin of the code but rather bind together the code with a contract. The contract will be bundled as part of application and will be accepted by the mobile device during deployment. At runtime, the contract will ensure that the code to be executed is authorized to do so. This is a significant step forward in assuring that only secure code can execute in the mobile device.

The other techniques are application sandboxing, signing and permissions.

- **Application Sandboxing:** Treats each application in isolation and is a critical architectural principle to minimize damage in case the application is compromised.
- **Application Signing:** Gives some amount of legitimacy; depending on how it is signed, the sandbox restrictions can be rigorous or more trusting.
- **Permissions:** Are closely related to sandboxes in that it determines that the applications can only access their files.
- **Buffer Overflows:** Should not leave any scope for intrusion.

Information Security and Bring Your Own Device (BYOD)

Cool new mobile devices invade the market regularly. They are not only just sleek and visually appealing; they are affordable as well. Life of the new generation of workers is inseparably woven around such devices. Fuelled by the affordable connectivity and the charming ways of the online social world, the new generation of workers has a strong digital life. Most young workers have built their identity with the devices and they would like to use the devices in work environment also. In 2011, 41% percent of workers used personal technology to access business applications, up from 31% in 2010. Attempting to ban BYOD will be anachronistic. In the new world, the end point is the user and not the fixed, enterprise provided

Table 5. Risk profile worksheet

Scenario	Information Security Risks	Likelihood of Occurrence (Target Devices greatly influence this)	Impact of Risk (Low/Medium/ High)

Figure 5. Secure by contract (SxC)

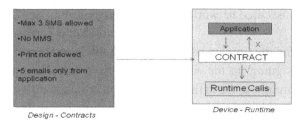

devices. Enterprises have realized the irreversible nature of this trend; they are increasingly formulating 'Bring Your Own Device' policies to their employees:

- Procter & Gamble is letting several hundred of its younger employees use their own laptops.
- Kraft Foods announced in May 2010 that it plans to let employees buy their own PCs.
- IBM is letting a significant portion of its work force bring their own devices to work.
- Citrix Systems Inc announced a reimbursable policy for employees to bring their devices.

Apart from employee satisfaction, the other drivers for BYOD include capacity constraint to manage infrastructure, lesser maintenance costs, employee productivity gains, a clear understanding of risks and having a sound mitigation plan. For enterprises, this opportunity if managed well, can lead to significant cost savings. In some cases, the enterprises have not just offered BYOD but rather encouraged by giving financial incentives for purchase of gadgets and/or data plans.

In the traditional way of doing things, the preferred way for managing security in enterprises is to arrest divergence and enforce conformance. IT will standardize on operating system, hardware; IT will do patch management, system upgrades; customizations are frowned upon. Even with such stringent policies enforced by IT, enterprises are routinely haunted with not-so glorious stories of data breaches. Adding BYOD to this will expose a higher level of security risk. BYOD impacts the heart of IT principles and the disarray is imaginable. Consider the following from an information security perspective:

- List of supported devices; Will all devices be supported?
- What type of support will be given?
- Encryption of enterprise data in private devices.
- Specify minimum requirement for hardware and software.
- How will the inventory of accessible devices maintained?

- How will access levels and information sensitivity be tagged?
- How patching and version upgrades will be managed?
- Compliance with regulatory authorities – the level of relevance for your business and how it is approached.
- Supporting multiple devices for a user.
- Clearly specify what actions will be taken on devices if they are lost or the employment is terminated.
- Policies for usage in unsecured networks.

There is a clear need for the employees to understand what they are signing up for when enterprises offer BYOD. Some questions to think through are: is the data in my device susceptible to automatic or remote deletion? What events trigger the automatic deletion? Does the company provide a way to recover the personal data deleted? Am I entitled to any reimbursement for the loss of personal content such as songs, videos or applications? Is remote deletion part of the standard employee termination process? Is my approval sought or required for the remote deletion? Is my personal data retained in case of automatic or remote wipe? (Cesare Garlati (2012))

This brings to a sensitive conjunction point of what is right and wrong. Ethics is a much debated subject even in clearer circumstances! As information systems take center stage in our daily existence, our identity in the digital world needs to be protected with the same degree of rigor as we would for our physical security.

Information Security: Federal Governments and Ethics/ Privacy Concerns

Sadly, the breach of information security is no longer uncommon news. In the year 2011 alone, there have been significant breaches that compromise personal information about consumers to hackers. The loss of customer records by Epsilon or the compromise of customer email address in Honda motors or Sony's shutdown of online gaming business due to breach in customer records are enough to convince even the diehard optimists of the lurking threat of consumer anger and loss of business goodwill should there be any security breach. Quite understandably, the consequences of the loss can be dreadful if it falls in the hands of unscrupulous persons. For instance, the breach of credit card information can cause enough agony even to the most peaceful minded consumers. The repercussions of any bad breach go much beyond the world of commerce.

Acutely aware of this, the Governments world over have started issuing regulations and directives aimed at safeguarding the interests of consumers and national security. *The need to protect identity and ethically handle sensitive information brings information security at an interdisciplinary conjunction point of how society deals with ethics and privacy and the role of the sensitive care keeper – the Governments.* We will discuss two instances of federal governments stepping in to shape information security policies to safeguard consumer interests.

Health Insurance Portability and Accountability Act (HIPAA)

This act was enacted by the US Congress and signed by the then President Bill Clinton in 1996. Title II of HIPAA is aimed at preventing healthcare abuse and sets civil and criminal penalties for willful violations (Thomas J Shaw (Ed) (2011)):

- **Privacy Rules:** Protects all *individually identifiable health information* held or transmitted by a covered entity or its business associate, in any form or media, whether electronic, paper, or oral. The Privacy Rule calls this information *"protected health information (PHI).*
- **Security Rules:** Establishes national standards to protect individuals' electronic

personal health information that is created, received, used, or maintained by a covered entity. The Security Rule requires appropriate administrative, physical and technical safeguards to ensure the confidentiality, integrity, and security of electronic protected health information.

The coverage of the HIPAA is quite extensive. The covered entities are:

- Covered Healthcare Providers
- Health Plans
- Healthcare Clearinghouses
- Medicare Prescription Drug Card Sponsors

Federal Trade Commission – Standards for Safeguarding Customer Information

Federal Trade Commission Act (FTCA) was enacted in 2003. This aims to protect consumer interests by mandating data providers to be sensitive about personal information. FTCA mandates that 'reasonable steps to protect data and personally identifiable information must be taken'. Combination of data elements that can be constructed back to represent a given individual is considered as personally identifiable information.

The objectives of the Safeguards Rule are to:

1. Ensure the security and confidentiality of customer information.
2. Protect against any anticipated threats or hazards to the security or integrity of such information.
3. Protect against unauthorized access to or use of such information that could result in substantial harm or inconvenience to any customer.

The Safeguards Rule requires that consideration is given to risks to customer information in all areas of the operation, with special emphasis on three critical areas: Employee Training and Management; Information Systems; Detecting and Managing System Failures. Table 6 summarizes some best practices from the act.

Mandates like these, have a great influence in shaping the information architecture. Besides, the ethics about appropriate activities on internet also influence information security. Ethics and culture are very closely linked with the geographical area where people live. With internet having no geographical boundary and often providing anonymity, the baser human tendencies have an unfortunately fertile ground to sprout. Apart from laws governing the usage and the associated deterrence for violations, the users themselves should have some etiquette and ethical value system. Many professions have explicit canons on what is ac-

Table 6. Best practices from FTCA

Employee Training and Management	Information Systems	Detecting and Managing System Failures
Check references prior to hiring	Store information in a secure area	Follow a written contingency plan
Train employees to maintain security, confidentiality and integrity of customer information	Dispose information secure	Regularly install patches to deal with vulnerabilities
Limit access of customer information	Securely transmit information	Backup data regularly
Regular remind and instruct employees on legal obligation to maintain information securely	Use appropriate oversights to detect improper usage or theft of customer information	Notify customers promptly if there is any breach
Promote strong password usage	Caution customers against sending sensitive data like credit card number through emails.	Maintain firewalls and anti virus softwares

ceptable. Bodies of lawyers and physicians have written rules to be followed; violating them will mean removing from the profession. Information technology field does not have such widely accepted principles as yet. The Computer Ethics Institute (Computer Ethics Institute, 2012) attempts to fill this gap, by suggesting the ten cardinal principles:

1. Thou shalt not use a computer to harm other people.
2. Thou shalt not interfere with other people's computer work.
3. Thou shalt not snoop around in other people's computer files.
4. Thou shalt not use a computer to steal.
5. Thou shalt not use a computer to bear false witness.
6. Thou shalt not copy or use proprietary software for which you have not paid.
7. Thou shalt not use other people's computer resources without authorization or proper compensation.
8. Thou shalt not appropriate other people's intellectual output.
9. Thou shalt think about the social consequences of the program you are writing or the system you are designing.
10. Thou shalt always use a computer in ways that ensure consideration and respect for your fellow humans.

On the other hand, the governments are using information systems to perform various essential functions from infrastructure to defense to tax collections. It is far more critical for Governments to enforce right information security measures. This has helped the enterprises in adopting policies experimented by Governments. Doing business on internet is doing business without geographical boundaries. It is fair to say that *information security is a global concern*. The world of information security standards and regulations has evolved actively due to the efforts of Governments.

INFORMATION SECURITY-STANDARDS AND REGULATIONS LANDSCAPE

The world of information security is rich in standards and regulations. While standards are guidance, regulations are mandated. The below is a partial listing of standards, regulations and organizations involved in information security.

Standards

- **ISO Standards ISO/IEC 27002:** Is an information security standard published by the International Organization for Standardization (ISO) and by the International Electrotechnical Commission (IEC). It contains 12 main sections all dealing with various facets of information security. Many countries have created equivalent standards based on this.
- **The Payment Card Industry Data Security Standard (PCI DSS):** Is an information security standard for organizations that handle cardholder information for the major debit, credit, prepaid, e-purse, ATM, and POS cards.
- **COBIT:** Control OBjectives for Information and related Technology - its mission is to research, develop, publish and promote an authoritative, up-to-date, international set of generally accepted information technology control objectives for day-to-day use by business managers, IT professionals and assurance professionals.
- **ITIL:** The Information Technology Infrastructure Library - is a set of best practices and guidelines that define an integrated, process-based approach for managing information technology services. ITIL seeks to ensure that effective information security measures are taken at strategic, tactical, and operational levels.

Regulations

- **SOX:** The Sarbanes-Oxley Act of 2002 affects executive management of publicly traded firms. This legislation seeks to improve the reliability and accuracy of financial reporting. The IT departments are tasked with the ensuring information security.
- **HIPAA:** Health Information Portability and Accountability Act.
- **21 CFR Part 11:** This deals with FDA guidelines on electronic records and electronic signatures in the United States. Part 11 requires information systems to be trustworthy to create electronic equivalents of paper documents. This has direct bearing on information security.
- **Federal Information Processing Standard (FIPS):** Is a publicly announced standardization developed by the United States federal government for use in computer systems by all non-military government agencies and by government contractors, when properly invoked and tailored on a contract.
- **Federal Information Security Management Act of 2002 (FISMA):** The act recognizes the importance of information security to the economic and national security interests of the United States. The act requires each federal agency to develop, document, and implement an agency-wide program to provide information security for the information and information systems that support the operations.

List of Organizations

- **ACM:** Association of Computing Machinery – www.acm.org
- **NIST:** National Institute of Standards and Technology – www.nist.gov
- **CSA:** Cloud Security Alliance - https://cloudsecurityalliance.org/
- Information Systems Audits and Control Association - www.isaca.org
- Information Systems Security Association - www.issa.org
- The International Information Systems Security Certification Consortium, Inc - www.isc2.org
- The Computer Ethics Institute - http://computerethicsinstitute.org/
- The Open Group – www3.opengroup.org

FUTURE RESEARCH DIRECTIONS

The contemporary research areas in information security are focused on the following (partial listing):

- Federal Governments, Ethics, Privacy
- Business Continuity and Risk Management
- Trust in Digital Life
- Digital Forensics
- Usability
- Secure Software Development
- New Era of Business: Fuzzy Boundaries, Clouds, Mobility, Social Media, Jurisprudence

We will look at two of the above themes to briefly understand the contours of research.

Research Topic: Digital Forensics and Information Security

With commerce increasingly conducted through internet, it is necessary to ensure that business is conducted in legally acceptable ways and fair to all involved. System of justice requires convincing evidence to prove guilt and malice. Such evidence is increasingly necessary to be built from information systems. Building of such evidence that can be used for legal purposes is digital forensics. Formal definition (Ken Zatyko (2007)):

The application of computer science and investigative procedures for a legal purpose involving the analysis of digital evidence after proper search authority, chain of custody, validation with mathematics, use of validated tools, repeatability, reporting, and possible expert presentation.

Consider the following scenario. SkinGlow Inc is selling its products through its web sites. The products are also sold through authorized agents in their web sites. SkinGlow of late is experiencing user dissatisfaction and increased complaints about their products. On investigation, SkinGlow found that a few unauthorized web sites operating in safe havens are selling spurious products using its label. SkinGlow wants collect necessary digital evidence to appeal in courts of law. This is an instance of digital forensics: the act of collecting digital evidence to substantiate its case for legal scrutiny (Brian Carrier, 2003).

Digital forensics is a maturing science that is used for serious purposes. How do we prove the integrity of digital evidence? What principles from the science of information security can be applied in this context? (Chet Hosmer, 2002)

- **Establish Digital Time:** Advance accuracy and trust of digital time.
- **Bind Events to Digital Time:** Digitally bind this trusted electronic time to digital events on a regular basis.
- Promote Standardization of this throughout the digital world.
- Establish relationship between Digital Time and Legal Time.

Other relevant and interesting challenges:

- **Use of Computers:** How to prove that computers were involved?
- **Linking digits to person:** Systems only store digits, how do we prove that it in fact, originating from the person suspected?

- **Event reconstruction:** How to reconstruct the events to prove the plausibility of occurrence?

Digital forensics needs must influence the design considerations of information systems. In many claim situations, the suing party may claim that the 'database is not reliable'. It will be the job of information security specialist to prove that every record in the database is reliable and can be traced to an event. Digital forensics coupled with information security specialist will have to work with the attorneys to establish the reliability of records in electronic form.

The basic process followed is to identify data sources – collect data - analyze data – build evidence – draw conclusions. It is very likely that the data volumes will be huge. Information integrity principles play a crucial role in building unassailable evidence.

Some of the research centers focusing on digital forensics are the University of Rhode Island (http://www.dfcsc.uri.edu/), Purdue University (http://www.cyberforensics.purdue.edu/), Coventry University, (http://wwwm.coventry.ac.uk/researchnet/digitalsecurityandforensics/Pages/DigitalSecurityandForensics.aspx). The annual 'International Conference on Digital Forensics & Forensics' is an excellent place to look for trends in this field.

Research Topic: Usability and Information Security

Information security breach occurs due to a variety of reason. Human error contributes to the most significant proportion of breaches. It is intriguing – systems are designed for human use yet a large number of breaches occur due to human negligence. Is there more than technology that has got to play a role in information security? If so, what is it and how can we positively influence to result in more secure information systems?

As discussed in the earlier part of this chapter, information systems started their evolution in defense and research context which was staffed by highly educated personnel. Hence, information security evolved without needing to bother about usability as the small community of well conversant people who used the system was anyway capable of figuring out what is happening and how to use.

Computer systems that are very secure are often intimidating for users. On the other hand, systems that offer poor security are unusable as they are too unsafe to use. Either way, systems are rendered useless if the proper balance between usability and security is not achieved (Lorrie Faith Cranor; Simson Garfinkel, 2005). To even think that security and usability are divergent themes is not quite true. Recent research efforts focus on achieving both by incorporating usability into security thoughts as the ultimate aim is to *use* systems securely.

Generally speaking, human desire is to take shortcuts. Complicated security procedures will be bypassed by the users. Human computer interaction principles should inform and guide information security. A good understanding of human psychology will be desirable to design systems. Some principles based on human psychology ("Human Factors", 2012):

- Complacency with familiar risks.
- Educating the users by emphasizing on the possible gains of following information security principles rather than focusing on the possible losses.
- **Risk Homeostatis:** People who accept a certain level of risk will maintain their tolerance at the same level; even if the risk chances are reduced, they will aggressively lower guard elsewhere to remain in the same risk level.

Usability must be factored right from requirements analysis: activities like task analysis and core task scenario, user profile, usability objectives should be carried out. The design and development phase, should include activities like simplicity of design, prototype development, usability tests (Simon Parkin; Aad van Moorsel; Philip Inglesan; M. Angela Sasse, 2010).

Information security can only be improved by progressing on several disciplines. Depending on the nature of systems, the organization and users who will use the system, the risk profile will vary. The solutions will therefore have to be dynamic. The field is an interesting, interdisciplinary discipline poised for significant breakthroughs from brilliant minds in the times to come.

CONCLUSION

In this chapter, we saw how information security has multiple forces of influence from technology innovations like mobile and cloud computing to federal regulations governing the use of digital information. Enterprises have to operate in 'boundaryless' world and securing information is the paramount concern in the emerging ways of doing business. Federated authentication, need to classify information assets, policies governing implementation and traceability of events are very important. Also covered in the chapter was how social media, mobility and cloud can be approached sensitively.

Security cannot be an afterthought – it has to be thoughtfully weaved into the software during the development process. Information security has to be seen holistically as most of the implementation principles trace their origin to enterprise business strategy. By developing such a holistic picture, one can clear understand the influencing forces and the realms of possibilities.

As businesses become more digitally conducted, the need for effective and ethical forensic techniques is important. During the next few years, we expect novel ways of accomplishing information security that blends some form of physical identification like biometrics. That information security is poised for very interesting times is evident from the wide array of ongoing, inter-disciplinary research involving sociology, computer science, business management, jurisprudence, human computer interaction and public administration.

REFERENCES

Australian Government, Department of Defense. (n.d.). *Human factors and information security: Individual, culture and security environment.* Retrieved 14 March, 2012, from http://www.dtic. mil/cgi-bin/GetTRDoc?AD=ADA535944

Bertino, E., & Takahashi, K. (2011). *Identity management – Concepts, technologies and systems.* Norwood, MA: Artech House.

Carrier, B. (2003). *Open source digital forensics tools - The legal argument.* Retrieved March 14, 2012, from http://www.digital-evidence.org/papers/opensrc_legal.pdf

Cloud Security Alliance. (n.d.). Retrieved 15 March, 2012, from https://cloudsecurityalliance. org/

Computer Ethics Institute. (n.d.). *Ten commandments of computer ethics.* Retrieved March 15, 2012, from http://computerethicsinstitute.org/publications/tencommandments.html

Cranor, L. F., & Garfinkel, S. (2005). *Security and usability - Designing secure systems that people can use.* O'Reilly Media.

Dwivedi, H., Clark, C., & Thiel, D. (2010). *Mobile application security.* The McGraw-Hill Company.

Freedictionary.com. (2012). *Information security.* Retrieved on 14 March, 2012, from http://www. thefreedictionary.com/information+security

Garlati, G. (2012). *The dark side of BYOD – Privacy, personal data loss and device seizure.* Retrieved March 14, 2012, from http://consumerization.trendmicro.com/consumerization-byod-privacy-personal-data-loss-and-device-seizure/

Holland, K. (2008). *Integrating information security into software development lifecycle.* Retrieved March 14, 2012, from http://msdn.microsoft.com/en-us/library/cc168643.aspx

Hosmer, C. (2002). Proving the integrity of digital evidence with time. *The International Journal of Digital Evidence, 1*(1). Retrieved March 14, 2012, from http://www.utica.edu/academic/institutes/ecii/publications/articles/9C4EBC25-B4A3-6584-C38C511467A6B862.pdf

Howard, M., & Lipner, S. (2006). *The security development lifecycle.* Redmond, WA: Microsoft Press.

ISACA. (n.d.). An introduction to business model for information security. Retrieved March 15, 2012, from http://www.isaca.org/Knowledge-Center/Research/ResearchDeliverables/Pages/An-Introduction-to-the-Business-Model-for-Information-Security.aspx

LeVeque, V. (2006). *Information security – A strategic approach.* Hoboken, NJ: John Wiley & Sons Inc.

Merkow, M., & Breithaupt, J. (2006). *Information security – Principles and practices.* Pearson Eduction Inc.

Parkin, S., van Moorsel, A., Inglesant, P., & Sasse, M. A. (2010). A stealth approach to usable security: Helping IT security managers to identify workable security solutions. In *Proceedings of the 2010 Workshop on New Security Paradigms* (NSPW '10), (pp. 33-50). New York, NY: ACM. DOI=10.1145/1900546.1900553

Shaw, T. J. (Ed.). (2011). *Information security and privacy: A practical guide for global executives, lawyers and technologists*. American Bar Association.

Whitman, M. E., & Mattord, H. J. (2012). *Principles of information security* (4th ed.). Course Technology.

Winkler, V. J. R. (2011). *Securing the cloud*. Waltham, MA: Elsevier Inc.

Zatyko, K. (2007). *Commentary: Defining digital forensics*. Retrieved March 14, 2012, from http://www.forensicmag.com/node/128

ADDITIONAL READING

Ahmed, M., & Ahamad, M. (2012). Protecting health information on mobile devices. In *Proceedings of the Second ACM conference on Data and Application Security and Privacy* (CODASPY '12), (pp. 229-240). New York, NY: ACM. DOI=10.1145/2133601.2133629

Alfawaz, S., Nelson, K., & Mohannak, K. (2010). Information security culture: A behaviour compliance conceptual framework. In C. Boyd & W. Susilo (Eds.), *Proceedings of the Eighth Australasian Conference on Information Security* (AISC '10), Vol. 105, (pp. 47-55). Darlinghurst, Australia: Australian Computer Society, Inc.

Allen, J. H., Barnum, S., Ellison, R. J., McGraw, G., & Mead, N. R. (2008). *Software security engineering: A guide for project managers*. Upper Saddle River, NJ: Addison Wesley Professional.

Anderson, R. (2008). *Security engineering – A guide to building dependable distributed systems*. Indianapolis, IN: Wiley Publishing.

Bala, D. (2008). Biometrics and information security. In *Proceedings of the 5th Annual Conference on Information Security Curriculum Development* (InfoSecCD '08), (pp. 64-66). New York, NY: ACM. DOI=10.1145/1456625.1456644

Casey, E. (2011). *Digital evidence and computer crime*. San Diego, CA: Academic Press.

de Leeuw, K., & Bergstra, J. (Eds.). (2007). *The history of information security – A comprehensive handbook*. Elsevier Inc.

Fried, S. (2010). *Mobile device security: A comprehensive guide to securing your information in a moving world*. Auerback Publications.

Friedman, J., & Hoffman, D. V. (2008). Protecting data on mobile devices: A taxonomy of security threats to mobile computing and review of applicable defenses. *Information and Knowledge Systems Management*, 7(1-2), 159–180.

Harwood, M., Goncalves, M., & Pemble, M. (2011). *Security strategies in web applications and social networking*. Sudbury, MA: Jones & Bartlett Learning.

Herzig, T. (Ed.). (2010). *Information security in healthcare: Managing risk*. Chicago, IL: HIMSS.

Krutz, R. L., & Vines, R. D. (2010). *Cloud security: A comprehensive guide to secure cloud computing*. Indianapolis, IN: Wiley Publishing Inc.

Lasey, D. (2009). *Managing the human factor in information security*. West Sussex, UK: John Wiley and Sons.

Matthys, E., & de Landtsheer, C. (2010). *Business continuity management: A practical guide to BS25999 & information security*. Retiarius Press.

Nemati, H. (2010). *Pervasive information security and privacy developments: Trends and advancements*. Hershey, PA: IGI Global. doi:10.4018/978-1-61692-000-5

Peltier, T. R. (2005). *Information security risk analysis*. Auerback Publishers.

Pfleeger, C. P., & Pfleeger, S. L. (2011). *Security in computing*. Upper Saddle River, NJ: Prentice Hall.

Satchell, C., Shanks, G., Howard, S., & Murphy, J. (2006). Beyond security: Implications for the future of federated digital identity management systems. In J. Kjeldskov & J. Paay (Eds.), *Proceedings of the 18th Australia Conference on Computer-Human Interaction: Design: Activities, Artefacts and Environments* (OZCHI '06), (pp. 313-316). New York, NY: ACM. DOI=10.1145/1228175.1228231

Smedinghoff, T. J. (2008). *Information security law: The emerging standards for corporate compliance*. Cambridgeshire, UK: IT Governance Ltd.

Solove, D. J. (2004). *The digital person – Technology and privacy in information age*. New York, NY: New York University Press.

Straub, D. W., Goodman, S., & Baskerville, R. L. (Eds.). (2008). *Information security – Policy, processes and practices*. Armonk, NY: ME Sharp Inc.

Vacca, J. (2009). *Computer and information security handbook*. Burlington, MA: Elsevier Inc.

Weiner, N. (1954). *The human use of human beings: Cybernetics and society*. Da Capo Paperback.

Werlinger, R., Hawkey, K., Botta, D., & Beznosov, K. (2009). Security practitioners in context: Their activities and interactions with other stakeholders within organizations. *International Journal of Human-Computer Studies, 67*(7), 584-606. DOI=10.1016/j.ijhcs.2009.03.002

Williams, P. A. H. (2008). In a 'trusting' environment, everyone is responsible for information security. *Information Security Technical Reports, 13*(4), 207-215. DOI=10.1016/j.istr.2008.10.009

Yong, L. E., Jun, L. H., & Sik, M. K. (2007). Study on information security strategy for ubiquitous society. In M. N. Katehakis, A. Zamora, & R. Alvarez (Eds.), *Proceedings of the 6th WSEAS International Conference on Information Security and Privacy* (ISP'07), (pp. 79-84). Stevens Point, WI: World Scientific and Engineering Academy and Society (WSEAS).

Zhang, X., Wuwong, N., Li, H., & Zhang, X. (2010). Information security risk management framework for the cloud computing environments. In *Proceedings of the 2010 10th IEEE International Conference on Computer and Information Technology* (CIT '10), (pp. 1328-1334). Washington, DC: IEEE Computer Society. DOI=10.1109/CIT.2010.501

KEY TERMS AND DEFINITIONS

Boundaryless/Deperimeterization: Absence of strong perimeter or boundary separating the enterprise from outside world.

Digital Identity: Ways of identifying an individual in electronic world.

Ethics: System of moral principles.

Federated Authentication: Honoring by all parties (of the federation) to authentication mechanisms and decisions by any party within the federation.

Information Assets Tag: Ways to analyzing the information data stores and labeling of data stores to indicate the sensitivity and other attributes about the information.

Security Token: Passing trust information from one domain to another.

Social Media: Means of easy communication by people through internet using social tools like Facebook, Twitter, etc.

Chapter 21
Constructive Knowledge Management Model and Information Retrieval Methods for Software Engineering

Zeyar Aung
Masdar Institute of Science and Technology, UAE

Khine Khine Nyunt
King Faisal University, Kingdom of Saudi Arabia

ABSTRACT

In this book chapter, the authors discuss two important trends in modern software engineering (SE) regarding the utilization of knowledge management (KM) and information retrieval (IR). Software engineering is a discipline in which knowledge and experience, acquired in the course of many years, play a fundamental role. For software development organizations, the main assets are not manufacturing plants, buildings, and machines, but the knowledge held by their employees. Software engineering has long recognized the need for managing knowledge and that the SE community could learn much from the KM community. The authors introduce the fundamental concepts of KM theory and practice and mainly discuss the aspects of knowledge management that are valuable to software development organizations and how a KM system for such an organization can be implemented. In addition to knowledge management, information retrieval (IR) also plays a crucial role in SE. IR is a study of how to efficiently and effectively retrieve a required piece of information from a large corpus of storage entities such as documents. As software development organizations grow larger and have to deal with larger numbers (probably millions) of documents of various types, IR becomes an essential tool for retrieving any piece of information that a software developer wants within a short time. IR can be used both as a general-purpose tool to improve the productivity of developers or as an enabler tool to facilitate a KM system.

DOI: 10.4018/978-1-4666-3679-8.ch021

1. KNOWLEDGE MANAGEMENT

Knowledge management is fundamentally corporate intellectual assets to improve the organization's effectiveness, as well as its business opportunity enhancement. Key to knowledge management is capturing tacit knowledge for the tangible benefits for the organization. The aim of knowledge management is to continuously improve an organization's performance in which sharing, creating, assimilating, disseminating, and applying knowledge throughout the organization. Knowledge management is a continuous process to understand the organization's knowledge needs, the location of the knowledge, and how to improve the knowledge.

1.1 Fundamental Concept of Theory and Practice

Knowledge is one of the organization's most important value and influencing its competitiveness. In this age of information organizations see their people as their key assets. The knowledge, skills and competencies of these people add to the growth of the organization.

The first section of this topic presents fundamental knowledge – the "tacit" or personal knowledge versus the "explicit" or organizational knowledge (Nonaka and Takeuchi, 1995). Tacit knowledge resides in individuals and teams which includes personal experiences, thinking, competence, perceptions, insights and know-how that are indicated but not actually expressed. Explicit knowledge that is codified and conveyed to other thought which will be transformed to data, information later documents, records and files.

As Nonaka and Takeuchi (1995) illustrate that there are four ways to transform the knowledge. Firstly, "Socialization" means to share experience from tacit knowledge to tacit knowledge. This process is first to share experience and then to exchange tacit knowledge. Thus, socialization is used in sharing learners' experience and know-how with other learners. The second concept is "externalization" that means the conversion of tacit knowledge into explicit knowledge. This process is to rationalize tacit knowledge and articulate it into explicit concept. Third one is "Internalization" that is a process of embodying explicit knowledge into tacit knowledge. Individual gained knowledge and experience through the explicit knowledge and individual can develop the new tacit knowledge internally. The fourth one is "Combination" that converts explicit knowledge into more complex and systematic sets of explicit knowledge. In this process, individuals combine and exchange different explicit knowledge to explicit knowledge with others.

The second section presents the Five Learning Cycles model of "organizational learning" (Sanchez, 2001). In this general model of learning processes in an organization, five kinds of learning cycles are identified that link of individuals, groups, and the overall organization in an organizational learning process.

Sanchez (2001) illustrates that the first learning cycle is "Individual Learning Cycle" whose individuals imagine alternative interpretive frame works and new kinds of knowledge. The second learning cycle is "Individual/Group Learning Cycle" who shares their new knowledge within groups to evaluate the new knowledge developed by individuals. The third learning cycle is "Group Learning Cycle" whose interact with other groups to determine whether new knowledge developed by a given group becomes accepted within the overall organization. In this stage managers or leaders are the domain expert of the learning. The fourth learning cycle is "Group/Organization Learning Cycle" in which new knowledge accepted at the organizational level which is embedded in new processes, systems, and the culture of an organization. The fifth learning cycle is "Organization Learning Cycle" which is new knowledge embedded in new processes, systems, and organizational culture which leads to new patterns of action by groups and individuals.

As Sanchez (2001) illustrates about basic assumptions in personal versus organizational knowledge management. Firstly, Personal knowledge in nature is very difficult to extract. In contrast, organizational knowledge can be articulated and codified to create as an organizational asset. As a result of this stage individuals knowledge can be articulated and transformed to explicit knowledge which can be references for others individuals. Secondly, personal knowledge must be transferred by people to people. In contrast, organizational knowledge can be disseminated through Information Technology to be transformed as an explicit knowledge such as documents, records and files.

Thirdly, Learning can be encouraged by bringing the right people in the right time in the personal knowledge. On the other hand, learning process can be created through definable and manageable knowledge explicitly throughout the organization. As a result, Organizational knowledge approach focus on designing organizational knowledge processes for generating, articulating, categorizing and leveraging throughout the organization.

1.2 Knowledge Management in Software Engineering

Software engineering is a knowledge intensive business and as such it could benefit from the ideas of knowledge management. The important question here is: where does knowledge resides in software engineering? Software engineering involves a multitude of knowledge-intensive tasks: analyzing user requirements for new software systems, identifying and applying best software development practices, collecting experience about software development process, project planning and risk management, and many others (Birk et. al., 1999).

In this section, we will present the perspective of KM for SE such as knowledge management support for core activities in SE, organizational memories for software development and classification of knowledge management tools relevant to SE.

1.2.1 Knowledge Management Support for Core Activity in Software Engineering

This section addresses major core KM activities in software engineering processes such as Document Management and Competence Management. Document Management system allows for the storing and uploading files, search and retrieval and the search for experts based on content. On the other hand, Competence Management represents the management of tacit knowledge is vital to the organization through as explicit knowledge.

- **Document Management:** Birk et al. (1999) illustrate the wide spectrum of software engineering processes that might occur in a typical software engineering project. A software development project involves a variety of document-driven processes and activities. Document Management is mainly focus on authoring, reviewing, editing, and using these documents which becomes the main sharing knowledge system throughout the organization. There are many tools to support DM system such as Hyperwave, Microsoft Sharepoint, Lotus Domino, and Xerox DocuShare which include features such as defining process workflows and finding experts. Therefore, document management is a basic activity toward supporting an organization's implementation of a knowledge management system.

- **Competence Management:** CM is more difficult to identify and difficult to manage tacit knowledge that resides in individual experts and team. It means that not all tacit knowledge can be transformed explicit knowledge. So, an organization must track who knows what to fully utilize undocumented knowledge. This process becomes the transformation of tacit knowledge to explicit knowledge which becomes the organization's assets. In general, we should form the small group to capture knowledge in fact larger group of people are exposed to the risk of "not knowing what other people know." An elaborated solution to this problem is competence management, skills management or expert network.

Initially, the main objective of Competence Management systems is to find individuals who have specific pieces of knowledge but later use to generate and edit their own profile by using CM tools such as Skillscape and Skillsoft.

1.2.2 Organizational Memory for Software Development

Organizational memory is both an individual- and organizational level construct (Walsh and Ungson, 1991). However, Individual memory is not sufficient and the entire organization needs a memory to explicitly record critical events. Software Engineers conduct their daily work often supports to create such a memory in the SE environment. There are many SE practices to build such memories such as version control, change management, documenting design decisions, and requirements traceability which will effect directly or indirectly to software development.

Version control system also known as Source Code Control System, represent a class of tools that indirectly create a project memory. The system recoded the information about who made the change, why need to be change and when they change. This memory helps the software's evolution after the project. Then domain expert has to identify to use this information for advanced analysis of software products and processes.

Design Rationale is an approach to capture the software design decision explicitly to avoid repeating mistake as well as create a product memory. This memory will definitely help engineers to test different technical solutions and make decision during the design process. But how engineers make decisions which are rarely captured because it difficult to understand the reason behind the solution.

Software requirements drive the development of software systems, but the connection between the final system and its requirements is fuzzy.

Traceability is an approach that explicitly connects the requirements and the final software system. This memory will help what type of requirements led to a particular of source code, what type of code did engineers develop to satisfy the particular requirement.

1.2.3 Classification of Knowledge Management Tools

In this section, we present types of commercial and academic KM tools. Most of the commercial tools are search and database maintenance, intranet features, FAQ lists, logged chat features, find-an-expert features, personalization, etc., which aid in knowledge-sharing within an organization. Some of the tools are Experience Management System, Case-Based Reasoning (CBR) for retaining and retrieving experience.

The tool named BORE (Building and Organizational Repository of Experiences) was developed by the University of Nebraska-Lincoln. BORE is case studies based tool which is related to real time problems solving experiences so that Software developers can use these solutions in future projects.

Mostly IT based tools that can help to fulfill KM goal. IT based tools are categorized as bellows:

- **Groupware Systems:** It is a supporting tool to determine the processes that take place in the organization as well as how knowledge is currently stored and distributed, and establish how certain functions would improve them. publishing and communication tools, collaborative management tools, video conferencing and informal communication tools provides facilities to create, share explicit knowledge as well to find the sources of the knowledge. One of the best examples of groupware tool is Lotus Notes.

- **Decision Support Systems:** The role of this system is to access and manipulate data based on Data Warehouse and Data Mining technology as well as online analytical processing system (OLAP). The goal is to enhance decision –making and solving problem.

- **Content Management Systems:** CMS is responsible for the creation, management, and distribution of content on the intranet, extranet, or a website which is relevant to knowledge management (KM). Although such systems deal almost exclusively with explicit knowledge, the sheer volume of documents that an organization has to deal with makes them useful and in some cases even mandatory.

1.3 Constructive Knowledge Management Model

This section presents our proposed "constrictive knowledge management" model that entails different methods/forms of KM for different steps of software engineering. The model makes clear how new knowledge developed by individuals in a software development organization must navigate each of the Five Learning Cycles (Sanchez, 2001) to become accepted by other people in the organization, and then how new knowledge becomes embedded in the organization and its way of working. In effect, the model shows at the macro level how personal knowledge is converted into organizational knowledge, and vice versa, in

processes for active and continuous organizational learning.

We start by showing in Figure 1, we understand by "organization" a company or a business unit within a company whose core business is to develop software and which carries out activities to improve its software practices and processes. we consider a software development project team which include Project Manager who lead the team, System Analyst - a specialist who studies the problems and needs of an organization to determine how people, data, processes, and information technology can best accomplish improvements for the business, System Designers - a technical specialist who translates system users' business requirements and constraints into technical solution, Developers who implements the software components, Test Engineers who performs unit and software integration testing, Technical Writers who produces and maintains the software design document and associated models, and R&D team for the post project evaluation. Our model is based on the five learning cycle to generate, disseminate and apply knowledge within the organization.

In the first cycle, individuals generate imaginary alternative interpretive frame works and new kinds of knowledge which is tacit knowledge. It can be any best practice of software development or new method of solving problem or new approach of software methodology, etc. In the second cycle, organization would have workshop or discussion for all individuals who share their new knowledge within groups to evaluate the new knowledge developed by individuals. In this section, group member would have open discussion about new idea can be accepted or rejected. In the third cycle, groups who interact with other groups to determine whether new knowledge developed by a given group becomes accepted within the overall organization. In this stage the domain experts (manager or leader) are the main player to emergence the new knowledge to the organization. The fourth cycle, group or organization have to select new knowledge accepted at the organizational level

Figure 1. Constructive knowledge management model

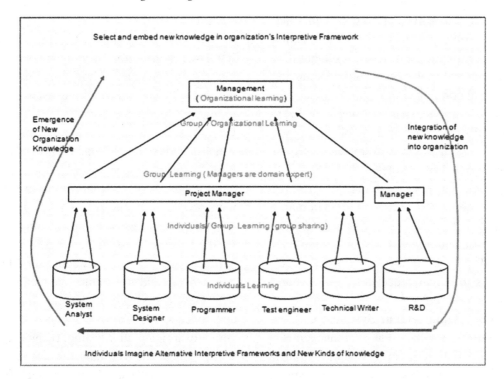

which is embedded in new processes, systems, and the culture of an organization's interactive framework. The fifth cycle, new knowledge is embedded in new processes, systems and organizational culture which lead to new patterns of action by groups and individuals. Finally, new knowledge would be integrated into the organization.

Then we introduced Figure 2, the detail model of how knowledge was articulate to the organization through Information Technology system and how IT system is being used for this regards.

After capturing the tacit knowledge from the individual, group or organization learning cycle was introduced to evaluate and defined the new knowledge which is approved by domain expert, mostly are managers and leaders. Then domain expert is responsible to enter scenarios to the information system by using standard format which is approved by organization. After storing new knowledge in the repository, we can generate the best practice and new organization knowledge by summarizing data, aggregate data by using

various analyzing tools and query on ontological meta data which is a back bone for providing and accessing knowledge sources. The word "ontology" is a terminology for the knowledge indexing and searching process. When you do comparison for key-word based indexing or searching, an ontology will be formalized, common and shared the description of a domain which is the main advantages of indexing and searching process. Then the output result will support for decision making and emergence of new organizational knowledge which must be integrate with business process and organizational culture.

Figure 3 shows the detail process of the main activities of our proposed model, from the initial definition of the objectives of knowledge and experiences that are intended to capture, until its end, when the new knowledge and best practices are identified and integrated to the software development process as well as project activities.

Firstly, organization defines a series of objectives for new knowledge creation for those software development practices and processes that the

Figure 2. General overview of constructive knowledge management model

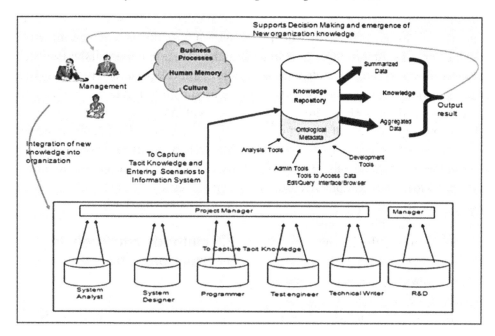

Figure 3. Detailed process of knowledge capturing

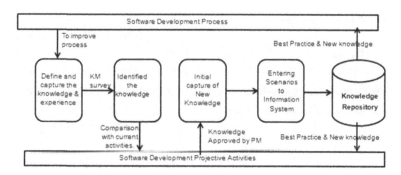

organization considers necessary to improve. Based on these objectives the "KM Survey" is developed, defined as a knowledge management which purpose is to capture new knowledge and experiences. The survey contains a series of questions or multiple choices so that individuals have an opportunity to share of the knowledge and experience in the KM workshop or particular discussion time which is officially set by organization.

Secondly, after survey has done, domain expert (manager or leader) has to verify the outstanding answers given by individuals. This is very initial stage to identify the new knowledge. This new knowledge should go for the group discussion to get opinions for other individuals whether accepted or rejected. Then domain expert are the main key person to do comparison with current practice and decide to adopt as a new knowledge to improve the software development process or project activities.

Thirdly, once these survey are elaborated, individuals are assigned to execute software development process or project tasks for a primary analysis for the initial identification of new knowledge and experiences captured in the answer which is to register their reflections and impressions, difficulties found, unforeseen facts and similar considerations related to the manner in which they carry out his/her tasks. At this stage, domain expert has responsible to monitor the outcomes.

Lastly, new knowledge and personal experiences will be incorporated into the Repository and these knowledge and experience will impact on how software process and project activities will be carried out in the future, and be the basis for future improvements to the software practices and processes used by the organization.

This sequence of activities is repeated iteratively in order to enable the organization to manage, in an incremental manner, the creation of knowledge. In this way, it is possible to gather more insights about their appropriateness and to allow the organization to continuously refine the knowledge and experience already captured.

2. INFORMATION RETRIEVAL

Information retrieval (IR) is a study of how to effectively and efficiently retrieve a piece of information that a user wants from any form of large-volume storage like a collection of files, documents, databases, knowledge bases, or ultimately the World Wide Web. Internet search engines like Google are popular examples of information retrieval tools. Large software development organizations has to deal with thousands or even millions of documents of a variety of types for every step of the software development life cycle — like feasibility reports, various design diagrams and reports, program source codes and comments, test scripts and reports, maintenance reports, etc. — for each of its software projects. (There may be hundreds of such projects in a big software house.) Thus, there is a pressing need for a tool to organize all of these documents in a systematic way and enable the retrieval of a piece

of information required by a software developer in an easy and efficient manner. A dedicated IR system for software engineering will be able to address these requirements and will help make the life of a developer easier. In fact, an IR system can be used both as a generic tool for retrieving any pieces of information that developers needs from a large corpus of documents in the development life cycle of a software project or as a facilitator tool to support a software engineering KM system (e.g., in retrieving a piece of encoded knowledge from a knowledge base).

2.1 Methods and Tools in Information Retrieval

In this section, we will present the methods and tools that are available in IR — especially those relevant to the SE business. We will explore the distinct yet interrelated IR techniques of corpus building, indexing, query evaluation, and evaluation of retrieval effectiveness.

Given a collection of documents, we have to transform them into a specific representational form, called a corpus, to facilitate easier handling, and then build an index on it for faster retrieval.

2.1.1 Corpus Building

Since the original documents are normally in free formats, like plain text files, pdf files, word processing (like MS Word) files, XML files, or program source code files, extracting useful textual information from them is an important exercise. Various file parsers and text segmentation tools (Choi, 2000), depending on the source file type, could be used for information extraction purpose. After the extracting textual information, we have to preprocess it in order to make it cleaner and more standardized.

In the preprocessing step, we usually convert a given text into a "bag of words". That means tokenizing (i.e., splitting) of the text strings into a set of bare words by removing punctuation marks. Then, non-informative stop words such as articles, conjunctions, and prepositions (for example, "a", "the", "who", "from", "this") are removed. After that, we carry out stemming, in which all the derived words are converted into their corresponding base words. For example, if the base word is "fish", the derived words are "fishing", "fished", "fish", and "fisher", etc.

After extracting the textual information from the original documents and preprocessing them, we build the resultant texts into a corpus. This involves storing them in a standardized "internal" format, which can be in the form of plain text files, tables in relational databases, or distributed file systems like MapReduce or Hadoop. These new files/records can be regarded as cleansed versions of their original documents. Each file/record in the corpus can be linked to its original document for back referencing in the future. The purpose of building the corpus is to enable easier manipulation of all the pieces of information in the IR system.

2.1.2 Indexing

After building a corpus, we usually construct an index on it with a view to faster retrieval. This step is essential when the number of documents in the corpus is large, usually containing thousands or even millions of documents, as in the case of a corpus for a big software house. An index can take one of many possible forms. One of the classical examples for document indexing is *inverted file indexing* (Baeza-Yates and Ribeiro-Neto, 2011). We store a main list of distinct words, and each word in that main list points to individual "posting lists" containing the IDs for the documents in which it occurs, its frequency in each document, and optionally, its positions of occurrences. Another type of document indexing is a *signature file*. Given a list of words of interest, a signature

for each document is a bit vector which encodes the presence (1) or absence (0) of each word in it. Usually, a hash coded version of that signature is stored in order to reduce the storage space. This hash-coded signature will serve as a mask to filter out many irrelevant documents during the query processing.

Another popular model for indexing and processing of documents is called a *vector space model* (Baeza-Yates and Ribeiro-Neto, 2011). Each document is regarded as a single data point in a high dimensional space (i.e., a data vector with a high number of attributes.) Each dimension in this model represents a distinct word in the corpus. That is, if there are t unique words in our corpus, each document is a t-dimensional data point (vector). In its simplest form, the attribute value for each dimension in a document vector is 1 if the corresponding word is present in the document and 0 if the word is not. In practice, more sophisticated mechanisms such as normalized word weights are used.

Since t can be a very large number for large corpuses, the techniques of dimensionality reduction (such as Principal Component Analysis) or unsupervised feature selection (like random feature projection) may be used to reduce the number of dimensions of a document vector. This is done in order to avoid the "curse of dimensionality", a phenomenon which negatively affects both speed and accuracy in query processing. Indexing techniques can be used to index the data points either in their original or reduced dimensional spaces. High dimensional indexing techniques like iDistance, kd-tree, and X-tree or filtering techniques VA-File can be used (Samet, 2006).

An enhance version of the vector pace model is known as the *latent semantic indexing* model (Deerwester et al., 1990). The vector space model assumes independence among words in a document. However, this does not reflect the reality. The latent semantic indexing utilizes the rich expressive power of natural language like English. It groups semantically related words into "concepts" using singular value decomposition. The resultant concepts are regarded as independent of each other.

2.1.3 Query Evaluation

The simplest form of queries for document retrieval is a *Boolean query*. A few key words and the Boolean operators between them are used to retrieve the documents that contain those words. Such queries are equivalent to normal database searches. For example, a query like *"renewable AND (power OR energy) AND (solar OR photovoltaic OR PV)"* will retrieve documents that contain information regarding renewable energy generation using solar panels.

For the *rank queries*, the documents in the corpus are ranked according to their putative relevance to the query key words (like Google does when we search our key words). The putative relevance is measured using the concept of "similarity" between the documents. "Distance" is the flip concept of similarity. We can merely measure either one of those concepts and the reaming one can be readily known. For example, if the similarity between two documents is in the range 0.0 (least similar) to 1.0 (most similar), the distance between these documents can be calculated as:

$$Distance = 1.0 - Similarity$$

Conversely, similarity can also be calculated from a normalized distance (ranged 0.0 to 1.0) as:

$$Similarity = 1.0 - Distance$$

A number of methods can be used to determine the similarity (and hence distance) between two given documents. Before giving the definitions of similarities, let's first look at the concept of "weight" of each word.

In general, the weight w of a word in a document is a combination of its local weight l, which is specific to that document, and global weight g, which is common for all the documents in the corpus (Marcus, 2011).

$$w = l \times g$$

One of the most common forms for local weight is the term frequency tf, which means the frequency (count) of this word in that given document.

$$l = tf$$

One of the most common forms for global weight is the inverse document frequency idf, which is the logarithm (base 2) of the ratio of the total number of documents in the corpus N to the number of documents f in which the word occurs.

$$g = idf = \log_2 \frac{N}{f}$$

It should be noted that the inverse document frequency idf for each word is independent of the query and can be calculated and stored in advance.

Therefore, the weight of a word is calculated as:

$$w = tf \times idf = tf \times \log_2 \frac{N}{f}$$

Now, we can calculate the similarity between the query Q represented as a vector of the normalized weights of the words it contains: $(Q = [w_1^q, w_2^q, \ldots, w_t^q])$ and a document D in the corpus also represented as a vector of the normalized weights of the words it contains:

$(D = [w_1^d, w_2^d, \ldots, w_t^d])$, where t is the number of all unique words in the corpus.

For the sake of clarity, let us denote $w_i^q = x_i$ and $w_i^d = y_i$, where $1 \leq i \leq t$.

The magnitudes of the vectors Q and D can be calculated as:

$$|Q| = \sqrt{\sum_{i=1}^{t}(x_i)^2} \quad and \quad |D| = \sqrt{\sum_{i=1}^{t}(y_i)^2}$$

It should be noted that $|D|$ can be pre-computed for all the documents in the corpus. The dot product of the two vectors Q and D is calculated as:

$$Q.D = \sum_{i=1}^{t} x_i.y_i$$

Some of the most common measures to calculate the similarity or the distance of Q and D are as follows:

Cosine Similarity:

$$Similarity(Q,D) = \frac{Q.D}{|Q|.|D|}$$

Jaccard Similarity:

$$Similarity(Q,D) = \frac{Q.D}{|Q|^2 + |D|^2 - Q.D}$$

Dice Similarity:

$$Similarity(Q,D) = \frac{2.Q.D}{|Q|^2 + |D|^2}$$

Normalized Euclidean Distance:

$$Distance(Q,D) = \sqrt{\frac{\sum_{i=1}^{t}(x_i' - y_i')^2}{2}}$$

where x_i' and y_i' are the normalized weights in the unit query vector $Q' = Q/|Q|$ and the unit document vector $D' = D/|D|$ respectively.

It should be noted that the indexing mechanisms discussed above are utilized in calculating the similarity of the query to every documents in the corpus.

For example, in inverted file indexing, for each word in the query (after removing stopped words and stemming), the posting list corresponding to that word is visited in order to calculate the values of $x_i.y_i$ for that word with respect to all the documents. In order words, the dot product $Q.D$ for every document is incrementally updated whenever a posting list corresponding to each word in the query is visited. After visiting all the concerning posting lists, the final value of $Q.D$ for every document is obtained. The term $|D|$ for every document has been usually pre-computed, and the term $|Q|$ for the query can be computed straightforwardly. Thus, at the final, based on the similarity measure of one's choice, the similarity of every document D in the corpus with respect to the query Q is obtained. Then, the documents are scored (ranked) according to their similarity values. The advantage of inverted file indexing is that we can compute the similarity between the query and the documents without actually visiting the documents in the corpus but by merely visiting the index. This is particularly useful when the documents are of large sizes.

In the vector space model, we can elect to use a distance measure such as normalized Euclidean distance and use a distance-based indexing technique like iDistance (Jagadish et al., 2005) in order to select any given k number of nearest (i.e., most similar) documents using a k nearest neighbors (kNN) algorithm.

2.1.4 Evaluation of Retrieval Effectiveness

The effectiveness of a retrieval exercise with regard to a query can be evaluated with the metrics of precision, recall, and F-measure. Suppose that for a given query, we rank the documents in the corpus using a similarity/distance measure of our choice. Then we retrieve the top k highest ranking documents as our answer. Among those k documents, some of them (say r of them) are "actually" relevant to query, but some may be not, unfortunately. (Those documents which are actually relevant must be identified by human experts beforehand.) Suppose that in the corpus, there are a total of R documents which are relevant to the query. The measures of precision and recall are defined as:

$$precision = \frac{r}{R}$$

$$recall = \frac{r}{k}$$

Both precision and recall range between 0.0 and 1.0. The higher the precision/recall is, the better the retrieval system is. Precision and recall tell us about the two different perspectives of accuracy and coverage regarding the retrieval exercise. In order to reflect those two perspectives simultaneously, F-measure is introduced.

$$F = 2 \times \frac{precision \times recall}{precision + recall}$$

2.1.5 Other Information Retrieval Techniques

In addition to the core task of document retrieval, other tasks and techniques that fall under the broader area of information retrieval are as follows:

- **String Matching:** To perform exact or approximate matching of one text (sub) string to another. This is useful in exactly pinpointing input search phrase(s) inside the documents that are highly ranked after executing a query (like Google does). String matching methods like Rabin-Karp algorithm, finite automata method, Knuth-Morris-Pratt algorithm etc. can be used for this task (Cormen et al., 2009).

- **Document Categorization:** To automatically categorize a set of documents into two or more distinct categories (like news reports, articles, scientific papers, etc.). It is a supervision learning task in which the desired categories must be predefined and some sample documents for each category must be available in the first place (Sebastiani, 2002).

- **Document Clustering:** To split a given set of documents into their respective groups. It is an unsupervised learning task in which the groups (categories) themselves are not predefined (Andrews and Fox, 2007). However, whether it is needed to predefine the required number of groups or not depends on the type of clustering algorithm used.

- **Duplicate Document Detection:** To detect the documents that are exactly the same or almost the same (Chowdhury et al., 2002). This is useful for storage space reduction, plagiarism detection, document versioning and control, etc.

- **Text data Mining:** To extract a specific type of information from a single or a set of documents (Cohen and Hunter, 2008). For example, from a set of scientific papers on chemistry, all the chemical reactions mentioned in them can be extracted using text mining techniques.

2.2 Information Retrieval for Software Engineering

In this section, we will provide the concrete examples of how IR techniques can be used to improve the productivity of software developers in general and how they can facilitate a software engineering KM system in particular.

We first have to build a corpus for a piece of software by parsing its program source codes and extracting key words from other documents (Marcus, 2011). As generally described on Section 2.1.1, this involves removing the stop words in English, standard function library names, programming language keywords, etc. After that, another preprocessing job is carried out to standardize the variable names, etc. For example, the variable names of *max_count, MaxCount, MaximumCount* in multiple source code files are now unified to a standard one (say *MaxCount*). (If the software house has a strict standardized naming convention, this preprocessing job will be much easier.) Then, stemming is done to convert derived words into their respective base words (like converting *MaxCounter* into *MaxCount*). Likewise, Lexical analysis can be performed to break up text strings into words or tokens (like splitting *MaxCount* into two words: Max and Count). In addition to the source code files, other types of documents such as feasibility reports, requirement specifications, system designs, program designs, test scripts, test reports, user complaints, maintenance reports, etc. are also to be processed and stored into their

respective corpuses or a centralized corpus. After building the corpus(es), any type of indexing of one's choice, as described in Section 2.1.2, is applied on it with a view to speeding up the processing of queries in the future.

2.2.1 IR for Software Engineering in General

In general, IR can be applied to some of the important problems in SE like the *concept localization* problem for discovering a point of change, the *traceability link recovery* problem for finding the links of documents associated with a proposed change in requirement, the *bug triage* problem for verification of bugs, assignment of severity level, and recommendation of relevant developer, etc., and the *software clustering* problem for organizing similar software entities into intrinsic groups (Marcus, 2011).

- **Concept Localization:** It means "discovering human oriented concepts and assigning them to their implementation instances within a program" (Biggerstaff et al., 1993). Concept location is needed whenever a modification is to be made to software at various design levels and/or at source code level. Thus, it must be within a well-defined context and level of abstraction. The locations of a particular concept (e.g., *Change Input Method*) may be different for the task undertaken by a high-level system designer and that by a developer. The user usually formulates a query and executes it to get the ranks of the corpus's documents that are relevant to his/her task in hand. Then, he/she can examine the results and make changes to the affected original documents accordingly. This procedure is repeated a couple of times with different queries. Concept location is also useful in determining the dependency and coupling of codes.

- **Traceability Link Recovery:** It means "the ability to describe and follow the life of a requirement, in both forwards and backwards direction (i.e., from its origins, through its development and specification, to its subsequent deployment and use, and through all periods of on-going refinement and iteration in any of these phases.)" (Gotel and Finklestein, 1994). This problem is related to the above concept location problem but the objective is different. Since it is desirable to discover as many documents that involve in the link in question as possible, a higher recall rate is much desirable. The user can review the traceability link reported by the IR system, validate it, and report his/her feedback on its relevance. Traceability link recovery is also useful in impact analysis of software bug/failure and in identification of reusable software components.

- **Bug Triage:** When a software bug occurs, the project in-charge has to verify the incoming bug report, assign a severity level to it, and allocate a developer to solve it (Marcus, 2011). It can be started by analyzing the contents of the bug report. The sub-problems for the bug triage process are: duplicate bug detection, developer recommendation, assignment of severity level, and detection of security bugs. We can use string matching, document classification, clustering, and duplication detection tools in order to automate this process.

- **Software Clustering:** The purpose is to group software entities into clusters such that the entities in the same cluster are similar to each other, and those in different clusters are different. Document clustering techniques (Andrews and Fox, 2007) can be utilized for this purpose. The cluster-

ing results can be evaluated using cluster quality measures like silhouette analysis (Rousseeuw, 1987). Software clustering is useful for software architecture recovery, identifying the topics implemented, detecting software clones, software re-modularization, program comprehension, etc. (Marcus, 2011).

2.2.2 IR for Proposed Constructive Knowledge Management Model

The primary role for an IR system in our proposed constructive knowledge management model for software development is to efficiently retrieve the knowledge mainly from the knowledge repository and its ontological metadata in some cases. Most pieces of knowledge stored in the repository will be in the form of highly standardized, concise and restricted-vocabulary textual information. Therefore, standard IR corpus building, indexing strategies and query processing techniques can be used to facilitate efficient and effective retrieval by an organizational knowledge user. For the retrieval from the ontological metadata, ontology-based retrieval methods like Vallet et al. (2005) could be used.

During the testing period, the effectiveness of the retrieval results for each query can be manually verified with regard to their actual relevance to the topic in question and then evaluated using the metrics of precision, recall, and F-measure. We can experiment with different combinations of IR models (like vector space or latent semantic) and similarity/distance measures (like Cosine, Jaccard, Dice, or normalized Euclidean), and select the one which gives us the best results.

CONCLUSION

The paradigm shift of Knowledge Management is growing very firstly in many of organizations nowadays. The fundamental concepts and processes discussed here reflect of growing shift in management thinking and practice today. This paradigm shift is from traditional management concept which is based on command and control to new concept of management which is more concerned with developing, supporting, connecting, leveraging and empowering employees as knowledge workers.

In Software Engineering environment, Knowledge Management is of interest to many software professionals and researchers and is being tested by many organizations as a potential solution repository related to software development problems. As we can see recent developments in IT definitely enable sharing documented knowledge independent of time and space. We can foresee that there will also be support for capturing and disseminating knowledge in various formats, enabling organizations and individuals to share knowledge on a world-wide scale in the future.

In addition to knowledge management, information retrieval also plays a crucial role in Software Engineering. IR can be used both as a general-purpose tool to improve the productivity of developers or as an enabler tool to facilitate a Knowledge Management system.

REFERENCES

Andrade, J., Ares, J., García, R., Rodríguez, S., & Suárez, S. (2006). A reference model for knowledge management in software engineering. *Engineering Letters*, *13*, 159–166.

Andrews, N. O., & Fox, E. A. (2007). *Recent developments in document clustering*. Technical Report TR-07-35, Virginia Polytechnic Institute and State University.

Baeza-Yates, R., & Ribeiro-Neto, B. (2011). *Modern information retrieval: The concepts and technology behind search* (2nd ed.). ACM Press.

Bertino, E., Ooi, B. C., Sacks-Davis, R., Tan, K. L., Zobel, J., Shilovsky, B., & Catania, B. (1997). *Indexing techniques for advanced database systems*. Kluwer Academic Publishers. doi:10.1007/978-1-4615-6227-6

Biggerstaff, T. J., Mitbander, B. G., & Webster, D. (1993). The concept assignment problem in program understanding. In *Proceedings of the 15th International Conference on Software Engineering (ICSE'93)*, (pp. 482-498).

Birk, A., Surmann, D., & Althoff, K.-D. (1999). Applications of knowledge acquisition in experimental software engineering. In *Proceedings of 11th European Workshop on Knowledge Acquisition, Modeling and Management (EKAW'99)*, (pp. 67-84).

Bjørnson, F. O., & Dingsøyr, T. (2008). Knowledge management in software engineering: A systematic review of studied concepts, findings and research methods used. *Information and Software Technology*, *50*, 1055–1068. doi:10.1016/j.infsof.2008.03.006

Choi, F. Y. Y. (2000). Advances in domain independent linear text segmentation. *Proceedings of the 1st Meeting of the North American Chapter of the Association for Computational Linguistics (ANLP-NAACL'00)*, (pp. 26–33).

Chowdhury, A., Frieder, O., Grossman, D., & McCabe, M. C. (2002). Collection statistics for fast duplicate document detection. *ACM Transactions on Information Systems*, *20*, 171–191. doi:10.1145/506309.506311

Cohen, K. B., & Hunter, L. (2008). Getting started in text mining. *PLoS Computational Biology*, *4*, e20. doi:10.1371/journal.pcbi.0040020

Cormen, T. H., Leiserson, C. E., Rivest, R. L., & Stein, C. (2009). *Introduction to algorithms* (3rd ed.). MIT Press.

Davenport, T. H., & Prusak, L. (1998). *Working knowledge: How organizations manage what they know*. Harvard Business School Press.

Deerwester, S., Dumais, S. T., Landauer, T. K., Furnas, G. W., & Harshman, R. A. (1990). Indexing by latent semantic analysis. *Journal of the Society for Information Science, 41*, 391–407. doi:10.1002/(SICI)1097-4571(199009)41:6<391::AID-ASI1>3.0.CO;2-9

Fischer, G., & Ostwald, J. (2001). Knowledge management: Problems, promises, realities and challenges. *IEEE Intelligent Systems, 16*, 60–72. doi:10.1109/5254.912386

Gotel, O. C. Z., & Finklestein, C. W. (1994). An analysis of the requirements traceability problem. In *Proceedings of the 1st International Conference on Requirements Engineering (ICRE'94)*, (pp. 94-101).

Jagadish, H. V., Ooi, B. C., Tan, K. L., Yu, C., & Zhang, R. (2005). iDistance: An adaptive B+-tree based indexing method for nearest neighbor search. *ACM Transactions on Database Systems, 30*, 364–397. doi:10.1145/1071610.1071612

LaBrie, R., & Louis, R. S. (2003). Information retrieval from knowledge management systems: Using knowledge hierarchies to overcome keyword limitations. In *9th Americas Conference on Information Systems (AMCIS'03)*, (pp. 2552-2563).

Manning, C. D., Raghavan, P., & Schütze, H. (2008). *Introduction to information retrieval*. Cambridge, UK: Cambridge University Press. doi:10.1017/CBO9780511809071

Marcus, A. (2011). *Information retrieval methods for software engineering*. In Canadian Summer School on Practical Analyses of Software Engineering Data (PASED'11), Montreal, Quebec, Canada, 2011. Retrieved from http://pased.soccerlab.polymtl.ca/materials/june-18-2011/PASED-06.18.2011-Slides.pdf

Nonaka, I., & Takeuchi, H. (1995). *The knowledge creating company*. Oxford, UK: Oxford University Press.

Rousseeuw, P. J. (1987). Silhouettes: A graphical aid to the interpretation and validation of cluster analysis. *Computational & Applied Mathematics, 20*, 53–65. doi:10.1016/0377-0427(87)90125-7

Samet, H. (2006). *Foundations of multidimensional and metric data structures*. Morgan Kaufmann Publishers.

Sanchez, R. (1997). Managing articulated knowledge in competence-based competition. In *Strategic learning and knowledge management* (pp. 163–187). John Wiley and Sons.

Sanchez, R. (2001). Managing knowledge into competences: The five learning cycles of the competent organization. In *Knowledge management and organizational competence* (pp. 3–37). Oxford University Press.

Sanchez, R. (2004). Creating modular platforms for strategic flexibility. *Design Management Review, 15*, 58–67. doi:10.1111/j.1948-7169.2004.tb00151.x

Sanchez, R., Heene, A., & Thomas, H. (Eds.). (1996). *Dynamics of competence-based competition: Theory and practice in the new strategic management*. Elsevier Pergamon.

Sebastiani, F. (2002). Machine learning in automated text categorization. *ACM Computing Surveys, 34*, 1–47.

Sindhgatta, R. (2006). Using an information retrieval system to retrieve source code samples. In *Proceedings of the 28th International Conference on Software Engineering (ICSE'06)*, (pp. 905-908).

Vallet, D., Fernández, M., & Castells, P. (2005). An ontology-based information retrieval model. In *Proceedings of the 2nd Annual European Semantic Web Conference (ESWC'05)*, (pp. 455-470).

Walsh, J. P., & Ungson, G. R. (1991). Organizational memory. *Academy of Management Review*, *16*, 57–91.

KEY TERMS AND DEFINITIONS

Information Retrieval: Information retrieval is the area of study concerned with searching for documents, for information within documents, and for metadata about documents, as well as that of searching structured storage, relational databases, and the World Wide Web (Wikipedia definition).

Knowledge: Knowledge is a familiarity with someone or something, which can include facts, information, descriptions, or skills acquired through experience or education (Wikipedia definition).

Knowledge Base: A knowledge base is a special kind of database for knowledge management. A knowledge base provides a means for information to be collected, organized, shared, searched and utilized (Wikipedia definition).

Knowledge Management: Knowledge management comprises a range of strategies and practices used in an organization to identify, create, represent, distribute, and enable adoption of insights and experiences (Wikipedia definition).

Knowledge Retrieval: Knowledge Retrieval seeks to return information in a structured form, consistent with human cognitive processes as opposed to simple lists of data items (Wikipedia definition).

Organizational Memory: Organizational memory (sometimes called institutional or corporate memory) is the accumulated body of data, information, and knowledge created in the course of an individual organization's existence (Wikipedia definition).

Software Engineering: Software engineering is the application of a systematic, disciplined, quantifiable approach to the development, operation, and maintenance of software, and the study of these approaches; that is, the application of engineering to software (Wikipedia definition).

Chapter 22
Modeling Transparency in Software Systems for Distributed Work Groups

A B Sagar
Hyderabad Central University, India

ABSTRACT

Software systems require ethics. Several systems fail due to lack of ethics built into them. So, every software engineer needs to have an idea on ethics, so that they can build them into the software systems. Ethics requires accountability. Accountability is to the organization, stakeholders, and to the society. This chapter discusses the ethical issue of transparency. In the previous decade, we have seen a very increased use of this term. Transparency is being considered an indispensable ingredient in social accountability and is necessary for preserving and guaranteeing ethical and fair processes. Transparency is related to visibility of information, and without it, the organization and stakeholders will be left in blind states. Ultimately, the lack of transparency leads to unpleasant surprises due to bad decisions, letdown, increasing doubts, uncertainty, failure, and the breakdown of faith and trust. This is bad for the organizations involved, the people investing in them, stakeholders, suppliers, and employees. It is also bad, as we have seen recently, for the economy. This is true for government agencies and functions just as for businesses and communities. The least transparent governments are the most dictatorial and secretive in their decision-making and governance. An informed citizenship is vital for healthy, free societies, just as informed investors are needed for a healthy, strong economy. The degree of transparency in the software systems, then, becomes a barometer for health and vitality in governments, leadership, and business. The growing importance to the requirement of transparency in all these domains was the motivation to the present chapter.

DOI: 10.4018/978-1-4666-3679-8.ch022

1. INTRODUCTION

Transparency policies have proven to be effective for resolving controversial issues by minimizing health and safety risks, fighting corruption, promoting civil rights, sustaining improvements to public services, etc. Recent observations revealed that there is an increase in societal attention to the issue of transparency and it was also predicted that transparency will become the required premise for gaining and maintaining customer trust and collaborative relationships with all stakeholders in all constructive software systems. This chapter studies transparency and provides a basis for implementing transparency in a software system. The work presented in this chapter can be used in any software system to facilitate transparency into the system. The objective of this chapter is to provide a rudimentary framework for transparency and also provide a few implementation details to facilitate implementation of transparency in any software system.

Doubts and uncertainty can lead to loss of faith and trust. Loss of faith and trust on a software system, leads to collapse of the system. Transparency – which can be defined as "the accessibility of information to stakeholders of a business, regarding matters that affect their interests" – can shape and revolutionize a software system. Transparency policies have proven to be effective for resolving controversial issues by minimizing health and safety risks, fighting corruption, promoting civil rights, sustaining improvements to public services, etc. Recent observations revealed that there is an increase in societal attention to the issue of transparency and it was also predicted that transparency will become the required premise for gaining and maintaining customer trust and collaborative relationships with all stakeholders in all constructive software systems.

2. TRANSPARENCY

Transparency means openness of decisions and actions. Put another way, it means a free flow of information about decisions and actions, from source to recipient. There are several categories that are considered under transparency. Publication: The software system simply provides some rudimentary information about a specific issue; citizens/users can get a basic insight into operations and personnel; Transaction: The software system automates some public sector processes to remove partly those processes from human control; Reporting: The software system provides specific details of public sector decisions and actions; these may be reported in the form of performance indicators; Openness: The software system not only provides details of current performance, but enables users to compare that performance against pre-set standards (may also be called benchmarks or targets). Thus transparency is related to both financial and non- financial reporting. Financial reporting includes tracking of monetary data and non-financial reporting includes task execution data. This section provides a theoretical basis for understanding transparency and the conclusion provides details needed for implementation of transparency in a work group.

A work group implies two or more individuals who routinely function like a team, and interdependent in achievement of a common goal, and may or may not work next to one another or in the same department. This kind of work groups are ever present in business domains or as software teams. They represent a part of a business or the business itself. Transparency implies visibility of information related to financial and non-financial matters of the work group and its stakeholders. Work groups are generally hierarchical in nature with one supervising over another i.e. higher levels supervise over lower levels. Hierarchies are a common structure in organizations. This is because they reflect a natural and common technique for human beings to deal with complexity. In business, the business owner traditionally occupied the pinnacle of the organization. In most modern large companies, there is now no longer a single dominant shareholder, and the collective power of the business owners is for most purposes delegated to a board of directors, which in turn delegates the day-to-day running of the company to a managing director or CEO. For example, a typical work group will be a Self Help Group and the hierarchical structure will be as given in Figure 1.

Transparency is related to both financial and non-financial reporting. Financial reporting includes tracking of monetary data and non-financial reporting includes task execution data. This section provides a theoretical basis for understanding transparency and the section 3 provides details needed for implementation of transparency in a work group.

2.1 Directions of Transparency

In the context of a software system for a business where several levels of administration are present, transparency may take four directions: upwards, downwards inwards, and outwards. One important question for the software system developer is to ask his/her own self what would happen if the hierarchy is not properly captured. If an organization has different structures for regional vs functional management, the developer needs to use a pair of hierarchies and transparency is to be designed for both these hierarchies (See Figure 2). In all these directions both the "operational transparency" and "transactional transparency" are implied.

- **Upwards Transparency:** Is meant to describe a hierarchical principal actor situation where the subordinate actor's actions

Figure 1. Hierarchical structure

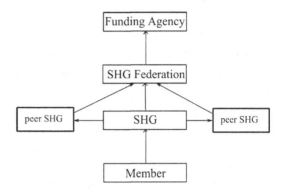

(or transactions) can be observed by the principal.

- **Downwards Transparency:** Is the opposite of upwards, ie. when the principal can be observed by subordinate actors.
- **Inwards Transparency:** Is the transparency for outsiders to see the inside of the organization.
- **Outwards Transparency:** Is the transparency it is seeing in all the outsiders (peers) of the organization.

2.2 Degrees of Transparency

We can classify transparency into three degrees: opaqueness, translucency and clarity. Two more degrees can be described namely "*black hole*" and "*dazzle*". They are used to describe the two extreme situations where no information is released by a work group or too much information is disclosed, respectively. Opaqueness is when a work group does not disclose any information to its stakeholders. A work group should not be maintaining opaqueness if it wants to be transparent. Translucency is when a work group discloses its information "*partially*". A work group cannot be transparent until it discloses *all* of the essential information. Clarity is when a work group discloses all of its information. Only the work group having clarity degree of transparency is the transparent work group.

Figure 2. Work group, subordinates, and supervisors

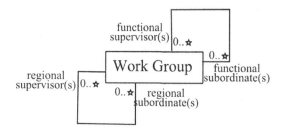

2.2 Dimensions of Transparency

Klotz *et al.* (2008) suggested nine dimensions of transparency. They stratified these nine dimensions into three distinctive groups – recognition, facilitation and enabling. Since three of the suggested dimensions are considered to be integral consequences of providing transparency in the first six dimensions, only six of Klotz et al's nine dimensions were adopted in our present model, and then they were stratified into the dimensions of time (pre, per, and post). Thus each activity (task) will have three phases viz. pre-activity, per-activity and post-activity and transparency is defined on these three phases.

For example, let '*w*' be the activity to be done by the work group and let wpre, wper, wpost be the pre-activity, per-activity and post-activity phases of the work *w*, and each phase requires communication with stakeholders. Suppose a work group's activity (*w*) is to irrigate and supply five tonnes of corn. Now, this activity can be divided into three phases: pre-activity (*wpre*), per-activity (*wper*) and post-activity (*wpost*). As per the discussion in the above subsection, each activity will have to maintain transparency in the four directions *viz.* upward, downward, inward and outward. That is, each activity involves communication with entities like governing bodies, subordinates, members, peers/competitors, etc. In *wpre*, communication with supervisor/governing bodies involves describing how much land they are going to use, expenditure estimates, how many members are going to

work in it, skills and experience possessed by the members, what fertilizers and chemicals are being used, what techniques are being employed, how waste is disposed, how much each member earns, delivery dates, other responsibilities undertaken by the work group, etc. And communication with the subordinates involves describing terms and conditions laid down by the supervising/governing bodies, number of hours each member should work, wages for the members, responsibilities of each member, skills and experience required in the members, etc. Communication with the peers and competitors include enquiring regarding problems that are faced in their experience, enquiring how they solved specific issues, seeking suggestions, viewing their data, reports, bills, etc. In *wper*, communications regarding status and problems are made. Similarly in the *wpost*, communications regarding feedback and performance understanding are carried on.

If the transparency of *w* is T_w, then it is the sum of transparencies of the three phases i.e. transparency of pre-activity (T_{wpre}), transparency of per-activity (T_{wper}) and transparency of post-activity (T_{wpost}).

$$T_w = T_{wpre} + T_{wper} + T_{wpost}$$

Interestingly, the degrees of transparency can be correspondingly mapped on to the phases of activity (See Figure 3). Prior to the pre-activity phase, the degree of transparency is opaque (or null). If the transparency conditions are met in the pre-activity phase, the degree of transparency becomes translucent. If the transparency conditions are met at per-activity phase and post-activity phases, then the degree of transparency becomes clear. As it is observed that after each activity phase, the degree of transparency is increasing, it is of interest to us to define the primary constituents of each activity phase which affect the degree of transparency. At each activity phase we define the transparency dimensions that are required. Though transparency dimensions are

Figure 3. Degrees of transparency

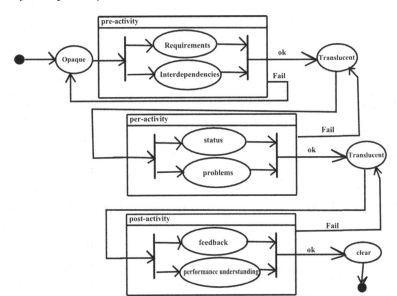

task- and situation-dependent, some dimensions are mandatory. Recognition of responsibilities and interdependencies are primarily of concern before the realization of a given activity (pre-activity). Recognition of status and problems are primarily related to transparency into an ongoing activity (per-activity). Similarly, understanding of performance and feedback are related to post-activity transparency.

2.3 Perspectives in Transparency

Three main perspectives can be observed in Transparency: static, dynamic and radical.

- **Static Transparency:** In Static Transparency, reporting information is standardized and is done in official formats — such as the financial statements required by various government agencies, comprehensible format for customers, etc. However this is not a very efficient type of transparency because in this type, information disclosure is *"telling"* rather than *"sharing"*, and the flow of information is

mainly unidirectional i.e. from the work group to stakeholders. Since there is no on demand display of information, it does not fully portray the meaning of transparency.

Let $_{static}T_w(G)$ represent static transparency of a work group 'G' over the activity 'w'. Since it is static, it suggests a unidirectional flow of information from 'G' to stakeholders 'S'.

$$_{static}T_w(G) \Rightarrow \forall info \in G, S \in stakeholders, flow(info,G,S) \wedge \neg flow(info,S,G)$$

flow(info, G, S) indicates that the information ('info') flows from work group 'G' to stakeholders 'S'. Since this is static transparency, the information flow can be unidirectional only i.e. G to S. But the converse, i.e. *flow(info,S, G)* does not hold true. That is, info could not flow from S to G. There is no information on demand, that is, stakeholders cannot request and obtain information of their choice. They only get what the work group chooses to reveal. This kind of transparency is also called selective transparency. Thus static transparency gives liberty to the work groups but not to the stakeholders. A work group adopts static transparency when its rules for reporting are all predefined (by the governing bodies), and it need not respond to stakeholder's queries.

- **Dynamic Transparency:** Is when the work group and its stakeholders can exchange, share and compare information and adapt its online behavior and electronic requests and queries to the answers and reactions of respective counterparts.

$$_{dynamic}T_w(G) \Rightarrow \forall info \in G, S \in stakeholders,$$

$$flow(info,G,S) \land flow(info,S,G)$$

- **Radical Transparency:** Refers to the capability of a work group to employ internet-based technologies, such as rss, blogs and collaborative websites, in order to create a direct and continuous dialogue with customers and other stakeholders.

$$_{radical}T_w(G) \Rightarrow \forall info \in G, S \in stakeholders,$$
$$stream(info,G,S) \land stream(info,S,G)$$

stream(info, G, S) is similar to the flow function as in dynamic perspective, but the difference is only that the info flow is continuous in streaming.

3. IMPLEMENTING TRANSPARENCY IN A WORK GROUP

To implement the above theoretical approach in a practical environment of work groups, a Work group Behavioral Model [WBM] and Task Execution Cycle [TEC] are proposed. WBM outlines the general behavior of every work group. WMB provides an imprint of generic behavior of each work group and TEC gives the different states of an executing activity (task). Relationship between WBM and TEC is that TEC is an integral part of ExTsk of the WBM.

3.1 Work Group Behavioral Model (WBM)

The behavior of a work group which is basically executing tasks assigned by a supervisor is modeled in Figure 4. Each work group, after receiving a task, checks for the feasibility of the task. If the task is feasible, then begins to execute the task. But if the task is infeasible, then assigns the task to another work group. When the task is assigned to others, the task goes into a sleep state. After completion of the task, receives a signal and wakes up from sleep, for any remaining work to be completed. All the execution details will be stored in the Repst for preserving transparency.

The primitives of the WMB are explained below:

- **TMonitor:** TMonitor is a continuously running process which keeps monitoring for items like tasks, acks, requests, reports, etc. When it receives an item it immediately forwards it to Rpt.
- **Rpt:** Rpt has varied functionalities depending on the item it receives. If the item is a task, it will notify the task sender through

Figure 4. Work group behavior model

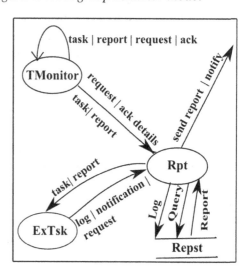

an ack about the receipt of the task. And it will forward the task to ExTsk to continue execution. If the item is an ack, it will store the ack in the Repst against the corresponding task it has dispatched. If the item is a request, it will query the Repst and generate a report and dispatch it to the requester. If the item is a report, it will store the report in the Repst against the corresponding task for which request was made.

- **ExTsk:** The functionality of ExTsk is to log the stages a task passes through as the work group executes the task. If the received task is feasible to that workgroup, execution is started. Else, if the task is partially feasible, then task is split into three portions (feasible part, assign part, remainder part) and the feasible part is executed. The assign part is assigned to a different work group. Soon after the report is received indicating the completion of the assign part, the remainder part is executed. After completing the execution of the whole task, ExTsk sends the task completed notification to Rpt to be forwarded to all the notification recipients. the notification recipients can be in any of the four directions given by the directions of transparency. Also, depending on the perspective of the transparency being followed, the messages are dispatched. If it is following static transparency, then the report is dispatched to the notification recipients only if the work group thinks it is essential. Else if it is following dynamic transparency, then it will dispatch if that report is demanded a priori. And if it is following radical transparency, then it will immediately dispatch the report into all its channels. While executing the task, ExTsk writes the intermediate task status to the store Repst through Rpt so that transparency is maintained regarding the status of task at every phase of execution of the task.

- **Repst:** Repst is a repository. Each activity (task) along with all related information is stored in Repst. Whenever a request is received at the TMonitor, it is forwarded to Rpt; Rpt makes a query to Repst and the query result is sent as response (report). All logs are also stored in Repst.

3.2 Task Execution Cycle (TEC)

The Task Execution Cycle (TEC) is integral part of ExTsk of WMB (See Figure 5). It has all the states that a task undergoes. The states are described below:

- **Recv:** The task is in Recvd state when it is just received. It will be in this state until the work group is ready to consider it for execution.
- **Initiate:** The task moves to Initiated state when the work group has considered to begin execution.
- **Execute:** The task moves to Executing state when the work group has started execution or is continuing execution after waking up from sleep.
- **Assign:** The task moves to assigned state if the task was assigned to a different work group.
- **Sleep:** The task moves to sleep state once the task was assigned.

Figure 5. Task execution cycle

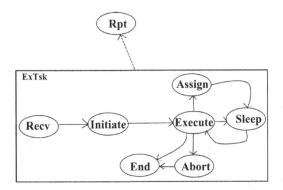

- **Abort:** If the task was found to be infeasible or if the assignment fails, then the task moves to aborted state.
- **End:** The final state of every task is the End state.

As discussed earlier, dynamic or radical transparencies involve duplex form of communication. A requester can make a request and the task executing work group is bound to send the details. This involves querying the Repst regarding the task, generating the report from the Repst, and forwarding the report to the requester. Now, implementation of transparency in all the activities like task execution, ack sending, request handling, etc can be done using transparency messages. Every activity has certain states as given in the Task Execution Cycle. For each state in the execution of the task, transparency messages are associated providing financial and non-financial information. When the task reaches a state, a transparency message is sent to the notification recipient based on the direction, degree, dimension and perspectives of the transparency being followed.

Paths taken by the activity in the TEC are:

1. Recvd $\rightarrow$ Initiate $\rightarrow$ Execute $\rightarrow$ End
2. Recvd $\rightarrow$ Initiate $\rightarrow$ Execute $\rightarrow$ Assign $\rightarrow$ Sleep $\rightarrow$ Execute $\rightarrow$ End
3. Recvd $\rightarrow$ Initiate $\rightarrow$ Execute $\rightarrow$ Abort $\rightarrow$ End
4. Recvd $\rightarrow$ Initiate $\rightarrow$ Execute $\rightarrow$ Assign $\rightarrow$ Sleep $\rightarrow$ Execute $\rightarrow$ Abort $\rightarrow$ End

3.3 Transparency Computation

Transparency can be finally represented as: Transparency (A,B,direction,degree,dimension,perspective) indicating transparency between any two entities A and B (representing a subordinate work group and supervisor work group, or a work group and its peer, etc), the direction of transparency (upwards, downwards, inwards, outwards), degree of transparency (opaque, translucent, clear) and perspective (static, dynamic, radical).

3.3.1 Direction of Transparency

There are four directions for transparency and notification recipient details will be specified in the task. If the transparency is maintained in all the directions, then the value is whole, otherwise it will be a ratio of number of directions in which transparency is maintained to the total directions i.e. four.

3.3.2 Degree of Transparency

This is easier to compute. The number of messages to be dispatched will be specified in the task specification. This value is taken as 100%. Now, depending on the number of messages that were dispatched, the ratio is computed which gives the degree.

3.3.3 Perspectives of Transparency

The different perspectives to be maintained by the work group for a task will be given in the task specification. If it is static perspective, then the work group need to send transparency messages only at the specified time periods. There will be no provision for stakeholders to get data on demand. If it is dynamic transparency, then the work group should provide a facility for stakeholders to make requests for information, and the work group should also have mechanism for receiving requests, generating required reports and sending them to the notification recipients. If it is radical transparency, then it should have mechanism to stream the information through various communication channels such RSS, Blogs, etc.

3.3.4 Dimensions of Transparency

The dimensions of transparency will be provided in the task specification. The transparency messages will be regarding recognition of responsibilities and interdependencies, recognition of status and problems, understanding of performance and feedback. However, transparency is not computed at a single instant. It is computed over the span of entire task. Since each task has three phases, viz. pre-activity, per-activity and post-activity, transparency is computed over all these phases. For each state of the TEC there is a corresponding transparency message providing the operational and transactional information. Also each transparency message is given a "value" based on its priority. Since each transparency messages is attributed with a value, depending on the number of messages sent and the value associated with the sent messages, transparency at that phase can be computed. The total transparency is a sum of transparencies of these three phases.

Transparency at a phase i is equal to the product of values of a messages v and number of transparency messages n.

$$T_i = \Sigma(v * n)_i$$

Thus, final Transparency is the sum of transparencies at pre-active phase, per-active phase and post-active phases.

$$T = T_{pre} + T_{per} + T_{post} = \Sigma(v * n)_{pre} + \Sigma(v * n)_{per} + \Sigma(v * n)_{post}$$

3.3.5 Timeliness

Timeliness is also important for transparency. For real time tasks, timeliness is very essential. The given algorithm helps in keeping check on timeliness of the work group. Consider a scenario where item designing task prevails only for a short time, while the supervision task persists through all subtasks and until the end of the task. We define goals depending on the number of subtasks completed. For each goal, a corresponding message is defined. If a goal is reached, then a success tag is added to the message and sent to the fault monitor. If the goal is not reached in time, then it will add a failed tag to the message and sends the message to the fault monitor. The failed message also carries the reason for failure allowing the fault monitor to initiate a repair action. Thus the fault monitor knows if there is a fault and the reason for the fault. Also, if no message has reached as per the schedule, then the fault monitor knows that some serious fault has occurred even preventing the message passing. The fault monitor ensures that message sending schedule is not forgotten by the work groups alerting them at regularly about their next message sending interval.

For example, suppose a task (along with task specification) was given to the work group G_1. The work group divides the task into subtasks and distributes the subtasks among its members. The task specification contains the goal and time intervals when the messages have to be reported. The fault monitor is also provided with this same information. So, the work group starts executing the subtasks and whenever the goal is reached or the prescribed time interval is reached, it will send the messages to the fault monitor. The fault detector will keep checking whether messages are arriving as per prescribed time intervals. If messages are not received as per the time interval then it starts suspecting a fault in the work group. Let p and q represent a work group and a fault monitor respectively. Let m_i be the message sent by p to q at a pre-specified time. p sends messages to q; when q receives a positive message, it trusts that there is no fault at p and starts a timer with a timeout value θ as per specification to wait for the next message. If the timer expires before q receives the next message from p, then q starts suspecting that a fault might have occurred at p. Instead of waiting until for θ time period every time before suspecting a fault, we can have a local fault monitor at each work group to continuously monitor the work group, and report to the central fault monitor as soon as a fault is identified. But each work group functions in its own way owing to the environment where it works, making it impossible to define a local monitor for each work group and its subtasks. So we come to a conclusion that though the work group does not follow a regular pattern for task execution, as long as it meets its goals in time there is no fault in it.

Let m_i and m_j be two messages to be sent by p to q at time intervals i and j $[i < j]$. Let $T(p)$ and $T(q)$ be the time lines of p and q. If message m_i is sent by p at time $T(p)_i$ and q receives it at $T(q)_i$, i.e. $T(p)_i = T(q)_i$, then there is no fault. Let θ_j be the timeout value to receive message m_j. If m_j does not arrive before θ_j expires, then q can start suspecting a fault in p. But if m_j arrives well before θ_j expires, then q concludes that p is doing very well in its task execution and is well ahead of deadlines. In this case, the new arrival time is $T(q)_{pre-j}$ and the earlierness is given by δ_j.

$$\delta_j = \theta_j - T(q)_{pre-j}$$

Now the next message mkmust arrive before the expiry of the timeout value θ_k. If it does not arrive, then the fault monitor senses a possibility of a fault since the usual timeout has expired, but still extends its timeout by δ_j before confirming a fault occurrence because work group's deadline is $T(p)_k$ but not $T(p)_k - \delta_j$. If mkdoes not arrive after $\delta_j + \theta_k$, then the fault monitor starts suspecting a fault in p. However, one more idea for verifying the possibility of a fault is by having fault monitor send a request to p at $T(p)_k - \delta_j$, if a reply is not received, then it can start suspecting a fault in p. This allows the fault monitor to identify a fault even before the prescribed time interval $T(p)_k$ by an earlierness of δ_j.

3.3.5.1 Algorithm for a Fault Detection()

1. *Initiation:*
2. *p: workgroup*
3. *q: FaultMonitor*
4. *T(q): Proposed arrival time of message at q*
5. *T(p): Proposed message sending time at p*
6. *AT(q): Actual arrival time of message at q*
7. *δ: earlierness of the message*
8. *for i ← 1 to n tasks*
9. *do*
10. *switch*
11.
12. *case $AT(q)_i = T(q)_i$:*
13. *suspect(p) ← false*
14. *δ ← 0;*
15. *return NoFault*
16.
17. *case $AT(q)_i < T(q)_i$:*
18. *suspect(p) ← false*
19. *δ ← δ + (T(q)_i − AT(q)_i)*
20. *return NoFault*
21.
22. *case $AT(q)_i > T(q)_i$:*
23. *If(AT(q)_i ≤ T(q)_i + δ)*
24. *δ ← δ − (AT(q)_i − T(q)_i)*
25. *suspect(p) ← false*
26. *If(AT(q)_i > T(q)_i + δ)*
27. *suspect(p) ← true*
28. *suspectlist ← suspectlist ∪ {p}*
29. *return FaultOccurred*

3.4 Task Design

Executing a task is the basic operation of a member or work group. Since task is the basic operation performed, task needs to be well defined. Every task, besides other attributes, has the following attributes:

Task_Id: Identification token of the task; *Parent_Task:* If the task is subtask of a bigger task, then this is the *id* of the parent task; *Transparency_Perspective:* Perspective of transparency to be followed for this task; *Transparency_Degree:* Degree of transparency to be maintained; *Transparency_Dimensions*: Dimensions of transparency; *Transparency_Directions:* Directions in which transparency is to be maintained; *IsPartitionable:* Yes, if the task can be split and distributed; No, if it has to be executed at only one place; *Risks:* Risks involved with the task. ; *Task_Type:* Whether the given task is technical or non-technical; *Creation_Date:* Date when the task was created. ; *Excluded_Executors:* Restricted executors list; *Task_Stakeholders*: All the stakeholders who are related to the task; *Task_Status*:

Status of the task, indicating how far the task was completed; *Skills_Needed:* List of skills needed to execute the task; *Skills_Levels_Needed*: Level of skills needed for executing the task; excellent, fair, medium, poor skill levels; *Task_Infrastructure*: Infrastructure that would be required for the execution of the task. ; *Task_Priority:* Priority of the task; Low, medium, high; *Start_By_Date*: The date by which one has to start the execution of the task. ; *Interdependencies*: Interdependencies of the task; *Task_Supervisor*: The member/work group in-charge of the task; *Complete_By_Date*: The date by which one has to complete the execution of the task; *Notification_Recipients*: Stakeholders that are to be notified about the status of the task; *Responsibilites:* Responsibilites that are to be undertaken by the task executor; *Task_Initiator*: Identity of the one who initiated the task; *Potential_Executors*: Executors for whom the task is meant ; *Cost_of_Task*: Cost of the task estimated using variables like the resources and skills it involves and its significance (priority).

Other operations related to tasks are sending reports, ack, requests, notifications,etc. When a request is received, it has to be processed and response (report) must be sent to the requester. When a task is received, an acknowledgment must be sent to the sender. During the execution of the task, task status is to be notified to the notification recipients and requeters. And when a log or report is received, it is stored in the repository. In WMB, each module has different functionalities.

3.5 Functionalities of Modules of WMB

The Functionalities of Modules of Workgroup Behavior Models are displayed in Table 1.

CONCLUSION

This paper defined and implemented Transparency. Work group Behavior Model (WMB) and Task Execution Cycle (TEC) corresponding to the work group scenario are defined. Primitives like transparency messages, task execution states, etc which required for the implementation are also defined. Degree of Transparency can be assessed using the number of transparency messages corresponding to a task. For e.g., if a task has hundred transparency messages associated with its execution, the task initiator can define custom thresholds for opaqueness, translucency and clarity. During execution of the task, as the task executor sends the transparency messages, the count of the messages gives the degree of transparency. The dimensions of transparency are realized by defining various transparency messages in the phases of the task i.e. pre-activity,

Table 1. Functionalities of modules of WMB

Module Function	Module Function	Module Function
TMonitor Receives Task	Rpt Receives Task	ExTsk Receives Task
Receives Report Forwards to Rpt	Sends Log	Sends Notification
Receives Ack	Sends Request	Sends Report
Receives Ack	Sends Report	Sends Query
Receives Request	Sends Notification	
Receives Log		
Receives Notification		

per-activity and post-activity phases. In the pre-activity phase, transparency messages related to requirements and interdependencies are defined. In the post-activity phase, transparency messages related to status and problems are defined. And in the post-activity phase, transparency messages related to feedback and performance understanding are defined. Thus the dimensions of Transparency are implemented. The perspectives of transparency are assessed based on the operational behavior of the task executor. If the task executor operates on simplex mode of communication, i.e. only sends messages but does not receive any queries from the stakeholders, then the transparency is static transparency. And, if the task executor maintains duplex mode i.e. not only sends messages but also receives queries and responds to them, then the transparency is dynamic transparency. Radical transparency is when the task executor streams the messages and maintains duplex mode of communication. Radical transparency is a form of static transparency with the interval between the transmission of messages being very small. Thus perspectives of transparency are implemented. A method for total transparency of a work group over a complete task is also derived. Thus the present paper successfully defines and outlines implementation of Transparency.

ACKNOWLEDGMENT

I am greatly thankful to *Prof. Hrushikesha Mohanty* for all his guidance and thoughts and for being the motive behind my research ideas.

REFERENCES

Andreas, O., Børge, L., Eva, A., & Andreas, S. (2010). *A framework for transparency: USAID, CARE, GTZ/NABARD.* 21st Annual Conference of the Production and Operation Management Society, Vancouver, Canada, May 07, 2010 - May 10, 2010.

Bertot, J. C., Robertson, S., & Nahon, K. (2012). *Introduction to the open government, transparency and citizen engagement.* Minitrack, 45th Hawaii International Conference on System Sciences, 2012.

de Biazzi, M. R., Muscat, A. R. N., & de Biazzi, J. L. (2009). Process management in the public sector: A Brazilian case study. *PICMET 2009 Proceedings.*

Koendjbiharie, S., Koppius, O., Vervest, P., & van Heck, E. (2010). *Network transparency and the performance of dynamic business networks.* 4th IEEE International Conference on Digital Ecosystems and Technologies (IEEE Dest 2010), 2010.

Madsen, P. (2010). Dynamic transparency, prudential justice, and corporate transformation: Becoming socially responsible in the Internet Age. *Journal of Business Ethics, 90,* 639–648. doi:10.1007/s10551-010-0597-8

Parikh, T. (2007). *Rural microfinance service delivery: Gaps, inefficiencies and emerging solutions* (2007). Vaccaro, A., & Madsen, P. (2009). Corporate dynamic transparency: The new ICT-driven ethics? *Ethics and Information Technology, 11,* 113–122.

Vaccaro, A., & Madsen, P. (2009). Transparency in business and society: introduction to the special issue. *Ethics and Information Technology, 11,* 101–103. doi:10.1007/s10676-009-9197-7

Chapter 23
Ontology Augmented Software Engineering

Qazi Mudassar Ilyas
King Faisal University, Saudi Arabia

ABSTRACT

Semantic Web was proposed to make the content machine-understandable by developing ontologies to capture domain knowledge and annotating content with this domain knowledge. Although, the original idea of semantic web was to make content on the World Wide Web machine-understandable, with recent advancements and awareness about these technologies, researchers have applied ontologies in many interesting domains. Many phases in software engineering are dependent on availability of knowledge, and the use of ontologies to capture and process this knowledge is a natural choice. This chapter discusses how ontologies can be used in various stages of the system development life cycle. Ontologies can be used to support requirements engineering phase in identifying and fixing inconsistent, incomplete, and ambiguous requirement. They can also be used to model the requirements and assist in requirements management and validation. During software design and development stages, ontologies can help software engineers in finding suitable components, managing documentation of APIs, and coding support. Ontologies can help in system integration and evolution process by aligning various databases with the help of ontologies capturing knowledge about database schema and aligning them with concepts in ontology. Ontologies can also be used in software maintenance by developing a bug tracking system based upon ontological knowledge of software artifacts and roles of developers involved in software maintenance task.

DOI: 10.4018/978-1-4666-3679-8.ch023

INTRODUCTION

Abran et al. (Abran 2004) define software engineering as:

Application of a systematic, disciplined, quantifiable approach to the development, operation, and maintenance of software, and the study of these approaches; that is, the application of engineering to software.

The development is a comprehensive term in this definition comprising of analysis, requirement specification, design, development, testing and integration of software. There are several other activities complementing the process of software development, operation and maintenance such as configuration management, process management, project management, software engineering tools and methods, and software quality assurance. W3C (World Wide Web Consortium) defines Semantic Web as:

The Semantic Web provides a common framework that allows data to be shared and reused across application, enterprise, and community boundaries.

Ontologies are backbone of semantic web application. They capture machine-understandable specifications of a domain of interest that can be used by software agents to understand concepts and relationships among concepts in that domain. Although originally introduced for semantic web applications, ontologies have now become a means to describe non-web based content too. These machine-understandable specifications can be used to support many non-web based tasks as well.

Most of the activities and processes mentioned in the definition of software engineering above can benefit from the power of description provided by ontologies and they can be used to describe problem domain in software development. They can also be used to describe software components to support component based software engineering and help developers find suitable components for their specific requirements. A number of other uses of ontologies have been considered by researchers such as use of ontologies in requirement engineering to find and fix incomplete, inconsistent and unfeasible requirements, in application integration by adding an ontology layer on top of various heterogeneous databases. In fact, semantic web technologies can help in many, if not all, phases of software development.

This chapter discusses the use of ontologies to support various phases of software analysis, design and development. After establishing a connection between software engineering and knowledge engineering domains, the chapter discusses the application of ontologies, the back bone of knowledge engineering, in various phases of software analysis, design and development. The use of ontologies to assist in software analysis, design, development, system evolution, system integration, and system maintenance is discussed. The chapter is closed with conclusions and further readings sections.

BACKGROUND

The domains of software engineering and knowledge engineering are very closely related to each other. Software engineering is highly dependent upon the availability, extraction, synthesis and production of knowledge. The early stages in software development such as analysis and requirement modeling require collection of the existing knowledge from the business in the form of business rules and user requirements. Design and development stages may require knowledge about existing libraries, components and code repositories. Test case scenarios can also make use of knowledge of user feedback and usage behavior. Lastly, after the software is put into operation, software maintenance and support requires knowledge from various stakeholders. Thus knowledge serves as backbone in all stages of software development life cycle.

Knowledge engineering discipline focuses on generation of knowledge to describe content for searching, extracting and interpreting this content when required. With the advent of semantic web technologies, ontologies have gained attraction of various communities that are dependent upon availability and processing of knowledge. As mentioned above, software engineering can also benefit from these technologies for various development tasks. Ontologies – the machine understandable descriptions of domains – are backbone of semantic web applications and they can help in supporting various phases and activities in the software development process as mentioned above.

Marrying software engineering and knowledge engineering technologies can help in reducing the time of development, improved quality and lesser number of errors shipped with the developed software.

ONTOLOGIES IN SOFTWARE ENGINEERING

As mentioned above, ontologies can be used to support almost all phases of software development. This section discusses how ontologies can be to support various stages of software development life cycle starting from problem description until software maintenance and support.

We broadly divide software development life cycle into five stages including system analysis, design, development, testing, and maintenance and discuss use of ontologies in these stages. The role of ontologies in all of these phases is discussed.

Ontologies in System Analysis

System analysis consists of various tasks such as fact finding, requirements discovery, requirements

modeling and use cases. Requirements are the first building block in software development. Bentley et al. (Bentley 2007) state that good software requirements should be:

- **Consistent:** No two requirements should have any conflict.
- **Complete:** System requirements must capture all possible system inputs and outputs.
- **Feasible:** It should be feasible to satisfy all requirements captured.
- **Required:** There should be no unnecessary requirements.
- **Accurate:** The requirements should be error-free.
- **Traceable:** A direct mapping must exist between requirements and system functions.
- **Verifiable:** All requirements should be stated in such a way as to be tested in testing phase.

Inconsistent, ambiguous and incomplete requirements are major reasons for failure of software systems. Several studies (e.g., More 2011) have proven that good requirements can play a key role in reducing the time of development, man hours of development and number of defects shipped in the software. Good software requirements also increase quality of software, user satisfaction and help in successful implementation and adoption of software systems.

Siegemund et al. (Siegemund 2011) summarize the drawbacks of existing requirements engineering approaches as follows:

- Background business knowledge required to come up with good enough requirements is not captured and analyzed.
- Relationship between various requirements can be very useful to identify incorrect, incomplete and inconsistent requirements but generally the relationships established

between requirements are limited or not captured at all.

- Conflicts and ambiguities in the requirements are not addressed properly.
- Basic properties of requirements such as completeness, accuracy and consistency are not verified.
- Abstraction level of requirements is relatively lower.

Taking a close look at these drawbacks reveals clearly to anyone having even basic knowledge of ontologies that these are the problems ontologies are meant to address and these problems are precisely the reason for existence of ontologies. The use of ontologies in requirements engineering process can be many folds. Some of the possible uses of ontologies are given below:

Ontologies can be used to capture domain knowledge for developing and understanding of the domain. This domain model would make it easier to understand the concepts, concept-subconcept relationship, constraints and other requirements in that domain. This knowledge will help at later stages to develop complete, consistent and accurate requirements.

Existing techniques to represent requirements include natural language, use cases, process models (data flow diagrams) or structured languages. Natural language has many inherent problems that may result in ambiguity. Use case models also use natural language hence they are not a good choice either. Process models are good at representing flow of data through business processes but there is no way to find inconsistencies in requirements. Structured languages are a step towards standardized way of representing complex requirements but they have limited and fixed level of expressiveness. Ontologies can be used to formally represent software requirements (Decker 2005) and can provide various levels of expressiveness to meet specific needs of various applications. Atkinson et al. (Atkinson 2011) propose to marry ontologies

with Unified Modeling Language (UML). They propose a potency based approach to multi-level modeling framework that enables ontologies to include various classification levels by treating classes, instances and meta-classes in a uniform way. This unified modeling approach helps in supporting exploratory and unbounded models in addition to constructive and bounded models.

Ontologies can also be used to develop Software Requirements Specifications (SRS). Ontologies can provide varying level of expressiveness to match a desired level for specification of requirements based upon the domain knowledge. These formal specifications can also help in requirements validation and management at later stages.

Requirements validation, management and traceability can benefit hugely from ontologies as ontologies can provide strong binding of the domain knowledge with the requirements specifications (Mayank 2004). This domain knowledge can be used to validate and check consistency of requirements using the reasoning support provided by the ontologies.

Ontologies in System Design and Development

With the recent adoption of component-based software engineering and object oriented paradigm, reuse has become the name of the game in software development. One of the key issues for software engineers in this regard is to find suitable components in software development fulfilling the unique requirements of the software. Currently, there is no standardized way of describing the software components to enable efficient searching of components. The other aspects of components such as, interfaces and other information also needs to be captured and maintained. Ontologies, in this regard can be used to describe interfaces of the components, component documentation, programming language and licensing information etc. Happel et al. (Happel 2006) identify two key issues in this regard namely low integration of artifact metadata and insufficient utilization of background knowledge and propose a three-layer architecture to address these issues:

1. A description of software artifacts such as interface, authorship and licensing. These artifacts are stored in a repository.
2. A knowledge layer on the top of repository layer consists of an ontology and reasoning support to enhance the repository layer. This component layer also consists of instance data of components that is generated with a shallow ontology residing between the two layers.
3. Finally, SPARQL queries can be used to query this knowledge base.

Another problem faced by software developers at coding stage is regarding the use of Application Programmer Interfaces (APIs). Currently, there is no standardized way of documenting APIs (Happel 2006). Eberhart et al. (Eberhart 2004) suggest the use of ontologies to create central repositories of annotations of API documentation and share them via public web servers to benefit software developers. They propose SmartAPI to create globally unique identifiers for concepts in APIs that can later be used even for complex tasks such as creating a sequence of calls to API to complete a task.

Ontologies in Systems Integration and Evolution

System integration is one of key challenges in software engineering. Also software systems evolve over time because of changing system requirements. This evolution requires changes in the database of software system. Previously Electronic Data Interchange (EDI) has been used to integrate systems and exchange data between them but it is not flexible and every new integration required

new wrappers to be written. eXtensible Markup Language (XML) was developed to provide this flexibility in data interchange but the expressive power of XML is limited. Since ontologies became popular, many researchers have proposed their use in system integration. They are also a natural choice to capture changes in system requirements to address system evolution.

Poggi et al. (Poggi 2008) identify numerous challenges in use of ontologies in system integration and data interchange. The first and foremost challenge is the famous expressivity-decidability dilemma of ontologies. Higher degree of expressiveness means low decidability and we are required to reduce expressiveness in order to ensure query answers in finite time. Reducing expressiveness means the complex concepts cannot be described appropriately. Scalability is another challenge that needs significant attention as it is hard for ontologies to match scalability provided by the latest database technologies such as relational databases. Another challenge is called impedance mismatch which means how to establish mapping between the concepts of ontology and semantics of data stored in the database. Lastly, query answering is the issue that needs to be addressed so that the users can give queries in a conceptual way based upon the ontologies and the system should translate these queries to reason about various data sources. To address these issue Poggi et al. (Poggi 2008) propose a new Description Logic (DL) language, DL_A that provides sufficient expressiveness without compromising the decidability. They have also developed querying mechanism based upon unfolding, a technique that translates the query on the basis of relationships in the relational database considering the mapping between these resources and the ontological concepts.

Curino et al. (Curino 2008a) propose ADAM (Advanced Data And Metadata Manager), a unified framework to deliver practical solutions to the problems of automatic schema mapping and assisted schema evolution. ADAM is based on

PRISM (Curino 2008b), a system used to support database administrator in schema evolution process. PRISM user captures all evolutions in the schema using Schema Modification Operators (SMO). These SMOs are used by ADAM to analyze proposed evolution with respect to information preservation and redundancy. The data is then migrated between different versions of schema. The mappings are established between various versions of schema. Finally, the system translates queries on the old schema to their equivalent on the current schema. Thus system helps in maintaining a machine-understandable version of schema evolution and integration.

Ontologies in Systems Maintenance

"Nothing but change is constant" is a famous saying. Software systems also change over time after they are put into operation. A system change request can be as simple as generating a new report without any change in the database or as complex as a new problem that needs complete analysis, design, development, and testing effect of this change on the existing system. Software bugs are the most important cause of system maintenance. Usually, all bugs are reported and related information is stored in a bug reporting system. Developers discuss the bug and make changes in the code to fix it. The problem is that the relationship the bug and any changes in the code do not have a clear relationship. It makes it very difficult to manage a large number of bugs.

Ankolekar et al. (Ankolekar 2006) propose the use of ontologies to support software maintenance task for online problem solving communities. The proposed system is base on three ontologies; one ontology for software artifacts, one for software bugs and one community ontology that describes roles of developers involved in bug fixing. This prototype can help in building full fledge systems for managing software bugs in a more systemic manner.

FUTURE RESEARCH DIRECTIONS

A number of applications of ontologies in software engineering domain have been introduced in this chapter. There are, however, a number of other aspects of software engineering that still need attention of knowledge engineering community. Software testing is one aspect where no significant applications of ontologies have been proposed. Evaluation of user interfaces is another area where ontologies can be applied. A number of other research areas are open in which knowledge engineering can help software engineering such as serviced oriented architecture, web services description, discovery and modeling, software project management etc.

CONCLUSION

This is relatively new area of research. Most of applications and systems proposed in marrying software engineering and knowledge engineering domains are in prototype stage. Semantic web is becoming mature with standardization in various aspects but faces challenges in ontology alignment, matching and mapping aspects. The applications of ontologies in software engineering highlighted in the chapter are tip of the iceberg. A huge amount of research is going on in this domain and we expect more and tangible applications of ontologies in software engineering.

REFERENCES

Abran, A., & Moore, J. W. (Eds.). (2004). *Guide to the software engineering body of knowledge, SWEBOK*. IEEE Computer Society.

Ankolekar, A., Sycara, K., Herbsleb, J., Kraut, R., & Welty, C. (2006). Supporting online problem solving communities with the Semantic Web. In *Proceedings of the 15th Int. Conference on World Wide Web,* Edinburgh, Scotland (pp. 575-584).

Atkinson, C., Bastian, K., & Björn, G. (2011). *Supporting constructive and exploratory modes of modeling in multi-level ontologies.* In The 7th International Workshop on Semantic Web Enabled Software Engineering Co-located with ISWC2011 Bonn, Germany.

Bentley, L. D., Whitten, J. L., & Randolph, G. (2007). *Systems analysis and design for the global enterprise.* McGraw-Hill Companies Inc.

Curino, C. A., Moon, H. J., & Zaniolo, C. (2008b). Graceful database schema evolution: The PRISM workbench. *Proceedings of the VLDB Endowment, 1*(1), 761–772.

Curino, C. A., Tanca, L., & Zaniolo, C. (2008a). *Information systems integration and evolution: Ontologies at rescue.* In International Workshop on Semantic Technologies for System Maintenance (STSM) co-located with the 16th IEEE International Conference on Program Comprehension (ICPC 2008) in Amsterdam, The Netherlands.

Decker, B., Rech, J., Ras, E., Klein, B., & Hoecht, C. (2005). Self-organized reuse of software engineering knowledge supported by semantic wikis. In *Proceedings of Workshop on Semantic Web Enabled Software Engineering* (SWESE).

Eberhart, A., & Argawal, S. (2004). SmartAPI - Associating ontologies and APIs for rapid application development. In *Proceedings of Workshop of Ontologien in der und für die Softwaretechnik,* Germany.

Happel, H.-J., Korthaus, A., Seedorf, S., & Tomczyk, P. (2006). KOntoR: An ontology-enabled approach to software reuse. In *Proceedings of the 18th International Conference on Software Engineering and Knowledge Engineering* (SEKE), San Francisco.

Mayank, V., Kositsyna, N., & Austin, M. (2004). *Requirements engineering and the Semantic Web, part II. Representation, management, and validation of requirements and system-level architectures. Technical Report. TR 2004-14.* University of Maryland.

More, N. T., Sapre, B. S., & Chawan, P. M. (2011). An insight into the importance of requirements engineering. *International Journal of Internet Computing, 1*(2).

Poggi, A., Lembo, D., Calvanese, D., Giacomo, G. D., Lenzerini, M., & Rosati, R. (2008). Linking data to ontologies. *Journal on Data Semantics,* 133–173.

Siegemund, K., Thomas, E. J., Zhao, Y., Pan, J., & Assmann, U. (2011). *Towards ontology-driven requirements engineering.* In The 7th International Workshop on Semantic Web Enabled Software Engineering Co-located with ISWC2011Bonn, Germany.

ADDITIONAL READING

Allemang, D., & Hendler, J. (2011). *Semantic Web for the working ontologist, second edition: Effective modeling in RDFS and OWL.* Morgan Kaufmann.

Antoniou, G., & Harmelen, F. V. (2008). *A Semantic Web primer.* The MIT Press.

Breitman, K., Casanova, M. A., & Truszkowski, W. (2010). *Semantic Web: Concepts, technologies and applications.* Springer.

Davies, J. (2006). *Semantic Web technologies: Trends and research in ontology-based systems.* Wiley. doi:10.1002/047003033X

Gaevic, D., Djuric, D., Devedic, V., Selic, B. V., & Bézivin, J. (2010). *Model driven engineering and ontology development.* Springer.

Liyang, Y. (2011). *A developer's guide to the Semantic Web*. Springer.

McComb, D. (2003). *Semantics in business systems: The savvy manager's guide*. Morgan Kaufmann.

Parreiras, F. S. (2012). *Integration of the Semantic Web and Model-Driven Software*. Wiley-IEEE Press. doi:10.1002/9781118135068

Passin, T. B. (2004). *Explorer's guide to the Semantic Web*. Manning Publications.

Pollock, J. T. (2009). *Semantic Web for dummies*. Wiley.

KEY TERMS AND DEFINITIONS

Description Logic: Description Logic is a family of formal knowledge representation languages that is used to model concepts, roles & individuals, and their relationships.

Knowledge Engineering: Knowledge Engineering: is an engineering discipline that involves integrating knowledge into computer systems in order to solve complex problems normally requiring a high level of human expertise.

Machine Understandability: The process whereby a software agent can understand the meaning of certain concepts to accomplish a task or take decision.

Ontology: A formal and explicit specification of a conceptualization.

Requirements Engineering: Identification, specification and documentation of requirement.

Semantic Web: It is not a separate Web but an extension of the current one, in which information is given well-defined meaning, better enabling computers and people to work in cooperation.

Software Component: A software package, a Web service, or a module that encapsulates a set of related functions (or data).

Software Engineering: Application of a systematic, disciplined, quantifiable approach to the development, operation, and maintenance of software, and the study of these approaches; that is, the application of engineering to software.

Compilation of References

1982 *Principles of information systems for management.* Dubuque, IO: William C. Brown.

Abrams, M. D., Heaney, J. E., King, O., LaPadula, L. J., Lazear, M. B., & Olson, I. M. (1991). Generalized framework for access control: Towards prototyping the ORGCON Policy. *Proceedings of the 14th National Computer Security* Conference, Baltimore, MD, USA.

Abran, A., & Moore, J. W. (Eds.). (2004). *Guide to the software engineering body of knowledge, SWEBOK.* IEEE Computer Society.

Abrial, J. R. (Ed.). (1996). *The B-Book: Assigning programs to meanings.* Cambridge, UK: Cambridge University Press. doi:10.1017/CBO9780511624162

Achterbergh, J., Beeres, R., & Vriens, D. (2003). Does the balanced score-card support organizational viability. *Kybernetes: The International Journal of Systems & Cybernetics, 32*(9/10), 1387–1404. doi:10.1108/03684920310493314

ACSI - Australian Communications – Electronic Security Instruction 33. (2012). *The Information Security Group of the Australian Government's Defense Signals Directorate.* Retrieved March 18, 2012, from www.dsd.gov.au/_lib/pdf_doc/acsi33/acsi33_u_0904.pdf

Agrawal, A., & Huang, X. (2008). Pairwise DNA alignment with sequence specific transition-transversion ratio using multiple parameter sets. *International Conference on Information Technology, 17-20,* 89–93.

Agrawal, A., & Khaitan, S. K. (2008). A new heuristic for multiple sequence alignment. *IEEE International Conference on Electro/Information Technology,* (pp. 215–217).

Ahituv, N., & Neumann, S. (1982). *Principles of information systems for management. Dubuque, IO: William C.* Brown.

Ahmad, M., & Mathkour, H. (2009). *A pattern matching approach for redundancy detection in bi-lingual and mono-lingual corpora.* IAENG 2009.

Ahmad, M., & Mathkour, H. (2009). Genome sequence analysis: A survey. *Journal of Computer Science, 5*(9), 651-660. ISSN 1549-3636

Ahmad, M., & Mathkour, H. (2009). *Multiple sequence alignment with GAP consideration by pattern matching technique.* International Conference on Signal Acquisition and Processing, Malaysia.

Ahmad, M., Khan, H. M., & Mathkour, H. (2009). An integrated statistical comparative analysis between variant genetic datasets of Mus musculus. *International Journal of Computational Intelligence in Bioinformatics and System Biology, 1*(2), 163-176. ISSN: 1755-8042

Ahmad, M., & Mathkour, H. (2009). *Genome sequence analysis by Matlab histogram comparison between Image-sets of genetic data.* Hong Kong: WCSET.

Ahmed, N. Y. P., & Vandenberg, A. (2005). Parallel algorithm for multiple genome alignment on the Grid environment. *Proceedings of 19th IEEE International Symposium on Parallel and Distributed Processing,* (p. 7).

Ahmed, I., & Ilyas, Q. M. (2012). Gleaning disaster related information from World Wide Web. *Journal of Theoretical and Applied Information Technology, 40*(2).

Ahuja, G. (2000). Collaboration networks, structural holes, and innovation: A longitudinal study. *Administrative Science Quarterly, 45*(3), 425–455. doi:10.2307/2667105

Akers, S. B. (1978). Binary decision diagrams. *IEEE Transactions on Computers, 27,* 509–516. doi:10.1109/TC.1978.1675141

Alalwan, J. A., & Weistroffer, H. R. (2012). Enterprise content management research: A comprehensive review. *Journal of Enterprise Information Management, 25*(4).

Albert, L. (2010). What agile can do for government. *Agilex Technologies.* Retrieved March 1, 2012, from http://gcn.com/articles/2010/10/15/what-agile-can-do-for-government.aspx

Alexander, I. (2003). Misuse cases: Use cases with hostile intent. *IEEE Computer Society, Focus Magazine.*

Al-Fatah Karasneh, A. (2012). Impact of BSC on financial performance: An empirical study on Jordanian bank. *European Journal of Economics. Finance and Administrative Sciences, 1*(46), 54–70.

Alger, J. I. (2001). *On assurance, measures, and metrics: Definitions and approaches.* Workshop on Information-Security-System Rating and Ranking, Williamsburg, Virginia, May 21-23.

Alhammouri, M. (2007). Lecture Notes in Computer Science: *Vol. 4680. Management of groups and group keys in multi-level security environments* (pp. 75–80). Berlin, Germany: Springer. doi:10.1007/978-3-540-75101-4_7

Alhammouri, M. (2008). A design of an access control model for multilevel-security documents. *Advanced Communication Technology, 2*(17-20), 1476–1481.

Alkussayer, A., & Allen, W. (2009). The ISDF framework: Integrating security patterns and best practice. *Journal of Information Processing Systems, 6*(1).

Alsmadi, I., & Dieri, M. (2009). Separation of concerns in teaching software engineering. In *Proceedings of CISSE 2009,* USA. Retrieved from http://conference.cisse2009.org/proceedings.aspx

Alvarez, M. (2006). *Second Life and school: The use of virtual world worlds in high education.* Trinity University, San Antonio, TX. Retrieved June 12, 2011, from http://www.trinity.edu/adelwich/worlds/articles/trinity.manny.alvarez.pdf

Anderson, R. J. (1996). A security policy for clinical information systems. *Proceedings of the IEEE Symposium on Security and Privacy.* ISBN: 0-8186-7417-2

Anderson, N. (2003). Applicant and recruiter reactions to new technology in selection: A critical review and agenda for future research. *International Journal of Selection and Assessment, 11*(2/3), 121–136. doi:10.1111/1468-2389.00235

Andrade, J., Ares, J., García, R., Rodríguez, S., & Suárez, S. (2006). A reference model for knowledge management in software engineering. *Engineering Letters, 13,* 159–166.

Andreas, O., Børge, L., Eva, A., & Andreas, S. (2010). *A framework for transparency: USAID, CARE, GTZ/NABARD.* 21st Annual Conference of the Production and Operation Management Society, Vancouver, Canada, May 07, 2010 - May 10, 2010.

Andrews, N. O., & Fox, E. A. (2007). *Recent developments in document clustering.* Technical Report TR-07-35, Virginia Polytechnic Institute and State University.

Ankolekar, A., Sycara, K., Herbsleb, J., Kraut, R., & Welty, C. (2006). Supporting online problem solving communities with the Semantic Web. In *Proceedings of the 15th Int. Conference on World Wide Web,* Edinburgh, Scotland (pp. 575-584).

Annotea. (2012). Retrieved from http://sourceforge.net/projects/metadata-net/files/

Annozilla. (2012). Retrieved from http://annozilla.mozdev.org/

Anthoney, S. F., & Armstrong, P. I. (2010). Individuals and environments: linking ability and skill rating with interests. *Journal of Counseling Psychology, 57*(1), 36–51. doi:10.1037/a0018067

Arbaugh, W. A., Fithen, W. L., & McHugh, J. (2000). Windows of vulnerability: A case study analysis. *Computer, 33*(12), 52–59. doi:10.1109/2.889093

Arkin, B., Stender, S., & McGraw, G. (2005). Software penetration testing. *IEEE Security & Privacy, 3*(1), 84–87. doi:10.1109/MSP.2005.23

Armstrong, C. J. (2007). Mapping information security curricula to professional accreditation standards. *Information Assurance and Security Workshop,* (pp. 30–35).

Arreguin, C. (2007). *Reports from the field: Second Life community convention 2007 education track summary*. Retrieved December 2, 2007, from http://www.holymeatballs.org/pdfs/VirtualWorldsforLearningRoadmap_012008.pdf

Arslan, A. N., & He, D. (2006). An improved algorithm for the regular expression constrained multiple sequence alignment problems. *Sixth IEEE Symposium on Bioinformatics and Bioengineering*, (pp. 121–126).

Arthur, W. Jr, Glaze, R. M., Villado, A. J., & Taylor, J. E. (2010). The magnitude and extent of cheating and response distortion effects on unproctored internet-based tests of cognitive ability and personality. *International Journal of Selection and Assessment*, *18*(1), 1–16. doi:10.1111/j.1468-2389.2010.00476.x

Arvey, R. D., Strickland, W., Drauden, G., & Martin, C. (1990). Motivational components of test taking. *Personnel Psychology*, *43*, 695–716. doi:10.1111/j.1744-6570.1990.tb00679.x

Aryee, S., & Budhwar, P. (2008). Human resource management and organizational performance. In Ashton Center for Human Resources (Eds.), *Strategic human resource management* (pp. 191-212). London, UK: Chartered Institute of Personnel and Development.

Ashby, W. R. (1956). *Introduction to cybernetics*. London, UK: Methuen.

Atkinson, C., Bastian, K., & Björn, G. (2011). *Supporting constructive and exploratory modes of modeling in multi-level ontologies*. In The 7th International Workshop on Semantic Web Enabled Software Engineering Co-located with ISWC2011 Bonn, Germany.

Auger, R. (2007). *Writing software security test cases*. Retrieved February 18, 2009, from http://www.qasec.com/cycle/securitytestcases.shtml

Australian Government, Department of Defense. (n.d.). *Human factors and information security: Individual, culture and security environment*. Retrieved 14 March, 2012, from http://www.dtic.mil/cgi-bin/GetTRDoc?AD=ADA535944

Badia, A. (2005). From conceptual models to data models. In van Bommel, P. (Ed.), *Transformations of knowledge, information and data: Theory and applications* (pp. 283–302). Hershey, PA: Idea Group Inc. doi:10.4018/978-1-59140-527-6.ch007

Baeza-Yates, R., & Ribeiro-Neto, B. (2011). *Modern information retrieval: The concepts and technology behind search* (2nd ed.). ACM Press.

Bailenson, J., & Yee, N. (2007). Virtual interpersonal touch: Haptic interaction and co-presence in collaborative virtual environments. *International Journal of Multimedia tools and Applications*, *37*(5), 5-14.

Baker, W. H. (2007). Is information security under control? *Investigating Quality in Information Security Management. Security & Privacy*, *5*(1), 36–44. doi:10.1109/MSP.2007.11

Baker, W. H., Hutton, A., Hylender, C. D., Novak, C., Porter, C., & Sartin, B. (2009). *The 2009 data breach investigations report*. Verizon Business RISK Team.

Bannister, B. D. (1986). Performance outcome feedback and attributional feedback: Interactive effects of recipient responses. *The Journal of Applied Psychology*, *71*(2), 203–210. doi:10.1037/0021-9010.71.2.203

Bansal, A. K. (1995). Establishing a framework for comparative analysis of genome sequences. *First International Symposium on Intelligence in Neural and Biological Systems*, (pp. 84–91).

Barab, S., & Duffy, T. (2000). From practice fields to communities of practice. In Jonassen, D., & Land, S. (Eds.), *Theoretical foundations of learning environments* (pp. 25–55). New Jersey: Lawrence Erlbaum Associates.

Barab, S., Thomas, M., Dodge, T., Carteaux, R., & Tuzun, H. (2005). Making learning fun: Quest Atlantis, a game without guns. *Educational Technology Research and Development*, *53*(1), 86–107. doi:10.1007/BF02504859

Barbaranelli, C., & Caprara, G. V. (2000). Measuring the Big Five in self-report and other ratings: A multitrait-multimethod study. *European Journal of Psychological Assessment*, *16*(1), 31–43. doi:10.1027//1015-5759.16.1.31

Barnett, R. (2008). *ModSecurity blog: Is your website secure? Prove it.* Retrieved May 16, 2009, from http://www.modsecurity.org/blog/archives/2008/01/is_your_website.html

Barnum, S., & McGraw, G. (2005). Knowledge for software security. *IEEE Security & Privacy, 3*(2), 74–78. doi:10.1109/MSP.2005.45

Barrick, M. R., & Mount, M. K. (1991). The Big Five personality dimensions and job performance: A meta-analysis. *Personnel Psychology, 44,* 1–25. doi:10.1111/j.1744-6570.1991.tb00688.x

Barrick, M. R., & Mount, M. K. (1996). Effects of impression management and self-deception on the predictive validity of personality constructs. *The Journal of Applied Psychology, 81*(3), 261–272. doi:10.1037/0021-9010.81.3.261

Barrick, M. R., Patton, G. K., & Haugland, S. N. (2000). Accuracy of interviewer judgments of job applicant personality traits. *Personnel Psychology, 53,* 925–951. doi:10.1111/j.1744-6570.2000.tb02424.x

Barros, H., Silva, A., Costa, E., Bittencourt, I. I., Holanda, O., & Sales, L. (2011). Steps, techniques, and technologies for the development of intelligent applications based on Semantic Web Services: A case study in e-learning systems. *Engineering Applications of Artificial Intelligence, 24*(8), 1355–1367. doi:10.1016/j.engappai.2011.05.007

Bartlett, L. M. (2003). Progression of the binary decision diagram conversion methods. *Proceedings of the 21st International System Safety Conference,* August 4-8, 2003, Ottawa, (pp. 116-125).

Bartlett, L. M., & Andrews, J. D. (2001). Comparison of two new approaches to variable ordering for binary decision diagrams. *Quality and Reliability Engineering International, 17*(3), 151–158. doi:10.1002/qre.406

Bartram, D. (2000). Internet recruitment and selection: kissing frogs to find princes. *International Journal of Selection and Assessment, 8*(4), 261–274. doi:10.1111/1468-2389.00155

Bartram, D. (2005). The great eight competencies: A criterion-centric approach to validation. *The Journal of Applied Psychology, 90*(6), 1185–1203. doi:10.1037/0021-9010.90.6.1185

Batchelder, B. (2008). *How we entered the cloud: Computing on the web.* First Annual Conference on Quality Software Development.

Bates, A., & Poole, G. (2003). *Effective teaching with technology in higher education.* San Francisco, CA: Jossey Bass.

Batini, C. Ceri, S., & Navathe, S. B. (1992). *Conceptual database design: An entity-relationship approach.* Redwood City, CA: Benjamin Cummings.

Bauer, T. N., Maertz, C. P. Jr, Dolen, M. R., & Campion, M. A. (1998). Longitudinal assessment of applicant reactions to employment testing and test outcome feedback. *The Journal of Applied Psychology, 83*(6), 892–903. doi:10.1037/0021-9010.83.6.892

Bauer, T. N., Truxillo, D. M., Tucker, J. S., Weathers, V., Bertolino, M., Erdogan, B., & Campion, M. A. (2006). Selection in the information age: The impact of privacy concerns and computer experience on applicant reactions. *Journal of Management, 32*(5), 601–621. doi:10.1177/0149206306289829

Beer, S. (1959). *Cybernetic and management.* London, UK: English Universities Press.

Beer, S. (1972). *Brain of the firm.* London, UK: Allen Lane, The Penguin Press.

Beer, S. (1979). *The heart of enterprise.* London, UK: John Wiley.

Belkadi, F., Bonjour, E., & Dulmet, M. (2007). Competency characterisation by means of work situation modelling. *Computers in Industry, 58,* 164–178. doi:10.1016/j.compind.2006.09.005

Bell, D., & LaPadulla, L. (1973). *Secure computer systems: Mathematical foundations,* Vol. 1. Technical Report MTR-2547. Bedford, MA: MITRE Corporation.

Bentley, L. D., Whitten, J. L., & Randolph, G. (2007). *Systems analysis and design for the global enterprise.* McGraw-Hill Companies Inc.

Berends, J. J., van der Bij, J. D. K., & Weggeman, M. (2006). Knowledge sharing mechanisms in industrial research. *Research and Development Management, 36*(1), 85–95.

Berinato, S. (2002). *CIO - Return on security spending*, (pp. 43–52).

Berio, G., & Harzallah, M. (2007). Towards an integrating architecture for competence management. *Computers in Industry*, *58*, 199–209. doi:10.1016/j.compind.2006.09.007

Bernard, E. V. (1993). *Essays on object-oriented software engineering*. Englewood Cliffs, NJ: Prentice-Hall.

Bertino, E., Ooi, B. C., Sacks-Davis, R., Tan, K. L., Zobel, J., Shilovsky, B., & Catania, B. (1997). *Indexing techniques for advanced database systems*. Kluwer Academic Publishers. doi:10.1007/978-1-4615-6227-6

Bertino, E., & Takahashi, K. (2011). *Identity management – Concepts, technologies and systems*. Norwood, MA: Artech House.

Bertot, J. C., Robertson, S., & Nahon, K. (2012). *Introduction to the open government, transparency and citizen engagement*. Minitrack, 45th Hawaii International Conference on System Sciences, 2012.

Bertrand, Y. (2005). *Contemporary theories and practice in education* (2nd ed.). Madison, WI: Atwood Publishing.

Bicycle and motorcycle dynamics. (n.d.). Wikipedia: The Free Encyclopedia. Retrieved from http://en.wikipedia.org/wiki/Bicycle_and_motorcycle_dynamics

Bigge, M., & Shermis, S. (1992). *Learning theories for teachers*. Harper Collins.

Biggerstaff, T. J., Mitbander, B. G., & Webster, D. (1993). The concept assignment problem in program understanding. In *Proceedings of the 15th International Conference on Software Engineering (ICSE'93)*, (pp. 482-498).

Bignell, S., & Parson, V. (2010). *Best practicing in virtual worlds: A guide using problem-based learning in Second Life*. Universities Derky & Aston and Higher Education Academy Psychology Network.

Birk, A., Surmann, D., & Althoff, K.-D. (1999). Applications of knowledge acquisition in experimental software engineering. In *Proceedings of 11th European Workshop on Knowledge Acquisition, Modeling and Management (EKAW'99)*, (pp. 67-84).

Birnbaum, Z. W. (1969). On the importance of different components in a multicomponent system. In Korishnaiah, P. R. (Ed.), *Multivariate analysis* (pp. 581–592).

Bischofberger, W. R., & Pomberger, G. (1992). *Prototyping- oriented software development–Concepts and tools*. New York, NY: Springer-Verlag. doi:10.1007/978-3-642-84760-8

Bishop, M. (2004). *Introduction to computer security* (1st ed.). Addison-Wesley Professional.

Bjørnson, F. O., & Dingsøyr, T. (2008). Knowledge management in software engineering: A systematic review of studied concepts, findings and research methods used. *Information and Software Technology*, *50*, 1055–1068. doi:10.1016/j.infsof.2008.03.006

Blumenthal, S. C. (1969). *Management information systems: A framework for planning and development*. Englewood Cliffs, NJ: Prentice-Hall.

Boateng, B. A., & Boateng, K. (2007). Issues to consider when choosing open source content management systems (CMSs). In St.Amant, K., & Still, B. (Eds.), *Handbook of research on open source software: Technological economic and social perspectives* (pp. 255–268). doi:10.4018/978-1-59140-999-1.ch020

Boehm, B. (1986). A spiral model of software development and enhancement. *SIGSOFT Software Engineering Notes*, *11*(4), 14–24. doi:10.1145/12944.12948

Boehm, B. W. (1988). A spiral model of software development and enhancement. *IEEE Computer*, *21*(5), 61–72. doi:10.1109/2.59

Boehm, B., & Basili, V. R. (2001). Software defect reduction top 10 list. *Computer*, *34*(1), 135–137. doi:10.1109/2.962984

Boehm, B., & Turner, R. (2003). *Balancing agility and discipline: A guide for the perplexed*. Boston, MA: Addison-Wesley.

Boellstorff, T. (2008). *Coming of age in Second Life*. Princeton, NJ: Princeton University Press.

Boer, N. I., Berends, J. J., & van Baalen, P. (2011). Relational models for knowledge sharing behavior. *European Management Journal*, *29*, 85–97. doi:10.1016/j.emj.2010.10.009

Boer, N. I., van Baalen, P. J., & Kumar, K. (2004). The implications of different models of social relations for understanding knowledge sharing. In Tsoukas, H., & Mylonopoulos, N. (Eds.), *Organizations as knowledge systems: Knowledge, learning and dynamic capabilities* (pp. 130–151). New York, NY: Palgrave MacMillan.

Boh, W. F. (2007). Mechanisms for sharing knowledge in project-based organizations. *Information and Organization*, *17*, 27–58. doi:10.1016/j.infoandorg.2006.10.001

Boiko, B. (2002). *Content management bible*. New York, NY: Hungry Minds.

Booch, G. (1994). *Object-oriented analysis and design with applications*. Benjamin Cummings.

Booch, G., Maksimchuk, R., Engle, M., Young, B., Conallen, J., & Houston, K. (2007). *Object-oriented analysis and design with applications* (3rd ed.). Reading, MA: Addison-Wesley Professional.

Boulos, M., Hetherington, L., & Wheeler, S. (2007). Second Life: An overview of the potential of 3-D virtual worlds in medical and health education. *Health Information and Libraries Journal*, *24*(4), 233–245. doi:10.1111/j.1471-1842.2007.00733.x

Bovy, R. C. (1981). Successful instructional methods: A cognitive information processing approach. *Educational Communications and Technology Journal*, *29*(4), 203–217.

Brereton, P., & Budgen, D. (2000). Component-based systems: A classification of issues. *IEEE Computers*, *33*(11), 54–62. doi:10.1109/2.881695

Brewer, D. F. C., & Nash, M. J. (1989). The Chinese Wall security policy. In *Proceedings of the 1989 IEEE Symposium on Security and Privacy*, (pp. 206-214).

Bricken, W. (1990). *Learning in virtual reality*. Technical report No. HITL-M-90-5, University of Washington.

Briggs, J. (1977). *Instructional design: Principles and applications*. Educational Technologies Publications.

Britain, S., & Liber, O. (1999). *A framework for pedagogical evaluation of virtual learning environments*. JTAP, JISC Technology Applications, Report 41. Retrieved from http://www.leeds.ac.uk/educol/documents/00001237.html

Broaddribb, S., & Carter, C. (2009). Using Second Life in human resource development. *British Journal of Educational Technology*, *40*(3), 547–550. doi:10.1111/j.1467-8535.2009.00950.x

Brocke, J., Simons, A., & Cleven, A. (2008). A business process perspective on enterprise content management: towards a framework for organisational change. *Proceedings of the 16th European Conference on Information Systems*, Galway, Ireland, (pp. 1680-1691).

Brocke, J., Simons, A., & Cleven, A. (2009). Towards a business process-oriented approach to enterprise content management: The ECM-blueprinting framework. *Information Systems and E-Business Management*, *9*(4), 1–22.

Bronack, S., Sanders, R., Cheney, A., Riedl, R., Tashner, J., & Matzen, N. (2008). Presence pedagogy: Teaching and learning in 3D virtual immersive world. *International Journal of Teaching and Learning in Higher Education*, *20*(1), 59–69.

Brooks, F. P. (1995). *The mythical man-month: Essays on software engineering, anniversary edition* (2nd ed.). Addison-Wesley Professional.

Brownsword, L., Carney, D., & Oberndorf, T. (1998). *The opportunities and complexities of applying commercial-off-the-shelf components*. SEI Interactive. Retrieved from http://www.sei.cmu.edu/interactive/Features/1998/June/Applying_COTS/Applying_COTS.htm

Bruckman, A. S. (1997). *MOOSE Crossing: Construction, community, and learning in a networked virtual world for kids*. Unpublished Doctoral Dissertation, Massachusetts.

Bruckman, A., & Bandlow, A. (2002). HCI for kids. In Jacko, J., & Sears, A. (Eds.), *The human-computer interaction handbook: Fundamentals, evolving technologies, and emerging applications*. Lawrence Erlbaum and Associates.

Bryant, R. E. (1986). Graph-based algorithms for Boolean functions using a graphical representation. *IEEE Transactions on Computers*, *35*(8), 677–691. doi:10.1109/TC.1986.1676819

Buchanan, J. R., & Linowes, R. G. (1980). Making distributed data processing work. *Harvard Business Review*, *58*(5), 143–161.

Buchanan, J. R., & Linowes, R. G. (1980). Understanding distributed data processing. *Harvard Business Review, 8*(4), 43–153.

Buchheim, R. (2006). The future of ECM. In R. Stalters (Ed.), *AIIM Expo, Conference and Exposition,* (pp. 3-9).

Buitelaar, P., Cimiano, P., & Magnini, B. (2005). *Ontology learning from text: Methods, applications and evaluation. Frontiers in Artificial Intelligence and Applications.* IOS Press.

Bull, G., & Kajder, S. (2004). Tapped in. *Learning and Leading with Technology, 31*(5), 34–37.

Burton, J. K., Niles, J. A., Lalik, R. M., & Reed, M. W. (1986). Cognitive capacity engagement during and following interspersed mathernagenic questions. *Journal of Educational Psychology, 78*(2), 147–152. doi:10.1037/0022-0663.78.2.147

Burt, R. S. (2000). Structural holes versus network closure as social capital. In Lin, N., Cook, K. S., & Burt, R. S. (Eds.), *Social capital: Theory and research* (pp. 1–30). Preprint.

Cai, L. D. J., & Liakhovitch, E. (2000). Evolutionary computation techniques for multiple sequence alignment. *Proceedings of the 2000 Congress on Evolutionary Computation,* Vol. 2, (pp. 829-835).

Caldwell, S. D., Herold, D. M., & Fedor, D. B. (2004). Toward an understanding of the relationships among organizational change, individual differences, and change in person-environment fit: A cross-level study. *The Journal of Applied Psychology, 89*(5), 868–882. doi:10.1037/0021-9010.89.5.868

Callaghan, M. J., McCusker, K., Lopez Losada, J., Harkin, J. G., & Wilson, S. (2009). Engineering education island: Teaching engineering in virtual worlds. *ITALICS, 8*(3). Retrieved June, 2011, from http://www.ics.hearacademy.ac.uk/italics/download_php?file=italics/vol8iss3/pdf/italicsVol8Iss3Nov2009Paper01.pdf

Callahan, R. E. (1962). *Education and the cult of efficiency.* Chicago, IL: University of Chicago Press.

Cannegieter, J. J., Heijstek, A., Linders, B., & van Solingen, R. (2008, November). *CMMI roadmaps: Software engineering process management.* Technical Note, CMUSEI.

Cannon, W. (1932). *The wisdom and the body.* New York, NY: Nerton.

Can, T. (2009). Learning & teaching languages online: A constructivist approach. *Novitas Royal, 3*(1), 60–74.

Capers Jones. (2012, January). Evaluating ten software development methodologies. *Software Magazine.*

Cardenas, A. F., & McLeod, D. (1990). *Research foundations in object-oriented and semantic database systems.* Englewood Cliffs, NJ: Prentice Hall.

Carrier, B. (2003). *Open source digital forensics tools - The legal argument.* Retrieved March 14, 2012, from http://www.digital-evidence.org/papers/opensrc_legal.pdf

Carvalho, B. de R., & Ferreira, M. T. (2001). Using information technology to support knowledge conversion processes. *Information Research, 7*(1).

CC - Common Criteria for Information Technology Security Evaluation v2.3. (2007). Retrieved from http://www.commoncriteriaportal.org/public/developer/index.php?menu=2

Ceri, S., & Fraternali, P. (1997). *Database applications with objects and rules.* Essex, UK: Addison Wesley Longman.

Chan, D., & Schmitt, N. (2004). An agenda for future research on applicant reactions to selection procedures: A construct-oriented approach. *International Journal of Selection and Assessment, 12*(1/2), 9–23. doi:10.1111/j.0965-075X.2004.00260.x

Chan, D., Schmitt, N., Sacco, J. M., & DeShon, R. P. (1998). Understanding pretest and posttest reactions to cognitive ability and personality tests. *The Journal of Applied Psychology, 83*(3), 471–485. doi:10.1037/0021-9010.83.3.471

Chang, Y. F., Chen, C. Y., Chen, H. W., Lin, I. H., Luo, W. X., & Yang, C. H. … Chang, C. H. (2005). Bioinformatics analysis for genome design and synthetic biology. *Proceedings of Emerging Information Technology Conference.*

Chang, R. Y., & Morgan, M. W. (2000). *Performance scorecards*. San Francisco, CA: Jossey-Bass.

Chapman, D. S., & Webster, J. (2003). The use of technologies in the recruiting, screening, and selection processes for job candidates. *International Journal of Selection and Assessment, 11*(2/3), 113–120. doi:10.1111/1468-2389.00234

Chebotarev, P. Y. (1994). Aggregation of preferences by the generalized row sum method. *Mathematical Social Sciences, 27,* 293–320. doi:10.1016/0165-4896(93)00740-L

Chen, Y. (2011). *A dream of software engineers, service orientation and cloud computing*. Keynote presentation in the 13th IEEE Joint International Computer Science and Information Technology Conference, and in the IEEE Joint International Information Technology and Artificial Intelligence Conference, Chongqing, China, August 20-22, 2011.

Chen, Y., Pan, Y., Chen, Y., & Liu, W. (2006). Partitioned optimization algorithms for multiple sequence alignment. *20th International Conference on Advanced Information Networking and Applications,* Volume 2, (p. 5).

Chen, J., & McQueen, R. J. (2009). Knowledge transfer processes for different experience levels of knowledge recipients at an offshore technical support center. *Information Technology & People, 23*(1), 54–79. doi:10.1108/09593841011022546

Chen, S., Langner, C. A., & Mendoza-Denton, R. (2009). When dispositional and role power fit: Implications for self-expression and self-other congruence. *Journal of Personality and Social Psychology, 96*(3), 710–727. doi:10.1037/a0014526

Chen, Y., & Cheng, L. (2010). An approach to group ranking decisions in a dynamic environment. *Decision Support Systems, 48,* 622–634. doi:10.1016/j.dss.2009.12.003

Chess, B. (2008). Space race. *My Security Planet Fortify blog*. Retrieved May 12, 2009, from http://rgaucher.info/planet/Fortify_blog/2008/08/13/

Chess, B., & McGraw, G. (2004). Static analysis for security. *IEEE Security & Privacy, 2*(6), 76–79. doi:10.1109/MSP.2004.111

Choi, F. Y. Y. (2000). Advances in domain independent linear text segmentation. *Proceedings of the 1st Meeting of the North American Chapter of the Association for Computational Linguistics (ANLP-NAACL'00),* (pp. 26–33).

Chowdhury, J. (2008). Enterprise content management system-revolution for data ware housing. Retrieved from http://www.karmayog.org/it/upload/During%20the%20era%20of%201980_1.doc

Chowdhury, A., Frieder, O., Grossman, D., & McCabe, M. C. (2002). Collection statistics for fast duplicate document detection. *ACM Transactions on Information Systems, 20,* 171–191. doi:10.1145/506309.506311

Christiansen, N. D., Goffin, R. D., Johnston, N. G., & Rothstein, M. G. (1994). Correction the 16PF for faking: Effects on criterion-related validity and individual hiring decisions. *Personnel Psychology, 47,* 847–860. doi:10.1111/j.1744-6570.1994.tb01581.x

Churchill, E., Snowdon, D., & Munro, A. (2001). Collaborative virtual environments: Digital places and spaces for interaction. In Churchill, E. F., Snowdon, D. N., & Munro, A. J. (Eds.), *Collaborative virtual environments digital places and spaces for interaction* (pp. 3–17). London, UK: Springer-Verlag Publisher.

Clarke, S., & Maher, M. (2001). *The role of place in designining a learner centered virtual learning enviroment*. Presentation from Computer Aided Architectural Design (CAAD). Retrieved April 20, 2008, from http://web.arch.usyd.edu.au/-mary/Pubs/2001pdf/CF2001.pdf

Clarke, J., Dede, C., Ketelhut, D. J., & Nelson, B. (2006). A design-based research strategy to promote scalability for educational innovations. *Educational Technology, 46*(3), 27–36.

Cloud Security Alliance. (n.d.). Retrieved 15 March, 2012, from https://cloudsecurityalliance.org/

CNSS Secretariat. (2006). *National information assurance (IA) glossary*. Committee on National Security Systems.

Coad, P., & Yourdon, E. (1991). *Object-oriented design*. Yourdon Press.

Coblentz, N. (2009). SAMM assessment interview template. *SAMM Assessment Interview Template*. Retrieved September 18, 2009, from http://spreadsheets.google.com/pub?key=rYpVqQR3026Zu4DNg8LBIwg&gid=3

Cohen, F. (2009). Load testing in the cloud with open source testing automation. *Beyond Testing Magazine, 1*.

Cohen, K. (2006). *Second Life offers students a virtually real education*. The Phoenix Media/Communications Group. Retrieved April 20, 2008, from http://thephoenix.com/Article.aspx?id=20561&page=1

Cohen, K. B., & Hunter, L. (2008). Getting started in text mining. *PLoS Computational Biology, 4*, e20. doi:10.1371/journal.pcbi.0040020

Coksel-Canbek, N., Mauromati, M., Makridou-Bousiou, D., & Demiray, U. (2009). *Lifelong learning through Second Life: Current trends, potentials and limitations*. Retrieved 12, June, 2011, from http://academia.edu.documents.s3.amazonaws.com/847924/Lifelong_learning_through_Second_Life.pdf

Cole, M., & Engestrom, Y. (1993). A cultural-historical approach to distributed cognition. In Salomon, G. (Ed.), *Distributed cognitions: Psychological and educational considerations*. New York, NY: Cambridge University Press.

Collins, H. M. (2001). Tacit knowledge, trust and the Q of sapphire. *Social Studies of Science, 31*(1), 71–85. doi:10.1177/030631201031001004

Comparison of project-management software. (n.d.) Wikipedia: The Free Encyclopedia. Retrieved December 31, 2011, from http://en.wikipedia.org/wiki/Comparison_of_project_management_software

Computer Ethics Institute. (n.d.). *Ten commandments of computer ethics*. Retrieved March 15, 2012, from http://computerethicsinstitute.org/publications/tencommandments.html

Content Manager. (2004). *ECM market to reach $9B in software and service*. Retrieved from http://www.contentmanager.net/magazine/article_445_ecm_market_software_services.html

Cormen, T. H., Leiserson, C. E., Rivest, R. L., & Stein, C. (2001). *Introduction to algorithms* (2nd ed., pp. 540–549). MIT Press and McGraw-Hill.

Cormen, T. H., Leiserson, C. E., Rivest, R. L., & Stein, C. (2009). *Introduction to algorithms* (3rd ed.). MIT Press.

Cornell, M. N. W., Paton, W. S., Goble, C. A., Miller, C. J., Kirby, P., & Eilbeck, K. … Oliver, S. G. (2001). GIMS-A data warehouse for storage and analysis of genome sequence and functional data. *Proceedings of the IEEE 2nd International Symposium on Bioinformatics and Bioengineering Conference*, (pp. 15–22).

Corporation, E. M. C. (2009). *EMC ranked leader in Gartner 2009 ECM magic quadrant*. Retrieved from https://community.emc.com/docs/DOC-5189

Cranor, L. F., & Garfinkel, S. (2005). *Security and usability - Designing secure systems that people can use*. O'Reilly Media.

Crawley, F. (1999). *16.882J: Systems architecture*. (Class notes). Cambridge, MA: MIT graduate course.

Crawley, J. N. (1999). Behavioural phenotyping of transgenic and knockout mice: Experimental design and evaluation of general health, sensory functions, motor abilities, and specific behavioural tests. *Brain Research, 835*, 18–26. doi:10.1016/S0006-8993(98)01258-X

Cronin, B., Morath, R., Curtin, P., & Heul, M. (2006). Public sector use of technology in managing human resources. *Human Resource Management Review, 16*, 416–430. doi:10.1016/j.hrmr.2006.05.008

Curino, C. A., Tanca, L., & Zaniolo, C. (2008). *Information systems integration and evolution: Ontologies at rescue*. In International Workshop on Semantic Technologies for System Maintenance (STSM) co-located with the 16th IEEE International Conference on Program Comprehension (ICPC 2008) in Amsterdam, The Netherlands.

Curino, C. A., Moon, H. J., & Zaniolo, C. (2008). Graceful database schema evolution: The PRISM workbench. *Proceedings of the VLDB Endowment, 1*(1), 761–772.

Curphey, A. (2006). Web application security assessment tools. *IEEE Security and Privacy Archive, 4*(4).

Dale, K., & Fox, M. L. (2008). Leadership style and organizational commitment: Mediating effect of role stress. *Journal of Managerial Issues, 20*(1), 109.

Damiani, E. (2000). Design and implementation of an access processor for XML documents. *Proceeding of the 9th International WWW Conference*, Amsterdam.

Damjanović, V. (2010). Semantic reengineering of business processes. *Information Systems, 35*(4), 496–504. doi:10.1016/j.is.2009.06.003

Dasiopoulou, S., Giannakidou, E., Litos, G., Malasioti, P., & Kompatsiaris, Y. (2011). A survey of semantic image and video annotation tools. In Paliouras, G., Spyropoulos, C. D., & Tsatsaronis, G. (Eds.), *Knowledge-driven multimedia information extraction and ontology evolution.* Springer Verlag. doi:10.1007/978-3-642-20795-2_8

Davenport, T. H., & Prusak, L. (1998). *Working knowledge: How organizations manage what they know.* Harvard Business School Press.

Davidson, A. (2001). A fast pruning algorithm for optimal sequence alignment, bioinformatics and bioengineering conference. *Proceedings of the IEEE 2nd International Symposium,* (pp. 49–56).

de Biazzi, M. R., Muscat, A. R. N., & de Biazzi, J. L. (2009). Process management in the public sector: A Brazilian case study. *PICMET 2009 Proceedings.*

de Freitas, S. (2008). *Serious virtual worlds: A scoping study.* Bristol, UK: Joint Information Systems Committee. Retrieved May 24, 2010, from www.jisc.ac.uk/publications/publications/seriousvirtualworldsreport.aspx.

de Freitas, S., Harrison, I., Magoulas, G., Mee, A., Mohamad, F., & Oliver, M. (2006). The development of a system for supporting the lifelong learner. *British Journal of Educational Technology, Special Issue, Collaborative E-Support for Lifelong Learning, 37*(6), 867-880.

De Lucia, A., Francese, R., Passero, A., & Tortora, G. (2009). Development & evaluation of a virtual campus on Second life: The case of second DMI. *Computers & Education, 52,* 220–233.

De Lucia, F. R., Passero, I., & Tortora, G. (2009). Second Life technological transfer to companies: The case study of the CC ICT sub centre. *Journal of E-Learning & Knowledge Society, 5*(3), 23–32.

Decker, B., Rech, J., Ras, E., Klein, B., & Hoecht, C. (2005). Self-organized reuse of software engineering knowledge supported by semantic wikis. In *Proceedings of Workshop on Semantic Web Enabled Software Engineering* (SWESE).

Dede, C. (2002). *No cliché left behind: Why education policy is not like the movies.* NCREL National Educational Technology Conference.

Deerwester, S., Dumais, S. T., Landauer, T. K., Furnas, G. W., & Harshman, R. A. (1990). Indexing by latent semantic analysis. *Journal of the Society for Information Science, 41,* 391–407. doi:10.1002/(SICI)1097-4571(199009)41:6<391::AID-ASI1>3.0.CO;2-9

DeRue, D. S., & Morgeson, F. P. (2009). Stability and change in person-team and person-role fit over time: The effects of growth satisfaction, performance, and general self-efficacy. *The Journal of Applied Psychology, 92*(5), 1242–1253. doi:10.1037/0021-9010.92.5.1242

Desai, L. (2003). *Oracle collaboration suite: An Oracle Technical White Paper.* July 2003.

Dewey, J. (1933). *How we think: A restatement of the relation of reflective thinking to the educative process.* Boston, MA: D. C. Heath. Brilliant.

Di Sessa, A. (1995). Epistemology and systems design. In diSessa, A., & Hoyles, C. (Eds.), *Computers and Exploratory Learning* (pp. 15–29). Springer Verlag. doi:10.1007/978-3-642-57799-4_2

Dia (Version 0.97.2) [Software]. (n.d.). Retrieved from from http://live.gnome.org/Dia/Download

Diagramming software (n.d.). Wikipedia: The Free Encyclopedia. Retrieved December 31, 2011, from http://en.wikipedia.org/wiki/Diagramming_software

Dickover, N. (1994). Reflection-in-action: Modeling a specific organization through the viable system model. *Journal of Systemic Practice & Action Research, 7*(1), 43–62.

Dick, W., & Cary, L. (1990). *The systematic design of instruction.* Harper Collins.

Dieterle, E., & Clark, J. (2006). *Multi-user environments for teaching and learning.* Retrieved June 12, 2011, from http://64.94.241.248/rivercityproject/documents/MUVE-for-TandL-Dieterle-Clarke.pdf

Dillenbourg, P. (1999). What do you mean by collaborative learning? In Dillenbourg, P. (Ed.), *Collaborative-learning: Cognitive and computational approaches.* Oxford, UK: Elsevier.

Dillenbourg, P. (2008). Integrating technologies into educational ecosystems. *Distance Education*, *29*(2), 127–140. doi:10.1080/01587910802154939

Documentation for Dia. (December 2010). Retrieved March 24, 2012, from http://live.gnome.org/Dia/Documentation

DOD - Department of Defense Standard. (1985). *Department of Defense trusted computer system evaluation criteria.* (DOD 5200.28-STD, GPO 1986-623-963, 643 0, Dec. 26).

Dolibarr ERP/CRM. (Version DoliWamp 3.1.1). [Software]. (n.d.). Retrieved from http://sourceforge.net/projects/dolibarr/files/Dolibarr%20ERP-CRM/3.1.1/

Dolibarr User Documentation. (March 2012). Retrieved March 24, 2012, from http://wiki.dolibarr.org/index.php/User_documentation

Donaldson, R. E. (1992). Cybernetics and human knowing: One possible prolegomenon. *Cybernetics & Human Knowing*, *1*(2/3), 11–13.

DotNet. (2012). *Dot net framework 3.5*. Retrieved March 5, 2012, from http://msdn.microsoft.com/enus/library/w0x 726c2.aspx

Driver, R. (1988). Theory into practice II: A constructivist approach to curriculum development. In Fensham, P. (Ed.), *Development and dilemmas in science education* (pp. 133–149). London, UK: The Falmer Press.

Due, R. T. (2000). The economics of component-based development. *Information Systems Management*, *17*(1), 92–95.

Duffy, J. (2001). The tools and technologies needed for knowledge management. *Information Management Journal*, *35*(1), 64–67.

Dunn, R., Szapkiw, A., Holder, D., & Hodgson, D. (2010). Of student teachers and avatars: Working towards an effective model for geographically distributed learning communities of pre-service educators using virtual worlds. In D. Gibson & B. Dodge (Eds.), *Proceedings of Society for Information Technology & Teacher Education International Conference 2010* (pp. 423-427). Chesapeake, VA: AACE.

Dunn, W. S., Mount, M. K., Barrick, M. R., & Ones, D. S. (1995). Relative importance of personality and general mental ability in managers' judgments of applicant qualifications. *The Journal of Applied Psychology*, *80*, 500–509. doi:10.1037/0021-9010.80.4.500

Dunwoodie, B. (2004). Global ECM market still likely to consolidate. *CMS Wire*. Retrieved from http://www.cmswire.com/cms/enterprise-cms/global-ecm-market-still-likely-to- consolidate-000301.php

Dwivedi, H., Clark, C., & Thiel, D. (2010). *Mobile application security*. The McGraw-Hill Company.

Dynamics, S. P. I. Inc. (2002). *Complete web application security: Phase 1–Building web application security into your development process*. SPI Dynamics, Inc. Retrieved from http://cnscenter.future.co.kr/resource/rsc-center/vendor-wp/Spidynamics/Webapp_Dev_Process.pdf

Earl, C.-M. (2005). Peace building and human security: A constructivist perspective. *International Journal of Peace Studies*, *10*(1), 69–86.

Eberhart, A., & Argawal, S. (2004). SmartAPI - Associating ontologies and APIs for rapid application development. In *Proceedings of Workshop of Ontologien in der und für die Softwaretechnik*, Germany.

Edmonds, G. S., Branch, R. C., & Mukherjee, P. (1994). A conceptual framework for comparing instructional design models. *Educational Research and Technology*, *42*(2), 55–72. doi:10.1007/BF02298055

Ein-Dor, P., & Segev, E. (1978). *Managing management information systems*. Lexington, MA: Lexington Books, D.C. Heath and Company.

Elliott, J. L. (2005). *AquaMOOSE 3D: A constructionist approach to math learning motivated by artistic expression*. Unpublished Doctoral Dissertation, Georgia Institute of Technology, Atlanta, GA.

Elliott, G., & Strachan, J. (2004). *Global business information technology* (p. 87).

Elmasri, R., & Navathe, S. B. (Eds.). (2003). *Fundamentals of database systems*. Addison-Wesley.

Endeavour Agile, A. L. M. (2011). *Endeavour software project management* (Version 1.25) [Software]. Retrieved from http://sourceforge.net/projects/endeavour-mgmt/files/endeavour-mgmt/endeavour-mgmt-1.25/

Epstein, J. (2009). *What measures do vendors use for software assurance? Build security in.* Carnegie Mellon University. Retrieved from https://buildsecurityin.us-cert.gov/daisy/bsi/articles/knowledge/business/1093-BSI.html

Espejo, R., & Harnden, R. (1989). *The viable system model.* New York, NY: John Wiley & Sons.

Esteves, M., Antunes, R., Fonceca, B., Morgado, L., & Martins, P. (2008). Lecture Notes in Computer Science: *Vol. 5411. Using Second Life in programming's communities of practice. Groupware: Design, Implementation, and Use* (pp. 99–106).

Esteves, M., Fonsecaa, B., Morgado, L., & Martins, P. (2009). Using Second Life for problem-based learning in computer science programming. *Journal of Virtual Worlds Research, 2*(1).

Fan, M., Stallaert, J., & Whinston, A. B. (2000). The adoption and design methodologies of component-based enterprise systems. *European Journal of Information Systems, 9*(1), 25–35. doi:10.1057/palgrave.ejis.3000343

Fernie, S., Green, S. D., Weller, S. J., & Newcombe, R. (2003). Knowledge sharing: context, confusion and controversy. *International Journal of Project Management, 21*, 177–187. doi:10.1016/S0263-7863(02)00092-3

Ferraiolo, D. F., & Kuhn, R. (1992). *Role-based access controls.* 15th National Computer Security Conference.

Ferraiolo, D. F., Sandhu, R., Gavrila, S., Kuhn, R., & Chandramouli, R. (2001). Proposed NIST standard for role-based access control. *ACM Transactions on Information and System Security, 4*(3). doi:10.1145/501978.501980

Fichman, R. G., & Kemerer, C. F. (2002). Activity based costing for component-based software development. *Information Technology Management, 3*(1-2), 137–160. doi:10.1023/A:1013121011308

Finch, D. M., Edwards, B. D., & Wallace, J. C. (2009). Multistage selection strategies: Simulating the effects on adverse impact and expected performance for various predictor combinations. *The Journal of Applied Psychology, 94*(2), 318–340. doi:10.1037/a0013775

FIPS - Federal Information Processing Standard (FIPS-PUB199) 199. (2004). *Standards for security categorization of federal information and information systems.* Retrieved March 2, 2012, from http://csrc.nist.gov/publications/fips/fips199/FIPS-PUB-199-final.pdf

Fischer, G., & Ostwald, J. (2001). Knowledge management: Problems, promises, realities and challenges. *IEEE Intelligent Systems, 16*, 60–72. doi:10.1109/5254.912386

Florac, W. A. (1998). *Practical software measurement: Measuring for process management and improvement.* Paper presented at conference SEPG98.

Fonseca, J., Vieira, M., & Madeira, H. (2007). Testing and comparing web vulnerability scanning tools for SQL injection and XSS attacks. *13th Pacific Rim International Symposium on Dependable Computing, PRDC 2007* (pp. 365–372).

Forrester, J. (1994). Policies, decisions and information sources for modeling. In Morecroft, J., & Sterman, J. (Eds.), *Modeling for learning organizations.* Portland, OR: Productivity.

Fowler, D. (2008). *Implementing enterprise content management using Microsoft SharePoint. Capstone Report.* University of Oregon.

Fox, J., Bailenson, J., & Binney, J. (2009). Virtual experiences, physical behaviors: The effect of presence on imitation of an eating avatar. *Presence (Cambridge, Mass.), 18*(4), 294–303. doi:10.1162/pres.18.4.294

Francis, L. (2009). *Cloud computing: Implications for enterprise software vendors.* ESV.

Freedictionary.com. (2012). *Information security.* Retrieved on 14 March, 2012, from http://www.thefreedictionary.com/information+security

Fujii, K., & Suda, T. (2006). Semantics-based dynamic Web service composition. *International Journal of Cooperative Information Systems, 15*(3), 293–324. doi:10.1142/S0218843006001372

Gagné, R. M., Briggs, L. J., & Wager, W. W. (1988). *Principles of instructional design.* New York, NY: Holt, Rinehart and Winston.

Gajendra, S., Sun, W., & Ye, Q. (2010). Second Life: A story of communication tool in social networking and business. *Information Teaching Journal, 9*(3), 524–534. doi:10.3923/itj.2010.524.534

GanttProject (Version 2.5) [Software]. (n.d.). Retrieved from http://www.ganttproject.biz/download

Gardiner, M., Scott, J., & Horan, B. (2008). Reflections on the use of Project Wonderland as a mixed-reality environment for teaching and learning. *Researching Learning in Virtual Environments International Conference Proceedings,* The Open University, UK.

Garlati, G. (2012). *The dark side of BYOD – Privacy, personal data loss and device seizure.* Retrieved March 14, 2012, from http://consumerization.trendmicro.com/consumerization-byod-privacy-personal-data-loss-and-device-seizure/

Gazzard, A. (2009). Teleporters, tunnels & time: Understanding warp devices in videogames. *Proceedings of the Digital Games Research Association* (DiGRA).

Gee, J. P. (2003). *What video games have to teach us about learning and literacy.* New York, NY: Palgrave Macmillan. doi:10.1145/950566.950595

Gellatly, I. R. (1996). Conscientiousness and task performance: Test of cognitive process model. *The Journal of Applied Psychology, 81*(5), 474–482. doi:10.1037/0021-9010.81.5.474

Genovese, J. (2003). *Piaget, pedagogy & evolutionary psychology.* Retrieved May 24, 2010, from http://www.epjournal.net/filestore/ep01127137.pdf.

Gevers, J. M. P., Rutte, C. G., & Eerde, W. (2006). Meeting deadlines in work groups: Implicit and explicit mechanisms. *Applied Psychology, 55,* 52–72. doi:10.1111/j.1464-0597.2006.00228.x

Gibbs, G. (2007). *Analyzing qualitative data.* London, UK: Sage.

Gibson, C. F., & Nolan, R. L. (1974). Managing the four stages of EPP growth. *Harvard Business Review, 52*(1), 76–88.

Gollmann, D. (1999). *Computer security* (1st ed.). New York, NY: John Wiley & Sons. Retrieved from http://www.wiley.com/legacy/compbooks/catalog/97844-2.htm

Gordon, J. E. (2006). *The new science of strong materials.* Penguin Books.

Gotel, O. C. Z., & Finklestein, C. W. (1994). An analysis of the requirements traceability problem. In *Proceedings of the 1st International Conference on Requirements Engineering (ICRE'94),* (pp. 94-101).

Graff, M. G., & Van Wyk, K. R. (2003). *Secure coding: Principles & practices.* O'ReillyPub.

Granovetter, M. S. (1973). The strength of weak ties. *American Journal of Sociology, 78*(6), 1360–1380. doi:10.1086/225469

Graubart, R. (1989). On the need for a third form of access control. In *Proceedings of the 12th National Computer Security Conference,* Baltimore, MD, USA, 10-13 Oct.

Greer, M., Rodriguez-Martinez, M., & Seguel, J. (2010). *Open source cloud computing tools: A case study with a weather application.* Florida: IEEE Open Source Cloud Computing.

Greguras, G. J., & Diefendorff, J. M. (2009). Different fits satisfy different needs: Linking person-environment fit to employee commitment and performance using self-determination theory. *The Journal of Applied Psychology, 94*(2), 465–477. doi:10.1037/a0014068

Gremillion, L. L., & Pyburn, P. (1983). Breaking the systems development bottleneck. *Harvard Business Review, 61*(2), 130–137.

Gruber, T. R. (1993). A translation approach to portable ontology specifications. *Knowledge Acquisition, 5*(2), 199–220. doi:10.1006/knac.1993.1008

Guélat, J.-C. (2009). *Integration of user generated content into national databases – Revision workflow at swisstopo*. 1st EuroSDR Workshop on Crowd Sourcing for Updating National Databases, Wabern, Switzerland.

Gueutal, H. G., & Falbe, C. M. (2005). eHR: Trends in delivery methods. In H. G. Gueutal & D. L. Stone (Eds.), *The brave new world of eHR* (pp. 226-254). San Francisco, CA: Jossey-Bass.

Gupta, A. K., & Govindarajan, V. (2000). Knowledge flows within multinational corporations. *Strategic Management Journal, 21*(4), 473–496. doi:10.1002/(SICI)1097-0266(200004)21:4<473::AID-SMJ84>3.0.CO;2-I

Gupta, M. (1996, November). Security classification for documents. *Computers & Security, 15*(1), 55–71. doi:10.1016/0167-4048(95)00023-2

Hamat, A., & Amin-Embi, M. (2010). Constructivism in the design of online learning tools. *European Journal of Educational Studies, 2*(3), 237–246.

Hammond, N., & Allison, L. (1989). Extending hypertext for learning: An investigation of access and guidance tools. In Sutcliffe, A., & Macaulay, L. (Eds.), *People and Computers V* (pp. 293–304). Cambridge, UK: Cambridge University Press.

Hand, B., & Treagust, D. (1995). Development of a constructivist model for teacher inservice. *Australian Journal of Teacher Education, 20*(2), 28–29.

Hani, S. U. (2009, December). *Impact of process improvement on software development predictions, for measuring software development project's performance benefits*. ACM Press. ISBM: 978-1-60558-642-7

Hani, S. U. (2012). *Impact of process improvement on software development predictions*. Unpublished doctorial research report, Graduate School of Engineering Science and Information Technology, Hamdard University, Pakistan.

Happel, H.-J., Korthaus, A., Seedorf, S., & Tomczyk, P. (2006). KOntoR: An ontology-enabled approach to software reuse. In *Proceedings of the 18th International Conference on Software Engineering and Knowledge Engineering* (SEKE), San Francisco.

Harrison, M., Ruzzo, W., & Ullman, J. (1976). Protection in Operating Systems [Aug.]. *Communications of the ACM, 19*(8), 461–471. doi:10.1145/360303.360333

Hausknecht, J. P., Day, D. V., & Thomas, S. C. (2004). Applicant reactions to selection procedures: An updated model and meta-analysis. *Personnel Psychology, 57*, 639–683. doi:10.1111/j.1744-6570.2004.00003.x

Haycock, K., & Kemp, J. (2008). Immersive learning environments in parallel universes: Learning through Second Life. *School Libraries Worldwide, 14*(2), 89–97.

He, S., Chang, H., & Wang, Q. (2009). Component library-based ERP software development methodology. *International Conference on Interoperability for Enterprise Software and Applications China*, (pp. 34-38).

Hefner, R. (2005, November). *Achieving the promised benefits of CMMI*. Presented at CMMI Technology Conference & User Group.

Heiner, M., Schneckenberg, D., & Wilt, J. (2001). *Online pedagogy – Innovative teaching and learning strategies in ICT-environments*. Workpackage 1, Working group 7/8 Pedagogy, 3453/ 001-001 EDU-ELEARN. Retrieved May 2, 2011, from http://www.cevu.org/reports/docs/WP1_WG7_8BP.pdf

Hempel, P. S. (2004). Preparing the HR profession for technology and information work. *Human Resource Management, 43*(2/3), 163–177. doi:10.1002/hrm.20013

Henri, F. (1994). Distance learning and computer-mediated communication: Interactive, quasi- interactive or monologue? In O'Malley, C. (Ed.), *Computer supported collaborative learning*. Berlin, Germany: Springer-Verlag.

Herring, C., & Kaplan, S. (2000). Viable systems: The control paradigm for software architecture revisited. *AS-WEC '00: Proceedings of the 2000 Australian Software Engineering Conference*, (p. 97). IEEE Computer Society.

Herrington, J., Oliver, R., & Reeves, T. C. (2003). Patterns of engagement in authentic online learning environments. *Australian Journal of Educational Technology, 19*(1), 59–71.

Heusinkveld, S., & Reijers, H. A. (2009). Reflections on a reflective cycle: Building legitimacy in design knowledge development. *Organization Studies*, 30, 865–886.

Higgins, K. J. (2009). The rocky road to more secure code. *DarkReading*. Retrieved September 18, 2009, from http://www.darkreading.com/security/app-security/showArticle.jhtml?articleID=216403548&pgno=1&queryText=&isPrev=

Highhouse, S. (2008). Stubborn reliance on intuition and subjectivity in employee selection. *Industrial and Organizational Psychology. Perspectives on Science and Practice*, 1(3), 333–342.

Hildreth, P., Kimble, C., & Wright, P. (1998). Computer mediated communications and international communities of practice. [The Netherlands: Erasmus.]. *Proceedings of Ethicomp*, 98, 275–286.

Hislop, D. (2005). *Knowledge management in organizations: A critical approach*. Oxford, UK: Oxford University Press.

Hoffer, J. A., George, J. F., & Valacich, J. S. (2003). *Modern system analysis and design* (p. 23). Pearson Education Asia.

Hoffer, J. A., George, J. F., & Valacich, J. S. (2005). *Modern systems analysis* (4th ed.). Upper Saddle, NJ: Prentice Hall.

Hogan, M. (2008). *Cloud computing and databases: How databases can meet the demands of cloud computing*. ScaleDB.

Holland, K. (2008). *Integrating information security into software development lifecycle*. Retrieved March 14, 2012, from http://msdn.microsoft.com/en-us/library/cc168643.aspx

Hong, D., Suh, E., & Koo, C. (2011). Developing strategies for overcoming barriers to knowledge sharing based on conversational knowledge management: A case study of a financial company. *Expert Systems with Applications*, 38(12). doi:10.1016/j.eswa.2011.04.072

Hope, P., McGraw, G., & Anton, A. I. (2004). Misuse and abuse cases: Getting past the positive. *IEEE Security & Privacy*, 2(3), 90–92. doi:10.1109/MSP.2004.17

Hopkins, J. (2000). Component primer. *Communications of the ACM*, 43(10), 27–30. doi:10.1145/352183.352198

Hosmer, C. (2002). Proving the integrity of digital evidence with time. *The International Journal of Digital Evidence, 1*(1). Retrieved March 14, 2012, from http://www.utica.edu/academic/institutes/ecii/publications/articles/9C4EBC25-B4A3-6584-C38C511467A6B862.pdf

Houa, X., Ong, S. K., Nee, A. Y. C., Zhang, X. T., & Liu, W. J. (2011). GRAONTO: A graph-based approach for automatic construction of domain ontology. *Expert Systems with Applications*, 38(9), 11958–11975. doi:10.1016/j.eswa.2011.03.090

Hough, L. M., Eaton, N. K., Dunnette, M. D., Kamp, J. D., & McCloy, R. A. (1990). Criterion-related validities of personality constructs and the effect of response distortion on those validities. *Journal of Applied Psychology Monograph*, 75(5), 581–595. doi:10.1037/0021-9010.75.5.581

Howard, M. (2009). *A conversation about threat modeling*. Retrieved May 16, 2009, from http://msdn.microsoft.com/en-us/magazine/dd727503.aspx

Howard, M., & LeBlanc, D. (2002). *Writing secure code*. Redmond, WA: Microsoft Press.

Howard, M., & LeBlanc, D. (2003). *Writing secure code*. Redmond, WA: Microsoft Press.

Howard, M., & Lipner, S. (2006). *The security development lifecycle*. Redmond, WA: Microsoft Press.

Howe, C., & Mercer, N. (2007). *The primary review: Research survey 2/1b, children's social development, peer interaction and classroom learning*. Cambridge University.

Howe, J. (2008). *Crowdsourcing: Why the power of the crowd is driving the future of business*. Crown Business.

Hughes, C., & Moshell, J. (1997). Shared virtual worlds for education: The ExploreNet experiment. *Multimedia Systems*, 5(2), 145–154. doi:10.1007/s005300050050

Hull, C. E., & Lio, B. H. (2006). Innovation in non-profit and for-profit organizations: Visionary, strategic, and financial considerations. *Journal of Change Management*, 6(1), 53–65. doi:10.1080/14697010500523418

Humphrey, W. (1989). *Managing the software process. Reading*. MA: Addison-Wesley.

Ibáñez, M. B., García, J. J., Galán, S., Maroto, D., Morillo, D., & Kloos, C. D. (2011). Design and implementation of a 3D multi-user virtual world for language learning. *Journal of Educational Technology & Society, 14*(4), 2–10.

IBM Software Group. (2009). *The value of cloud computing to outsourcers and their clients*. IBM. Retrieved from ftp://ftp.software.ibm.com/software/uk/rational/cloud_computing_white_paper.pdf

IDC. (2012). *Software appliances ease cloud application deployment*. IDC Technology Spotlight.

IEEE ANSI/IEEE Standard 1008-1987. (1986). *IEEE standard for software unit testing*.

IEEE Standard 610.12-1990. (1990). *IEEE standard glossary of software engineering terminology*.

Ilyas, Q. M., Kai, Y. Z., & Talib, M. A. (2004). A conceptual architecture for semantic search engine. In *8th IEEE International Multi-topic Conference* (INMIC2004), Lahore, Pakistan (pp. 606-610).

Ilyas, Q. M., & Ahmad, I. (2010). A conceptual architecture of SAHARA - A semantic disaster management system. *World Applied Sciences Journal, 10*(8), 980–985.

Ilyas, Q. M., Kai, Y. Z., & Talib, M. A. (2004). A journey from information to knowledge: Knowledge representation and reasoning on the web. *Information Technology Journal, 3*(2), 163–167. doi:10.3923/itj.2004.163.167

Information Security. (n.d.). Wikipedia: The Free Encyclopedia. Retrieved from http://en.wikipedia.org/wiki/Information_security

ISACA. (n.d.). An introduction to business model for information security. Retrieved March 15, 2012, from http://www.isaca.org/Knowledge-Center/Research/ResearchDeliverables/Pages/An-Introduction-to-the-Business-Model-for-Information-Security.aspx

ISO. IEC 17799 - International Organization for Standardization, BS ISO/IEC 17799:2000 - Information technology. (2012). *Code of practice for information security management,* 1st Edition, 2000-12-01.

ITSEC - Information Technology Security Evaluation Criteria. (1991). *Commission European Communities*.

Jackson, M. (2000). *Systems approaches to management* (pp. 69-71, 272-279). New York, NY: Kluwer Academic.

Jacobson, I., Booch, G., & Rumbaugh, J. (1999). *The unified software development process*. Addison Wesley Publication.

Jagadish, H. V., Ooi, B. C., Tan, K. L., Yu, C., & Zhang, R. (2005). iDistance: An adaptive B+-tree based indexing method for nearest neighbor search. *ACM Transactions on Database Systems, 30*, 364–397. doi:10.1145/1071610.1071612

Jain, H., Vitharana, P., & Zahedi, F. M. (2003). An assessment model for requirements identification in component-based software development. *The Data Base for Advances in Information Systems, 34*(4), 48–63. doi:10.1145/957758.957765

Jarmon, L., Keating, E., & Toprac, P. (2008). Examining the societal impacts of nanotechnology through simulation: Nano scenario. *Simulation & Gaming, 39*(2), 168–181. doi:10.1177/1046878107305610

Jarmon, L., Traphagan, T., & Mayrath, M. (2008). Understanding project-based learning in Second Life with a pedagogy, training, and assessment trio. *Educational Media International, 45*(3), 157–176. doi:10.1080/09523980802283889

Jarvilehto, T. (1999). The theory of the organism environment system III: Role of effect influences on receptors in the formation of knowledge. *Integrative Psychological & Behavioral Science, 34*(2), 90–100. doi:10.1007/BF02688715

Jayaram, K. R., & Aditya, P. M. (2005). *Software engineering for secure software - State of the art: A survey* (CERIAS TR 2005-67). Purdue University. Retrieved from https://www.cerias.purdue.edu/apps/reports_and_papers/view/2884

Jenkins, T. (2004). *Enterprise content management: What you need to know*. Open Text Corporation.

Jensen, R., & Veloso, M. M. (2000). OBDD-based universal planning for synchronized agents in non-deterministic domains. *Journal of Artificial Intelligence Research, 13*, 189–226.

Jinglun, Z., & Quan, S. (1998). Reliability analysis based on binary decision diagrams. *Journal of Quality in Maintenance Engineering, 4*(2), 150–161. doi:10.1108/13552519810213707

Jiwani, K., & Zelkowitz, M. (2004). Susceptibility matrix: A new aid to software auditing. *IEEE Security and Privacy, 2*(2), 16–21. doi:10.1109/MSECP.2004.1281240

Johnson, A., Roussos, M., Leigh, J., Barnes, C., Vasilakis, C., & Moher, T. (1998). The NICE project: Learning together in a virtual world. In *Proceedings of IEEE Virtual Reality Annual International Symposium* (pp. 176-183). Albuquerque, USA.

Johnson, K. A., & Kulpa, M. (2010, March). *Agile CMMI®: Obtaining real benefits from measurement and high maturity*. Presented at conference SEPG-2010.

Johnson, A., Moher, T., Ohlsson, S., & Gillingham, M. (1999). The Round Earth Project – Collaborative VR for conceptual learning. *IEEE Computer Graphics and Applications, 19*(6), 60–69. doi:10.1109/38.799741

Johnson, D. W., & Johnson, R. T. (1996). Cooperation and the use of technology. In Jonassen, D. (Ed.), *Handbook of research for educational communications and technology* (pp. 1017–1044). New York, NY: Macmillan.

Jonassen, D. H. (1991). Objectivism versus constructivism: Do we need a new philosophical paradigm? *Educational Technology Research and Development, 39*(3), 5–14. doi:10.1007/BF02296434

Jonassen, D., & Rohrer-Murphy, L. (1999). Activity theory as a framework for designing constructivist learning environments. *Educational Technology Research and Development, 47*(1), 61–79. doi:10.1007/BF02299477

Jones, A., Lipton, R., & Snyder, L. (1976). A linear-time algorithm for deciding security. In *Proceedings of the 17th Symposium on the Foundations of Computer Science*, (pp. 33-41).

Kafai, Y. B. (2006). Playing and making games for learning: Instructionist and constructionist perspectives for game studies. *Games and Culture, 1*(1), 36–40. doi:10.1177/1555412005281767

Kajava, J. (2006). Information security standards and global business. *IEEE International Conference on Industrial Technology (ICIT),* (pp. 2091–2095).

Kallonis, P., & Sampson, D. (2010). Implementing 3D virtual classroom simulation for teachers' continuing professional development. *Proceedings of the 18th International Conference on Computers in Education*. Putrajaya, Malaysia: Asia-Pacific Society for Computers in Education.

Kamel, S. (2003). *Introduction to business information system: Internet marketing: Corporate and business unit strategy*. Lecture presented at the American University in Cairo.

Kampffmeyer, U. (2006). Enterprise content management. DMS EXPO 2006 in Köln.

Kan, P. (2004). *Structuring specifications of reactive systems using B*. PhD Thesis, Kings College, University of London.

Kaner, C., Falk, J., & Nguyen, H. Q. (1999). *Testing computer software* (p. 42). Wiley Computer Publishing.

Kappen, C., & Salbaum, J. M. (2003). Comparative genome annotation for mapping, prediction and discovery of genes. *Proceedings of the 36th Annual Hawaii International Conference on System Sciences*.

Kaput, J., & Roschelle, J. (2000, October). *Shifting representational infrastructures and reconstituting content to democratize access to the math of change & variation: Impacts on cognition, curriculum, learning and teaching*. Paper presented at the workshop to Integrate Computer-based Modeling & Scientific Visualization into K-12 Teacher Education Programs, Ballston, VA.

Keen, P. G. W., & Morton, S. (1978). *Decision support systems: An organizational perspective* (p. 93). Reading, MA: Addison-Wesley, Inc.

Kehoe, J. F., Dickter, D. N., Russell, D. P., & Sacco, J. M. (2005). E-selection. In Gueutal, H. G., & Stone, D. L. (Eds.), *The brave new world of eHR* (pp. 54–103). San Francisco, CA: Jossey-Bass.

Keller, R. T. (2001). Cross-functional project groups in research and new product development: Diversity, communication, job stress and outcomes. *Academy of Management Journal, 44*(3), 547–555. doi:10.2307/3069369

Kemp, J. (2007). A critical analysis into the use of enterprise content management systems in the IT industry. Retrieved from www.aiimhost.com/whitepapers/James-Kemp_ECMReport.pdf

Kemp, J., & Livingstone, D. (2009). *Putting a Second Life "metaverse" skin on learning management systems.* Retrieved 12, June, 2011, from: http://www.sloodle.com/whitpaper.pdf

Kettunen, P. (2011). *Rethinking software-intensive new product development: From product push to value evolution.* Retrieved from cloudsoftwareprogram.com

Khan, I. (2006). *Software quality assurance through metrics.* Presented at training session, Business Beam, Pakistan.

Khan, S., Ilyas, W. M., & Anwar, W. (2009). *Contextual advertising using Semantic Web approach.* International Conference on Frontiers of Information Technology, Abbottabad, Pakistan.

Kieffer, K. M., Schinka, J. A., & Curtiss, G. (2004). Person-environment congruence and personality domains in the prediction of job performance and work quality. *Journal of Counseling Psychology, 51*(2), 168–177. doi:10.1037/0022-0167.51.2.168

Kim, B. K., & Beak, Y. (2010). Exploring ideas and possibilities of second life as an advanced elearning environment. In Hao Yang, H., & Yen Yuen, S. C. (Eds.), *Handbook of research on practices and outcomes in e-learning: Issues and trends* (pp. 165 181). Hershey, PA: Information Science Reference.

Kim, F., & Skoudis, E. (2009). *Protecting your web apps: Two big mistakes and 12 practical tips to avoid them.* SANS Institute.

Kim, I., Bae, D., & Hong, J. (2007). A component composition model providing dynamic, flexible, and hierarchical composition of components for supporting software evolution. *Journal of Systems and Software, 80*(11), 1797–1816. doi:10.1016/j.jss.2007.02.047

Kluemper, D. H., & Rosen, P. A. (2009). Future employment selection methods: Evaluating social networking web sites. *Journal of Managerial Psychology, 24*(6), 567–580. doi:10.1108/02683940910974134

Knoodl. (2012). Retrieved from http://www.knoodl.com/ui/home.html;jsessionid=0129154041003C2F75412AD22293E146

Knowles, M. (1984). *Andragogy in action. Applying modern principles of adult education.* San Francisco, CA: Jossey-Bass.

Koendjbiharie, S., Koppius, O., Vervest, P., & van Heck, E. (2010). *Network transparency and the performance of dynamic business networks.* 4th IEEE International Conference on Digital Ecosystems and Technologies (IEEE Dest 2010), 2010.

Kolas, L., & Stampe, A. (2004). *Implementing delivery methods by using pedagogical design patterns.* Retrieved 29 May, 2011, from www2.tisip.no/E-LEN/papers/ED-MEDIA/SymposiaNTNU.pdf

Kolawa, A., & Huizinga, D. (2007). *Automated defect prevention: Best practices in software management* (p. 75). Wiley-IEEE Computer Society Press.

Koleva, B. N., Schnadelbach, H. M., Benford, S. D., & Greenhalgh, C. M. (2000). Developing mixed reality boundaries. In *Proceedings of Designing Augmented Reality Environments* (DARE 2000) (pp.155–157). Elsinore, Denmark.

Koltai, B., Warnick, J., Agbaji, R., & Nilan, S. (2001). Test driven development. *ACM Transactions on Computational Logic, 5*(50), 1–21.

Koster, R. (2004). *A virtual world by any other name?* [Msg 21]. Message posted to http://terranova.blogs.com/terra_nova/2004/06/a_virtual_world.html

Kotlarsky, J. I., Oshri, J., van Hillegersberg, K., & Kumar, K. (2007). Globally distributed component-based software development: An exploratory study of knowledge management and work division. *Journal of Information Technology, 22*(2), 161–173. doi:10.1057/palgrave.jit.2000084

Kozulin, A. (1999). The concept of activity in Soviet psychology: Vygotsky, his disciples and critics. In Lloyd, P., & Fernyhough, C. (Eds.), *Lev Vygotsky- Critical assessments: Vygotsky's theory* (Vol. I, pp. 179–202). New York, NY: Routledge.

Krishni, N. (2001). *How to check compliance with your security policy*. Retrieved from http://www.sans.org/infosecFAQ/policy/compliance.htm

Kroenke, D. (2009). Information systems for competitive advantage. In Laudon, K. C., Laudon, J. P., & Brabston, M. E. (Eds.), *Using management information systems: Managing a digital firm* (2nd ed.). London, UK: Prentice Hall.

Krogstie, J., Terry, H., & Siau, K. (Eds.). (2005). *Information modeling methods and methodologies*. Hershey, PA: Idea Group Publishing.

Kruchten, P. (2003). *The rational unified process: An introduction* (3rd ed.). Boston, MA: Addison-Wesley Longman Publishing Co., Inc.

Kutsikos, K., & Makropoulos, D. (2006). Distribution-collaboration networks (DCN): A network-based infrastructure for e-government services. *International Journal of Applied Systemic Studies, 1*, 1.

Kvale, S., & Brinkmann, S. (2009). *Interviews: Learning the craft of qualitative research interviewing* (2nd ed.). London, UK: Sage.

LaBrie, R., & Louis, R. S. (2003). Information retrieval from knowledge management systems: Using knowledge hierarchies to overcome keyword limitations. In *9th Americas Conference on Information Systems (AMCIS'03)*, (pp. 2552-2563).

Lampson, B. (1974). Protection. *ACM Operating Systems Review, 8*(1), 18–24. doi:10.1145/775265.775268

Landon, B. (1999). *Online educational delivery applications: A web tool for comparative analysis*. Retrieved June 12, 2011, from http://www.ctt.bc.ca/landonline/index.html

Land, S., & Hannafin, M. (2000). Student-centered learning environments. In Jonassen, D., & Land, S. (Eds.), *Theoretical foundations of learning environments* (pp. 1–23). Lawrence Erebaum Associates.

Landwher, C. E., Bull, A. R., McDermott, J. P., & Choi, W. S. (1994). A taxonomy of computer program security flaws, with examples. *ACM Computing Surveys, 3*(26).

Lano, K. (2005). *Advanced system design in Java*. London, UK: Butterworth-Heinman.

Lanowitz, T. (2005). *Now is the time for security at the application level*. Gartner Group. Retrieved from http://www.sela.co.il/_Uploads/dbsAttachedFiles/GartnerNow-IsTheTimeForSecurity.pdf

Larman, C., & Basili, R. V. (2003). Iterative and incremental development: A brief history. *IEEE Computer, 36*(6), 47–56. doi:10.1109/MC.2003.1204375

Laudon, K. C., & Laudon, J. P. (2011). Information systems, organizations, and strategy. In *Using management information systems: Managing a digital firm* (2nd ed.). London, UK: Pearson Education Inc. Prentice Hall.

Lave, J., & Wenger, E. (1991). *Situated leaning: Legitimate peripheral participation*. Cambridge, UK: Cambridge University Press. doi:10.1017/CBO9780511815355

Lee, Z.-J., & Lee, C.-Y. (2005). An intelligent system for multiple sequences alignment. *IEEE International Conference on Systems, Man and Cybernetics,* Vol. 2, (pp. 1042–1047).

Lee, C. Y. (1959). Representation of switching circuits by binary decision diagrams. *Bell System Technology, 38*, 985–999.

Lee, T. B., Hendler, J., & Lassila, O. (2001). The Semantic Web, a new form of web content that is meaningful to computers will unleash a revolution of new possibilities. *Scientific American.*

Lei, D., Hitt, M. A., & Bettis, R. (1996). Dynamic core competences through meta-learning and strategic context. *Journal of Management, 22*(4), 549–569. doi:10.1177/014920639602200402

Leontiev, A. N. (1978). *Activity, consciousness and personality*. Prentice-Hall.

Lepak, D. P., & Snell, S. A. (1998). Virtual HR: Strategic human resource management in the 21st century. *Human Resource Management Review, 8*(3), 215–234. doi:10.1016/S1053-4822(98)90003-1

Lesser, E., & Prusak, L. (1999). *Communities of practice, social capital and organizational knowledge*. Retrieved January 15, 2010, from http://www.providersedge.com/docs/km_articles/Cop_-_Social_Capital_-_Org_K.pdf

Lethbridge, T. C., & Laganière, R. (2001). *Object oriented software engineering: Practical software development using UML and Java* (1st ed.). Maidenhead, UK: McGraw Hill.

LeVeque, V. (2006). *Information security – A strategic approach*. Hoboken, NJ: John Wiley & Sons Inc.

Liber, O. (1999). *A pedagogical framework for the evaluation of virtual learning environments*. Bangor, University of Wales. Retrieved January 15, 2010, from http://www.jtap.ac.uk

Liber, O. (2004). *A framework for the pedagogical evaluation of e-learning environment*. Retrieved January 15, 2010, from http://www.pgce.seton.ac.uk/IT/School_ICT/VLEusage/VLEpedagogy.pdf

Liber, O. (1998). Structuring institutions to exploit learning technologies: A cybernetic model. *Association for Learning Technology Journal*, *6*(1), 13–18. doi:10.1080/0968776980060103

Lievens, F., & Harris, M. M. (2003). Research on internet recruiting and testing: Current status and future directions. *International Review of Industrial and Organizational Psychology*, *18*, 131–165.

Li, J., Conradi, R., Slyngstad, O. P., Torchiano, M., Maurizio, M., & Bunse, C. (2008). A state-of-the- practice survey of risk management in development with off-the-shelf, software components. *IEEE Transactions on Software Engineering*, *34*(2), 271–286. doi:10.1109/TSE.2008.14

Lin, B., & Hsieh, C. (2001). Web-based teaching and learner control: a research view. *Computers & Education*, *37*, 377–386.Macedo, A., & Morgado, L. (2009). *Learning to teach in Second Life*. Retrieved 15 January, 2010, from http://www.eden-online.org/contents/conferences/OCRC's/Porto/AM_LM.pdf

Lipner, S., & Howard, M. (2005). The trustworthy computing security development lifecycle. *Microsoft Developer Network*. Retrieved September 24, 2009, from http://msdn.microsoft.com/en-us/library/ms995349.aspx

List of Unified Modeling Language tools. (n.d.). Wikipedia: The Free Encyclopedia. Retrieved December 31, 2011, from http://en.wikipedia.org/wiki/List_of_Unified_Modeling_Language_tools

Liu, M. Y., & Traore, I. (2004). UML-based security measures of software products. In *Proceedings of the 4th International Conference on Application of Concurrency to System Design (ACSD-04)*, Hamilton, Ontario, Canada, June.

Liu, R.-L. (2008). Interactive high-quality text classification. *Information Processing & Management*, *44*(3), 1062–1075. doi:10.1016/j.ipm.2007.11.002

Liu, W., Schmidt, B., Voss, G., & Muller-Wittig, W. (2007). Streaming algorithms for biological sequence alignment on GPUs. *IEEE Transactions on Parallel and Distributed Systems*, *18*(9), 1270–1281. doi:10.1109/TPDS.2007.1069

Li, X., & Parsons, J. (2011). Assigning ontological semantics to unified modeling language for conceptual modeling. In Siau, K., Chiang, R., & Hardgrave, B. (Eds.), *Systems analysis and design: People, processes, and projects* (pp. 180–194). AMIS.

Locke, E. A., & Latham, G. P. (2002). Building a practically useful theory of goal setting and task motivation: a 35-year odyssey. *The American Psychologist*, *57*(9), 705. doi:10.1037/0003-066X.57.9.705

Locuratolo, E. (1998). *ASSO: Portability as a methodological goal*. (Technical Report, IEI:B4-05-02).

Locuratolo, E. (2009). *An approach to the evolution of conceptual methods*. (ISTI-TR-007).

Locuratolo, E. (2011). *Meta-modeling to design the structure database schema*. In K. Siau, R. H. L. Chiang, & B. C. Hardgrave (Eds.), *Systems analysis and design: People, processes, and projects*, Vol. 1 (pp. 195–215). (Advances in Management Information Systems, vol. 18). United States of America: M E. Sharpe.

Locuratolo, E., & Palomäki, J. (2012). *Construction of concepts and decomposition of objects*. (Technical report TR-02-2011, ISTI-TR-02-2011).

Locuratolo, E., Loffredo, M., & Signore, O. (1998). Database reengineering for quality. In *Proceedings of the 6th Re-engineering Forum*, Firenze.

Locuratolo, E. (2005). Model transformations in designing the ASSO methodology. In van Bommel, P. (Ed.), *Transformations of knowledge, information and data: Theory and applications* (pp. 283–302). Hershey, PA: Idea Group Inc.doi:10.4018/978-1-59140-527-6.ch013

Locuratolo, E. (2009). Database design based on B. In Erickson, J. (Ed.), *Database technologies: Concepts, methodologies, tools, and applications* (pp. 400–456). Hershey, PA: Information Science Reference. doi:10.4018/978-1-60566-058-5.ch028

Locuratolo, E., & Matthews, B. (1999). On the relationship between ASSO and B. In Jaakkola, H., Kangassalo, H., & Kawaguchi, E. (Eds.), *Information modelling and knowledge bases X* (pp. 235–253). Amsterdam, The Netherlands: IOS Press.

Locuratolo, E., & Palomäki, J. (2008). Extensional and intensional aspects of conceptual design. In Jaakkola, H., Kiyoki, Y., & Tokuda, T. (Eds.), *Information modelling and knowledge bases XIX* (pp. 160–169). Amsterdam, The Netherlands: IOS Press.

Locuratolo, E., & Palomäki, J. (2013in press). Ontology for database preservation. In Nazir, M., Colomb, R. M., & Abdullah, M. S. (Eds.), *In Ontology-based applications for enterprise systems and knowledge management*. Hershey, PA: IGI Global.

Locuratolo, E., & Rabitti, F. (1998). Conceptual classes and system classes in object databases. *Acta Informatics*, *35*(3), 181–210. doi:10.1007/s002360050118

Lodderstedt, T., Basin, D. A., & Doser, J. (2002). SecureUML: A UML-Based Modeling Language for Model-Driven Security. *In Proc. of the 5th International Conference on the Unified Modeling Language (UML '02)*, Springer-Verlag London, UK, ISBN:3-540-44254-5.

Lucas, H. C. (1975). *Why information systems fail*. New York, NY: Columbia University Press.

MacFarland, L. A., Yun, G. J., Harold, C. M., Viera, L., & Moore, L. G. (2005). An examination of impression management use and effectiveness across assessment center exercises: The role of competency demands. *Personnel Psychology*, *58*, 949–980. doi:10.1111/j.1744-6570.2005.00374.x

Maciaszek, L. A., & Liong, B. L. (2005). *Practical software engineering*. Addison Wesley Publications.

Madey, G., Freeh, V., & Tynan, R. (2002). *The open source software development phenomenon: An analysis based on social network theory*. AMCIS.

Madsen, P. (2010). Dynamic transparency, prudential justice, and corporate transformation: Becoming socially responsible in the Internet Age. *Journal of Business Ethics*, *90*, 639–648. doi:10.1007/s10551-010-0597-8

Magoutas, B., & Mentzas, G. (2010). SALT: A semantic adaptive framework for monitoring citizen satisfaction from e-government services. *Expert Systems with Applications*, *37*(6), 4292–4300. doi:10.1016/j.eswa.2009.11.071

Maher, M., & Bilda, G. (2006). Studying design behavior in collaborative virtual environments. In R. N. Pikaar, A. P. Komihgsreld, & J. M. Settels (Eds.), *Proceedings of 16th World Congress on Ergonomics* (IEA 2006 Congress). Maastricht, The Netherlands: Elsevier. Retrieved 15 January, 2010, from http://www.web.arch.usyd.edu.au/-mary/Pubs/2006pdf/Maher-1248.pdf

Malik, S., Wang, A. R., Brayton, R. K., & Vincentelli, A. S. (1988). Logic verification using binary decision diagrams in logic synthesis environment. In *Proceedings of the IEEE International Conference on Computer Aided Design*, ICCAD'88. Santa Clara CA, USA, (pp. 6–9).

Mall, R. (2008). *Fundamentals of software engineering* (p. 32). PHI.

Manninen, T. (2000). Interaction in networked virtual environments as communicative action - social theory and multi-player games. In *Proceedings of CRIWG2000 Workshop*, October 18-20, Madeira, Portugal, IEEE Computer Society Press.

Manning, C. D., Raghavan, P., & Schütze, H. (2008). *Introduction to information retrieval*. Cambridge, UK: Cambridge University Press. doi:10.1017/CBO9780511809071

Marcus, A. (2011). *Information retrieval methods for software engineering*. In Canadian Summer School on Practical Analyses of Software Engineering Data (PASED'11), Montreal, Quebec, Canada, 2011. Retrieved from http://pased.soccerlab.polymtl.ca/materials/june-18-2011/PASED-06.18.2011-Slides.pdf

Marjanovic, O. (2005). Process-oriented CRM enabled by component-based workflow technology. *Proceedings of the 18th Bled eConference*, Bled, Slovenia, June 6-8.

Marmor-Squires, A. B., & Rougeau, P. A. (1988). Issues in process models and integrated environments for trusted systems development. *Proceedings of the 11th National Computer Security Conference* (pp. pp. 109–113). United States Government Printing Office.

Martin, J. (1991). *Rapid application development*. Indianapolis, IN: Macmillan Publishing Co., Inc.

Mason, R., & Rennie, F. (2008). *E-learning and social networking handbook: Recourses for higher education.* New York, NY: Routledge.

Matthews, B., & Locuratolo, E. (1999). In Woodcock, J., & Davis, J. (Eds.), *Formal development of databases in ASSO and B* (pp. 388–410). Lecture Notes in Computer Science.

Matzler, K., Renzl, B., Müller, J., Herting, S., & Mooradian, T. A. (2008). Personality traits and knowledge sharing. *Journal of Economic Psychology, 29*, 301–313. doi:10.1016/j.joep.2007.06.004

Mayank, V., Kositsyna, N., & Austin, M. (2004). *Requirements engineering and the Semantic Web, part II. Representation, management, and validation of requirements and system-level architectures. Technical Report. TR 2004-14.* University of Maryland.

Mayrath, M., Sanchez, J., Traphagan, T., Heikes, J., & Trivedi, A. (2007). Using Second Life in an English course: Designing class activities to address learning objectives. In C. Montgomerie & J. Seale (Eds.), *Proceedings of World Conference on Educational Multimedia, Hypermedia and Telecommunications 2007* (pp. 4219-4224). Chesapeake, VA: AACE.

Ma, Z. (2006). Database modeling of engineering information. In *Database modeling for industrial data management emerging technologies and applications* (pp. 35–61). Hershey, PA: Idea Group Publishing. doi:10.4018/978-1-59140-684-6.ch001

McAdams, D. P. (2009). *The person-an introduction to the science of personality psychology.* Hoboken, NJ: John Wiley and Sons, Inc.

McCollum, C. J., Messing, J. R., & Notargiacomo, L. (1990). Beyond the Pale of MAC and DAC - Defining New Forms of Access Control. *In Proc. of the Symposium on Security and Privacy*, Oakland, CA, USA.

McConnell, D. (1994). *Implementing computer supported cooperative learning.* London, UK: Kogan Page.

McConnell, S. (1995). *Rapid development*. Redmond, WA: Microsoft Press.

McCrae, R. R., Stone, S. V., Fagan, P. J., & Costa, P. T. Jr. (1998). Identifying causes of disagreement between self-reports and spouse ratings of personality. *Journal of Personality, 66*, 286–313. doi:10.1111/1467-6494.00013

McFarlan, F. W. (1981). Portfolio approach to information systems. *Harvard Business Review, 59*(5), 142–150.

McFarlan, F. W., McKinney, J. L., & Pyburn, P. (1983). The information archipelago Plotting a course. *Harvard Business Review, 61*(1), 145–156.

McGraw, G. (1998). Testing for security during development: Why we should scrap penetrate-and-patch. *IEEE Aerospace and Electronic Systems, 13*(4), 13–15. doi:10.1109/62.666831

McGraw, G. (2004). Software security. *IEEE Security & Privacy, 2*(2), 80–83. doi:10.1109/MSECP.2004.1281254

McGraw, G. (2006). *Software security: Building security in.* Addison-Wesley Professional.

McGraw, G., Chess, B., & Migues, S. (2009). *Building security in maturity model*. Fortify & Cigital.

McGrenere, J. L. (1996). *Design: Educational electronic multi-player games. A Literature Review.* Department of Computer Science, The University of British Columbia.

McKenney, J. L., & McFarlan, F. W. (1982). The information archipelago-Maps and bridges. *Harvard Business Review, 60*(5), 109–119.

McManus, M. A., & Ferguson, M. W. (2003). Biodata, personality, and demographic differences of recruits from three sources. *International Journal of Selection and Assessment, 11*(2/3), 175–183. doi:10.1111/1468-2389.00241

Mead, N. R., & Allen, J. H. (April 2009). *Making the business case for software assurance*. Special Report, Software Engineering Institute, Carnegie Mellon University.

Mead, N. R., & McGraw, G. (2003). *The DIMACS Workshop on Software Security*. DIMACS Center.

Meftah, B. (2008). *Business software assurance: Identifying and reducing software risk in the enterprise.* Presented at the 9th Semi-Annual Software Assurance Forum. Retrieved from https://buildsecurityin.us-cert.gov/swa/downloads/Meftah.pdf

Meira, L. (1998). Making sense of instructional devices: The emergence of transparency in mathematical activity. *Journal for Research in Mathematics Education, 29*(2), 121–142. doi:10.2307/749895

Mell, P., Bergeron, T., & Henning, D. (2005). Creating a Patch and Vulnerability Management Program. *Computer Security Division, National Institute of Standards and Technology (NIST) Special Publication 800-40 Version 2.0,* Gaithersburg, MD, USA, 75 pages.

Mennecke, B., Triplett, J., Hassall, L., Heer, R., & Jordan-Conde, Z. (2008). *Embodied social presence theory.* Retrieved January 15, 2010, from http://www.papers.ssrn.com/abstract=1286281

Merkow, M., & Breithaupt, J. (2006). *Information security – Principles and practices.* Pearson Eduction Inc.

Metrick, S., & Epstein, A. (1999). *Emerging technologies for active learning, part 1: Multi- user virtual environments.* LNT Perspectives. Retrieved 12, June, 2011, from http://www2.edc.org/LNT/news/Issue10/feature3a.htm

Miao, Y., Pinkwart, N., & Hoppe, H. U. (2007). A collaborative virtual environment for situated learning of car driving. *International Journal on Advanced Technology for Learning, 3*(4), 233–240.

Michailidou, A., & Economides, A. A. (2003). E learn: Towards a collaborative educational virtual environment. *Journal of Information Technology Education, 2,* 131–152.

Microsoft Corporation. (2008). *Microsoft security development lifecycle (SDL) version 3.2.* Microsoft Corporation.

Microsoft Corporation. (2009). *The microsoft security development lifecycle* (SDL). Retrieved March 23, 2009, from http://msdn.microsoft.com/en-us/security/cc448177.aspx

Microsoft Corporation. (2009). SDL process template. *MSDN.* Retrieved May 22, 2009, from http://msdn.microsoft.com/en-us/security/dd670265.aspx

Mohamed, A. A., Orife, J. N., & Wibowo, K. (2001). The legality of key word search as a personnel selection tool. *Employee Relations, 24*(5), 516–522. doi:10.1108/01425450210443285

Mon, L. (2009). Questions and answers in a virtual world: Educators and librarians as information providers in Second Life. *Journal of Virtual Worlds Research, 2*(1).

Mooney, A. (2007). Core competence, distinctive competence, and competitive advantage: What is the difference? *Journal of Education for Business,* (November/December): 110–115. doi:10.3200/JOEB.83.2.110-115

Moore, A. P., Ellison, R. J., & Linger, R. C. (2001). *Attack modeling for information security and survivability.* (Technical Note CMU/SEI-2001-TN-001).

More, N. T., Sapre, B. S., & Chawan, P. M. (2011). An insight into the importance of requirements engineering. *International Journal of Internet Computing, 1*(2).

Moret, B. M. E. (1982). Decision trees and diagrams. *Computing Surveys, 14,* 413–416. doi:10.1145/356893.356898

Mount, M. K., Judge, T. A., Scullen, S. E., Sytsma, M. R., & Hezlett, S. A. (1998). Trait, rater, and level effects in 360-degree performance ratings. *Personnel Psychology, 51,* 557–576. doi:10.1111/j.1744-6570.1998.tb00251.x

Munkvold, B. E., Päivärinta, T., Hodne, A. K., & Stangeland, E. (2006). Contemporary issues of enterprise content management: The case of Statoil. *Scandinavian Journal of Information Systems, 18,* 69–100.

Murata, M. (2003). XML access control using static analysis. *Proceedings of the 10th ACM Conference on Computer and Communications Security,* Washington DC, USA.

Murhpy, K. R., & DeShon, R. (2000). Interrater correlations do not estimate the reliability of job performance ratings. *Personnel Psychology, 53,* 873–900. doi:10.1111/j.1744-6570.2000.tb02421.x

Nahar, N., Hamel, L., Popstova, M. S., & Gogarten, J. P. (2007). GPX: A tool for the exploration and visualization of genome evolution. *Proceedings of the 7th IEEE International Conference on Bioinformatics and Bioengineering,* (pp. 1338–1342).

Nasser, S., Vert, G. L., Nicolescu, M., & Murray, A. (2007). Multiple sequence alignment using fuzzy logic. *IEEE Symposium on Computational Intelligence and Bioinformatics and Computational Biology*, (pp. 304–311).

NCSC. (1987). *A guide to understanding discretionary access control in trusted systems*. National Computer Security Center (NCSC). *NCSC-TG, 003*(Sept), 30.

Nemirovsky, R., Tierney, C., & Wright, T. (1998). Body motion and graphing. *Cognition and Instruction, 16*(2), 119–172. doi:10.1207/s1532690xci1602_1

Ng, K. (March 2008). *Framework to communicate the impact and benefits of software process initiative: The MSC Malaysia perspective*. SEPG 2008, Tampa Florida, USA.

Nicosia, L. (2008). *Adolescent literature and Second Life: Teaching young adult texts in the digital world. New literacies: A professional development wiki for educators. Improving Teacher Quality Project (ITQP)*. Federally Funded Grant.

Nie, M., Roush, P., & Wheeler, M. (2010). Second Life for digital photography: An exploratory study. *Contemporary Educational Technology, 1*(3), 267-280.

Nielsen, F. (2000). *Approaches to security metrics*. NIST and CSSPAB Workshop, Washington, DC, June 13-14.

NIST. (2004). *Security considerations in the information SDLC*. (NIST Special Publication SP 800-64 Rev. 1). Retrieved March 2, 2012, from http://www.iwar.org.uk/comsec/resources/security-life-cycle/index.htm

Nonaka, I., & Takeuchi, H. (1995). *The knowledge creating company: how Japanese companies create the dynamics of innovation* (p. 284). New York, NY: Oxford University Press.

Nonaka, I., & von Krogh, G. (2009). Perspective-tacit knowledge and knowledge conversion: Controversy and advancement in organizational knowledge creation theory. *Organization Science, 20*(3), 635–652. doi:10.1287/orsc.1080.0412

Nordheim, S., & Paivarinta, T. (2006). Implementing enterprise content management: From evolution through strategy to contradictions out-of-the-box. *European Journal of Information Systems, 15*(6), 648–662. doi:10.1057/palgrave.ejis.3000647

Noy, N. F., & McGuinness, D. L. (2001). *Ontology development 101: A guide to creating your first ontology*. Stanford Knowledge Systems Laboratory Technical Report KSL-01-05 and Stanford Medical Informatics Technical Report SMI-2001-0880.

O'Brien, J. (1999). *Management information systems – Managing information technology in the internetworked enterprise*. Boston, MA: Irwin McGraw-Hill.

Okada, M., Yamada, A., Tarumi, H., Yoshida, M., & Moriya, K. (2003). DigitalEE II: RV-augmented interface design for networked collaborative environmental learning. In *Proceedings of the International Conference on Computer Support for Collaborative Learning* (pp. 265-274). Illinois, Chicago.

O'Leary-Kelly, A. M., Martocchio, J. J., & Frink, D. D. (1994). A review of the influence of group goals on group performance. *Academy of Management Journal, 37*(5), 1285–1301. doi:10.2307/256673

O'Reilly, C. A. III, Chatman, J., & Caldwell, D. F. (1991). People and organizational culture: A profile comparison approach to assessing person-organization fit. *Academy of Management Journal, 34*(3), 487–516. doi:10.2307/256404

O'Brien, J. A. (2003). *Introduction to information systems: Essentials for the e-business enterprise*. Boston, MA: McGraw-Hill.

O'Callaghan, R., & Smits, M. A. (2005). Strategy development process for enterprise content management. *Proceedings of the 13th European Conference on Information Systems*, Regensburg, Germany, (pp. 1271-1282).

Oliveira, M., Mortensen, J., Jordan, J., Steed, A., & Slater, M. (2003). Considerations in the design of virtual environment systems: A case study. *Proceedings 2nd International Conference on Application and Development of Computer Games*, Hong Kong, January 2003. Retrieved 15 January, 2010, from http://www.cs.ucl.ac.uk/research/w/Dive

O'Loughlin, M. (1992). Rethinking science education: Beyond Piagetian constructivism toward a socio-cultural model of teaching and learning. *Journal of Research in Science Teaching, 29*, 791–820. doi:10.1002/tea.3660290805

OMG. (2012). *The Object Management Group*. Needham, MA: Author. Retrieved March 5, 2012, from http://www.omg.org/

Ostroff, C., & Aumann, K. A. (2004). Person-environment fit. In Spielberger, C. (Ed.), *Encyclopedia of applied psychology* (*Vol. 3*, pp. 19–28). doi:10.1016/B0-12-657410-3/00746-7

Ott, D. (1999). *Collaboration dans un environnement virtuel 3D: Influence de la distance à l'objet référencé et du "view awareness" sur la résolution d'une tâche de "grounding". Travail de mémoire pour l'obtention du Diplôme "Sciences et Technologie de l'Apprentissage et de la Formation"*. Université de Genève Faculté de Psychologie et des Sciences de l'Education.

OWASP - The Open Web Application Security Project. (2009). Retrieved March 18, 2012, from https://www.owasp.org/index.php/Category:OWASP_Project

OWASP Foundation. (2006). *OWASP - CLASP* (1.2 ed.). OWASP Foundation. Retrieved from http://www.owasp.org/index.php/Category:OWASP_CLASP_Project

Palmer, S. R., & Felsing, J. M. (2002). *A practical guide to feature-driven development*. Prentice Hall International.

Papert, S., & Resnick, M. (1995). *Technological fluency and the representation of knowledge. Proposal to the National Science Foundation*. MIT Media Laboratory.

Parikh, T. (2007). *Rural microfinance service delivery: Gaps, inefficiencies and emerging solutions* (2007). Vaccaro, A., & Madsen, P. (2009). Corporate dynamic transparency: The new ICT-driven ethics? *Ethics and Information Technology*, *11*, 113–122.

Parkin, S., van Moorsel, A., Inglesant, P., & Sasse, M. A. (2010). A stealth approach to usable security: Helping IT security managers to identify workable security solutions. In *Proceedings of the 2010 Workshop on New Security Paradigms* (NSPW '10), (pp. 33-50). New York, NY: ACM. DOI=10.1145/1900546.1900553

Parnas, D., & Clements, P. C. (1986). A rational design process: How and why to fake it. *IEEE Transactions on Software Engineering, 12*(2), 251-256. ISSN: 098-5589

Parsaye, K., & Chignell, M. (1988). *Expert systems for experts* (p. 365). Hoboken, NJ: Wiley.

Paulhus, D. L., & Reid, D. B. (1991). Enhancement and denial in socially desirable responding. *Journal of Personality and Social Psychology*, *60*(2), 307–317. doi:10.1037/0022-3514.60.2.307

Paulk, M. (2001). Extreme programming from a CMM perspective. *IEEE Software*, (November-December): 19–26. doi:10.1109/52.965798

Peachey, A., & Herman, C. (2011). Presence for professional development: Students in the virtual world. *Learning Technology*, *13*(4), 11–14.

Peeters, M. A. G. (2006). *Design teams and personality: Effects of team composition on processes and effectiveness*. Dissertation, Technische Universiteit Eindhoven.

Pellas, N. (2010). *Using CVEs (collaborative virtual environments) in K-12 education*. Virtual Worlds - Best Practices in Education. 1st International Conference in Second Life.

Pellas, N. (2011). *Distance learning in the virtual world of Second Life*. Athens, Greece: Free Publishing. (In Greek)

Pellas, N. (2012). Towards a beneficial formalization of cyber entities' interactions during the e-learning process in the virtual world of "Second Life". In Renna, P. (Ed.), *Production and manufacturing system management: Co-ordination approaches and multi-site planning*. Hershey, PA: IGI Global.

Peña, J., McGlone, M., Jarmon, L., & Sanchez, J. (2009, November). *The influence of visual stereotypes and rules on language use in virtual environments*. Paper to be presented at the annual meeting of the National Communication Association.

Pereira, M., Harris, A., Duncan Davidson, R., & Niven, J. (2000). *Building a virtual learning space for C&IT staff development*. Centre for Open and Distance Learning. The Robert Gordon University. Paper presented at the European Conference on Educational Research, Edinburgh. Retrieved 15 January, 2010, from http://www.leeds.ac.uk/educol/documents/00001651.html

Pfleeger, C. P., & Pfleeger, S. L. (2003). *Security in computing* (3rd ed.). Prentice Hall.

PhD Thesis. (2007). *Accessible and Usable Internet System*. Kings College, University of London.

Piaget, J. (1970). *Structuralism*. New York, NY: Basic Books.

Piaget, J. (1971). *Genetic epistemology*. New York, NY: Harper & Row.

Piaget, J. (1985). *The equilibration of cognitive structures: The central problem of intellectual development*. Chicago, IL: University of Chicago Press.

Poggi, A., Lembo, D., Calvanese, D., Giacomo, G. D., Lenzerini, M., & Rosati, R. (2008). Linking data to ontologies. *Journal on Data Semantics*, 133–173.

Poole, M. (2008). Blue skies: Education in Second Life. *Christian Perspectives in Education, 1*(2). Retrieved 15 January, 2010, from http://digitalcommons.liberty.edu/cpe/vol1/iss2/4

Potter, B., & McGraw, G. (2004). Software security testing. *IEEE Security & Privacy, 2*(5), 81–85. doi:10.1109/MSP.2004.84

Potter, N., & Sakry, M. (2011). *Making process improvement work: A concise action guide for software managers and practitioners*. Report by the process. *Group*.

Prahalad, C. K., & Hamel, G. (1990). The core competence of the corporation. *Harvard Business Review, 68*, 79–91.

Prasolova-Førland, E., Sourin, A., & Sourina, O. (2006). Cyber campuses: Design issues and future directions. *The Visual Computer, 22*(12), 1015–1028. doi:10.1007/s00371-006-0042-2

Pravir, C. (2009). *Software assurance maturity model: A guide to building security into software development* (1.0 ed.). OpenSAMM Project. Retrieved from http://www.opensamm.org/

Pressman, R. S. (1996). *A manager's guide to software engineering*. New York, NY: McGraw-Hill.

Quatre Group LLC. (2009). *5pm* [Software]. Retrieved from https://demo.5pmweb.com/login.php

Rajko, S., & Aluru, S. (2004). Space and time optimal parallel sequence alignments. *IEEE Transactions on Parallel and Distributed Systems, 15*(12), 6. doi:10.1109/TPDS.2004.86

Rappa, N., Yip, D., & Baey, S. (2009). The role of teacher, student & ICT in enhancing student engagement in multi-user environments. *British Journal of Educational Technology, 40*(1), 61–69. doi:10.1111/j.1467-8535.2007.00798.x

Rashid, N. A. A., Abdullah, R., Talib, A. Z. H., & Ali, Z. (2006). Fast dynamic programming based sequence alignment algorithm. *The 2nd International Conference on Distributed Frameworks for Multimedia Applications*, (pp. 1–7).

Rauscher, K. F., Krock, R. E., & Runyon, J. P. (2006). Eight ingredients of communications infrastructure: A systematic and comprehensive framework for enhancing network reliability and security. *Bell Labs Technical Journal, 11*(3), 73–81. doi:10.1002/bltj.20179

Raymond, E. S. (1998). The cathedral and the bazaar. *First Monday, 3*(3).

Read, S., Miller, L., Appleby, P., Nwosu, M., Reynaldo, S., Lauren, A., & Putcha, A. (2006). Socially optimized learning in a virtual environment: Reducing risky sexual behavior among men who have sex with men. *Journal of Human Communication Research, 32*(1), 1–34. doi:10.1111/j.1468-2958.2006.00001.x

Redfern, S., & Naughton, N. (2002). Collaborative virtual environments to support communication and community in internet-based distance education. *Journal of Information Technology Education, 1*(3), 201–211.

Reed, J. (2011). *Cloud computing for law firms*. Advologix.com.

Reeve, L., & Han, H. (2005). *Survey of semantic annotation platforms*. ACM SAC 2005, Santa Fe, New Mexico.

Richardson, R. (2003). *CSI/FBI computer crime and security survey. Technical Report*. CSI.

Ritter-Guth, B., & Nicosia, L. Pasteur, E. (2008). Literature alive! *EDUCAUSE Review, 43*(5). Retrieved 3 December, 2010, from http://www.educause.edu/educause+review/educausereviewmagazinevolume43/literaturealive/163184

Robbins, S. (2007). A futurist's view of Second Life education: A developing taxonomy of dynamic spaces *Second Life Education Workshop 2007: Part of the Second Life Community Conversation* (pp. 27-33). Chicago, IL: Hilton.

Rockley, A. (2006). *Content management 2006: Market directions and trends*. The Rockley Bulletin.

Rohm, H., & Malinoski, M. (2012). *Strategy-based balanced scorecards for technology companies*. Retrieved from www.balancescorecard.org

Romiszowski, A. (1974). *Selection and use of instructional media*. London, UK: Kogan Page.

Romiszowski, A. J. (1990). The hypertext/hypermedia solution—But what is exactly the problem? In Jonassen, D. H., & Mandl, H. (Eds.), *Designing hypermedia for learning* (pp. 321–354). Heidelberg, Germany: Springer. doi:10.1007/978-3-642-75945-1_19

Romme, A. G., & Endenburg, G. (2006). Construction principles and design rules in the case of circular design. *Organization Science*, *17*(2), 287–297. doi:10.1287/orsc.1050.0169

Rosemann, M., Vessey, I., Weber, R., & Wyssusek, B. (2004). On the applicability of the Bunge–Wand–Weber ontology to enterprise systems requirements. *Proceedings of the 15th Australasian Conference on Information Systems*.

Rosse, J. G., Miller, J. L., & Stecher, M. D. (1994). A field study of job applicants' reactions to personality and cognitive ability testing. *The Journal of Applied Psychology*, *79*(6), 987–992. doi:10.1037/0021-9010.79.6.987

Rothwell, W., & Katanas, C. (1998). *Mastering the instructional design process: A systemic approach*. San Francisco, CA: Jossey Bass Publishers.

Rotibi, B., & Murphy, I. (2012). *Creative shorts: Twelve lifecycle management principles for world class cloud development*. Creative Intellect Consulting.

Rotmans, J., & Rothman, D. (Eds.). (2003). *Scaling issues in integrated assessment*. Lisse, The Netherlands: Swets & Zeitlinger.

Rousseeuw, P. J. (1987). Silhouettes: A graphical aid to the interpretation and validation of cluster analysis. *Computational & Applied Mathematics*, *20*, 53–65. doi:10.1016/0377-0427(87)90125-7

Royce, W. (1970). Managing the development of large software systems. *Proceedings of IEEE Wescon* (pp. 1–9).

RTI. (2002). *Planning Report 02-3 The economic impacts of inadequate infrastructure for software testing*. NIST. Retrieved from http://www.nist.gov/director/prog-ofc/report02-3.pdf

Ruël, H., Bondarouk, T., & Looise, J. K. (2004). *E-HRM: innovation or irritation? An exploration of web-based human resource management in large companies*. Utrecht, The Netherlands: Lemma Publishers.

Rufer-Bach, K. (2009). *The Second Life grid*. Canada: Wiley Publishing, Inc.

Rumbaughj, J., Jacobson, I., & Booch, G. (1999). *The unified modeling languages reference manuals*. New York, NY: Addison-Wesley.

Rune, J., Jensen, M., Bryant, R. E., & Veloso, M. M. (2002). SetA*: an Efficient BDD-based heuristic search algorithm. In *Proceedings of AAAI-2002*, Edmonton, Canada.

Ryan, A. M., & Ployheart, R. E. (2000). Applicants' perceptions of selection procedures and decisions: A critical review and agenda for the future. *Journal of Management*, *26*, 565–606. doi:10.1177/014920630002600308

Ryan, A. M., Sacco, J. M., McFarland, L. A., & Kriska, S. D. (2000). Applicant self-selection: Correlates of withdrawal from a multiple hurdle process. *The Journal of Applied Psychology*, *85*, 163–179. doi:10.1037/0021-9010.85.2.163

Ryan, A. M., & Tippins, N. T. (2004). Attracting and selecting: What psychological research tells us. *Human Resource Management*, *43*(4), 305–318. doi:10.1002/hrm.20026

Ryan, R. M., & Deci, E. L. (2000). Self-determination theory and the facilitation of intrinsic motivation, social development and well-being. *The American Psychologist*, *55*(1), 68–78. doi:10.1037/0003-066X.55.1.68

Sackett, P. R., & Lievens, F. (2008). Personnel selection. *Annual Review of Psychology*, 419–450. doi:10.1146/annurev.psych.59.103006.093716

Sadana, V. (n.d.). *A survey based software quality model*. Department of Computer Science. *University of Missouri-Rolla*.

SAFECode. (2008). *Fundamental practices for secure software development*. SAFECode. Retrieved from http://www.safecode.org/publications.php

SAFECode. (2008). *Software assurance: An overview of current industry best practices*. SAFECode. Retrieved from http://www.safecode.org/publications.php

SAFECode. (2009). *Security engineering training*. SAFECode. Retrieved from http://www.safecode.org/publications.php

Sajadi, S., & Khan, T. (2011). An evaluation of constructivist approaches to eLearning for learners with ADHD: Development of a constructivist pedagogy for special needs. *European, Mediterranean & Middle Eastern Conference on Information Systems* (pp. 656-671). Athens, Greece.

Salomon, G. (1995). No distribution without individual's cognition: A dynamic interactional view. In *Distributed cognitions: Psychological and educational considerations* (pp. 111–137). New York, NY: Cambridge University Press.

Saltzer, J., & Schroeder, M. (1975). The protection of information in computer systems. *Proceedings of the IEEE*, *63*(9), 1278–1308. doi:10.1109/PROC.1975.9939

Samet, H. (2006). *Foundations of multidimensional and metric data structures*. Morgan Kaufmann Publishers.

Sanchez, J. (2007). A socio-technical analysis of second life in an undergraduate English course. In C. Montgomerie & J. Seale (Eds.), *Proceedings of World Conference on Educational Multimedia, Hypermedia and Telecommunications 2007* (pp. 4254-4258). Chesapeake, VA: AACE

Sanchez, R. (1997). Managing articulated knowledge in competence-based competition. In *Strategic learning and knowledge management* (pp. 163–187). John Wiley and Sons.

Sanchez, R. (2001). Managing knowledge into competences: The five learning cycles of the competent organization. In *Knowledge management and organizational competence* (pp. 3–37). Oxford University Press.

Sanchez, R. (2004). Creating modular platforms for strategic flexibility. *Design Management Review*, *15*, 58–67. doi:10.1111/j.1948-7169.2004.tb00151.x

Sanchez, R., Heene, A., & Thomas, H. (Eds.). (1996). *Dynamics of competence-based competition: Theory and practice in the new strategic management*. Elsevier Pergamon. Sebastiani, F. (20020. Machine learning in automated text categorization. *ACM Computing Surveys*, *34*, 1–47.

Sandhu, R. J., & Samarati, P. (1994). Access control: Principles and practice. *IEEE Communications*, 32(9).

Sandhu, R. S. (1992). The typed access matrix model. In *Proceedings of the 1992 IEEE Computer Society Symposium on Research in Security and Privacy*, Oakland, CA, USA, (pp. 4-6).

Sandhu, R. S. (1992). Expressive power of the schematic protection model. *Journal of Computer Security*, *1*(1), 59–98.

Sandhu, R. S., & Park, J. (2003). *Usage control: A vision for next generation access control*. MMM-ACNS. doi:10.1007/978-3-540-45215-7_2

SANS Institute. (2007). *Information security policy - A development guide for large and small companies*. SANS Institute, InfoSec Reading Room.

Saraçoğlu, R. (2008). A new approach on search for similar documents with multiple categories using fuzzy clustering. *Expert Systems with Applications*, *34*(4), 2545–2554. doi:10.1016/j.eswa.2007.04.003

Savenkov, R. (2008). *How to become a software tester* (p. 386). Roman Savenkov Consulting.

Schellnhuber, H. J., Crutzen, P. J., Clark, W. C., Claussen, M., & Held, H. (Eds.), *Earth system analysis for sustainability: Dahlem Workshop report 91*. Cambridge, MA: MIT Press.

Schmeil, A., & Eppler, M. (2008). Knowledge sharing & collaborative learning in Second Life: A classification of Virtual 3D group interaction scripts. *Journal of Universal Campus Sciences, 14*(3), 665–677.

Schmidt, F. L., & Hunter, J. E. (1998). The validity and utility of selection methods in personnel psychology: Practical and theoretical implications of 85 years of research findings. *Psychological Bulletin, 124*(2), 262–274. doi:10.1037/0033-2909.124.2.262

Schmidt, F. L., Viswesvaran, C., & Ones, D. S. (2000). Reliability is not validity and validity is not reliability. *Personnel Psychology, 53*, 901–912. doi:10.1111/j.1744-6570.2000. tb02422.x

Schmitt, N., & Oswald, F. L. (2006). The impact of corrections for faking on the validity of noncognitive measures in selection settings. *The Journal of Applied Psychology, 91*, 613–621. doi:10.1037/0021-9010.91.3.613

Schneider, B., Kristof-Brown, A., Goldstein, H. W., & Smith, D. B. (1997). What is this thing called fit? In Anderson, N., & Herriot, P. (Eds.), *International handbook of selection and assessment* (pp. 393–412). Chichester, UK: Wiley.

Schoeffler, S., Buzzell, R. D., & Heany, D. F. (1974). Review: Impact of strategic planning on profit performance. *Harvard Business Review*, (March-April): 137–145.

Schuh, P. (2005). *Integrating agile development in the real world*. Hingham, MA: Charles River Media.

Schutte, G. (1997). *Virtual teaching in higher education: The new intellectual superhighway or just another traffic jam?* Retrieved 15 January, 2010, from http://www.csun. edu/sociology/virexp.html

Schwaber, K., & Beedle, M. (2002). *Agile software development with Scrum*. Upper Saddle River, NJ: Prentice-Hall.

Sebok, A., & Nystad, E. (2004). Design and evaluation of virtual reality systems: A process to ensure usability. *Proceedings of 'Virtual Reality Design and Evaluation Workshop 2004*. University of Nottingham. Retrieved 15 January, 2010, from http://www.view.iao.fraunhofer.de/ Proceedings/papers/sebok.PDF

Security Classification. PUBLIC. (2011). *Information security policy*, Version 2.1. Ministry of Labour, Citizens' Services and Open Government, British Columbia, Canada. Retrieved from http://www.cio.gov.bc.ca/local/ cio/informationsecurity/policy/isp.pdf

Security, A. (2009). *Web vulnerability scanners comparison*. Retrieved from http://anantasec.blogspot. com/2009/01/web-vulnerability-scanners-comparison. html

Securosis. (2009). *Building a web application security program*. Securosis. Retrieved from http://securosis.com/ research/publication/building-a-web-application-security-program/

Sharan, S. (1980). Cooperative learning in small groups: Recent methods and effects on achievement, attitudes and ethnic relations. *Review of Educational Research, 50*(2), 241–271.

Sharma, S., Sugumaram, V., & Rajagopalan, B. (2002). A framework for creating hybrid-open source software communities. *Information Systems Journal, 12*(1), 7. doi:10.1046/j.1365-2575.2002.00116.x

Sharp, J., & Ryan, S. (2010). A theoretical framework of component-based software development phases. *SGMIS Database, 41*(1), 56–75. doi:10.1145/1719051.1719055

Shaw, T. J. (Ed.). (2011). *Information security and privacy: A practical guide for global executives, lawyers and technologists*. American Bar Association.

Sheehy, K., Ferguson, R., & Clough, G. (2008). Learning in the panopticon: Ethical and social issues in building a virtual educational environment. *International Journal of Social Science, Special Edition: Virtual Reality in Distance Education, 2*(2), 89-97.

Shelly, G. B., Cashman, T. J., & Vermaat, M. E. (2008). *Discovering computers*. Boston, MA: Thomson Course Technology. ISBN 10: 1 -4239-1205-5

Shepherdson, J. W., Lee, H., & Mihailescu, P. (2007). mPower -- A component-based development framework for multi-agent systems to support business processes. *BT Technology Journal, 25*(3-4), 260–271. doi:10.1007/ s10550-007-0083-8

Shrivastava, P. (1987). Rigor and practical usefulness of research in strategic management. *Strategic Management Journal, 8*, 77–92. doi:10.1002/smj.4250080107

Siegemund, K., Thomas, E. J., Zhao, Y., Pan, J., & Assmann, U. (2011). *Towards ontology-driven requirements engineering*. In The 7th International Workshop on Semantic Web Enabled Software Engineering Co-located with ISWC2011Bonn, Germany.

Sierpinska, A. (1993). The development of concepts according to Vygotsky. *Focus on Learning Problems in Mathematics, 15*(2 & 3), 87–107.

Silver, E. A., Pike, D. F., & Peterson, R. (1998). *Inventory management and production planning schedules* (3rd ed.). Hoboken, NJ: John Wiley and Sons Inc.

Silver, M. S., Markus, M. L., & Beath, C. M. (1995). The information technology interaction model: A foundation for the MBA core course. *Management Information Systems Quarterly, 19*(3), 361–390. doi:10.2307/249600

Simpson, S. (2008). *Fundamental practices for secure software development: A guide to the most effective secure development practices in use today*. Retrieved March 18, 2012, from http://www.safecode.org

Sindhgatta, R. (2006). Using an information retrieval system to retrieve source code samples. In *Proceedings of the 28th International Conference on Software Engineering (ICSE'06)*, (pp. 905-908).

Sindre, G., & Opdahl, A. L. (2001). Templates for misuse case description. In *Proceedings of the 7th International Workshop on Requirements Engineering, Foundation for Software Quality (REFSQ'2001)*, Interlaken, Switzerland, June 4-5.

Sivan, Y. (2009). Overview: State of virtual worlds standards in 2009. *Technology, Economy, and Standards, 2*(3). Retrieved 15 January, 2010, from https://journals.tdl.org/jvwr/article/view/671/539

Slavin, R. E. (1983). *Cooperative learning*. New York, NY: Longman.

Smith, M. A., Farnham, S. D., & Drucker, S. M. (2000). The social life of small graphical chat spaces. *Proceedings of the Conference on Human Factors in Computing Systems* (CHI'00) (pp. 462-469). Hague, The Netherlands: ACM Press.

Smith, H. A., & McKeen, J. D. (2003). Developments in practice VIII: Enterprise content management. *Communications of the Association for Information Systems, 11*(33), 647–659.

Software Engineering Research Laboratory. (2008). Institute of Electrical and Electronics Engineers, Inc. Retrieved from www.swebok.org

Soloway, E. (1990). Quick, where do the computers go? *Communications of the ACM, 34*(2), 29–33. doi:10.1145/102792.102797

Sommerville, I. (2010). *Software engineering* (9th ed.). Addison Wesley.

Sorensen, E. (2006). Learning to learn: A meta-learning perspective on pedagogical design of e-learning. In Center of Research on Lifelong Learning (Eds.). *Learning to learn network meeting report* (pp.48-53). Isra, Italy: European Commission.

Spagnolo, A. M. (2000). *Incrementare la qualità in ambito Basi di Dati*. Tesi di Laurea, Università degli studi di Pisa, Corso di laurea in Scienze dell'Informazione.

Spector, P. E. (2008). *Industrial and organizational psychology* (5th ed.). Hoboken, NJ: John Wiley and Sons Inc.

Spence, J. (2008). Demographics of virtual worlds. *Virtual Worlds Research: Consumer Behavior in Virtual Worlds, 1*(2). Retrieved 15 January, 2010, from http://journals.tdl.org/jvwr/article/download/360/272

Sprague, R. H., & Carlson, E. D. (1982). *Building effective decision support systems*. Englewood Cliffs, NJ: Prentice-Hall.

Sprott, D. (2000). Componentizing the enterprise application packages. *Communications of the ACM, 43*(3), 63–69. doi:10.1145/332051.332074

Steed, A., & Tromp, J. (1998). Experiences with the evaluation of CVE applications. [University of Manchester, UK.]. *Proceedings of Collaborative Virtual Environments CVE, 98*, 123–130.

Steinkuehler, A., & Williams, D. (2006). Where everybody knows your (screen) name: Online games as "third places.". *Journal of Computer-Mediated Communication, 11*, 885–909. doi:10.1111/j.1083-6101.2006.00300.x

Stewart, G. L., Darnold, T. C., Zimmerman, R. D., Parks, L., & Dustin, S. L. (2010). Exploring how response distortion of personality measures affects individuals. *Personality and Individual Differences, 49*, 622–628. doi:10.1016/j.paid.2010.05.035

Stolovitch, D., & La Rocque, G. (1983). *Introduction a la technique de l' instruction.* Prefontaine Editions: St. Jean sur Richelieu.

Stone, D. L., Stone-Romero, E. F., & Lukaszweski, K. (2003). The functional and dysfunctional consequences of using technology to achieve human resource system goals. In Stone, D. L. (Ed.), *Research in human performance and cognitive engineering technology* (*Vol. 3*, pp. 37–68). Greenwich, CT: JAI.

Stone-Romero, E. F. (2005). The effects of HR system characteristics and culture on system acceptance and effectiveness. In Gueutal, H. G., & Stone, D. L. (Eds.), *The brave new world of eHR* (pp. 226–254). San Francisco, CA: Jossey-Bass.

Strauss, A. M., & Corbin, J. (1990). *Basics of qualitative research.* Newbury Park, CA: Sage.

Strijbos, J. W., Martens, R. L., & Jochems, W. (2004). Designing for interaction: Six steps to designing computer-supported group-based learning. *Computers & Education, 42*, 403–424.

Strohmeier, S. (2007). Research in e-HRM: Review and implications. *Human Resource Management Review, 17*, 19–37. doi:10.1016/j.hrmr.2006.11.002

Sugumaran, V., & Storey, V. C. (2003). A semantic-based approach to component retrieval. *The Data Base for Advances in Information Systems, 34*(3), 8–24. doi:10.1145/937742.937745

Sukumar, K., Vecchiola, C., & Buyya, R. (2004). The structure of the new IT frontier: Aneka platform for elastic cloud computing applications. *Computing, 342*(1), 261–273. Retrieved from www.buyya.com/papers/Aneka-MagazineArticle3.pdf

Sun Microsystems, Inc. (2001). *Enterprise JavaBeans specification*, Version 2.0. Retrieved March 18, 2012, from http://java.sun.com/ejb/docs.html

Sun Microsystems, Inc. (2001). *How to develop a network security policy: An overview of internetworking site security.* Retrieved March 18, 2012, from http://www.sun.com/software/whitepapers/wp-security-devsecpolicy

Sylva, H., & Mol, S. T. (2009). E-recruitment: a study into applicant perceptions of an online application system. *International Journal of Selection and Assessment, 17*(3), 311–323. doi:10.1111/j.1468-2389.2009.00473.x

Szulanski, G. (1996). Exploring internal stickiness: Impediments to the transfer of best practices within the firm. *Strategic Management Journal, 17*, 27–43.

Talib, M. A., Kai, Y. Z., & Ilyas, Q. M. (2006). A framework towards web services composition modeling & execution. *International Journal of Web and Grid Services, 2*(1), 25–49. doi:10.1504/IJWGS.2006.008878

Tan, S. (2008). An empirical study of sentiment analysis for Chinese documents. *Expert Systems with Applications, 34*(4), 2622–2629. doi:10.1016/j.eswa.2007.05.028

Taylor, D., & McGraw, G. (2005). Adopting a software security improvement program. *IEEE Security & Privacy, 3*(3), 88–91. doi:10.1109/MSP.2005.60

Tesluk, P., Mathieu, J. E., Zaccaro, S. J., & Marks, M. (1997). Task and aggregation issues in the analysis and assessment of team performance. In Brannick, M. T., Salas, E., & Prince, C. (Eds.), *Team performance assessment and measurement* (pp. 197–224). Mahwah, NJ: Lawrence Erlbaum.

Thomas, R., & Sandhu, R. S. (2004). Towards a multi-dimensional characterization of dissemination control. *Proceedings of the IEEE International Conference on Policies for Distributed Networks and Systems.*

Thompson, H. H. (2003). Why security testing is hard. *IEEE Security and Privacy, 1*(4), 83–86. doi:10.1109/MSECP.2003.1219078

Thuy, P. T. T., Lee, Y. K., & Lee, S. (2012). (in press). S-trans: Semantic transformation of XML healthcare data into OWL ontology. [Corrected Proof]. *Knowledge-Based Systems.* doi:10.1016/j.knosys.2012.04.009

Tiến, L. N. (2010). *Information systems analyses and design.* Retrieved through http://tienhuong.files.wordpress.com/2010/03/slides.ppt

Tippins, N. T., Beaty, J., Drasgow, F., Gibson, W. M., Pearlman, K., Segall, D. O., & Shepherd, W. (2006). Unproctored internet testing in employment settings. *Personnel Psychology*, *59*, 189–225. doi:10.1111/j.1744-6570.2006.00909.x

Tomas, D. (1995). Feedback and cybernetics: Reimagining the body in the age of cyborg. In M. Featherstone & R. Burrows (Eds.), *Cyberspace/cyberbodies/cyberpunk: Cultures of technological embodiment* (pp. 21-43). London, UK: Sage.

Topbraid. (2012). Retrieved from http://www.topquadrant.com/products/TB_Composer.html

Tran, V., & Liu, D. (1997). A procurement-centric model for engineering component-based software systems. *Proceedings of the 5th International Symposium on Assessment of Software Tools and Technologies*, (pp. 70-80).

Traore, I. (2009). *Course notes: ELEC 567 advanced network security and forensics*. Graduate course offered at the Department of Electrical and Computer Engineering, University of Victoria, B.C. Canada, Spring.

Traore, I., & Aredo, D. B. (2004). Enhancing structured review using model-based verification. *IEEE Transactions on Software Engineering*, *30*(11). doi:10.1109/TSE.2004.86

Truchon, M. (2008). Borda and the maximum likelihood approach to vote aggregation. *Mathematical Social Sciences*, *55*, 96–102. doi:10.1016/j.mathsocsci.2007.08.001

Truxillo, D. M., Bauer, T. N., Campion, M. A., & Paronto, M. E. (2002). Selection fairness information and applicant reactions: A longitudinal field study. *The Journal of Applied Psychology*, *87*, 1020–1031. doi:10.1037/0021-9010.87.6.1020

Tsiporkova, E., & Boeva, V. (2006). Multi-step ranking of alternatives in a multi-criteria and multi-expert decision making environment. *Information Sciences*, *176*, 2673–2697. doi:10.1016/j.ins.2005.11.010

Tsoukas, H. (1996). The firm as a distributed knowledge system: A constructionist approach. *Strategic Management Journal, 17*(winter special issue), 11-25.

Tyndale, P. (2002). A taxonomy of knowledge management software tools: Origins and applications. *Evaluation and Program Planning*, *25*(2), 183–190. doi:10.1016/S0149-7189(02)00012-5

Tyrväinen, P., Päivärinta, T., Salminen, A., & Iivari, J. (2006). Characterizing the evolving research on enterprise content management. *European Journal of Information Systems*, *15*(6), 627–634. doi:10.1057/palgrave.ejis.3000648

US-CERT - United States Computer Emergency Readiness Team. (2012). Retrieved March 18, 2012, from http://www.kb.cert.org/vuls

Vacca, J. R. (2009). *Computer and information security handbook*. Elsevier.

Vaccaro, A., & Madsen, P. (2009). Transparency in business and society: introduction to the special issue. *Ethics and Information Technology*, *11*, 101–103. doi:10.1007/s10676-009-9197-7

Vallet, D., Fernández, M., & Castells, P. (2005). An ontology-based information retrieval model. In *Proceedings of the 2nd Annual European Semantic Web Conference (ESWC'05)*, (pp. 455-470).

Van Aken, J. E. (2005). Management research as a design science. *British Journal of Management*, *16*, 19–36. doi:10.1111/j.1467-8551.2005.00437.x

Van Aken, J. E., Berends, J. J., & van der Bij, J. D. (2007). *Problem solving in organizations: a methodological handbook for business students*. Cambridge, UK: Cambridge University Press. doi:10.1017/CBO9780511618413

Van den Hooff, B., & Huysman, M. (2009). Managing knowledge sharing: Emergent and engineering approaches. *Information & Management*, *46*, 1–8. doi:10.1016/j.im.2008.09.002

Van Eerde, W., & Thierry, H. (1996). Vroom's expectancy models and work-related criteria: A meta-analysis. *The Journal of Applied Psychology*, *81*(5), 575–586. doi:10.1037/0021-9010.81.5.575

Van Iddekinge, C. H., Raymark, P. H., & Roth, P. L. (2005). Assessing personality with a structured employment interview: Construct-related validity and susceptibility to response inflation. *The Journal of Applied Psychology*, *90*, 536–552. doi:10.1037/0021-9010.90.3.536

Van Iddekinge, C. H., Raymark, P. H., Roth, P. L., & Payne, H. S. (2006). Comparing the psychometric characteristics of rating of face-to-face and videotaped structured interviews. *International Journal of Selection and Assessment, 14*(4), 347–359. doi:10.1111/j.1468-2389.2006.00356.x

Van Manen, M. (1990). *Researching lived experience: Human science for an action sensitive pedagogy.* Ontario, Canada: Althouse press.

Van Strien, P. J. (1997). Towards a methodology of psychological practice. *Theory & Psychology, 7*(5), 683–700. doi:10.1177/0959354397075006

Vasileiou, V., & Paraskeva, F. (2010). Teaching role-playing instruction in Second Life: An exploratory study. *Journal of Information Technology & Organizations, 5,* 25–50.

Vaughn, R. B. (2001). *Are measures and metrics for trusted information systems possible?* Workshop on Information-Security-System Rating and Ranking, Williamsburg, Virginia, May 21-23.

Verdon, D., & McGraw, G. (2004). Risk analysis in software design. *IEEE Security & Privacy, 2*(4), 79–84. doi:10.1109/MSP.2004.55

Vidgen, R. (1998). Cybernetics & business processes: Using the viable system model to develop entire process architecture. *Knowledge & Process Management: The Journal of Corporate Transformation, 5,* 118–131. doi:10.1002/(SICI)1099-1441(199806)5:2<118::AID-KPM19>3.0.CO;2-3

Viega, J., & McGraw, G. (2001). *Building secure software.* USA: Addison-Wesley.

Vitari, C., Ravarini, A., & Rodhain, F. (2006). An analysis framework for the evaluation of content management systems. *Communications of the Association for Information Systems, 18*(37), 782–803.

Vitharana, P., Jain, H., & Zahedi, F. (2004). Strategy-based design of reusable business components. *IEEE Transactions on Systems, Man and Cybernetics. Part C, Applications and Reviews, 34*(4), 460–474. doi:10.1109/TSMCC.2004.829258

Vitharana, P., Zahedi, F. M., & Jain, H. (2003). Design, retrieval, and assembly in component-based software development. *Communications of the ACM, 46*(11), 97–102. doi:10.1145/948383.948387

Vogel, R. M., & Feldman, D. C. (2009). Integrating the levels of person-environment fit: the roles of vocational fit and group fit. *Journal of Vocational Behavior, 75,* 68–81. doi:10.1016/j.jvb.2009.03.007

Vosinakis, S., Koutsabasis, P., Zaharias, P., & Belk, M. (2010). *Problem-based learning in virtual worlds: A case study in user interface design.* Experiential Learning in Virtual Worlds - Exploring the Complexities, Interdisciplinary Press. Retrieved 12 June, 2011, from http://www.inter-disciplinary.net/wp-content/uploads/2011/02/vosinakisepaper.pdf

Vosniadou, S. (1996). Learning environments for representational growth and cognitive flexibility. In Vosniadou, S., DeCorte, E., Glaser, R., & Mandl, H. (Eds.), *International perspectives on the design of technology supported learning environments* (pp. 13–24). Hillsdale, NJ: Lawrence Erlbaum Associates, Inc.

Vrasidas, C. (2000). Constructivism versus objectivism: Implications for interaction, course design, and evaluation in distance education. *International Journal of Educational Telecommunications, 6*(4), 339–362.

Vrellis, I., Papachristos, N. M., Natsis, A., & Mikropoulos, T. A. (2010). *Measuring presence in a collaborative physics learning activity in Second Life.* 7th Pan-Hellenic Conference with International Participation "ICT in Education", September 23-26, Korinthos, Greece.

Vygotsky, L. (1935/1978). *Mind in society: The development of higher psychological processes.* Cambridge, MA: Harvard University Press.

Vygotsky, L. (1987). *The collected works of L.S. Vygotsky, 1. Problems of general psychology (including Thinking and Speech- Minick N., transl.).* New York: Plenum.

Vygotsky, L. S. (1997). *The collected works of L.S. Vygotsky (Vol. 3).* (Rieber, R. W., & Wollock, J., Trans.). New York, NY: Plenum Press.

Waguespack, L., & Schiano, W. T. (2004). Component-based IS architecture. *Information Systems Management*, *21*(3), 53–60. doi:10.1201/1078/44432.21.3.20040601/82477.8

Walsh, J. P., & Ungson, G. R. (1991). Organizational memory. *Academy of Management Review*, *16*, 57–91.

Wang, S., & Hsu, H. (2009). Using the ADDIE model to design Second Life activities for online learners. *TechTrends*, *53*(6), 76–81. doi:10.1007/s11528-009-0347-x

Wang, S., & Noe, R. A. (2010). Knowledge sharing: A review and directions for future research. *Human Resource Management Review*, *20*, 115–131. doi:10.1016/j.hrmr.2009.10.001

Wayner, P. (2000). *Free for all*. New York, NY: HarperCollins.

Webb, D. (2008). *Why the Cisco i-Prize is so powerful*. ComputerWorld Canada. Retrieved from http://www.itworldcanada.com/a/Daily-News/563ea3a9-deab-4536-8b24-819f8de1c3d4.html

Wei, Y., Wang, R., Hu, Y., & Wang, X. (2012). From web resources to agricultural ontology: A method for semi-automatic construction. *Journal of Integrative Agriculture*, *11*(5), 775–783. doi:10.1016/S2095-3119(12)60067-7

Welk, D. (2006). The trainer's application of Vygotsky's "zone of proximal development" to asynchronous, online training of faculty facilitators. *Online Journal of Distance Learning Administration, 9*(4). Retrieved 15 January, 2010, from http://www.westga.edu/~distance/ojdla/winter94/welk94.htm

Werr, A., & Stjernberg, T. (2003). Exploring management consulting firms as knowledge systems. *Organization Studies*, *24*(6), 881–908. doi:10.1177/0170840603024006004

Wertsch, J., & Stone, A. (1985). The concept of internalization in Vygotsky's account of the genesis of higher mental functions. In Wertsch, J. (Ed.), *Culture, communication, and cognition: Vygotskian perspectives* (pp. 162–179). New York, NY: Cambridge University Press.

Weusijana, B., Svihla, V., Gawel, D., & Bransford, J. (2007). Learning about adaptive experience in multi-user virtual environments. *Second Life Education Workshop 2007 Part of the Second Life Community Convention* (pp. 34-39). Chicago, IL: Hilton.

Weusijana, B., Svihla, V., Gawel, D., & Bransford, J. (2009). MUVE's and experimental learning: Some examples. *Innovate: Journal of Online Education, 5*(5). Retrieved 12 June, 2011, from http://www.edutek.net/Kofi/MUVEs_and_Experiential_Learning-Some_Examples.pdf

Whipple, W. R. (1987). Collaborative learning. *AAHE Bulletin*, *40*(2), 3–7.

WhiteHat Security Inc. (2008). *WhiteHat website security statistic reports* (No. 6th Edition). WhiteHat Security Inc. Retrieved from http://www.whitehatsec.com/home/resource/stats.html

Whitman, M. E., & Mattord, H. J. (2012). *Principles of information security* (4th ed.). Course Technology.

Wiener, N. (1948). *Cybernetics or control and communication in the animal and the machine*. Cambridge, MA: MIT Press.

Wiesmann, A., Curphey, M., van der Stock, A., & Stirbei, R. (2005). *A guide to building secure web applications and web services, V2.0.1*. OWASP Foundation. Retrieved from http://www.owasp.org/index.php/Developer_Guide

Williams, J. (2008). *Establishing a security API for your enterprise (ALPHA version)*. OWASP Foundation.

Winkler, V. J. R. (2011). *Securing the cloud*. Waltham, MA: Elsevier Inc.

Wolf Frameworks. (2011). *Developing applications using platform-as-a-service: A paradigm shift in application development*. Retrieved from www.wolfframeworks.com

Wong, M., & Raulenson, P. (1974). *A guide to systematic instructional design*. NJ: Educational Technology Publications.

Woolley, R., & Fletcher, D. (2007). *Research summary: Enterprise content management*. White paper, Department of Technology Services.

Wright, P., & Dyer, L. (2000). *People in the e-business: New challenges, new solutions*. Working paper 00-II, Center for advanced human resource studies, Cornell University.

Xie, M., Tan, K. C., Goh, K. H., & Huang, X. R. (2000). Optimum prioritisation and resource allocation based on fault tree analysis. *International Journal of Quality & Reliability Management, 17*(2), 189–199. doi:10.1108/02656710010304591

Yackel, E., Rasmussen, C., & King, K. (2000). Social and socio-mathematical norms in advanced undergraduate mathematics course. *The Journal of Mathematical Behavior, 19*, 275–287. doi:10.1016/S0732-3123(00)00051-1

Yang, H. L., & Wu, T. C. T. (2008). Knowledge sharing in an organization. *Technological Forecasting and Social Change, 75*, 1128–1156. doi:10.1016/j.techfore.2007.11.008

Yang, J. T. (2007). Knowledge sharing: Investigating appropriate leadership roles and collaborative culture. *Tourism Management, 28*, 530–543. doi:10.1016/j.tourman.2006.08.006

Yang, J. T. (2008). Individual attitudes and organisational knowledge sharing. *Tourism Management, 29*, 345–353. doi:10.1016/j.tourman.2007.03.001

Yara, P., Ramachandran, R., Balasubramanian, G., Muthuswamy, K., & Chandrasekar, D. (2009). Global software development with cloud platforms: Software engineering approaches for offshore and outsourced development. *Proceedings of SEAFOOD 2009, Lecture Notes in business Information Processing*.

Yuan, J. (2006). Semantic-based dynamic enterprise information integration. In Ma, Z. (Ed.), *Database modeling for industrial data management emerging technologies and applications* (pp. 35–61). Hershey, PA: Idea Group Publishing. doi:10.4018/978-1-59140-684-6.ch006

yWorks (2012). *yEd* (Version 3.9.1) [Software]. Retrieved from http://www.yworks.com/en/products_yed_download.html

Zahedi, M. (2011). *Agile service networks for cloud computing*. Master thesis. Retrieved June 1, 2012, from http://www.idt.mdh.se/utbildning/exjobb/files/TR1191.pdf

Zaid, B., Jamaludin, R., & Hosam, A. (2011). Perceived satisfaction levels and student learning performance towards Second Life virtual environment for learning the Islamic concepts. *Australian Journal of Basic and Applied Sciences, 5*(9), 1860–1864.

Zatyko, K. (2007). *Commentary: Defining digital forensics*. Retrieved March 14, 2012, from http://www.forensicmag.com/node/128

Zhang, X., Park, J., Parisi-Presicce, F., & Sandhu, R. (2004). A logical specification for usage control. *Proceedings of the 9th ACM Symposium on Access Control Modules and Technologies*.

Zhao, Y., Ma, P., Lan, J., Liang, C., & Ji, G. (2008). An improved ant colony algorithm for DNA sequence alignment. *International Symposium on Information Science and Engineering*, Vol. 2, (pp. 683–688).

Zielke, M. A., Roome, T. C., & Krueger, A. B. (2009). A composite adult learning model for virtual world residents with disabilities: A case study of virtual ability Second Life Island. *Journal of Virtual Worlds Research, 2*(1), 4–20.

About the Contributors

Khalid A. Buragga is an Associate Professor of Information Systems department in the college of Computer Sciences and Information Technology at King Faisal University, Hofuf, Saudi Arabia. He received his B.Sc. in Computer Information Systems from King Faisal University. And, he received his M.Sc. in Computer Information Systems from University of Miami, USA, and the PhD in Information Technology from George Mason University, USA. His research interests include software design, software development, software quality, software reliability, E-Commerce and web development, Business Process Re-engineering (BPR), communications, networking and signal processing, and integrating systems.

Noor Zaman acquired his Degree in Engineering in 1998, and Master's in Computer Science at the University of Agriculture Faisalabad Pakistan in 2000. His academic achievements further extended with a PhD in Information Technology at University Technology PETRONAS (UTP), Malaysia. He is currently working as a Faculty member in the College of Computer Science and Information Technology, King Faisal University, in Saudi Arabia. He takes care of versatile operations including teaching, research activities, information technology management and leading ERP projects. He headed the Department of Information Technology (IT), and administered the prometric center in the Institute of Business and Technology (BIZTEK), in Karachi Pakistan. He has worked as a consultant for Network and Server Management remotely in Apex Canada USA base Software house and call center. Dr. Noor Zaman has authored several research papers in internationally recognized index journals and well reputed conferences. He Authored and edited several books, has many publications to his credit. He is an Associate Editor, Regional Editor, and Reviewer for a number of reputed international research journals around the world. He has completed several international research grants and currently involved with different funded projects in different countries. His area of interest include Wireless Sensor Network (WSN), Mobile Computing, Cloud Computing, Network and Communication, Software Engineering, Green technology, Artificial Intelligence, Operating system, Unix, and Linux.

* * *

Muneer Ahmad received his MSc and PhD degrees from COMSATS University Pakistan and University Technology PETRONAS Malaysia. He has vast teaching experience at university level and holds numerous publications in many international journals and conferences. He has served as a reviewer for many famous journals and conferences.

Jaffar Ahmad Alalwan is an Assistant Professor at the Institute of Public Administration in the eastern province of Saudi Arabia. He holds a PhD from Virginia Commonwealth University in Information Systems, an MBA from the University of Scranton in Management Information Systems and Marketing, and a BS in Business Administration from King Abdul Aziz University. Alalwan has published research in the areas of strategic information systems planning, enterprise content management systems, electronic government, and the Semantic Web.

Izzat Mahmoud Alsmadi is an Assistant Professor in the department of Computer Information Systems at Yarmouk University in Jordan. He obtained his PhD degree in Software Engineering from NDSU (USA). His second Master's is in Software Engineering from NDSU (USA) and his first Master's is in CIS from University of Phoenix (USA). He had BSc degree in Telecommunication Engineering from Mutah University in Jordan. He has several published books, journals, and conference articles largely in software engineering and information retrieval fields.

Zeyar Aung received his Bachelor of Computer Science (Honors) degree from University of Computer Studies, Yangon, Myanmar in 1999, and his PhD in Computer Science from the National University of Singapore in 2006. He is currently an Assistant Professor at the Computing and Information Science Program of Masdar Institute of Science and Technology, Abu Dhabi, United Arab Emirates. Prior to that, he worked as a Research Fellow at the Data Mining Department of the Institute for Infocomm Research (I2R), A*STAR, Singapore. Dr. Aung's current research interests include cyber security, smart grids, data mining, information retrieval, and wireless sensor networks. His past research interests were in bioinformatics and chemoinformatics. As of July 2012, he has published 23 research articles in various scientific journals and conferences. He has received a total of 130+ citations for his publications.

Tanya Bondarouk is Associate Professor of Human Resource Management at the University of Twente, the Netherlands. She serves as the European Regional Editor for the *Personnel Review* journal. Since 2002 she has been busy with the emerging research area of Electronic HRM, and has edited a number of special issues in international journals on this topic. Her main publications concern an integration of Human Resource Management and social aspects of Information Technology Implementations and appear in the *International Journal of HRM*, *Personnel Review*, *European Journal of Management*, and *European Journal of Information Systems*. Her research covers both private and public sectors and deals with a variety of areas such as the implementation of e-HRM, management of HR-IT change, HRM contribution to IT projects, roles of line managers in e-HRM, implementation of HR Shared Service Centers. She has conducted research projects with the Dutch Ministry of Interior and Kingdom Relations, Dow Chemical, Ford, IBM, ABN AMRO bank, and Shell. Among her current research projects are Implementation of HR Shared Service Centers at the Dutch Ministry of Defense, a large non-academic hospital, and the Belgian Federal Public Health Service. Since 2006 she is involved in organizing European Academic Workshops on e-HRM, and International Workshops on HRIS.

Partha Chakraborty is the Sr, Director & Head of Global Delivery R&D Practice in Cognizant Life Sciences (www.cognizant.com). He is a BTech from Indian Institute of Technology (IIT), Kharagpur. He has worked with large healthcare providers and multiple large global pharmaceuticals globally and led IT transformation in Clinical & Safety as well as the implementation of critical engagements. He has presented his point of view in FDA Science Congress, CDISC Interchange, International Society of Pharmacovigilance (ISOP) and DIA. He is instrumental in creating the 1st certificate course, in Pharmacovigilance in India, launched by Symogen, UK. He has written a chapter, called "Role of Information Technology on Drug Safety" in a recently published book "Elements of Pharmacovigilance"; "Statistical Methods Applied in Drug Safety" in a recently published book "Handbook of Research on Pharmacoinformatics."

José Fonseca received his PhD in Informatics Engineering from the University of Coimbra in 2011. Since 2005, he has been with the Centre for Informatics and Systems of the University of Coimbra (CISUC) as a researcher. He teaches computer related courses in the Polytechnic Institute of Guarda since 1993. He is the author or co-author of more than a dozen papers in refereed conferences and he has acted as referee for many international conferences in the dependability and security areas. His research on vulnerability and attack injection was granted with the DSN's William Carter Award of 2009, sponsored by the IEEE Technical Committee on Fault-Tolerant Computing and IFIP Working Group on Dependable Computing and Fault Tolerance (WG 10.4).

Fausto Pedro García Márquez got the European Doctorate on Engineering at the School of Industrial Engineers (ETSII) of Ciudad Real, University of Castilla-La Mancha (UCLM, Spain), March 2004. He is Engineering from University of Cartagena in Murcia, Spain, (September 1998) and Technical Engineer from the Polytechnic University School at UCLM (September 1995), and recently, he got the degree in Business Administration and Management at the Faculty of Law and Social Sciences at UCLM (December 2006). He also holds the titles of Supper Technician in Labor Risks Prevention by UCLM (July 2000) and Transport Specialist at the Polytechnic University of Madrid, Spain, (June 2001). As a complement to his education, he has 32 courses with more than 1300 hours.

Syeda Umema Hani is currently about to finish her PhD research work in Software Engineering field with an interest in area of "Software Development Process Improvement" from Graduate School of Engineering Science and IT, Hamdard University. She has seven national and international level publications in her profile. She is a registered member of Pakistan Engineering Council and has been a part of INMIC technical committee. She has previously worked as a Software Engineer and Project Manager in Software Houses. Currently she is working as an Asst. Professor in Sir Syed University of Engineering and Technology and teaching Software Engineering, Relational Database Management Systems, Computer Programming and Problem Solving, and Data structures. Her professional interests also include requirement engineering, project management, strategic management, process improvement frameworks CMMI and COBIT5, and Six Sigma methodology.

Qazi Mudassar Ilyas, having started his career in academia more than a decade ago and serving for the most prestigious universities of Pakistan including University of the Punjab, Lahore and Ghulam Ishaq Institute, Topi, joined King Faisal University as a faculty member in 2010. He earned Bachelor's in Engineering from University of Agriculture, Pakistan with a Gold Medal, Master's in Computer Science from the same university and PhD in Information and Communication Engineering from Huazhong University of Science and Technology, China with Excellent Student Award. His research interests include Semantic Web, knowledge engineering, machine learning, and human computer interaction.

He is approved supervisor for PhD thesis by Higher Education Commission of Pakistan and member of scientific bodies including IEEE, Internet Society and Pakistan Engineering Council. He is also a member of editorial/reviewer boards of several scientific journals and conferences.

Runa Jesmin, currently a Technical Educator at Global Heart Forum (Imperial College London, Royal Brompton and Harefield Hospital London) UK obtained her A Level (including general and advanced mathematics) from Waltham Forest College London, UK; BSc in Mathematics, Statistics and Computing, with Management Sciences from University of East London, UK and PhD from King's College London (completed 3 years earlier than target year); UK. Dr. R. Jesmin has taught different areas of Computer Science [with Internet Science], Information System, Distance and e-Learn areas at different universities within the UK including King's College London (University of London); Manchester Metropolitan University, and at University of Leeds. She also worked as a post-doc researcher for Department of Music, King's College London in association with University of Oxford. She has participated as a member of numerous top-rated conference programmes and organising committees, reviewed a range of highly prestigious journals and book chapters, and participated in variety of publications and top-class presentation worldwide. Dr. Jesmin would welcome all research, teaching or Enterprise oriented project proposals within her scope.

Low Tang Jung obtained his Bachelor's degree in Computer Technology from Teesside University, UK in 1989, MSc IT from National University of Malaysia in 2001and PhD in IT from University Teknology PETRONAS UTP in 2011. Low has been in the academic line for the past 21 years as Senior Lecturer in various public and private institutes of higher learning. He teaches various engineering and ICT courses. He is currently a Senior Lecturer in Computer and Information Sciences Department, Universiti Teknologi PETRONAS, Malaysia. His research interests include wireless technology, embedded systems, wireless sensor networking, and robotics. Some of his current ongoing R&D projects and other completed projects have been recognized at national as well as international level by winning medals and awards at various national and international exhibitions/competitions. Low has his research works published in various conference proceedings and journals.

Elvira Immacolata Locuratolo graduated in Mathematics in 1978 at the University of Naples and carried out post-degree research at the "Istituto di Elaborazione dell'Informazione" of the National Research Council at Pisa (IEI-CNR). Since 1982, she has been a researcher at IEI- CNR and at the "Istituto di Scienze e Tecnologie dell'Informazione" of the National Research Council at Pisa (ISTI – CNR) Pisa. She is the author of numerous articles in books and journals. Her activity has been focused on algorithms and implementations of mapping from conceptual to logical database models, on model transformations and on meta-modelling. The main results obtained consist in the introduction of formal methods of conceptual database design, database re-engineering, approaches to data mining, ontology for database preservation and semantics for image databases. Recent research has regarded the transportation of some of these methods to the new scientific area of concept theory. Among her collaborations include those with the Rutherford Appleton Laboratory at Oxford and with the Tampere University of Technology at Pori, Finland.

Alberto Pliego Manguran got the Industial Engineering degree at the School of Industrial Engineers (ETSII) of Ciudad Real, University of Castilla-La Mancha (UCLM, Spain), 2012. He is Technical Engineer from the UCLM (2009).

Pellas S. Nikolaos is a PhD Candidate at the Department of Product and Systems Design Engineering, University of the Aegean, Greece. He obtained a Master's degree in Education with ICT, in the field of e-Learning through virtual worlds in 2010, at the Aristotle University of Thessaloniki. His thesis was about the handling of organizational complexity and flexibility interactions and the educational value-added of the qualitative or quantitative assessment of virtual worlds. In 2011, he also was written a research book about the pedagogical value of the e-learning process in virtual environments. Nowadays, he starts his dissertation research, which addresses in configuring and using virtual worlds for learning applications with the "Jigsaw" teamwork technique to investigate the engagement factors and assortment learning presence of trainees' users. He has an extensive experience in education, especially in adult groups. His research interests include the use of ICT in education, with emphasis on learning through "Metaverse" skin or "Open-source" virtual worlds and contemporary learning methods.

Khine Khine Nyunt received her Bachelor of Science (Honors) Mathematics degree from University of Yangon, Myanmar in 1991 and her Master's in Computer Science from Institute of Computer Science & Technology, Yangon, Myanmar in 1995 and her second Master in Management of Technology from National University Singapore in 2008. She is currently holding a Lecturer position at King Faisal University, Kingdom of Saudi Arabia. Prior to that, she worked as a Lecturer at Management Development Institute of Singapore, Curtin University of Technology, Multimedia University, Malaysia and Institute of Computer Science and Technology, Myanmar with over ten years of teaching experience in course of Computer Science subjects. Her current research interests include knowledge management, information retrieval and data mining.

Krishnamurthy Raghuraman is a Chief Architect in Cognizant's Life Sciences Business Unit's Technology Consulting Group. Raghu's current interest areas include enterprise architecture, information security, collaboration oriented architectures, mobility applications, and big data. He has worked with several major pharmaceuticals in envisioning and leading transformational initiatives. He has presented papers at conferences and was recently named a senior member of the prestigious Association of Computing Machinery (ACM). Raghu enjoys solving complex technical problems and is an advocate of systems thinking. He likes to spend time with academia in sharing knowledge and learning. He was invited for guest lecturers in the Indian Institute of Technology, Chennai. Raghu holds a Master's degree from the Indian Institute of Technology, Mumbai, and is a TOGAF-certified enterprise architect.

Rizaldy Rapsing has more than 20 years of combined experience in the education sector and IT industries. He was first trained in the EDP of a telecommunications company. From 1993 to 2001, he maintained working in universities and Software Development companies simultaneously, an experience that allowed him to develop skills both in programming, analysis, and communication. In 2001, after months of becoming IT Head, he focused on one job alone. In 2006, he decided to explore working abroad, initially in Salalah College of Technology in Oman for more than 5 years and now in King Faisal University of Saudi Arabia. Currently, the College of Computer Sciences and Information Technology has entrusted him to concentrate on students' research projects to align their research activities and address specific issues from the directives of the industry, the opportunity to offer alternative systems, or the proposal to solve problems relating to current procedures.

Huub Ruël is a Professor of International Business at Windesheim University of Applies Sciences, the Netherlands. He holds a Master in Work and Organisational Psychology, and a PhD in Business Administration/Human Resource Management. His thesis focused on implementation of IT's in office-environments based upon Adaptive Structuration Theory-ideas. After that his main research focus became e-HRM, combining IT and HRM knowledge. In 2004 he published a book *E-HRM: Innovation or Irritation?* in which the results of e-HRM implementation in five large international companies were described. Articles derived from this e-HRM study have been published in academic and professional journals.

Saqib Saeed is an Assistant Professor in the department of Graduate Studies and Applied Sciences at Bahria University Islamabad, Pakistan. He obtained his PhD in Information Systems from University of Siegen, Germany. He had a Master's degree in Software Technology from Stuttgart University of Applied Science Germany. His areas of interest lie in software engineering, human computer interaction, computer supported cooperative work, and ICT4D.

A B Sagar is a research scholar in the Department of Computers & Information Sciences, University of Hyderabad, India. His research interests include micropayment schemes, ethics in information technology, etc. His research work is aimed towards development of an information system for the Self Help Groups of India with ethical values in it. He has published his work in several national and international journals and conferences. He is grateful to his research guide Prof H Mohanty for his guidance in the research work.

Monika Sethi holds MCA degree from Punjab Technical University, Jalandhar, India. She is Faculty in GGDSD College Chandigarh, India and pursuing PhD in the area of Cloud Computing from the Thapar University, Patiala, India. Her areas of interests include cloud computing, software engineering, and software reusability.

Anju Sharma holds MSc (I.T.) degree from Punjab University Chandigarh and PhD from Thapar University, Patiala, India. She is Faculty in School of Mathematics and Computer Application, Thapar University, Patiala, India. Her areas of interests include parallel and distributed computing, grid computing, resource management, resource discovery, and peer to peer networks.

Arshad Siddiqi has completed all his education in USA with BS in Computer Sciences, MBA in Management, and PhD in System Sciences. He has 30 years of upper level management experience in the ICT industry in many countries, presently working as Director ICT at Institute of Business Administration, Karachi, implementing Green Technology and Tier III Data Center/DRC.

Paul Timmermans is a researcher at the University of Twente. While aspiring towards a career as a strategic business consultant, he is a trainee at a consultancy firm specialized in psychological testing and assessments, and psychodiagnostics. He holds a Master's in Industrial Engineering and Management Sciences, and a Master in Industrial and Organizational Psychology. His first Master's thesis concerned the establishment and reinforcement of deadline commitment at an automotive company, whereas his second Master's thesis focused on determining the requirements of e-selection. In line with both of his Master's theses, he is mainly interested in topics on the cross section of industrial engineering and management sciences, and I/O psychology.

Issa Traore obtained a PhD in Software Engineering in 1998 from Institute Nationale Polytechnique (INPT)-LAAS/CNRS, Toulouse, France. He has been with the faculty of the Department of Electrical and Computer Engineering of the University of Victoria since 1999. He is currently an Associate Professor and the Coordinator of the Information Security and object Technology (ISOT) Lab at the University of Victoria. His research interests include biometrics technologies, computer intrusion detection, network forensics, software security, and software quality engineering. He has published over 100 technical papers in computer security in the last 10 years. He is currently serving as Associate Editor for the *International Journal of Communication Networks and Distributed Systems* (IJCNDS).

Marco Vieira is an Assistant Professor at the University of Coimbra, Portugal. Marco Vieira is an expert on dependability benchmarking and his research interests also include experimental dependability evaluation, fault injection, security benchmarking, software development processes, and software quality assurance, subjects in which he has authored or co-authored more than one hundred of papers in refereed conferences and journals. He has participated in many research projects, both at the national and European level. Marco Vieira has served on program committees of the major conferences of the dependability area and acted as referee for many international conferences and journals in the dependability and databases areas.

Isaac Woungang received his MSc & PhD degrees in Mathematics from the Université de la Méditerranée-Aix Marseille II, France, and Université du Sud, Toulon-Var, France in 1990 and 1994, respectively. In 1999, he received a MSc. degree from the INRS-Materials and Telecommunications, University of Quebec, Montreal, Canada. From 1999 to 2002, he worked as a Software Engineer at Nortel Networks. Since 2002, he has been with Ryerson University, where he is now an Associate Professor of Computer Science and Coordinator of the Distributed Applications and Broadband (DABNEL) Lab at Ryerson University. His current research interests include network security, and computer communication networks. Dr. Woungang has published six (6) book chapters and over seventy (70) refereed technical articles in scholarly international journals and conferences. He edited six (6) books in the areas of wireless networks, published by reputed publishers such as Springer, Elsevier, and Wiley.

Index